TROUBLE FREE C

(Book for C-Programming)

By

HARI MOHAN PANDEY

Lecturer, CS & IT Deptt. MPSTME, NMIMS
University, Mumbai, Maharastra

UNIVERSITY SCIENCE PRESS

(An Imprint of Laxmi Publications Pvt. Ltd.)

BANGALORE • CHENNAI • COCHIN • GUWAHATI • HYDERABAD
JALANDHAR • KOLKATA • LUCKNOW • MUMBAI • RANCHI

NEW DELHI

Published by :
UNIVERSITY SCIENCE PRESS
(*An Imprint of Laxmi Publications Pvt. Ltd.*)
113, Golden House, Daryaganj,
New Delhi-110002
Phone : 011-43 53 25 00
Fax : 011-43 53 25 28
info@laxmipublications.com
www.laxmipublications.com

First Edition : 2009

OFFICES

© **Bangalore**	080-26 61 15 61	© **Chennai**	044-24 34 47 26
© **Cochin**	0484-237 70 04, 405 13 03	© **Guwahati**	0361-254 36 69, 251 38 81
© **Hyderabad**	040-24 65 23 33	© **Jalandhar**	0181-222 12 72
© **Kolkata**	033-22 27 43 84	© **Lucknow**	0522-220 95 78
© **Mumbai**	022-24 91 54 15, 24 92 78 69	© **Ranchi**	0651-221 47 64

UTF-9265-395-TROUBLE FREE C **C—16082/08/07**

Typesetted at : Shubham Composer, N. Delhi. printed at : Repro Knowledgecast Limited, Thane

TROUBLE FREE C

(Book for C-Programming)

CONTENTS

PREFACE

It gives me immense pleasure in presenting the first edition of the book **"Trouble Free C"** primarily intended for engineering/non-engineering students. This book has been written to meet the requirement of the students who want to acquaint themselves with lots of programming examples written in a lucid manner.

The subject matter of this book has been divided into 17 chapters. Each chapter has been written and developed with immense simplified programs, which will clear the core concepts of C language. This book is especially for those students who are tyro in the field of C programming. Inside the book you will find numerous programs instead of just code snippet to illustrate even the basic concept. The book assumes no previous exposure to the C programming language. It also contains some good programming examples, which might be useful for experienced programmers. All the programming examples given in this book have been tested on Turbo C 3.0.

Though there are many books available on C programming but the present book has its own unique quality. I do not claim the originality of the subject matter but I am confident to say that the presentation of the subject matter with complete explanation is my original contribution.

All effort has been made to keep this book error free. However, there is possibility that some errors might have crept in inadvertently. I would, therefore be grateful if such oversight are pointed out by the readers. Suggestions for improvement of the text from readers are welcomed.

—Author

ACKNOWLEDGEMENT

First of all, I would like to say thanks to "BABA VISVNATH" for their constant bless in writing this book. As understanding of the study like this is never the outcome of the efforts of a single person, rather it bears the imprint of a number of people who directly or indirectly helped me in completing this book. I would be failing in my duty if I don't say a word of thanks to all those whose sincere advice to make this book a real educative, effective, and pleasurable. I would like to acknowledge My Father Dr. V.N. Pandey, My Mother Smt. Madhuri Pandey and My sisters Ms. Anjana Pandey, and Ms. Ranjana Pandey and My brother Mr. Man Mohan Pandey.

I have immense pleasure in expressing my whole hearted gratitude to Prof. RR Sedamkar (Associate Dean, MPSTME), Prof R.M. Samant, Prof. S.B. Patil, Miss Varsha Nemade (Lecturer), Mr. Vivek Sharma (Lecturer), Miss Malvika Sharma (Lecturer), Mr. B. Salendra(Senior Lecturer), Er. Ruchika Arora (Infosys Pvt. Ltd.) for providing helps and guidance during the writing of this book.

I also thanks my lots of student whose conceptual queries have always helped me in digging the subject matter deep.

I am thankful to all the employees of MPSTME, NMIMS University especially Mr. D. K. Das for their parental support throughout the writing of this book. I also thankful to Mr. Bharat Thodji and Mr. Mahendra Joshi who have been supported me in all types of Lab activities during the writing of this book.

How will I forget my close buddy Asst. Prof. Saurabh Banerjee who suggests me the title of the book. I also thanks to the librarian of MPSTME at Shirpur Mr. Anand Gawdekar who provided each and every good book on C timely.

—Author

1

SETTING THE BASE FOR 'C' PROGRAMMING

If you have no prior idea of programming, software, translators, RAM etc. then you must not skip this chapter. This chapter sets your base for the programming.

The introduction part and section 1.2 gives you an idea of human language and computer language. It tells you how they are different and discuss all different types of computer languages like machine, assembly and high level.

Overview of programming discuss the fundamentals of programming like data, instruction and program, what a problem is from programming point of view, problem solving techniques: algorithms, pseudo code, flow charts etc. It also discusses subroutines and functions, programming methodology: bottom up and top down approach, types of programming: procedural, structured, object oriented etc.

A detailed discussion of translators like assembler, compiler and interpreter is given in section 1.4. Types of software, role of RAM in program execution, basic memory measuring units and brief introduction of Number system is given.

1.1 INTRODUCTION

A language is system of communication. We use many languages like English, Hindi or any other language to express our views, ideas, thoughts etc. to any other person. Similarly when we write programs for the computer there should be a language by means of which computer express our views and ideas. There are two types of language—a computer language and a natural language. A computer language has limited and restricted vocabulary whereas a natural language is rich in vocabulary.

Every language has got certain rules which govern the formation of valid sentences. Every language also defines certain symbols which are permissible in that language. The rules of using symbols as per the given language are known as **syntax rules** for that language. The syntax rules are called the rules of the grammar for that language. The meaning of the grammar is called **semantics**. Whenever we write any computer program we must follow syntax for the programming language which we are using for writing the computer program.

1.2 CLASSIFICATION OF COMPUTER LANGUAGES

All computer language can be classified into three major categories. Machine and Assembly together can be put into "Low-Level" language.

1. Machine Language
2. Assembly Language
3. High-Level Language.

1.2.1 Machine Language

Machine language is called the language of the computer as computer understands only this language which is language consists of sequence of 0's and 1's. Using this language whatever you want to input to computer has to be supplied in the form of strings of 0's and 1's. For example character 'A' may be represented as 01100101, 0 itself may be represented as 01001000 and so on.

Features of this Language are:

1. Consists of strings of 0's and 1's.
2. Natural language of computer.
3. Internally 0 and 1 are converted into electric signals.
4. Each and every command or operation must be stated in the form of 0's and 1's.
5. Execution of program is very fast as machine instructions are directly understood by the computer.
6. They are machine dependent.
7. Difficult to program, modify and are error-prone.
8. No translator is required.

1.2.2 Assembly Language

Assembly language, commonly called assembly, asm or symbolic machine code, is a human-readable notation for the machine language that specific computer architecture uses. Machine language, a pattern of bits encoding machine operations, is made readable by replacing the raw values with symbols called mnemonics.

For example, a computer with the appropriate processor will understand this X86 machine language:

1011000001100001

For programmers, however, it is easier to remember the equivalent assembly language representation:

MOV AL, 061H

Which means to move the hexadecimal value 61(97 decimal) into the processor register with the name "AL". The mnemonic "MOV" is short for "move", and a comma-separated list of arguments or parameters follows it; this is a typical assembly language statement. Transforming assembly into machine language is accomplished by an assembler, and the reverse by a dissembler.

Some more examples of mnemonics are given in the following table:

Table 1.1 ***Mnemonics & their Meaning***

Mnemonic	*Meaning*
LDA X	Load accumulator with X
ADD X	Add the contents of memory X to the contents of accumulator.
MUL X	Multiply the contents of memory X to the contents of accumulator
STA 1200H	Store contents of accumulator to memory location 1200H

Features of this Language are:

1. Use of mnemonics to write programs which are small words specific to machine to denote a specific operation like ADD, SUB, MUL which represent the operations addition, subtraction, multiplication respectively.
2. For writing programs set of mnemonics are made fixed for a specific type of machine. The programs are written using these mnemonics but internally a translator called assembler converts them into machine language form.
3. Assembler is any system software which is specific for a specific machine.
4. Easier to understand and modify.
5. Easy to locate and correct errors.

1.2.3 High-Level Language

We have seen that assembly and machine language require deep knowledge of computer hardware whereas in higher language you have only the instructions in English words and logic of the problem irrespective of the type of computer you are using. Higher level languages are simple languages that use English and Mathematical symbols like +, –, *, /, % etc. for its program construction. High-level language enables programmers to concentrate more on the logic and less on the intricacies of the particular computer on which users are working.

Use of high-level languages makes program easy to read, write and understand. Any higher level language has to be converted into machine language for the computer to understand and for that a translator is required which is specific for a specific high-level language. For example a translator for a 'C' programming language will be different from a translator for FORTRON language.

Features of this Language are:

1. Program is written in simple English like language.
2. Lets the programmer to concentrate on logic rather worry about hardware configurations.
3. Every instruction from a program is translated into corresponding machine language program by a translator which may be compiler or interpreter.
4. Easy to use and modify.
5. Very less error prone.
6. For each different HLL a separate translator is required.

1.3 OVERVIEW OF PROGRAMMING

Programming now-a-days has become synonymous with computers. A large number of software companies are involved in the development of computer software (collection of computer programs) which are used by almost any where in the whole world. Satellite and space shuttle technology, weather forecasting, oil-exploration, internet, intranet, e-commerce, accounting etc. have been made easy by all these software.

All computer programs are meant to solve problems encountered in day-to-day life, that's why a better quality of program has to be planned and achieved. Therefore program development is not a merely learning the syntax of programming language or formulating group of statements but creating programs that will function accurately for an indefinite period of time.

In this section we will understands the basics of programming, tools used for the conversion, programming methodology etc.

1.3.1 Data, Instruction and Program

DATA : A data is any raw fact related with a physical/non physical entity like name of a person, color of a chair, salary of an employee.

INSTRUCTION : An instruction is made when we arrange the data in a meaningful way or order.

A PROGRAM : A program is a collection of a number of instructions arranged in a meaningful order.

In short

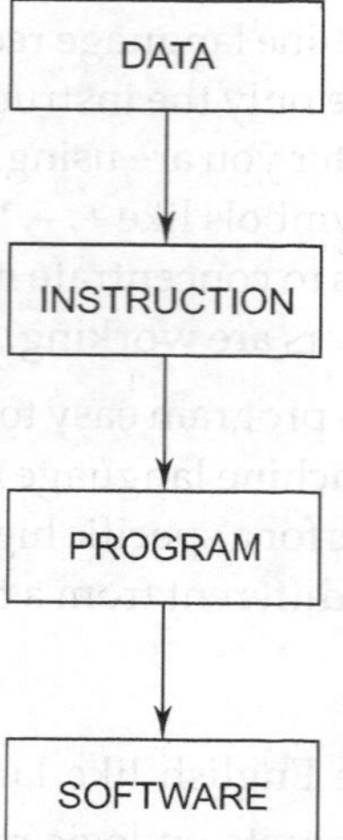

Fig. 1.1 *Relation among data, instruction, program and software.*

The arrow upper to lower side presents many to one operation. That is many data together constitute an instruction and many instructions together constitute a program and many programs together constitute software.

1.3.2 Problem Definition

Every problem has to be defined before finding a solution for it. Defining the problem is done by the end-user or client in such a way that is easily understood by the computer. The problem has to be converted by the computer programmer into computer understandable form. As an example consider the problem of **max of three numbers:**

The input is to be supplied by the user and computer will find out the maximum of three numbers and will present the user maximum number as output.

Therefore in case of problem definition, the input data has to be supplied at time of execution of program or before and the computer should give the expected output. The solution of the problem has also to be determined manually for a set of input data. Therefore problem definition has two parts *i.e.* input data and an output. If these are well defined, the problem is defined.

1.3.3 Problem-Solving Techniques (Designing the Program)

For better designing of a program, a systematic planning must be done to code it into the high-level language. Prior planning of program helps programmer as instructions can be correlated and errors can be minimized.

There are various techniques available for mapping the program logic like algorithms, flowchart and pseudo code etc. We will have a brief study of all these tools.

Algorithm

In mathematics and computing, an algorithm is a procedure (a finite set of well-defined instruction) for accomplishing some tasks which, given an initial state, will terminate in a defined end-state. The computational-complexity and efficient implementation of the algorithm are important in computing, and this depends on suitable data structures.

'Knuth' has given a list of five properties that are widely accepted as requirements for an algorithm:

(*a*) **FINITENESS:** An algorithm must always terminate after a finite number of steps.

(*b*) **DEFINITENESS:** Each step of an algorithm must be precisely defined; the actions to be carried out must be rigorously and unambiguously specified for each case.

(*c*) **INPUT:** Quantities which are given to it initially before the algorithm begins. These inputs are taken from specified sets of objects.

(*d*) **OUTPUT:** Quantities which have a specified relation to the inputs

(*e*) **EFFECTIVENESS:** All of the operations to be performed in the algorithm must be sufficiently basic that they can in principle be done and in a finite length of time by a man using paper and pencil.

Advantages of Algorithm:

(*a*) It is independent of programming language.

(*b*) It is easy to debug, *i.e.* errors can be pointed out easily.

(*c*) Each step of algorithm can be easily coded into high-level language.

(*d*) Easy to understand and modify.

Examples of algorithm:

A. Max of two numbers
   1. INPUT A, B, C
   2. IF A > B THEN
   3. PRINT "MAX is", A
   4. ELSE
   5. PRINT "MAX is", B
   6. RETURN

B. Sum and Average of three numbers.
   1. INPUT A, B, C
   2. SUM = (A + B + C)
   3. AVG = SUM/3
   4. PRINT "SUM is" SUM
   5. PRINT "AVG is", AVG
   6. RETURN.

Pseudo Code

It is a program analysis tool that is used for planning program logic. Pseudo Code refers to imitated or false code. Each code or English like sentence represent one logical operation of the program being designed. Pseudo code is a written statement of an algorithm using a restricted and well-defined vocabulary.

Example 1. *Sum and difference of two numbers.*

```
INPUTE Number_1
INPUT Number_2
Sum = Number_1+Number_2
Difference = Number_1 - Number_2
Display Sum
Display Difference.
```

Advantages of Pseudo Code

(*a*) Converting a pseudo code to a programming language is much easier than converting a flowchart to a programming language.

(*b*) Writing of pseudo code involves much less time than drawing an equivalent flow chart are few and syntax is quite similar to programming languages.

(*c*) Modification of pseudo code is easier.

Flow Chart

It is one of the methods of program design. A flowchart is a pictorial representation of an algorithm that uses boxes of different shapes to denote different types of instructions. The boxes contain actual instructions which are to be executed. The boxes are connected to each other with solid lines to indicate the flow of the operation. Because of pictorial flow of the program any error can be detected easily prior to running the program. Basically a flowchart is the picture of the logic of the program which we can make prior to write the program in any of the computer programming language.

If you are a beginner to the programming it is advisable to create a flow chart of the program first before you start writing the actual program. Once you are accustomed to the programming then you can directly write the program.

Flow Chart Symbols

The instructions of the program are illustrated in the flow chart with the help of some symbols/ boxes which are the standard symbols that is use of a particular symbol denote a specific type of operation.

The various symbols used in the flow chart are given below:

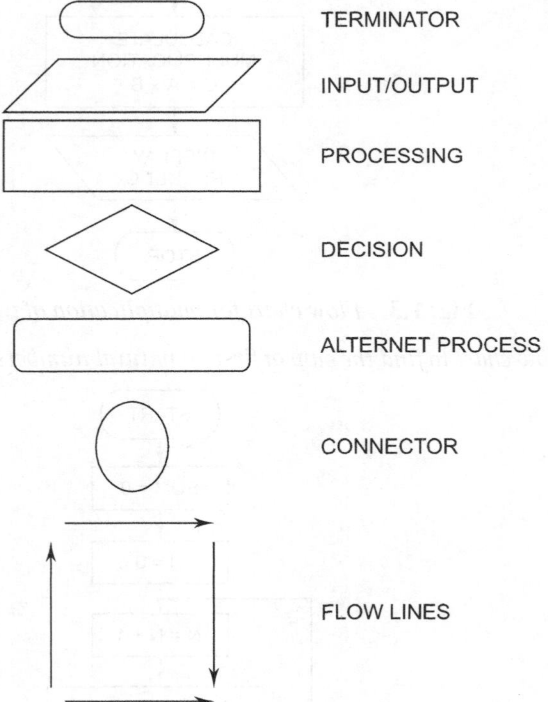

Fig. 1.2 *Symbols used for flowchart.*

The meaning of the various symbols shown above is mentioned below:

1. **TERMINATOR:** It is used to indicate the beginning (START), ending (STOP) and pauses (HLT) in the program logic flow.
2. **INPUT/OUTPUT:** Any function of input/output device is put in this box. For example reading from keyboard and display on to the monitor.
3. **PROCESSING:** It contains all types of instructions which process data like arithmetic, logical, data movement or any other type of calculations on to the data.

4. **DECISION:** This symbol is used in the flow chart to indicate a decision statement and this symbol presents two branches: one when condition is true and another for false condition.
5. **CONNECTORS:** In case your flow chart becomes long and does not fit in a single page, instead of using flow lines to connect flow chart from one page to other connectors can be used.
6. **FLOW LINES:** They represent the flow of operation. Normal flow is from top to bottom. They are mostly required in case of loop.

Example. *Multiplication of two numbers.*

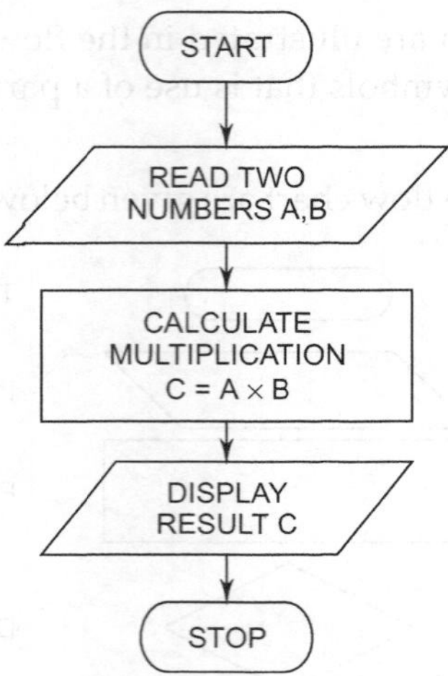

Fig. 1.3 *Flow chart for multiplication of two numbers.*

Example. *Draw a flow chart to find the sum of first 50 natural numbers.*

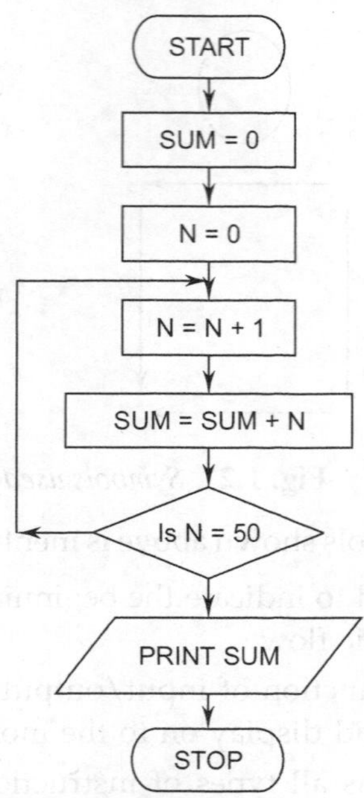

Fig. 1.4 *Flowchart for computing the sum of first 50 natural numbers.*

1.3.4 Subroutines/ Procedure and Functions

Subroutines are small block of codes which are once written can be used at number of places in other programs, as many number of times as required without rewriting. A subroutine is invoked in other programs by the use of CALL statements followed by subroutine name with parameters if any. (Some languages do not require CALL statements to call a subroutine like C, C++, VC++ and java). Procedure is another name given to subroutine.

As an example consider finding a factorial of a number at many places in the program. You won't be writing the logic at all places in the program. Instead you can write the logic in subroutine and can call the subroutine at places where ever required.

Functions are similar to subroutines with the difference that they return a value to the place from which they are called.

All the languages provide number of subroutines and functions pre-built into the language which can be used directly by the programmer in their code where ever required. For example all types of mathematical functions like sin, cos, log, POW etc, input/output functions, string manipulations routines and functions etc.

1.3.5 Programming Methodology

1. Bottom up and Top Down Approach

Any problem can be dealt with any two ways, viz, top down or bottom up. A simple example is given here to illustrate the output. Sorting an array of numbers involves the following:

(*a*) Comparison
(*b*) Exchange

At the top level, an algorithm has to be formulated to carry out sorting using the above operations. Once the algorithm is confirmed, then the algorithm for comparison and exchange are formulated, before implementation of the entire algorithm. Therefore in this approach one begins from the top level without bothering about the minute details for implementation to start with.

The bottom up approach is just the reverse. The lower level tasks are first carried put and are then integrated to provide the solution. In this method lower level structures of the program are developed first then progressively higher level structures are created. Here the algorithms for exchange and comparison will be formulated before formulating the algorithm for the whole problem.

In any case, dividing the problem into small tasks and then solving each task provides the solution. Therefore, either the top down or bottom up methodology has to be adopted for finding the problem into smaller modules and then solving it. In the top down methodology, the overall structure is defined before getting into details, but in the bottom up approach, the details are worked out first before defining the overall structure.

Important Points about Bottom up Approach

1. In bottom up design individual part of the system are specified in details. The parts are then linked together to form larger components, which are in turn linked until a complete system is formed.

2. Bottom up design yields programs which are smaller and more agile. A shorter program doesn't have to be divided into so many components means program which are easier to read or modify.
3. Bottom up design promotes code re-use. When you write two more programs, many of the utilities you wrote for the first program will also be useful in the succeeding ones. That's why re-usability of code is one of the main benefits of the bottom-up approach.
4. Bottom up design makes programs easier to read.
5. Working bottom-up helps to clarify your ideas about the design of your program.
6. Bottom up programming may allow for unit testing, but until more of the system comes together none of the system can be tested as whole, often causing complications near the end of the project.
7. An example of programming which uses this approach is C++ and java.

Important Points About Top-Down Approach

1. In the top down model an overview of the system is formulated, without going into details for any part of it. Each part of the system is then refined by the designing it in more detail.
2. Each new part may then be refined again, defining it in yet more detail until the entire specification is detailed enough to validate the model.
3. Top-down approaches emphasize planning and a complete understanding of the system. It is inherent that no coding can begin until a sufficient level of detail has been reached in the design of at least some part of the system.
4. Top-down programming is programming style, the mainstay of traditional procedural language, in which design begins by specifying complete pieces and then dividing them into successively smaller pieces.
5. The technique for writing a program using top down methods is to write a main procedure that names all the major functions/ subroutines it will need. When all the various functions/ subroutines have been coded the program is done.
6. Top-down programming may complicate testing, since nothing executable will exist until near the end of the project.
7. An example of programming which uses this approach is C and Pascal

1.3.6 Why Study Programming Language?

There are numbers of reasons for the above question. Six of them are:

1. To improve your ability to develop efficient algorithm.
2. To improve your use of existing programming language.
3. To increase your vocabulary of useful programming language.
4. To allow a better choice of programming language.
5. To make easier to learn a new language.
6. To make easier to design a new language.

1.4 TRANSLATOR

A translator is a system software which converts a program written in HLL or is an assembly language into machine language. In general there can be three types of translators:

1. Assembler
2. Compiler
3. Interpreter.

1. Assembler

An assembler is a program which converts a program written in assembly language into machine language. An assembler takes the assembly language code written in a file saved with **.asm** extension and translates into the machine code of the computer. The assembler is written by the programmer who have sound knowledge of instruction formats and addressing modes of the machine for which assembler is to be written. Apart from converting assembly code into corresponding machine code, the assembler "assembles" the machine code into the memory of the computer and makes it ready for execution. The code produced by the assembler is actually not pure machine language code and is called object code. The code is used by the linker system software which produces as output the pure machine language in .exe format.

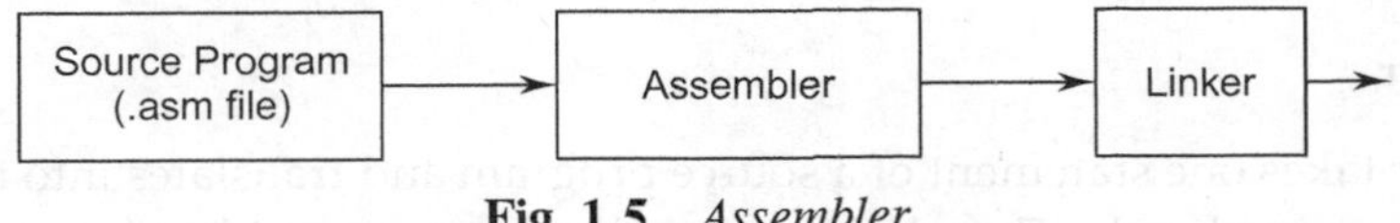

Fig. 1.5 *Assembler.*

In the first step **.asm** file is passed to assembler which generates **.obj file** as output. In the second step this **.obj** act as input to the linker which produces .exe file as output.

2. Compiler

A compiler is a translator which translates a program written in **HLL** into machine language similar to assembler the output produced is a **.obj** file which is known as object module. This object module is passed to the linker which links the necessary files to the object module and generates executable file (.exe file).

For different types of high-level language there are different types of compiler. For example to compile a Pascal program you will require a Pascal compiler, for C a C compiler and so on. This is because a compiler understands the specific language only.

The compilation process is usually a two-step process. (Better say two pass)

(*a*) **PASS 1 of the compiler:** The pass1 can be further divided into three parts:

1. Lexical Analysis
2. Syntax Analysis
3. Semantic Analysis

- In the lexical analysis the compiler divides the input stream into valid lexical units or tokens. For example in a C language various tokens may be keywords, identifiers, operators, constants etc. The various tokens are put into their respective classes. The program which does this lexical analysis is called LEXER.

- In syntax analysis it is checked whether the valid lexical units are in a proper order or not according to some production rules. For example in C if we write

  C= *a* + *b*;

  Then the input stream *c* = *a* + *b*; is divided into number of tokens which are *c* = *a* + *b* ;**(a total of 6 tokens).**

  According to C assignment rules the input stream is ok as ***a* + *b*** will be assigned to ***c***. If we write ***a* + *b* = *c*;** then it will generate syntax error. Syntax analysis is also called **PARSING** and the program which does the syntax analysis is called **PARSER** or **SYNTAX ANALYZER.**

- The semantic analysis part concerns with the meaning of the statements or instructions. For example the C statement ***c* = *a* + *b*;** tells the semantic analysis part to first evaluate value of ***a* + *b*** (taking into consideration the type of ***a*** and ***b***) and assign the value to the variable *c*.

  The error generated by the compiler are known as syntax error and compilation errors which are displayed if any error occurs during lexical analysis or syntax analysis. The compiler cannot catch logical errors.

(*b*) **PASS2 of the compiler :** The pass2 of the compiler concern with code generation and memory allocation. For the C instruction internal codes are generated which are understandable by the machine. Memory is allocated to the variables, arrays etc.

3. Interpreter

An interpreter takes one statement of a source program and translates into the machine language which executes immediately. The whole program is not converted first into machine language form instead translation and execution alternates for every statement of the program. The compiler is not involved in the execution of the programmer. This task is done by the linker. In case of interpreter no executable file is generated.

Difference Between Compiler and Interpreter

1. In compiler the whole program is converted into machine language whereas in interpreter one statement is translated at a time.
2. No involvement of compiler during execution of the program, Interpreter itself is responsible for the execution of the program.
3. The object code produced in the compilation process is saved and can be used for future use; this is not in case with the interpreter.
4. As compared to interpreter, compiler is a complex program.
5. Interpreter is slow compared to compiler as each statement must be translated every time the program is to be executed.
6. Compiler gives fast response to changes in the program.

1.5 INTRODUCTION TO NUMBER SYSTEM

Since hands are the most convenient tools nature has provided, human beings have always tended to use them in counting. The decimal number system followed naturally from this usage. The binary number system and digital codes are fundamental to computers and to digital electronics in general. In this chapter we will discuss, the binary number system and its relationship to another number system such as decimal, hexadecimal, and octal is the principal focus. Also, digital codes such as binary coded decimal (BCD), the gray code, and the ASCII are covered. The parity method for detecting errors in codes is introduced.

1.6 TYPES OF NUMBER SYSTEM

Number system comes in two flavor which are defined by the figure given below:

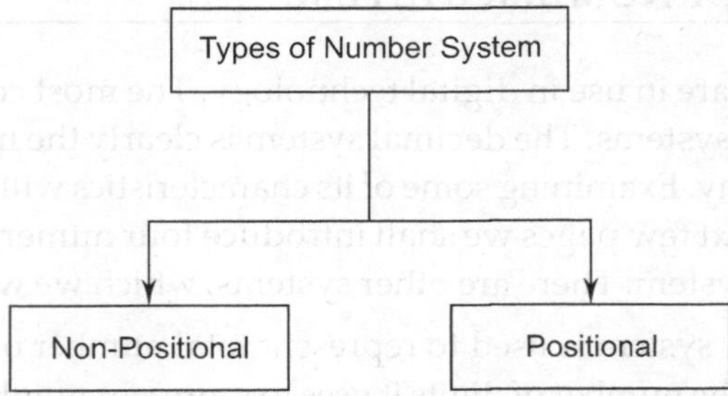

Fig. 1.6 *Different types of number system.*

1.6.1 Non-Positional Number Systems

In the beginning human being counted on figure, when ten figures were not adequate stones or sticks used to indicate values. This method of counting uses an additive approach or the non-positional number system.

In non-positional number system, we have symbols such as:

Numbers	*Symbols*
1	I
2	II
3	III
4	IIII
5	IIIII

Fig. 1.7 *Symbols used for non-positional number systems.*

From the above table it is noticeable that each symbol represents the same values regardless of its position in the number and the symbols are simply added to find out the value of a particular number since it is very difficult to perform any of the arithmetic operation.

1.6.2 Positional Number Systems

In **"positional number system"** there are only a few symbols called digits, and these symbols represent different values depending on the position they occupy in the number .The value of each digit in such a number is determined by three considerations:

(a) The digit itself.
(b) The position of the digit in the number.
(c) The base of the number system (where base is defined as the total number of digits available in the number system).

The number system that we use in our day-to-day life is called the decimal number system. In this number system, the base is equal to 10 because there are altogether ten symbols or digits (0, 1, 2, 3, 4, 5, 6, 7, 8, 9) used in this system.

1.7 BASE OF RADIX NUMBER SYSTEM

Many number systems are in use in digital technology. The most common are the decimal, binary, octal, and hexadecimal systems. The decimal system is clearly the most familiar to us because it is a tool that we use every day. Examining some of its characteristics will help us to better understand the other systems. In the next few pages we shall introduce four numerical representation systems that are used in the digital system. There are other systems, which we will look at briefly.

Base of radix number system is used to represent total number of digits available in any number system *i.e.* it defined as the number of digits it uses to represent numbers in the system. Therefore, the decimal number uses ten digits, from 0 to 9, so its base or radix is 10 and so on.

There are four types of number system:

1. Binary Number System
2. Octal Number System
3. Decimal Number System
4. Hexadecimal Number System.

1.8 RULES FOR REPRESENTATION OF NUMBER SYSTEMS

There are three rules given for representation of any number system. These three rules are given below:

Rule 1: Total number of digits available which we called **"Base"** of the number system.

Rule 2: First digit is always is zero (0).

Rule 3: We can find last digit by using the formula **"Last digit = Base-1"**.

Now, we will implement all the three rules to show number systems.

Table 1.1. ***The rules used for representation of number system***

1. Binary Number System:		
Rule 1:	Base	= 2
Rule 2:	First digit	= 0
Rule 3:	Last digit	= Base − 1
		= 2 − 1
		= 1

⇨ Final digits = 0, 1

2. Decimal Number System:

Rule 1: Base = 10

Rule 2: First digits = 0

Rule 3: Last digit = Base –1

= 10 – 1

= 9

⇨ Final digit = 0, 1, 2, 3, 4, 5, 6, 7, 8, 9

3. Octal Number System:

Rule 1: Base = 8

Rule 2: First digit = 0

Rule 3: Last digit = Base – 1

= 8 – 1

= 7

⇨ Final digits = 0, 1, 2, 3, 4, 5, 6, 7

4. Hexadecimal number system:

Rule 1: Base = 16

Rule 2: First digit = 0

Rule 3: Last digit = Base – 1

= 16 – 1

= 15

⇨ Final digits = 0, 1, 2, 3, 4, 5, 6, 7, 8, 9, A , B, C, D, E, F

The meaning of A, B, C, D, E, F in hexadecimal number system are shown below:

Table. 1.2 ***The symbols used in hexadecimal number system.***

Symbols	*Value*
A	10
B	11
C	12
D	13
E	14
F	15

1.9 CONVERSION FROM ONE NUMBER SYSTEM TO OTHERS

We can convert one number system to another number system. Since the input and final output values are to be in decimal. Most of the computer professionals are often required to convert numbers into other number systems.

There are mainly following conversions occur:

1. Decimal to Binary
2. Binary to Decimal
3. Binary to Octal
4. Octal to Binary.
5. Binary to Hexadecimal
6. Hexadecimal to Binary
7. Decimal to Octal
8. Octal to Decimal.

Now we are going to show step-by-step conversion procedure.

1.9.1 Decimal To Binary Conversion

In this section we will discuss how to convert a decimal number to the equivalent binary number. Here we will discuss two methods to achieve our goal .The two methods are given below:

(*i*) Sum of weight method (*ii*) Repeated division methods.

1.9.1.1 Sum of Weight Methods

In this method to find the binary number that is equivalent to a given decimal number is to determine the set of binary weights whose sum is equal to the decimal number.

An easy way to remember binary weights is that the lowest is 1, which is 2^0 and that by doubling any weight you get the next higher weight.

Example. *Find the equivalent binary number of the decimal number* $(25)_{10}$

Solution:

$$25 = 16 + 8 + 1$$
$$= 2^4 + 2^3 + 2^0$$

That is placing 1's in the appropriate weight positions, 2^4, 2^3 and 2^0 and 0's in the 2^2, and 2^1 position s determine the binary number for the decimal 25.Therefore,

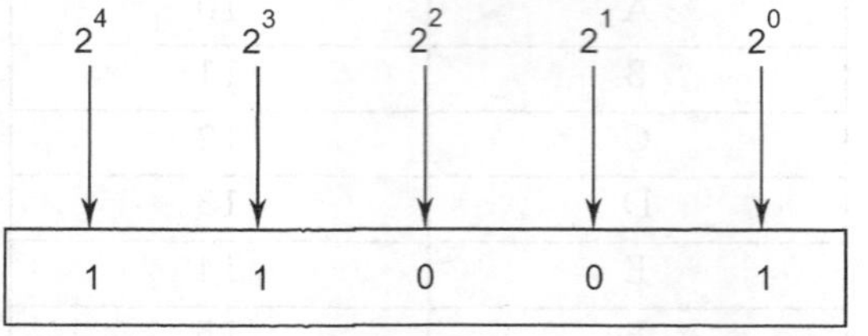

Example. *Find the equivalent binary number*

(*a*) $(58)_{10}$ (*b*) $(9)_{10}$ (*c*) $(13)_{10}$ (*d*) $(12)_{10}$

Solution:

(*a*)

$$58 = 32 + 16 + 8 + 2$$
$$= 2^5 + 2^4 + 2^3 + 2^1$$

Therefore binary equivalent of the decimal $(58)_{10}$ is:

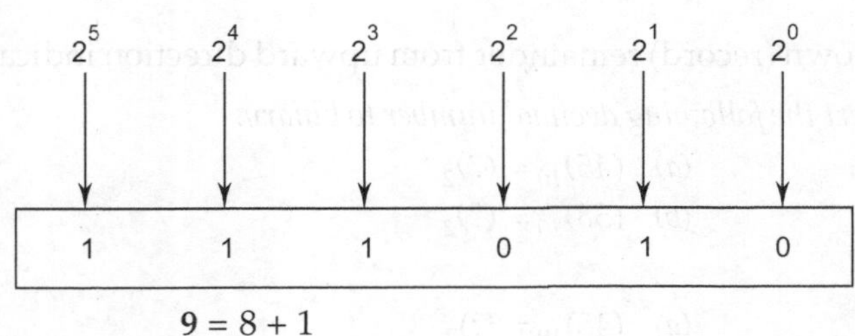

(*b*)

$$9 = 8 + 1$$
$$= 2^3 + 2^0$$

Therefore binary equivalent of the decimal $(9)_{10}$ is:

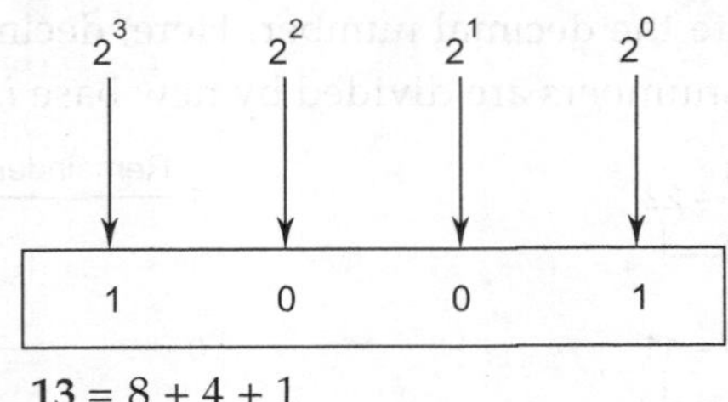

(*c*)

$$13 = 8 + 4 + 1$$
$$= 2^3 + 2^2 + 2^1$$

Therefore binary equivalent of the decimal $(13)_{10}$ is:

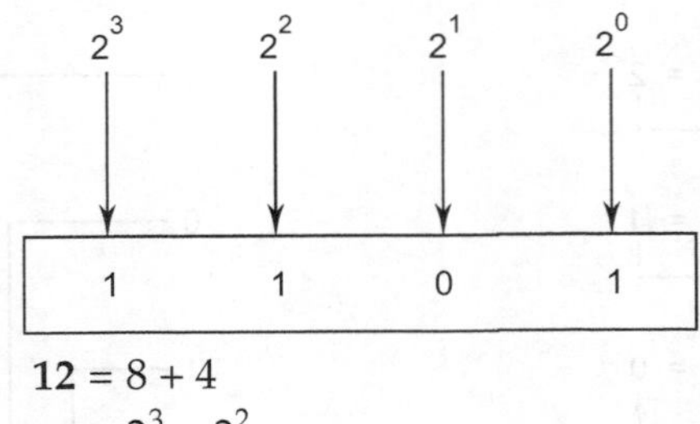

(*d*)

$$12 = 8 + 4$$
$$= 2^3 + 2^2$$

Therefore binary equivalent of the decimal $(12)_{10}$ is:

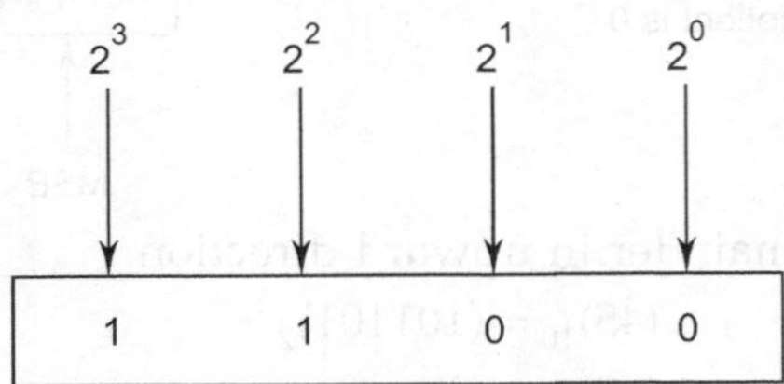

1.9.1.2 Repeated Division Method

This is the systematic method of converting whole numbers from decimal to binary is the repeated division by 2 processes.

The following rules are followed: to convert the decimal number to binary number

Rules to convert a decimal number to equivalent binary number

Rule 1: First of all select the decimal number.

Rule 2: These decimal numbers are divided by new base (*i.e.* 2) until the integer position is '0'.

Rule 3: Noted down (record) remainder from upward direction indicated by arrow mark.

Example. *Convert the following decimal number to binary.*

(a) $(45)_{10} = (?)_2$

(b) $(58)_{10} = (?)_2$

Solution:

(a) $(45)_{10} = (?)_2$

For getting the binary equivalent of the given decimal number here we apply **"Repeated Division Method"**. Therefore:

Rule 1: First of all write the decimal number, Here, decimal number is $(45)_{10}$

Rule 2: These decimal numbers are divided by new base *i.e.* 2 until the integer position is '0'

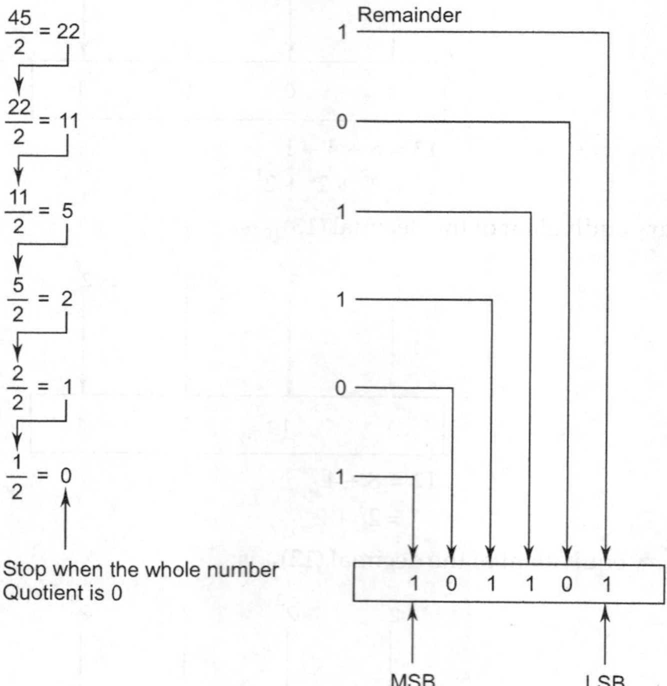

Rule 3: Note down remainder in upward direction

i.e. $(45)_{10} = (101101)_2$

(b) $(58)_{10} = (?)_2$

2	58	
2	29	0
2	14	1
2	7	0
2	3	1
2	1	1
	0	1

Record remainder in upward direction

Therefore binary equivalent of $(58)_{10}$ is $(111010)_2$

Example: *Convert the following decimal number to binary.*

(a) $(19)_{10} = (?)_2$

(b) $(69)_{10} = (?)_2$

(c) $(12)_{10} = (?)_2$

(d) $(50)_{10} = (?)_2$

Solution:

(a) $(19)_{10} = (?)_2$

2	19	
2	9	1
2	4	1
2	2	0
2	1	0
	0	1

Record remainder in upward direction

Therefore binary equivalent of $(19)_{10}$ is $(10011)_2$

(b) $(69)_{10} = (?)_2$

2	69	
2	34	1
2	17	0
2	8	1
2	4	0
2	2	0
2	1	0
	0	1

Record remainder in upward direction

This implies that $(69)_{10} = (1000101)_2$

(c) $(12)_{10} = (?)_2$

2	12	
2	6	0
2	3	0
2	1	1
	0	1

Record remainder in upward direction

This implies that $(12)_{10} = (1100)_2$

(d) $(50)_{10} = (?)_2$

2	50	
2	25	0
2	12	1
2	6	0
2	3	0
2	1	1
	0	1

Record remainder in upward direction

This implies that $(50)_{10} = (110010)_2$

1.9.2 Converting Decimal Fraction Number to Binary Number

Here we will discuss a procedure for fractional conversions. An easy way to remember fractional binary weights is the most significant weight is 0.5, which is 2^{-1}, and that by halving any weight ,we get the next lower weight ,thus a list of four fractional binary weight would be 0.5, 0.25, 0.125, 0.0625.

Here also two methods given for converting decimal fraction number to binary number:

1. Sum of weights
2. Repeated multiplication by 2.

1.9.2.1 Sum of Weight Method

The sum of weight method can be applied to fractional decimal number in the following manner as given below:

Example. Show the sum of weight method and find binary equivalent of the decimal number $(0.625)_{10}$

Solution:

$$0.625 = 0.5 + 0.125$$
$$= 2^{-1} + 2^{-3}$$

Therefore

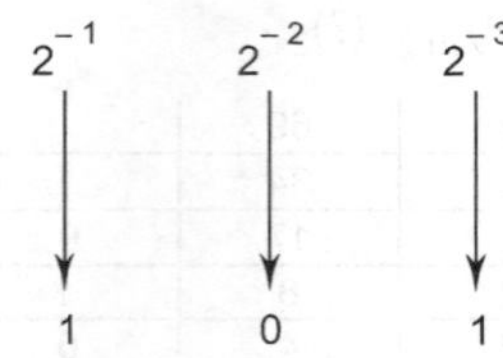

Hence, $(0.625)_{10} = (0.101)_2$

There is a 1 in the 2^{-1} position, a 0 in the 2^{-2} position, and a 1 in the 2^{-3} position.

1.9.2.2 Repeated Multiplication By 2 Method

As we see, decimal whole numbers can be converted to binary by repeated division by 2. Decimal fractions can be converted to binary by repeated multiplication by 2.

To convert the decimal fraction number to binary number, the following steps are applied:

Steps to convert decimal fraction number into binary number

Step 1: First of all select the decimal fractional number.

Step 2: These number are multiplied by 2 and carry binary number be noted down.

Step 3: If the decimal fraction becomes same or approximate nearly then stop implementation.

Step 4: Noted down binary numbers in downwards by arrow direction

Example: *Convert the following decimal numbers to binary:*

(a) $(0.3125)_{10} = (?)_2$

Solution:

Step 1: First of all select the decimal fraction number.

Here, given decimal fraction number is $(0.3125)_{10}$

Step 2: These numbers are multiplied by 2 and carry binary number be noted down.

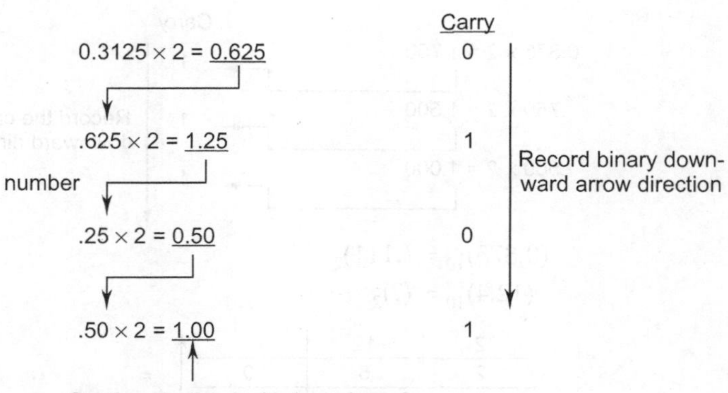

Thus, $(0.3125)_{10} = (.0101)_2$

Example: *Convert the following decimal number to binary number system.*

(a) $(45.4)_{10} = (?)_2$

(b) $(0.875)_{10} = (?)_2$

(c) $(12.4)_{10} = (?)_2$

Solution:

(a) $(45.4)_{10} = (?)_2$

(*a*) $(45.4)_{10} = (?)_2$

First of all we convert $(45)_{10} = (?)_2$

and then we will covert $(0.4)_{10} = (?)_2$

2	45	
2	22	1
2	11	0
2	5	1
2	2	1
2	1	0
	0	1

Record remainder in upward direction

i.e. $(45)_{10} = (101101)_2$

Now, find $(04)_{10} = (?)_2$

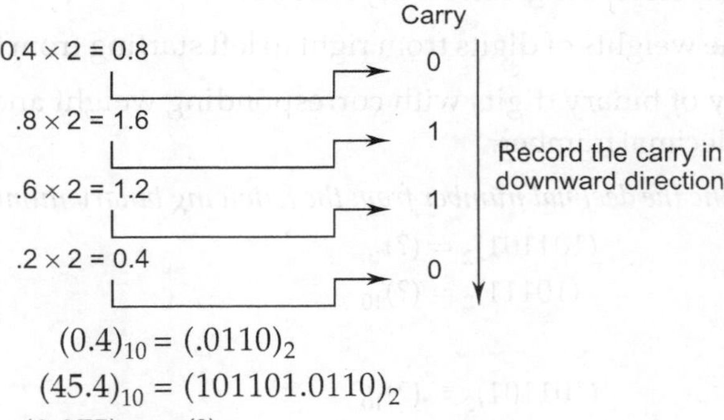

i.e. $(0.4)_{10} = (.0110)_2$

Hence, $(45.4)_{10} = (101101.0110)_2$

(*b*) $(0.875)_{10} = (?)_2$

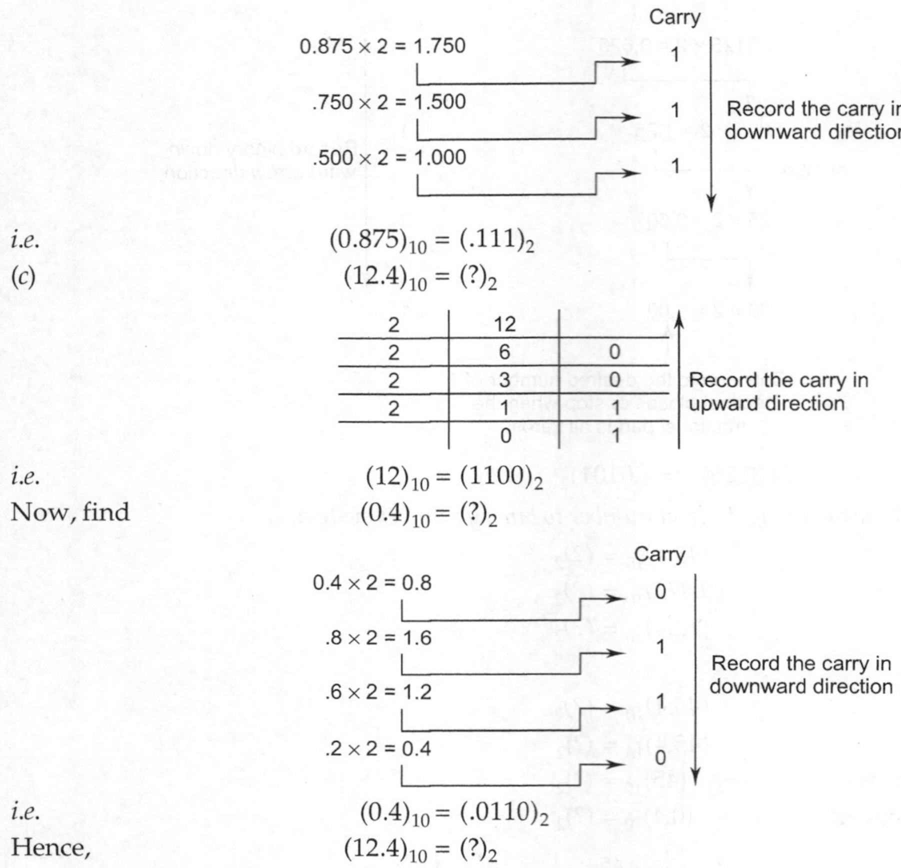

i.e. $(0.875)_{10} = (.111)_2$

(*c*) $(12.4)_{10} = (?)_2$

i.e. $(12)_{10} = (1100)_2$

Now, find $(0.4)_{10} = (?)_2$

i.e. $(0.4)_{10} = (.0110)_2$

Hence, $(12.4)_{10} = (?)_2$

1.9.3 Converting Binary Number To Decimal Number

Here we will show step-by-step procedure used for converting binary number to equivalent decimal number system.

The following given steps used for this conversion:

Steps used for the conversion of the binary number to decimal number

Step 1: First of all select the given binary number.

Step 2: Write the weights of digits from right to left starting from 0 to upward.

Step 3: Multiply of binary digits with corresponding weight and added it .This gives the required decimal number.

Example. *Determine the decimal number from the following binary number:*

(*a*) $(101101)_2 = (?)_{10}$

(*b*) $(10111)_2 = (?)_{10}$

Solution:

(*a*) $(101101)_2 = (?)_{10}$

Step 1: First of all select the given binary number
Here, binary number is $(101101)_2$

Step 2: Write the weights of digits from right to left starting from 0 to upward.

Binary Number:	1	0	1	1	0	1
Weight:	5	4	3	2	1	0

Step 3: Multiply of binary digit with corresponding weight and add it:

Binary Number:	1	0	1	1	0	1
Weight:	5	4	3	2	1	0

$$= 1 \times 2^5 + 0 \times 2^4 + 1 \times 2^3 + 1 \times 2^2 + 0 \times 2^1 + 1 \times 2^0$$
$$= 2^5 + 0 + 2^3 + 2^2 + 0 + 1$$
$$= 32 + 0 + 8 + 4 + 0 + 1$$
$$= 45$$

This implies that : $(101101)_2 = (45)_{10}$

(b) $(10111)_2 = (?)_{10}$

Here again we apply the same procedure as for above example which we will show below:

Binary Number:	1	0	1	1	1
Weight:	4	3	2	1	0

$$= 1 \times 2^4 + 0 \times 2^3 + 1 \times 2^2 + 1 \times 2^1 + 1 \times 2^0$$
$$= 16 + 0 + 4 + 2 + 1$$
$$= 23$$

Thus, $(10111)_2 = (23)_{10}$

1.9.4 Converting Binary Fractional Number to Decimal Number

The following given steps are used for such type of conversion:

Steps used to convert binary fractional number to decimal number

Step 1: Write the given binary number.

Step 2: Write the weight of the digits starting from left to right starting from '–1' and upward.

Step 3: Multiplying of binary digits with corresponding weight and added it. This gives us an equivalent decimal number.

Example. *Determine the decimal number from the following given binary number*

(a) $(.10101)_2 = (?)_{10}$

(b) $(.011)_2 = (?)_{10}$

(c) $s(1001.0101)_2 = (?)_{10}$

Solution:

(a) $(.10101)_2 = (?)_{10}$

Step 1: Write the given binary number
Here given binary number is $(.10101)_2$

Step 2: Write the weight of the digits starting from "left to right", starting from – 1 and upward.

Binary Number:	1	0	1	0	1
Weight:	– 1	– 2	– 3	– 4	– 5

Step 3: Multiplying of binary digit with corresponding weight and added it:

Binary Number:	1	0	1	0	1
Weight:	– 1	– 2	– 3	– 4	– 5

$= 1 \times 2^{-1} + 0 \times 2^{-2} + 1 \times 2^{-3} + 0 \times 2^{-4} + 1 \times 2^{-5}$

$= 0.5 \quad + 0 \quad + 0.125 \quad + 0 \quad + 0.03125$

$= (0.65625)_{10}$

(*b*) $(.011)_2 = (?)_{10}$

Binary Number:	0	1	1
Weight:	– 1	– 2	– 3

$= 0 \times 2^{-1} + 1 \times 2^{-2} + 1 \times 2^{-3}$

$= 0 \quad + .25 \quad + 0.125$

$= (.375)_{10}$

(*c*) $(1001.0101)_2 = (?)_{10}$

Here, we first find $(1001)_2 = (?)_{10}$

and then $(.0101)_2 = (?)_{10}$

Binary Number:	1	0	0	1
Weight:	3	2	1	0

$= 1 \times 2^3 + 0 \times 2^2 + 0 \times 2^1 + 1 \times 2^0$

$= 8 \quad + 0 \quad + 0 \quad + 1$

$= (9)_{10}$

Now find $(.0101)_2 = (?)_{10}$

Binary Number:	0	1	0	1
Weight:	– 1	– 2	– 3	– 4

$= 0 \times 2^{-1} + 1 \times 2^{-2} + 0 \times 2^{-3} + 1 \times 2^{-4}$

$= 0 + .25 + 0 + 0.0625$

$= (0.3125)_{10}$

This implies that the result will be:

$(1001.0101)_2 = (9.3125)_{10}$

1.9.5 Binary To Hexadecimal Conversion

Converting a binary number to hexadecimal is a very straight forward procedure. That is simply break the binary number into 4-bit groups, starting at the right most bit and replace each 4-bit group with the equivalent hexadecimal symbols.

Here, we will also give step-by-step procedure for finding hexadecimal numbers. The steps are:

Steps used to convert binary number to hexadecimal number

Step 1: Again, first of all write the give binary number.

Step 2: Apply partition of the binary number in to group of four bits each from right to left.

Step 3: Record the decimal equivalent of each group.

Step 4: Write A for 10, B for 11, C for 12, D for 13, E for 14 and F for 15.

Step 5: Combine these decimal equivalents and it gives the required hexadecimal numbers.

Example: *Find the hexadecimal equivalent for the binary number* $(111111000101101001)_2$

Solution:

Step 1: Write binary number

1 1 1 1 1 1 0 0 0 1 0 1 1 0 1 0 0 1

Step 2: Partition the given binary numbers in to group of four bits each from right to left.

0011 1111 0001 0110 1001

Step 3: Write down decimal equivalent of each group

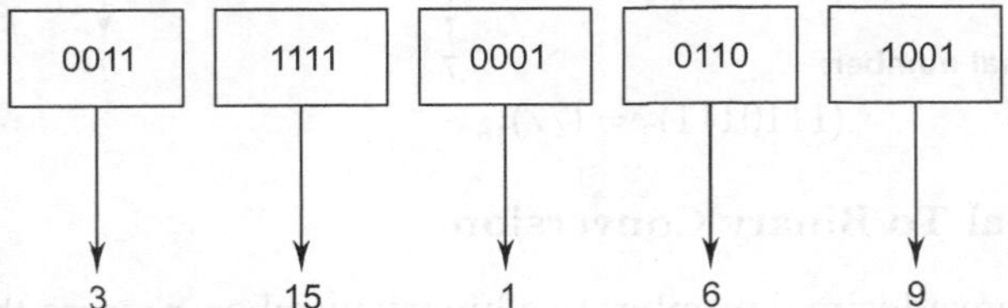

Step 4: Write F for 15

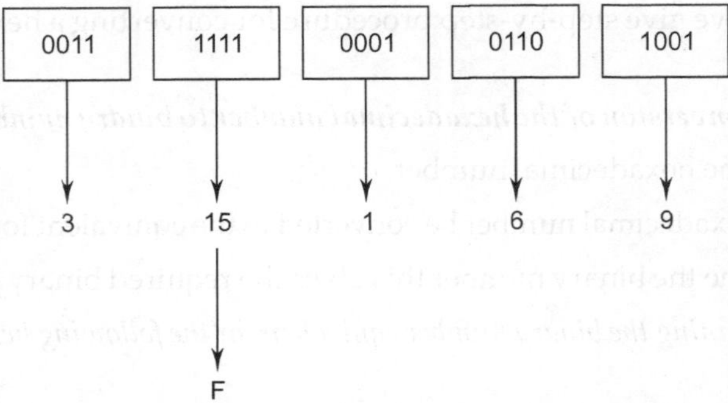

Step 5: Combine all together gives hexadecimal number *i.e.* $(3F169)_{16}$

Thus, $(111111000101101001)_2 = (3F169)_{16}$

Example: *Convert the following binary number to hexadecimal number system:*

(a) $(11011.01101101)_2 = (?)_{16}$

(b) $(1110111)_2 = (?)_{16}$

Solution:

(a) $(11011.01101101)_2 = (?)_{16}$

For the given example we first convert $(11011)_2$ into hexadecimal and then we will convert $(.01101101)_2$ in hexadecimal form.

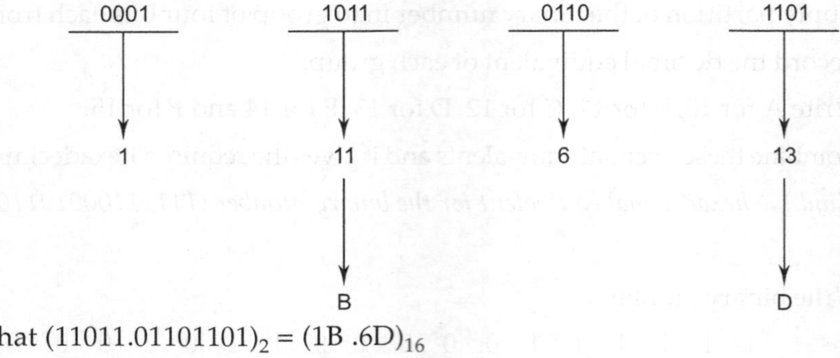

This implies that $(11011.01101101)_2 = (1B.6D)_{16}$

(*b*) $(1110111)_2 = (?)_{16}$

Binary number: 0111 0111

Decimal number: 7 7

i.e. $(1110111)_2 = (77)_{16}$

1.9.6 Hexadecimal To Binary Conversion

To convert from a hexadecimal number to a binary number, reverse the process and replace each hexadecimal symbol with the appropriate group of four bits binary number.

Now here again we give step-by-step procedure for converting a hexadecimal number to binary number.

Steps used for the conversion of the hexadecimal number to binary number

Step 1: Write the hexadecimal number.

Step 2: Each hexadecimal number be converted to the equivalent four bit binary number.

Step 3: Combine the binary number this gives the required binary number.

Example: *Determining the binary number equivalent for the following hexadecimal number* $(CF8E)_{16}$

Solution:

Step 1: Write the hexadecimal number

Here, the given hexadecimal number is $(CF8E)_{16}$

Step 2: Convert each hexadecimal number to its equivalent 4-bit binary number.

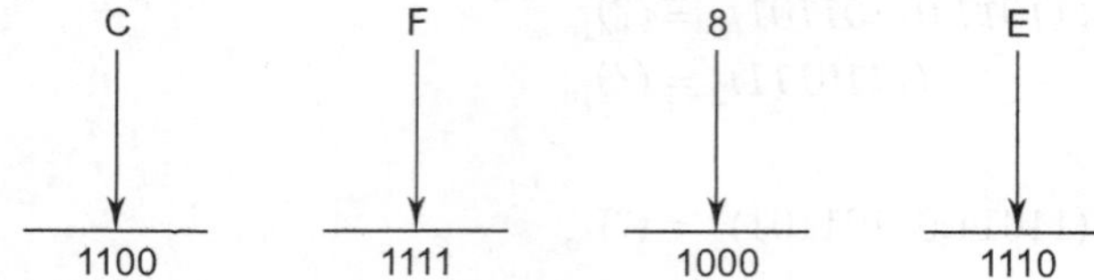

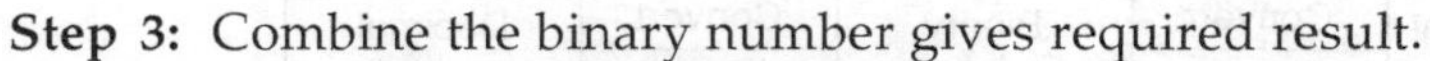

Step 3: Combine the binary number gives required result.

i.e. $(CF8E)_{16} = (1100111110001110)_2$

Example: Convert the following hexadecimal number to its equivalent binary number.

(*a*) $(2C6B.F2)_{16} = (?)_2$

(*b*) $(CA57)_{16} = (?)_2$

(*c*) $(307.DA)_{16} = (?)_2$

Solution:

(*a*) $(2C6B.F2)_{16} = (?)_2$

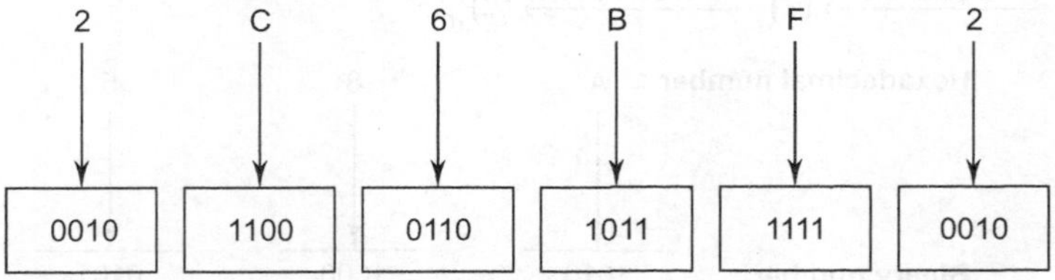

2	C	6	B	F	2
0010	1100	0110	1011	1111	0010

i.e. $(2C6B.F2)_{16} = (1011000101011111110010)_2$

(*b*) $(CA57)_{16} = (?)_2$

C	A	5	7
1100	1010	0101	0111

Hexadecimal number

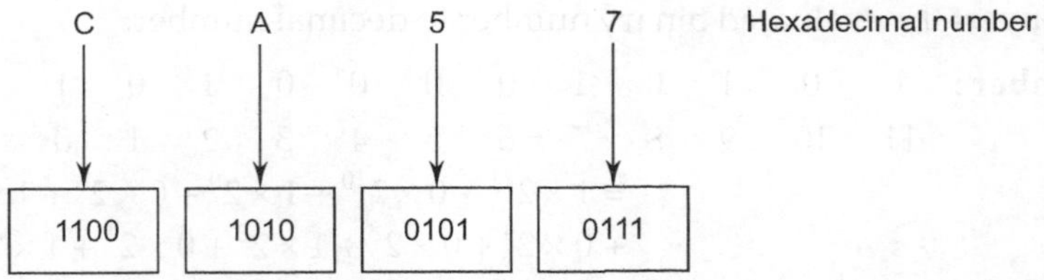

i.e. $(CA57)_{16} = (1100101001010111)_2$

(*c*) $(307.DA)_{16} = (?)_2$

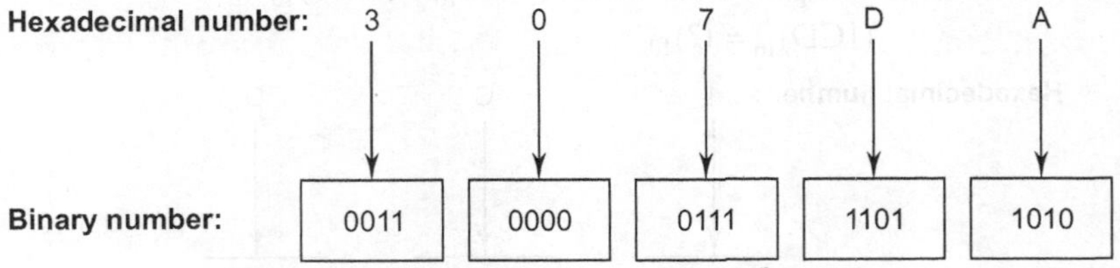

Hexadecimal number:	3	0	7	D	A
Binary number:	0011	0000	0111	1101	1010

i.e. $(307.DA)_{16} = (110000011111011010)_2$

1.9.7 Hexadecimal To Decimal Conversion

We have two approaches to convert hexadecimal number to decimal number.

Approach 1

In this approach to find the decimal equivalent of a hexadecimal number is to first convert the hexadecimal number to binary and then convert from binary to decimal.

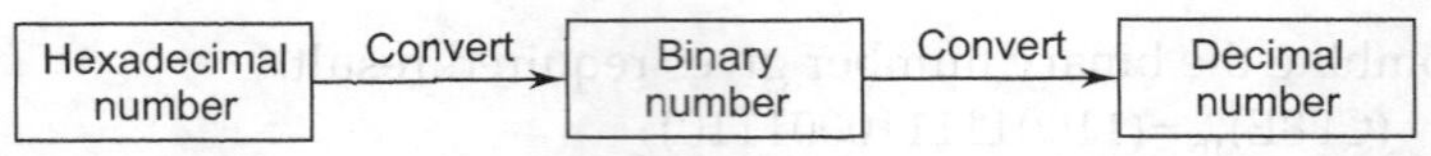

Fig. 1.8 *Conversion from hexadecimal number to decimal number*

Example: *Convert the following hexadecimal number to equivalent decimal number.*

(a) $(A85)_{16}$

(b) $(1CD)_{16}$

Solution:

(a) $(A85)_{16} \xrightarrow{\text{Convert}} (?)_2 \xrightarrow{\text{Convert}} (?)_{10}$

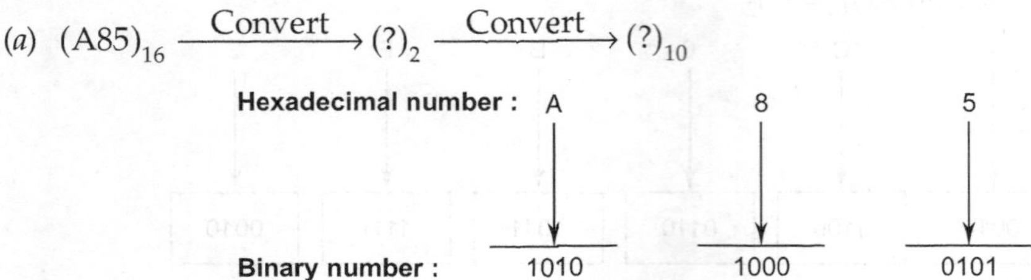

i.e. $(A85)_{16} \xrightarrow{\text{Convert}} (101010000101)_2 \xrightarrow{\text{Convert}} (?)_{10}$

Now, we convert the evaluated binary number to decimal number:

Binary number :	1	0	1	0	1	0	0	0	0	1	0	1
Weight :	11	10	9	8	7	6	5	4	3	2	1	0

$$= 1\times2^{11} + 0\times2^{10} + 1\times2^{9} + 0\times2^{8} + 1\times2^{7} + 0\times2^{6} + 0\times2^{5} + 0\times2^{4} + 0\times2^{3} + 1\times2^{2} + 0\times2^{1} + 1\times2^{0}$$

$$= 2048 + 512 + 128 + 4 + 1$$

$$= 2693$$

This shows that the required result *i.e.* $(A85)_{16} = (2693)_{10}$

(b) $(1CD)_{16} = (?)_{10}$

Hexadecimal number : 1 C D

Binary number : 1010 1100 1101

Now we assign weight for the binary numbers:

Binary number :	0	0	0	1	1	1	0	0	1	1	0	1
Weight :	11	10	9	8	7	6	5	4	3	2	1	0

$$= 0\times2^{11} + 0\times2^{10} + 0\times2^{9} + 1\times2^{8} + 1\times2^{7} + 1\times2^{6} + 0\times2^{5} + 0\times2^{4} + 1\times2^{3} + 1\times2^{2} + 0\times2^{1} + 1\times2^{0}$$

$$= 256 + 128 + 64 + 8 + 4 + 1$$

$$= (461)_{10}$$

Approach 2

In this approach to convert a hexadecimal number to its decimal equivalent is to multiply the decimal value of each hexadecimal digit by its weight and then take the sum of these products.

The weights of a hexadecimal number are increasing powers of 16 from right to left, for a 4-digit hexadecimal number weights are:

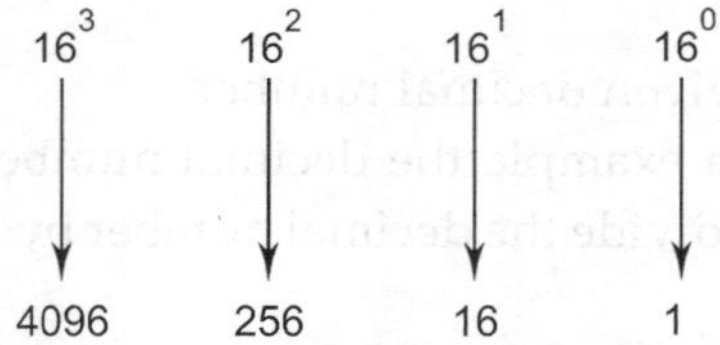

Example. *Convert the following hexadecimal numbers to decimal number:*

(a) *(B2F8)16*

(b) *(65A)16*

Solution:

(*a*) $(B2F8)_{16} = (?)_{10}$

Hexadecimal number :	B	2	F	8
Weight :	3	2	1	0

$$= (B \times 16^3) + (2 \times 16^2) + (F \times 16^1) + (8 \times 16^0)$$
$$= (B \times 1096) + (2 \times 256) + (F \times 16) + (8 \times 1)$$
$$= (11 \times 4096) + 512 + (15 \times 16) + 8$$
$$= 45056 + 512 + 240 + 8$$
$$= 45816$$

Thus, the result is given as:

$$(B2F8)_{16} = (45816)_{10}$$

(*b*) $(65A)_{16} = (?)_{10}$

Hexadecimal number :	6	5	A
Weight :	2	1	0

$$= (6 \times 16^2) + (5 \times 16^1) + (A \times 16^0)$$
$$= (6 \times 256) + (5 \times 16) + (10 \times 1)$$
$$= 1536 + 80 + 10$$
$$= 1626$$

Thus, the result is given as:

$$(65A)_{16} = (1626)_{10}$$

1.9.8 Decimal To Hexadecimal Conversion

In this section we will discuss the conversion of decimal number system to hexadecimal system.

To find the hexadecimal number from the equivalent decimal number we apply repeated division of a decimal number by 16 that will produce the equivalent hexadecimal number, which is formed by the remainders of the divisions.

Working Rules:

Step 1: First of all write down the decimal number

Step 2: Repeatedly divide the decimal number by 16 until when whole number quotient is zero.

Step 3: Record the remainder in upward direction.

Example: *Convert the decimal number 650 to hexadecimal equivalent number.*

Solution:

Step 1: Write down the given decimal number

Here in the given example the decimal number is $(650)_{10}$

Step 2: Now, repeatedly divide the decimal number by 16 until when whole number quotient is zero

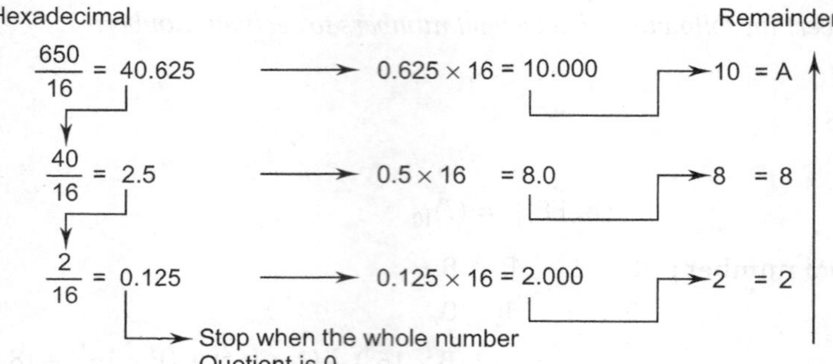

Step 3: Record remainder in upward direction. Hence required result will be:

$$(650)_{10} = (28A)_{16}$$

1.9.9 Octal to Decimal Conversion

In this section we will discuss how one can convert an octal number to decimal number. Since the octal number system has a base of eight, each successive digit position is an increasing power of eight, beginning in the right-most column with 8^0.

Working Rules: For the evaluations of an octal number in terms of it's accomplished by multiplying each digit by its weight and summing products

Example: *Convert the octal number to decimal number system* $(2374)_8$

Solution:

Octal number :	2	3	7	4
Weight :	3	2	1	0

$$= 2 \times 8^3 + 3 \times 8^2 + 7 \times 8^1 + 4 \times 8^0$$
$$= 2 \times 512 + 3 \times 64 + 7 \times 8 + 4 \times 1$$
$$= 1024 + 192 + 56 + 4$$
$$= (1276)_{10}$$

1.9.10 Decimal to Octal Conversion

A method of converting a decimal number to an octal number is the repeated division by-8 method, which is similar to the method used in the conversion of decimal numbers to binary or to hexadecimal.

Working Rules:

Step 1: Write down the given decimal number.

Step 2: Repeatedly divide the decimal number by new base i.e., 8 until whole number quotient is zero.

Step 3: Record the remainder by upward arrow i.e. first remainder generated the LSD

1.9.11 Octal to Binary Conversion

It is very easy to convert from octal number system to binary number system because each digit can be represented by a 3-bit binary number.

Working Rules:

Step 1: Write down the given octal number.

Step 2: All octal numbers are converted to three bits binary equivalents.

Step 3: Combine all the binary numbers and this gives the required result.

1.9.12 Binary to Octal Conversion

This is the reverse process of the octal conversion. The procedure is as follows: Start with the right -most group of three bits and moving from right to left, convert 3-bit group to the equivalent octal digit. If there are not three bits available for the left most group, add either one or two zeros to make a complete group. These leading zeros do not affect the value of binary number.

Working Rules:

Step 1: First of all write down the given binary number.

Step 2: Partition of the given binary number into group of three digits each starting from right to left.

Step 3: Write the decimal equivalent of each group.

Step 4: Combine these decimal equivalent (digit) this gives required result.

1.9.13 Octal to Hexadecimal Conversion

Octal to hexadecimal conversion is two-step processes which are given below:

Step 1: First of all convert octal number to equivalent binary number

Step 2: Then convert binary number to hexadecimal number

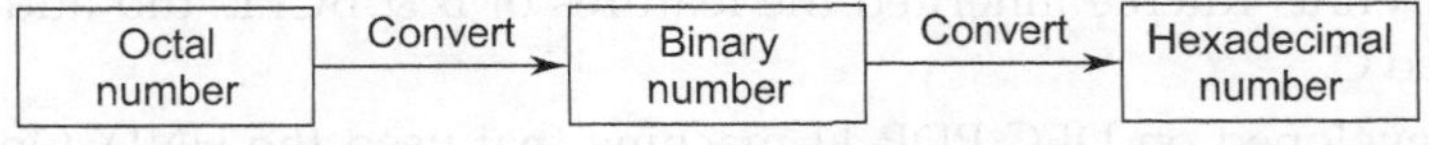

Fig. 1.9 *The conversion of octal number to hexadecimal number.*

2

INTRODUCTION TO 'C'-BASICS

2.1 C-OVERVIEW

C is a programming language developed at AT & T's bell laboratory of USA in 1972. It was designed and written by Dennis Ritchie. C is a general purpose programming language with lots of features. It is called middle level language because it reduces the gap between high-level language and low-level language and at the same time incorporating the best elements of high-level language with the control and functionality of assembly language. As a middle level language C allows the manipulation of bits and bytes & addresses the basic building block elements with which the computer functions. It provides a relatively good programming efficiency and relatively good machine efficiency.

C is a structured programming language which allows variety of programs in small modules. Modular programming reduces burden of debugging testing and maintenance. The user is required to think of a problem in terms of function/ modules. By combining different modules a complete program can be developed.

2.2 HISTORICAL DEVELOPMENT OF C

(*a*) In the 1960 Combined Programming Language (CPL) was developed at Cambridge University.

(*b*) Later on Basic Combined Programming Language (BCPL) was developed by Martin Richards at Cambridge University.

(*c*) A new language called B invented by Ken Thompson came into existence.

(*d*) In 1970 Dennis Ritchie inherited the features of B & BCPL, did add some new features & developed C.

(*e*) C was developed on DEC PDP-11 machine that used the UNIX Operating System.

(*f*) In 1978 it was first described in the book "The C Programming Language" by Dennis Ritchie and Brain Kernighan.

(*g*) The ANSI (American National Standard Institute) was finally adopted it in Dec 1989 with the first copy available in early 1990.

2.3 C-CHARACTER SET

A 'C' program is a collection of number of instructions written in a meaningful order. Further instructions are made up of keywords, variables, functions etc. which uses the C character set defined by C. It is a collection of various characters, digits and symbols which can be used in a C program.

It comprises following:

S. No.	*Elements of C character Set*
1	Upper case letters: A to Z
2	Lower case letters: a to z
3	Digits : 0 to 9
4	Symbols(see below)

Table 2.1 ***C Character Set***

Symbol	*Name*	*Symbol*	*Name*
~	Tilde	>	Greater than
<	Less than	&	Ampersand
|	Or/pipe	#	Hash
>=	Greater than equal	<=	Less than equal
= =	Equal	=	Assignment
!=	Not equal	^	Caret
{	Left brace	}	Right brace
(	Left parenthesis	)	Right parenthesis
[	Left square bracket	]	Right square bracket
/	Forward slash	\	Backward slash
:	Colon	;	Semicolon
+	Plus	-	Minus
*	Multiply	/	Division
%	Mod	,	Comma
'	Single quote	"	Double quote
>>	Right shift	<<	Left shift
.	Period	_	Underscore

2.4 'C' TOKENS

The smallest individual unit in a C program is called C Token. C defines six types of tokens:

1. Keywords
2. Identifiers
3. Constants
4. String Constants
5. Special Symbols
6. Operators

1. Keywords

Keywords are those words that meaning has already been known to the compiler. That is meaning of each keyword is fixed. You can simply use the keyword for its intended meaning .You cannot change the meaning of the keywords. Also you cannot use keywords as name for variables, function, arrays etc. All keywords are written in small case letters.

There are **32** keywords in C. Following figure lists all keywords available in C.

Table 2.2 *C keyword*

auto	Break	Case	char	const
Continue	Default	Do	double	else
Enum	Extern	Float	for	goto
if	Int	Long	register	return
Short	Signed	Sizeof	static	struct
Switch	Typedef	Union	unsigned	void
Volatile	While			

2. Identifier

Identifiers are names given to various program elements like variables, array, functions, structures etc.

Rules For Writing Identifiers

(*a*) First letter must be an alphabet or underscore (_).
(*b*) From second character onwards any combination of digits, alphabets or underscore is allowed.
(*c*) Only digits, alphabets, underscore are allowed. No other symbol is allowed.
(*d*) Keywords cannot be used as an identifier.
(*e*) For ANSI (American National Standard Institute) C maximum length of identifier is 32 but many compiler support more than 32.

EXAMPLES OF VALID AND INVALID IDENTIFIERS (ON THE BASIS OF ABOVE RULES)

VALID:

order_no	name	_err	_123
xyz	radius	a23	int_ rate

INVALID:

order-no	12name e rr	int	
x $	s name	akash + 45	123

3. Constants

Constants in C refer to fixed values that do not change during the execution of a program. There are various types of constants in C. They are classified into the following categories as given below:

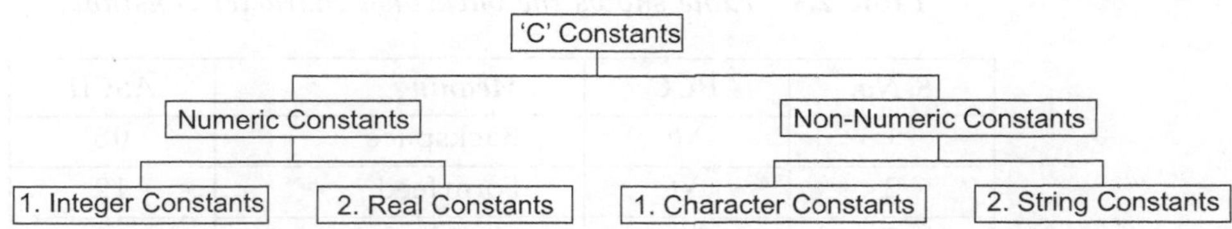

Fig. 2.1 *C constants.*

(*i*) **INTEGER CONSTANTS :** They are of three types:

(*a*) **Decimal Constants:** They are sequence of digits from 0 to 9 without fractional part. It may be negative, positive or zero.

Example: 12, 455, – 546, 0 etc.

(*b*) **Octal Constant:** They have sequence of numbers from 0 to 7 and first digit must be 0

Example: 034, 0, 0564, 0123 etc.

(*c*) **Hex Constant:** They have sequence of digits from 0 to 9 and A to F (represents 10 to 15). They start with 0x or 0X.

Example: 0x34, 0xab3, oX3E etc.

(*ii*) **REAL CONSTANT :** They are the number with fractional part. They also known as floating point constants.

Example: 34.56, 0.67, 1.23 etc.

Real constants can also be represented in exponential or scientific notation which consists of two parts. For example the number 212.345 can be represented as **2.12345e + 2** where ***e* + 2** means **10 to the power 2.** Here the portion before the *e* that is **2.12345** is known as **mantissa** and **+2** is the **exponent.** Exponent is always an integer number which can be written either in lower case or upper case.

(*iii*) **SINGLE CHARACTER CONSTANTS :** They are enclosed in single quote. They consist of single character or digit.

Example: '4', 'A', '*n*' etc.

Character constants have integer value known as ASCII (American Standard Code for Information Interchange) values. For example ASCII value for A is 65.

(*iv*) **STRING CONSTANTS :** They are sequence of characters, digits or any symbol enclosed in double quote.

Example: "hello", "23twenty three", "& ^ ABC". "2.456" etc.

(*v*) **BACKSLASH CONSTANTS :** C defines several backslash constants which are used for special purpose. They are called so because each backslash constant starts with backslash (\\). They are represented with 2 characters whose general form is **\\char** but treated as single character. They are also called escape **sequence.** Given below the list of backslash character (escape sequence) character constants:

Table 2.3 *Table shows the backslash character constant*

S. No.	*BCC*	*Meaning*	*ASCII*
1	\b	Backspace	08
2	\f	Form feed	12
3	\n	New line	10
4	\r	Carriage return	13
5	\"	Double quote	34
6	\'	Single quote	39
7	\?	Question mark	63
8	\a	Alert	07
9	\t	Horizontal tab	09
10	\v	Vertical tab	11
11	\0	Null	00

(*vi*) **SPECIAL SYMBOLS:** They are also known as separator and they are square brackets [], braces { }, parenthesis ( ) etc. They [ ] used in array and known as subscript operator, the symbol ( ) is known as function symbols.

2.4.1 Variables

A variable is a named location in memory that is used to hold a value that can be modified in the program by the instruction. All variables must be declared before they can be used. They must be declared in the beginning of the function or block (except the global variables). The general form of variable declaration is:

data type variable [list];

Here list denotes more than one variable separated by commas;

Example:

int *a;*

float *b, c;*

char *p, q;*

Here ***a*** is a variable of type int, ***b*** and ***c*** are variable of type float, and *p, q* are variables of type char, int, float and char are data types used in C. The rule for writing variables are same as for writing identifiers as a variables is nothing but an identifier.

2.4.2 Counting Tokens

1. **int** *a, b, c;*
   (*i*) int is a keyword. (1)
   (*ii*) *a, b* and *c* variables. (3)
   (*iii*) comma (,) is operator. (2)

(*iv*) ; is delimiter. (1)

So, total number of tokens (1 + 3 + 2 + 1= 7)

2. $c = a + b - 10;$

(*i*) a, b and c variables.(3)

(*ii*) +, =, – are operators (3)

(*iii*) ; is delimiter (1)

(*iv*) 10 is integer constant. (1)

So, total number of tokens (3 + 3 + 1 + 1 = 8)

2.5 DATA TYPES

C defines several data types which can be used under different programming situations like an int data type can be used to represent whole numbers as an age of a person, roll number etc. or float data type can be used to represent salary of a person, interest rate etc. Following is the list of all data types available in C along with their range, and number of bytes they require in memory.

Table 2.4 ***Data Type and Their Range***

S. No.	*Data Type*	*Size(in byte)*	*Range*
1	int or short	2	– 32768 to 32767
2	Unsigned int	2	0 to 65535
3	Long int	4	– 2147483648 to 2147483647
4	Float	4	3.4e-38 to 3.4e+38
5	Char	1	– 128to127
6	Unsigned char	1	0 to 255
7	Unsigned long	4	0 to 4294967295
8	Double	8	1.7e-308 to 1.7e+308
9	Long double	10	3.4e-4932 to 3.4e+4932

For the calculation of range of data types we have a fixed formula:

- For a signed data types if it takes n bits in memory then the range of values a particular variable of this data type can take is

$$-2^{(n-1)} \text{ to } 2^{(n-1)} - 1$$

Example. for $n = 16$(int) the range is

$$-2^{15} \text{ to } 2^{15} - 1$$

And for char data type $n = 8$ the range is

$$-2^{7} \text{ to } 2^{7} - 1$$

- For an unsigned data types if it takes n bits in memory then the range of values a particular variables of this data type can take is

$$0 \text{ to } 2^{n} - 1$$

- Apart from these inbuilt data types C also provides derived data types which are array, enum, struct and union.
- They are called so as they help in deriving new data types or user defined data types.
- C also has one special data type which is void and has its own importance in various programming situations.

2.6 YOUR FIRST 'C' PROGRAM

Lot's of theory! Now let's put all the theory into action by writing few programs which will clarify your concepts studied so far.

So let gets on with our first program which simply prints **Hello C** on to the screen

```
/* Prog 2.1 Printing Hello C on the screen */
#include <stdio.h>
  main( )
{
  printf("Hello C");
}
Output:
  Hello C
```

EXPLANATION: Whatever written inside **/*and */** is treated as comment, and is ignored by the C compiler. You may also comment multiple lines as we will see in the coming programs. We use comments to write which program we are going to make or to write some remarks about instruction for better understanding.

#include is the preprocessor directive.**stdio.h** is the standard input output header file (due to **.h** extension) which is to be included in every C program. There may be space between **#include** and **<stdio.h>.** Next line is the function **main( ) due to symbol ( )** which is known as function symbol. This function must be present in every C file you make because execution of your C program starts from this **main ( ).** { is the opening brace for main function and } is the closing brace. All statements, instructions are written inside the main function. **printf( )** is the inbuilt function (pre built in C compiler) which parts whatever written inside " " on to the screen, so the output. C is **case-sensitive** programming language, so what ever you use that is in-built in C has to be in lower case.

The declaration of **printf** function is given in the header file **stdio.h**. Every statement in C program has to end with **;(semicolon).**

2.6.1 Compilation and Execution

- Open a new file and type your program in it.
- Save your file by pressing **F2** or by opening File menu then choosing write to in Turbo C or save in Turbo C++ with **.c** extension say **first.c**
- Compiled by pressing **Alt+F9** combination and then execute using **Ctrl+F9** combination.
- If you want you can directly press **Ctrl+F9** key combination.
- Provide there are no errors you can view the output by pressing **Alt+F5** key combination.

Compilation Process

- Compilation is the process in which your c source program is checked for any syntactical or syntax errors like missing semicolon, comma, double quotes etc.
- If everything is ok then the compiler generates a **.obj file** which contains object code with the same name.
- In the above case the compiler generated file would be **first.obj.**
- It generates one more file with the same name **first.bak** which stands for backup file.
- Actually backup file is a copy of the C source file.
- The purpose of this file is that if by any case your source file (first.c) is deleted or lost you may get the whole program from this file.
- The compiler generated **file.obj** is passed to the linker who does the job of linking the necessary files to your program and generates an .exe version of your program.
- In short we can say that when you press **Ctrl+F9,3 files** are generated:

  (*a*) **.obj file** (*b*) **.bak file and** (*c*) **.exe file**

2.7 STRUCTURE OF A 'C' PROGRAM

The general structure of any C program is as given below. It simply states that a standard C program may look like according to various sections presents in the structure.

Documentation
Header files
Symbolic Constants
Global variables, functions
main( ) {.........}
Global function definitions

Fig. 2.2 *Basic structure of a C program.*

The first section Documentation is optional and is used to put comments for the program usually the program heading as we have given.

In second section we include various header files required by our C program. Symbolic constants and global variable, functions are defined after that if required.

The main ( ) function must be present in every C program. It contains all the statements which are to be executed. All statements are put inside the braces and terminate with the semicolon.

A full fledge C program is given below. Don't worry if you do not understand extra stuff at this point. This is just to give you an idea of structure of a C program.

```
/*Documentation*/
/*Prog 2.2 Demo program for C structure, does not serve any purpose
except demonstration */
#include<stdio.h> /* header file inclusion*/
#include<conio.h>
```

```
int x; float y; char z; /* global variables*/
int sum (int, int); /* Global function*/
void show ( ); /* global function*/
main ( ) /* main function*/
{
     printf("Demo program \n");
     void demo  ( ); /* local function in main*/
     x= 10;
     y= 34.56;
     z= 'p';
     x= sum(10,20);
     show ();
}
/*global function definitions*/
int sum(int x, int y)
{
     return x+y;
}
     void show  ( )
{
     printf("in show \n");
}
```

2.8 PROGRAMMING EXAMPLE PART-1

```
/* PROG 2.3 A C program with two printf */
#include<stdio.h>
main ()
{
   printf("Hello C");
   printf("Second Program");
}
```

Output:

```
              Hello C Second Program
```

EXPLANATION: We have used two **printf** statements in the program. By default the output is produced on the same line. If we want output to be placed on the next line we can do so as this is done in the next program.

```
/* Prog 2.4 Demo of new line character ver1*/
#include<stdio.h>
main ( )
{
```

```
    printf("Hello C \n");
    printf("Second Program");
 }
```

Output:

```
        Hello C
        Second Program
```

EXPLANATION: After printing **Hello C** on the first line, line is changed by the inclusion of new line character **\n.** It can also placed in the beginning of second **printf** statement as **printf ("\n Second Program"). Note** the "\" is known as backslash and "/" is known as forward slash. The usual mistake committed by beginners is to write "/" instead of "\"

```
/* Prog 2.5 Demo of new line character ver 2*/
#include<stdio.h>
   main ( )
   {
        printf ("Hello C");
        printf("\n");
        printf ("Second Program");
   }
```

Output:

```
            Hello C
            Second Program
```

EXPLANATION: The \n can be put in a single printf. Rest is similar to previous program.

```
/* Prog 2.6 Demo of tab*/
   #include<stdio.h>
      main ( )
      {
           printf("Hello C \t");
           printf("" Second Program ");
```

Output:

```
                        Hello C                     Second Program
```

EXPLANATION: The program prints **Hello C,** leaves a tab and prints **Second Program** due to \t (horizontal tab) on the same line. The tab is equal to 7 or 8 spaces. The net effect of writing \t is to leave 7 or 8 space at once. The tab is system defined and can be changed. Similar to \n the \t can be placed in the beginning of second printf as printf("\t Second Program").

```
/* Prog 2.7 program to print student detail */
 #include<stdio.h>
   main( )
   {
        printf("Name =\t Hari Mohan Pandey\n");
        printf("Year = \t First Year\n");
```

```
        printf("Discipline = \t Comp. Engg.");
    }
```

Output:

```
            Name = Hari Mohan Pandey
            Year = First Year
            Discipline = Comp. Engg.
```

EXPLANATION: The program is self-explanatory.

```
/* Prog 2.8 Demo of carriage return \r ver 1*/
#include<stdio.h>
 main( )
 {
     printf("First Line \n");
     printf("Second Line \r");
 }
```

Output:

```
            First Line
```

EXPLANATION: Due to \r backslash constant second printf statement will not return *i.e.* "First Line".

```
/* Prog 2.9 Demo of carriage return \r ver 2*/
#include<stdio.h>
 main( )
 {
     printf("First Line\n");
     printf("Second Line\r");
     printf("Third Line");
 }
```

Output:

```
            First Line
            Third Line
```

EXPLANATION: Due to \r (carriage return) second line won't be printed as explained in the previous program but this does not affect the remaining printf statements.

```
/* Prog 2.10 Demo of carriage return \r ver 3*/
    #include<stdio.h>
      main ( )
      {
          printf ("First Line\n");
          printf ("Second Line\r\n");
          printf ("Third Line");
      }
```

Output:

```
First Line
Second Line
Third Line
```

EXPLANATION: The backslash character constants \r\n translates into \n, so the output.

```
/* Prog 2.11 Demo of Beep */
#include<stdio.h>
 main( )
 {
   pritnf ("This will give you a beep sound \a");
 }
```

Output:

```
A beep sound
```

EXPLANATION: The backslash character constant \a produces a beep out from PC speaker. Get your ear closer to the PC speaker you will hear a beep.

Suppose you want to print **"Hey! I'm learning C".** You just can't write inside printf as **printf(""Hey! I'm learning C""). To achieves** this see the program below.

```
/*Prog 2.12 Demo of \" */
#include<stdio.h>
main( )
{
     printf("\" Hey ! I'm learning C");
 }
```

Output:

```
"Hey! I'm learning C
```

EXPLANATION: To print a double quote "you have to use \". On the similar basis you can use \' to print single quote, \\ to print single back slash using printf.

```
/*Prog 2.13 Demo of \b*/
#include<stdio.h>
   main( )
   {
      printf("Using Backspace \b\b");
   }
```

Output:

```
Using Backspace
```

EXPLANATION: Note in the output cursor will be at *c* in the word *b* **Backspace.** This is due to two **\b constants.**

Earlier all the program have explained to you the way of writing C program as well as how to use character constants in your program. Now I introduce variables in C programs.

2.9 USING VARIABLE IN C PROGRAM

A variable is named location in memory. Before using a variable it must be declared. The various data type discussed above can be used to declare different types of variables depending upon requirement. All variables must be declared in the beginning of the program.

```
/* Prog 2.14 Program to print an int variable */
#include<stdio.h>
main ( )
 {
        int a;
        printf("Using variables\n");
        printf("value of a= %d", a);
 }
Output:
                Using variables
                Value of a = -1243
```

EXPLANATION: Through the statement int a we are declaring ***a*** a variable of type int, this is called variable declaration. A variable declaration allocates a fixed amount of storage during compilation. In this case 2bytes (in Turbo C for int data type) are allocated for variable ***a*** during compilation as we have not assigned any value to the variable ***a,*** compiler assigns some garbage value which may be anything. On my PC it is as shown in the output. On your PC it may be some other value. %d is called format specifier and used to print integer values. Here the value of a will be printed.

List of Format Specifier for All the Data Types

Table 2.5 ***Data types & Corresponding Format Specifier.***

S.No	*Data Type*	*Format Specifier*
1.	Int	%d or %i
2.	Float	%g or %f
3	Char	%c
4	Unsigned int	%u
5	Long int	%ld
6	Unsigned long int	%lu
7	Double	%lf
8	Long double	%Lf

```
/* Prog 2.15 printing of float value */
#include<stdio.h>
 main( )
{
      float a;
      a = 5.5;
      printf("Value of a = %f\n",a);
}
```

Output:

```
      Value of a = 5.500000
```

EXPLANATION: Here we have printed a real value using %f format specifier. Real values are represented by using **float** data types and value is known as floating point data. They represent a precision of 6 digits after decimal point (single precision). If you use double data type same %**f is** used for printing the value but they provide a precision of 14 digits after decimal point. **(Double precision).** These precision are default. If you want more precision you can use field width for printing the floating point data or any type of data.

```
/* Prog 2.16 input int type value from user */
   #include<stdio.h>
   #include<conio.h>
      void main( )
      {
            int x;
            clrscr( );
            printf("Enter an integer value");
            scanf("%d",&x );
            printf("You entered %d\n ",x);
            getch( );
      }
```

Output:

```
            Enter an integer value
               21
            You entered 21.
```

EXPALNATION: The scanf function is used to take the value from keyboard. The syntax of this function:

scanf("format specifier", address of variables);

Here %d denotes we want to take an integer value from keyboard and denotes address of a variable *x* at which this value will be stored. The & is known as ampersand or address operator.

Two new functions have been introduced in this program. **clrscr ()** function clear the screen and **getch( )** function gets a character from screen without echoing it on to the screen. The overall effect of these functions is that when our program executes it first clear the screen and after taking input from the user it immediately prints the output. The declaration of these two functions is given in the header file **<conio.h>**. If you don't write **getch ( )** you will have press **Alt + F5** to see the output.

/*Prog 2.17 Use of wrong format specifier ver1*/

```
#include<stdio.h>
#include<conio.h>
 void main()
{
    float f;
   clrscr();
   printf("Enter a float value\n");
   scanf("%d",&f);
   printf("f = %f \n", f);
   getch();
}
```

Output:

```
Enter a float value
   4.7
    f= 0.000000
```

EXPLANATION: If you have by mistake written %d or %i for scanning **float** value you will not get any error but input value won't be scanned and you will get a zero stored in the variable. So always use correct format specifier in the **scanf.**

/*Prog 2.18 Use of Wrong format specifier ver2*/

```
#include<stdio.h>
#include<conio.h>
  void main ()
  {
     int a;
     clrscr();
     printf("Enter an int value \n");
     scanf("%f", &a);
     printf("a= %d\n",a);
     getch();
  }
```

Output:

```
Enter an int value
   scanf: floating point formats not linked
   abnormal program termination
```

EXPLANATION: This is due to %f in **scanf** instead of %d or %i .The explanation of the error can not be stated here. The program even does not wait for taking an input.

2.10 INTRODUCTION TO QUALIFIERS

Qualifiers qualify the meaning of data types. Unsigned, signed, short and long are the 4 qualifiers available in C. The manner in which they are used as follows:

signed int *x*, *y*, *b*;

unsigned int *p*, *q*;

long int num;

short int *n*;

long int is a data type as mentioned earlier and short int is same as signed int or simply int on most of the C compilers. Signed qualifier is used where we want to work with both positive and negative values. Unsigned qualifier can be used where we want with only positive values. They can be used only with char and interger data types. The available range increases in positive when we use unsigned say for example range of signed char or simply char –128 to 127 where as for unsigned char it is 0 to 255. Same holds for int/ or long int. Apart from these two important keywords are also used as qualifiers constant and volatile. The constant qualifier is used to declare a variable as a constant for example const int $x = 10$; declare a constant *x* of type int with constant value. For more about constant see in the next chapter.

2.11 PROGRAMMING EXAMPLES PART-2

From program 13 to17 we have initialized those variables by providing values in the program itself. What if we want user to provide values through keyboard. The next few programs illustrate how to take input of various types from user.

```
/*Prog 2.19 input int type value from user*/
#include<stdio.h>
#include<conio.h>
 void main()
 {
      int x;
      clrscr();
      printf("Enter an interger value\n");
      scanf("%d",&x);
      printf("You entered %d\n",x);
      getch();
 }
```

Output:

```
 Enter an interger value
345
You entered 345
```

EXPLANATION: The scanf function is used to take input from keyboard. The syntax of this function is given as:

scanf("format specifier", address of variable);

Here in the program %**d** denotes we want to take an integer values from the keyboard and **&x** denotes address of variable *x* at which this value will be stored. The **&** is known as **ampersand or address operator.**

Two new functions **clrscr ()** function is clear the screen and **getch ()** function gets a character from screen without echoing it on to the screen. The overall effect of these functions is that when our program executes it first clear the screen and after taking input from user it immediately prints the output. The declaration of these two functions is given in the header file **<conio.h>.** If don't write **getch()** you will have to press **Alt + F5** to see the output.

```
/*Prog 2.20 Input more than one int type value ver1*/
#include<stdio.h>
#include<conio.h>
 void main()
 {
    int x,y;
    clrscr();
    printf("Enter integer value for x\n");
    scanf("%d",&x);
    printf("Enter integer value for y\n");
    scanf("%d",&y);
    printf("x=%d\ty=%d\n",x,y);
    getch();
 }
```

Output:

```
Enter integer value for x
12
Enter integer value for y
34
x=12 y=34
```

EXPLANATION: There is nothing new in this program except that we have taken two integer values by one for ***x* and *y*** respectively. The next program shows how to take integer value with a single **scanf.**

```
/*Prog 2.21 Input more than one int type value ver 2*/
#include<stdio.h>
#include<conio.h>
 void main()
 {
    int x,y;
```

```
    clrscr();
    printf("Enter integer values for x and y\n");
    scanf("%d%d",&x,&y);
    printf("x=%d\tY=%d",x,y);
    getch();
  }
```

Output:

Enter integer values for x and y

12 45

x=12   Y=45

EXPLANATION: It's simple to take two integer values using a single scanf. Don't forget to put comma between &*x* and &*y*. There may be space between two %**d's** . While inputting two numbers, if mistaken or intentionally you enter Spaces, Tab or Enter key then all these are ignored by the **scanf.**

/*Prog 2.22 Reading mix data types*/

```
#include<stdio.h>
#include<conio.h>
 void main()
 {
    int x;
    char ch;
    float f;
    clrscr();
    printf("Enter an int, a char and a float value\n");
    scanf("%d%c%f",&x,&ch,&f);
    printf("x=%d\tch=%c\tf=%f",x,ch,f);
    getch();
 }
```

Output:

```
Enter an int, a char and a float value
12 e 34.56
x=12     ch=e    fa=34.560000
```

EXPLANATION: The program is simple and easy to understand.

/*Prog 2.23 Conversion of decimal to octal and hex */

```
#include<stdio.h>
#include<conio.h>
 void main()
 {
    int a;
    clrscr();
```

```
    printf("Enter an int value\n");
    scanf("%d",&a);
    printf("Octal representation is %o\n",a);
    printf("Hex representation is %x\n",a);
    getch();
 }
```

Output:

```
Enter an int value
23
Octal representation is 27
Hex representation is 17
```

EXPLANATION: In the program we have taken an integer value from the user and have displayed its octal and hex equivalent using %o and %x format specifier.

/*Prog 2.24 printing ASCII value of char input*/

```
#include<stdio.h>
#include<conio.h>
 void main()
 {
    char a;
    clrscr();
    printf("Enter a character value \n");
    scanf("%c",&a);
    printf("ASCII value is %d\n",a);
    getch();
 }
```

Output:

```
Enter a character value
f
ASCII value is 102
```

EXPLANATION: The program is self-explanatory

POINTS TO PONDER

In this section you have learned the following points.

- Some header files should be included at the beginning of your C program.
- Header files, such as **stdio.h** and **stdlib.h,** contain the declarations for functions used in your C program; for example, the **printf ()** and **exit ()** functions.
- Comments in your C programs are needed to help you document your programs. You can put comments anywhere you like in your programs.
- In **ANSI C,** a comment starts with the opening comment mark, /*, and ends with the closing comment mark, */.

- Every C program should have one but only one **main ()** function. The program execution starts and ends with the **main ()** function.
- The sequence of a carriage return and a line feed is carried out when the computer sees the newline character, **\n.**
- The return statement can be used to return a value to indicate to the operating system whether an error has occurred. The **exit ()** function terminates a program; the argument to the function indicates the error status, too.
- The void data type can be used to modify the type of a return value for a function. Applying void to **main ()** tells the operating system that the **main ()** function does not return any value after termination.
- Compiling and linking are consecutive steps that have to be finished before an executable file is produced.
- Everybody, including you, makes mistakes in programming. Debugging is a very important step in your program design and coding
- Different types of C compilers available today are: **Quick C, Turbo C, Microsoft C, Borland C, Lattice C, Power C, Objective C etc.**
- C is a **structured/ Modular/ Procedural** programming language which follows **top-down programming** approach.
- A declaration of variable does not allocate memory space, whereas definition does allocate memory space.
- C is free form language i.e. the following code will work:

```
(a) main(){ printf("Hello\n");}
(b) main(){clrscr(),printf("hello\n")getch();}
```

- A header file is a file, which contains declaration of various built-in functions. It also contains declaration of various constant, macros etc which a programmer can use in its program. It's not that header file are built-in, you can create your own header files and use them as per your requirement. Some of the common header files are **stdio.h, conio.h, process.h, math.h, dos.h, limits.h, string.h, ctype.h, io.h etc.**
- Features of main function:
  - (*i*) Declared by C compiler, defined by user.
  - (*ii*) Only one main function in a C program
  - (*iii*) Default return type int is assumed.
  - (*iv*) Take arguments.
  - (*v*) First function to be called when program executed.
- The C keywords reserved in the C language
- The **char** data type and the %**c** format specifier
- The **int** data type and the %**d** format specifier
- The **float** data type and the %**f** format specifier
- Floating-point numbers can be suffixed **with f or F** to specify float. A floating-point number without suffix is double by default.
- The possible ranges of the char, int, and float data types
- Scientific notation and the %**e and** %E format specifiers

QUESTIONS AND ANSWERS

Q1. *Why do you need to put comments into your programs?*

Ans: Comments help us document what a program, or a special portion of a program, does. Especially when a program becomes very complex, we need to write comments to mark different parts in the program.

Q2. *Why is the main () function needed in your program?*

Ans: The execution of a C program starts and ends with the **main ()** function. Without the **main ()** function, the computer does not know where to start to run a program.

Q3. *What does the #include directive do?*

Ans: The **#include** directive is used to include header files that contain the declarations to the functions used in your C program. In other words, the **#include** directive tells the C preprocessor to look into directories and find the specified header file.

Q4. *Why do you need a linker?*

Ans: After compiling, some function code may still be missing in the object file of a program. A linker must then be used to link the object file to the C standard library or other user-generated libraries and include the missing function code so that an executable file can be created.

EXERCISES

A. Answer the following questions:

1. What are the salient features of C?
2. What is the purpose of a variable and a constant in a programming language?
3. What is the basic difference between primary data types and secondary data types?
4. Why the C language is called middle level language?
5. What is the difference between an interpreter and a compiler?
6. Write the rule of writing C program?
7. Elaborate the different sections of C program?
8. What is the role of curly braces ({}) in C program?
9. What is token? List the different types of C tokens?
10. What is a variable in C? How are they different from keywords?
11. Why do we use qualifiers? What is their significance?
12. What are the identifiers in any programming language? Discuss rules for writing identifiers.
13. Is **main** a keyword? Explain.
14. List any five keyword with there uses.
15. What do you mean by type conversion? Why is it necessary?
16. Write about space requirement for variables of different data type.

B. Fill in the blanks:

1. A variable declaration fixes ____________ and ____________ of the variables.

2. A ____________ may precede a data type in a data type declaration.
3. To print a float number without decimal part we use ____________ in printf.
4. An octal constant is preceded by ____________.
5. Variables are also known as ____________.
6. A hex constant is preceded by ____________.
7. The total number of files produced after compilation & execution (including source file) is ____________.
8. Nested comments are ____________ in C.

C. Match the following:

1. int data type	(*a*) 2 bytes
2. Type of token in C	(*b*) 6
3. Constant	(*c*) 10 bytes
4. Long double data type	(*d*) precedes a data type.
5. Qualifier	(*e*) backslash constant
6. Escape sequence	(*f*) value does not changes.

D. Write true or false against each sentence:

1. The data type **char** is an integral data type.
2. C was developed by **Ken Thompson.**
3. The constant **0234** is equal to **234**
4. The first character for and identifier must be underscore.
5. **ANSI C** supports **33** keywords.
6. **C** was developed at **Microsoft Corporation.**
7. %g and %f both are used to represent **float** numbers.
8. **tab (\t)** is not a white space character.
9. C allows **long float** data type.

3

INTRODUCTION TO OPERATORS & EXPRESSIONS IN 'C'

This chapter lets acquaint with the basic fundamental operators available in C. It starts with the introduction and tells you what is the basic operator and expression in C. It then gives you an idea of unary and binary operators in C. All the primitive operators like **Arithmetic, Logical, Relational, Assignment, Increment/decrement, and Bitwise** are explained in full detail with lots of programming examples. It also illustrates ternary operator? : available in C. One special operator which is also act as function *i.e.* **sizeof** operator is also discussed. The comma operator is also given special mention. The Chapter also gives precedence table of all the operators in C with their associatively. Approximately 15 fully solved programs are given which makes your concepts better about the precedence of operators.

After the operator and expressions, all different types of methods which are used to declare constants are discussed. Use of **macro,** keyword **const** and **enum** have been explained in detail. Macro and enum are used to declare symbolic constant and const is a keyword. The usage of these is clarified with the help of examples.

Meaning of types conversion in C is explained with code snippets. Both the conversion *i.e.* **implicit type** and **explicit type** conversion is explained. A brief introduction of **typedef** is also given at the end which is used to create new data type in C.

3.1 INTRODUCTION

For performing different kinds of operations, various types of operators are required. An operator denotes an operation to be performed on some data that generates some value. For example plus operator (+) 2 and 3 generates 5. Here 2 and 3 are called operands.

'C' is very rich in built-in operators. There are four main classes of operators:

(*a*) Arithmetic
(*b*) Relational
(*c*) Logical
(*d*) Bitwise

Apart from these four classes there are some other operators. The whole list of operators provided by C is given in the table below:

Table 3.1 *Operators in 'C'.*

S. No.	*Operator*	*Symbol Representation*
1.	Arithmetic	+, -, *, /,%
2.	Logical	&&, | |, !
3	Relational	>, <, >=, <=, = =, !=
4	Assignment	=
5	Increment	+ +
6	Decrement	--
7	Comma	,
8	Conditional	? :
9	Bitwise	&, |, ^, !,>>, <<
10	Special operator	sizeof

3.1.1 Binary Operators

All the operators which require two operands to operate on are known as binary operators. For example as shown in the above table all the arithmetic, relational, logical (except! (NOT) operator), comma, assignment, bitwise (except ~ operator) operators etc. are binary operators.

EXAMPLE: 2+4, 34 > 45, x = 23, 2 & 5

3.1.2 Unary Operators

Unary operators are those operators which require only one operands to operate on are known as unary operators. For example as shown in which in the above table increment/ decrement! (NOT), ~ (1's complement operator), **sizeof** etc are unary operators. C also provides unary plus and unary minus i.e. +20 and -34.Here + and - are known as unary plus and unary minus operators.

EXAMPLE: +4, -3, ++x, sizeof (int), sizeof(2.0).

Note: ?:operator is known as ternary operator as it requires three operands to operate on. One before?, Second after ? and third after:

3.2 EXPRESSIONS

Operator together with operands constitutes an expression or a valid combination of constants, variables, and operators forms an expression is usually recognized by the type of operator used with in the expression. Depending upon that you may have integer expression, floating point expression, relational expression etc. You may have different types of operators in an expression which is a mixed mode expression. See the table given below for few examples.

Table 3.2 *Types of Expressions.*

S. No.	*Expression*	*Type of Expression*
1.	2+3*4/6-7	Integer Arithmetic
2.	2.3*4.7/6.0	Real Arithmetic
3.	a>b!=c	Relational
4.	X && 10 || y	Logical
5.	2>3+x && y	Mixed

3.3 ARITHMETIC OPERATORS

As given in Table 3.3 there are mainly five arithmetic operators in C. They are +, -, *, / and % which are used for addition, subtraction, multiplication, division and remainder respectively. See the table given below:

Table 3.3 *Arithmetic Operators.*

S. No.	*Operator*	*Meaning/used for*
1.	+	Addition
2.	–	Subtraction
3.	/	Division
4.	*	Multiplication
5.	%	Remainder

The remainder operator can be used only with integers. For all other operators if one of the operand is **float** and second one is **int** then result will be in **float.**

Let's write some programs which illustrate use of these operators:

```
/* Prog 3.1 Sum of two numbers*/
   #include<stdio.h>
   #include<conio.h>
   void main( )
   {
      float a,b,c;
      clrscr();
      printf("Enter two numbers\n");
      scanf("%f%f",&a,&b);
      c=a+b;
      printf("Sum of %f and %f is %f\n", a,b,c);
      getch();
 }
```

```
Output:
Enter the float numbers
3.4     5.7
Sum of 3.400000 and 5.700000 is 9.100000
```

EXPLANATION: The program is very simple. It accepts two **float** numbers from the user and generates the sum which is stored in variable ***c***. We can directly write the sum without using third variable as:

printf("Sum of %f and %f is %f\n", a,b,a+b);

As clear from the output of the program that precision from the **float** data type i.e. numbers of digits after decimal point is 6?

```
/* Prog 3.2 Sub and Mul of two float numbers ver1*/
#include<stdio.h>
#include<conio.h>
 main()
 {
      float a,b,c,d;
      clrscr();
      printf("Enter the two numbers\n");
      scanf("%f%f", &a,&b);
      c= a-b;
      d=a*b;
      printf("Sub of %f and %f is %f\n",a,b,c);
      printf("Mul of %f and %f is %f\n",a,b,d);
      getch();
 }
Output:
Enter the float numbers
 3.4  2.3
Sub of 3.400000 and 2.300000 is 1.100000
Mul of 3.400000 and 2.300000 is 7.820000
```

EXPLANATION: The * (asterisk) symbol is used for multiplication of two numbers. Rest is self-explanatory.

```
/* Prog 3.3: Sub and Mul of two float numbers ver2*/
 #include<stdio.h>
 #include<conio.h>
    void main()
    {
       float a,b;
       clrscr();
```

```
    printf("Enter the two numbers\n");
    scanf("%f%f",&a,&b);
    printf("Sub of %f and %f is %f\n",a-b);
    printf("Mul of %f and %f is %f \n", a*b);
    getch();
  }
```

Output:

```
Enter the float numbers
3.4 2.3
Sub of 3.400000 and 2.300000 is 1.100000
Mul of 3.400000 and 2.300000 is 7.820000
```

EXPLANATION: If you do need multiplication and subtraction of ***a*** and ***b*** later in the program no need to use *c* and *d* variables unnecessary as this was done in the previous program.

/* Prog 3.4: Division of two int numbers */

```
  #include<stdio.h>
  #include<conio.h>
    void main( )
    {
       int a,b,c;
       clrscr();
       printf("Enter two integer numbers\n");
       scanf("%d%d", &a,&b);
       c=a/b;
       printf("Division of %d and %d is %d\n",a/b);
       getch();
    }
```

Output:

```
Enter two integer number
6  3
Division of 6 and 3 is 2
```

EXPLANATION: The operator "/" called forward slash is used for division operation. The division of two integer number always yields an integer. If any of the number is **float** then result will be a **float** value.

/* Prog 3.5: Division of two float numbers*/

```
 #include<stdio.h>
 #include<conio.h>
   void main()
   {
      float a,b, c;
```

```
    clrscr();
    printf("Enter two numbers\n");
    scanf("%f%f", &a,&b);
    c=a/b;
    printf("Division of %f and %f is %f\n",c);
    getch();
  }
```

```
Output:
Enter two float numbers
13 5
Division of 13.000000 and 5.000000 is 2.600000
```

EXPLANATION: As explained in the previous program division of two **float** numbers will be a float value?

```
/* Prog 3.6: Division of an int with float constant*/
   #include<stdio.h>
   #include<conio.h>
     void main( )
     {
        int a;
        clrscr();
        printf("Enter an integer number \n");
        scanf("%d",&a);
        printf("Division of %d by %f is %f\n",a,3.0,a/3.0);
        getch();
     }
```

```
   Output:
   Enter an integer number
   13
   Division of 13 by 3.000000 is 2.666666
```

EXPLANATION: If any of the operand is **float** the output will be a float value. Division by zero is not permitted. If you do so you will get the following error:

Floating point error: Divide by 0
Abnormal program termination

The error can be avoided by checking first whether denominator is zero or not through **if** condition which we will see in the next Chapter.

```
/* Prog 3.7: Demo of mod operator % ver 1*/
   #include<stdio.h>
   #include<conio.h>
     void main()
     {
```

```
        int a,b,r,q;
        clrscr();
        printf("Enter two integer numbers\n");
        scanf("%d%d",&a,&b);
        q=a/b;
        r=a%b;
        printf("a=%d\tb=%d\n",a,b);
        printf("quotient = %d\t remainder = %d \n",q,r);
        getch();
    }
```

Output:

```
Enter two integer numbers
15 4
a= 15 b= 4
q= 3 r = 3
```

EXPLANATION: The percentage symbol"%" is used for modulus of a number. **a/b** produces quotient and **a%b** where % is called remainder operator produces remainder when **a** is divided by **b**. The mathematical behind remainder operator is:

a % b = a - (a / b) *b **(where a/b is integer division)**

% operator works only with integer operands. Never use **float** operands. C does not allow float operand with % operator.

```
/* Prog 3.8: Demo of mod operator 5 ver 2 */
#include<stdio.h>
#include<conio.h>
 void main()
 {
    clrscr() ;
    printf("%d/%d=%d\t%d%%%d=%d\n",17,5,17/5,17,5,17%5);
    printf("%d/%d=%d\t%d%%%d=%d\n",-17,5,-17/5,-17,5,-7%5);
    printf("%d/%d=%d\t%d%%%d=%d\n",17,-5,17/-5,17,-5,17%-5);
    printf("%d/%d=%d\t%d%%%d=%d\n",-17,-5,-17/-5,-17,-5,-17%- 5);
    getch();
}
```

Output:

```
        17/5 = 3        17%5= 2
        -17/5 = -3      -17%5= -2
        17/-5 = -3      17%-5 = 2
        -17/-5= 3       -17%-5 = -2
```

EXPLANATION: In order to print % in the printf use % twice. Using % operator if the numerator is -ve answer will be negative. This can be verified by the formula given in the previous program for **– 17 and 5.**

$$
\begin{aligned}
-17 \% 5 &= -17 - (-17/5) * 5 \\
&= -17 - (-3) *5 \\
&= -17 + 15 \\
&= -2
\end{aligned}
$$

3.4 CONDITIONAL & RELATIONAL OPERATORS

Table 3.4 *Relational Operators.*

S. No.	*Operator*	*Meaning/used for*
1.	>	Greater than
2.	<	Less then
3.	>=	Greater than equal to
4.	<=	Less then equal to
5.	= =	Equal to
6.	!=	Not equal to

The two symbol? : together are called ternary or conditional operator. Before? condition is specified with the help of relational operators which may be any one operator as given in the table above. If the condition specified before? is true any expression or statement after ? is executed. If condition is false then statement or expression after : (colon) is evaluated. The general syntax is:

(condition)? True part : false part;

All relational operators yield Boolean values i.e. true or false. A true value is represented by 1and false value by 0. In expression any non-zero value is terminated as true value.

See programs for more explanation.

```
/* Prog 3.9 Demo of ? : and relational operator == ver1*/
#include<stdio.h>
#include<conio.h>
   void main()
   {
       int a= 0;
       clrscr();
       a==0?printf("a is zero\n");:printf("a is not zero\n");
       getch();
   }
```

Output:

```
                 a is zero
```

EXPLANATION: ? : operator is known as conditional operator (also called as ternary operator) works as follows:

The condition which is to be checked (here *a* = = 0) written before?. On success of condition the action which is to be performed written after ? In this case the statement printf **("*a* is zero*n*").** On failure of condition the action which is to be taken written after: In this case the statement **printf("*a* is not zero*n*").** In the condition it is being checked whether value of ***a*** is equal to **0** or not. The operator = = is called equality operator. It checks both the operands on either side of it are equal or not. If equal then condition is true else it is false. Try changing value of ***a*** and you will get different output.

NOTE: Conditional operator always works with relational operators.

```
/*Prog 3.10: Demo of? : and relational operator ver 2*/
#include<stdio.h>
#include<conio.h>
 void main( )
 {
    int a= 5, b=6,x;
    clrscr( );
    x=(a==b);
    x?printf("Both are equal\n"):printf("Both are not equal");
    getch( );
 }
Output:
             Both are not equal
```

EXAPLANATION: As the expression **a = = b** gives false, **0** is stored in *x*. If it were true **1** would be stored in *x*. Before? value is zero due to **0** in *x* which means false so the output.

```
/* Prog 3.11 : Demo of relational operators*/
   #include<stdio.h>
   #include<conio.h>
     void main( )
   {
        int a=5,b=6,c,d,e,f,g;
        clrscr( );
        c=a>b;
        d=a<b;
        e=(4!=3);
        f=(8>=17);
        g= (123<=123);
        printf("value of c=%d\n",c);
        printf("value of d=%d\n",d);
        printf("value of e=%d\n",e);
```

```
    printf("value of g=%d\n",g);
    getch( );
}
```

Output:

```
        value of c=0
        value of d=1
        value of e=1
        value of f=0
        value of g=1
```

EXPLANATION: If the condition is true value returned is **1** else **0**, so the output. For truth a value of **1** is assumed, for falsify a value of **0** is assumed by C.

/*Prog 3.12: Max of two numbers*/

```
#include<stdio.h>
#include<conio.h>
 void main( )
 {
     int a,b,c;
     clrscr( );
     printf("Enter the two integer numbers\n");
     scanf("%d%d", &a,&b);
     c=a>b?a:b;
     printf("max of %d and %d is %d \n",a,b,c);
     getch( );
 }
```

Output:

```
        Enter the two integer numbers
        34   56
         max of 34 and 56 is 56
```

EXPLANATION: If **a** is greater than **b** then **a** is assigned to **c** else **b** is assigned to **b.** In any case maximum of two is stored in **c** which is printed by the **printf.** Condition of equality of two numbers is not checked in the program which is shown in the modified program below.

/* Prog 3.13: Max of two numbers ver2 */

```
#include<stdio.h>
#include<conio.h>
 main()
 {
   int a,b;
   clrscr();
   printf("Enter two integer numbers\n");
```

```
   scanf("%d%d",&a,&b);
   (a==b)?printf("%d is equal to %d",a,b):(a>b)
   ?printf("%d is max\n",a):printf("%dis max\n",b);
 getch();
 }
```

Output:

```
          (first run)
          Enter two integer numbers
          34   34
          34 is equal to 34
          (second run)
          Enter two integer numbers
          34   35
          35 is max
```

EXPLANATION: Observe carefully the above program. Nesting of ternary operator (one inside another) is done to achieve the goal. If the first condition fails, then in the colon(:) part we check whether **a > b**. If this is true then statement after? (after a>b) executes i.e. In the failure part of the ternary operator we have one more ternary operator. This is known as nesting of ternary operators.

```
/* Prog 3.14 To check whether a number is +ve ,-ve or zero */
#include<stdio.h>
#include<conio.h>
 void main()
 {
      int a;
      clrscr();
      printf("Enter an integer number\n");
      scanf("%d",&a);
      (a==0)?printf("number is zero"):(a>0)
      ?printf("number is +ve"):printf("number is -ve");
      getch();
 }
```

Output:

```
            (First run)
            Enter an integer number
            0
            number is zero
            (second run)
            Enter an integer number
            -45
            number is -ve
```

EXPLANATION: The program is self-explanatory.

```
/* Prog 3.15: Max of three numbers */
#include<stdio.h>
#include<conio.h>
void main
{
    int a,b,c,d,max;
    clrscr();
    printf("Enter the three integer numbers\n");
    scanf("%d%d%d",&a,&b,&c);
    d=a>b?a:b;
    max=c>d?c:d;
    printf("max of %d,%d and %d is %d\n", a,b,c, max);
    getch();
}
```

Output:

```
Enter the three integer numbers
23    45      67
 Max of 23, 45 and 67 is 67
```

EXPLANATION: The solution of finding maximum of three numbers ***a, b, c*** is reduced to finding maximum of two numbers. First max of ***a*** and ***b*** is found out (which is ***d*** in this case), then max of ***d*** and ***c*** is found out, which results in max of ***a, b, c.***

The above program can be minimized by nesting of ternary operators.

```
/* Prog 3.16: Max of three numbers version 2*/
#include<stdio.h>
#include<conio.h>
    void main( )
    {
        int a,b,c,max;
        clrscr( );
        printf("Enter the three integer numbers\n");
        scanf("%d%d%d",&a,&b,&c);
        max=(a>b?(a>c?a:c): (b>c? b:c));
        printf("max of %d,%d and %d is %d \n",a,b,c,max);
        getch( );
    }
```

Output:

```
Enter the three integer numbers
23      45          67
max of 23, 45 and 67 is 67
```

EXPLANATION: We explain the program as:

max = (a>b?(a>c? a:c): (b>c?b:c))

A1 A2

Here we assume two names for the expressions A1 and A2 as shown above. In the nested condition when *a* > *b* is true **A1** executes and **A2** is skipped. This means that *a* is greater then *b* so next we will have to check whether *a* > *c*. This is what **A1** represents. If *a* > *c* maximum is *a* else maximum is *c*, which is assigned to max.

If *a* > *b* fails it means *b* is greater than *a* , then **A1** is skipped and **A2** executes. Falsity of *a* > *b* means *b* is greater then or equal to *a* so next have to check whether *b* > *c* this is what **A2** represents. In **A2** if *b* > *c* then maximum is *c* which is assigned to max.

```
/*Prog 3.17: max of 4 numbers*/
#include<stdio.h>
#include<conio.h>
   void main()
   {
      int a,b,c,d,m;
      clrscr( );
      printf("Enter the four integer numbers\n");
      scanf("%d%d%d%d",&a,&b,&c,&d);
      m=(a>b?(a>c?(a>d?a:d):(c>d?c:d)):(b>c?(b>d?b:d):
         (c>d?c:d));
      printf("Max of %d,%d,%d and %d is %d\n",a,b,c,d,max);
      getch();
   }
Output:
         Enter the four integer numbers
         23     43    56    6
         Max of 23, 43, 56 and 6 is 56
```

EXPLANATION: Observe the logic by pondering over it. It is not difficult to understand. If you have got the previous program then it will be easy for you to understand this one too. To assist some help we can write the statement as:

m=(a>b?(a>c?(a>d?a:d):(c>d?c:d)) : (b>c?(b>d?b:d):(c>d?c:d));

← A1 →← A2 →← A3 →← A4 →

If *a* > *b* is true **A1** executes else **A3** executes. In **A3** if *b* > *c* is true **A4** executes. In **A1** if **a > c** is true its true part that is **(*a* > *d*? *a*: *d*)** executes else **A2** executes. On the same basis try yourself max of 5 numbers using ternary operator.

3.5 LOGICAL OPERATORS

Logical operators are used to check logical relation between two expressions. Depending upon the truth or falsehood of the expression they are assigned value1 **(true)** and **0(false).** The expressions may be variables, constants, functions etc. See the table given below:

Table 3.5 *Logical Operators.*

S. No.	Symbol	Meaning
1.	&&	AND
2.	||	OR
3.	!	NOT

The **&&** and | | are binary operators. For **&&** to return true value both of its operand must yield true value. For | | to yield true value at least one of the operand yield true value. The **NOT (!)** operator is unary operator. It negates its operand i.e. if operand is true it convert it into false and vice-versa.

3.5.1 Logical and (&&)

The operator works with two operands which may be any expression, variable, constant or function. It checks both of its operand returns true value or not. If they it returns true value (*i.e.* a decimal 1). If either of its operand is false, false value is returned (*i.e* a decimal 0).

Table 3.6 *Truth table of Logical AND (&&)*

Operand1	Operand 2	Returned value
False	False	False
False	True	False
True	False	False
True	True	True

```
/* Prog 3.18: Demo of Logical Operator &&(AND) ver 1*/
#include<stdio.h>
#include<conio.h>
 void main()
{
    int res, a=10, b= 20;
    clrscr();
    res=(a>=10 && b = = 20);
    printf("Returned value in res=%d\n",res);
    getch();
}
```

Output:-

```
        resturned value is res= 1
```

EXPLANATION: The && is called **AND** operator. On both side of this operator condition is specified. If both the conditions are true the returned value is true is **1** else false value is returned that is **0**. In the above program both the conditions in the expression are true so **res** contains 1 as result.

```
/* Prog 3.19: Demo of Logical operator && (AND) ver 2*/
#include<stdio.h>
#include<conio.h>
 void main()
 {
    int res,a=0,b=2;
    clrscr();
    res=(a!=0 && b<=2);
    printf("Returned value in res = %d\n", res);
    getch();
 }
```

Output:

```
        Returned value in res= 0
```

EXPLANATION: In the expression the condition before **&&** is false and after **&&** it is true so overall value of the expression is false so a 0 is assigned to **res**.

3.5.2 Logical or (||)

The operator works with two operands which may be any expression, variable, constant or function. It checks any of its operand returns true value or not. If they it returns true value i.e. a decimal 1.If both of its operands are false, a false value is returned *i.e.* a decimal 0.

Table 3.7 *Truth table of OR.*

Operand1	*Operand 2*	*Returned value*
False	False	False
False	True	True
True	False	True
True	True	True

```
/*Prog 3.20: Demo of Logical Operator */
#include<stdio.h>
#include<conio.h>
   void main()
   {
     int res,a = 100,b=120;
     clrscr();
```

```
      res=(a>=100 || b<0)
      printf("Returned value in res =%d \n",res);
      getch();
   }
```

Output:

returned value is res =1

EXPLANATION: The || is called **OR operator.** On both side of this operator condition is specified. If any of the condition is true the returned value that is **1** else **0**. In the above program first condition in the expression is **true** but second is false so **res** contains **1** as result.

3.5.3 Logical Not (!)

The operator convert a **true** value into false and vice-versa. Again the operand may be any expression, constant, variable or function.

Table 3.8 *Truth Table of Not.*

Operand	Return Value
False	True
True	False

```
/* Prog 3.21: Demo of Logical Operator! (NOT) ver 1*/
#include<stdio.h>
#include<conio.h>
    void main()
     {
        int res, a=1;
        clrscr();
        res = !a;
        printf("Returned value in res=%d\n",res);
        getch();
     }
```

Output:

Returned value in res=0

EXPLANATION: The ! Is called **NOT** or **negation operator.** It is an **unary operator** meaning only one operand is required to operate on it. If operand's value is nonzero it is converted into false value, *i.e.* 0 and vice-versa. Similarly, if a true condition is specified it will be turned into false and vice-versa. Try changing value of a to zero, returned value in **res** will be **1.**

```
/* Prog 3.22: Demo of Logical Operators (NOT ! operator) ver2*/
# include<stdio.h>
#include<conio.h>
  void main()
```

```
{
  int res;
  clrscr();
  res= !(10>=5 && -4<=1);
  printf("Returned value in res=%d\n", res);
  getch();
}
```

Output:

```
        returned value is res=0
```

EXPLANATION: Both conditions in && operator are true so whole inner expression is true, after negation the returned value will be 0.

3.6 ASSIGNMENT OPERATOR

The = operator is called assignment operator. We have seen several instances of this operator in many of the earlier program. One more use of this operator is the shortening of following types of expressions:

$$x = x + 1, \quad y = y^* (x - 5), \quad a = a/10, \quad t = t\% \; 10;$$

In all the above expressions the variable on both side of = operator is same so we can change the above expression in shorter form as follows

$$x = x + 1 \quad => \quad x += 1$$
$$y = y^* (x - 5) \quad => \quad y^* = (x - 5)$$
$$a = a/10 \quad => \quad a/ = 10$$
$$t = t\% \; 10 \quad => \quad t\% = 10$$

This form **op=** where operator may be any operator is called **compound operator** or **shorthand assignment operator.**

3.7 INCREMENT OPERATOR (+ +) AND DECREMENT OPERATOR (--)

The operators ++ is known as increment operator and the operator--is known as decrement operator. Both are unary operators. The ++ increment the value of its operand by 1 and – decrement the value of its operands by 1. For example ++ *x* becomes 11 (assume *x* = 10 prior to the operation ++ *x* and -- *x*) and –*x* becomes 9.

See the program given below for more explanation.

```
/* Prog 3.23: Demo of ++ operator ver 1*/
#include<stdio.h>
#include<conio.h>
 void main()
{
```

```
  int x;
  clrscr();
  x=10;
  printf("before increment x=%d\n",x);
  x++;
  printf("after increment x=%d\n",x);
  getch();
}
```

Output:

```
        before increment x= 10
        after increment x= 11
```

EXPLANATION: The ++ operator is called increment operator. It is an unary operator that is it requires only one operand to operate which increment the value of operand by 1 *i.e.* x ++ is equivalent to $x = x + 1$. If ++ is written before operand *i.e.* ++ x it is known as **pre increment** and if ++ is written after operand *i.e.* x++ it is known as **post increment.** In the above program we have used post increment operator. Had we have used pre increment the output would be same. For distinction between two check out next program.

```
/*Prog 3.24:Demo of ++ operator ver2*/
#include<stdio.h>
#include<conio.h>
 void main()
 {
   int x,y;
   clrscr();
   x=10;
   y=x++;
   printf("x=%d\n",x);
   printf("y=%d\n",y);
   getch();
}
```

Output:

```
        x=11
        y=10
```

EXPLANATION: In the above program we have used post-increment operator with x and we are assigning the value to y. Due to post increment first x will be assigned to y and x will be incremented by 1 that is $y = x$++ is equivalent to the following statement:

$$y = x;$$
$$x = x++;$$

```
/* Prog 3.25 Demo of ++ operator ver 3 */
#include<stdio.h>
```

```
#include<conio.h>
  void main()
    {
      int x,y;
      clrscr();
      x=10;
      y =++x;
      printf("x=%d\n",x);
      printf("y=%d\n",y);
      getch();
    }
```

output:

```
              x= 11
              y= 11
```

EXPLANATION: In the above program we have used pre-increment operator with *x* and we are assigning the value to the *y*. Due to pre-increment first *x* will be incremented by 1 and the same incremented value will be assigned to $y = ++x$ is equivalent to the following two statements:

$$x = x + 1;$$
$$y = x;$$

NOTE: There is only ++ operator which is used to increment the value of the operand by one. There is no such operator as +++ or ++++ which increment the value by 2 or 3.

Similar to increment operator we have decrement operator (--) which is again may be of two types: pre-decrement operator and post-decrement operator.

```
/*Prog 3.26: Demo of ++ and - operator ver 1*/
#include<stdio.h>
#include<conio.h>
void main ()
{
     int x,y;
     clrscr();
     x=10;
     y=++x;
     --x;
     y--;
     x=y++;
     y=--x;
     x=y++;
     printf("x=%d\n",x);
     printf("y=%d\n",y);
     getch();
```

```
}
```

Output:

```
        x=9
        y=10
```

EXPLANATION: For explanation observe the following table:

Statement	Value of x	Value of y
Y = ++x	11	11
--x	10	11
y --	10	10
X = y ++	10	11
Y = --x	09	09
X = y ++	09	10

```
/*Prog 3.27 Demo of ++ and - Operator ver 2*/
#include<stdio.h>
#include<conio.h>
  void main( )
  {
        int x;
        clrscr( );
        x=10;
        printf("%d%d%d%d%d\n",--x,++x,x,x++,x--);
        getch( );
  }
```

Output:

```
        10   11   10   9    10
```

EXPLANATION: The output will be determined from right of **printf** statement:

Statement	*Value of x*	*Explanation*
x--	10	Value of xwill be printed then decremented
x++	09	Value of x will be printed then incremented
X	10	Value of x will be printed
++x	11	Value of x will be incremented then printed
--x	10	Value of x will be decremented then printed

So the output is 10 11 10 9 10 ++ and – are known as unary operators as said earlier because they require only one operand to operate. Similar to this if we write +2 or –2 or with variables say +a or –a then these operators are also known as unary plus and unary minus. Unary minus changes the sign of the operand where as unary plus has no affect on to the operand.

3.8 BITWISE OPERATORS

They are called so because they operate on bits. They can be used for the manipulation of bits. All these operators are extensively used when interfacing with the hardware and for setting of bits in registers of the device. C provides total 6 types of bitwise operators. They are as follows:

Table 3.9 *Bitwise Operators*

S.No.	*Operator*	*Meaning/Used for*
1.	&	Bitwise AND
2.	|	Bitwise OR
3.	^	Bitwise XOR
4.	~	One's complement
5.	>>	Right shift
6.	<<	Left shift

For all the following programs we consider only first 4 bits of the number for explanation purpose. So range of possible numbers is -7 to 8 in case of signed numbers (-2^{14} to -2^{41}-1) and (0 to -2^4-1) in case of unsigned numbers. In case you assume 8 bits for the numbers then use full **8** bits for the number even if it can be using 4 bits for example 10 can be written using 4 bits as 1010 and using 8 bits as 00001010.

3.8.1 Bitwise and (&)

It takes two bits as operand and returns the value **1** if both are **1.** If either of them is **0,** the result is **0.**

Table 3.10 *Truth table of Bit wise AND.*

First bit	*Second bit*	*Result*
0	0	0
0	1	0
1	0	0
1	1	1

```
/*Prog 3.28: Demo of bitwise operator & (AND)*/
#include<stdio.h>
#include<conio.h>
    void main()
    {
        int a=2,b=3;
        int c;
        clrscr();
        c=a&b;
```

```
        printf("c=%d\n",c);
        getch();
    }
```

Output:

```
        C=2
```

EXPLANATION: Binary values of $a = 2$ is 0010 and $b = 3$ is 0011 **Bitwise AND** of those values is performed as follows:

```
0 0 1 0
0 0 1 1
-------
0 0 1 0        (output in c will be 2 in decimal)
-------
```

If both bit are **1** output bit will be 1 using **&** operator else **0.**

3.8.1.1 Masking Using Bitwise and

The **AND** operator is used for **masking** purpose. For example we have a binary number 1010**1101.** We want to preserve the right most 4 bit (shown in italics) and make the remaining bits to zero. For this purpose we choose a binary number **00001111. We choose one's (1) for those bits which we want to preserve and zero for which we do not want to preserve.** Then we perform Bitwise AND operation of these two binary numbers .That is:

```
1 0 1 0 1 1 0 1        (Original Number)
0 0 0 0 1 1 1 1        (Mask)
---------------
0 0 0 0 1 1 0 1
---------------
```

This is known as masking. The number together with we perform Bitwise **AND is known as Mask.** As another example say you want to preserve bit number 0, 1, 4, 6(0th bit is the rightmost). So mask will be **01010101.**

```
1 0 1 0 1 1 0 1        (Original Number)
0 1 0 1 0 1 0 1        (Mask)
---------------
0 0 0 0 0 1 0 1
---------------
```

3.8.2 Bitwise Or (|)

It takes two bits as operand and returns the value **1** if at least one is **1.** If both are **0** only then result is **0** else it is **1.**

Table 3.11 *Truth table of Bitwise OR*

First bit	*Second bit*	*Result*
0	0	0
0	1	1
1	0	1
1	1	1

```
/* Prog 3.29 Demo of bitwise operator | (OR) */
#include<stdio.h>
#include<conio.h>
  void main()
  {
    int a=12,b=7;
    int c;
    clrscr();
    c=a|b;
    printf("c=%d\n",c);
    getch();
  }
Output:
                C=15
```

EXPLANATION: Binary value of *a* = **12 is 1100 and** *b* **= 7 is 0111 OR** of these two values is performed as follows:

1 1 0 0
0 1 1 1
---
1 1 1 1 **(Output in c will be 15 in decimal)?**

If any of the bit 1 output will be 1 using OR operator.

3.8.3 Bitwise Xor (^)

This operator takes at least two bits (may be more than two). If number of **1's** are odd then result is **1** else result is **0**

Table 3.12 *Truth table of Bitwise XOR*

First bit	*Second bit*	*Result*
0	0	0
0	1	1
1	0	1
1	1	0

```
/* Prog 3.30: Demo of bitwise operator ^(XOR)*/
#include<stdio.h>
#include<conio.h>
  void main()
  {
     int a=5,b=6;
     int c;
```

```
    clrscr();
    c=a^b;
    printf("c=%d\n",c);
    getch();
  }
```

Output:

C=3

EXPLANATION: Binary values of ***a* = 5 is 0101 and *b* = 6 is 0110 XOR** of these two values is performed as follows:

```
  0101
  0110
  ----
  0011      (output in c will be 3 in decimal)
```

If odd number of 1's are there output will be one otherwise output will be 0 using XOR operator.

3.8.4. 1's Complement (˜)

The symbol (~) denotes one's complement. It is a unary operator and complements the bits in its operand *i.e.* **1** is converted to **0** and **0** is converted to **1.**

```
/*Prog 3.31 Demo of bitwise operator ~ (1's complement) */
#include<stdio.h>
#include<conio.h>
 void main()
 {
   int a=5,b;
   b=~a;
   clrscr();
   printf("b=%d\n",b);
   getch();
 }
```

Output:

b=10

EXPLANATION: Binary value of *a* = 5 is 0101

In one's complement we invert the bit values *i.e.* **0** is inverted into **1** and vice-versa. So the output will be:

***b* = 10 (in binary 1010)**

If you get the output **– 6** don't get puzzled. What I've said is correct also but the computer has given the answer in 2's complement form.

To reverse check that your answer **10(in decimal)** or **1010(in binary)** is correct read the following matter carefully:

Binary value of 6 → 0110

1's complement of 6→ 1001

2's complement of 6 → 1's complement of 6 + 1

1001

0001(1 + 1 = 0 1 and carry 1) 1010 (which is our answer)

3.8.5 Left Shift Operator (<<)

The operator is used to shift the bits of its operand. It is written as *x* << **num;** which means shifting the bits of *x* towards left by **num** number of times. A new zero is entered in the least significant Bit (LSB) position. (See the programs given below)

```
/* Prog 3.32 Demo of bitwise operator << (left shift) ver1*/
#include<stdio.h>
#include<conio.h>
 void main()
 {
     int a=2,b;
     b=a<<1;
     clrscr();
     printf("b=%d\n",b);
     getch();
 }
```

Output:

```
b=4
```

EXPLANATION: ***a*** **<< 1** means shifting the contents of a towards left by **1** position. If we represent the number **2** in binary as:

b3	*b2*	*b1*	*b0*
0	0	1	0

Where ***b0*** is the first bit from left which is called **Least Significant Bit (LSB)** and *b3* is called **Most Significant Bit (MSB).** Shifting left by **1Bit** position results in *b3* losing its value and taking from *b2*, *b2* getting from **b1** and **b1** form ***b0*****,** a new zero is inserted at ***b0*****.** So the resultant bit pattern will be:

b3	*b2*	*b1*	*b0*
0	1	1	0

Which is 4 in decimal.

NOTE: Shifting the bits left once multiplies the number by 2.

```
/* Prog 3.33 Demo of bitwise operator << (left shift) ver 2 */
#include<stdio.h>
#include<conio.h>
```

```
void main()
{
    int a=2,b;
    b=a<<2;
    clrscr();
    printf("b=%d\n",b);
    getch();
}
Output:
                b= 8
```

EXPLANATION: ***a* << 2** means shifting the contents of **a** twice towards left.

Original value in **a = 0010**

b3	*b2*	*b1*	*b0*
0	0	1	0

Shifting one

b3	*b2*	*b1*	*b0*
0	1	0	0

(4 in decimal)

Shifting the value obtained in first step

b3	*b2*	*b1*	*b0*
1	0	0	0

Which is 8 in decimal and this is the final output.

3.8.6 Right Shift Operator (>>)

The operator is used to shift the bits of its operand. It is written as *x* >> **num;** which means shifting the bits of *x* towards right by **num** number of times. A new zero is entered in the **Most significant Bit (MSB)** position.

See the program given below:

```
/* Prog 3.34 Demo of bitwise operator >> (right shift) ver1*/
#include<stdio.h>
#include<conio.h>
void main()
{
   int a=8,b;
   b=a>>1;
   clrscr();
   printf("b=%d\n",b);
```

```
    getch();
}
```

Output:

b=4

EXPLANATION: ***a* >> 1** means shifting the contents of ***a*** towards right by **1** bit position. If we represent the number **8** in binary as:

*b*3	*b*2	*b*1	*b*0
1	0	0	0

Shifting right by **1 bit** position results in ***b*0** losing its value and taking from ***b*1, *b*1** getting from ***b*2** and ***b*2** from ***b*1,** new zero is inserted in ***b*3.** So the resultant bit pattern will be:

*b*3	*b*2	*b*1	*b*0
0	1	0	0

NOTE: Shifting the bits right once divides the number by 2.

```
/* Prog 3.35 Demo of bitwise operator >> (right shift) ver 2*/
#include<stdio.h>
#include<conio.h>
void main()
{
    int a=8,b;
    clrscr();
    b=a>>2
    printf("b=%d\n",b);
    getch();
}
```

Output:

b=2

EXPLANATION: ***a* >> 2** means shifting the contents of a twice towards right.

Original value in ***a* = 1000**

*b*3	*b*2	*b*1	*b*0
1	0	0	0

Shifting once

*b*3	*b*2	*b*1	*b*0
0	1	0	0

(4 in decimal)

Shifting the value obtained in first step.

b3	b2	b1	b0
0	0	1	0

Which is 2 in decimal and is the final output.

3.9 SIZEOF OPERATOR

This operator is used to find size in bytes a particular variable of a particular type or a constant takes up in memory. This is the only operator which also works as a function.

```
/* Prog 3.36: Demo of sizeof operator ver 1*/
#include<stdio.h>
#include<conio.h>
void main()
{
    int a;
    float b;
    char c;
    double d;
    clrscr();
    printf("Size of int variable a=%d\n", sizeof (a));
    printf("Size of float variable b=%d\n", sizeof (b));
    printf("Size of char variable c=%d\n", sizeof (c));
    printf("Size of double variable d=%d\n", sizeof (d));
    getch();
}
```

Output:

```
Size of int variable a = 2
Size of float variable b = 4
Size of char variable c= 1
Size of double variable d = 8.
```

EXPLANATION: The program gives the amount of memory in bytes taken by variables of different types. Size of int variable in Turbo C is 2 bytes where as in Windows it is of 4 bytes.

```
/* Prog 3.37: Demo of size of operator ver 2*/
#include<stdio.h>
#include<conio.h>
void main()
{
```

```
    clrscr();
    printf("Size of char constant   = %d\n",sizeof('V'));
    printf("Size of int constant    = %dbytes\n",sizeof (4));
    printf("size of float constant = %d bytes\n",sizeof(34.5));
    getch();
}
```

Output:

```
        Size of char constant = 2
        Size of int constant  = 2
        Size of float constant = 8
```

EXPLANATION: Instead of writing variables we have used constants here. The result differs in case of **float** constant. **A character constant is treated as integer and a float constant is treated as double so the output.** If you want a float constant to be treated as float constant not double suffix *f* of F after float constant *i.e.* in the above case if you write sizeof(4.3*f*) or sizeof(4.3F) the size returned will be 4.

```
/* Prog 3.38 Demo of sizeof operator ver 3*/
#include<stdio.h>
#include<conio.h>
  void main()
  {
     int x;
     clrscr();
     printf("size of x =%d\n",sizeof x);
     printf("size of int =%d\n",sizeof(int));
     getch();
  }
```

Output:

```
     Size of x = 2
     Size of int = 2
```

EXPLANATION: sizeof is called operator because we can write **sizeof** *x* where *x* is any variable of any type, whereas we cannot write **sizeof int** or **sizeof float etc** this results in compilation error. Try yourself and see the error.

3.10 THE COMMA (,) OPERATOR

This is most important operator in C yet overlooked by most of the programmers. But understanding how this operator works is must in C. The operator works from left to right and in expressions separated by commas rightmost expression becomes the operand for this operator.

See the example given below:

```
/* Prog 3.39: Demo of comma operator ver 1*/
#include<stdio.h>
#include<conio.h>
  void main()
  {
     int a=2,b=3,c=4,x=2;
     clrscr();
     x=(a,b,c);
     printf("x=%d\n",x);
     getch();
  }
```

Output:

```
x=4
```

EXPLANATION: The associativity (see next section) of comma operator is from left to right and the rightmost value is given to *x i.e.* value of *c* in the above program.

```
/* Prog 3.40 Demo of comma operator ver 2*/
#include<stdio.h>
#include<conio.h>
 void main()
 {
    int a=2,b=3,c=4,x=2;
    clrscr();
    x=(c--,c++,++a);
    printf("x=%d\tc=%d\n",x,c);
    getch();
 }
```

Output:

```
x=3
c=4
```

EXPLANATION: As stated earlier comma operators works from left to right. So value of *c* becomes 3 after *c*--, after *c* ++ it becomes 4 again. Value of a becomes 3 due to ++ *a* and this value is assigned to *x*, so the output.

The above were the just two examples of comma operator. You will find more examples of this operator in coming Chapters.

3.11 PRECEDENCE OF OPERATORS

Table 3.13 *Precedence of operators.*

Operators	*Associativity*	*Priority*
+, -, ++,!,&, ~, sizeof	Right to left	1
*, /, %	Left to right	2
+, -	Left to right	3
<<, >>	Left to right	4
<, <=, > ,>=	Left to right	5
==, !=	Left to right	6
&	Left to right	7
^	Left to right	8
|	Left to right	9
&&	Left to right	10
||	Left to right	11
?:	Right to left	12
=	Right to left	13
,	Left to right	14

NOTE: In the first row + and – are unary operator.

Precedence tells in an expression which operation should be performed first depending upon priority of operators. Associativity means when two or more operators have same priority then from which side (left or right) we operate. For example if we write ***a*b/c***

Then in this expression * and / has got same priority so whether we perform ***a*b*** first or ***b/c*** first or in other way we should consider ***b*** as part of sub expression ***b/c*** or part of sub-expression ***a*b.***

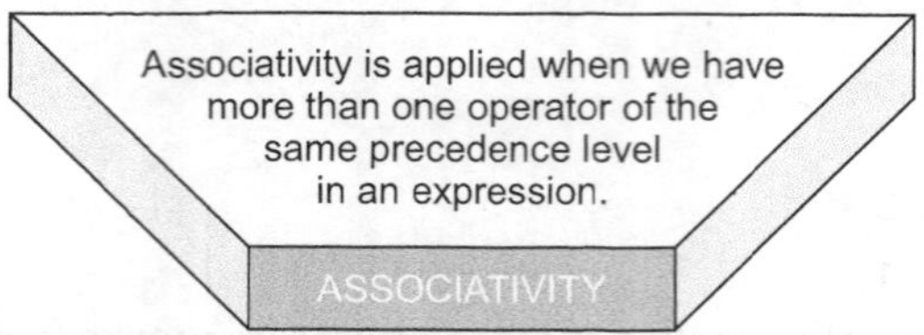

Fig. 3.1 *Associativity used in precedence of operator.*

As we know associativity of * and / is from left to right so sub-expression ***a*b*** will performed first then the result of ***a*b*** will be divided by ***c.***

The following programs will solidify your concepts of the precedence & associativity of operators.

```
/* Prog 3.41: Demo precedence of operators (arithmetic) ver 1*/
#include<stdio.h>
#include<conio.h>
 void main()
```

```
{
   int a=2,b=3,c=4,d;
   clrscr();
   d=a*4/b+c-10%3;
   printf("d=%d\n",d);
   getch();
}
```

Output:

```
                d=4
```

EXPLANATION: As priority of say **opr1 (*, /, %)** is higher than say **opr2 (+, –)** so expression involving **opr1** are evaluated first. Again at the same level the associativity of **opr1** is from left to right, so evaluation will proceed as:

$$
\begin{aligned}
d &= 2 * 4 / 3 + 4 - 10 \% 3 \\
&= 8 / 3 + 4 - 10 \% 3 \\
&= 2 + 4 - 10 \% 3 \\
&= 2 + 4 - 1 \\
&= 6 - 1 \\
&= 5
\end{aligned}
$$

```
/* Prog 3.42: Precedence of operators (arithmetic) ver 2*/
#include<stdio.h>
#include<conio.h>
 void main()
 {
   float a=12,b=3,c=4,d;
   clrscr();
   d=(a-b)/c;
   printf("d=%f\n",d);
   getch();
 }
```

Output:

```
                d=2.250000
```

EXPLANATION: We want to evaluate difference of *a* and *b* divided by *c*. For that we have to write *(a – b)/c*. As precedence of / is more than – if we write *a – b/c* then initially *b/c* will be evaluated that we don't want. So whenever we want to evaluate an expression irrespective of the priority of the operator we write the expression within parenthesis.

```
/*Prog 3.43: Precedence of operators (arithmetic ++) ver 3*/
#include<stdio.h>
#include<conio.h>
 void main()
 {
```

```
    int a=4,b=3,c=2,d;
    clrscr();
    d=a*b/c-++c;
    printf("d=%d\n",d);
    getch();
  }
```

Output:

d=1

EXPLANATION: The priority of ++ is higher so *c* because **3** because of **++*c*.** This value of *c* is used in the whole expression. The expression is evaluated as:

d= 4 *3 /3 – 3
= 12 / 3 – 3
= 4 – 3
= 1

```
/* Prog 3.44: precedence of operators (arithmetic, sizeof, and NOT) ver 4*/
#include<stdio.h>
#include<conio.h>
  void main()
  {
      int a=4,b=0,c=2,d;
      clrscr();
      d=!b*sizeof(c)%a/c;
      printf("d=%d\n",d);
      getch();
  }
```

Output:

d=1

EXPLANATION: Priority of ! and **sizeof** is same so they are evaluated from left to right. Similarly, priority of % and / is same but less than ! and **sizeof** so they are evaluated from left to right after **! and sizeof.**

d = 1 * sizeof (2) % 4 / 2
= 1 * 2 % 4 / 2
= 2 % 4 / 2
= 2 / 2
= 1

```
/* Prog 3.45: Precedence of operators (arithmetic, logical, relational, increment) ver 5*/
#include<stdio.h>
#include<conio.h>
```

```
void main()
{
   int a=4,b=4,c=2,d;
   clrscr();
   d=a*2 && b>c - ++c;
   printf("d=%d\n",d);
   getch();
}
```

Output:

```
        d=1
```

EXPLANATION: First ++*c* is evaluated so *c* becomes **3.** The rest of the expression is evaluated as:

$$\begin{aligned} d &= (4 * 2) \&\& 4 > 3 - 3 \\ &= 4 \&\& 4 > (3 - 3) \\ &= 8 \&\& (4 > 0) \\ &= 8 \&\& 1 \\ &= 1 \end{aligned}$$

In relational operators expression will be either true or false. **1** denotes true **0** denotes false. In logical operators operands are compared with **0.** If they are non zero then condition is interpreted as true. In the above case as **4 > 0** is true so **1** is assumed at this place. In the next step **8** is non zero as well as **1** is nonzero. As both conditions of logical **AND** are true, the whole expression is true and a **1** is assigned to **d.**

```
/* Prog 3.46: Precedence of operators (arithmetic, relational) ver 6 */
#include<stdio.h>
#include<conio.h>
  void main()
  {
     int a=2,b=3,x;
     clrscr();
     x=a>10+b>0-1;
     printf("x=%d\n",x);
     getch();
  }
```

Output:

```
        x = 1
```

EXPLANATION: The expression is evaluated as:

$$\begin{aligned} x &= 2 > (10 + 3) > 0 - 1 \\ &= 2 > 13 > (0 - 1) \\ &= 0 > -1 \\ &= 1 \end{aligned}$$

```
/* Prog 3.47: Precedence of operators (use of ( )) ver 7 */
#include<stdio.h>
#include<conio.h>
  void main()
  {
      int a=2,b=3,x;
      clrscr();
      x=(a>10)+(b>0);
      printf("x=%d\n",x);
      getch();
  }
```

Output:

```
                x = 1
```

EXPLANATION: The expression inside the parenthesis will evaluated first. So the expression evaluated as:

$$x = (2 > 10) + (3 > 0)$$
$$= (0) + (1)$$
$$= 1.$$

```
/*Prog 3.48: Precedence of operators (unary + and -) ver 8*/
  #include<stdio.h>
  #include<conio.h>
 void main()
 {
     int a=-2,b=-3,x;
     clrscr();
     x=+a*-b+!(b>12);
     printf("x=%d\n",x);
     getch();
 }
```

Output:

```
                x = -5
```

EXPLANATION: Unary + does not serve any purpose. So +*a* does not have any effect on the value of *a*. The expression is evaluated as:

$$x = -2 * -(-3) + !(-3 > 12)$$
$$= -2 * 3 + !(0)$$
$$= (-2 * 3) + 1$$
$$= -6 + 1$$
$$= -5$$

```
/* Prog 3.49: Precedence of operators (left, right shift) ver 9 */
#include<stdio.h>
```

```
#include<conio.h>
  void main()
  {
      int a=2,b=2,x;
      clrscr();
      x=a>>1<<b;
      printf("x=%d\n",x);
      getch();
  }
```

Output:

```
            x = 4
```

EXPLANATION: As the priority of >> (right shift) and << (left shift) is same. The expression is evaluated from left to right as:

$$x = (2 >> 1) << 2$$
$$= 1 << 2$$
$$= 4$$

```
/* Prog 3.50: Precedence of operator ver 10 */
#include<stdio.h>
#include<conio.h>
 void main()
 {
    int a=2,b=2,c=1,x;
    clrscr();
    x=a>>1>b+c%3<<2 * ++c;
    printf("x=%d\n",x);
    getch();
 }
```

Output:

```
            x = 0
```

EXPLANATION: The expression is evaluated as (c is 2 due to ++)

$$x = 2 >> 1 > 2 + (2 \% 3) << 2 * 2$$
$$= 2 >> 1 > 2 + 2 << (2 * 2)$$
$$= 2 >> 1 >> 2 + 2 << 4$$
$$= (2 >> 1) > 4 << 4$$
$$= 4 > (4 << 4)$$
$$= 4 > 64$$
$$= 0$$

```
/*Prog 3.51: Precedence of operators (short hand assignment) ver 11*/
#include<stdio.h>
#include<conio.h>
```

```
void main()
{
    int a=2,b=3,c=4,x=2;
    clrscr();
    x+=a*b+c/3-++a;
    printf("x=%d\n",x);
    getch();
}
```

Output:

```
x=9
```

EXPLANATION: The expression is evaluated as (++*a* is evaluated first so it will be 3).

$$x += (3*3) + 4 / 3 - 3$$
$$x += 9 + (4 / 3) - 3$$
$$x += (9 + 1) - 3$$
$$x += 10 - 3$$
$$x += 7$$
$$x = x + 7$$
$$x = 2 + 7$$
$$x = 9$$

/* Prog 3.52: Precedence of operators (( ) and comma) ver 12 */

```
#include<stdio.h>
#include<conio.h>
void main()
{
    int a=2,b=3,c=4,x=2;
    clrscr();
    x+=(a,c,b);
    printf("x=%d\n",x);
    getch();
}
```

Output:

```
x= 5
```

EXPLANATION: In comma (,) operator rightmost value is assigned to variable when values are within parenthesis. So expression becomes $x += c$ which is $x = x + c$.

/*Prog 3.53: Precedence of operators (logical AND) ver 13*/

```
#include<conio.h>
#include<stdio.h>
void main()
{
    int a=0,b=3,c=4,x=2;
```

```
     clrscr();
     x=a++ && --c;
     printf("x=%d\n",x);
     printf("a=%d\n",a);
     printf("a=%d\n",c);
     getch();
  }
```

Output:

```
x = 0
a = 1
c = 4
```

EXPLANATION: In the logical AND operation if the first value is false, second value is not evaluated. Second value is evaluated only when the first value is true. Here *a* is zero and **post increment** on *a*. Due to ***a* = 0** the first condition is false and – *c* is not evaluated.

```
/* Prog 3.54: Precedence of operators (logical OR) ver 14 */
#include<stdio.h>
#include<conio.h>
 void main()
 {
  int a=0,b=3,c=4,x=2;
  clrscr();
  x= a++ || --c;
  printf("x=%d\n",x);
  printf("a=%d\n",a);
  printf("a=%d\n",c);
  getch();
 }
```

Output:

```
x= 1
a= 1
c= 3
```

EXPLANATION: In the logical **OR** irrespective of the truth value of first operand i.e. whether it is true or false the second operand is evaluated. So the output.

3.12 DECLARING CONSTANTS

A constant is a value which cannot be changed. For example value of π ***(pi)* is 22/7 or 3.14** which is a constant. To use constants in our programs C defines mainly three ways of declaring constants. We discuss each of them one by one.

3.12.1 Use of #Define Directive

#define preprocessor directive can be used to declare a constant. Its general syntax is given as:

#define constant_name value

There must be at least a single space between **#define** and **constant_name.** For example: **#define PI 3.14** which declares a constant (actually it is a macro constant) named **PI** with value **3.14.** There should be no assignment operator (=) between **PI** and **3.14.** Each macro constant must be declared on separate line. Macro constants are also known as **symbolic constant as we use string symbols to define constants.**

```
/* Prog 3.55 Demo of constant using #define */
#define PI 3.14
#define H "hello\n"
#define MC "macro constant\n"
#include<stdio.h>
#include<conio.h>
 void main()
 {
   clrscr();
   printf(H);
   printf(MC);
   printf("value of PI is %f\n",PI);
   getch();
 }
```

Output:

```
hello
macro constant
value of PI is 3.14
```

EXPLANATION: We have used three symbolic constants in the program named **PI , H and MC.** First one (PI) is a float constant and other two are string constants. Before compilation they are processed by a special program called preprocessor which replaces all the occurrences of macro constant by their value. Each macro constant is return in upper case, it is not necessary but to distinguish macro name from variables we declare macro in upper-case and variables in lower-case.

In the above program if we write PI = **PI + 1 or PI = 343** *i.e.* try to change the value of **PI** an error is flashed which states that we cannot change the constant value.

3.12.2 Use of Const Keyword to Define Constant

The second way of declaring constant is to use const keyword. Its syntax is given as follows:

Const data_type var_name=value;

EXAMPLE: **const int x = 100;**

1 2 3 4

1. **const → KEYWORD**
2. **int → data type**
3. ***x* → variable**
4. **100 → value**

That is *x* as a constant and assign a value **100** to it. Later in the program we cannot change the value of *x*.

```
/* Prog 3.56 Demo of const keyword */
#include<stdio.h>
#include<conio.h>
 void main()
 {
    const int X=100;
    const float PI=3.14;
    const char*S="constant";
    const char C='C';
    clrscr();
    printf("int constant X=%d\n",X);
    printf("float constant PI=%f\n",PI);
    printf("string constant S=%s\n",S);
    printf("char constant C=%c\n",C);
    getch();
 }
```

Output:

```
int constant X=100
float constant PI=3.140000
string constant S=constant
char constant C=C
```

EXPLANATION: For string constant we have use **char** pointer variable. Rest is self explanatory.

3.12.3 Use of Enum to Declare Constant

We understand the use of **enum** with the help of an example:

```
enum my_cons
{
    MIN;
    MID;
    MAX;
};
```

The above declaration creates new data type **my_cons** with the help of **enum** keyword. The declaration statements within { } creates three **int type** constants, **MIN, MID and MAX** which are known as **enumeration constants.** By default the value of **MIN** is **0, MID is 1 and MAX is 2.** As they are constant they cannot be changed inside the program. They can only be of type **int** and **char.** No other type is allowed .Take one more example.

```
enum colors
{
    RED;
    GREEN=25;
    BLUE;
};
```

In this example value of **RED** will be **0, GREEN** will have **25** and **BLUE** will have value **26.** The keyword **enum** is used to create enumeration constants, also known as symbolic constants. After the creation of enumeration constants enumeration type variable can be created for example:

enum colors col1, col2;

These enumeration variable **col1** and **col2** can be assigned enumeration constants created earlier like:

col1 = RED; col 2= BLUE;

Although the variables **col 1** and **col 2** can be assigned any integer value but usually they are assigned enumeration constants. That is the following is also valid **col 1=34; col2= 45;**

We give some programming examples.

```
/* Prog 3.57 Demo of enumeration constants ver 1*/
#include<stdio.h>
#include<conio.h>
 void main()
 {
    enum colors
    {
      red,green,blue
    };
    enum OS
    {
      dos=1,linux,windows=5,unix
    };
    clrscr();
    printf("red=%d\t green=%d\t blue =%d\n",red,green,blue);
    printf("dos=%d\t linux=%d\t",dos,linux);
    printf("windows=%d\t unix=%d\n",windows,unix);
    getch();
 }
```

```
Output:
red=0    green=1   blue =2
dos=1    linux=2   windows=5    unix=6
```

EXPLANATION: The program is self-explanatory.

The enumeration constants are basically used in switch-case construct.

NOTE THE FOLLOWING POINTS ABOUT ENUMERATORS

(*i*) The values of enumerators need not be distinct in the same enumeration type.
(*ii*) The names of enumerators in different enumeration types must be distinct.
(*iii*) The names of the enumerators must be different from other normal variables.
(*iv*) Enumerators are treated only as integer constants by the compiler.

3.13 TYPE CONVERSION

Sometimes in expression we require to convert the data type of a variable or a constant say from **float to int** or **int to float** etc. Two types of conversions C supports:

1. **Implicit type conversion.**
2. **Explicit type conversion.**

3.13.1 Implicit Type Conversion

In this type of conversion the compiler internally converts the type depending upon expression without letting user to know. For example if you write

int num = 34.56;

Then **num** will be assigned the value **34 not 34.56** is treated as **double** and internal conversion occurs from **double** to **float** and from **float** to **int** and **34 is** assigned to the variable **num.**

As another example consider the following code snippet.

int a **= 10;**
float b **= 2.5,** c**;**
$c = a + b$**;**

In the expression $c = a + b$, type of a and b is not same. According to size float is greater than int so variable a in internally converted into float and then addition is performed so the result obtained will also be in float.

The conversion is always done from lower data type to higher data type. For example a char can be converted to *int, long int, float, double and long double.* Similarly, an int can be converted into float, long int and long double and so on.

3.13.2 Explicit Type Conversion

In this type of conversion (also known as type **casting**) we explicitly convert the variable's or constant's data type from one to another. For example

int a **= 10;**
float $x = a/3$**;**

In the above expression $x = a/3$ both **x and 3** are type **int** so output will be 3.000000 and not **3.333333** even though type of x is **float.** To get the required result we type cast a as float by writing

x = (float) *a*/3;

Also we could have written a/3.0 to get the same result.

POINTS TO PONDER

In this section you have learned the following points:

- The assignment operator (=), which has two operands on each side. The value of the right-side operand is assigned to the operand on the left side.
- The arithmetic assignment operators, +=, –=, *=, /=, and %=, which are the combinations of the arithmetic operators with the assignment operator.
- The unary minus operator (–), which returns the negation of a numeric value.
- The two versions of the increment operator, ++. You know that in ++*x*, the ++ operator is called the pre-increment operator; and in *x*++, ++ is the post-increment operator.
- The two versions of decrement operator, --. You have learned that, for example, in -- *x*, the -- operator is the pre-decrement operator, while in *x*--, -- is called the post-decrement operator.
- The six relational operators in C: == (equal to), != (not equal to), > (greater than), < (less than), >= (greater than or equal to), and <= (less than or equal to).
- How to change the type of data by prefixing a cast operator to the data.
- The sizeof operator returns the number of bytes that a specified data type can have. You can use the operator to measure the size of a data type on your machine.
- The logical AND operator (&&) returns 1 only if both its two operands (that is, expressions) are TRUE. Otherwise, the operator returns 0.
- The logical OR operator (| |) returns 0 only if both its two operands are FALSE. Otherwise, the operator returns 1.
- The logical negation operator (!) reverses the logical value of its operand.
- There are six bit-manipulation operators: the bitwise AND operator (&), the bitwise OR operator (|), the bitwise XOR operator (^), the bitwise complement operator (~), the right-shift operator (>>), and the left-shift operator (<<).
- The conditional operator (?:) is the only operator in C that can take three operands.

QUESTIONS AND ANSWERS

Q1. *What is the difference between the pre-increment operator and the post-increment operator?*

Ans: The pre-increment operator increases the operand's value by 1 first, and then returns the modified value. On the other hand, the post-increment operator stores a copy of the operand value in a temporary location and then increases the operand value by 1. However, the copy of the unmodified operand value is returned in the expression. For instance, given *x* = 1, the ++*x* expression returns 2, while the *x*++ expression returns 1.

Q2. *Is the unary minus operator (–) the same as the subtraction operator (–)?*

Ans: No, they are not the same, although the two operators share the same symbol. The unary minus operator is used to change the sign of a value. In other words, the unary minus operator returns the negation of the value. The subtraction operator is an arithmetic operator that performs subtraction between its two operands.

Q3. *Which one has a higher precedence, a relational operator or an arithmetic operator?*

Ans: An arithmetic operator has a higher precedence than a relational operator. For instance, the $x * y + z > x + y$ expression is interpreted as $((x * y) + z) > (x + y)$.

Q4. *What does a relational expression return?*

Ans: A relational expression returns either 0 or 1. If the relationship indicated by a relational operator in an expression is true, the expression returns 1; otherwise, the expression returns 0.

Q5. *Why do we need the sizeof operator?*

Ans: The sizeof operator can be used to measure the sizes of all data types defined in C. When you write a portable C program that needs to know the size of an integer variable, it's a bad idea to hard-code the size as 16 or 32. The better way to tell the program the size of the variable is to use the sizeof operator, which returns the size of the integer variable at runtime.

Q6. *What's the difference between | and ||?*

Ans: | is the bitwise OR operator that takes two operands. The | operator compares each bit of one operand to the corresponding bit in another operand. If both bits are 0, 0 is placed at the same position of the bit in the result. Otherwise, 1 is placed in the result.

On the other hand, ||, the logical OR operator, requires two operands (or expressions). The operator returns 0 (that is, FALSE) if both its operands are false. Otherwise, a nonzero value (that is, TRUE) is returned by the || operator.

Q7. *Why is 1 << 3 equivalent to $1 * 2^3$?*

Ans: The 1 << 3 expression tells the computer to shift 3 bits of the operand 1 to the left. The binary format of the operand is 0001. (Note that only the lowest four bits are shown here.) After being shifted 3 bits to the left, the expression returns 1000, which is equivalent to $1 * 2^3+0 * 2^2+0 * 2^1+0 * 2^0$; that is, $1 * 2^3$.

Q8. *What can the conditional operator (?:) do?*

Ans: If there are two possible answers under certain conditions, you can use the ?: operator to pick up one of the two answers based on the result made by testing the conditions. For instance, the expression (age > 65) ? "Retired" : "Not retired" tells the computer that if the value of age is greater than 65, the string of Retired should be chosen; otherwise, Not retired is chosen.

EXERCISES

A. Answer the following questions:

1. Explain different types of operator available in C?
2. Explain various unary operators in C?
3. Describe logical operators with their return values.

4. What are the relational operators?
5. Explain ternary operator in C?
6. What is the difference between '=' and '= ='?
7. Explain the precedence of operators in arithmetic operations?
8. Why bitwise operators are useful? Explain where they are applicable?
9. Why is the need of type conversion?
10. What do you understand by type casting? Give examples of implicit and explicit type casting?
11. What are the uses of comma (,) and conditional (?) operators?
12. What is the difference between division and modular division operations?
13. What are the ASCII codes? List the codes for digits 1 to 9, A to Z and a to z?

B. Brain Drill

1. Write a program to enter a number (<100 and >15). Display the number in reverse order using % and / operator?
2. Write a program to convert entered temperature from Celsius to Fahrenheit?
3. Write a program to enter a four digit number and find out sum of its digit using % and / operator.
4. Write a program to display number all alphabets (upper and lower) along with their ASCII values.
5. Write a program to enter two numbers and do comparison of them. If first one is greater then find out division of two numbers else find out multiplication of two numbers.
6. Write a program to print whether entered number is even or odd using ternary operator.
7. Write a program to evaluate the expression 2X + 3Y-10. Value for X and Y should be taken from the user side.
8. Write a program to multiply two floating point numbers and print the product as a double in exponential notation.
9. Write a program to complement the bits starting from R and ending at S, of a given number and print the value of the manipulated number in binary, octal and hexadecimal form.
10. Write a program for binary addition with carry of 8 bit numbers.
11. Write a program to shift a number by 4 bits by storing bits to another number. The program should print out the values of the number formed by shifted bits, in decimal and binary forms.
12. Write a program to entered two numbers and find the smallest out of them. Use conditional operator.
13. Write a program to shift the entered numbers by three bits right and display the result.
14. Write a program to shift the entered number by three bits left and display the result.

C. Write True or False against each statement:

1. The expression ++ (4 + 6) is a valid.

2. +++p increment s value of p by 2.
3. A char data type always occupies two bytes in memory.
4. Assignment operation is performed during execution of the program
5. The expression ++(x + y) is a valid one.
6. The one's complement ~ is a binary operator.
7. The assignment a*1 = b; is a valid one.
8. The sizeof is a keyword but not a function.

D. Match the following columns:

I	II
1. >>	(*a*) Type Coercion.
2. a & b	(*b*) Arithmetic expression.
3. a >> = b	(*c*) Masking
4. x/y % z	(*d*) Assignment
5. (int) (x + 5)	(*e*) Operator.

E. Fill in the blanks:

1. The expression (double (22/7)) yields ____________________.
2. The modulus-operator can be applied only to _________ types.
3. Left shifting a number is equivalent to ___________.
4. The second operator of the operator % and / must be _________.
5. Assignment operator uses the Associativity of ____________.
6. The expression (float (22/7)) yields ____________________.
7. The symbol for bitwise AND is _____ and symbol for logical AND is ______.

F. Predict the output of the following programs:

1.
```
main()
{
    int x = 5, y = -10, z;
    int a = 4, b = 2;
    z = x + + + y * b / a;
}
```

2.
```
main ()
{
    int x =3, y = 4;
    x = x ^ y;
    y = y ^ x;
    x = x ^ y;
    printf("x=%d\ty=%d\n",x,y);
}
```

```
3. main ()
   {
      int i;
      i = 1;
      i = i + 2 * i + +;
      printf("%d", i);
   }
4. main()
   {
      int i=0, j=1;
      printf("%d%d%d\n"i++ &&++j,i,j);
   }
5. main()
   {
      int x=0,y=1;
      x = y++;
      x = ++y;
      x = y--;
      x = --y;
      printf("x=%d\ty=%d\n",x,y);
   }
6. main()
   {
      enum {A,B,C,D=100,E=5};
      printf("%d%d%d\n",B-C,D*E,D-C);
   }
7. enum color{green, orange, blue, red, white};
   main()
   {
      green = green + 1;
      printf("%d,%d\n",green, red);
   }
8. #define scanf "%s is string"
   main()
   {
      printf(scanf,scanf);
   }
```

9.
```
main()
{
    int x = 5;
    printf("%d %d %d \n",x,x<<2,x>>2);
}
```

10.
```
#define PRINT(int)printf("%d",int)
main()
{
    int x,y,z;
    x = 03, y=-1, z=01;
    PRINT (x^x);
    Z<<=3;
    PRINT(z);
    y>>=3;
    PRINT(y);
}
```

4

DECISION MAKING AND BRANCHING IN 'C'

The chapters discuss the basics of decision making and branching in C. Decision making is achieved in C with the help of **if-else** construct. All different forms of this selective construct are discussed. The simple **if, if-else,** nesting of **if-else** and **else-if ladder,** all are discussed in detail by first giving the syntaxes of each then illustrating them numerous programming examples.

An alternative of **else-if ladder,** another selective construct **switch-case** is explained with lots of examples.

Chapter input/output was discussed using **printf** and **scanf** in the chapter2 .Here in the section 4.7 built -in character oriented function like **getchar ( ), putchar ( ), getch ( ), getche ( )** are covered. Header file **ctype.h** is explored which contains various character manipulation functions and macros.

Concept of branching is introduced in the **section 4.8** with the help of **goto** construct which is used for branching in C. Its reason for negligence in the programming arena has also been discussed. Its usefulness is certain programming situations is also covered.

4.1 INTRODUCTION

Decision-making statements are needed to alter the sequence of the statements in the program depending upon certain circumstances. In the absence of decision-making statements a program executes in the **serial fashion** statement basis. We have seen examples in the programs given in earlier chapters. In this chapter we are going to write statements which control the flow of execution on the basis of some decision. Decision can be made on the basis of success or failure of some logical condition. They allow us to control the flow of our program. These conditions can be placed in the program using decision-making statements.

C language supports the following decision-making control statements:

(*a*) The if statement

(*b*) The if-else statement

(*c*) The if-else-if ladder statement

(*d*) The switch-case statement.

All these decision-making statements checks the given condition and then executes its **sub block** if the condition happens to be true. On falsify of condition the block is skipped. **(A block is a set of statements enclosed within the opening and closing brace {and}).** All control statement uses a combination of relational and logical operators to form conditions as per the requirement of the programmer.

4.2 THE IF STATEMENT

The general syntax of **if** statement is as:

```
if(condition)
{
      Statements;
      Statements;
      Statements;
      ........;
}
```

The **if** statement is used to execute /skip a block of statements on the basis of truth or falsify of a condition. The condition to be checked is put inside the parenthesis which is preceded by keyword **if**

We present numbers of programs to illustrate the working of if statement.

```
/* Prog 4.1 Demo of if statement */
#include<stdio.h>
#include<conio.h>
  void main()
  {
     int x;
     clrscr();
     x=10;
     if(x>0)
     printf("x is greater than 0");
     getch();
  }
Output:
       x is greater than 0
```

EXPLANATION: IF is a conditional execution statement. It's a keyword. The condition to be checked is put inside parenthesis. If the condition is true the first statement after **if gets executed,** else it is skipped. In the above program the condition inside parenthesis is true so the output.

```
/*Prog 4.2 Demo of if statement ver2*/
#include<stdio.h>
#include<conio.h>
 void main()
 {
    int x;
    clrscr();
    x=1;
    if(x==0)
        printf("x is equal to zero");
 }
```

Output:

```
        (Blank screen)
```

EXPLANATION: The **if** condition is false and there is only one statement just after if which will be skipped due to false condition, so the output.

```
/* Prog 4.3 Demo of if statement ver3 */
#include<stdio.h>
#include<conio.h>
 void main()
 {
    int x;
    clrscr();
    x=51;
    if(x<40)
    printf("x is less than 40");
    printf("x is greater or equal to forty");
    getch();
 }
```

Output:

```
x is greater or equal to forty
```

EXPLANATION: If the **if** condition is false only the first statement after **if** will be skipped and rest others following the first statement will be executed. As in this program the **if** condition is false so the output. If it were true then both **printf** statement would get executed. If you want to put more than one statement dependent on **if** condition then put all such statements inside curly braces { } *i.e.* from a block of statements dependent on **if** as shown in the next program.

```
/* Prog 4.4 Demo of if statement ver4*/
#include<stdio.h>
#include<conio.h>
 void main()
```

```
{
 int x;
 clrscr();
 printf("Enter the value of x\n");
 scanf("%d",&x);
 if(x>=100)
   {
     printf("x greater or equal to 100\n");
     printf("you think high\n");
 }
 printf("x less than 100");
 getch();
}
```

Output:

```
Enter the value of x
275
x greater or equal to 100
you think high
x less than 100
```

EXPLANATION: You can put any number of statements inside curly braces after **if** and all will be dependent on **if** condition.

```
/* Prog 4.5 Demo if statement ver5*/
#include<stdio.h>
#include<conio.h>
 void main()
 {
   int x;
   clrscr();
   x=12;
   if(x)
   printf("x is non zero");
   getch();
 }
```

Output:

```
 X is non zero
```

EXPLANATION: In the above program **if(*x*)** expands to **if(!*x* = 0)** This syntax of checking a variable against non zero is used quite often, be sure you do remember this. The **if** condition is true so the output.

```
/*Prog 4.6 Demo of if statement ver 6*/
#include<stdio.h>
```

```
#include<conio.h>
 void main()
 {
      int x;
      clrscr();
      x=0;
      if(!x)
         printf("x is zero");
      getch();
 }
```

Output:

```
      X is zero
```

EXPLANATION: In the above program **if(!*x*) expands to if (!(*x*! = 0))** whose real meaning is **if (*x* == 0).** Again similar to the previous this syntax is used quite often in the programming. The condition is true so the output.

```
/* Prog 4.7 Demo of if statement ver7*/
#include<stdio.h>
#include<conio.h>
 void main()
 {
   int x;
   clrscr();
   x=10;
   if(x=10)
       printf("x is equal to 10");
   getch();
}
```

Output:

```
      X is equal to 10
```

EXPLANATION: In the above program, instead of equal to operator = = we have used assignment operator so the meaning of if statement will be:

if(x=10) =>> if(10)→if(10!=0)

and this condition will always remain true irrespective of the value of *x* so it will always print **"*x* is equal to 10"** irrespective of the value of *x*.

4.3 THE IF-ELSE STATEMENT

In all the above program we didn't write the other side of **if** condition i.e. we didn't take the action when the condition fails. The **if-else** construct allows us to do this.

Its general syntax is:

```
if(condition)
{
        Statements;
        Statements;
        Statements;
        ........;
}
else
  {
        Statements;
        Statements;
        Statements;
        ........;
  }
```

If the condition within **if** true all the statements within the block following **if** are executed else they are skipped and **else** part get executed.

```
/* Prog 4.8 program to check number is even or odd*/
#include<stdio.h>
#include<conio.h>
 void main()
 {
   int num;
   clrscr();
   printf("Enter any number\n");
   scanf("%d",&num);
   if(num%2==0)
                  printf("number is even \n");
   else
                  printf("number is odd\n");
   getch();
 }
```

Output:

(First run)

Enter any number

```
12
number is even
```

(Second run)

```
Enter any number
17
number is odd
```

EXPLANATION: The priority of % is higher than **==,** so *a* % **2** is compared to **0.** If this is true then the number is even else number is not even. The **else** part executes only when **if** part is false and vice-versa. In the program both **if** and **else** part contains just one statement to be dependent upon them so braces are not needed, however if you put there won't be any harm. The condition could be written in the following manner also:

```
if(num%2!=0)
    printf("number is odd\n");
else
    printf("number is evev\n");
```

```
/*Prog 4.9 To check whether a number is +ve or -ve */
#include<stdio.h>
#include<conio.h>
 void main()
 {
   int num;
   clrscr();
   printf("Enter any number\n");
   scanf("%d",&num);
   if(num>0)
        printf("number is +ve\n");
   else
        printf("number is -ve\n");
   getch();
 }
```

Output:

(First run)

```
Enter any number
-89
number is -ve
```

(Second run)

```
Enter any number
13
number is +ve
```

EXPLANATION: If the number is greater than zero the number is positive and if the number is less than zero then number is negative.

If the user supplies zero (0) as input, **if** condition is false and **else** part get executed which prints **"number is –ve".** But in reality number is zero not negative so we modify the above program and give you the next program which handles this.

```
/*Prog 4.10 To check whether a number is +ve, -ve or zero */
#include<stdio.h>
#include<conio.h>
 void main()
 {
   int num;
   clrscr();
   printf("Enter any number\n");
   scanf("%d",&num);
   if(num==0)
          printf("number is zero\n");
   if(num>0)
          printf("number is +ve\n");
   else
          printf("number is -ve\n");
   getch();
 }
```

Output:

```
          (first run)
          Enter any number
          -12
          number is -ve
          (second run)
          Enter any number
          0
          number is zero
          number is -ve ← wrong result
```

EXPLANATION: There is one small change in the program from the previous one. We have added a simple **if** condition which check whether number is zero or not.

The above program works finite but is less efficient. If the input happens to be zero then we need not check the later **if** condition. Out of the two **if** and **else** part we want only one part should get executed.

There are few solution to make the above program more efficient one is to terminate the program when the first **if** condition happens to be true. The program may be modified as:

```
if(a==0)
{
        printf("number is zero\n");
        exit(0);
}
```

exit () is the in-built function to terminate the program. Any positive integer number may be given as argument. As prototype for this function header file either **stdlib.h** or **process.h** has to be included. As

```
/* Prog 4.11 for the solution of the problem generated in above program
*/
#include<stdio.h>
#include<conio.h>
#include<stdlib.h> /*used for exit()function */
 void main()
 {
    int num;
    clrscr();
    printf("Enter any number\n");
    scanf("%d",&num);
    if(num==0)
    {
        printf("number is zero\n");
        exit(0);/*presentin stdlib.h or process.h*/
    }
    if(num>0)
      printf("number is +ve\n");
    else
      printf("number is -ve\n");
    getch();
 }
```

Output:

```
(First run)
Enter any number
0
number is zero
(Second run)
Enter any number
12
number is +ve
```

```
(Third run)
Enter any number
-14
number is -ve
```

```
/*Prog 4.12 Maximum of two numbers */
#include<stdio.h>
#include<conio.h>
 void main()
 {
    int a,b,c;
    clrscr();
    printf("Enter the two numbers\n");
    scanf("%d%d",&a,&b);
    if(a>b)
        printf("%d is greater\n",a);
    else
        printf("%d is greater \n",b);
   getch();
 }
```

```
Output:
Enter the two numbers
345 567
567 is greater
```

EXPLANATION: The program is self explanatory.

```
/* Prog 4.13 To calculate gross salary of the person. Given basic
salary(bs) as input. If bs is >5000 da 55% of bs and hra = 15% of bs else
da = 45% of bs and har=10 % of bs */
#include<stdio.h>
#include<conio.h>
 void main()
 {
    float bs,gs,hra,da;
    clrscr();
    printf("Enter your basic salary\n");
    scanf("%f",&bs);
    if(bs<=5000)
    {
        da=(bs*45)/100;
        hra=(bs*10)/100;
```

```
    }
    else
    {
        da=(bs*55)/100;
        hra=(bs*15)/100;
    }
    gs=bs+da+hra;
    printf("Basic salary is %f\n",bs);
    printf("HRA is %f\n",hra);
    printf("DA is %f\n",da);
    printf("Gross salary is %f\n",gs);
    getch();
}
```

Output:

```
Enter your basic salary
16000
Basic salary is 16000.000000
HRA is 2400.000000
DA is 8800.000000
Gross salary is 27200.000000
```

EXPLANATION: We input the basic salary in **bs.** Through **if** condition we check basic salary **bs** against **5000.** Depending upon whether **if** condition is true or false **hra** and **da** are calculated as per the condition specified in the problem.

4.4 NESTING OF IF-ELSE'S

Nesting of **if-else** means one **if-else** or simple **if** as the part of another **if-else** or simple **if** statement. There may be various syntaxes of nesting of **if-else** We present few of them:

SYNTAX-1

```
if(condition)
{
    If(condition)
        {
            Statements;
            Statements;
            Statements;
            .........................
        }
    else
```

```
        {
           Statements;
           Statements;
           Statements;
        }
}
```

In the above case there is no **else** part of the first **if.**

SYNTAX-2

```
if(condition)
{
     if(condition)
        {
           Statements;
           Statements;
           Statements;
        }
     else
        {
           Statements;
           Statements;
           Statements;
        }
 }
else
 {
           Statements;
           Statements;
           Statements;
 }
```

SYNTAX-3

```
if(condition)
{
    if(condition)
       {
           Statements;
           Statements;
           Statements;
       }
    else
```

```
        {
             Statements;
             Statements;
             Statements;
        }
}
else
{
    if(condition)
        {
             Statements;
             Statements;
             Statements;
        }
else
        {
             Statements;
             Statements;
             Statements;
        }
}
```

We give numbers of examples of nesting of **if-else's** which are based on the above syntaxes.

```
/* Prog 4.14 to check whether a year is leap or not ver 1*/
#include<stdio.h>
#include<conio.h>
 void main()
 {
    int year;
    clrscr();
    printf("Enter any year:-\n");
    scanf("%d",&year);
    if(year%100 ==0)
    {
        if(year %400==0)
            printf("The given year is not a leap year\n");
        else
            printf("The given year is not a leap year\n");
    }
    else
```

```
    {
        if(year%4==0)
            printf("The given year is leap year");
        else
            printf("The given year is not a leap year\n");
    }
    getch();
}
```

Output:

(First run)

```
Enter any year:-
1999
The given year is not a leap year
```

(Second run)

```
Enter any year:-
2000
The given year is a leap year
```

EXPLANATION: A year is leap year if it is completely divisible by 100 and 400 or not divisible by 100 but divisible by 4. Initially if the **year %100** is zero, the inner **if** checks if the **year %400** is zero. If this is so the year is leap else the year is not leap. If the outer **if** fails its corresponding **else** part executes in which we check **year % 4 ==0,** If this is true the year is leap else year is not leap.

```
/*Prog 4.15 To check whether a year is leap or not ver 2*/
#include<stdio.h>
#include<conio.h>
 void main()
 {
  int year,t1,t2;
  clrscr();
  printf("Enter any year\n");
  scanf("%d",&year);
  t1=(year%100==0)&&(year%400==0);
  t2=(year%100!=0)&&(year%4==0);
  if(t1||t2)
      printf("The given year is leap year\n");
  else
      printf("The given year is not a leap year");
  getch();
 }
```

Output:

(first run)

```
Enter any year
2000
The given year is leap year
(second run)
Enter any year
1999
The given year is not a leap year
```

EXPLANATION: The use of && and || operator have reduced the length of the program as well as has made readable and efficient. *t*1 and *t*2 are temporary variables introduced. If any of them is 1 the **if** condition is true and year is leap year else year is not leap year.

```
/*Prog 4.16 Maximum of three numbers ver1 */
#include<stdio.h>
#include<conio.h>
 void main()
 {
    int a,b,c,max;
    clrscr();
    printf("Enter the three numbers\n");
    scanf("%d%d%d",&a,&b,&c);
    if(a==b && b==c)
      printf("All the three numbers are equal");
    else
    {
     if(a>b)
       {
        if(a>c)
                    max=a;
       }
     else
       {
        if(b>c)
                    max=b;
     else
                    max=c;
 }
     printf("%dis greater \n",max);
    }
    getch();
 }
```

```
Output:
(First run)
Enter the three numbers
567 234 198
567is greater
(Second run)
Enter the three numbers
120 120 120
All the three numbers are equal
```

EXPLANATION: If all the numbers are not equal we check **if** $a > b$, if this is true it means a is greater than b, we then check $a > c$ if this so then a is the greatest else c is greatest. If $a > b$ is false initially it means b is greater than a b, we then check whether $b > c$, if this is so then b is greatest else c is greatest.

4.5 ELSE-IF LADDER

The general syntax of **else-if ladder** is given below:

```
if (condition)
         Statements;
            else if(condition)
                            Statements;
                                 else if(condition)
                                              Statements;
                                              .............;
                                              .............;
                                              .............;
```

If the first **if** condition is satisfied, then all its related statements are executed and all other **else-if's** are skipped. The control reaches to first **else-if** only if the first **if** fails. Same for second, third and other **else-if's** depending upon what your program required. **That is out of this else-if ladder only one if condition will be satisfied.**

We present number of programs to illustrate **else-if** ladder construct.

```
/*Prog 4.17 Maximum of three numbers ver2 */
#include<stdio.h>
#include<conio.h>
 void main()
 {
    int a,b,c,max;
    clrscr();
    printf("Enter the three numbers\n");
    scanf("%d%d%d",&a,&b,&c);
```

```
    if((a==c)&&(a==c))
        printf("All three are equal\n");
        else if(a>b&&a>c)
             printf("maximum is %d\n",a);
             else if(b>a&&b>c)
                  printf("maximum is %d\n",b);
    else
        printf("maximum is %d\n",c);
    getch();
  }
```

```
Output:
Enter the three numbers
12 34 56
maximum is 56
```

EXPLANATION: In the above program if all three inputs are equal, first **if** condition is satisfied and after executing its set of statements control reaches directly to **getch().** If first **if** fails it is checked whether ***a*** is greater or ***b*** is greater by the subsequent two **if** conditions using logical **AND** operator else ***c*** is found to be the maximum. The logical operator **&&** have been used for finding maximum of three numbers.

```
/*Prog 4.18 Arrange three numbers in Ascending order ver 1*/
#include<stdio.h>
#include<conio.h>
 void main()
 {
   int a,b,c,min,max,mid;
   clrscr();
   printf("Enter the three numbers\n");
   scanf("%d%d%d",&a,&b,&c);
   if(a>b&&a>c)
     max=a;
     else if(b>a && b>c)
          max=b;
          else if(c>a && c>b)
               max=c;
   if(a<b && a<c)
     min=a;
     else if(b<a && b<c)
          min=b;
          else if(c<a && c<b)
               min=c;
```

```
   mid=(a+b+c)-(min+max);
   printf("Ascending order %d\t%d\t%d\n",min,mid,max);
   getch();
 }
```

Output:

```
Enter the three numbers
23 456 78
Ascending order 23 78 456
```

EXPLANATION: In the variable **max** we have stored the maximum among three and in the variable **min** we have stored the minimum among three. The **mid** is calculated by subtracting **(min + max)** from the sum of ***a, b, c i.e.* (*a* + *b* + *c*).**

This program can also be made using conditional operator and is quite easy in writing as well as requires less amount of code.

See the next program

```
/*Prog 4.19 Arrange three numbers in Ascending order ver 2*/
#include<stdio.h>
#include<conio.h>
  void main()
  {
    int a,b,c,min,max,mid;
    clrscr();
    printf("Enter the three numbers\n");
    scanf("%d%d%d",&a,&b,&c);
    max=a>b?(a>c?a:c):(b>c?b:c);
    min=a<b?(a<c?a:c):(b<c?b:c);
    mid=(a+b+c)-(min+max);
    printf("Ascending order of %d %d %d \n",min,mid,max);
    getch();
  }
```

Output:

```
Enter the three numbers
23 43 12
Ascending order of 12 23 43
```

EXPLANATION: Through nesting of conditional operator we have found min and max among three and rest is same as explained in the previous program.

```
/*Prog 4.20 To determine the status of entered character */
#include<stdio.h>
#include<conio.h>
 void main()
```

```
 {
    char c;
    clrscr();
    printf("Enter a character\n");
    scanf("%c",&c);
    if(c>=65 && c<=90)
       printf("U entered uppercase letter\n");
       else if(c>=97 && c<=122)
              printf("U entered lowercase letter\n");
                   else if(c>=48 && c<=57)
                          printf("U entered a digit\n");
    else
    {
       printf("U entered a special symbol\n");
    }
    getch();
 }
```

Output:

(First run)

```
Enter a character
D
U entered uppercase letter
```

(second run)

```
Enter a character
f
U entered lowercase letter
```

(third run)

```
Enter a character
#
U entered a special symbol
```

EXPLANATION: The ASCII values for lowercase alphabets is from **97 to 122 (inclusive both)** and for uppercase it is from **65 to 97(inclusive both).** It is checked whether the entered character is within these two ranges using **else-if ladder.** Similarly ASCII values for digits are from **48 to 57 (inclusive both)** so character entered is also checked with this range. If all three conditions fail then the character entered must be a special symbol.

```
/* Prog 4.21 Program for case conversion */
#include<stdio.h>
#include<conio.h>
 void main()
 {
```

```
  char c;
  clrscr();
  printf("Enter a character\n");
  scanf("%c",&c);
  if(c>=65 && c<=90)
    printf("Lower case equivalent is %c\n",c+32);
         else if(c>=97 && c<=122)
               printf("Upper case equivalent is %c\n",c-32);
  else
      printf("Not a character\n");
      getch();
  }
```

Output:

(First run)

```
Enter a character
f
Upper case equivalent is F
```

(Second run)

```
Enter a character
D
Lower case equivalent is d
```

Explanation: Difference between ASCII values of uppercase and lower case alphabet is 32 i.e.

$$\text{'A'} + 32 = \text{'}a\text{'}$$

Or

$$\text{'}a\text{'} - 32 = \text{'A'}$$

As stated above characters are treated as integers so arithmetic operation can be performed on them.

/*Prog 4.22 To determine grade of student based on its percentage*/

```
#include<stdio.h>
#include<conio.h>
#include<stdlib.h>
  void main()
  {
     float m1,m2,m3,per;
     clrscr();
     printf("Enter the marks in three subjects (max 100)\n");
     scanf("%f%f%f",&m1,&m2,&m3);
     if((m1<1 && m1>100)||(m2<1 && m2>100) ||(m3<1 && m3>100))
```

```
    {
        printf("Marks must be within the range 0 to 100 \n");
        getch();
        exit(0);
    }
       per=(m1+m2+m3)/3;
       if(per>=90)
        printf("Grade is A\n");
         else if(per>=80 && per<90)
           printf("Grade is B\n");
             else if(per>=70 && per<80)
               printf("Grade is C\n");
                 else if(per>=60 && per<70)
                   printf("Grade is D\n")
                     else if(per>=50 && per<60);
                       printf("Grade is E\n");
       else
                       printf("Fail\n");
      getch();
   }
```

Output:

```
Enter the marks in three subjects
89 87 90
Grade is B
```

EXPLANATION: Initial **if** condition ensures that user enters marks range **0 to 100.** On the basis of percentage we display the grade of the student. For calculation of percentage we have reduced **(*a* + *b* + *c*)/100*300** to just **(*a* + *b* + *c*)/3.** If **per>=90** we display **grade A** else for **per** in between **80 to 90** the **grade is B** and so on. In the initial **if** you do not write **getch()** program will terminate immediately without letting you to see the execution of **printf** statement.

```
/*Prog 4.23 To determine roots of the quadratic equation */
#include<stdio.h>
#include<conio.h>
 void main()
 {
   float a,b,c,r1,r2,dis;
   clrscr();
   printf("Enter the value of a,b,and c\n");
   scanf("%f%f%f",&a,&b,&c);
   dis=b*b-4*a*c;
```

```
   if(dis<0)
      printf("Roots are imaginary\n");
   else if(dis==0)
   {
         printf("Roots are equal\n");
         printf("Root1=%f\n",-b/(2*a));
         printf("Root2=%f\n",-b/(2*a));
   }
   else
   {
         printf("Roots are unequal\n");
         r1=(-b+sqrt(dis))/(2.0*a);
         r2=(-b-sqrt(dis))/(2.0*a);
         printf("Root1=%f\n",r1);
         printf("Root2=%f\n",r2);
   }
   getch();
}
```

Output:

(First run)

```
Enter the value of a,b,and c
2 3 4
Roots are imaginary
```

(Second run)

```
Enter the value of a,b,and c
2 5 3
Roots are unequal
Root1=8182.750000
Root2=-8185.250000
```

(Third run)

```
Enter the value of a,b,and c
4 4 1
Roots are equal
Root1=-0.500000
Root2=-0.500000
```

EXPLANATION: The **quadratic equation** in mathematics is given as:

$$AX^2 + BX + C = 0$$

Where A, B, and C are constants. The solution of the equation comprises of two roots as power of X is 2.

$$R1 = (-B + \sqrt{} B*B - 4 *A *C) / 2* A$$
$$R2 = (-B - \sqrt{} B*B - 4 *A *C) / 2* A$$

The expression **B*B – 4 *A*C** is known as **discriminant (say dis)** and on the basis of its value the roots are determined as equal **(dis= = 0) imaginary (dis<0) or unequal (dis>0)** as shown in the above program.

In the program we take as input the three constant's value using A, B, and C and calculate the value of **dis.**

4.6 SWITCH-CASE STATEMENT

Switch-case statement can be used to replace **else-if ladder** construct. Its general syntax is as follows:

```
switch(expression)
{
   case choice1:
                    statements;
                    break;
   case choice2:
                    statements;
                    break;
   case choice3:
                    statements;
                    break;
   ..................................
   ..................................
   ..................................
   default:
}
```

The **expression** may be any **integer** or **char** type which yield only **char or integer** as result. **choice 1, choice 2, and choice *n*** are the possible values which we are going to test with the expression. In case none of the values from **choice 1** to **choice *n*** matches with the values of **expression** the **default** case is executed.

Some Points for Switch-case Statements

- The switch statement is a multi-way branch statement.
- If there is a possibility to make a choice from a number of options, this structured selection is useful.
- The switch statement evaluates expression and then looks for its value among the case constant.
- If the value matches with case constant, this particular case statement is executed. If not default is executed.

- Switch, case and default are reversed keywords.
- The break statement used in switch ( ) passed control outside the switch ( ) block. By mistake if no break statements are given all the cases following it are executed.

```
/* Prog 4.24 Demo of switch-case ver 1 */
#include<stdio.h>
#include<conio.h>
 void main()
 {
   int num;
   clrscr();
   printf("Enter 0,1,or 2\n");
   scanf("%d",&num);
   switch(num)          /*Switch statement start*/
   {
      case 0:
               printf("U entered zero\n");
               break;
      case 1:
               printf("U entered one\n");
               break;
      case 2:
               printf("U entered two\n");
               break;
      default:
               printf("Other than 0,1,2\n");
   }
   getch();
 }
```

Output:

(First run)

```
Enter 0,1,or 2
0
U entered zero
```

(Second run)

```
Enter 0,1,or 2
1
U entered one
```

(Third run)

```
Enter 0,1,or 2
```

```
2
U entered two
(Fourth run)
Enter 0,1,or 2
3
Other than 0,1,2
```

EXPLANATION: The condition to be checked is placed inside **switch** enclosed in parenthesis. The different values against which condition is checked is put using **case** statement. In the first case value is checked against **0.** This is similar to writing **if(num = = 0).** The colon: after **case** gets executed. Similarly, if the value of **num** is **zero** then first case matches and all the statement under that **case** gets executed. Similarly if the value of **num** is **1** second **case** gets executed and same for the rest of the **case** statements. A **break** statement is needed to ignore the rest of the **case** statements and come out from **switch** block in case a match is found. If none of the **case** matches then **default** gets executed. Writing **default** is optional.

```
/*Prog 4.25 Demo of switch-case ver 2*/
#include<stdio.h>
#include<conio.h>
 void main()
 {
  int num;
  clrscr();
  printf("Enter 0,1,or 2\n");
  scanf("%d",&num);
  switch(num)
  {
   case 0:
                printf("U entered zero \n");
                break;
   case 1:
                printf("U entered one \n");
   case 2:
                printf("U entered two\n");
                break;
   default:
                printf("other than 0,1,2\n");
  }
  getch();
 }
Output:
(First run)
```

```
Enter 0, 1, or 2
0
U entered zero
(Second run)
Enter 0, 1, or 2
1
U entered one
U entered two
```

EXPLANATION: There is no **break** statement in **case 1** and **case 2** are assumed to be true so the output. In fact due to the absence of **break** statement in the second case rest of the statements are considered part of the second **case** till a **break** is not found. **break in case 2** causes control to come out from **switch.** If break were not in **case 2,** also then **default** would got executed too.

```
/* Prog 4.26 To check given character is vowel or not using switch case
ver 1*/
#include<stdio.h>
#include<conio.h>
 void main()
 {
    char ch;
    clrscr();
    printf("Enter any character \n");
    scanf("%c",&ch);
    switch(ch)
    {
       default:
                   printf("Not a vowel\n");
                   break;
       case'a':
       case'e':
       case'i':
       case'o':
       case'u':
                   printf("It is a vowel\n");
                   break;
    }
    getch();
 }
Output:
(first run)
Enter any character
```

```
a
It is a vowel
(second run)
Enter any character
f
Not a vowel
```

EXPLANATION: As stated earlier only characters and integers can be used within **switch. default can be put anywhere in the switch block.** For this **break** statement has to be written. If you put **default** statement at the end of **switch block** then writing **break is optional.** For five different cases only one statement executes i.e. out of five cases if any of the case is true **printf** executes. There is no other way of combining all cases al-together.

There is one limitation of the above program. This program works only for vowels that are input in lower case as lower and upper case are treated differently in C. For handling upper case also see the next example.

```
/* Prog 4.27 To check given character is vowel or not using switch case
ver 2*/
#include<stdio.h>
#include<conio.h>
  void main()
  {
      char ch;
      clrscr();
      printf("Enter any character\n");
      scanf("%c",&ch);
      switch(ch)
      {
         default:
                   printf("It is not vowel\n");
                   break;
         case'A':
         case'a':
         case'E':
         case'e':
         case'I':
         case'i':
         case'O':
         case'o':
         case'U':
         case'u':
                   printf("It's a vowel");
```

```
                break;
        }
        getch();
    }
```

```
Output:
Enter any character
A
It's a vowel
```

EXPLANATION: In the program irrespective of what we input **'a' or 'A'** the output will be same. You can put multiple **case** statements in this manner. There is no limit on number of **case** statements a **switch block** may have.

4.7 HANDLING CHARACTER INPUT\OUTPUT

We have seen only few programs which dealt with character input and output. Also input of character from keyboard was done through scanf with %*c* format specifier and same %*c* was used for printing character using **printf** onto the screen.

C provides several built-in functions for handling input / output as well as for other operations on characters. In this section we will discuss the use of these functions through numbers of program.

```
/* Prog 4.28 Demo of getchar ()and putchar () */
#include<stdio.h>
#include<conio.h>
 void main()
 {
   char ch;
   clrscr();
   printf("Enter any character\n");
   ch=getchar();
   printf("U entered \n");
   putchar(ch);
   getch();
 }
```

```
Output:
Enter any character
f
U entered
f
```

EXPLANATION: The function **getchar( )** is used to take input a single character from keyboard. It takes no argument but returns the character which in **ch.** The function **putchar ( )** is used to print a single character onto the screen. This function takes just one argument, the character to be displayed in this case it is **ch.**

```
/* Prog 4.29 checking case of given character using built-in functions
*/
#include<stdio.h>
#include<conio.h>
#include<ctype.h>
 void main()
 {
   char ch;
   clrscr();
   printf("Enter a character\n");
   ch=getchar();
   printf("U entered\n");
   putchar(ch);
   if(isupper(ch))
     printf("\nThe character is in uppercase\n");
   else
     printf("\nThe character is in lowercase\n");
   getch();
 }
```

Output:

(First run)

```
Enter a character
D
U entered
D
The character is in uppercase
```

(Second run)

```
Enter a character
d
U entered
d
The character is in lowercase
```

EXPLANATION: The function **isupper** checks whether the character **ch** is in upper case or not. If it is so it returns a non-zero value and **if** condition is true. On the similar basis you can use **islower** function to check for character in lower case. Both of these functions are declared in **ctype.h** so this file must be included in your program.

```
/* Prog 4.30 case conversion using built-in function */
#include<stdio.h>
#include<conio.h>
#include<ctype.h> /*for tolower and toupper functions*/
```

```
void main()
{
   char ch;
   clrscr();
   printf("Enter a character\n");
   ch=getchar();
   printf("U entered \n");
   putchar(ch);
   printf("\nReverse case is \n");
   if(isupper(ch))
      putchar(tolower(ch));
   else
      putchar(toupper(ch));
   getch();
}
```

Output:

(First run)

```
Enter a character
A
U entered
A
Reverse case is
a
```

(Second run)

```
Enter a character
a
U entered
a
Reverse case is
A
```

EXPLANATION: If the character entered is in upper case we convert the same in lower case using in-built function **tolower.** If the **if** condition is not true it means character entered is in lower case so we convert it into upper case using in-built function **toupper.** Similar to **isupper** we also have macro **islower.** Again both of these are declared in file **ctype.h** so don't forget to include the file.

4.7.1 getch ( ), getche ( ) and getchar ( )

Here we discuss the differences and similarity between the three functions **getch, getche and getchar.** The use of **getchar( )** and **getch ( )** we have seen earlier but use of **getche( )** to input character and displaying was not discussed.

1. **getch ( ):** Reads a single character from the keyboard without echoing it on the screen *i.e.* it doesn't wait. As soon as key is pressed it returns. That's why we have been using this function to display results of our program when we press **ctrl+F9** key.
2. **getche( ):** This function is similar to **getch( )** with the difference that echoes the entered character on to the screen.
3. **getchar( ):** It takes a character and waits for the user to press **Enter** key

   Here we present a small program to show the effects of these functions.

```
/*Prog 4.31 Demo of getch( ), getche()and getchar()*/
#include<stdio.h>
#include<conio.h>
 void main()
 {
    char a,b,c;
    clrscr();
    printf("Enter any character (getch() version)\n");
    a=getch();
    printf("\n Enter any character(getche()version)\n");
    b=getche();
    printf("\n Enter any character(getchar()version)\n");
    c=getchar();
    printf("\n Entered characters are %c %c %c\n",a,b,c);
    getch();
 }
Output:
Enter any character (getch() version)
Enter any character(getche()version)
s
Enter any character(getchar()version)
d
Entered characters are a s d
```

EXPLANATION: In the first character input we entered a but it was not displayed due to **getch ( ),** but character was stored in variable ***a*** successfully. In the second case character entered was ***s,*** it was echoed and stored in variable ***b*** due to **getche ( ).** In third case the character entered was ***d.*** After entering *d,* **getchar ( )** waited for user to press **Enter key.** The entered characters were displayed then.

4.8 UNCONDITIONAL BRANCHING USING GOTO

The goto statement is used to transfer control of program from one point to other. In fact it make program control to jump to the statement specified by a lable. This type of **unconditional transfer of control using goto is called branching.** The label must be in the same function in which **goto** is used.

The general syntax for goto statement is as follows:

goto label;

We understand the use of **goto** using a program.

```
/* Prog 4.32 Demo of goto ver1 */
#include<stdio.h>
#include<conio.h>
#include<math.h>
 void main()
 {
  int x;
  clrscr();
  start:              /* defined a label*/
  printf("Enter a +ve number\n");
  scanf("%d",&x);
  if(x<0)
  goto start;/*ifcondition true backward jump to label start*/
  printf("sqrt of number is %f\n",sqrt(x));
  getch();
 }
Output:
(First run)
Enter a +ve number
28
sqrt of number is 5.291503
(Second run)
Enter a +ve number
-25
Enter a +ve number
25
sqrt of number is 5.000000
```

EXPLANATION: The **start :** is terminated as a label. The start is a label name which must be followed by a colon. Any valid identifier name can be taken as label name .When a –ve number is entered **if** condition returns true and control is transferred back to **start** using **goto start;** statement. In the program the jump is backward here the control is being transferred previous to the **goto start;** statement hence it is **backward jump.** If it were ahead of **goto start;** then it would be a **forward jump.**

```
/*Prog 4.33 Demo of goto over 2*/
#include<stdio.h>
#include<conio.h>
 void main()
```

```
{
   clrscr();
   goto start2;
   start1:
          printf("I'm at the start1 label \n");
   start2:
          printf("I'm at the start2 label \n');
   getch();
}
```

Output:

```
I'm at the start2 label
```

EXPLANATION: In the program we have two labels named **start1** and **start2.** The first label is skipped by transferring control directly to label 2 *i.e.* **start2.** This is forward jump.

In the above program if we have to reach at **start2 first** then **start1** and then simply at the end of program we could modify the program as shown below.

```
/*Prog 4.34 Demo of got over 3*/
#include<stdio.h>
#include<conio.h>
 void main()
 {
   clrscr();
   goto start2;
   start1:
          printf("I'm at the label1\n");
          goto end;
   start2:
          printf("I'm at the label2 \n");
          goto start1;
   end:
          printf("Terminating the program\n");
   getch();
 }
```

Output:

```
I'm at the label2
I'm at the label1
Terminating the program
```

EXPLANATION: The program is self explanatory.

```
/*Prog 4.35 Loop creation using goto */
#include<stdio.h>
```

```
#include<conio.h>
 void main()
 {
     int n=0;
     clrscr();
     printf("Loop starts\n");
     loop: n++;
     printf("n=%d\n",n);
     if(n<5)
                    goto loop;
     printf("Loop ends\n");
     getch();
 }
```

Output:

```
Loop starts
n=1
n=2
n=3
n=4
n=5
Loop ends
```

EXPLANATION: Initial value of ***n*** is **0.** It is incremented at label **loop** and then printed. The value of ***n*** is checked against **5** using **if.** If ***n*** **< 5** then control is transferred back to **loop** label *i.e.* same set of codes are repeated for a finite number of time (here number is 5). This is looping which we have achieved using **goto** and **if.**

POINTS TO PONDER

In this section you have learned the following points.

- An important task of a program is to instruct the computer to jump to a different portion of the code according to the specified branch conditions.
- The if statement is a very important statement for conditional branching in C.
- The if statement can be nested for making a series of decisions in your program.
- The if-else statement is an expansion of the if statement.
- The switch statement helps you to keep your program more readable when there are more than just a couple decisions to be made in your code.
- The case and default keywords, followed by a colon (:) and an integral value, are used in the switch statement as labels.
- The break statement can be used to exit the switch construct or a loop (usually, an infinite loop).

- The continue statement is used to let you stay within a loop while skipping over some statements.
- The goto statement enables the computer to jump to some other spots in your computer. Using this statement is not recommended because it may cause your program to be unreliable and hard to debug.

QUESTIONS AND ANSWERS

Q1. *How many expressions are there in the if statement?*

Ans: The if statement takes only one expression to hold the conditional criteria. When the expression is true (that is, the conditions are met), the statements controlled by the if statement are executed. Otherwise, the next statement following the if statement block is executed.

Q2. *Why is the if-else statement an expansion of the if statement?*

Ans: When the conditional expression in the if statement is false, the program control flow is returned back to the original track. However, when the conditional expression in the if-else statement is false, the program control flow branches to the statement block under the else keyword and returns to its original track after the statements controlled by else are executed. In other words, the if statement allows a single statement block to be executed or skipped entirely, whereas the if-else statement executes one of the two statement blocks under the control of the if-else statement.

Q3. *Why do you normally need to add the break statement into the switch statement?*

Ans: When one of the cases within the switch statement is selected, the program control will branch to the case and execute all statements within the selected case and the rest of the cases that follow it. Therefore, you might get more results than you expected. To tell the computer to execute only the statements inside a selected case, you can put a break statement at the end of the case so that the program control flow will exit the switch construct after the statements within the case are executed.

Q4. *What can the continue statement do inside a loop?*

Ans: When the continue statement inside a loop is executed, the program control is branched back to the beginning of the loop so that another iteration can be started. Inside the loop, any statements following the continue statement will be skipped over each time if the continue statement is executed.

EXERCISES

A. Answer the following questions:

1. What are the limitations of switch-case statement?
2. Is it possible to use multiple else with if statement?
3. Can we use multiple default statement in switch-case in C?
4. Can we put default statement anywhere in the switch-case structure?
5. Give the reason for avoidance of goto statement?

6. Why break statement is essential in switch-case structure? Which other functions or keywords can be used in place of the break statement?
7. Write the use of else and default statements in if ...else and switch case statements respectively.
8. Explain the break and goto with the help of examples?
9. Why use of goto statement is discouraged in programming?

B. Brain Drill

1. Write a program to check whether a voter is eligible for voting or not? If his/her age is equal to or greater 18 display "Eligible" else display "Not eligible".
2. Write a program to check whether a triangle can be formed with three positive integers supplied.
3. Write a program to check whether a triangle is right-angled or not.
4. Write a program which will find whether a number is divisible by 2,3,4,5 and 6.
5. Write a program in C to find out largest of 10 numbers using if and goto only.
6. Write a program in C that will read the values of x and evaluate the following function.

   1 for x > 0

   Y = 0 for x = 0

   – 1 for *x* < 0

7. Write a program to calculate the amount of the bill for the following jobs.
   (*a*) Scanning and hardcopy of a passport photo Rs. 5/-.
   (*b*) Scanning and hardcopies (more than 10) Rs. 3/-.
8. Write a program to calculate bill of Internet browsing. The conditions are given below:
   (*a*) 1 Hour – 20 Rs.
   (*b*) ½ Hour – 15Rs.
   (*c*) Hours – 90Rs.

   The owner should enter number of hours spent by customer.
9. Write a program to calculate the sum of remainders obtained by dividing with modular division operations by 2 on 1 to 9 numbers.

C. Match the following columns:

I	II
1. **break**	(*a*) can be put anywhere in switch-case
2. **branching**	(*b*) used for early exit.
3. **typedef**	(*c*) used for creating new data type.
4. **getche()**	(*d*) echo the character
5. **getch()**	(*e*) goto is used
6. **default**	(*f*) does not echo the character.

D. Write True and False against each statement:

1. The construct **if *a>b;*** is correct syntax for **if**.
2. C supports **if-else-then** construct.
3. **if (*x*)** means **if(*x* = 0)**

4. **switch-case** is selective control struct.
5. For decision making in C **if-else-endif** is used.
6. **continue** can be used inside **switch-case.**
7. **goto** is used inside **switch-case.**
8. **getchar()** can be used to read an integer.

E. Fill in the blanks:

1. In C there are ____________ ways to declare constants.
2. **if(!*x*)** is equal to ____________.
3. The ____________ can be placed anywhere in the switch-case statement
4. In switch only ____________ expression can be used
5. **if** is used for ____________ in C.
6. The use of ____________ should be avoided in programming
7. In else-if ladder only ____________ condition can be used at a time.
8. For character manipulation functions header file used is ____________.

F. Predict the output of the following programs:

```
1. main()
   {
       if(!3.14)
             printf("Hello PI\n");
       else
             printf("bye bye \n");
   }
2. main()
   {
       unsigned int x=-10; int y=10;
       if(y<=x)printf("I'm good\n");
       if(y==(x=-10))printf("Rama is better\n");
       if((int)x==y)printf("We are the best\n");
   }
3. main()
   {
       int a=2,b=4,c=8,x=4;
       if (x==b)
       x=a;
       else
       x=b;
       if(x!=b)
       c = c + b;
       else
```

```
    c = c + a;
    printf("c=%d \n",c);
  }
4. main()
  {
    int x=2,y=2,z=1;
    if(x = y % 2)
    z + = 10;
    else
    z + = 20;
    printf("x=%d",x);
  }
5. main()
  {
    int sc = 4;
    switch(sc)
    {
      default: ;
      case 3:
                  sc + = 5;
                  if(sc == 8)
                  {
                    sc++;
                    if(sc==9)break;
                    sc *=2;
                  }
                  sc -= 4;
                  break;
      case 8:
                  sc+=5;
                  break;
    }
      printf("sc=%d\n",sc);
    }
6. main()
  {
    int i=0;
    switch(i)
    {
      case 0: i++;
```

```
        case 1: i+++2;
        case 2: ++i;
    }
    printf("%d",i++);
}
```

7. main()

```
{
    int x=10,y=0;
    if (x && y++)
    printf("x=%d\ty=%d\n",x++,--y);
}
```

8. main()

```
{
    int x=0,y=10;
    if(x||y++)
    printf("x=%d\ty=%d\n",x++,--y);
}
```

5

INTRODUCTION TO LOOPING STRUCTURE IN 'C'

The Chapter takes you to a long journey of one of the most important and very useful programming construct, the loop. A basic introduction to loop is given in the beginning of the Chapter. Introduction to all different types of loops **while, for and do-while** available in C is given.

While loop is explained in detail with the help of lot of programming examples in the step-by-step manner *i.e.*, starting from basic small programs up to complex programs have been explained in a lucid manner. Common programming errors in the usage are also pin pointed through small programs. Use of **break** and **continue** statement is illustrated with examples.

The most frequently used **for** loop is explained in greater length with programming examples ranging from factorial, prime number, to pattern displaying programs with the help of nesting of **for** loops. Additional programming examples have been given as two parts. In the **section 5.10 do-while** loop is discussed with its unique features of executing at least once even condition is false. Differences between **do-while** loop and **while** loop are discussed.

Points to ponder section presents some key points of the Chapter.

5.1 INTRODUCTION

Looping is a process in which set of statements are executed repeatedly for a finite or infinite number of times. C provides three ways to perform looping by providing three different types of loop. Looping can be called synonymously iteration of repetition. Loops are the most important part of almost all the programming language such as C, C++, java, VB, C#, Delphi etc.

In our practical life we see lots of examples where some repetitive tasks has to be performed like finding average marks of students of a class, finding maximum salary of group of employees, counting numbers etc.

A loop is a block of statements with which are executed again and again till a specific condition is satisfied. C provides three loops to perform repetitive action.

1. **while**
2. **for**
3. **do-while**

To work with any types of loop three things have to be performed:

- Loop control variable and its initialization.
- Condition for controlling the loop.
- Increment / decrement of control variable.

LOOPS: C gives you a choice of three types of loop, while, do while and for.

- The **while loop** keeps repeating an action until an associated test returns false. This is useful where the programmer does not know in advance how many times the loop will be traversed.
- The **do while** loops is similar, but the test occurs after the loop body is executed. This ensures that the loop body is run at least once.
- The **for** loop is frequently used, usually where the loop will be traversed a fixed number of times. It is very flexible, and novice programmers should take care not to abuse the power it offers.

Let's work first with the while loop.

5.1.1 The While Loop

The syntax of the while loop is simple:

```
while (condition)
{
    Statements;
    Statements;
    ..........................;
}
```

The statements inside { } is called body of the **while** loop. If no braces are there then only the first statement after **while** is constructed as the body of the **while** loop. All the statements within the body are repeated till the condition specified in the parenthesis in **while** is satisfied. As soon as condition becomes false the body is skipped and control is transferred to the next statement outside the loop. There should be no semicolon after the **while.** We will see what happens when you do so.

Let's write few programs to understand the **while** loop better.

```
/*Prog 5.1 Demo of while loop (printing number 1 to 10) ver 1*/
#include<stdio.h>
#include<conio.h>
void main()
{
  int t=1;
```

```
    clrscr();
    while(t<=10)
    {
      printf("t=%d\n",t);
      t++;
    }
    getch();
  }
```

Output:

```
t=1
t=2
t=3
t=4
t=5
t=6
t=7
t=8
t=9
t=10
```

EXPLANATION: In the **while** loop we have stated the condition ***t* < = 10.** *t* is called loop control variable. Initially value of *t* is **1.** This value of *t* is compared with 10 which is true so control reaches into the while loop and printf statement within loop executes which prints the value of ***t.*** Then *t* is incremented by **1** *i.e.,* becomes **2.** Control reaches back to the condition of the while loop which is true. This process continues. When value of **t** becomes **11**, which causes condition in the while loop to becomes false and control comes out of loop. As there is no statement outside the loop so program terminates.

```
/*Prog 5.2 Demo of while loop (printing number 1 to 10) ver 1*/
#include<stdio.h>
#include<conio.h>
 void main()
 {
    int t=1;
    clrscr();
    while(t<=10)
    printf("t=%d\n",t++);
    getch();
 }
```

Output:

```
t=1
t=2
t=3
t=4
t=5
t=6
t=7
t=8
t=9
t=10
```

EXPLANATION: This program is similar to previous one but the coding is reduced. The braces are not necessary because there is only statement after while so the body comprises only one statement. First **t** printed then incremented which is checked for the condition and loop continues till condition returns true.

```
/* Prog 5.3 Printing number 5 to 1 using while loop ver 1*/
#include<stdio.h>
#include<conio.h>
 void main()
 {
   int t=5;
   clrscr();
   while(t>=1)
   printf("t=%d\n",t--);
   getch();
 }
```

Output:

```
t=5
t=4
t=3
t=2
t=1
```

EXPLANATION: This program is simple. Here we have printed the value from **5 to 1** by decrementing the control variable ***t* by 1** in each successive iteration till **t > = 1** condition satisfied.

```
/*Prog 5.4 printing numbers 5 to 1 using while loop ver 2*/
#include<stdio.h>
#include<conio.h>
 void main()
 {
```

```
   int t=5;
   clrscr();
   while(t-->=1)
   printf("%d\t",t);
   getch();
 }
```

Output:

```
4    3    2    1    0
```

EXPLANATION: This program does not produce the intended output. Where the fault does lies? In the expression *t-->=1* first **t** is tested against **1** then *t* is decremented. Initially **t** is 5 so condition is true now t becomes 4 which is printed. In the next iteration 4 is compared with 1 which is true then t decremented by 1 resulting the value 3 which is printed and so on. If you want output 5 to 1 then simply make *t* = 6.

```
/*Prog 5.5 Thing not to be done */
#include<stdio.h>
#include<conio.h>
 void main()
 {
    int t=5;
    clrscr();
    while(t>=1);      /* Wrong things */
    printf("t=%d\t",t--);
    getch();
 }
```

Output:

Infinite loop

EXPLANATION: The **semicolon (;)** after the while is called empty statement which is also the body of the while loop since no braces are there. Empty statement means doing nothing so while loop does nothing and keeps checking value of *t* against 1 as t is 5 initially so condition remains true forever, so the infinite loop.

```
/*Prog 5.6 printing all even number between 1 to 30 */
#include<stdio.h>
#include<conio.h>
 void main()
 {
    int t=1;
    clrscr();
    while(t<30)
    {
       if(t%2==0)
```

```
  printf("t=%d\t",t);
  t++;
    }
    getch();
 }
```

Output:

```
t=2     t=4     t=6     t=8     t=10    t=12    t=14    t=16    t=18
t=20    t=22    t=24    t=26    t=28
```

EXPLANATION: This program simply checks remainder when t is divided by 2. If it is 0 *i.e.,* even number the value of t is printed. This continues till t is less than 30.

```
/* Prog 5.7 printing all odd numbers between 1 and 30*/
#include<stdio.h>
#include<conio.h>
 void main()
 {
    int t=1;
    clrscr();
    while(t<30)
    {
       if(t%2==1)
  printf("t=%d\t",t);
  t++;
    }
    getch();
 }
```

Output:

```
t=1     t=3     t=5     t=7     t=9     t=11    t=13    t=15    t=17
t=19    t=21    t=23    t=25    t=27    t=29
```

EXPLANATION: This program is similar to previous one with the difference that it prints all odd numbers between **1** (inclusive) and **30.**

With one small change in the program and what you get.

```
/*Prog 5.8 printing all odd numbers between 1 and 30 ver 2*/
#include<stdio.h>
#include<conio.h>
 void main()
 {
  int t=1;
  clrscr();
  while(t<=30)
```

```
    if(t%2==1)
       printf("t=%d\t",t++);
  getch();
 }
```

Output:

```
t=1 (infinite loop)
```

EXPLANATION: For the first time **t** =1 and condition in the while loop is true. Body of the while loop is the if conditional statement only as there are no braces around the while loop. The if condition is true so **1** is printed and t is incremented, **t** becomes 2 now. Condition in the while loop is tested which is true but this time condition in the if is false so printf is skipped and control reaches back to while. Condition is true as 2<=30 but if condition fails again and this continues for infinite number of times as t remains 2 forever.

```
/*Prog 5.9 printing numbers between 1 and 100 which are completely
divisible by 3 and 5 */
#include<stdio.h>
#include<conio.h>
 void main()
 {
    int t=1;
    clrscr();
    while(t<=100)
    {
    if(t%3==0 && t%5==0)
       printf("%d\t",t);
       t=t+1;
    }
    getch();
 }
```

Output:

```
15     30    45    60    75    90
```

EXPLANATION: If remainder divided by 3 is zero then number is completely divisible by 3. Same is true for 5 so we have combined the two conditions by **&& (logical AND)** operator so if remainder in both the cases is zero than && condition will hold true and that number will be printed

```
/*Prog 5.10 printing numbers 10 20 .....100 */
#include<stdio.h>
#include<conio.h>
 void main()
 {
    int t=10;
    clrscr();
```

```
   while(t<=100)
   {
     printf("t=%d\t",t);
     t=t+10;
   }
   getch();
 }
```

Output:

```
t=10    t=20    t=30    t=40    t=50    t=60    t=70
t=80    t=90    t=100
```

EXPLANATION: This program tests the condition *t<=100* and in the body increments *t* by **10** thus prints value from **10 to 100.**

```
/*Prog 5.11 generation of table of any given number*/
#include<stdio.h>
#include<conio.h>
 void main()
 {
  int n,t=1,value;
  clrscr();
  printf("Enter any +ve number\n");
  scanf("%d",&n);
  printf("Table for the enterd number is given below\n");
  while(t<=10)
  {
   value=n*t;
   printf("%d * %d = %d\n",n,t,value);
   t++;
  }
  getch();
 }
```

Output:

```
Enter any +ve number
7
Table for the enterd number is given below
7 * 1 = 7
7 * 2 = 14
7 * 3 = 21
7 * 4 = 28
7 * 5 = 35
7 * 6 = 42
```

```
7 * 7 = 49
7 * 8 = 56
7 * 9 = 63
7 * 10 = 70
```

EXPLANATION: Any +ve number is taken as input .The number *n* is multiplied by 1 through 10 inside the while loop and the loop counter, number and value is displayed by formatting as to produce the desired output.

```
/* Prog 5.12 maximum of n elements */
#include<stdio.h>
#include<conio.h>
 void main()
 {
    int n,max,t=1,m;
    clrscr();
    printf("Enter how many numbers \n");
    scanf("%d",&n);
    printf("Enter the number\n");
    scanf("%d",&m);
    max=m;
    while(t<n-1)
    {
       printf("Enter the number\n");
       scanf("%d",&m);
       if(max<m)
        max=m;
        t++;
    }
    printf("maximum element is %d\n",max);
    getch();
}
```

Output:

```
Enter how many numbers
5
Enter the number
12
Enter the number
34
Enter the number
5
Enter the number
```

```
1212
maximum element is 1212
```

EXPLANATION: Initially numbers of elements are taken is ***n***. The first number is taken outside the loop and assumed to be maximum; this number is stored in **max.** Then remaining numbers are taken inside the loop. On each iteration the number is compared with the **max,** if the max is less than number taken then number will be the maximum one. This is checked through if statement. In the end when control comes out from while loop max is displayed.

```
/* Prog 5.13 to reverse the number ver 1 */
#include<stdio.h>
#include<conio.h>
 void main()
 {
    int orig,rev=0,r;
    clrscr();
    printf("Enter the number\n");
    scanf("%d",&orig);
    while(orig!=0)
    {
       r=orig%10;
       rev=rev*10+r;
       orig=orig/10;
    }
    printf("Reverse Number =%d\n",rev);
    getch();
 }
```

Output:

```
Enter the number
3456
Reverse Number =6543
```

EXPLANATION: The logic to reverse a number is quite simple. Let's understand it step by step inside the loop:

Suppose orig => original number entered by programmer.

```
            rev => reverse of the orig.
               r => remainder
            while(orig!=0)
            {
               r=orig%10;
               rev = rev *10 +r;
               orig= orig /10;
```

```
        }
```

Let's understand step-by-step procedure inside the loop.

Initially set r=0

Suppose orig = 3456

Then while (3456! = 0) **(condition given inside while loop is true)**

S1:	orig =3456	r = 3456 % 10 = 6	rev = 0*10 +6= 6	orig =3456/10 =345
S2	orig = 345	r = 345 %10= 5	rev =6*10 +5 =65	orig =345/10= 34
S3	orig =34	r = 34%10 = 4	rev = 65*10 + 4 =654	orig =34/10=3
S4	orig =3	r =3%10 = 3	rev = 654 *10 + 3 = 6543	orig = 3/10=0
S5	orig=0			

As **orig =0** so condition inside the **while** loop is false and control comes out of loop. The reverse number is variable **rev which is printed.**

```
/*Prog 5.14 to reverse the number ver2*/
#include<stdio.h>
#include<conio.h>
 void main()
 {
   int orig,r;
   clrscr();
   printf("Enter the number\n");
   scanf("%d",&orig);
   printf("Reverse Number=");
   while(orig!=0)
   {
     r=orig%10;
     printf("%d",r);
     orig/=10;
   }
   getch();
 }
```

Output:

```
Enter the number
2345
Reverse Number=5432
```

EXPLANATION: This program simply finds remainder by **10** of the entered number **orig** prints it. It then removes the last digit from original number by dividing the original number **orig** by 10 and storing it back in the original number. This continues till number **orig** does not become zero.

```
/*Prog 5.15 To check whether a number is Armstrong or not */
#include<stdio.h>
```

```
#include<conio.h>
 void main()
 {
    int num,r,save,newnum=0,count=0;
    clrscr();
    printf("Enter the number\n");
    scanf("%d",&num);
    save=num;
    while(num!=0)
    {
       num=num/10;
       count++;
    }
    num=save;
    while(num!=0)
    {
       r=num%10;
       newnum=newnum+pow(r,count);
       num=num/10;
    }
    if(newnum==save)
       printf("Number %d is Armstrong\n",save);
    else
       printf("Number %d is not Armstrong\n",save);
    getch();
 }
```

Output:

(First run)

```
Enter the number
1234
Number 1234 is not Armstrong
```

(Second run)

```
Enter the number
153
Number 153 is not Armstrong
```

EXPLANATION: A number is called Armstrong if sum of count number of power of each digit is equal to the original number. For e.g., to check 153 is Armstrong number or not we see that number of digits are 3 then:

$$1^3 + 5^3 + 3^3 => 1 + 125 + 27 => 153$$

Which is equal to the original number so number 153 is Armstrong.

Let's see a four-digit number **1653.**

$$1^4 + 6^4 + 5^4 + 3^4 = 1 + 1296 + 81 + 256 = 1653$$

So program proceeds as follows:

First while loop: First find out number of digits, before doing this **save** the number in the save variable. Now number of digits are stored in the **count** variable. At this stage num **is 0** so copy the value from **save** to **num. POW** is a library function whose prototype is given in header file **math.h** It return to the number to the power where first argument is number and second is the power for *e.g.*, **pow(2,3) gives** $2^3 = 8$, pow(3,2) = $3^2 = 9$.

Second while loop: Steps of second while loop are as follows:

Initially num = 153 newnum = 0 count = 3

S1 r =153%10 = 3 newnum = 0 + pow (3, 3) = 0 + 3^3 = 27 num = 153/10 = 15

S2 r = 15 %10 = 5 newnum = 27 + pow (5, 3) =27 + 5^3 = 152 num = 15/10 = 1

S3 r = 1%10 = 1 newnum = 152 + pow (1, 3) =152 + 1 = 153 num = 1/10 = 0

As newnum contains 153 which is compared with the original number stored in save. We get output 153 is Armstrong number.

In the previous program how did I come to know that 153 or 1634 is Armstrong number? Simply by writing a program which told me which number between 1 and 1000 are Armstrong numbers. The same is given below.

```
/*Prog 5.16 all Armstrong numbers between 1 and 10000 */
#include<stdio.h>
#include<conio.h>
#include<math.h>
 void main()
 {
    int num,save,count=0,r,sum=0,i=1;
    clrscr();
    while(i<=10000)
    {
     num=i;
     while(num!=0)
     {
      num/=10;
      count++;
      }
      num=i;
      while(num!=0)
      {
        r=num%10;
        sum=(int)(sum+(int)pow(r,count));
```

```
        num=num/10;
    }
    if(i==sum)
        printf("\n%d\n\t",i);
        count=0;
        sum=0;
        i++;
        }
        getch();
    }
```

Output:

```
1       2       3       4       5       6       7       8
9       153     370     371     407     1634    8208    9474
```

EXPLANATION: The logic remains same but with one change the whole logic has been put into the third **while** loop where **i** is the loop counter which runs from **1 to 10000.** Each iteration of this while loop gives new input number to both inner loop which checks whether the number is Armstrong or not if it is the number is printed. Note **count** and **sum** has to be initialized to zero at the end of each iteration otherwise they would carry values for the next iteration.

5.1.1.1 *The Infinite While Loop*

You can make a while loop infinite by putting **1** in the expression field, like this:

```
while (1)
{
    statement1;
    statement2;
    ............................;
    ........................ . .;
}
```

Because the expression **always returns 1,** the statements inside the statement block will be executed over and over—that is, the while loop will continue forever. Of course, you can set certain conditions inside the while loop to break the infinite loop as soon as the conditions are met.

The C language provides some statements, such as if and break statements, that you can use to set conditions and break the infinite while loop if needed.

5.1.1.2 *Break Statement*

Break statement is used to come out early from loop without waiting for the condition to become false. We have seen one such usage of break in the **switch-case** statements. When the **break** statement is encountered in the **while** loop or any of the loops which will see later, the control immediately transfers to first statement out of the loop *i.e.,* loop is exited prematurely. If there is nesting of loops the *break* will exit only from the current loop containing it.

Let's write some programs which make use of **break** statement.

```
/* Prog 5.17 demo of break statement*/
#include<stdio.h>
#include<conio.h>
 void main()
 {
  int x=1;
  clrscr();
  while(x<5)
  {
    if(x==3)
       break;
        printf("\nInside the loop x=%d\t",x);
        x++;
  }
  printf("\nOutside the loop x=%d\n",x);
  getch();
}
```

Output:

```
Inside the loop x=1
Inside the loop x=2
Outside the loop x=3
```

EXPLANATION: When x is 3 if condition becomes true, the body of the if statement is single break statement so all the statement in the loop following the break are skipped and control is transferred to the first statement after the loop which is printf which prints outside the loop $x = 3$.

```
/*Prog 5.18 square of numbers */
#include<stdio.h>
#include<conio.h>
 void main()
 {
    long int num;
    clrscr();
    while(4)
    {
       printf("Enter any number(-99 to quit)\n");
       scanf("%ld",&num);
       if(num==-99)
```

```
 break;
      printf("Square of number is %ld \n",num*num);
   }
   getch();
 }
```

Output:

```
Enter any number(-99 to quit)
5
Square of number is 25
Enter any number(-99 to quit)
6
Square of number is 36
Enter any number(-99 to quit)
7
Square of number is 49
Enter any number(-99 to quit)
Enter any number(-99 to quit)
3
Square of number is 49
Enter any number(-99 to quit)
-99
```

EXPLANATION: The statement **while(4)** interprets as **while(4!=0)** which is always true so our loop runs for infinite number of times. Instead of **4** any **+ve or –ve** number may be given except zero. **To break** out from loop we ask user to enter number **– 99** which is checked through **if** condition and if it is true then we come out from loop through **break** else prints square of the number entered.

```
/*Prog 5.19 To check number is prime or not ver 1*/
#include<stdio.h>
#include<conio.h>
 void main()
 {
   int num,flag=0,c=2;
   clrscr();
   printf("Enter the number\n");
   scanf("%d",&num);
   while(c<=num/2)
   {
      if(c%2==0)
      {
```

```
            flag=1;
            break;
         }
         c++;
      }
      if(flag)
         printf("Number is prime\n");
      else
         printf("Number is not prime\n");
      getch();
   }
```

Output:

(First run)

```
Enter the number
11
Number is prime
```

EXPLANATION: A number is prime if it completely divisible by 1 and itself e.g., 1, 3, 5, 7, 11, 13,17,19,23 etc. To check whether a number is prime or not we start from a counter ***c*=2**(every number divided by 1) continues till ***c*<=num/2 since no number is completely divisible by a number which is more than half of that number.** For *e.g.*, **12** is not divisible by **7, 8, 9, 10, 11** which are more than **6.** So we check if the number is divisible by any number **<=num/2** then it cannot not be prime we set **flag =1** and come out from the loop. The **flag** was initialized to **0** in the beginning so **if *c*%2==0** is true control sets **flag =1** which means number is not prime else **flag** remains zero which means control never transferred to **if** block *i.e.*, number is prime. So outside the loop we check this value of **flag** and prints accordingly.

The same program can be written in a different manner as shown in the next program.

```
/*Prog 5.20 To check number is prime or not ver 2*/
#include<stdio.h>
#include<conio.h>
#include<stdlib.h>
 void main()
 {
    int num,c=2;
    clrscr();
    printf("Enter the number\n");
    scanf("%d",&num);
    while(c<=num/2)
    {
 if(c%2==0)
 {
```

```
      printf("Number is not prime\n");
      getch();
      exit(0);
   }
   c++;
   }
   printf("Number is prime\n");
     getch();
   }
```

Output:

```
Enter the number
24
Number is not prime
```

EXPLANATION: if *c*%2 = =0 is true we simply print Number is not prime and exit from the program, courtesy **exit(0)** function from **stdlib.h** header file. **if** *c*%2==0 is never true during the loop then at the end when loop exit maturely then we print **number is prime.**

5.1.1.3 The Continue Statement

The continue statement causes the remainder of the statements following the continue to be skipped and continue with the next iteration of the loop. So we can use ***continue*** statement to bypass certain number of statements in the loop on the basis of some condition given by *if* generally.

The syntax of continue statement is simply

continue;

Lets write a program to illustrate **continue** statement

```
/*Prog 5.21 Demo of continue statement */
#include<stdio.h>
#include<conio.h>
 void main()
 {
    int t=0;
    clrscr();
    while(t<=10)
    {
       t++;
       if(t%2)
 continue;
       printf("%d\n",t);
    }
```

```
   getch();
 }
```

Output:

```
2
4
6
8
10
```

EXPLANATION: When **t** is an odd number **continue** in the body of the **if** condition causes loop to continue with next iteration of loop skipping **printf** statement. If number is even the number is simply printed as **continue** itself is skipped.

In the coming part of this program as well as in other Chapters you will see lots of examples of ***continue*** statement. The above program was just to give an idea how **continue** statement works in loop.

5.1.2 The for Loop

This is the second loops which are going to examine in this section. The **for** loop is most frequently used by programmers just because of its simplicity. The syntax of **for** loop is given here:

```
for (initialization; condition; increment/decrement)
{
        Statements;
        Statements;
        ..........................;
}
```

There are various other syntaxes of **for loop** which we will see in a short while.

Now, let's write some program to illustrate the functioning of this loop.

```
/*Prog 5.22 demo of for loop ver1*/
#include<stdio.h>
#include<conio.h>
 void main()
 {
   int t;
   clrscr();
   for(t=1;t<=10;t++)
   printf("t=%d\n",t);
   getch ();
 }
```

```
Output:
t=1
t=2
t=3
t=4
t=5
t=6
t=7
t=8
t=9
t=10
```

EXPLANATION: The first part of **for** loop ***t*=1** is the initialization *i.e.,* we are providing an initial value of 1 loop counter ***t***. Next statement ***t*<=10** is the testing condition for which this loop runs if condition is true. The last part is increment of loop works by first making ***t*=1** and then checking the condition whether ***t*<=10** if so it executes the next statement following **for *i.e.* printf.** Recall as there is no braces after **for** loop only first statement is considered the body of the **for** loop. It then goes to the increment the value of ***t*,** checks the test condition and executes the **printf.** This continues till the condition ***t*<=10** is true. As soon as the condition becomes false in this case ***t*=11** control comes out from loop and program terminates.

```
/*Prog 5.23 demo of for loop ver 2*/
#include<stdio.h>
#include<conio.h>
 void main()
 {
    int t;
    clrscr();
    for(t=5;t!=0;t--)
    printf("t=%d\n",t);
    getch();
 }
Output:
t=5
t=4
t=3
t=2
t=1
```

EXPLANATION: In the program **for** loop runs from 5 to 1 each time decrementing the value of *t* by one. When it becomes zero condition ***t*! =0** becomes false and loop terminates.

```
/*Prog 5.24 demo of for ver3*/
#include<stdio.h>
```

```
#include<conio.h>
 void main()
 {
    int t;
    clrscr();
    for(t=5;t;t--)
 printf("t=%d\n",t);
    getch();
 }
```

Output:

```
t=5
t=4
t=3
t=2
t=1
```

EXPLANATION: Simply writing ***t*** in the condition part means ***t*! =0.** Rest is same as in the above program.

```
/*Prog5.25 demo of for loop, odd number between 1 and 10*/
#include<stdio.h>
#include<conio.h>
 void main()
 {
    int t;
    clrscr();
    for(t=1;t<=10;t=t+2)
    printf("t=%d\n",t);
    getch();
 }
```

Output:

```
t=1
t=3
t=5
t=7
t=9
```

EXPLANATION: Here the increment in the loop counter ***t*** is by **2.** So the loop prints the value of ***t*** and increment ***t*** by **2** in every iteration, checks condition and if it is true then prints again. This continues till ***t*<=10** remains true.

```
/*Prog 5.26 Demo of for loop, odd numbers between 30 to 3*/
#include<stdio.h>
#include<conio.h>
```

```
 void main()
 {
    int t;
    clrscr();
    for(t=30;t>=1;t=t-3)
    printf("t=%d\n",t);
    getch();
 }
```

Output:

```
t=30
t=27
t=24
t=21
t=18
t=15
t=12
t=9
t=6
t=3
```

EXPLANATION: In this program we are printing number from **30 to 3** with decrementing ***t*** in every iteration by **3.**

There are various **syntaxes** of writing the **for loop** see the next few program

```
/*Prog 5.27 For loop syntax 1 ver 1*/
#include<stdio.h>
#include<conio.h>
 void main()
 {
    int t;
    t=10;
    clrscr();
    for(;t<=100;t+=10)
    printf("%d\n",t);
    getch();
 }
```

Output:

```
10
20
30
40
```

```
50
60
70
80
90
100
```

EXPLANATION: In this program we have left the initialization part and have put this before the **for** loop, still semicolon (;) is must in the **for loop.**

The general syntax for such type of for loop as given in the above program is given below:

```
for(;condition;increment/decrement)
{
   Statements;
}
```

```
/*Prog 5.28 for loop syntax 2 ver1*/
#include<stdio.h>
#include<conio.h>
 void main()
 {
   int t;
   clrscr();
   for(t=1;t<=10;)
   {
      printf("t=%d\n",t);
      t++;
   }
   getch();
}
```

Output:

```
t=1
t=2
t=3
t=4
t=5
t=6
t=7
t=8
t=9
t=10
```

EXPLANATION: In this program we have written within braces. Note braces are must because you are having two statements which we want to make as body of the **for** loop.

The general syntax is given as:

```
for(initialization;condition;)
{
    Statements;
    Increment/decrement;
}
```

```
/*Prog 5.29 To print and find sum of series 1+2+3+4+5+.....*/
#include<stdio.h>
#include<conio.h>
 void main()
 {
    int n,sum=0,t;
    clrscr();
    printf("Enter the number of terms:-\n");
    scanf("%d",&n);
    for(t=1;t<=n;t++)
    {
       printf("%d + ",t);
       sum=sum+t;
    }
    printf("Sum of series is:=%d",sum);
    getch();
 }
```

Output:

```
Enter the number of terms:-
6
1 + 2 + 3 + 4 + 5 + 6 + Sum of series is:=21
```

EXPLANATION: The number of terms is taken in the variable *n*. We run the loop from **1** to ***n*** with increment of **1.** The sum is stored in the variable sum initialized to **0** in the beginning.

```
/*Prog 5.30 To print and find sum of series 1-2+3-4+5-.....*/
#include<stdio.h>
#include<conio.h>
 void main()
 {
    int n,sum=0,t,k=1;
    clrscr();
```

```
   printf("Enter the number of terms\n");
   scanf("%d",&n);
   for(t=1;t<=n;t++)
   {
      if(t%2)
 printf("%d-",t);
      else
 printf("%d+",t);
      sum=sum+(t*k);
      k=k*(-1);
   }
   printf("Sum of series is %d",sum);
   getch();
 }
```

Output:

```
Enter the number of terms
8
1-2+3-4+5-6+7-8+Sum of series is -4
```

EXPLANATION: In the series to be generated odd numbers are **+ve** and even numbers are **–ve.** We take one variable *k*=1.*k* is multiplied by – 1 inside the loop in each iteration of the **for** loop.

Initially **sum=0 + (1 * 1)** gives **sum = 1** then *k* becomes *k* = **1* – 1 = – 1** which is used in the second iteration of the loop. In the second iteration sum becomes **sum = 1 + (2* – 1)** *i.e.*, **sum = 1 – 2= – 1** and value of *k* changes to **1** again **(– 1 * – 1 = 1)** and this continues for *n* times.

```
/*Prog 5.31 to print and find sum of series 1^2 + 2^2 +3^2 +....(^ stand
s for power)*/
#include<stdio.h>
#include<conio.h>
 void main()
 {
   long int n,sum=0,t;
   clrscr();
   printf("Enter the number of terms:-\n");
   scanf("%ld",&n);
   for(t=1;t<=n;t++)
   {
      printf("%d^%d+ ",t,2);
      sum=sum+(long int)pow(t,2);
   }
   printf("Sum of series is %ld",sum);
   getch();
```

```
 }
```

Output:

```
Enter the number of terms:-
7
1^0+ 2^0+ 3^0+ 4^0+ 5^0+ 6^0+ 7^0+ Sum of series is 49
```

EXPLANATION: pow is standard library function which returns power of first argument to second number *i.e.,* **pow (2, 3)** returns **2** to the power **3** ***i.e.,* 8.** We take number of terms in the n and run for loop from 1 to n. On each iteration we **found 2** to power t and ad it to sum. **pow** returns double so it is **type casted to long int.**

```
/*Prog 5.32 To print and find sum of series 1+x +x^2+x^3+.....*/
#include<stdio.h>
#include<conio.h>
#include<math.h>
 void main()
 {
   long int n,t,sum=1,x;
   clrscr();
   printf("Enter the number of terms \n");
   scanf("%ld",&n);
   printf("Enter the value of x\n");
   scanf("%ld",&x);
   printf("%ld+",1);
   for(t=1;t<=n;t++)
   {
     printf("%ld^%ld +",x,t+1);
     sum=sum+(long int)pow(x,t+1);
   }
   printf("\nSum of series is %ld",sum);
   getch();
 }
```

Output:

```
Enter the number of terms
4
Enter the value of x
2
1+2.000000+2.000000^2+2.000000^3+
Sum of series is 15.000000
```

EXPLANATION: As we have done in all series program number of terms is taken in the variable *n*. We do take value x also in the variable *x*. As power starts from *x* to the **power 2** we **write** $t + 1$ in the **pow** function and initializes **sum = 1.** Rest is self-explanatory.

```
/*Prog 5.33 Printing odd numbers using continue */
#include<stdio.h>
#include<conio.h>
 void main()
 {
  int t;
  clrscr();
  for(t=1;t<=10;t++)
  {
    if(t%2)
 continue;
 printf("%d\n",t+1);
  }
  getch();
 }
```

Output:

```
3
5
7
9
11
```

EXPLANATION: As stated earlier **continue** statement cases **continue the loop** with the next iteration by leaving all the statements after the continue statement. Thus whenever we have an odd number we continue with the next iteration of loop which causes ***t*** to be incremented by **1** and continue the **for** loop

```
/*Prog 5.34 Converting 0 through 15 to hex numbers */
#include <stdio.h>
#include <conio.h>
 void main()
 {
   int i;
   clrscr();
   printf("Hex(uppercase) Hex(lowercase) Decimal\n");
   for (i=0; i<16; i++)
   {
     printf("%X %x %d\n", i, i, i);
   }
```

```
    getch();
}
```

Output:

```
Hex(uppercase) Hex(lowercase) Decimal
0              0              0
1              1              1
2              2              2
3              3              3
4              4              4
5              5              5
6              6              6
7              7              7
8              8              8
9              9              9
A              a              10
B              b              11
C              c              12
D              d              13
E              e              14
F              f              15
```

EXPLANATION: Now, let's have a look at the code given in **program 5.34.** As you know, **line 2** includes the header file **stdio.h** for the **printf ()** function used later in the program. Inside the body of the **main ()** function, the statement in **line 6** declares an integer variable, ***i*. Line 8** displays the headline of the output on the screen. **Lines 9_11** contain the **for** statement. Note that the first expression in the for statement is ***i* = 0,** which is an assignment expression that initializes the integer variable ***i* to 0.**

The second expression in the **for** statement is ***i* < 16,** which is a relational expression. This expression returns **1** as long as the relation indicated by the less-than operator (<) holds. As mentioned earlier, the second expression is evaluated by the for statement each time after a successful looping. If the value **of *i*** is less than **16,** which means the relational expression remains true, the **for** statement will start another loop. Otherwise, it will stop looping and exit.

The third expression in the for statement is ***i*++** in this case. This expression is evaluated and the integer variable ***i*** is increased by **1** each time after the statement inside the body of the **for** statement is executed. Here it doesn't make a big difference whether the **post-increment operator (*i*++)** or the **pre-increment operator (++*i*)** is used in the third expression. In other words, when the for loop is first encountered, ***i*** is set to **0**, the expression

```
i<16
```

is evaluated and found to be true, and therefore the statements within the body of the for loop are executed. Following execution of the for loop, the third expression *i*++ is executed incrementing *i* to 1, and *i*<16 is again evaluated and found to be true, thus the body of the loop is executed again. The looping lasts until the conditional expression *i*<16 is no longer true.

There is only one statement inside the for statement body, as you can see in **line 10.** The statement contains the **printf()** function, which is used to display the hex numbers (both uppercase and lowercase) converted from the decimal values by using the format specifiers, %**X and** %*x.*

Here the decimal value is provided by the integer variable ***i***. As explained, ***i*** contains the initial value of **0** right before and during the first looping. After each looping, ***i*** is increased by 1 because of the third expression, ***i++***, in the for statement. The last value provided by i is **15.** When ***i*** reaches **16,** the relation indicated by the second expression, ***i*** **< 16,** is no longer true. Therefore, the looping is stopped and the execution of the for statement is completed.

5.1.2.1 *The Null Statement*

As you may notice, the **for** statement does not end with a semicolon. The **for** statement has within it either a statement block that ends with the closing brace (**}**) **or a single statement that ends with a semicolon.** The following **for** statement contains a single statement:

```
for (i=0; i<8; i++)
        sum += i;
```

Now consider a statement such as this:

```
for (i=0; i<8; i++);
```

Here the **for** statement is followed by a semicolon immediately. **In the C language, there is a special statement called the null statement.** A null statement contains nothing but a semicolon. In other words, a null statement is a statement with no expression.

Therefore, when you review the statement for ($i = 0; i < 8; i$++);, you can see that it is actually a for statement with a null statement. In other words, you can rewrite it as

```
for (i=0; i<8; i++);
```

Because the **null statement** has no expression, the **for** statement actually does nothing but loop.

5.1.2.2 *How to Add More Expressions Into for Loop*

The C language allows you to put more expressions into the three expression fields in the for statement. Expressions in a single expression field are separated by commas.

For instance, the following form is valid in C:

```
for (i=0, j=10; i<10, j>0; i++, j--)
{
     /* statement block */
}
```

Here, in the first expression field, the two integer variables, ***i*** and ***j***, are initialized, respectively, with **0** and **10** when the **for** statement is first encountered. Then, in the second field, the two relational expressions, ***i*<10 and *j*>0,** are evaluated and tested. If one of the relational expressions **returns 0,** the looping is stopped. After each iteration and the statements in the statement block are executed successfully, ***i* is increased by 1, *j* is reduced by 1** in the third expression field, and the expressions ***i*<10 and *j*>0** are evaluated to determine whether to do one more looping.

```
/*Prog 5.35 Demo of multiple expressions in a single for loop*/
#include <stdio.h>
#include <conio.h>
 void main()
 {
    int i, j;
    clrscr();
    for (i=0, j=8; i<8; i++, j--)
    printf("%d + %d = %d\n", i, j, i+j);
    getch();
 }
```

Output:

```
0 + 8 = 8
1 + 7 = 8
2 + 6 = 8
3 + 5 = 8
4 + 4 = 8
5 + 3 = 8
6 + 2 = 8
7 + 1 = 8
```

EXPLANATION: Here in the shown program **line 6** declares two integer variables, ***i* and *j*,** which are used in a **for** loop. In **line 8, *i*** is initialized with **0** and ***j*** is set to **8** in the first expression field of the **for** statement. The second expression field contains a condition, ***i*<8,** which tells the computer to keep looping as long as the value of ***i*** is less than **8.**

Each time, after the statement controlled by **for in line 8** is executed, the third expression field is evaluated, and ***i*** is increased by **1** while ***j*** is reduced by **1.** Because there is only one statement inside the **for** loop, no braces ({and}) are used to form a statement block.

The statement in **line 9** displays the addition of ***i* and *j*** on the screen during the looping, which outputs eight results during the looping by adding the values of the two variables, ***i* and *j*.**

```
/*Prog 5.36 Demo of multiple expressions ver2 */
#include <stdio.h>
#include <conio.h>
 void main()
 {
   int i, j;
   clrscr();
   for (i=0, j=1; i<8; i++, j++)
```

```
    printf("%d - %d = %d\n", j, i, j - i);
    getch();
 }
```

Output:

```
1 - 0 = 1
2 - 1 = 1
3 - 2 = 1
4 - 3 = 1
5 - 4 = 1
6 - 5 = 1
7 - 6 = 1
8 - 7 = 1
```

EXPLANATION: Note that in **line 8,** there are two assignment expressions, ***i*=0 and *j*=1,** in the first expression field of the **for** statement. These two assignment expressions initialize the ***i* and *j*** integer variables, respectively. There is one relational expression, ***i*<8,** in the second field, which is the condition that has to be met before the looping can be carried out. Because ***i*** starts at **0** and is incremented by **1** after each loop, there are a total of eight loops that will be performed by the **for** statement. The third expression field contains two expressions, ***i*++ and *j*++,** that increase the two integer variables by **1** each time after the statement in **line 9** is executed. **The printf()** function in **line 9** displays the subtraction of the two integer variables, ***j* and *i*,** within the **for loop.** Because there is only one statement in the statement block, the braces (**{and}**) are discarded.

```
/*Prog 5.37 for loop syntax 3 ver1*/
#include<stdio.h>
#include<conio.h>
 void main()
 {
    int t;
    t=1;
    clrscr();
    for(;t<=10;)
    printf("t=%d\n",t++);
    getch();
 }
```

Output:

```
t=1
t=2
t=3
t=4
t=5
```

```
t=6
t=7
t=8
t=9
t=10
```

EXPLANATION: In this program we have left both initialization and increment /decrement part, still semicolon is necessary on both sides.

The general syntax is:

```
initialization;
for ( ; condtion ; )
 {
      Statements;
      Increment/decrement;
 }
```

5.1.2.3 *Nesting of for Loop*

Nesting of **for loop** is used most frequently in many programming situations and one of the most important usage in displaying various patterns which we will see in the coming programs.

The syntax for nesting of for loop is given here:

```
for(initialization; condition; increment/decrement)
{
     for(initialization; condition; increment/decrement)
     {
          Statements;
     }
   Statements;
}
```

For each iteration of first **for** loop (outer **for loop**) inner for loop runs as it is part of the body of outer **for** loop. The inner **for** loop has its own set if statements which executes till the condition for inner **for** loop is true.

See numbers of programs given below:

```
/*Prog 5.38 Nesting of for loop ver1*/
#include<stdio.h>
#include<conio.h>
 void main()
 {
   int a,b;
   clrscr();
   for(a=1;a<=3;a++)
```

```
    {
      for(b=1;b<=4;b++)
    printf("%d\t",a*b);
      printf("\n");
    }
    getch();
  }
```

Output:

```
1       2       3       4
2       4       6       8
3       6       9       12
```

EXPLANATION: The body of the first **for** loop (outer) contains three statements. The inner **for** loop's body has got only statement. Initially ***a* is 1** and condition ***a*<=3** in the outer loop is true. First statement inside outer **for** loop is inner **for** loop which initializes ***b*=1**. Now this **for loop** runs for **1 to 4** for value of ***a*=1.** When this loop terminates on reaching a value of ***b*=5,** control is transferred to third statement **printf ("\n");** which leaves a line on the output screen. Now control is transferred to outer loop which increments value of ***a* by 1** which becomes **2.** The process repeats with value of ***b*** **from 1 to 4** for value of ***a*=2,** till ***a*<=3 remains true.**

```
/* Prog 5.39 Demonstrating nested loops */
#include <stdio.h>
#include <conio.h>
 void main()
 {
   int i, j;
   clrscr();
   for (i=1; i<=3; i++) /* outer loop */
   {
   printf("The start of iteration %d of the outer loop.\n", i);
   for (j=1; j<=4; j++) /* inner loop */
   printf("Iteration %d of the inner loop.\n", j);
   printf("The end of iteration %d of the outer loop.\n", i);
   }
   getch();
 }
```

Output:

```
The start of iteration 1 of the outer loop.
    Iteration 1 of the inner loop.
    Iteration 2 of the inner loop.
    Iteration 3 of the inner loop.
```

```
    Iteration 4 of the inner loop.
The end of iteration 1 of the outer loop.
The start of iteration 2 of the outer loop.
    Iteration 1 of the inner loop.
    Iteration 2 of the inner loop.
    Iteration 3 of the inner loop.
    Iteration 4 of the inner loop.
The end of iteration 2 of the outer loop.
The start of iteration 3 of the outer loop.
    Iteration 1 of the inner loop.
    Iteration 2 of the inner loop.
    Iteration 3 of the inner loop.
    Iteration 4 of the inner loop.
The end of iteration 3 of the outer loop.
```

EXPLANATION: In program, two **for** loops are **nested** together. The **outer for loop** starts in **line 8** and ends in **line 13,** while the **inner for loop starts in line 10 and ends in line 11.**

The inner loop controls one statement that prints out the iteration number according to the numeric value of the integer variable ***j***. As you see in **line 10,** ***j*** is initialized with **1,** and is increased by **1** after each looping (that is, iteration). The execution of the inner loop stops when the value of ***j*** is greater than **4.**

Besides the inner loop, the outer loop has two statements in **lines 9 and 12,** respectively. The **printf ()** function in **line 9** displays a message showing the beginning of an iteration from the outer loop. An ending message is sent out in **line 12** to show the end of the iteration from the outer loop.

From the output, you can see that the inner loop is finished before the outer loop starts iteration. When the outer loop begins iteration, the inner loop is encountered and run again. The output from the program clearly shows the execution orders of the inner and outer loops.

```
/*Prog 5.40 to print the following pattern, input is number of lines
1
2 2
3 3 3
4 4 4 4
*/
#include<stdio.h>
#include<conio.h>
 void main()
 {
    int line,row,col;
    clrscr();
    printf("Enter the Number of lines\n");
```

```
    scanf("%d",&line);
    for(row=1;row<=line;row++)
    {
      for(col=1;col<=row;col++)
      printf("%d ",row);
      printf("\n");
    }
    getch();
  }
```

```
Output:
Enter the Number of lines
5
1
2 2
3 3 3
4 4 4 4
5 5 5 5 5
```

EXPLANATION: We have used two **for** loops in the program. One is to control the number of rows and second is to control number of cols. Initially assume **line =4** so outer **for** loop runs four times. In the first run **row=1** and inner loop runs only once. The **printf("\n")** statement is within the second **for** loop so this leaves new after printing 1.When control reaches second time inside outer **for loop** value of row is 2, inner loop starts again by setting the value of **col = 1,** this time inner loop runs twice printing the value of **row** which is **2** twice. This continues till **row<=4.**

```
/*Prog 5.41 To print the following pattern, input is number of lines
A
B B
C C C
D D D D
*/
#include<stdio.h>
#include<conio.h>
 void main()
 {
    int line,row,col;
    char ch='A';
    clrscr();
    printf("Enter the number of lines\n");
    scanf("%d",&line);
    for(row=1;row<=line;row++)
    {
```

```
        for(col=1;col<=row;col++)
    printf("%c",ch);
        printf("\n");
        ch++;
    }
    getch();
 }
```

Output:

```
Enter the number of lines
5
A
BB
CCC
DDDD
EEEEE
```

EXPLANATION: We do increment value of ch in the inner for loop but before the start of next iteration of outer for loop we set back value of ch='A'.

```
/*Prog 5.42 To print the following pattern, input is number of lines
1
1 2
1 2 3
1 2 3 4
1 2 3 4 5 */
#include <conio.h>
#include <stdio.h>
 void main()
 {
    int line,row,col;
    clrscr();
    printf("Enter the number of lines \n");
    scanf("%d",&line);
    printf("The pattern is shown below:");
    for(row=1;row<=line;row++)
    {
       for(col=1;col<=row;col++)
       {
          printf("%d",col);
       }
       printf("\n");
```

```
    }
    getch();
  }
```

```
Output:
Enter the number of lines
6
The pattern is shown below:
1
12
123
1234
12345
123456
```

EXPLANATION: This program is similar to previous program but instead of printing the value of row we have printed the value of col to get the desired output.

```
/*Prog 5.43 to print the following pattern, input is number of lines
A
B C
D E F
G H I J */
#include<stdio.h>
#include <conio.h>
 void main()
 {
    int line,row,col;
    char ch='A';
    clrscr();
    printf("Enter the number of line \n");
    scanf("%d",&line);
    printf("The pattern is shown below:\n");
    for(row=1;row<=line;row++)
    {
       for(col=1;col<=row;col++)
       {
          printf("%c",ch);
          ch++;
       }
    printf("\n");
 }
```

```
 getch();
}
```

Output:

```
Enter the number of line
5
The pattern is shown below:
A
BC
DEF
GHIJ
KLMNO
```

EXPLANATION: This program is similar to the previous program with the difference that instead of printing integer value we are printing alphabet as **char** data type.

```
/*Prog 5.44 to print the following pattern, input is number of lines
1
22
333
4444
55555 */
#include<stdio.h>
#include<conio.h>
 void main()
 {
   int line, row,col,b;
   clrscr();
   printf("Enter the number of lines \n");
   scanf("%d",&line);
   printf("The pattern is shown below\n");
   for(row=1;row<=line;row++)
   {
    for(b=1;b<=line-row;b++)
 printf(" ");
  for(col=1;col<=row;col++)
   printf("%d",row);
     printf("\n");
   }
   getch();
 }
```

```
Output:
Enter the number of lines
5
The pattern is shown below
        1
       22
      333
     4444
    55555
```

EXPLANATION: To get the above output note before printing 1 we have to leave 3 spaces (line-row). Similarly, 2 spaces for 2, 1 space for printing b and no space for printing 4. This has been achieved by inserting one more for loop between outer and inner loop. Prior to printing the values we leave the spaces through for loop.

```
/*Prog 5.45 To print the following pattern, input is number of lines
                    *
                 *     *
              *     *     *
           *     *     *     *
        *     *     *     *     *
     *     *     *     *     *     *
  *     *     *     *     *     *     *
*     *     *     *     *     *     *     *
*/
#include<stdio.h>
#include<conio.h>
 void main()
 {
   int line,row,col,b;
   clrscr();
   printf("Enter the number of lines\n");
   scanf("%d",&line);
   printf("The pattern is shown below:\n");
   for(row=1;row<=line;row++)
   {
    for(b=1;b<=line-row;b++)
 printf(" ");
 for(col=1;col<=row;col++)
 printf(" *");
   printf("\n");
  }
```

```
  getch();
 }
```

Output:

```
Enter the number of lines
8
The pattern is shown below:
                   *
                 *   *
               *   *   *
             *   *   *   *
           *   *   *   *   *
         *   *   *   *   *   *
       *   *   *   *   *   *   *
     *   *   *   *   *   *   *   *
```

EXPLANATION: While printing value through third for loop we have intentionally left one space before asterisk (*). This can be done after asterisk (*) also. .Rest of the part is same as the earlier programs.

```
/*Prog 5.46 To print the following pattern, input is number of lines
     ********
      *******
       ******
        *****
         ****
          ***
           **
            *
*/
#include<stdio.h>
#include<conio.h>
 void main()
 {
    int line,row,col,b;
    clrscr();
    printf("Enter the number of lines\n");
    scanf("%d",&line);
    printf("The pattern is shown as:\n");
    for(row=line;row>=1;row--)
    {
       for(b=line-row;b>=1;b--)
        printf(" ");
        for(col=row;col>=1;col--)
```

```
        printf("*");
        printf("\n");
      }
    getch();
    }
```

Output:

```
Enter the number of lines
8
The pattern is shown as:
     ********
      *******
       ******
        *****
         ****
          ***
           **
            *
```

EXPLANATION: Nothing new in this program except that we start from line no and decrement row by one in each iteration till **row>=1.** The logic for printing space has also been changed because this time we leave no space for printing first row, one space for printing second row and so on.

```
/*Prog 5.47 To print the following pattern, input is number of lines
            *
          *   *
        *   *   *
      *   *   *   *
    *   *   *   *   *
      *   *   *   *
        *   *   *
          *   *
            *
*/
#include<stdio.h>
#include<conio.h>
 void main()
 {
    int line,row,col,b;
    clrscr();
    printf("Enter the number of lines\n");
    scanf("%d",&line);
    printf("The pattern is shown below:\n");
    for(row=1;row<=line;row++)
```

```
    {
       for(b=1;b<=line-row;b++)
        printf(" ");
          for(col=1;col<=row;col++)
 printf(" *");
  printf("\n");
    }
    for(row=line;row>=1;row--)
    {
       for(b=line-row;b>=1;b--)
        printf(" ");
        for(col=row;col>=1;col--)
        {
 if(row==line)
  continue;
  printf(" *");
        }
        if(row==line)
          continue;
          printf("\n");
    }
    getch();
  }
```

```
Output:
Enter the number of lines
5
The pattern is shown below:
         *
        * *
       * * *
      * * * *
     * * * * *
      * * * *
       * * *
        * *
         *
```

EXPLANATION: Here we have combined the two logic given in earlier program. The first block of for loop prints asterisk (*) in descending order and second block of for loop prints them in ascending order. Note the two statements.

```
if( row ==line)
    continue;
```

ensures that when second block of for loop executes we don't get repeated pattern of line no of asterisk in the first iteration of outer for loop.

```
/*Prog 5.48 To print the following pattern, input is number of lines
1
0 1
1 0 1
0 1 0 1
1 0 1 0 1
*/
#include <stdio.h>
#include <conio.h>
 void main()
 {
  int line,row,col;
  clrscr();
  printf("Enter the number of lines\n");
  scanf("%d",&line);
  printf("The pattern is shown below:\n");
  for(row=1;row<=line;row++)
  {
    for(col=1;col<=row;;col++)
     if(row%2==0)
       printf("%d",!(col%2));
     else
       printf("%d",(col%2));
     printf("\n");
  }
  getch();
 }
Output:
Enter the number of lines
6
The pattern is shown below:
1
01
101
0101
10101
010101
```

EXPLANATION: Observe the pattern carefully. On even number of lines we have a different pattern and on odd number of line we have a different pattern. On even number of lines *i.e.*, for row=2, 4, 6,….. if we print the complement of col %2 we get the desired pattern. On row=1, 3, 5,…… we simply print the col%2.

```
/*Prog 5.49 To print the following pattern, input is number of line
1
232
34543
4567654
567898765
67891011109876
*/
#include<stdio.h>
#include<conio.h>
 void main()
 {
    int line, row, col, val, b;
    clrscr();
    printf("Enter the number of lines\n");
    scanf("%d",&line);
    printf("The pattern is \n");
    for(row=1;row<=line;row++)
    {
     val=row;
     for(col=1;col<2*row+1;col+=2)
        printf("%d",val++);
        val=val-2;
        for(b=1;b<=row-1;b++)
 printf("%d", val--);
 printf("\n");
    }
    getch();
}
```

Output:

```
Enter the number of lines
6
The pattern is
1
232
```

```
34543
4567654
567898765
67891011109876
```

EXPLANATION: We assume the pattern itself consists of two sub patterns. The first pattern assume up to the numbers shown in bold. Rest of numbers is part of second pattern. For each iteration of the outer for loop we store row number into **val** variable and print this till **col<2*row +1** remains true. We have chosen this condition as for **row=1, 2, 3, 4** we get **2*row+1 as 3, 5, 7, 9** which are the bold letters shown in pyramid.

For second half of pattern, we note that in the second line we have to print just one number **(2),** in the third line two numbers **(4, 3)** and so on wich is controlled by **row-1.** To print the number we subtract **2** from **val** and decrement on each iteration.

```
/*Prog 5.50 Comma operator in for loop ver 1*/
#include <stdio.h>
#include <conio.h>
 void main()
 {
    int i,j;
    clrscr();
    for(i=1,j=10;i<=5,j>=1;i++,j--)
     printf("%d\t%d\t%d\t\n",i,j,i*j);
    getch();
 }
```

Output:

```
1     10    10
2     9     18
3     8     24
4     7     28
5     6     30
6     5     30
7     4     28
8     3     24
9     2     18
10    1     10
```

EXPLANATION: This program demonstrate how you can use two control variables in the for loop. We have used *i* and *j* whose initial values are 1 and 10 respectively. In this way you can as many control variable as you want but each must be separated by comma, and last one must be terminated by semicolon (;). In the condition part when I becomes 6 condition *i*<=5 turns out to be false but due to comma operator which always checks the rightmost expression (here *j*>=1) so even though *i*<=5 condition is false loop runs with the values of I an *j* till *j*>=1 does not become false. Recall one use of comma, operator we used with if in chapter-3.

```
/*Prog 5.51 To find the factorial of a number */
#include <stdio.h>
#include <conio.h>
 void main()
 {
   int num,t;
   long int fact=1;
   clrscr();
   printf("Enter a +ve integer number\n");
   scanf("%d",&num);
   for(t=1;t<=num;t++)
    fact=fact*t;
   printf("The factorial of %d is %ld\n",t,fact);
   getch();
 }
```

Output:

```
Enter a +ve integer number
6
The factorial of 7 is 720
```

EXPLANATION: The factorial of number say 5 is calculated by multiplying 5*4*3*2*1 or by multiplying 1*2*3*4*5 which will be 120. Initially fact is 1. We run the loop from 1 to num; it may be from num to 1 also. In each iteration value of fact is multiplied by t and stored back in fact which is used in the next iteration. For better understanding lets take num = 4.

```
S1    t = 1    fact = 1 * 1 => 1
S2    t = 2    fact = 1 * 2 => 2
S3    t = 3    fact = 2 * 3 => 6
S4    t = 4    fact = 6 * 4 => 24
```

```
/*Prog 5.52 To check a number is perfect or not */
#include <stdio.h>
#include <conio.h>
 void main ()
 {
   int num, t, sum=0;
   clrscr();
   printf("Enter a +ve integer number \n");
   scanf("%d",&num);
   for(t=1;t<=num/2;t++)
   {
     if(num%t==0)
```

```
     sum=sum + t;
   }
   if(sum==num)
     printf("The number is perfect \n");
   else
     printf("The number is not a perfect number\n");
     getch();
   }
```

Output:

```
Enter a +ve integer number
4
The number is perfect
```

EXPLANATION: A number is called perfect if sum of its factor is equal to the number itself for e.g., 6, its factor are 1, 2, 3 and sum of its factor is 6 which is equal to the number 6 so it is a perfect number. Similarly 28 is a perfect number. In the loop we initialize sum to 1 and run the loop for num/2 as for any number say t which is more than num/2, num%*t* won'*t* be zero(excluding num itself.)

/*Prog 5.53 All perfect numbers between 1 and 1000 */

```
#include <stdio.h>
#include <conio.h>
 void main()
 {
   int num=1,sum=0,t;
   clrscr();
   printf("Perfect numbers are \n");
   while(num<=1000)
   {
     for(t=1;t<=num/2;t++)
     {
       if(num%t==0)
         sum=sum+t;
     }
    if(sum==num)
     printf("%d",sum);
     sum=0;
     num++;
    }
    getch();
   }
```

Output:

```
Perfect numbers are
6 28 496
```

EXPLANATION: The while loop controls numbers from 1 to 1000 and for loop tests number for perfect. The sum must be initialized to 0 before next iteration of while loop.

5.1.3 Do-while Loop

The last loop is the **do-while** loop. Its syntax is as follows:

```
do
{
      Statements;
      Statements;
      Statements;
      ...............;
      ...............;
} while(condition);
```

It is similar to **while** loop with the difference that condition is checked at the end, instead of checking it at the beginning.

Let's write some programs to illustrate the functionality of this loop

```
/*Prog 5.54 demo of do-while loop ver 1*/
#include<stdio.h>
#include<conio.h>
 void main()
 {
    int t=1;
    clrscr();
    do
    {
       printf("%d\n",t);
       t++;
    }while(t<=10);
 getch();
}
```

Output:

```
1
2
3
4
```

```
5
6
7
8
9
10
```

EXPLANATION: The **do-while** loop is similar to the **while** loop with the difference that the **condition is checked at the end.** The loop starts with a **do** following the block and at the end of block the condition is writing using **while.** The **while** is part of the **do-while loop** and it must be terminated by **semicolon;.** Initially the value of ***t*** is **1** which is printed through **printf** then ***t*** becomes **2.** At the end of the block the condition is **true,** control transfer back to do block and process continues.

Some Important Points Regarding DO-While Loop

- **It** is also called **bottom testing loop or exit controlled loop** as condition at the bottom of the loop.
- Regardless of the condition given at the end of block the loop runs at least once.
- The **do-while** loop is mostly used for writing menu driven programs.

```
/* Prog 5.55 Demo of using a do-while loop */
#include <stdio.h>
#include <conio.h>
 void main()
 {
    int i;
    clrscr();
    i = 65;
    do
    {
     printf("The numeric value of %c is %d.\n", i, i);
      i++;
    } while (i<91);
    getch();
}
```

Output:

```
The numeric value of A is 65.
The numeric value of B is 66.
The numeric value of C is 67.
The numeric value of D is 68.
The numeric value of E is 69.
The numeric value of F is 70.
The numeric value of G is 71.
```

```
The numeric value of H is 72.
The numeric value of I is 73.
The numeric value of J is 74.
The numeric value of K is 75.
The numeric value of L is 76.
The numeric value of M is 77.
The numeric value of N is 78.
The numeric value of O is 79.
The numeric value of P is 80.
The numeric value of Q is 81.
The numeric value of R is 82.
The numeric value of S is 83.
The numeric value of T is 84.
The numeric value of U is 85.
The numeric value of V is 86.
The numeric value of W is 87.
The numeric value of X is 88.
The numeric value of Y is 89.
The numeric value of Z is 90.
```

EXPLANATION: The statement in **line 8** of the above program initializes the integer variable *i* **with 65.** The integer variable is declared in **line 6.**

Lines 9_12 contain the **do-while** loop. The expression *i*<91 is at the **bottom of the loop** in **line 12.** When the loop first starts, the two statements in **lines 10 and 11** are executed before the expression is evaluated. Because the integer variable **i** contains the initial value of **65**, the **printf ()** function in **line 10** displays the numeric value as well as the corresponding character **A** on the screen.

After the integer variable i is increased by **1 in line 11,** the program control reaches the **bottom** of the **do-while** loop. Then the expression *i*<**91** is evaluated. If the relationship in the expression still holds, the program control jumps up to the top of the **do-while** loop, and then the process is repeated.

```
/*Prog 5.56 Demo of do-while loop */
#include <stdio.h>
#include <conio.h>
 void main()
 {
  int t=5;
  clrscr();
  do
  {
   printf("%d\n",t);
   t--;
```

```
  }while(t>0);
 getch();
 }
```

Output:

5

4

3

2

1

EXPLANATION: The program is self-explanatory.

```
/*Prog 5.57 To find number of digits in a given number till single digit
*/
#include <stdio.h>
#include <conio.h>
 void main()
 {
   long int num;
   int count=0,sum=0,save,r;
   clrscr();
   printf("Enter the number \n");
   scanf("%d",&num);
   do
   {
      sum=0;
      while(num!=0)
      {
         r=num%10;
         sum=sum+r;
         num=num/10;
      }
      if(sum>9)
      num=sum;
   }while(num>9);
   printf("Sum of digits up to single digits is %d\n",sum);
   getch();
 }
```

Output:

```
Enter the number
4275
Sum of digits up to single digit is 9.
```

EXPLANATION: For example number is 4275 then sum of digits is 4+2+7+5=18. As 18 is more than 9 we repeat the process and get the result 1+ 8 =9. This time answer is in single digit so we stop the process. In the program for finding sum of digits we have used while loop but for sum of digits up to single digit we have used do-while loop. When sum>9, sum is assigned to num and for this num, sum of digits are determined using do-while.

POINTS TO PONDER

In this section you have learned the following points:

- Looping can be used to perform the same set of statements over and over until specified conditions are met.
- Looping makes your program concise.
- There are three statements, **for, while,** and **do-while,** that are used for looping in C.
- There are three expression fields in the **for** statement. The second field contains the expression used as the specified condition(s).
- The **for** statement does not end with a **semicolon.**
- The empty **for(; ;)** statement can be used to form an **infinite loop.**
- Multiple expressions, separated by commas, can be used in the **for** statement.
- There is only one expression field in the while statement, and the expression is used as the specified condition.
- The while statement does not end with a semicolon.
- The **while (1)** statement can create an **infinite loop.**
- The **do-while** statement places its expression at the **bottom** of the loop.
- The **do-while** statement does end with a semicolon.
- The **inner loop** must finish first before the outer loop resumes its iteration in nested loops.

QUESTIONS AND ANSWERS

Q1. *How does a for loop work?*

Ans: There are three expression fields in the for statement. The first field contains an initializer that is evaluated first and only once before the iteration. The second field keeps the conditional expression that must be tested before the statements controlled by the for statement are executed. If the conditional expression returns a nonzero value, which means the specified condition is met, one iteration of the for loop is carried out. After each iteration, the expression in the third field is evaluated, and then the expression in the second field is reevaluated. The process (that is, looping) is repeated until the conditional expression returns 0.

Q2. *What is the difference between the while and do-while statements?*

Ans: The main difference is that in the while statement, the conditional expression is evaluated at the top of the loop, while in the do-while statement, the conditional expression is evaluated at the bottom of the loop. Therefore, the statements controlled by the do-while statements are executed at least once.

Q3. *Can the while statement end with a semicolon?*

Ans: By definition, the while statement does not end with a semicolon. However, it's legal in C to put a semicolon right after the while statement like this: while (expression);, which means there is a null statement controlled by the while statement. Remember that the result will be quite different from what you expect if you accidentally put a semicolon at the end of the while statement.

Q4. *If two loops are nested together, which one must finish first, the inner loop or the outer loop?*

Ans: The inner loop must finish first. Then the outer loop will start another iteration if the specified condition is still met.

EXERCISES

A. Answer the following questions:

1. What is loop? Why is it necessary in the program?
2. What happens if you create a loop that never ends?
3. What is the difference between (!0) and (!1). How while loop works with these values?
4. Is it possible to nest while loop within for loops?
5. How do you choose between while and for loop?
6. Is it possible to create a for loop that is never executed?
7. Is it possible to use multiple while statement with do statement?
8. Give the syntax of for loop and explain the functionality of for loop?
9. Explain the difference between break and continue?
10. Explain the difference between looping and branching?

B. Brain Drill:

1. Write a program to display alphabets as given below:
   az by cx dw ev fu gt ir jq kp lo mn nm ol pk qj ri sh tg uf ve wd xc yb za
2. Write a program to calculate sum of the first and last number from 1 to 20.example (1 + 20, 2 + 19, 3 + 18, …….)
3. Write a program to find sum of first 50 numbers.
4. Write a program to find total number of votes in favor of person 'X' and 'Y'. Assume 20 voters will be casting their votes to these persons. Count the number of votes gained by 'X' and 'Y'. User can enter her choice by pressing only 'X' and 'Y'.
5. Write a program to check entered data for the following. Whenever input is nonzero or positive display numbers from 1 to that number otherwise display message "Negative or zero". The program is to be performed for 10 numbers.
6. Write a program to display 11, 22, 33, 44, …….., 99 using ASCII values and any loop.

7. Print multiplication of digits of any number. For example number 345, multiplication is 3 * 4 * 5 = 60. Use do-while loop.
8. Write a program to enter an integer number and find the largest and the smallest digit of that number.
9. Write a program in C to reverse a negative number.
10. Assume that in s sequence the next number is obtained by adding the last four numbers repeatedly; write a program to generate the first 20 numbers of the sequence given that the first four numbers are 0, 0, 1 and 1.
11. Write a program to read a positive integer number *'n'* and perform the squares of the individual digits. For example if n = 234 the n answer should be 4 9 16.
12. Write a program to read a positive integer *'n'* and generate the numbers in the following way. If the entered number is 4 the output will be as follows. OUTPUT: 4!3!2!1!01!2!3!4!5!.
13. Write a program to enter a two integer values through the keyboard .Using while loop, perform the product of the two integers. In case product is zero (0), loop should be terminated otherwise loop will continue.
14. Enter 10 numbers through keyboard and sort them in ascending and descending order using do-while loop.
15. Write a nested for loop that prints a 5 X 10 pattern of 0s.

C. Match the following columns:

I	II
1. continue	(*a*) causes an early exit.
2. top testing loop	(*b*) do-while loop
3. bottom testing loop	(*c*) executes at lest once.
4. do-while loop	(*d*) takes control to the beginning of the loop.
5. break	(*e*) while loop.

D. Write True and False against each statements:

1. In do-while semicolon is put after the while which is must.
2. In while semicolon is put after while is must.
3. One type of loop can be nested in other type of loop.
4. A continue and break cannot be used together in a loop.
5. Maximum number of initialization that can be put in a for loop is 2 only.
6. A continue statement causes an early exit for the loop.
7. C support repeat-until loop.
8. Loops are used for controlling the execution of the program.

E. Predict the output of the following programs:

```
1. main ( )
   {
      int count =11;
      while (--count + 1);
```

```
      printf("count down is %d\n", count);
   }
2. main ( )
   {
      int x = 0;
      for (; ;)
      {
          if (++x = =4) break;
          continue;
       }
      printf("x=%d\n",x);
   }
3. main ( )
   {
      unsigned int I;
      for (i=10; i>=0; i--)
      printf("%d",i);
   }
4. main ( )
    {
      char ch = 'A';
      while(ch<='F')
      {
      switch(ch)
      {
       case 'A':case 'B':case 'C':case 'D':ch++; continue;
       case 'E': case 'F': ch++;
      }
     putchar (ch);
    }
   }
5. main ( )
   {
      int i=3;
      while (i--)
      {
         int i= 100;
         i --;
         printf("%d....",i);
```

```
        }
    }
6. main ( )
    {
        int i=0;
        for(i=0;i<=10;i++)
        {
                switch(i)
                {
                    case 0: i+=5;
                    case 1: i+=2;
                    case 5: i+= 5;
                    default : i+=4;
                    break;
                }
                printf("%d",i);
        }
7. main()
    {
        while(!0)
        {
            printf("\n Hello");
        }
    }
8. main()
    {
        while(!1)
        {
            printf("\nHello");
        }
    }
9. main()
    {
        while(" ")
        {
            printf("\n %s","Hello");
        }
    }
```

6

WORKING WITH ARRAYS IN 'C'

6.1 INTRODUCTION

An array is a data structure which can store multiple elements of same data type (homogeneous) under one name. In another way we say that array is a collection of variables of same type all of which are referred by a common name. Specific element of an array is accessed by an index. The declaration of an array is done as:

data_type variable_name [size];

e.g., int arr [5];

By the above statement we are declaring an array named as arr and which can store 5 integer elements .The size is specified in [] square bracket (subscript operator). Size must be given when an array is declared. Array name is an identifier which follows the rules of writing an identifier. Because each integer element takes 2 bytes so this array declaration reverses 10 bytes of memory for the array during compilation. All the elements of an array are stored in contiguous locations with the first element accessed as **array name [0], second as array name [1]** and so on. In our case It will be arr [0], arr [1] upto arr [4]. **The first element of an array starts at index 0 and last element at index arraysize-1.**

Each variable stored in memory has got some address; similarly array has also got an address. In the following figure we assume that array location starts at address 2040. As our array is of integer type each element will be stored at address 2 plus the previous address.

2040	2042	2044	2046	2048
arr[0]	arr[1]	arr[2]	arr[3]	arr[4]

6.1.1 How is Array Different from Variable?

One single variable can store only one value at a time. When we have to work with multiple data items at the same time all of which have some common features for example age of all the students, salary of all the employees etc. then instead of creating separate variable for each data item we can use array.

6.2 SOME IMPORTANT POINTS ABOUT ARRAY

1. Array is a homogeneous data structure which stores elements of similar type *i.e.*, 5 elements of **int** type, **10 elements of float type, and 20 elements of char types etc.**
2. All the elements share the same name and each can be modified individually for *e.g.*,

   int *a*[5] ;
   a[0] = 30;
   a[2] = 56;

   Now changing value is ***a*[0]** does not affect the value of all other elements.
3. Though each element uses the common name of array but each element is treated separately and stored at separate memory location.
4. The array name gives the base address of the array. Given its base address we can reach to address of any element and can find out its value.
5. The amount of storage required by an array depends upon its type and its size.

   The formula can be stated as:

   Total number of bytes = sizeof (type) *length of array

   For example:

   int arr[5]; float[4];

   As integer data type takes **2 byte** in memory here we declare array **arr of size 5.** This implies that the total number of bytes require for int a [5] is:

   Total number of bytes = sizeof(int)*5
   = 2 *5
   = 10

   For float array

   Total number of bytes = sizeof(float)*4
   = 4*4
   = 16
6. In C there is no bound checking on array. It's your responsibility to check end of the array.
7. The number of subscript determines the dimensionality of array. For *e.g.*, **int a[5]** is declaration of one dimension array written as **1-D.** Similarly **int a[4][4]** declares **2-D** array.

   Let's gets you familiar with the concepts through programming examples.

6.3 PROGRAMMING EXAMPLES (PART-1)

```
/*Prog 6.1 input 5 element array and display it ver 1*/
#include<stdio.h>
#include<conio.h>
#define s 5
 void main()
 {
```

```
   int a[5];
   int i;
   clrscr();
   for(i=0;i<s;i++)
   {
     printf("\n Enter a[%d] element:",i);
     scanf("%d",&a[i]);
   }
   printf("Array elements are \n");
   for(i=0;i<s;i++)
    printf("a[%d]= %d\n",i,a[i]);
   getch();
 }
```

Output:

```
 Enter a[0] element:10
 Enter a[1] element:12
 Enter a[2] element:13
 Enter a[3] element:14
 Enter a[4] element:2
Array elements are
a[0]= 10
a[1]= 12
a[2]= 13
a[3]= 14
a[4]= 2
```

EXPLANATION: This program declares an array of size **5** of name ***a*** and loads the array with **5** values entered by the user. To store the five values we have used a **for** loop which runs from **0 to 4.** On each iteration it prompts you to enter the next element of the array and it stores at the location which is denoted by its address **&** ***a[i]*** where ***i*** **will run from 0 to 4.** Then all the elements of the array are displayed one by one through **for** loop. In the program we have used a **macro template S** which denotes size of the array. It is preferable to use macro when giving size of an array because later when you want to change size of the array you will have to go to every place in the program where you used the array and change the size explicitly. Macro saves this effort because you can simply change the value of S which will be automatically expanded to the place where you have used it.

```
/*Prog 6.2 input 5 element array and display it ver2*/
#include<stdio.h>
#include<conio.h>
```

```
#define s 5
 void main()
 {
    int a[s];
    int i;
    clrscr();
    printf("Enter %d numbers \n",s);
    for(i=0;i<s;i++)
    scanf("%d",&a[i]);
    printf("Array element are\n");
    for(i=0;i<s;i++)
    printf("%d\t",a[i]);
    getch();
 }
```

Output:

```
Enter 5 numbers
12 23 34 45 56
Array elements are
12        23        34        45        56
```

EXPLANATION: This program is similar to the previous one but here user is not prompted to enter each element in turn, instead all the numbers are entered at once and scanned through **scanf** one by one which are then displayed through second **for** loop. The numbers can be separated by space or by new line character ***\n***.

/*Prog 6.3 initialization of array ver1 */

```
#include<stdio.h>
#include<conio.h>
 void main()
 {
    int a[]={34,56,78,89,67};
    int i;
    clrscr();
    printf("Array element are \n");
    for(i=0;i<5;i++)
    printf("a[%d]=%d\n",i,a[i]);
    getch();
 }
```

Output:

```
Array elements are
a[0]=34
a[1]=56
```

```
a[2]=78
a[3]=89
a[4]=67
```

EXPLANATION: In all the above programs we were taking input from user for array elements except the previous one. But in this program array elements are initialized as:

int *a*[] = { 34,56,78,89,67};

We initialize the array within opening and closing braces { } and separate the elements by comma, . The size of array in subscript operator [] is optional.

```
/*Prog 6.4 initialization of array ver 2*/
#include<stdio.h>
#include<conio.h>
 void main()
 {
  int a[]={34,56,78,89,67};
  int i;
  clrscr();
  const int s=sizeof(a)/sizeof(int);
  printf("Array elements are \n");
  for(i=0;i<s;i++)
   printf("a[%d]=%d\n",i,a[i]);
  getch();
 }
Output:
Array elements are
a[0]=34
a[1]=56
a[2]=78
a[3]=89
a[4]=67
```

EXPLANATION: The program is similar to previous one except we have determined the number of elements i.e. size of array and stored it into a constant **s**. Size of array ***a*** will be **10** as total **5** elements are there in the array and array is of **int** type and size of **int** is 2 in **turbo C so s=10/2=5.**

The array could also be written as:

int *a*[5] = {34,56,78,89,67};

```
/*Prog 6.5 Accessing elements beyond boundary*/
#include<stdio.h>
#include<conio.h>
 void main()
 {
```

```
    int a[8]={34,56,78,89,67};
    int i;
    clrscr();
    const int s=sizeof(a)/sizeof(int);
    printf("Array elements are\n");
    for(i=0;i<s;i++)
    printf("a[%d]=%d\n",i,a[i]);
    getch();
 }
```

output:

```
Array elements are
a[0]=34
a[1]=56
a[2]=78
a[3]=89
a[4]=67
a[5]=0
a[6]=0
a[7]=0
```

EXPLANATION: When not all the elements are specified for the array the rest are assumed to be zero.

What happen if you declare array in this manner?

int *a*[3] = {34,56,78,89,67};

Here you will get compilation error:

Too many initializes

```
/*Prog 6.6 Output of uninitialized array */
#include <stdio.h>
#include <conio.h>
#define S 5
 void main()
 {
    int a[S];
    int i;
    clrscr();
    printf("Array elements are\n");
    for(i=0;i<S;i++)
    {
       printf("%d\n",a[i]);
    }
```

```
    getch();
  }
```

Output:

```
Array elements are
64
3291
-29146
12803
-28684
```

EXPLANATION: As can be seen from the output that when array elements are not defined *i.e.,* not given values they contain garbage value. Garbage value is any computer generated values and it will be different on different execution of same program. On your PC you may get some other

```
/*Prog 6.7 Counting number of +ve, -ve and zero elements in array */
#include <stdio.h>
#include <conio.h>
 void main()
 {
   Float a[]={34,56,67,-56,-98,0,2,-58,0,0,0,-80,-16,-17,36};
    int i, nop=0,non=0,zero=0;
    clrscr();
    const int S=sizeof(a)/sizeof(float);
    clrscr();
    printf("Array elements are \n");
    for(i=0;i<S;i++)
    {
      printf("%f\t",a[i]);
      if(a[i]>0)
           nop+=1;
           else if(a[i]<0)
                 non+=1;
                 else
                    zero+=1;
    }
   printf("No. of positive elements=%d\n",nop);
   printf("No. of negative elements=%d\n",non);
   printf("No.of zero elements=%d\n",zero);
   getch();
 }
```

```
Output:
Array elements are
34.000000 56.000000 67.000000 -56.000000 -98.000000
0.000000 2.000000 -58.000000 0.000000 0.000000
0.000000 -80.000000 -16.000000 -17.000000 36.000000
No. of positive elements=5
No. of negative elements=6
No. of zero elements=4
```

EXPLANATION: In the program we have initialized a **float** array *a* with **15** element. We are counting number of positive, negative and zero elements in the array by using simple if condition. On each iteration we check element against positive, negative or zero and increment the corresponding counter by one. When all elements are scanned we print them. Instead of initializing array, the element may be taken from user through **scanf**.

```
/*Prog 6.8 Displaying even and odd elements of array separately */
#include <stdio.h>
#include <conio.h>
#define S 6
 void main()
 {
    int arr[S];
    int i;
    clrscr();
     for(i=0;i<S;i++)
     {
       printf("\n Enter the arr[%d] element: ",i);
       scanf("%d",&arr[i]);
     }
     printf("Even Elements\n");
     for(i=0;i<S;i++)
     if(arr[i]%2==0)
     printf("%d\t",arr[i]);
     printf("\n Odd Elements \n");
     for(i=0;i<S;i++)
     if(arr[i]%2!=0)
     printf("%d\t",arr[i]);
     getch();
 }
```

```
Output:
Enter the arr[0] element: 23
Enter the arr[1] element: 45
```

```
Enter the arr[2] element: 12
Enter the arr[3] element: 56
Enter the arr[4] element: 78
Enter the arr[5] element: 90
Even Elements
12 56 78 90
Odd Elements
23 45
```

EXPLANATION: Program is self-explanatory.

```
/*Prog 6.9 Counting even and odd elements of array separately and their
sum */
#include <stdio.h>
#include <conio.h>
#define S 8
 void main()
 {
   int arr[S];
   int i,c_odd=0,c_even=0,s_odd=0,s_even=0;
   clrscr();
   for(i=0;i<S;i++)
   {
     printf("\n Enter the arr[%d] element:",i);
     scanf("%d",&arr[i]);
   }
   printf("Array elements \n");
   for(i=0;i<S;i++)
    printf("%d\t",arr[i]);
   for(i=0;i<S;i++)
   {
     if(arr[i]%2!=0)
     {
       c_odd=c_odd+1;
       s_odd=s_odd+arr[i];
     }
     else
     {
       c_even=c_even+1;
       s_even=s_even+arr[i];
     }
   }
```

```
    printf("\n Number of odd elements=%d\n",c_odd);
    printf("Number of even elements=%d\n",c_even);
    printf("Sum of odd elements=%d\n",s_odd);
    printf("Sum of even elements=%d\n",s_even);
    getch();
   }
```

Output:

```
Enter the arr[0] element:2
 Enter the arr[1] element:34
 Enter the arr[2] element:12
 Enter the arr[3] element:7
 Enter the arr[4] element:9
 Enter the arr[5] element:4
 Enter the arr[6] element:6
 Enter the arr[7] element:9
Array elements
2     34     12     7     9     4     6     9
 Number of odd elements=3
Number of even elements=5
Sum of odd elements=25
Sum of even elements=58
```

EXPLANATION: In this program we are counting all even elements of the array in the variable ***c_even,*** number of odd elements in variable ***c_odd,*** sum of all odd elements ***s_odd,*** sum of all even elements in ***s_even.***

```
/*Prog 6.10 min and max element of array */
#include <stdio.h>
#include <conio.h>
#define S 6
 void main()
 {
   int arr[S];
   int i,max,min;
   clrscr();
   for(i=0;i<S;i++)
   {
     printf("\n Enter the arr[%d] elements:",i);
     scanf("%d",&arr[i]);
   }
   max=arr[0];
   min=arr[0];
```

```
printf("Array elements\n");
for(i=0;i<S;i++)
printf("%d\t",arr[i]);
for(i=0;i<S;i++)
{
   if(min>arr[i])
      min=arr[i];
   if(max<arr[i])
      max=arr[i];
}
printf("\n \n Max element is %d\n",max);
printf("\n Min element is %d\n",min);
getch();
}
```

Output:

```
 Enter the arr[0] elements:34
 Enter the arr[1] elements:67
 Enter the arr[2] elements:8
 Enter the arr[3] elements:9
 Enter the arr[4] elements:23
 Enter the arr[5] elements:76
Array elements
34     67     8     9     23     76
Max element is 76
Min element is 8
```

EXPLANATION: To find the maximum element of an array we have assumed that first element of array is maximum element by storing the first element in the variable max. Then we are comparing this max variable with remaining elements of the array. If max is less than any other element of the array then that element is assigned to max. For finding minimum element of array again we assume that first element is minimum element and store it in variable min. We check if min is greater than any other element of the array, if so then that element is assigned to min.

```
/*Prog 6.11 Insertion of an element into array*/
#include <stdio.h>
#include <conio.h>
#define S 6 // macro used for declaration in global declaration section
 void main()
 {
   int arr[10];
   int i,pos,num,j;
```

```
    clrscr();
/* Apply for loop to enter elements into the array*/
    for(i=0;i<S;i++)
    {
      printf("\n Enter arr[%d] element:",i);
      scanf("%d",&arr[i]);
    }
    clrscr();
    printf("\n\n Array is \n\n");
    for(i=0;i<S;i++)
    printf("arr[%d]=%2-d\n",i,arr[i]);
    printf("\n Enter the element which u want to insert\n");
    scanf("%d",&num);
    printf("Enter the position(first should be 0)\n");
    scanf("%d",&pos);
/*MAIN LOGIC OF THE PROGRAM */
    if(pos>0 && pos<9)
    {
      for(j=S;j>pos;j--)
  arr[j]=arr[j-1];
  arr[j]=num;
    }
    else
    {
      printf("Wrong position selected\n");
      getch();
      exit(1);
    }
    printf("Array after insertion\n");
    for(i=0;i<S+1;i++)
    printf("arr[%d]=%d\n",i,arr[i]);
    getch();
  }
```

Output:

```
Array is
arr[0]=12
arr[1]=13
arr[2]=14
arr[3]=15
arr[4]=16
```

```
arr[5]=17
Enter the element which u wants to insert
19
Enter the position (first should be 0)
3
Array after insertion
arr[0]=12
arr[1]=13
arr[2]=14
arr[3]=19
arr[4]=15
arr[5]=16
arr[6]=17
```

EXPLANATION: The program inserts an element in the array. Initial size of the array ***a*** is **10** but we store only **6** elements in it. You may store maximum **9** elements as to run the program correctly space for element should be there in the array. In order to insert the element we are taking the position **pos** where the user wants to insert the element along with the element to be inserted. For insertion at the supplied position we have to shift the entire element downward by **pos** number of times starting from number of elements actually stored in the array. When the loop quits we store element at ***j*** position.

Inserting Element into the Array

There are two types of approaches:

1. **At the end of the array** 2. **At required position.**

1. **At the end of the array:** Inserting the element at the last position of the array is not very complex process. Just put the element at the last vacant position of the array.
2. **Insertion at required position:** Insertion of any element at the required position is very simple process. The procedure which we follow is: shift the element below at the position where new element to be inserted.

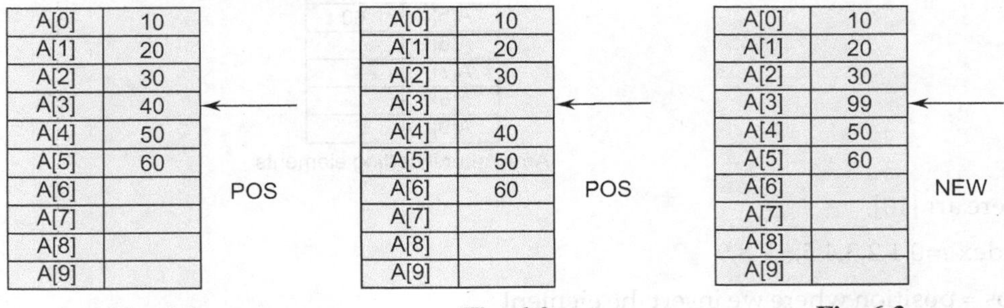

Fig. 6.1 **Fig. 6.2** **Fig. 6.3**

Description of Figures:

Fig-1 Initial array

Fig-2 After shifting element one position down

Fig-3 Insert the element 99 at required position

Working style of the program (DISCUSSION OF MAIN LOGIC)

Here the size of array is **10** because **arr [10].**

And we want to insert **6** element initially that's why we set **s=6 by #define** macro

Before entering element into the array **arr [10]** array is look like as:

A[0]	
A[1]	
A[2]	
A[3]	
A[4]	
A[5]	
A[6]	
A[7]	
A[8]	
A[9]	

Array arr [10]

After inserting the element arr[0]= 10

```
Arr[1]  = 20
Arr[2]  = 30
Arr[3]  = 40
Arr[4]  = 50
Arr[5]  = 60
```

A[0]	10
A[1]	20
A[2]	30
A[3]	40
A[4]	50
A[5]	60
A[6]	
A[7]	
A[8]	
A[9]	

Array after inserting elements

Here arr [10],

index *i*=0,1,2,3,4,5,6,7,8,9

pos = position where we insert the element

j =index to find the position

num = new element which we want to insert.

Now we set an example we want to insert 99 at position 3

I1. Check the condition for insertion at pos=3 num =99

```
                    If (pos>=0 && pos <=9)                    TRUE
    Apply for loop as:
        for (j=s; j>pos; j--)
for j=6
       → for (j= 6; j> 6; j--)                               TRUE
       → arr[j]=arr[j-1]
         arr [6] = arr[6-1] = arr[5]
i.e.     arr[6] = arr[5]
and      arr[j] = num
i.e      arr[6]
that is assign the value of pos 5 to pos 6.
           a[6] = a[5] = 60
Similarly,  a[5] = a[4] =50
           a[4] = a[3] =40
           a[3] = new num=99
```

/*Prog 6.12 Deleting from an array*/

```
#include <stdio.h>
#include <conio.h>
#define S 6
 void main()
 {
   int arr[S];
   int i,pos,num,j;
   clrscr();
/* Apply for inserting the elements of the array*/
   for(i=0;i<S;i++)
   {
     printf("\n Enter a[%d] element:",i);
     scanf("%d",&arr[i]);
   }
   printf("\n\n Array is \n\n");
/*Apply for loop to display the elements of the array*/
   for(i=0;i<S;i++)
   {
     printf("arr[%d]=%2d\n",i,arr[i]);
   }
   printf("\n Enter the position of the element");
   printf(" Which element you want to delete\n");
```

```
    scanf("%d",&pos);
/*Main logic of the program*/
    if(pos>=0 && pos<S)
    {
       for(j=pos;j<S;j++)
          arr[j]=arr[j+1];
    }
    else
    {
       printf("Wrong position selected \n");
       getch();
       exit(1);
    }
    printf("Array after deletion \n");
    for(i=0;i<S-1;i++)
     printf("arr[%d]=%d\n",i,arr[i]);
    getch();
    }
```

Output:

```
 Enter a[0] element:12
 Enter a[1] element:13
 Enter a[2] element:14
 Enter a[3] element:15
 Enter a[4] element:16
 Enter a[5] element:17
 Array is
arr[0]=12
arr[1]=13
arr[2]=14
arr[3]=15
arr[4]=16
arr[5]=17
Enter the position of the element which element you want to delete
2
Array after deletion
arr[0]=12
arr[1]=13
arr[2]=15
arr[3]=16
arr[4]=17
```

EXPLANATION: The logic for deletion is similar to logic for insertion in the array. Starting from the pos given by the user of element to be deleted, we shift all elements upward as to cover up the place of the deleted element.

Deletion of Element From the Array

There are also two approaches for deletion from the array:

1. **Deletion at the last** 2. **Deletion at required position.**

1. **Deletion at the last:** Deletion at the last position is very simple process just remove the element at the last position, which is shown in the figure below.

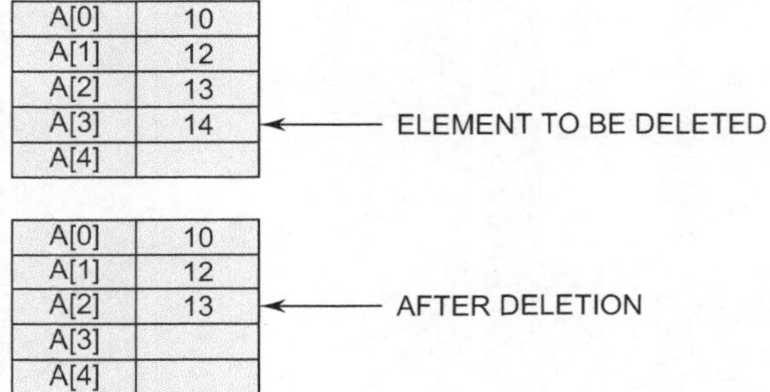

Fig. 6.4 *Deletion of the last.*

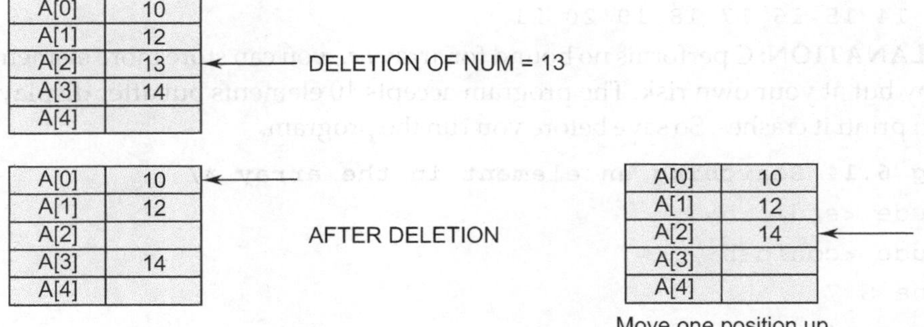

Fig. 6.5 *Deletion from specific position.*

```
/*Prog 6.13 Storing more than capacity*/
#include <stdio.h>
#include <conio.h>
 void main()
 {
   int a[5];
   int i;
   clrscr();
   printf("Enter 10 array elements\n");
   for(i=0;i<10;i++)
      scanf("%d",&a[i]);
```

```
    printf("Array elements \n");
   for(i=0;i<10;i++)
    printf("%d",a[i]);
   getch();
 }
```

Output:

```
Enter 10 array elements
12
13
14
15
16
17
18
19
20
21
Array elements
12 13 14 15 16 17 18 19 20 21
```

EXPLANATION: C performs no bound for array *i.e.,* you can store more element than the size of the array but at your own risk. The program accepts 10 elements but after displaying 10 elements through printf it crashes. So save before you run the program.

```
/*Prog 6.14 Searching an element in the array */
#include <stdio.h>
#include <conio.h>
#define S 7
 void main()
 {
   int arr[S], num, flag=0;
   int i;
   clrscr();
   printf("Enter %d array elements \n",S);
   for(i=0;i<S;i++)
   scanf("%d",&arr[i]);
   printf("Array elements are \n");
   for(i=0;i<S;i++)
   printf("a[%d]=%d",i,arr[i]);
   printf("Enter the element which u want to search\n");
   scanf("%d",&num);
   for(i=0;i<S;i++)
```

```
    {
      if(arr[i]==num)
      {
        flag=1;
        break;
      }
    }
    if(flag==1)
    printf("Element exist at location %d",i);
    else
    printf("Element does not exist in the array\n");
    getch();
  }
```

Output:

```
Enter 7 array elements
12
13
14
15
16
17
18
Array elements are
a[0]=12
a[1]=13
a[2]=14
a[3]=15
a[4]=16
a[5]=17
a[6]=18
Enter the element which u wants to search
12
Element exist at location 0
```

EXPLANATION: The element to be searched is taken in the num. Variable **flag** is initialized to **0** in the beginning. In the **for** loop num is compared with each element of the array and if a match occurs we make **flag =1** and quit from the loop. Value of **flag =1** ensures that a match has occurred. Outside the loop we check the value of flag and display the result accordingly. The program does not take into account how many times num appears in the array. It simply searches whether num is either in the array or not.

Searching of Element in the Array Working Proceudre

There are two ways for searching of any element in the array working procedure:

1. **Linear Searching** 2. **Binary Searching**

1. **Linear Searching:** In case of linear searching we search element one by one, if match if found then search is successful otherwise not getting the element.
2. **Binary Searching:** In case of binary search first of all we will find the value of first element, last element and then by applying the formula we will find out the value of mid:

$$MID = (int)\frac{FIRST + LAST}{2}$$

Now, start checking **`mid = key mid<key or mid>key`**

Elements <mid	mid	Elements >mid

EXAMPLE:

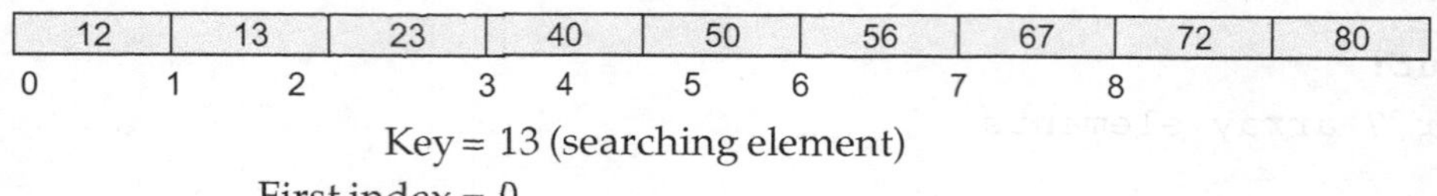

Key = 13 (searching element)

First index = 0

Last index = 8

Then mid element is evaluated as:

Mid = (int) (first + last) / 2

i.e., mid = (int) ((0+8)/2)

= (int) ((8)/2)

= 4

Element at position 4 *i.e.,* a [mid] =a [4] =50

Now compare a [mid] with searching element

12	13	23	40	50	56	67	72	80

0 1 2 3 Mid (4) 5 6 7 8

SUB ARRAY-1 SUB ARRAY-2

Since 50>13 searching in first half of the array (sub array 1)

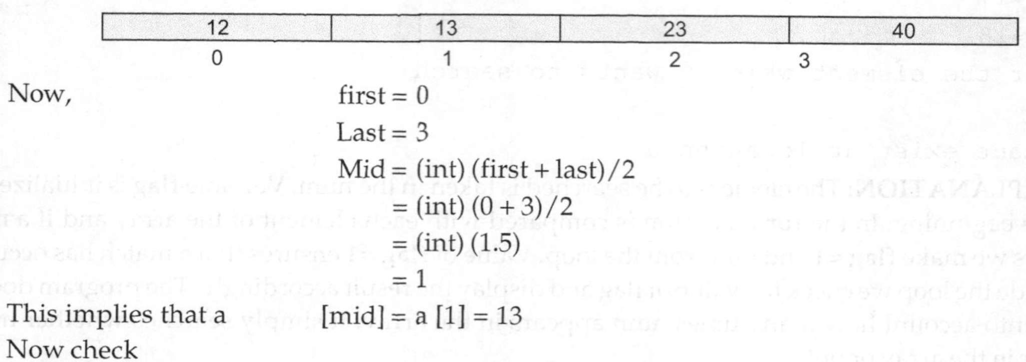

Now, first = 0

Last = 3

Mid = (int) (first + last)/2

= (int) (0 + 3)/2

= (int) (1.5)

= 1

This implies that a [mid] = a [1] = 13

Now check

Here a [mid] = a [1] = 13= searching element

Therefore, search is successful.

```
*Prog 6.15 Square of array elements in new array */
#include <stdio.h>
#include <conio.h>
#define S 7
 void main()
 {
    int arr1[S], arr2[S];
    int i;
    clrscr();
    printf("Enter %d array elements \n",S);
    for(i=0;i<S;i++)
    scanf("%d",&arr1[i]);
    printf("Array elements are \n");
    for(i=0;i<S;i++)
    printf("a[%d]=%d\n",i,arr1[i]);
    for(i=0;i<S;i++)
    arr2[i]=arr1[i]*arr1[i];
    printf("Square of array elements \n");
    for(i=0;i<S;i++)
    printf("a[%d]=%d\n",i,arr2[i]);
    getch();
 }
```

Output:

```
Enter 7 array elements
12
13
14
15
16
17
19
Array elements are
a[0]=12
a[1]=13
a[2]=14
a[3]=15
a[4]=16
a[5]=17
```

```
a[6]=19
Square of array elements
a[0]=144
a[1]=169
a[2]=196
a[3]=225
a[4]=256
a[5]=289
a[6]=361
```

EXPLANATION: The program is self-explanatory.

```
/*Prog 6.16 Sorting of element of array */
#include <stdio.h>
#include <conio.h>
#define S 6
 void main()
 {
  int a[S];
  int i,j,t;
  clrscr();
  for(i=0;i<S;i++)
  {
   printf("\n Enter a[%d] element:",i);
   scanf("%d",&a[i]);
  }
  clrscr();
  printf("Original Array\n");
  for(i=0;i<S;i++)
   printf("%d\t",a[i]);
   for(i=0;i<S;i++)
   for(j=i+1;j<S;j++)
    if(a[i]>a[j])
    {
       t=a[i];
       a[i]=a[j];
       a[j]=t;
    }
    printf("\n \nSorted Array\n");
    for(i=0;i<S;i++)
     printf("%d\t",a[i]);
```

```
    getch();
  }
```

Output:

```
 Enter a[0] element:12
 Enter a[1] element:4
 Enter a[2] element:56
 Enter a[3] element:2
 Enter a[4] element:59
 Enter a[5] element:3
Original Array
12          4     56     2     59     3
Sorted Array
2           3     4      12    56     59
```

EXPLANATION: Sorting means arrangement of array elements in either ascending order or descending order. In the program we sort in ascending order.

In order to understand the logic behind the program we take 5 elements of array and trace the logic as:

4	0	3	1	2
a [0]	a [1]	a [2]	a [3]	a [4]

For ***i*=0**, inner **for** loop runs **for *j*=1 to *j*=4** and it compares ***a*[0]** with all other elements of the array *i.e.*, ***a*[1], *a*[2], *a*[3], *a*[4].** If any of the elements is greater than *a* [0] then both the elements are swapped. For example *a*[0] is 4 and *a*[1] is 0, if condition turns out to be true then *a*[0] and *a*[1] are swapped. Now array becomes:

0	4	3	1	2
a [0]	a [1]	a [2]	a [3]	a [4]

For *j*=2 to *j*=4 if condition is false and array does not change. This completes one iteration of outer for loop. We can check that after the first iteration of outer for loop the smallest element of array occupies first place in the array. Continuing in this manner for *i*=1 and running *j*=2 to 4 we see that for *i*=1 and *j*=2 if condition is satisfied and *a*[1] and *a*[2] are swapped. Then array becomes

0	3	4	1	2
a [0]	a [1]	a [2]	a [3]	a [4]

For *i* =1 and *j* =3 if condition and *a*[1] and *a*[3] are swapped array becomes:

0	1	4	3	2
a [0]	a [1]	a [2]	a [3]	a [4]

So after the end of the inner for loop array will be:

0	3	4	1	2
a [0]	a [1]	a [2]	a [3]	a [4]

That is second number is at the second place in the array. So when the outer loop finishes the array will be stored in ascending order.

```
/*Prog 6.17 Counting frequencies of elements of array */
#include <stdio.h>
#include <conio.h>
#define S 12
 void main()
 {
    int a[S],freq[S];
    int i,j,k,n=S;
    clrscr();
    for(i=0;i<S;i++)
    {
       printf("\n Enter a[%d] element:",i);
       scanf("%d",&a[i]);
       freq[i]=1;
    }
    clrscr();
    printf("Original Array \n");
    for(i=0;i<S;i++)
    printf("%d\t",a[i]);
    for(i=0;i<n;i++)
    for(j=i+1;j<n;j++)
    {
       if(a[i]==a[j])
       {
          for(k=j;k<n;k++)
 a[k]=a[k+1];
 freq[i]++;
 n--;
       }
    }
    printf("\n Array with freq\n");
    printf("\nElement\tfreq\n");
    for(i=0;i<n;i++)
     printf("%d\t%d\n",a[i],freq[i]);
     getch();
 }
```

Output:

```
Original Array
12      13      14      15      12      13      14      15      11      20
12      13
```

```
Array with freq
Element  freq
12       3
13       3
14       2
15       2
11       1
20       1
```

EXPLANATION: The logic is similar to one which was used in array sorting program with few additions. We start with the first element of the array and compare this element with all the other elements of the array. If any other element of the array is same (say at position **j**) we shift all elements upwards starting with this **j** position and decrement size of array by one. Initially we assume that the frequency of each element is 1 and for that an array freq is used of same size as of the original array. If *a*[*i*] matches with any of the *a*[*j*] element that freq[*i*] is incremented by one. In the end we display the array along with their frequencies:

For example we take array:	3	2	3	11	2	5
And initial freq array:	1	1	1	1	1	1

$n = 6$; for $i = 0$ and $j = 2$ $a[i]$ and $a[j]$ are equal so freq [0] is incremented by one and array elements are shifted upward so:

array now becomes:	3	2	11	2	5	5
freq array becomes :	2	1	1	1	1	1

$n = 5$;

next no element matches with $a[0]$ so we now compare $a[1]$ with all remaining elements $a[1]$ matches with $a[3]$

array now becomes:	3	2	11	5	5	5
freq array becomes:	2	2	1	1	1	1

$n = 4$;

next for $a[2]$ and $a[3]$ there will be no matching and their frequency will remain one.

```
/*Prog 6.18 Checking and removal of duplicate elements of array */
#include <stdio.h>
#include <conio.h>
#define S 6
#define true 1
#define false 0
 void main()
 {
   int a[S];
   int i,j,k,n=S,dup_found=false;
```

```
clrscr();
for(i=0;i<S;i++)
{
  printf("\n Enter a[%d] element:",i);
  scanf("%d",&a[i]);
}
clrscr();
printf("Original array \n");
for(i=0;i<S;i++)
printf("%d",a[i]);
for(i=0;i<n;i++)
for(j=i+1;j<n;j++)
{
  if(a[i]==a[j])
  {
for(k=j;k<n;k++)
a[k]=a[k+1];
n--;
dup_found=true;
  }
}
if(dup_found==true)
  printf("\n Array contains duplicate element\n");
else
{
 printf("\n Array does not contains duplicte element \n");
 getch();
 exit(0);
}
 printf("\n Array after removing duplicte elements \n");
 for(i=0;i<n;i++)
 printf("%d",a[i]);
 getch();
}
```

Output:

```
Original array
12 13 15 17 18 12
Array contains duplicte element
Array after removing duplicte elements
12 13 15 17 18
```

EXPLANATION: The program is quite similar to previous program. We have removed the frequency array and to check whether array contains duplicate element we have taken one variable **dup_found** whose initial value is false. If control reaches to if block its value is changed to true.

6.4 TWO-DIMENSIONAL (2-D) ARRAY

A two-dimensional array can be thought of a matrix with rows and columns. For example if we declare a 2-D array as:

int arr[3] [4];

Then this declaration means a **2-D arr of 3 rows and 4columns** which can be represented as follows:

	Col 1	Col2	Col3	Col4
Row1	arr[0][0]	arr[0][1]	arr[0][2]	arr[0][3]
Row2	arr[1][0]	arr[1][1]	arr[1][2]	arr[1][3]
Row3	arr[2][0]	arr[2][1]	arr[2][2]	arr[2][3]

The first row and column starts at **0.** Inter section of row and column becomes the position of element of the 2-D array **for e.g., first row(0) and second column(1) element will be arr[0][1].**

```
/*Prog 5.19 demo of 2-D array ver 1*/
#include<stdio.h>
#include<conio.h>
 void main()
 {
   int arr[3][4];
   int i,j;
   clrscr();
   for(i=0;i<3;i++)
   {
      for(j=0;j<4;j++)
      {
  printf("\n Enter the arr[%d][%d] element:",i,j);
  scanf("%d",&arr[i][j]);
      }
   }
   printf("Array elements are\n");
   for(i=0;i<3;i++)
```

```
    {
      for(j=0;j<4;j++)
  printf("%d",arr[i][j]);
      printf("\n");
    }
  getch();
}
```

Output:

```
 Enter the arr[0][0] element:1
 Enter the arr[0][1] element:2
 Enter the arr[0][2] element:3
 Enter the arr[0][3] element:4
 Enter the arr[1][0] element:5
 Enter the arr[1][1] element:6
 Enter the arr[1][2] element:7
 Enter the arr[1][3] element:8
 Enter the arr[2][0] element:9
 Enter the arr[2][1] element:1
 Enter the arr[2][2] element:2
 Enter the arr[2][3] element:3
Array elements are
1     2     3     4
5     6     7     8
9     1     2     3
```

EXPLANATION: As we are dealing with two-dimensional array we have to first store all the elements (depends upon number of columns) for first row, then for second row up to total number of rows. For this we require two loops one which controls rows and one for columns. Through this we have first taken the values for 2-D array and later displayed them in the form of matrix.

```
/*Prog 6.20 demo of 2-D array ver2*/
#include<stdio.h>
#include<conio.h>
 void main()
 {
   int arr[3][3]={{1,2,3},{4,5,6},{7,8,9}};
   int i,j;
   clrscr();
   printf("Array elements are\n");
   for(i=0;i<3;i++)
   {
     for(j=0;j<3;j++)
```

```
    printf("%d\t",arr[i][j]);
    printf("\n");
    }
    getch();
 }
```

Output:

```
Array elements are
1      2    3
4      5    6
7      8    9
```

EXPLANATION: This program demonstrates how to initialize a 2-D array. A two-dimensional array is a collection of 1-D array so enclosed each 1-D array in braces though this is not necessary but provides better understandability *i.e.,* you may write in this manner also.

int arr[][] = {1,2,3,4,5,6,7,8,9}

```
/*Prog 6.21 Demo of 2-D array ver 3*/
#include <stdio.h>
#include <conio.h>
 void main()
 {
    int arr[][3]={{1,2,3},{4,5,6},{2,3,4}};
    int i,j;
    clrscr();
    printf("Array element are \n");
    for(i=0;i<3;i++)
    {
       for(j=0;j<3;j++)
        printf("%d",arr[i][j]);
       printf("\n");
    }
    getch();
 }
```

Output:

```
Array elements are
1 2 3
4 5 6
2 3 4
```

EXPLANATION: This program is similar to previous one but it tells you something new about 2-D array. You can omit row size while declaring a 2-D array but you cannot leave column size field why? Simple by counting number of elements for each row *i.e.,* column size the number of row can be calculated but by without knowing how many elements for each row a 2-D array cannot be allocated. So, the following will result in an error.

```
int arr[3][] = {{1,2,3},{4,5,6},{2,3,4}};
```

```
/*Prog 6.22 Demo of 2-D array ver4 */
#include <stdio.h>
#include <conio.h>
 void main()
 {
   int arr[][3]={{1,2,3},{4,3,6},{2,3,4}};
   int i,j,row,col=3;
   clrscr();
   row=sizeof(arr)/(col*sizeof(int));
   printf("Array elements are\n");
   for(i=0;i<row;i++)
   {
      for(j=0;j<col;j++)
      printf("%d",arr[i][j]);
      printf("\n");
   }
   getch();
 }
```

Output:

```
Array elements are
1  2  3
4  3  6
2  3  4
```

EXPLANATION: This program is simple with one change we have not given the size of row while declaring array instead we have determined it through calculation.

Sizeof (arr) = 18 (as 9 int elements are there in the array)

Col = 3 and sizeof (int) = 2

So row = 18 /(3*2) = 3

```
/*Prog 6.23 Transpose of a matrix */
#include <stdio.h>
#include <conio.h>
 void main()
 {
   int arr[3][3];
   int i,j;
   clrscr();
   printf("Enter the 6 elements of matrix:\n");
```

```
 for(i=0;i<3;i++)
   for(j=0;j<3;j++)
     scanf("%d",&arr[i][j]);
   printf("The matrix is \n");
   for(i=0;i<3;i++)
   {
     for(j=0;j<3;j++)
        printf("%d",arr[i][j]);
        printf("\n");
   }
   printf("The transpose Matrix is \n");
   for(i=0;i<3;i++)
   {
     for(j=0;j<3;j++)
        printf("%d",arr[j][i]);
        printf("\n");
   }
   getch();
}
```

Output:

```
Enter the 6 elements of matrix:
12
13
14
15
16
17
18
19
20
The matrix is
12 13 14
15 16 17
18 19 20
The transpose Matrix is
12 15 18
13 16 19
14 17 20
```

EXPLANATION: The transpose of a matrix with its row and column interchanged. For example if the matrix is written in C:

int a[3][2] = {{1,2},{3,4},{5,6}};

Diagrammatically it is represented as:

1	2
3	4
5	6

The transpose matrix is given as:

int a[2][3] = {{1,3,4},{2,4,6}};

That is to print the transpose of a matrix simply change the row and column and while printing interchange i and j.

```
/*Prog 6.24 Find max of each row of 3*4 matrix*/
#include <stdio.h>
#include <conio.h>
 void main()
 {
    int a[3][4];
    int i,j,max[3];
    clrscr();
    for(i=0;i<3;i++)
    {
       for(j=0;j<4;j++)
       {
        printf("\n Enter a[%d][%d] element:",i,j);
        scanf("%d",&a[i][j]);
       }
    }
    printf("\n\n Matrix is \n");
    for(i=0;i<3;i++)
    {
     for(j=0;j<4;j++)
       printf("%2d",a[i][j]);
     printf("\n");
    }
    for(i=0;i<3;i++)
    {
       max[i]=a[i][0];
       for(j=1;j<4;j++)
       {
```

```
        if(max[i]<a[i][j])
          max[i]=a[i][j];
      }
    }
    printf("Max of each row is as follows\n");
    for(i=0;i<3;i++)
    printf("Row %d:%d\n\n",i+1,max[i]);
    getch();
  }
```

Output:

```
Enter a[0][0] element:11
Enter a[0][1] element:12
Enter a[0][2] element:13
Enter a[0][3] element:14
Enter a[1][0] element:15
Enter a[1][1] element:16
Enter a[1][2] element:17
Enter a[1][3] element:18
Enter a[2][0] element:19
Enter a[2][1] element:20
Enter a[2][2] element:21
Enter a[2][3] element:22
Matrix is
11 12 13 14
15 16 17 18
19 20 21 22
Max of each row is as follows
Row 1:14
Row 2:18
Row 3:22
```

EXPLANATION: Finding max of each row of a 2-D array is quite simple. Assume each row as a 1-D array and apply the same logic to find max of 1-D array. To store the max element of each row we have taken 1-D array of size equal to row size of 2-D array under problem.

Actually there are two ways of implementing 2-D array in memory which are given as:

1. **Row-major implementation.**
2. **Column-major implementation.**

In this program we assume the row-major implementation and according to the row major implementation compiler control row wise that first complete row then second complete row and so on.

Row/column	C1	C2	C3
R1	1	2	3
R2	4	5	6
R3	7	8	9

Fig. 6.6 *A 2-D array of order a[3][3]*

Diagrammatically row-major implementation can be represented as:

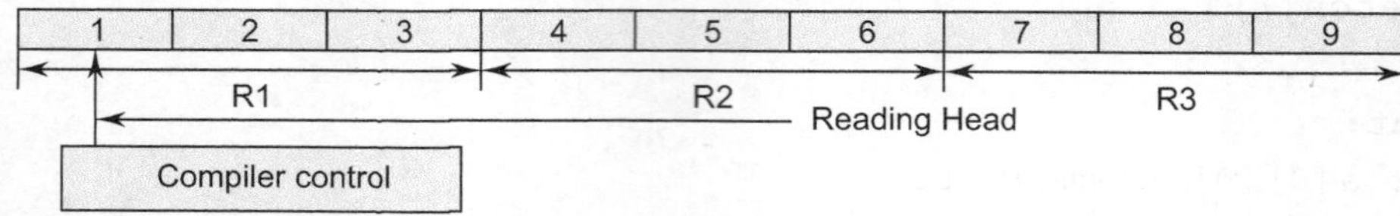

Fig. 6.7 *Row-major implementation of 2-D array.*

```
/*Prog 6.25 Find max of each col of 3*4 matrix */
#include <stdio.h>
#include <conio.h>
 void main()
 {
    int a[3][4];
    int i,j,max[4];
    clrscr();
    for(i=0;i<3;i++)
    {
     for(j=0;j<4;j++)
     {
       printf("\n Enter a[%d][%d] element:",i,j);
       scanf("%d",&a[i][j]);
     }
    }
   printf("\n\n Matrix is \n\n");
   for(i=0;i<3;i++)
   {
     for(j=0;j<4;j++)
     {
        printf("%2d",a[i][j]);
     }
     printf("\n");
   }
   for(j=0;j<4;j++)
   {
```

```
      max[j]=a[0][j];
      for(i=1;i<3;i++)
      {
         if(max[j]<a[i][j])
    max[j]=a[i][j];
      }
    }
    printf("Max of each col is as follows \n");
    for(i=0;i<4;i++)
    printf("Col %d:%d\n\n",i+1,max[i]);
    getch();
 }
```

Output:

```
Enter a[0][0] element:11
Enter a[0][1] element:12
Enter a[0][2] element:13
Enter a[0][3] element:14
Enter a[1][0] element:15
Enter a[1][1] element:16
Enter a[1][2] element:17
Enter a[1][3] element:18
Enter a[2][0] element:19
Enter a[2][1] element:20
Enter a[2][2] element:21
Enter a[2][3] element:22
Matrix is
11121314
15161718
19202122
Max of each col is as follows
Col 1:19
Col 2:20
Col 3:21
Col 4:22
```

EXPLANATION: This program is similar to previous one with the difference is that instead of finding out max element of each row we have found max element of each column.

```
/*Prog 6.26 sum of diagonal elements of a square matrix */
#include <stdio.h>
#include <conio.h>
```

```
void main()
{
   int a[3][3];
   int i,j,dsum=0;
   clrscr();
   for(i=0;i<3;i++)
   {
      for(j=0;j<3;j++)
      {
         printf("\n Enter a[%d][%d] element:",i,j);
         scanf("%d",&a[i][j]);
      }
   }
    printf("\n\n Matrix is \n");
    for(i=0;i<3;i++)
    {
      for(j=0;j<3;j++)
   printf("%2d",a[i][j]);
   printf("\n");
    }
    for(i=0;i<3;i++)
    for(j=0;j<3;j++)
      if(i==j)
      dsum=dsum+a[i][j];
    printf("Sum of diagonal elements is %d\n",dsum);
    getch();
}
```

Output:

```
Enter a[0][0] element:3
Enter a[0][1] element:4
Enter a[0][2] element:5
Enter a[1][0] element:6
Enter a[1][1] element:7
Enter a[1][2] element:8
Enter a[2][0] element:9
Enter a[2][1] element:1
Enter a[2][2] element:2
Matrix is
3 4 5
6 7 8
```

```
9 1 2
Sum of diagonal elements is 12
```

EXPLANATION: The diagonal element of a 2-D array can be calculated only if number of rows and columns are same and that matrix is called a square matrix. Diagonals elements of matrix are those elements where row and column are same such as **row 0 col 0, row 1, col1** and so on. **To find sum of diagonal elements we have checked if row is equal to column and if it is then sum it up. For the given matrix sum of diagonal elements would be 12.**

3	4	5
6	7	8
9	1	2

Fig. 6.8 *A 2-D matrix diagonal elements are shown bold.*

```
/*Prog 6.27 Sum of reverse diagonal elements of a square matrix */
#include <stdio.h>
#include <conio.h>
 void main()
 {
   int a[3][3];
   int i,j,dsum=0,k;
   clrscr();
   for(i=0;i<3;i++)
   {
      for(j=0;j<3;j++)
      {
         printf("\n Enter a[%d][%d] element:",i,j);
         scanf("%d",&a[i][j]);
      }
   }
   printf("\n\n Matrix is \n");
   for(i=0;i<3;i++)
   {
      for(j=0;j<3;j++)
      printf("%2d",a[i][j]);
      printf("\n");
   }
   i=0,j=2;
   for(k=0;k<3;k++)
   {
      dsum=dsum+a[i++][j--];
   }
```

```
   printf("\n Sum of diagonal elements:=%d\n",dsum);
   getch();
}
```

Output:

```
Enter a[0][0] element:1
Enter a[0][1] element:2
Enter a[0][2] element:3
Enter a[1][0] element:4
Enter a[1][1] element:5
Enter a[1][2] element:6
Enter a[2][0] element:7
Enter a[2][1] element:8
Enter a[2][2] element:9
Matrix is
1 2 3
4 5 6
7 8 9
Sum of diagonal elements: =15
```

EXPLANATION: This program is very similar to the previous one with the difference that instead of finding out sum of diagonal elements we have found sum of reverse diagonal elements. Logic is quite simple. The first element at (0,2), for second element increment row and decrement col and so on.

The second logic may be:

```
for(i=0;i<3;i++)
for(j=0;j<3;j++)
if(i+j = =3)
dsum + = a[i][j];
```

1	**2**	**3**
4	**5**	**6**
7	**8**	**9**

For the given matrix sum of the reverse diagonal elements would be **15.**

```
/*Prog 6.28 Sum of two matrices*/
#include <stdio.h>
#include <conio.h>
 void main()
 {
   int a[2][2], b[2][2], c[2][2];
   int i,j;
```

```
clrscr();
printf("Enter the elements of first matrix\n");
for(i=0;i<2;i++)
{
   for(j=0;j<2;j++)
   {
      printf("\n Enter a[%d][%d] element:",i,j);
      scanf("%d",&a[i][j]);
   }
}
printf("Enter elements of the second matrix\n");
for(i=0;i<2;i++)
{
 for(j=0;j<2;j++)
 {
  printf("\n Enter b[%d][%d] elements:",i,j);
  scanf("%d",&b[i][j]);
 }
}
printf("\n\n First matrix is given as\n");
for(i=0;i<2;i++)
{
   for(j=0;j<2;j++)
   {
      printf("%3d",a[i][j]);
   }
   printf("\n");
}
printf("\n Second matrix is given as:\n");
for(i=0;i<2;i++)
{
   for(j=0;j<2;j++)
   {
    printf("%3d",b[i][j]);
    }
   printf("\n");
}
printf("Sum of two matrix is \n");
for(i=0;i<2;i++)
{
```

```
    for(j=0;j<2;j++)
    {
      c[i][j]=a[i][j]+b[i][j];
      printf("%3d",c[i][j]);
    }
    printf("\n");
   }
   getch();
 }
```

Output:

```
Enter the elements of first matrix
 Enter a[0][0] element:1
 Enter a[0][1] element:2
 Enter a[1][0] element:3
 Enter a[1][1] element:4
Enter elements of the second matrix
 Enter b[0][0] elements:5
 Enter b[0][1] elements:6
 Enter b[1][0] elements:7
 Enter b[1][1] elements:8
 First matrix is given as
  1 2
  3 4
 Second matrix is given as:
  5 6
  7 8
Sum of two matrix is
  6 8
 10 12
```

EXPLANATION: The sum of two matrixes can be obtained only when dimensions of both are same *i.e.,* number of row and col of first matrix match with the second metric's row and col. Then sum can be calculated by summing element at the same row and col position. For example:

First matrix a [2] [2]

1	2
3	4

Second matrix b [2] [2]

5	6
7	8

Then the sum of two matrices will be matrix c [2] [2]

6	8
10	12

On the similar basis you can calculate the subtraction of two matrices.

```
/*Prog 6.29 Multiplication of two matrices */
#include <stdio.h>
#include <conio.h>
 void main()
 {
    int a[3][3],b[3][3],c[3][3];
    int i,j,k;
    clrscr();
    printf("Enter elements of first matrix \n");
    for(i=0;i<3;i++)
    {
       for(j=0;j<3;j++)
       {
          printf("\n Enter a[%d][%d] element:=",i,j);
          scanf("%d",&a[i][j]);
       }
    }
    clrscr();
    printf("Enter element of second matrix \n");
    for(i=0;i<3;i++)
    {
       for(j=0;j<3;j++)
       {
          printf("\n Enter b[%d][%d] element:=",i,j);
          scanf("%d",&b[i][j]);
       }
    }
    clrscr();
    printf("\n First Matrix is given below:\n");
    for(i=0;i<3;i++)
    {
       for(j=0;j<3;j++)
       printf("%4d",a[i][j]);
       printf("\n");
    }
```

```
    printf("\n\n Second Matrix is given below:\n");
    for(i=0;i<3;i++)
    {
       for(j=0;j<3;j++)
       printf("%4d",b[i][j]);
       printf("\n");
    }
/*Main logic starts here */
    for(i=0;i<3;i++)
    {
     for(j=0;j<3;j++)
     {
       c[i][j]=0;
       for(k=0;k<3;k++)
 c[i][j]=c[i][j]+a[i][k]*b[k][j];
     }
    }
/ *Main logic ends here */
    printf("\n\n Multiplication of two matrices is \n\n");
    for(i=0;i<3;i++)
    {
       for(j=0;j<3;j++)
          printf("%4d",c[i][j]);
       printf("\n");
    }
    getch();
  }
```

Output:

```
Enter elements of first matrix
 Enter a[0][0] element:=1
 Enter a[0][1] element:=2
 Enter a[0][2] element:=3
 Enter a[1][0] element:=4
 Enter a[1][1] element:=5
 Enter a[1][2] element:=6
 Enter a[2][0] element:=7
 Enter a[2][1] element:=8
 Enter a[2][2] element:=9
Enter element of second matrix
 Enter b[0][0] element:=1
```

```
Enter b[0][1] element:=2
Enter b[0][2] element:=3
Enter b[1][0] element:=4
Enter b[1][1] element:=5
Enter b[1][2] element:=6
Enter b[2][0] element:=7
Enter b[2][1] element:=8
Enter b[2][2] element:=9
First Matrix is given below:
        1   2   3
        4   5   6
        7   8   9
Second Matrix is given below:
        1   2   3
        4   5   6
        7   8   9
Multiplication of two matrices is
       30  36  42
       66  81  96
      102 126 150
```

EXPLANATION: For matrix multiplication of two matrices the number of col of first matrix must be equal to the number of row of second matrix *i.e.*, if dimension of first matrix is m by n then dimension of second matrix must be n by p and the resultant matrix will be of order m by p. The logic is as follows:

We take two matrices of order 3 by 3, suppose the order of first matrix is m by n and that of second matrix is n by p.

1	2	3		2	4	5		29	11	23
4	3	2		6	2	3	=	36	24	37
2	5	6		5	1	4		64	24	49

Fig. 6.9 *Procedure for matrix multiplication*

In the main logic the first loop runs from 0 to m. Second inner loop runs from 0 to p and third inner loop runs from 0 to n (common column of first matrix and row of second matrix). As the direction of arrow shows initially first row is chosen for value of $i = 0$ then for value of $j = 0$, k runs from 0 to 3 so we get:

$$C[0][0] = 0;$$
$$i = 0, j = 0, k = 0;$$
$$C[0][0] = c[0][0] + a[0][0] * b[0][0];$$
$$= 0 + 1*2;$$

= 2;

K = 1;

C [0] [0] = c [0] [0] + a [0] [1] * b [1] [0];

= 2 + 2 * 6;

= 2 + 12;

= 14;

K = 2;

C [0] [0] = c [0] [0] + a [0] [2] * b [2] [0];

= 14 + 3 * 5;

= 14 + 15;

= 29;

This is the value is first element of the result first column and first row of the resultant matrix.

After this third inner loop finishes. Now we have to chosen second column of second matrix so j becomes I and for value of $i = 0, j = 1, k$ again from 0 to 3.

C [0] [1] = 0;

$i = 0, j = 1, k = 0$;

C [0] [1] = c [0][1] + a[0][0] * b[0][1];

= 0 + 1*4;

= 4;

K = 1;

C [0] [1] = c [0] [1] + a [0] [1] * b [1] [1];

= 4 + 2 * 2;

= 4 + 4;

= 8;

K = 2;

C [0] [1] = c [0][1] + a[0][2] * b [2][1];

= 8 + 3 * 1;

= 11;

This is the value of first row and second column of resultant matrix.

After this third inner loop finishes. Now we have to choosen third column of second matrix so j becomes 2 and for value of $i = 0, j = 2, k$ again runs from 0 to 3.

C [0] [2] = 0;

I = 0; $j = 2$; $k = 0$;

C [0] [2] = c [0] [2] + a [0] [0] * b [0] [2];

= 0 + 1 * 5;

= 5;

K = 1;

C [0] [2] = c [0] [2] + a [0] [1] * b [1] [2];

= 5 + 2 * 3;

= 5 + 6;

= 11;

$$K = 2;$$
$$C[0][2] = c[0][2] + a[0][2] * c[2][2];$$
$$= 11 + 3*4;$$
$$= 11 + 12;$$
$$= 23;$$

This is the value of first row and third column of resultant matrix. After this value of *j* exhausts and value of I now becomes 1 and process repeat.

```
/*Prog 6.30 To insert an element in 2-Dimensional array*/
#include<stdio.h>
#include<conio.h>
#include<string.h>
#define R 10
#define C 15
/********** Function Declaration begins **********/
int insert(char[][C],int,int,char[]);
void traverse(char[][C],int);
/********** Function Declaration ends **********/
 void main()
 {
  int i=1,n,pos;
  char emp[R][C],item[R];
  clrscr();
   printf("\n\t Prgram to insert an employee name in 2-Dimensional
array:");
  printf("\n\n\t How many name you want to store in the array:");
  scanf("%d",&n);
  while(i<=n)
  {
     printf("\n Enter employee name:");
     scanf("%s",&emp[i]);
     i++;
  }
  traverse(emp,n);
  printf("\nEnter the position to insert new name:");
  scanf("%d",&pos);
  printf("\n Enter the employee name:");
  scanf("%s",&item);
  n = insert(emp,n,pos,item);
  traverse(emp,n);
  getch();
```

```
  }
  /********** Traversing array elements **********/
  /********** Function Definition begins **********/
   void traverse(char emp[][C], int n)
   {
     int i=1;
     printf("\n Employee names are:\n");
     while(i<=n)
     {
       printf("%d.",i);
       printf("%s\n",emp[i]);
       i++;
     }
     printf("\n");
   }
/********** Function Definition ends **********/
/********** Inserting array element **********/
/********** Function Definition begins **********/
 int insert(char emp[][C], int n, int pos, char item[])
 {
   int i;
   i=n;
   while(i>=pos)
   {
    strcpy(emp[i+1],emp[i]);
    i--;
   }
   strcpy(emp[pos],item);
   n= n+1;
   return n;
}
/********** Function Definition ends **********/
```

Output:

```
Program to insert an employee name in 2-Dimensional array:
How many names you want to store in the array:6
 Enter employee name:Vijay
 Enter employee name:Madhuri
 Enter employee name:Anajana
 Enter employee name:Manmohan
 Enter employee name:Hari
```

```
 Enter employee name:Ranjana
 Employee names are:
1.Vijay
2.Madhuri
3.Anajana
4.Manmohan
5.Hari
6.Ranjana
Enter the position to insert new name:5
Enter the employee name:HariMohan
Employee names are:
1.Vijay
2.Madhuri
3.Anajana
4.Manmohan
5.HariMohan
6.Hari
7.Ranjana
```

/*Prog 6.31 To Traverse elements from 2-Dimensional array*/

```
#include<stdio.h>
#include<conio.h>
#define R 10
#define C 15
/********** Function Declaration begins **********/
void traverse(char[][C],int);
/********** Function Declaration ends **********/
void main()
{
 int i=1,n;
 char emp[R][C];
 clrscr();
 printf("\n\t Program to traverse 2-Dimensional array having name of
employees:");
 printf("\n\t How many employees you want to store in the array:");
 scanf("%d",&n);
 while(i<=n)
 {
      printf("\n Enter employee name:");
      scanf("%s",&emp[i]);
```

```
      i++;
 }
 traverse(emp,n);
 getch();
}
/********** Traversing array elements **********/
/********** Function Definition begins **********/
void traverse(char emp[][C], int n)
{
 int i=1;
 printf("\n Employee name are:");
 while(i<=n)
 {
      printf("\n %d.",i);
      printf("%s\n",emp[i]);
      i++;
 }
 printf("\n");
}
/********** Function Definition ends **********/
```

Output:

```
Program to traverse 2-Dimensional array having name of employees:
How many employees you want to store in the array:6
 Enter employee name:Vijay
 Enter employee name:Madhuri
 Enter employee name:Anjana
 Enter employee name:Manmohan
 Enter employee name:HariMohan
 Enter employee name:Ranjana
 Employee name are:
 1.Vijay
 2.Madhuri
 3.Anjana
 4.Manmohan
 5.HariMohan
 6.Ranjana
```

```
/*Prog 6.32 To Delete element from 2-Dimensional array*/
#include<stdio.h>
#include<conio.h>
#include<string.h>
```

```
#define R 10
#define C 15
/********** Function Declaration begins **********/
int deletion(char[][C],int,int);
void traverse(char[][C],int);
/********** Function Declaration ends **********/
void main()
{
 int i=1,n,pos;
 char emp[R][C];
 clrscr();
 printf("\n\t Program to delete an employee name from 2-Dimensional
array:");
 printf("\n\n\t How many employees name you want to store in the
array:");
 scanf("%d",&n);
 while(i<=n)
 {
      printf("\n Enter employee name:",i);
      scanf("%s",&emp[i]);
      i++;
 }
 traverse(emp,n);
 printf("\n Enter the position to delete employee name:");
 scanf("%d",&pos);
 n = deletion(emp,n,pos);
 traverse(emp,n);
 getch();
}
/********** Traversing array elements **********/
/********** Function Definition begins **********/
void traverse(char emp[][C], int n)
{
 int i=1;
 printf("\n Employee names are");
 while(i<=n)
 {
      printf("\n%d.",i);
      printf("%s\n",emp[i]);
      i++;
```

```
 }
 printf("\n");
}
/********** Function Definition ends **********/
/********** Deleting array element **********/
/********** Function Definition begins **********/
int deletion(char emp[][C], int n, int pos)
{
 char item[C];
 strcpy(item,emp[pos]);
 printf("\nDeleted   employee   name   from   the   position   %d   is
:%s\n",pos,item);
 while(pos<=n)
 {
      strcpy(emp[pos],emp[pos+1]);
      pos++;
 }
 n= n-1;
 return n;
}
```

Output:

```
Program to delete an employee name from 2-Dimensional array:
How many employees name you want to store in the array:6
 Enter employee name:vijay
 Enter employee name:Madhuri
 Enter employee name:Anajna
 Enter employee name:Manmohan
 Enter employee name:Harimohan
 Enter employee name:Ranjana
 Employee names are
1.vijay
2.Madhuri
3.Anajna
4.Manmohan
5.Harimohan
6.Ranjana
Enter the position to delete employee name:5
Deleted employee name from the position 5 is :Harimohan
Employee names are
1.vijay
```

```
2.Madhuri
3.Anajna
4.Manmohan
5.Ranjana
```

6.5 3-DIMENSIONAL ARRAYS

A 3-dimensional array can be thought of a collection of 2-D array which can against be thought of 1-D array. For example we have a 3-D array declaration.

int arr [2][3][4];

We can think of the above declaration as array of 2-elements where each element is a 2-D array of size 3 by 4. These are usually not occurring in practice we will only present programs to demonstrate how to initialize and print them.

```
/*Prog 6.33 Demo of 3-D array */
#include<stdio.h>
#include<conio.h>
 void main()
 {
   int a[2][3][2]={{{1,2},{2,3},{3,4}},{{3,2},{2,5},{7,2}}};
   int i,j,k;
   clrscr();
   for(i=0;i<2;i++)
   {
    printf("2-D Array %d\n",i+1);
      for(j=0;j<3;j++)
      {
         for(k=0;k<2;k++)
         printf("%d\t",a[i][j][k]);
         printf("\n");
      }
    printf("\n");
   }
   getch();
 }
```

Output:

```
2-D Array 1
1        2
2        3
3        4
```

```
2-D Array 2
3        2
2        5
7        2
```

EXPLANATION:

```
int a[2][3][2]={{{1,2},{2,3},{3,4}},{{3,2},{2,5},{7,2}}};
```

The above declaration of a 3-D array with initialization can be understood as:

{1,2} represents **1-D** array with 2 elements. {{1,2},{2,3},{3,4}} represents 1st **2-D** array. Any element of this array will be represented by *a*[0][*j*][*k*] (j from 0 to 2 and *k* from 0 to 1). Similarly any element of 2nd 2-D array will be represented as *a*[1][*j*][*k*] (*j* from 0 to 2 and *k* from 0 to 1). To take input from user the code can be changed as:

```
for(i=0;i<2;i++)
{
    printf("Enter elements for the 2-D array %d\n",i+1);
    for(j=0;j<3;j++)
    {
        for(k=0;k<2;k++)
        {
            printf("Enter a[%d][%d][%d] element:",i,j,k);
            scanf("%d",&a[i][j][k]);
        }
    }
}
```

POINTS TO PONDER

In this section you have learned the following points:

- An array is a collection of variables that are of the same data type.
- In C, the index to an array starts at 0.
- You can initialize each individual element of an array after the declaration of the array, or you can place all the initial values into a data block surrounded by { and } during the declaration of an array.
- The memory storage taken by an array is determined by the product of the size of the data type and the dimensions of the array.
- A pointer is said to refer to an array when the address of the first element in the array is assigned to the pointer. The address of the first element in an array is also called the start address of the array.
- To assign the start address of an array to a pointer, you can either put the combination of the address-of operator (&) and the first element name of the array, or simply use the array name, on the right side of an assignment operator (=).

- A character array is considered a character string in C if the last element in the array contains a null character (\0).
- The null character (\0) marks the end of a string. C functions, such as printf(), will stop processing the string when the null character is encountered.
- C supports multi-dimensional arrays, too. A pair of brackets (the array subscript operator—[and]) indicates a dimension.
- The compiler can automatically calculate the memory space needed by an unsized array.
- To represent two-dimensional array in memory, there are two ways:
  (*a*) Row-major order.
  (*b*) Column-major order.

QUESTIONS AND ANSWERS

Q1. *Why do you need to use arrays?*

Ans: In many cases, you need to declare a set of variables that are of the same data type. Instead of declaring each variable separately, you can declare all the variables collectively in the format of an array. Each variable, as an element of the array, can be accessed either through the array element reference or through a pointer that references the array.

Q2. *What is the minimum index in an array?*

Ans: In C, the minimum index of a one-dimensional array is 0, which marks the first element of the array. For instance, given an integer array,

```
int  array_int[8];
```

the first element of the array is **array_int[0]**. Likewise, for a multi-dimensional array, the minimum index of each dimension starts at **0.**

Q3. *How do you reference an array by using a pointer?*

Ans: You can use a pointer to reference an array by assigning the start address of an array to the pointer. For example, given a pointer variable **ptr_ch** and a character array **array_ch,** you can use one of the following statements to reference the array by the pointer:

```
ptr_ch  =  array_ch;
ptr_ch  =  &array_ch[0];
```

Q4. *What can the null character do?*

Ans: The null character **(\0)** in C can be used to mark the end of a string. For instance, the **printf()** function puts the next character on the screen when the null character is encountered. Also, the null character always returns **FALSE** in a logical test.

EXERCISES

A. Answer the followings questions:

1. Array name contains the base address of the array? Can we change the base address of array?
2. Can we store value and addresses in the same array? Explain.
3. What are arrays? Why do we need them?

4. How do we initialize array elements?
5. What do you understand by 2-D arrays? Also discuss multidimensional array?
6. Is 2-D array be the combination of 1-D array? If yes explain with the help of suitable example?
7. How compiler control read the elements of 2-D array?
8. What do you understand by row-major implementation and column-major implementation of 2-D array?

B. Match the following columns:

I	II
1. Array	(*a*) Must be mentioned.
2. Left most dimensions in a	(*b*) can be omitted Multidimensional array.
3. Vector	(*c*) 1-D array.
4. Declaration of an array	(*d*) Allocating of memory at compile
5. Right most dimension in a time multidimensional array	(*e*) Derived data type.

C. Write True and False against each statement:

1. Matrix is an array of 1-D array.
2. C does not check array boundary.
3. Array name and subscript variables are same.
4. If the size of an array is less that the number of elements initialized, the size grows dynamically.
5. The two arrays can be assigned as arr1 =arr2.
6. A single array can be used to represent both int and float values.
7. The expression arr [*i*, *j*] and *a*[*i*][*j*] are same.
8. Numerical array elements can be read as a single entity.

D. Fill in the blanks:

1. Array name represents the __________ of the starting location.
2. __________ storage representation is used in a matrix.
3. Number of elements in a 2-D array having 4 rows and 6 columns is __________.
4. The array subscript must always start at __________.
5. The ________ of an array are stored in consecutive memory locations.
6. Missing elements of partially initialized array are set to __________.
7. The expression arr[5] and __________ are identical.
8. C has no check on __________.
9. A 1-D array is also known as __________.
10. A 2-D array is known as __________.

E. Brain Drill

1. Write a program to replace the zero with successive number in the following array

   int *x*[ ] = {1,0,3,0,5,0,7,0};
2. Write a program to read 10 integers in an array. Sort them out on the basis of number of digits in each element.

3. Write a program to read a number containing five digits. If number of digits is not 5 then an error should be flashed. If the number is 23453 output should be 0409162509.
4. Write a program to check whether the diagonal elements of a (4*x* 4) matrix are all zeros.
5. Write a program to shift all zero elements in an array towards end of the array.
6. Consider a matrix of 0's and 1's . A sequence of successive 1's along a row, or a column or a diagonal to be on a line. The number of 1's in a line is called its length. Write a C program to find out the line with the maximum length in such a matrix.
7. Write a program to read the text. Find out number of lines in it.
8. Write a program to read any three characters. Find out all the possible combinations.
9. Read the marks of five subjects in as examination. Display the top two student codes and their marks.
10. Write a program to read 10 integers in an array. Find the largest and smallest numbers.

F. Predict the output of the following programs:

1.
```
main ( )
{
    int a[10];
    printf("%d",((a+3) +(a+2));
}
```

2.
```
main ( )
{
    int a[3][4] = { {1,2},{4, 8, 15}};
    printf("%d",a[0][2]);
}
```

3.
```
main ( )
{
    int a[ ] = (1,2,3,4,5};
    int x = &a[5] - &a[1];
    printf("%d",x);
}
```

4.
```
main ( )
{
    int i,j;
    int m[3][3] = {1,2,3,4,5,6,7,8,9};
    for(i=2;i>=0;i--)
    for(j=2;j>=0;j--)
    printf("%d",*(m+j)+i);
}
```

5.
```
main ( )
{
    int arr[ ] = {1,2,3,4,5,6,7};
```

```
    char c[] = {'a','b','c','d','e'};
    printf("%d\t%d",(&arr[3]-&arr[0]),(&c[3] - &c[0]));
}
```

G. Answer the following:

1. What does the following statement do?

```
int array_int[4] = {12, 23, 9, 56};
```

2. Given an array, int data[3], what's wrong with the following initialization?

```
data[1]=1;
data[2] = 2;
data[3] = 3;
```

3. How many dimensions do the following arrays have?
   - o char array1[3][19];
   - o int array2[];
   - o float array3[][8][16];
   - o char array4[][80];

4. What's wrong with the following declaration?

```
char list_ch [] [] ={
                    'A', 'a',
                    'B', 'b',
                    'C', 'c',
                    'D', 'd',
                    'E', 'e'};
```

7

INTRODUCTION TO FUNCTIONS IN 'C'

The chapter teaches you the building block of the C programming language, the function. The chapter starts with the introduction to the functions, function definition, how and where they are used, types of function on the basis of creation and on the basis of argument and return type they take. Difference between user defined and library functions have also been discussed. A brief note on the **main** function is also given.

Next four sections are entirely devoted to functions which belong to one of the categories on the basis of whether they take argument or not, whether they return value or not. Many programming examples are given in all the **4** categories of the functions.

Recursion the most powerful programming technique used in functions discussed in with **10 fully explained programs.** One of the most widely used puzzle The tower of Hanoi used to each recursion to the beginners is represented as a separate section.

7.1 INTRODUCTION

A function is a self contained block of code written once for a particular purpose but can be used again. A function is a basic entity for C programming language. Even the execution of our program starts from the main function. They are the basic building blocks for the modular programming.

Depending upon the parameters and return type (discuss later on) functions are classified into 4 categories:

1. No return type and no arguments / parameters
2. No return type but arguments/ parameters
3. Return type but no arguments / parameters
4. Return type with arguments/ parameters

There are number of functions which we have so far like **printf (), scanf (), clrscr (), getch (), strlen () etc.** All these functions are library functions or built-in functions *i.e.,* they are already there in the

C programming language and we can use them in our programs. Again each of these functions belong to one of the categories given above. The limitations of these functions are that their code cannot be known, we can simply use them, and no modification can be done.

All the built-in functions have their prototype or declaration stored in their respective header files. For example function declaration of **printf and scanf** is stored in header file **stdio.h.** The definition of all the functions *i.e.,* the actual function code (what they do) is stored in compiled code is in **.obj** files and are linked to the program during compilation and linking. The compiled code is stored in **.obj** file. Thus we can simply use built-in functions in our program but we cannot modify them as their code is not available to the programmer.

We can write our own functions depending upon requirements and all those functions will be called user-defined functions as they are defined by the user and be put in any of the categories given below.

One important point to note is that **main ()** is not a library function. It is simply a restriction from C compiler that we have to use this function for our programming as execution starts from this function. So this can be put into the user defined function. Our whole discussion will be totally based on user defined functions.

Now, we start our discussion with the first category of the functions.

7.2 NO RETURN TYPE AND NO ARGUMENTS/PARAMETERS

The general syntax of this category of function is as follows:

```
Declaration of function:
         Void function_name (void);
Definition of function:
          Void function_name (void)
          {
            Statements;
            Statements;
            ..........................;
          }
```

For discussion of the above see the program given below.

Let's understand the working of the function with the help of some programs.

```
/*Prog 7.1 Demo of function ver1*/
#include<stdio.h>
#include<conio.h>
 void main()
 {
      void show(void); /* Declaration of function*/
```

```
     show();
 }
     void show(void)   /* Definition of function*/
     {
      printf("Hello from show function\n");
     }
```

Output:

```
Hello from show function
```

EXPLANATION: The line **void show (void)** is called declaration or prototype of the function. The general syntax is as given above:

```
void function_name (void);
```

In the above context **void** is the return type, **show** is the function name and **void** inside **show** indicates that this **show** function does not take any arguments. Whenever you have **()** after any name then that is a function. Obviously you may have arguments within **(). A function prototype tells the compiler three things about function:**

(*a*) its name (function name)

(*b*) return type.

(*c*) Number of arguments.

Here **void** means that function does not take any arguments and does not return any value. The function declaration must end with semicolon.

Actual working of the function is done by the definition of the function which is

```
void show(void)
{
   printf ("Hello from show function\n");
  }
```

The function definition starts with the same syntax as given for declaration but it does not end with semicolon and actual work which the function performs written in the form of C statements within { }. All the statements within { } of the function is called body of the function.

When we write **show ( )** it means we are calling the function **show ( ).** Whenever **show ( )** statement is encountered then control is transferred to the body of the function and all the statements written within the body of the function gets executed. When closing braces of the function is encountered then function returns to the next statement after from where the function was called. In this case it is **getch ( ).** In C every function will be called from some other function. Here we have called **show ( )** from within **main( ).** So **main( )** is called **calling** function and **show( )** is called **called/ callee** function.

```
/*Prog 7.2 demo of function ver 2 */
#include<stdio.h>
#include<conio.h>
 void main()
 {
```

```
    void show(void);
    printf("In main\n");
    show();
    printf("Back in main\n");
  }
    void show(void)
    {
    printf("In show function\n");
    }
```

```
Output:
In main
In show function
Back in main
```

EXPLANATION: There is small change in this program from the previous one. First line is as it is the declaration of function **show ( ).** As the program executes control goes to **printf** which prints **In main** on the screen. Then when **show ()** is encountered control is transferred to the definition of **show ( )** and executes all the statements within the body, here it prints **In show** function. As stated in the previous explanation that whenever a function returns it goes back to the next statement after from where it was called and here the next statements is **printf** which displays **Back in main** on to the screen and program terminates.

```
/*Prog 7.3 working with function */
#include<stdio.h>
#include<conio.h>
 void main()
 {
   void show();
   void disp();
   printf("In main\n");
   show();
   disp();
   printf("Back in main\n");
 }
   void show()
   {
      printf("In show function\n");
   }
   void disp()
   {
    printf("In disp function\n");
   }
```

```
Output:
 In main
 In show function
 In disp function
 Back in main
```

EXPLANATION: Here we are working with two functions. Again a prototype is given in the beginning. As clear from the output initially first **printf** in **main ()** is executed then **show( )** is called and **printf** within **show( )** is executed. When **show( )** returns **disp( )** is called and **printf** within **disp( )** is executed. When **disp ()** is returned second **printf** in **main( )** is executed, following which **getch( ),** executes and in the end program terminates.

```
/*Prog 7.4 working with three function */
#include<stdio.h>
#include<conio.h>
 void main()
 {
   void fun1();
   void fun2();
   void fun3();
   clrscr();
   printf("In main \n");
   printf("Going in function 1\n");
   fun1();
   fun2();
   fun3();
   printf("Back in main\n");
   getch();
 }
   void fun1()
   {
     printf("In fun1 function \n");
   }
   void fun2()
   {
     printf("In fun2 function\n");
   }
   void fun3()
   {
     printf("In fun3 function\n");
   }
```

Output

```
In main
Going in function 1
In fun1 function
In fun2 function
In fun3 function
Back in main
```

EXPLANATION: Not much is there to explain in this program. We have three functions which are called one by one.

```
/*Prog 7.5 Nesting of function*/
#include<stdio.h>
#include<conio.h>
 void main()
 {
   void fun1();
   void fun2();
   clrscr();
   printf("In main\n");
   printf("Going in function 1\n");
   fun2();
   printf("Back in main \n");
   fun1();
   getch();
 }
   void fun2()
   {
     printf("In fun2 function,called from fun1\n");
     printf("Returning from fun2\n");
   }
   void fun1()
   {
     printf("In fun1 function \n");
     printf("Going in fun2\n");
     fun2();
     printf("Back in fun1, going back to main\n");
   }
```

Output:

```
In main
Going in function 1
```

```
In fun2 function,called from fun1
Returning from fun2
Back in main
In fun1 function
Going in fun2
In fun2 function,called from fun1
Returning from fun2
Back in fun1, going back to main
```

EXPLANATION: In this program we have called **fun1( )** from **main( )** and inside **fun1( )** we have called **fun2( )**. When **fun2( )** returns control returns to the next **printf** statement following which **fun1( )** returns.

Now, I think at this stage you must have understood the first type of functions *i.e.,* which does not take any argument and which does not return any value. Now we turn our attention towards second category of function.

7.3 NO RETURN TYPE BUT ARGUMENTS

The general syntax of this category of function is as follows:

```
Declaration of function:
          void function_name (data_type arg,........);
Definition of function:
          void function_name (data_type arg,.......);
          {
                 Statements;
                 Statements;
                 ..........................;
          }
```

```
/*Prog 7.6 to display of integer through function ver1*/
#include<stdio.h>
#include<conio.h>
 void main()
 {
   void show(int);
   int a;
   clrscr();
   printf("Enter a number\n");
   scanf("%d",&a);
   show(a);
   getch();
```

```
}
void show(int x)
{
   printf("U entered =%d\n",x);
}
```

Output:

```
Enter a number
45
U entered =45
```

EXPLANATION: The declaration **void show (int)** states that function **show** does not return any value but accepts an argument/ parameter of **int** type *i.e.,* an **int** variable or an **int constant** will be passed to this function. When we call the function we pass an **int** value as shown by statement **show (*a*).** Here we are calling the function **show** and passing ***a*** as argument. **This is known as call by value as we are calling the function and passing value of the variable *a*.** The ***a*** value sent must be collected in some variable in the function definition. We collect this value in variable ***x*.** Note the type and number of arguments must match when defining the function. Variable ***a*** in function **main** is called **actual argument** and variable *x* in function **show** is called **formal argument** when we pass ***a*** to the function **show** a copy of ***a* is** sent which is collected in *x*. In the function we simply print the value of *x*.

```
/*Prog 7.7 display of integer through function ver2*/
#include<stdio.h>
#include<conio.h>
void main()
{
   void show(int);
   int a;
   clrscr();
   printf("Enter a number\n");
   scanf("%d",&a);
   show(a);
   printf("Number is %d\n",a);
   getch();
}
void show(int x)
{
   printf("U entered =%d\n", x);
   x=x+10;
}
```

Output:

```
Enter a number
45
```

```
U entered =45
Number is 45
```

EXPLANATION: In the **show** after printing *x* we have incremented it by **10.** When function returns (when closing brace is encountered) we print the value of *a* in the main. The value of *a* remains same as it was prior to sending to the function **show. Any change performed on the formal parameter does not reflect back in the actual parameters when functions are called by value *i.e.,* when value of actual parameters is send to the function.** This is vary important concept which will be discussed in detail when we study pointers.

```
/*Prog 7.8 function with two argument an int and char */
#include<stdio.h>
#include<conio.h>
 void main()
 {
   void show(int,char);
   int a;
   char ch;
   clrscr();
   printf("Enter an int and a char\n");
   scanf("%d\t%c",&a,&ch);
   show(a,ch);
   getch();
 }
   void show(int x,char y)
   {
      printf("a=%d\tch=%c\n",x,y);
   }
Output:
Enter an int and a char
23 r
a=23    ch=r
```

EXPLANATION: The declaration **void show (int, char)** tells the compiler that **show** is a function which accepts two arguments first one from left is of **int** type and second is of **char** type. We accept an **int** and a **char** from user **pass** the same to the function **show.** In the definition of show we simply show the variables on to the screen.

```
/*Prog 7.9 sum of two float numbers using function */
#include<stdio.h>
#include<conio.h>
 main()
 {
       void sum(float,float);
```

```
        float a,b;
        printf("Enter the two numbers\n");
        scanf("%f%f",&a,&b);
        sum(a,b);
        getch();
}
        void sum(float x,float y)
        {
               float t;
               t=x+y;
               printf("x=%f\ty=%f\n sum=%f\n",x,y,t);
               }
```

Output:

```
Enter the two numbers
2.3 4.5
x=2.300000      y=4.500000
sum=6.800000
```

EXPLANATION: The declaration **void sum(float, float)** tells the compiler that it is a function which accepts two arguments of **float** data type and returns nothing because of **void** before function name **sum**. If you want you may also write declaration in this manner **void sum(float *x*, float *y*).** Though this is optional in declaration but mandatory in definition as value passed to the function has to be stored in the formal parameters. We input two numbers in *a* and *b* from user and pass the same to function **sum.** The actual argument *a* and *b* are collected in formal argument *x* and *y*. Inside **sum** we declare a local variable *t* and store the sum *x* + *y* in *t*. In the end we display *x*, *y* **and sum** through **printf.**

The definition may be written using small number of statements as:

```
               void sum(float x, float y)
               {
                 printf("x=%f \n y=%f\n sum=%f\n", x, y, sum);
               }
```

```
/*Prog 7.10 max of two float numbers using function */
#include<stdio.h>
#include<conio.h>
 main()
 {
      void max(float,float);
      float a,b;
      clrscr();
      printf("Enter two numbers\n");
      scanf("%f%f",&a,&b);
```

```
     max(a,b);
     getch();
 }
     void max(float x,float y)
     {
          float t;
          t=x>y?x:y;
          printf("x=%f\ny=%f\nmax=%f\n", x, y, t);
     }
```

Output:

```
Enter the two numbers
4.3   2.5
X= 4.300000           y= 2.500000          max= 4.300000
```

EXPLANATION: In the program we are finding the max numbers using function. We accept the two numbers from user and pass to the function. In the function body we have found out max using **ternary operator? :** and stored the same in ***t*** which is displayed through the **printf.** Instead of ternary operator we could use **if-else** also in the following manner.

```
     void max(float x, float y)
     {
        float t;
        if (x>y)
           t=x;
        else
           t=y;
           printf("x=%f\t y=%f\n max=%f\n", x,y,t);
     }
```

Again we could have shortened the code as:

```
     void max(float x, float y)
     {
        printf("x=%f \t y=%f\n max=%f\n", x, y, x>y?x:y);
     }
```

```
/*Prog 7.11 maximum of three float numbers */
#include<stdio.h>
#include<conio.h>
 void main()
 {
   void max(float,float,float);
   float a,b,c;
   clrscr();
   printf("Enter three numbers\n");
```

```
    scanf("%f%f%f",&a,&b,&c);
    max(a,b,c);
    getch();
  }
    void max(float x,float y, float z)
    {
       float t,t1;
       t=x>y?x:y;
       t1=t>z?t:z;
       printf("x=%f\ty=%f\tz=%f\n",x,y,z);
       printf("max=%f\n",t1);
    }
```

Output:

```
Enter three numbers
12.3 6.7 190.3
x=12.300000     y=6.700000      z=190.300003
max=190.300003
```

EXPLANATION: The logic to find out maximum of three numbers has been written into the function **max** which accepts three arguments of **int** type and finds the maximum number using **ternary operator?:.** The logic has been explained earlier. The logic can also be written using **if-else** as:

```
Void max(float x, float y, float z)
{
    float m;
    if(x>y)
       if(x>z)
          m=x;
       else
          m=z;
    else
          if(y>z)
             m=z;
          else
               m=z;
    printf("x=%f\t y=%f\t z=%f\n max=%f\n", x, y, z, max);
}
```

```
/*Prog 7.12 program to check number is even or odd using function*/
#include<stdio.h>
#include<conio.h>
 void main()
```

```
{
 void checkEO(int);
 int num;
 clrscr();
 printf("Enter an integer number\n");
 scanf("%d",&num);
 checkEO(num);
 getch();
}
   void checkEO(int x)
   {
    if(x%2==0)
       printf("number is even\n");
    else
       printf("number is odd\n");
   }
```

Output:

```
Enter an integer number
198
number is even
```

EXPLANATION: We input an integer number from user and pass it to function **checkEO** which checks whether number is even or odd. The logic has been explained earlier also. The only difference here is that we have put the logic into the function so we can use it any where we want .It could be written in this manner also:

```
Void chekEO(int x)
{
 (x%2==0)?printf("no. is even\n"):printf("no. is odd\n");
}
```

```
/*Prog 7.13 convert case of character using function */
#include<conio.h>
#include<stdio.h>
 void main()
 {
    void convertcase(char);
    char ch;
    clrscr();
    printf("Enter a character \n");
    scanf("%c",&ch);
    convertcase(ch);
    getch();
```

```
}
   void convertcase(char ch)
   {
      char temp;
      printf("Original Case=%c\n",ch);
      if(ch>='a' && ch<='z')
       ch=ch-32;
       else if(ch>='A' && ch<='Z')
             ch=ch+32;
      printf("Reverse case=%c\n",ch);
   }
```

Output:

(First run)

```
Enter a character
A
Original Case=A
Reverse case=a
```

(Second run)

```
Enter a character
w
Original Case=w
Reverse case=W
```

EXPLANATION: In the function **convertcase** we pass a single character. The character is collected in formal parameter **ch.** In the function we check the value of **ch** if it is in between ***'a'* and *'z'*** we subtract **32** from it to get upper case equivalent . If **ch** falls between **'A' and 'Z'** then we add **32** in it to get lowercase equivalent. The function could be written in this manner also:

```
void convercase(char ch)
{
   char temp;
   printf("Original case=%c\n",ch);
   if(ch>=97 && ch<=122)
      ch=ch-32;
      else if(ch>=65 && ch<=90)
            ch=ch+32;
   printf("Reverse case=%c\n", ch);
}
```

/*Prog 7.14 Display decorated name using function*/

```
#include<stdio.h>
#include<conio.h>
 void main()
```

```
{
   void line(int,char);
   char str[20];
   clrscr();
   printf("Enter your name \n");
   gets(str);
   line(40,'=');
   printf("\n\t Welcome %s\n",str);
   line(40,'=');
   getch();
}
   void line(int n, char p)
   {
      int i;
      printf("\n");
      for(i=1;i<=n;i++)
      printf("%c",p);
   }
```

Output:

```
Enter your name
HARI MOHAN PANDEY
                ========================================
                    Welcome HARI MOHAN PANDEY

                ========================================
```

EXPLANATION: The function **line** accepts two parameters first one is an integer and second is a character. The function prints the second argument, first number of times *i.e.,* in the above program when function **line (30,'=')** is called it first leaves a blank line then using **for** loop prints'=' **30 times.** Depending upon your requirement you may put any value for the parameters.

```
/*Prog 7.15 print Fibonacci series using function*/
#include<stdio.h>
#include<conio.h>
 void main()
 {
   void fibbo(int);
   int num;
   clrscr();
   printf("Enter number of terms \n");
   scanf("%d",&num);
   fibbo(num);
   getch();
```

```
}
  void fibbo(int n)
  {
  int i,a=0,b=1,c;
  printf("%d",a);
  printf("%d",b);
  for(i=1;i<=n-2;i++)
  {
    c=a+b;
    printf("%d",c);
    a=b;
    b=c;
  }
}
```

Output:

```
Enter number of terms
9
01123581321
```

EXPLANATION: Fibonacci series were explained earlier. In function we pass the number of terms for which Fibonacci series is to be displayed. The same logic we introduced earlier has been used here.

Now, we move on to the fourth category of the functions first *i.e.*, **function with parameters and return type.** Third category will be discussed later on.

7.4 FUNCTION WITH PARAMETERS AND RETURN TYPE

The general syntax of this category of function is as follows:

```
Declaration of function:
      return_type function_name (data_type arg,.........);
Definition of function:
      return_type function_name (data_type arg,.........)
      {
            Statements;
            Statement;
            ......................;
            return data;
      }
```

For the discussion of the above see the program given below.

```
/*Prog 7.16 compute square of function and return using function*/
#include<stdio.h>
#include<conio.h>
 void main()
 {
    int sqr(int);
    int num,s;
    clrscr();
    printf("Enter the number\n");
    scanf("%d",&num);
    s=sqr(num);
    printf("num=%d\n Square of number=%d\n",num,s);
    getch();
 }
    int sqr(int x)
    {
       int t;
       t=x*x;
       return t;
    }
```

Output:

```
Enter the number
6
num=6
Square of number=36
```

EXPLANATION: The declaration of **int sqr(int)** tells the compiler that **sqr** is a function which accepts an argument of type **int** and the **int** before function name **sqr** represent return type of function **sqr** *i.e.*, an **int** value will be returned from function **sqr** through **return** statement. In the definition/ body of the function we calculate *x*x* into *t* and return the value of *t* through statement **return *t*.** When this happens the *t* returns at the place from where the function **sqr** was called so the statement *s* = **sqr(num)** becomes *s* = *t*. If value of *x* happens to be **5,** *t* will have **25** when it returns and the same will be assigned to ***t*.**

Alternative function definition may be written as:

```
int sqr (int x)
{
   return x*x;
}
```

NOTE: The default return type for a function in C is int and a function in C is int and a function with no arguments, not even void can take many arguments without declaring in function. As an example consider the given definition without declaration of function:

```
fun (int x, float b, char c,.........)
{
    Statements;
    Statements;
}
```

The return type of function is assumed as **int** and it can take any number of arguments of any type.

```
/*Prog 7.17 Area of circle using function*/
#include<stdio.h>
#include<conio.h>
 void main()
 {
    float area(float);
    float r,a;
    clrscr();
    printf("Enter the radius \n");
    scanf("%f",&r);
    a=area(r);
    printf("Radius =%f\t  Area=%f\n",r,a);
    getch();
 }
    float area(float r)
    {
        float t;
        t=3.14*r*r;
        return r;
    }
```

Output:

```
Enter the radius
3
Radius =3.000000              Area=28.260000
```

EXPLANATION: The declaration **float area (float)** tells the compiler that area is a function which accepts one argument of **float** type and returns one argument of float type and return one argument of **float** type. Inside the function we pass the radius of **float** type which we input from user in the **main.** The function calculates the area of the circle and return the area from the function which is collected in the variable ***a*** in the **main.**

Alternative code listing which you may write in the above function is as follows:

```
float area(float r)
{
    return(3.14*r*r);
}
```

```
/*Prog 7.18 Maximum of two numbers using function*/
#include<stdio.h>
#include<conio.h>
 void main()
 {
    int max(int,int);
    int m,a,b;
    clrscr();
    printf("Enter the two numbers\n");
    scanf("%d%d",&a,&b);
    m=max(a,b);
    printf("Max is %d\n",m);
    getch();
 }
    int max(int x, int y)
    {
      return x,y;
    }
```

Output:

```
Enter the two numbers
34 89
Max is 89
```

EXPLANATION: The program is quite simple. It finds max of two number using function **max** which accepts two arguments of type **int** and return max of two **int** variable.

```
/*Prog 7.19 Maximum of three number from a function which find maximum
of two numbers*/
#include<stdio.h>
#include<conio.h>
 void main()
 {
  int max (int, int);
  int m,a,b,c,t;
  clrscr();
  printf("Enter the three numbers\n");
  scanf ("%d%d%d", &a,&b,&c);
  m=max(a,max(b,c));
  printf ("Max is %d\n",m);
  getch();
 }
  int max(int x,int y)
```

```
{
  return (x,y);
}
```

Output:

```
Enter the three numbers
13 7 9
Max is 13
```

EXPLANATION: In the expression *m* = **max (*a*, max (*b*, *c*))** first **max (*b*, *c*)** is called and when this returns call **max(*b*, *c*)** is replaced by the maximum of two either ***b*** or ***c*** say ***t*** (assume). Then again function **max** is called which returns max of ***a* and *t*.** Note how we have calculated maximum of three numbers with a function which finds maximum of two number only.

On the similar basis you can calculate max of 4 numbers by writing

m = max (max (*a*, *b*), max(*c*, *d*));

```
/*Prog 7.20 To find factorial of a given number using function*/
#include<stdio.h>
#include<conio.h>
 void main()
 {
    long int fact(int);
    long int f;
    int num;
    clrscr();
    printf("Enter an integer number\n");
    scanf("%d",&num);
    f=fact(num);
    printf("factorial is %ld\n",f);
    getch();
 }
  long int fact(int n)
  {
    long int ans=1;
    int i;
    for(i=1;i<=n;i++)
    ans=ans*i;
    return ans;
  }
```

Output:

```
Enter an integer number
4
factorial is 24
```

EXPLANATION: The logic for finding factorial was explained earlier. Here we have put whole of the logic in the function **fact.** In the function we pass the number whose factorial is to be finding out. The function calculates the factorial and returns the factorial of the number. The return type of function is taken as **long int** as factorial may be large which may be out of range if return type is taken as **int.**

```
/* Prog 7.21 to check whether given number is prime or not using
function*/
#include<stdio.h>
#include<conio.h>
 void main()
 {
    int prime(int);
    int num,f;
    clrscr();
    printf("Enter the number\n");
    scanf("%d",&num);
    f=prime(num);
    f=0?printf("Number is prime\n"):printf("Number is not prime");
    getch();
 }
    int prime(int n)
    {
       int c=2,flag=0;
       while(c<=n/2)
       {
            if(n%c==0)
            {
               flag=1;
               break;
            }
               c++;
       }
    }
Output:
Enter the number
45
Number is not prime
```

EXPLANATION: The number to be checked for a prime is passed to function **prime** which checks whether number is prime or not. If it is prime then **flag** which is returned contains **0** and if it is not then **flag** return **1.** In the **main** this value is received in *f* and depending upon **0 or 1** we display appropriate output on to the screen.

```
/*Prog 7.22 To find number of digits in a given number using function*/
#include<stdio.h>
#include<conio.h>
  void main()
  {
     int no_of_digits(long int);
     long int num;
     int ans;
     clrscr();
     printf("Enter the number \n");
     scanf("%ld",&num);
     ans=no_of_digits(num);
     printf("Number of digits in number %ld is %d\n",num,ans);
     getch();
  }
     int no_of_digits(long int n)
     {
       int count=0;
       while(n!=0)
     {
        n=n/10;
        count++;
     }
    return count;
}
```

Output:

```
Enter the number
23456
Number of digits in number 23456 is 5
```

EXPLANATION: In the function we pass a parameter of **long int** type the number of which we want to find number of digits. We keep on dividing the number by **10** and increment the **count by 1.** On each iteration after dividing by **10** we assign the same to the ***n***. In the end we return the **count** to **main.**

```
/*Prog 7.23 to check whether a given three digit number is armstrong or
not using function*/
#include<stdio.h>
#include<conio.h>
 void main()
 {
    int armstrong(int);
```

```
int no_of_digit(int n);
int num,f;
clrscr();
printf("Enter a three digit number\n");
scanf("%d",&num);
if(no_of_digit(num)!=3)
{
  printf("Not a 3 digit number \n");
  getch();
  exit(0);
}
f=armstrong(num);
f==1?printf("Number   is   armstrong\n"):printf("Number   is   not
armstrong\n");
getch();
}
int no_of_digit(int n)
{
  int count=0;
  while(n!=0)
  {
    n=n/10;
    count++;
  }
return count;
}
int armstrong (int n)
{
  int s=0,r,m=n;
  while(n!=0)
  {
    r=n%10;
    s=s+r*r*r;
    n=n/10;
  }
if(s==m)
  return 1;
else
  return 0;
  }
```

```
Output:
(First run)
Enter a three digit number
153
Number is armstrong
(Second run)
Enter a three digit number
145
Number is not armstrong
```

EXPLANATION: In the program we have used two functions. To check that only three digits is entered by the user we have used the function **no_of_digit** which was explained in the previous program. In number of digits in not three then we display error and quit the program. In case the number is of **3 digit** we check whether it is Armstrong or not and display the result accordingly.

```
/*Prog 7.24 To find reveres of a given number using a function*/
#include<stdio.h>
#include<conio.h>
 void main()
 {
    long int reverse(long int);
    long int num,ans;
    clrscr();
    printf("Enter the number\n");
    scanf("%ld",&num);
    ans=reverse(num);
    printf("Reverse Number is %ld\n",ans);
    getch();
 }
    long int reverse(long int);
    {
      int rev=0,r;
      while(n!=0)
      {
    r=n%10;
    rev=rev*10+r;
    n=n/10;
      }
    return rev;
 }
```

```
Output:
Enter the number
2345
Reverse Number is 5432
```

EXPLANATION: The logic to find reverse of a number has been given earlier. The same is presented over here but within function. We simply pass the number and the function return the reverse of the number.

/*Prog 7.25 to check whether a given number is palindrome or not using function*/

```
#include<stdio.h>
#include<conio.h>
 void main()
 {
   int palindrome(long int);
   long int num;
   int f;
   clrscr();
   printf("Enter the number \n");
   scanf("%ld",&num);
   f=palindrome(num);
   f==1?printf("Number  is  palindrome\n"):printf("Number  is  not
palindrome\n");
   getch();
 }
   int palindrome(long int n)
   {
      int rev=0,r,m=n;
      while(n!=0)
      {
         r=n%10;
         rev=rev*10+r;
         n=n/10;
      }
      if(m==rev)
         return 1;
      else
         return 0;
   }
```

```
Output:
(First run)
Enter the number
```

```
1221
Number is palindrome
(Second run)
Enter the number
1345
Number is not palindrome
```

EXPLANATION: In the function **palindrome** we check whether number is palindrome or not .We first reverse the number and check the original and reverse number is same or not. If they then we return **1** else return **0.** This returned value is checked in the **main** and appropriate result is displayed to the user.

```
/*Prog 7.26 To check whether a given number is perfect or not using function ver 1*/
#include<stdio.h>
#include<conio.h>
 void main()
 {
    int perfect(long int);
    long int num;
    int f;
    clrscr();
    printf("Enter the number \n");
    scanf("%ld",&num);
    f=perfect(num);
    f==1?printf("Number   is   perfect\n"):printf("Number   is   not perfect\n");
    getch();
 }
    int perfect(long int n)
    {
       int sum=0,c=2;
       while(c<=n/2)
       {
          if(n%c==0)
          sum=sum+c;
          c++;
       }
       if(sum==n)
       return 1;
       else
       return 0;
 }
```

```
Output:
Enter the number
28
Number is perfect
```

EXPLANATION: If the sum of factor of a number is equal to the number then the number is called perfect. The logic presented here is same as was presented in **chapter-4.** But here if the number is perfect within the function we return **1** from function perfect else we return **0.** This returned value is collected in *f* and through ternary operator we display the result accordingly

We can make above program by using if-else statement also which is given below:

```
/*Prog 7.27 To check whether a given number is perfect or not using
function ver2*/
#include<stdio.h>
#include<conio.h>
 void main()
 {
   int perfect(long int);
   long int num;
   int f;
   clrscr();
   printf("Enter the number \n");
   scanf("%ld",&num);
   f=perfect(num);
   if(f==1)
        printf("Number is perfect\n");
   else
        printf("Number is not perfect\n");
   getch();
 }
   int perfect(long int n)
   {
      int sum=0,c=2;
      while(c<=n/2)
      {
         if(n%c==0)
         sum=sum+c;
         c++;
      }
      if(sum==n)
```

```
    return 1;
    else
    return 0;
}
```

Output:

```
Enter the number
28
Number is perfect
```

EXPLANATION: Very similar to the above program.

/*Prog 7.28 To check whether a given number is +ve ,-ve or zero using function*/

```
#include<stdio.h>
#include<conio.h>
 void main()
 {
   char num_status(long int);
   long int num;
   char ans;
   clrscr();
   printf("Enter the number\n");
   scanf("%ld",&num);
   ans=num_status(num);
   switch(ans)
   {
     case'p':
           printf("Number is positive\n");
           break;
     case'z':
           printf("Number is zero");
           break;
     case'n':
           printf("Number is negative");
           break;
   }
   getch();
 }
   char num_status(long int n)
   {
     if(n>0)
```

```
      return 'p';
       else if(n<0)
            return 'n';
              else
                   return 'z';
   }
```

```
Output:
(First run)
Enter the number
12
Number is positive
(Second run)
Enter the number
-12
Number is negative
(Third run)
Enter the number
0
Number is zero
```

EXPLANATION: In the function **num_status** we return ***'p'***, ***'n'***, **or** ***'z'*** if the number happens to be positive, negative or zero respectively. This returned value is collected in the **ans** variable and this value of **ans** is checked against ***'p'***, ***'n'***, ***'z'*** with the help of **switch-case.**

```
/*Prog 7.29 to find power of a given number using function ver 1*/
#include<stdio.h>
#include<conio.h>
 void main()
 {
   long int power(int,int);
   long int ans;
   int base,exp;
   clrscr();
   printf("Enter the base\n");
   scanf("%d",&base);
   printf("Enter the exponent\n");
   scanf("%d",&exp);
   ans=power(base,exp);
   printf("Result is %ld\n",ans);
   getch();
 }
   long int power(int b,int e)
```

```
{
    int i=1;
    long int res=1;
    while(i<=e)
    {
  res=b*res;
  i++;
    }
    return res;
}
```

Output:

```
Enter the base
5
Enter the exponent
3
Result is 125
```

EXPLANATION: In order to find power of a given number from user. The first one is **base (say 5)** and second is **exp (say 3)** and passes the same to the function **power.** The function calculates **3 to the power 4** and returns the result back to the **main in variable ans** which is displayed at the terminal. This program has got one limitation. The result is not correct if we supply negative exponent. This limitation is removed in the next program given below.

```
/* Prog 7.30 To find power of a given number using function ver 2*/
#include<stdio.h>
#include<conio.h>
 void main()
 {
  double power(int,int);
  double ans;
  int base,exp;
  clrscr();
  printf("Enter the base \n");
  scanf("%d",&base);
  printf("Enter the exp");
  scanf("%d",&exp);
  ans=power(base,exp);
  printf("Result is %lf\n",ans);
  getch();
 }
  double power(int b, int e)
```

```
{
    int i=1;
    double res=1.0;
    int exp_neg=0;
    if(e<0)
    {
      e=e*(-1);
      exp_neg=1;
    }
    while(i<=e)
    {
      res=b*res;
      i++;
    }
  if(exp_neg==1)
    return(1.0/res);
  else
    return res;
}
```

```
Output:
(First run)
Enter the base
5
Enter the exp-3
Result is 0.008000
(Second run)
Enter the base
5
Enter the exp3
Result is 125.000000
```

EXPLANATION: In the function power we check for negative exponent. If it is negative we make it positive by multiplying it by –1 and make **exp_neg=1.** We calculate power in the usual manner as given in the previous program. At the end of function we do not check the value of **exp_neg** if it is equal to **1** then exponent was negative so we return **(1.0/res)** else we return **res b to the calling function.**

```
/*Prog 7.31 to find lcm of two numbers using function*/
#include<stdio.h>
#include<conio.h>
 void main()
 {
```

```
    int a,b,lcm;
    int find_lcm(int,int);
    clrscr();
    printf("Enter two numbers \n");
    scanf("%d%d",&a,&b);
    lcm=find_lcm(a,b);
    printf("The lcm of %d and %d is %d\n",a,b,lcm);
    getch();
}
     int find_lcm(int p,int q)
     {
       int t;
       int sa=p,sb=q;
       for(; ;)
       {
          t=p;
          q=abs(p-q);
          p=t;
          if(q==0)
       break;
       }//for loop terminated here
       return((sa*sb)/p);
     }
```

Output:

```
Enter two numbers
3 6
The lcm of 3 and 6 is 6
```

EXPLANATION: We first find **hcf** of two numbers. Assume two numbers are **24 and 9.** Then **hcf** is calculated as:

24 9 15 6 9 3 6 3 3 0

Subtract **9** from **24** and write 15 next to 9 then subtract 9 from 15 and write 6 next to 15 and so on. When you get zero in the end stop this process and the number before zero will be the **hcf** of two numbers. Note that we write the absolute value of the subtraction of two numbers in each iteration. In the function when ***q*=0** we break from loop and the **hcf** we get in the variable ***p***. LCM is returned as **((sa*sb)/*p*).** Note initially we have to store the number in the new variables ***sa* and *sb*** as when we come out from the loop ***p*** contains **hcf and *q*** becomes zero so saving ***p*** and ***q*** is must.

Enough examples of fourth category of function. Let's march toward third category of function.

7.5 FUNCTIONS WHICH RETURNS BUT NO PARAMETERS

If functions do not accept any parameters then one question comes in our mind how can they return some value and on what data they will do the processing? These types of functions work with global data which is available to all the functions.

The general syntax of this category of function is as follows:

Declaration of function:

```
return_type function_ name (void);
```

Definition of function:

```
return_type function_name (void)
    {
        Statements;
        Statements;
        Statements;
        ..............................;
    }
```

For the discussion of the above see the program given below.

Let's work with some of the example of these type of functions.

```
/*Prog 7.32 Area of square using function with global data*/
int s=10;
#include<stdio.h>
#include<conio.h>
 void main()
 {
   int sqr();
   int ans;
   clrscr();
   ans=sqr();
   printf("Side=%d\nSquare=%d\n",s,ans);
   getch();
 }
  int sqr()
  {
    return s*s;
  }
```

Output:

```
Side=10
Square=100
```

EXPLANATION: Any variable declared outside the main is treated as global variable. It can be used any where in the whole program. As *s* is global it can be accessed at any place in the program. The function **sqr** uses this value of *s* and returns the square of number *s* to the **main.** Any global value can be used in this manner. However if more then one function manipulates the value of *s,* then problem may arise as *s* may be changed by any function without letting other function to know that value of *s* has been changed.

```
/*Prog 7.33 sum and mul of two global data*/
int a,b;
#include<stdio.h>
#include<conio.h>
 void main()
 {
  int sum();
  int mul();
  clrscr();
  printf("Enter the two numbers\n");
  scanf("%d%d",&a,&b);
  printf("a=%d\tb=%d\n",a,b,sum());
  printf("a=%d\tb=%d\n mul=%d\n",a,b,mul());
  getch();
 }
  int sum()
  {
    int c=a+b;
    a++;b++;
    return c;
  }
  int mul ()
  {
    return a*b;
  }
```

```
Output:
Enter the two numbers
3 4
a=4 b=5
sum=7
a=4 b=5 mul=20
```

EXPLANATION: As can be seen from the output of the program. The function **sum** performs sum of two numbers originally supplied by the user. These numbers are changed by the **sum** as they are global. When the **mul( )** calculates multiplication it performs the same on changed ***a*** and ***b***.

7.6 RECURSION

Recursion is a programming technique in which a function calls itself for a number of times until a particular condition is satisfied. It's a very important technique to understand and once understood many long listing of code can be reduced to a few number of lines. Recursion basically a word mostly used in mathematics to state a new terms in previous term such as:

$$X_{n+1} = X_n + 1 \text{ for } n >= 1 \text{ and } X_1 = 1$$

Then we can calculate X_2 in terms of X_1, X_2 in terms of X_2 and so on.

When solving a problem through recursion two conditions must be satisfied.

1. The problem must be expressed in recursive manner.
2. There must be a condition which stops the recursion otherwise there would be a stack overflow.

Let's write few programs which illustrate how recursion works.

```
/*Prog 7.34 demo of recursion */
#include<stdio.h>
#include<conio.h>
 void main()
 {
   static int t;
   if(t==5)
   {
     printf("Quit");
     getch();
     exit(0);
   }
   printf("hello from main%d\n",++t);
   main();
   getch();
 }
```

```
Output:
hello from main1
hello from main2
hello from main3
hello from main4
hello from main5
```

EXPLANATION: A **static** variable persists even when function execution comes to an end and its default initial value is **0.** When **main ()** executes for the first time value of *t* is 0. **if** condition fails and **printf** after **if** executes. When control reaches at **main()** the recursion starts as we are calling **main** from **main.** The **main** starts again for this call with value of ***t*=1.** Note **static int *t*;** statement is executed only once.**printf** after **if** gets executed and **main ()** is called again, this with value ***t*=2.** This continues until *t* does not become **5.** When *t* becomes **5, if** condition satisfies and recursion stops.

If we do not take ***t* as static** in the program our program will be put into an infinite loop as there will be no condition which stops recursion. As each time **main** is called a new *t* will be initialized with a new value, so there will be no effect of incrementing *t* in the **printf** statement

```
/*Prog 7.35 factorial of a number using recursion*/
#include<stdio.h>
#include<conio.h>
 void main()
 {
   long int fact(int);
   long int ans;
   int num;
   clrscr();
   printf("Enter an integer number\n");
   scanf("%d",&num);
   ans=fact(num);
   printf("Factorial is %d\n",ans);
   getch();
 }
  long int fact(int n)
  {
    return(n<1?1:n*fact(n-1));
  }
```

Output:

```
Enter an integer number
5
Factorial is 120
```

EXPLANATION: Assume **n is 4,** now recursion works as:

N	function returns
4	4 * fact (3)
3	4 * (3 * fact (2))
2	4 * (3 * (2 * fact (1)))
1	4 * (3 * (2 * 1))

When recursion starts each call to function **fact** creates new set of variables here only one. When ever recursion starts the recursive function calls does not executes immediately (in reality function addresses are put). They are saved inside the stack along with the value of variables. **(A stack is a data structure which grows upward from max_limit to 1. Each new item is "pushed" in the stack takes its place above the previously entered item. The items are "popped " out in the reverse**

order in which they were entered item. That's why they are called LIFO (last in first out). This process is called **winding** in the recursion context. When recursion is stopped in the above program when **n becomes 1** and function return the value **1, all the function call saved inside the stack are popped out from the stack in the reverse order and get executed *i.e.,* fact (1) returns to fact (2) fact (2) retruns to fact (3) and in the end fact (3) returns to fact (4)** which ultimately return to the **main.** This process is called **unwinding.**

You get the output within a fraction of second but this is the actual process occurs internally. If you want to have a feel of this winding and unwinding run your program by pressing **F7** in turbo C/ C++ editor.

```
/*Prog 7.36 display array element using recursion*/
#include<stdio.h>
#include<conio.h>
#define s 6
 void main()
 {
  void print(int,int[]);
  int a[s],i;
  clrscr();
  for(i=0;i<s;i++)
  {
   printf("\n Enter a[%d] element: ",i);
   scanf("%d",&a[i]);
  }
  printf("Array elements are \n");
  print(0,a);
  getch();
 }
  void print(int x, int p[])
  {
   if(x>=0 && x<s)
   {
     printf("%d",p[x]);
     print(++x,p);
   }
   else
     return ;
   }
```

Output:

```
 Enter a[0] element: 23
 Enter a[1] element: 24
```

```
 Enter a[2] element: 25
 Enter a[3] element: 26
 Enter a[4] element: 27
 Enter a[5] element: 28
Array elements are
23 24 25 26 27 28
```

EXPLANATION: In the function **print** we pass two values first is the starting index of the array and second is the array itself. The function prints the value of array through recursion. Using **if** we are assured that we print array elements within the range. Initially *x* **is 0** so first element of array is printed, and then we increment the *x* and call the function **print.** This starts the recursion process. In each function call **printf** print the array based on what is the value of *x* and call print. The recursion stops when *x* becomes **S+1.**

```
/*Prog 7.37 Display the entered number using recursion */
#include<stdio.h>
#include<conio.h>
 void main()
 {
    void show(int);
    int num;
    clrscr();
    printf("Entera number\n");
    scanf("%d",&num);
    printf("U entered \n");
    show(num);
    getch();
 }
    void show(int n)
    {
     if(n/10==0)
     {
       printf("%d",n%10);
       return;
     }
       show(n/10);
       show(n%10);
    }
Output:
Enter a number
9845
```

```
U entered
9845
```

EXPLANATION: The program prints the number entered but this is done through recursion. Assume the number is **234.**We understand the process step by step as follows:

Step1: **n=234** the **if** condition is false recursion starts here by calling **show (234/10)** *i.e.,* **show (23).**

Step2: **n=234 if** condition is false, now **show (23/10)** is called *i.e.,* **show (2)** is called.

Step3: **n=2 if** condition is true this time **2** is printed on the screen and function returns. As function returns for the value of **n= 23** it returns to next statement from where it was called is **show (23%10)** *i.e.,* **show (3)** is called.

Step4: **n=3** if condition is true and 3 is printed. When function returns it has executed all the statements of show function for **n=23** and it returns to **show (n%10)** statement for **n=234.** This time **show (4)** is called.

Step5: **n=4 if** condition is true and **4** is printed and function returns to **main.**

```
/*Prog 7.38 Fibonacci series using recursion*/
#include<stdio.h>
#include<conio.h>
 void main()
 {
   void fibbo_series(int,int,int);
   int num;
   clrscr();
   printf("Enter the number of terms\n");
   scanf("%d",&num);
   printf("Fibonacci series up to %d terms \n",num);
   fibbo_series(0,1,num);
   getch();
 }
   void fibbo_series(int a, int b, int n)
   {
    if(n!=0)
    {
     printf("%d",b);
     fibbo_series(b,a+b,--n);
    }
    else
      return;
   }
```

Output:

```
Enter the number of terms
7
Fibonacci series up to 7 terms
0 1 1 2 3 5 8
```

EXPLANATION: The program prints the Fibonacci series up to the given nth term. In the function **fibbo_series** we pass three parameters. First two are the values from which next term of the series will be evaluated and last parameter is the number of term. Assume value of ***n* is 5.** When the function is called from **main** the **value of a is 0, b is 1 and n is 5.**

Step1: **n=5 if** condition is true and value of **b** is printed *i.e.*, **1** and recursion starts by calling **fibbo_series (1, 1, 4)**

Step2: **n=4** if condition is true and again **1** is printed, **fibbo_series (1, 2, 3)** is called.

Step3: **n=3** if condition is true and **2** is printed, **fibbo_series (2, 3, 2)** is called.

Step4: **n=2** if condition is true and **3** is printed, **fibbo_series (3, 5, 1)** is called.

Step5: **n=1** if condition is true and **5** is printed, **fibbo_series (5, 8, 0)** is called.

Step6: **n=0** if condition is false and function returns.

```
/*Prog 7.39 nth term of fibonacci series using recursion */
#include<stdio.h>
#include<conio.h>
 void main()
 {
   int fib_ser_term(int);
   int num;
   clrscr();
   printf("Enter the number of terms \n");
   scanf("%d",&num);
   printf("%dthterm of series is %d",num,fib_ser_term(num));
   getch();
 }
   int fib_ser_term(int n)
   {
     if(n==1 || n==2)
       return 1;
     else
       return fib_ser_term(n-1)+fib_ser_term(n-2);
   }
```

Output:

(First run)

```
Enter the number of terms
```

```
7
7th term of series is 13
(Second run)
Enter the number of terms
6
6th term of series is 8
```

EXPLANATION: The program finds **nth** Fibonacci series term through recursion. The function **fib_ser_term** works as follows assume ***n* is 6** so series will be:

1 1 2 3 5 8 and 6th term will be 8.

Step1: **n=6** recursion starts as **fib_ser_term (5) +fib_ser_term (4);**

Step2: In the **step 1** the function is called twice one with value of **5** and another with value of **4.** Function call **fib_ser_term (5)** results in **fib_ser_term (4) + fib_ser_term (3)** and **fib_ser_term (4)** results in **fib_ser_term (3) + fib_ser_term (2).**

Step3: Continuing in this manner when call **fib_ser_term (1) and fib_ser_term (0)** occurs then function return 1.

IN SHORT TO GET THE RESULT WE SHOW IN THE FOLLOWING MANNER:

Fib_ser_term (3) = fib_ser_term (2) +fib_ser_term (1)
= 1+1
= 2

Fib_ser_term (4) = fib_ser_term (3) + fib_ser_term (2)
= 2 + 1
= 3

Fib_ser_term (5) = fib_ser_term (4) +fib_ser_term (3)
= 3 + 2
= 5

Fib_ser_term (6) = fib_ser_term (5) +fib_ser_term (4)
= 5 + 3
= 8

This last result **8** is returned to the **main** when unwinding finishes.

```
/*Prog 7.40 power of a number using resursion*/
#include<stdio.h>
#include<conio.h>
 void main()
 {
    float base,powe;
    float res;
    float power(float,float);
    clrscr();
    printf("Enter the base\n");
```

```
    scanf("%f",&base);
    printf("Enter the power\n");
    scanf("%f",&powe);
    res=power(base,powe);
    printf("%f to the power %f is %f\n",base,powe,res);
    getch();
}
    float power(float b,float p)
    {
        if(p>0)
        return(b*power(b,p-1));
              else if(p<0)
                      return(power(b,p+1)/b);
                      else
                         return 1;
    }
```

```
Output:
(First run)
Enter the base
5
Enter the power
3
5.000000 to the power 3.000000 is 125.000000
(Second run)
Enter the base
24
Enter the power
7
24.000000 to the power 7.000000 is 4586471424.000000
```

EXPLANATION: The function **power** finds power of a given number through recursion. There are two different cases we do consider. First when power is negative and second when power is positive. We consider both the case one by one. Assume **base is 2** and **power is 4.** Then function proceeds as follows:

Step1: **b=2, p=4** first **if** condition is true function return **2*power (2, 3),** recursion starts here as well as winding.

Step2: **b=2, p=3** first **if** condition is true function returns **2*power (2, 2)**

Step3: **b=2, p=2** first **if** condition is true function returns **2* power (2, 1)**

Step4: **b=2, p=1** first **if** condition is true function returns **2*power (2, 0)**

Step5: **b=2, p=0** this time both **if** conditions are false and function returns **1** at the place **power (2, 0).** Unwinding starts here.

In short we explain the unwinding process in the following manner:

power (2, 0) = 1

power (2,1)= 2*power(2,0)= 2*1=2

power (2 ,2)= 2*power(2,1)= 2*2=4

power (2, 3) = 2* power (2,2) = 2* 4= 8

power (2, 4) = 2* power(2, 3) = 8 * 2 = 16

The final value **16** is returned to the calling function *i.e.,* **main**

Now, assume **base is 2** and **power is -4**

Step1: b=2, p=–4 second **if** condition is true function returns **power (2,–3)/2,** recursion starts here as well as winding.

Step2: b=2, p=–3 second **if** condition is true function returns **power (2, –2)/2**

Step3: b=2, p=–2 second **if** condition is true function returns **power (2, –1)/2.**

Step4: b=2, p=–1 second **if** condition is true function returns **power (2, 0)/ 2**

Step5: b=2, p=0 this time both **if** conditions are false and function return **1** at the place power **(2, 0).** Unwinding starts here.

In short we explain the unwinding process in the following manner:

power (2, 0) = 1

power (2, –1) = power (2, 0) / 2 = 1/2 = 0.5

power (2, –2) = power(2, –1) / 2 = 0.5/2 = 0.250

power (2, –3) = power (2, –2) /2 = 0.250 / 2 = 0.125

power (2, –4) = power (2, –3)/ 2= 0.125/2= 0.625

The final value **.625 is** returned to the calling function *i.e.,* **main ()**

```
/*Prog 7.41 HCF of two numbers using recursion */
#include<stdio.h>
#include<conio.h>
 void main()
 {
   int a,b;
   int ans;
   int hcf(int,int);
   clrscr();
   printf("Enter the first number\n");
   scanf("%d",&a);
   printf("Enter the second number\n");
   scanf("%d",&b);
   ans=hcf(a,b);
```

```
    printf("HCF of two number is %d\n",ans);
    getch();
  }
    int hcf(int a,int b)
    {
    if(b==0)
     return a;
     else
       return hcf(b,a%b);
    }
```

Output:

(First run)

```
Enter the first number
4
Enter the second number
6
HCF of two number is 2
```

(Second run)

```
Enter the first number
48
Enter the second number
34
HCF of two number is 2
```

EXPLANATION: The recursive method of finding the **HCF** of two number was given by renowned mathematician **Euclid.** We have used the same method in our function. The working is as follows:

Step 1: a=4, b=6 if condition is false, function returns **hcf(6,4%6) is hcf (6,4)**

Step 2: a=6, b=4 if condition is false, function returns **hcf(4,6%6) is hcf (4,2).**

Step 3: a=4, b= 2 if condition is false, function returns **hcf(2,4%2) is hcf (2,0).**

Step 4: a=2, b=0 if condition is true, function returns ***a i.e.,* 4 band this is our desired answer.**

```
/*Prog 7.42 Reverse a string using recursion*/
#include<stdio.h>
#include<conio.h>
 void main()
 {
  char str[20];
  void rev(char *);
  printf("Enter a string\n");
```

```
  gets(str);
  printf("The reverse string is \n");
  rev(str);
  getch();
 }
    void rev(char *p)
    {
       if(*p)
       {
          rev(++p);
          printf("%c",*(--p));
       }
    }
```

Output:

(First run)

```
Enter a string
HARI MOHAN PANDEY
The reverse string is
YEDNAP NAHOM IRAH
```

(Second run)

```
Enter a string
NMIMS UNIVERSITY SHIRPUR CAMPUS
The reverse string is
SUPMAC RUPRIHS YTISREVINU SMIMN
```

EXPLANATION: As we have used pointer in the program. Better you get clear your concepts of pointers by studying the **pointers.** In the winding process each individual character is pushed into the stack until **\0** is not encountered. As ***p** contains **\0** recursion stops and unwinding starts. This display characters in reverse order.

/*Prog 7.43 sum of series 1+2+3+4+5+.....n through recursion*/

```
#include<stdio.h>
#include<conio.h>
 void main()
 {
   int sum(int);
   int s,n;
   clrscr();
   printf("Enter the number of terms\n");
   scanf("%d",&n);
   s=sum(n);
   printf("Sum of series up to %d terms is %d\n",n,s);
```

```
    getch();
  }
   int sum(int term)
   {
    if(term>0)
     return(term+sum(term-1));
   }
```

Output:

```
Enter the number of terms
5
Sum of series up to 5 terms is 15
```

EXPLANATION: The function **sum** is quite easy to understand. Assume ***n* is 5,** then the function will be returned as follows:

5 + sum (4)

5 + 4 + sum(3)

5 + 4 + 3 + sum(2)

5 + 4 + 3 + 2 + sum(1)

5 + 4 + 3 + 2 + 1

The last expression will be summed up and returned to the calling function *i.e.,* main when unwinding finishes.

```
/*Prog 7.44 sum of series 1+3+5+7+9+...+n through recursion*/
#include<stdio.h>
#include<conio.h>
 void main()
 {
    int sum(int);
    int s,n;
    clrscr();
    printf("Enter the number of terms\n");
    scanf("%d",&n);
    s=sum(n);
    printf("Sum of series up to %d terms is %d \n",n,s);
    getch();
 }
    int sum(int term)
    {
     if(term>0)
      return (2*term-1+sum(term-1));
```

```
}
```

Output:

```
Enter the number of terms
4
Sum of series up to 4 terms is 16
```

EXPLANATION: The function **sum** again quite easy to understand like the previous one. Assume *n* **is 4,** then the function will be returned as:

2 * 4 –1 + sum (3)

7 + (2 * 3 –1 + sum (2))

7 + 5 + (2 * 2 –1 + sum (1))

7 + 5 + 3 + 1

The last expression is summed up and returned to the calling function *i.e.,* **main** when unwinding finishes.

7.7 THE TOWER OF HANOI PUZZLE

The **Tower of Hanoi or Towers of Hanoi** is a mathematical game or puzzle. The puzzle was invented by the French Mathematician **Edouard Lucas** in 1883. It consists of three pegs, and a number of discs of different sizes which can slide onto any peg. The puzzle starts with the discs neatly stacked in order of size on one peg, smallest at the top, thus making a conical shape.

The object of the game is to move the entire stack to another peg, obeying the following rules: **only one disc may be moved at a time no disc may be placed on the top of a smaller disc.**

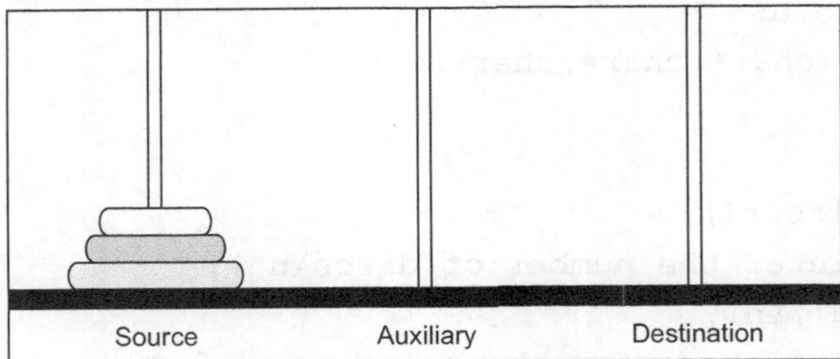

Tower of Hanoi (3 pegs)

Solution As Recursive Algorithm

- Label the pegs A, B, C- these labels may move at different steps
- Let *n* be the total number of discs.
- Number the discs from 1 (smallest, topmost) to n (largest, bottommost).

To move *n* discs from peg A to peg B:

1. Move ***n*-1** discs from A to C. This leaves disc **#*n*** alone on peg A.
2. Move disc **#*n*** from A to B.
3. Move ***n*-1** disc from C to B so they sit on disc **#*n*.**

The above is a recursive algorithm: to carry out steps 1 and 3, apply the same algorithm again for *n*-**1**. The entries procedure is a finite number of steps, since at some point the algorithm will be required for *n*=**1**. This step, moving a single disc from peg A to peg B, is trivial.

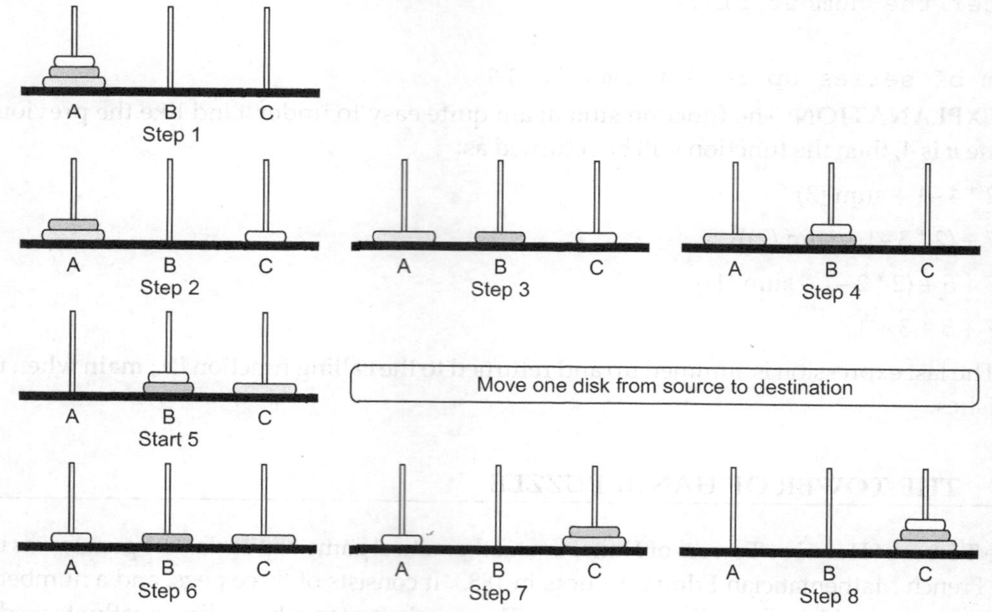

Solution of Tower of Hanoi puzzle

```
/*Prog 7.45 Recursive solution of tower of Hanoi problem*/
#include<stdio.h>
#include<conio.h>
 void TOW_HON(char*,char*,char*,int);
 void main()
 {
    int n; clrscr();
    printf("Enter the number of discs\n");
    scanf("%d",&n);
    printf("The steps for the solution are\n");
    TOW_HON("Peg1","Peg2","Peg3",n);
    getch();
 }
    void TOW_HON(char*p1,char*p2,char*p3,int n)
    {
      if(n<0)
     printf("ERROR!!!,INVALID DISC NUMBER \n");
     if(n==1)
        printf("\n Move disc from %s to %s\n",p1,p2);
     else
```

```
        {
          TOW_HON(p1,p3,p2,n-1);
          TOW_HON(p1,p2,p3,1);
          TOW_HON(p2,p1,p3,n-1);
        }
     }
```

Output:

(First run)

```
Enter the number of discs
3
The steps for the solution are
 Move disc from Peg1 to Peg2
 Move disc from Peg1 to Peg3
 Move disc from Peg3 to Peg1
 Move disc from Peg1 to Peg2
 Move disc from Peg2 to Peg3
 Move disc from Peg2 to Peg1
 Move disc from Peg1 to Peg2
```

(Second run)

```
Enter the number of discs
4
The steps for the solution are
 Move disc from Peg1 to Peg3
 Move disc from Peg1 to Peg2
 Move disc from Peg2 to Peg1
 Move disc from Peg1 to Peg3
 Move disc from Peg3 to Peg2
 Move disc from Peg3 to Peg1
 Move disc from Peg1 to Peg3
 Move disc from Peg1 to Peg2
 Move disc from Peg2 to Peg1
 Move disc from Peg2 to Peg3
 Move disc from Peg3 to Peg2
 Move disc from Peg2 to Peg1
 Move disc from Peg1 to Peg3
 Move disc from Peg1 to Peg2
 Move disc from Peg2 to Peg1
```

EXPLANATION: The program is purely based on the algorithm. Its not possible here to fully explain the working of the program for that even for ***n*=3,** there are **2-**level of recursion. In short we explain the steps as:

1. Move disc a to peg 1
2. Move disc 2 to disc 2.
3. Move disc 1 from 2 to 3, so it sits on 2.

You now have 2 disc stacked correctly on peg 3, peg 2 is empty again.

1. Move disc 3 to peg 2.
2. Repeat the first 3 steps above to move 1 &2 to sit on top of 3

Each time you re-build the tower from disc ***i* up to 1,** move disc ***i* + 1** from peg 1, the starting stack, and move the working tower again.

You can check that the solution presented as output is correct.

The total number of discs movement for the solution to come out is $\mathbf{2^n}$**-1** where n is the number of discs

POINTS TO PONDER

In this section you have learned the following points.

- A function declaration alludes to a function that is defined elsewhere, and specifies what type of arguments and values are passed to and returned from the function as well.
- A function definition reserves the memory space and defines what the function does, as well as the number and type of arguments passed to the function.
- A function can be declared to return any data type, except an array or a function.
- The return statement used in a function definition returns a single value whose type must be matched with the one declared in the function declaration.
- A function call is an expression that can be used as a single statement or within other expressions or statements.
- The void data type is needed in the declaration of a function that takes no argument.
- To declare a function that takes a variable number of arguments, you have to specify at least the first argument, and use an ellipsis (...) to represent the rest of the arguments passed to the function.
- va_start(), va_arg(), and va_end(), all included in stdarg.h, are needed in processing a variable number of arguments passed to a function.
- time(), localtime(), and asctime() are three time functions provided by C. They can be used together to obtain a character string that contains information of local date and time based on the calendar time.

QUESTIONS AND ANSWERS

Q1. *What is the main difference between a function declaration and a function definition?*

Ans: The main difference between a function declaration and a function definition is that the former does not reserve any memory space, nor does it specify what a function does. A function declaration only alludes to a function definition that is placed elsewhere. It also specifies what type of arguments and values are passed to and returned from the function. A function definition, on the other hand, reserves the memory space and specifies tasks the function can complete.

Q2. *Why do we need function prototypes?*

Ans: By declaring a function with prototypes, you specify not only the data type returned by the function, but also the types and names of arguments passed to the function. With the help of a function prototype, the compiler can automatically perform type checking on the definition of the function, which saves you time to debug the program.

Q3. *Can a function return a pointer?*

Ans: Yes. In fact, a function can return a single value that can be any data type except an array or a function. A pointer value—that is, the address—returned by a function can refer to a character array, or a memory location that stores another type of data. For instance, the C library function asctime() returns a character pointer that points to a character string converted from a date-time structure.

Q4. *Can you use top-down programming and bottom-up programming together to solve a problem?*

Ans: Yes. In practice, you can find that it's actually a good idea to combine the top-down and bottom-up programming approaches to solve problems. Using the two types of structured programming can make your program easy to write and understand.

EXERCISES

A. Answer the following questions.

1. Write the definition of a function. Indicate the types of functions available in C?
2. Differentiate between library and the user defined function?
3. How does a function works? Explain how arguments are passed and results are returned?
4. What are actual and formal arguments? Explain with suitable example?
5. What are void functions?
6. Why is return statement not necessary when function is called by reference?
7. What is recursion? Explain its advantages?
8. Explain the types of recursion?
9. Is it possible to call library function recursively?
10. Does the function prototype match with function definition?
11. What is the main ( ) in C? Why is it necessary in each program?

B. Match the following columns:

I	II
1. Formal parameter	(*a*) return nothing.
2. Actual parameter	(*b*) stack.
3. main () function	(*c*) calling function.
4. Recursion	(*d*) .obj file
5. Library function	(*e*) called function.
6. void	(*f*) starting function.

C. Write True or False against each statements:

1. The function main ( ) is built-in function.
2. All math functions return long as return type.
3. Function prototype and declaration is same thing.
4. A function definition must end with semicolon.
5. Two functions can have the same name in a single program.
6. A function can be called from more than one place in the program.
7. A function declared but not defined causes linking error.
8. One function cannot be defined within another function.
9. Recursion some times causes overflow of stack.
10. A function cannot return more than one value.

D. Fill in the blanks:

1. The function main can only return ________ as its return data type.
2. The header file contains ________ function.
3. We can manipulate the code for ________ function.
4. ________ are used to communicate the values between the functions.
5. A function uses ________ parameter passing mechanism.
6. Function declaration ends with ________.
7. The default return type for the function is ________.
8. ________ means returning no value.
9. The first calling function in any C program is ________ function.
10. Use of ________ converts large code into smaller ones.

E. Brain Drill:

1. Write a program to compute the total amount payable with annual interest for given number of years. The inputs are principle amount, rate of interest and number of years. Attempt the program with or without recursion.
2. Write user defined function for performing the following tasks.
3. Write a program to count for how many times a function called. Create a user defined function.
4. Write a C program using a function roots to calculate and display all roots of the quadratic $AX^2 + BX + C = 0$.
5. Write a C program which displays word equivalent of a number of only 3 digits *e.g.*, 123 should be displayed as one hundred twenty three.

6. Write a function that reads a number in binary form and converts it into hexadecimal form. Hexadecimal values must be stored also.
7. Write a program to calculate average temperature of five days. Create temp ( ) function.
8. Write a program to add return value of three functions.

F. Predict the output of the following programs:

1.
```
main ( )
    {
        int n= 10;
        int func(int);
        printf("%d",func(n));
    }
    int func(int c)
    {
        if(n>0) return (n+func(n-2));
        else return 0;
    }
```

2.
```
main ( )
    {
        int newval (int);
        int arr[] = {12,24,45,0};
        int I;
        int sum = 0;
        for (i=0;arr[i];i++);
        sum+=newval(arr[i]);
        printf("sum=%d ",sum);
     }
     int newval(int x)
   {
       static int div = 1;
       return (x/div++);
   }
```

3.
```
main()
   {
      int i=2;
      void twice(int);
      twice(2);
      printf("%d",i);
    }
    void twice(int x)
    {
       x=x*2;
```

```
   }
4. main()
   {
      int *f1();
      void f();
      f();
   }
   int *f1( )
   {
      int a=5;
      return &a;
   }
   void f()
   {
      int *b = f1();
      int c= *b;
      printf("%d",c);
    }
5. void func(int x)
   {
      if(x>0)func(--x);
      printf("%d",x);
   }
   int main()
   {
      func(5);
      return 0;
   }
6. main()
   {
      void fun(int,int);
      int i=10;
      f(i,i++);
   }
   void fun(int i, int j)
   {
      if(i>50)
      return ;
      i+=j;
      f(i,j);
      printf("%d",i);
   }
```

8

WORKING WITH STRING IN 'C'

The chapter starts with the introduction of strings which is nothing but at an array of characters terminated with null character. In the introduction part definition of string, declaration and defining them in C is given. The next section follows presents number of programming examples of strings which makes your concepts of strings better.

Array of strings is covered in section 8.3 with lots of programming examples. Small programs like reading and displaying the array of strings are given, program for sorting the string and many other programs are covered.

Discussion of few built-in library functions for string manipulation is presented in the last section. The most frequently used functions for string manipulation are covered only. A brief idea of other useful functions is given in the form of tables for the user so he can check out the functions by referring Turbo C help.

As string is closely related with pointers so programs and theory related with strings is also covered in the chapter-9 pointers. Reader may refer chapter-9 for the same time.

8.1 INTRODUCTION

We have studied arrays in the last chapter. Strings in C are character arrays with the last the last character is the null character represented by **"\0". A string constant in C is a group of characters, digits, symbols enclosed within double quote marks.** Strings are used for the manipulation of words and sentences. Few examples of C strings are **"A book", "This is HARI MOHAN PANDEY", etc.** We see number of examples of C strings in our daily life. Name of a person, subject name, course name, color of any object etc. It's not necessary that a string should only contain characters, it may contain any symbol but only within double quotes in case of constant strings (*i.e.*, not taken from user through keyboard) as stated earlier.

To declare a string in C we write as

char carr [] = "string";

Or

char carr [ ] = {'s','t','r','i','n','g'}

As string is simply a collection of characters terminated with **'\0' (null character, ASCII value is 0),** it is stored in memory in contiguous location with array name is the base address of string. We present a small example.

```
/* Prog 8.1 Demo of C string ver 1*/
#include<stdio.h>
#include<conio.h>
void main()
{
   char str[]="PANDEY";
   clrscr();
   printf("Hello %s\n",hari);
   getch();
}
```

Output:

```
Hello PANDEY
```

EXPLANATION: This is a pretty straight forward program to give you the demo of the C strings. A C string is a collection of characters stored in adjacent memory locations and terminated with a null character **'\0'.** You can call it a character array with the last character in array is '\0' whose ASCII value is **0.** In this short program we have declared and defined a string variable **str** whose content are **"PANDEY".** The length of the string is the number of characters contained within it. The size of the **str** is not mentioned while declaring the **str** but this will be calculated by the compiler even if you give it does not do any harm. As I just mentioned the **length of the string as the number of characters within it, the size of string is the total amount of memory allocated in terms of bytes.** In the above size of array was not specified so compiler will automatically allocate enough memory to store **"PANDEY"** along with null character "\0". So size of string **str** will be **7.** In the memory the string is represented as shown below. Recall from chapter array the name of array represents base address of array same holds for string so base address of string **str is 1024** in this case. First character **P is given by str[0], second by str[1] so on.**

Index	str[0]	str[1]	str[2]	str[3]	str[4]	str[5]	str[6]
	P	A	N	D	E	Y	\0
Base address	1024	1025	1026	1027	1028	1029	1030

8.2 WHAT IS STRING?

As introduced in chapter-6 (Introduction of array) **"Storing Similar Data Items,"** a ***string*** **is a character array terminated by a null character (\0).** For instance, a character array, array_ch, declared in the following statement, is considered a character string:

```
char array_ch[7] = {'H', 'e', 'l', 'l', 'o', '!', '\0'};
```

In C, the null character can be used to mark the end of a string, or to return logical FALSE. C treats \0 as one character. **Each character in a string takes only 1 byte.**

A series of characters enclosed in double quotes ("") is called a *string constant*. The C compiler can automatically add a null character (\0) at the end of a string constant to indicate the end of the string.

For example, the character string "A character string" is considered a string constant; so is "Hello!".

8.3 INITIALIZING STRINGS

As given earlier, a character array can be declared and initialized like this:

```
char arr_str[6] = {'H', 'e', 'l', 'l', 'o', '!'};
```

Here the array **arr_str** is treated as a character array. However, if you add a null character (\0) into the array, you can have the following statement:

```
char arr_str[7] = {'H', 'e', 'l', 'l', 'o', '!', '\0'};
```

Here the array arr_str is expanded to hold seven elements; the last element contains a null character. Now, the character array arr_str is considered a character string because of the null character that is appended to the array.

You can also initialize a character array with a string constant. For example, the following statement initializes a character array, **str** with a string constant, **"Hello!"**:

```
char str[7] = "Hello!";
```

The compiler can automatically append a **null character (\0) to the end of the array,** and treat the character array as a character string. Note that the size of the array is specified to hold up to seven elements, although the string constant has only six characters enclosed in double quotes. The extra space is reserved for the null character that the compiler will add later.

You can declare an unsized character array if you want the compiler to calculate the total number of elements in the array. For instance, the following statement

```
char str[] = "I like C.";
```

Initializes an unsized character array, **str,** with a string constant. Later, when the compiler sees the statement, it will figure out the total memory space needed to hold the string constant plus an extra null character added by the compiler itself.

If you like, you can also declare a char pointer and then initialize the pointer with a string constant. The following statement is an example:

```
char *ptr_str = "I teach myself C.";
```

WARNING!!!!?

Don't specify the size of a character array as too small. Otherwise, it cannot hold a string constant plus an extra null character. For instance, the following declaration is considered illegal:

```
char str[4] = "text";
```

Note that many C compilers will not issue a warning or an error message on this incorrect declaration. The runtime errors that could eventually arise as a result could be very difficult to debug. Therefore, it's your responsibility to make sure you specify enough space for a string.

The following statement is a correct one, because it specifies the size of the character array str that is big enough to hold the string constant plus an extra null character:

```
char str[5] = "text";
```

8.4 STRING CONSTANTS VERSUS CHARACTER CONSTANTS

As you know, a string constant is a series of characters enclosed in double quotes (" "). On the other hand, a character constant is a character enclosed in single quotes (' ').

When a character variable ch and a character array **str** are initialized with the same character, **x**, such as the following,

```
char ch = 'x'; // 1BYTE SPACE RESERVED
char str[] = "x";//2BYTE SPACE RESERVED
```

1 byte is reserved for the character variable ch, and two bytes are allocated for the character array str. The reason that an extra byte is needed for **str** is that the compiler has to **append a null character to the array.**

Another important thing is that a string is interpreted as a **char pointer.** Therefore, you can assign a character string to a pointer variable directly, like this:

```
char *ptr_str;
    ptr_str = "A character string.";
```

However, you can not assign a character constant to the pointer variable, as shown in the following:

```
ptr_str = 'x'; /* It's wrong. */
```

In other words, the character constant 'x' contains a right value, and the pointer variable ptr_str expects a left value. But C requires the same kind of values on both sides of an assignment operator =. It's legal to assign a character constant to a dereferenced char pointer like this:

```
char *ptr_str;
    *ptr_str='x';
```

Now the values on both sides of the = operator are of the same type.

```
/* Prog 8.2 Demo of C string ver2 */
#include<stdio.h>
#include<conio.h>
 void main()
 {
   char hari[]="Mohan";
   int i=0;
```

```
   clrscr();
   printf("Hello");
   while(hari[i]!='\0')
   printf("%c",hari[i++]);
   getch();
}
```

Output:

Hello Mohan

EXPLANATION: As explained in the previous program, individual characters of strings are stored at index **0, 1 ....length-1** and last character is the null character **\0** which designates end of the string. So we display each character with the help of **while** loop till null character is not encountered.

```
/*Prog 8.3 String versus character array */
#include<stdio.h>
#include<conio.h>
void main()
{
   char str[]={'m','o','h','a','n'};
   clrscr();
   printf("Hello %s\n",str);
   getch();
}
```

Output:

Hello mohanÅ

↑

(Some garbage data)

EXPLANATION: When we display the string we give simply the name of string to print its value and that is called its starting address or base address, recall from array discussion. The compiler starts displaying character from this address and continues till it encounters a null character which is a type of signal to stop. In the first program it was ok because null character was added by C compiler. But when we define the string in the above manner using each single character, we will have to supply the null character at the end. If you do not provide then C compiler cannot detect end of the string and display garbage values afterwards. So the output of the program.

The str is the above case is simply a char array of characters but not a string. To make it a string just adds '\0' at the end in this manner:

```
char str[ ] = {'m','o','h','a','n','\0'};
```

You may also write in this manner:

```
char str[8] = " Mohan";
```

If you write **`char str[2] = "Mohan"`** then you will get compilation error

Too many initializers

8.5 READING AND WRITING STRINGS

Let's focus on how to read or write strings with the standard input and output streams—that is, **stdin** and **stdout.** In C, there are several functions you can use to deal with string reading or writing. The following subsections introduce some of the functions:

THE gets () AND puts () FUNCTIONS

The **gets ()** function can be used to read characters from the standard input stream.

The syntax for the gets () function is

```
#include <stdio.h>
char *gets (char *s);
```

Here the characters read from the standard input stream are stored in the character array identified by *s*. The **gets ()** function stops reading, and appends a null character **\0** to the array, when a newline or **end-of-file (EOF)** is encountered. The function returns *s* if it concludes successfully. Otherwise, a null pointer is returned.

The **puts ()** function can be used to write characters to the standard output stream (that is, stdout).

The syntax for the **puts ()** function is

```
#include <stdio.h>
int puts (const char *s);
```

Here *s* refers to the character array that contains a string. The **puts ()** function writes the string to the **stdout.** If the function is successful, it **returns 0.** Otherwise, a nonzero value is returned.

The **puts ()** function appends a newline character to replace the null character at the end of a character array.

```
/*Prog 8.4 for showing the demo of gets and puts */
#include <stdio.h>
#include<conio.h>
 void main()
 {
   char str[80];
   int i,delt ='a'-'A';
   clrscr();
   printf("Enter a string less than 80 characters:\n");
   gets( str );
   i = 0;
   while (str[i]){
      if ((str[i] >= 'a') && (str[i] <= 'z'))
      str[i] -= delt; /* convert to upper case */
      ++i;
```

```
    }
    printf("The entered string is (in uppercase):\n");
    puts( str );
    getch();
}
```

Output:

```
Enter a string less than 80 characters:
hari mohan pandey
The entered string is (in uppercase):
HARI MOHAN PANDEY
```

EXPLANATION: The program given above is self-explanatory

8.6 HOW LONG IS A STRING?

Sometimes, you need to know how many bytes are taken by a string. In C, you can use a function called **strlen ()** to measure the length of a string.

THE strlen () FUNCTION

Let's have a look at the syntax of the **strlen ()** function.

The **syntax** for the **strlen ()** function is

```
#include <string.h>
size_t strlen (const char *s);
```

Here *s* is a **char** pointer variable. The return value from the function is the number of bytes. **size_t** is a data type defined in the **string.h header file.** The size of the data type depends on the particular computer system. Note that **string.h** has to be included in your program before you can call the **strlen ()** function.

```
/*Prog 8.4 finding length of string using strlen*/
#include<stdio.h>
#include<conio.h>
#include<string.h>
 void main()
 {
    char str[10];
    int len,size;
    clrscr();
    printf("Enter you name \n");
    scanf("%s",&str);
    printf("Hello %s\n",str);
    len=strlen(str);
```

```
    printf("Length=%d\n",len);
    printf("Size =%d\n",sizeof(str));
    getch();
  }
```

Output:

```
Enter you name
Madhuri
Hello Madhuri
Length=7
Size =10
```

EXPLANATION: strlen is the built-in function for finding out the length of the string. Its prototype is defined in the header file **"string.h"** so you will have to include this header file to use this function. The function takes just one argument, the string whose length is to be finding out. There are number of other string manipulation functions in the header file **"string.h"** which we will see in the coming programs.

```
/*Prog 8.5 length of string without strlen ver 1*/
#include<stdio.h>
#include<conio.h>
 void main()
  {
    char str[10];
    int i;
    clrscr();
    printf("Enter your name\n");
    scanf("%s",&str);
    printf("Hello %s\n",str);
    for(i=0;str[i]!=0;i++);
    printf("Length=%d\n",i);
    getch();
  }
```

Output:

```
Enter your name
HARI
Hello HARI
Length=4
```

EXPLANATION: This program demonstrate how you can find length of a string without the use of **strlen.** You can start checking simply each character of the string whether it is equal to null character **'\0' or 0 (ASCII** value of null character). If it is not, just increment control variable and in the end display its value which will be the length of string. **Note semicolon after for loop, the semicolon serves as empty statement here.** If the input is "Hari Mohan" then length will be only 4.

This is because while inputting strings, **the scanf function breaks at the first space encountered so only "Hari" will be stored in the string str.** To overcome this limitation of **scanf** simply use **gets** function as shown in the following program .The body of the for loop is; which server as empty statement and does nothing in each iteration of for loop. When loop terminates ***i*** contains the length of the string.

```
/*Prog 8.6 Length of string ver 2*/
#include<stdio.h>
#include<conio.h>
 void main()
 {
    char str[30];
    int i;
    clrscr();
    printf("Enter your name \n");
    gets(str);
    printf("Hello %s\n",str);
    for(i=0;str[i]!=0;i++);
    printf("Length =%d\n",i);
    getch();
 }
```

```
Output
Enter your name
Hari Mohan Pandey faculty of NMIMS University Mumbai
Hello Hari Mohan Pandey faculty of NMIMS University Mumbai
Length =52
```

EXPLANATION: The program is very similar to previous one with the change that we have used **gets** function to accept the string from the user.

```
/*Prog 8.7 Display of string and length counting ver1*/
#include<stdio.h>
#include<conio.h>
 void main()
 {
    char str[30];
    int i=0;
    clrscr();
    printf("Enter your name \n");
    gets(str);
    printf("Hello");
    while(str[i]!='\0')
    {
```

```
        printf("%c",str[i]);
        i++;
      }
    printf("\nLenght=%d\n",i);
    getch();
  }
```

Output

```
Enter your name
Mr. Hari Mohan Pandey
Hello Mr. Hari Mohan Pandey
Length=21
```

EXPLANATION: In this program we have printed the whole string character by character basis till we do not encounter the null character which denotes the end of the string. Printing string as shown in the above program can also be achieved if we know the length of the string, see the next program.

```
/*Prog 8.8 Display of string using length */
#include<stdio.h>
#include<conio.h>
#include<string.h>
 void main()
 {
    char str[30];
    int i=0,len;
    clrscr();
    printf("Enter your name \n");
    gets(str);
    len=strlen(str);
    printf("Hello ");
    while(i<len)
    {
        printf("%c",str[i]);
        i++;
    }
    getch();
 }
```

Output:

```
Enter your name
Vijay Nath Pandey
Hello Vijay Nath Pandey
```

EXPLANATION: **len** gives length of string for *e.g.*, for string **"Hari" len is 4** so **while** loop runs from **0 to 3** *i.e.*, len-1

```
/*Prog 8.9 Changing case of string characters */
#include<stdio.h>
#include<conio.h>
#include<string.h>
 void main()
 {
    char str[30];
    int i=0,len;
    clrscr();
    printf("Enter any string\n");
    gets(str);
    len=strlen(str);
    printf("\n Original string%s\n",str);
    printf("\n string with case changed \n");
    while(i<len)
    {
       if(str[i]>='a' && str[i]<='z')
             printf("%c",str[i]-32);
              else if(str[i]>='A' && str[i]<='Z')
                       printf("%c",str[i]+32);
    }
    getch();
 }
```

Output:

```
Enter any string
This is demo
Original string
This is demo
String with case changed
THIS IS STRING
```

EXPLANATION: We examine each character of string and change from lower to upper and vice versa.

```
/*Prog 8.10 reversing a string*/
#include<stdio.h>
#include<conio.h>
#include<string.h>
 void main()
```

```
{
    char stro[30],strr[30];
    int i=0,len,j;
    clrscr();
    printf("Enter any string\n");
    gets(stro);
    len=strlen(stro);
    printf("Original string%s\n",stro);
    printf("Reverse string\n");
    for(i=0,j=len-1;i<len,j>=0;i++,j--)
    {
        strr[j]=stro[i];
        }
    strr[j]='\0';
    printf("%s",strr);
    getch();
}
```

Output

```
Enter any string
hari
Original stringhari
Reverse string
irah
```

EXPLANATION: Logic to reverse to the string is quite simple. We take the last character from the end and put it at the starting position of the new reverse string. Then we decrement the counter for original and increment for the reverse string (*i.e., i*++ **and** *j*—**in this case).** As we are reversing the string character by character basis we will have to add null character when copying finishes.

8.7 STRCMP FUNCTION

In C you cannot directly compare the value of 2 strings in a condition like **if (string1 = = string2).** Most libraries however contain the **strcmp()** function, which returns a zero if 2 strings are equal, or a non zero number if the strings are not the same.

The syntax of **strcmp()** is given below:

strcmp(string1, string2)

String1 & **string2** may be string variables or string constants. **String1** & **string2** may be string variables or string constants some computers return a negative if the string1 is alphabetically less than the second and a positive number if the string is greater than the second.

Let's see some examples for better understanding point of view:

- **strcmp("Newyork", "Newyork")** will return zero because 2 strings are equal.
- **strcmp("their", "there")** will return a 9 which is the numeric difference between ASCII *'i'* and ASCII *'r'*.
- **strcmp("The", "the")** will return 32 which is the numeric difference between ASCII "T" & ASCII *"t"*.

```
/*Prog 8.11 string comparison */
#include<stdio.h>
#include<conio.h>
#include<string.h>
 void main()
 {
    char str1[]="hari";
    char str2[]="Mohan";
    int c;
    clrscr();
    c=strcmp(str1,str2);
    if(c<0)
    {
      printf("%s is greater than %s\n",str1,str2);
      }
        else if(c==0)
        {
         printf("%s is less than %s\n",str1,str2);
        }
          else if(c>0)
          {
            printf("%s and %s are equal\n",str1,str2);
        }
    getch();
 }
```

```
Output
hari and Mohan are equal
```

EXPLANATION: strcmp compares two strings and returns a +ve value if first string is greater than second string, -ve value if first is smaller than second string and a zero value if both strings are equal. What is the +ve or –ve value? Actually **strcmp** returns the ASCII difference of the first unmatched characters. In this case it returns – 7 (65 ASCII value of A) –72(ASCII value of H).

Let's take some more examples to build your concepts better:

1. **str1[]="vikas" and str2[] ="vikas"** here the value of *c* will be 32.
2. **str[]="deepa" and str2[]="Deepak";** here value of *c* will be – 75 (0 – 75 = – 75)

In this case first five characters are equal and then **str1** ends but **str2** not so difference between 0 and 75 is returned.

NOTE: Here it is noticeable that all this discussion is valid for **TURBOC2** only. If you check the value returned by **strcmp** in VC++ compiler you will get values **+1, 0** and **– 1** for **str1>str2, str1==str2** and for **str1<str2**

Therefore return value for strcmp follow the following rule:

strcmp returns an int value:

1. **< 0 if s1 < s2**
2. **==0 if s1==s2**
3. **>0 if s1>s2**

```
/*Prog 6.12 to check string for palindrome*/
#include<stdio.h>
#include<conio.h>
#include<string.h>
 void main()
 {
    char stro[30],strr[30];
    int i=0,len,j;
    clrscr();
    printf("Enter any string\n");
    gets(stro);
    len=strlen(stro);
    printf("Original string \n%s\n",stro);
    printf("Reverse string with \n");
    for(i=0,j=len-1;i<len,j>=0;i++,j--)
    strr[j]=stro[i];
    strr[j]='\0';
    printf("%s\n",strr);
    if(strcmp(stro,stro)==0)
       printf("string is palindrome\n");
    else
       printf("string is not palindrome\n");
    getch();
 }
```

Output:

```
Enter any string
Hari Mohan Pandey
Original string
```

```
Hari Mohan Pandey
Reverse string with
yednaP nahoM iraH
string is palindrome
```

EXPLANATION: A string is called palindrome if it is same on reversal *i.e.*, peep, sos etc. We have simply reversed the string and checked whether the original and reverse are the same using **strcmp** function as explained in the previous program.

8.8 COPYING STRINGS WITH STRCPY ()

If you want to copy a string from one array to another, you can copy each item of the first array to the corresponding element in the second array, or you can simply call the C function strcpy () to do the job for you.

The syntax for the strcpy () function is given as follows:

```
#include <string.h>
char *strcpy (char *dest, const char *src);
```

Here the content of the string **src** is copied to the array referenced by **dest.** The **strcpy ()** function returns the value of **src** if it is successful. The header file **string.h** must be included in your program before the **strcpy ()** function is called.

```
/*Prog 6.13 Demo of string copy using strcpy*/
#include<stdio.h>
#include<conio.h>
#include<string.h>
 void main()
 {
    char str1[]="I am Pandey";
    char str2[20];
    clrscr();
    strcpy(str2,str1);
    printf("string 1=%s\n",str1);
    printf("string 2=%s\n",str2);
    getch();
 }
Output:
string 1=I am Pandey
string 2=I am Pandey
```

EXPLANATION: strcpy is the function for copying one string into another. Its prototype as given in the string .h header file is char*strcpy (char*des, const chr*src); First argument is the source string in which you want to copy, second string is the destination string from which you want to copy. The second argument may be a string variable or a string constant *i.e.,* you may write strcpy (str2,"Ranjana"). The size of the destination string must be large enough to hold the source string.

```
/*Prog 8.14 demo of string copy without using strcpy */
#include<stdio.h>
#include<conio.h>
#include<string.h>
 void main()
 {
    char str1[30];
    char str2[30];
    int i=0;
    clrscr();
    printf("Enter the source string\n");
    gets(str1);
    while(str[i]!='\0')
    {
      str2[i]=str1[i];
      i++;
    }
    str2[i]='\0';
    printf("string1=%s\n",str1);
    printf("string2=%s\n",str2);
    getch();
 }
```

Output:

```
Enter the source string
Ruchika Arora
string1=Ruchika Arora
string2=Ruchika Arora
```

EXPLANATION: We copy from source string **str1** one character at a time into the target string **str2** till null character of source string **str1** is not found. In the end we append null character at the end of target string **str2.**

```
/*Prog 8.15 Behaviour of ctrcpy */
#include<stdio.h>
#include<conio.h>
#include<string.h>
 void main()
 {
    char str[]="Man Mohan Pandey";
```

```
    clrscr();
    printf("size before=%d\n",sizeof(str));
    strcpy(str,"Hari Mohan");
    printf("string=%s\n",str);
    printf("size after=%d\n",sizeof(str));
    getch();
  }
```

Output:

```
size before=17
string=Hari Mohan
size after=17
```

EXPLANATION: When **str** was declared and assigned the string **"Man Mohan pandey"** compiler allocated size as **17 bytes** during compilation and this size remains same for the whole program. Now storing **"Hari Mohan Pandey"** in the **str** doesn't mean that only first ten character will changed and **"Pandey"** of **"Man Mohan Pandey"** will remain as it. The size of **str** remain same but contents changes completely. Try giving a string more than **7 bytes** and your program **crashes** or **halts.** Remedy you know, simply give enough size to **str** when declaring, in this case say **char str[20].**

```
/*Prog 8.16 String comparison without strcmp*/
#include<stdio.h>
#include<conio.h>
#include<string.h>
 void main()
 {
    char str1 [30]; char str2 [30];
    int l1,l2,l,i,c;
    clrscr();
    printf("Enter first string \n");
    gets(str1);
    printf("Enter second string \n");
    gets(str2);
    l1=strlen(str1);
    l2=strlen(str2);
    l=l1>l2?l1:l2;
    for(i=0;i<l;i++)
    {
       if(str1[i]!=str2[i])
       break;
    }
    c=str1[i]-str2[i];
```

```
    if(c>0)
      printf("%s is greater than %s\n",str1,str2);
      else if(c<0)
       printf("%s is greater than %s\n",str2,str1);
    else
      printf("Both are equal\n");
    getch();
  }
```

```
Output:
(First run)
Enter first string
hari
Enter second string
hari
Both are equal
(Second run)
Enter first string
Hari
Enter second string
Ruchika
Ruchika is greater than Hari
```

EXPLANATION: We first find the length of both strings and store the maximum in the variable 1. We run the loop from **0 to 1** and break at the first mismatch character of both the strings. Rest is self-explanatory.

8.9 STRCAT() FUNCTION

When you combine two strings, you add the characters of one string to the end of other string. This process is called **concatenation.** The **strcat()** function joins 2 strings together. It takes the following form (syntax for **strcat ( )** function):

```
strcat(string1,string2)
```

string1 & string2 are character arrays. When the function **strcat** is executed **string2** is appended to **string1.** The string at **string2** remains unchanged.

EXAMPLE

```
strcpy(string1,"sri");
strcpy(string2,"Bhagavan");
printf("%s", strcat(string1,string2);
```

From the above program segment the value of **string1** becomes **sribhagavan.** The string at **str2** remains unchanged as **bhagawan.**

```
/*Prog 8.17 String concatenation using strcat*/
#include<stdio.h>
#include<conio.h>
#include<string.h>
 void main()
 {
    char fname[7],lname[7],cname[15];
    clrscr();
    printf("Enter your first name \n");
    scanf("%s",&fname);
    printf("Enter your last name \n");
    scanf("%s",&lname);
    strcpy(cname, fname);
    strcat(cname,lname);
    printf("Your complete name is %s \n",cname);
    getch();
 }
```

Output:

```
Enter your first name
Hari
Enter your last name
Mohan
Your complete name is HariMohan
```

EXPLANATION: strcat is the function for string concatenation *i.e.,* it adds two string. In this program first we have the **fname** string into **cname** using **ctrcpy** function the using strcat we have concatenated the second string **lname** with **cname.** The original contents of source string **cname** are not destroyed rather new contents are added just after it. Note in the program both name are added without leaving a space in between. To make it appear as **HariMohan** just add this line after **strcpy strcat(cname," ").** Figure shows contents of string **cname** after each operation of **strcpy and strcat.**

After strcpy (cname, fname);

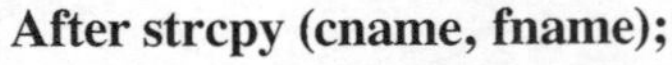

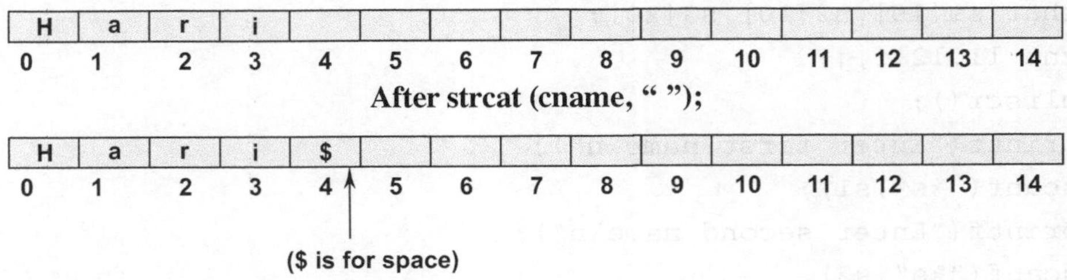

After strcpy (cname, lname);

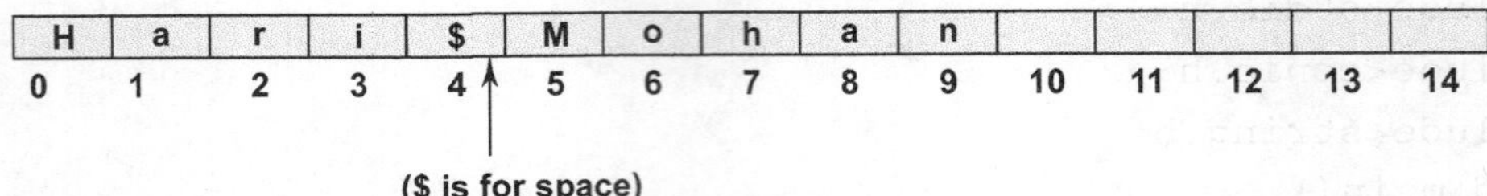


```
/*Prog 8.18 Concatenation using constant strings */
#include<stdio.h>
#include<conio.h>
#include<string.h>
 void main()
 {
    char str[50] =" ";
    clrscr();
    strcat(str,"\t\t You are Learning");
    strcat(str," String in C Programming ");
    printf("string is %s\n",str);
    getch();
 }
```

Output:

```
string is          You are Learning String in C Programming
```

EXPLANATION: Without the use of **strcpy** we have copied **"You are Learning"** into **str.** This is possible only when **str** was initialized to empty string **""**. If you do the same without initializing **str** you may get some weird output and program **crashes.** The reason is simple, you tried to concatenate **"You are Learning"** to the **garbage data** which was in the string **str.**

```
/*Prog 8.19 String concatenation without using strcat */
#include<stdio.h>
#include<conio.h>
#include<string.h>
 void main()
 {
    char s1[10],s2[10],s3[20];
    int l1,l2,i,j;
    clrscr();
    printf("Enter first name\n");
    scanf("%s",s1);
    printf("Enter second name\n");
    scanf("%s",s2);
    l1=strlen(s1);
    l2=strlen(s2);
    for(i=0;i<l1;i++)
```

```
    s3[i]=s1[i];
  s3[i]=' ';
  for(j=i+1,i=0;j<l1+l2,i<l2;j++,i++)
    s3[j]=s2[i];
  s3[j]='\0';
  printf("Your full name is %s\n",s3);
  getch();
}
```

Output:

```
Enter first name
Hari
Enter second name
Mohan
Your full name is Hari Mohan
```

EXPLANATION: We have copied characters from both string s1 and s2 in order. Firstly we have checked the length of first string and copied all characters for 0 to index l1-1, and then intentionally we have given a space. For copying s2 we start from index where s1 has finished fro *e.g.*, if s1 = "Hari" then including a space we start from 6th position in the s3. In the end as we are copying character by character we have to terminate the s3 by null character

```
/* Prog 8.20 String input using getchar ()*/
#include<stdio.h>
#include<conio.h>
#include<string.h>
 void main()
 {
  char str[30];char ch;
  int i=0;
  clrscr();
  printf("Enter a string\n");
  ch=getchar();
  while(i<30)
  {
    str[i]=ch;
    ch=getchar();
    if(ch=='\n')
    break;
    i++;
  }
  str[i]='\n';
```

```
  printf ("String is %s\n",str);
  printf("length is %d\n",i);
  getch();
 }
```

Output

```
Enter a string
work hard
String is work hard
length is 8
```

EXPLANATION: getchar ( ) function takes a single character as input, recall from chapter-3. When we enter a string say **"work hard"** first character that **w** is accepted in **ch** and from **ch** it is assigned to **str [0]** then I is incremented and loop continues. **Note C does not check array boundaries so if you input a string of length more than 30 characters your program crashes.** For the problem we have checked the condition in the loop so even if you enter a **30+ character** string only first **29** characters will be accepted. Also if you enter a **'\n'** ***i.e.,*** **Enter key,** all characters before Enter key will be accepted. Apart from **scanf** and **gets** this is another way of taking string from user.

8.10 ARRAY OF STRINGS

Similar to 2-D array of integers, float etc. we can have 2-D array of characters which is called as array of strings. A 2-D array of strings is declared as:

char str [5][10];

This declaration means that we are creating an array of **5** strings named **str** and each string may store max **10** characters (actually **9** one for **\0**). First string is accessed as **str [0],** second is **str [1]** and so on.

```
/*Prog 8.21 Array of string*/
#include<stdio.h>
#include<conio.h>
#include<string.h>
 void main()
 {
   char str[4][10];
   int i;
   clrscr();
   for(i=0;i<4;i++)
   {
      printf("\n Enter the name%d:",i+1);
      scanf("%s",str[i]);
   }
   printf("\n Name are \n");
```

```
   for(i=0;i<4;i++)
    printf("%s\n",str[i]);
   getch();
 }
```

Output:

```
 Enter the name1: Hari
 Enter the name2: Ruchika
 Enter the name3: Vijay
 Enter the name4: Anjana
 Name are
Hari
Ruchika
Vijay
Anjana
```

EXPLANATION: In the case of 2-D array of integer or float etc. we run two loops, one for row and second for the column but as the whole string is taken at once using gets or scanf we run only one loop for taking different strings. The same strings are displayed.

```
/*Prog 8.22 swapping of two strings */
#include<stdio.h>
#include<conio.h>
#include<string.h>
 void main()
 {
  char s1[10],s2[10],temp[10];
  clrscr();
  printf("Enter first name\n");
  scanf("%s",s1);
  printf("Enter second name\n");
  scanf("%s",s2);
  printf("Before swapping \n");
  printf("s1=%s\t s2=%s\n",s1,s2);
  strcpy(temp,s1);
  strcpy(s1,s2);
  strcpy(s2,temp);
  printf("After swapping\n");
  printf("s1=%s\t s2=%s\n",s1,s2);
    getch();
 }
```

```
Output:
Enter first name
NMIMS
Enter second name
MPSTME
Before swapping
s1=NMIMS        s2=MPSTME
After swapping
s1=MPSTME       s2=NMIMS
```

EXPLANATION: As we swapped two numbers with the help of third temporary number, we require a third temporary string here also. Again we cannot write **temp=** ***s1***, ***s1*****=*****s2***, ***s2*** **= temp** as this is not allowed on strings declared as chapter array. We have to use **strcpy** function for this purpose.

```
/*Prog 8.23 Strings sorting */
#include<stdio.h>
#include<conio.h>
#include<string.h>
 void main()
 {
   char str[4][10];
   int i,j;
   clrscr();
   for(i=0;i<4;i++)
   {
     printf("\n Enter name %d:",i+1);
     scanf("%s",str[i]);
   }
   printf("\n original order\n");
   for(i=0;i<4;i++)
    printf("%s\t",str[i]);
   for(i=0;i<4;i++)
   {
     for(j=i-1;j<4;j++)
      if(strcmp(str[i],str[j])>0)
      {
     strcpy(temp,str[i]);
     strcpy(str[i],str[j]);
     strcpy(str[j],temp);
      }
   }
```

```
    printf("\n sorted order \n");
    for(i=0;i<4;i++)
     printf("%s\t",str[i]);
    getch();
 }
```

Output:

```
Enter name 1: Akshay
Enter name 2: Purvi
Enter name 3: Piya
Enter name 4: Chinku
Original Order
Akshay   Purvi   Piya Chinku
Sorted Order
Akshay   Chinku  Piya Purvi
```

EXPLANATION: Using **strcmp** we compare whether first string is greater than second one, if so we swap the two strings. Swapping logic was given in the previous program. Sorting logic is same as was used for array sorting, difference is only that we are sorting string over here

8.11 STRREV () FUNCTION

This function reverses the characters in a string.

Syntax

strrev (string);

EXAMPLE: strrev ("program") reverses the characters in a string into "margrop".

```
/*Prog 8.24 String reversal using strrev*/
#include<stdio.h>
#include<conio.h>
#include<string.h>
 void main()
 {
    char str[10];
    clrscr();
    printf("Enter the string \n");
    scanf("%s",str);
    printf("Original string %s\n");
    printf("Reverse string %s \n",strrev(str));
    getch();
 }
```

Output:

```
Enter the string
```

```
MPSTME
Original string
Reverse string EMTSPM
```

EXPLANATION: strrev ( ) reverses the string given as its parameter. Its prototype is given in **string.h**

8.12 STRLWR () FUNCTION

This function converts all characters in a string from uppercase to lowercase.

syntax

strlwr (string);

For example: strlwr ("EXFORSYS") converts to Exforsys.

```
/* Prog 8.25 Conversion to lower case */
#include<stdio.h>
#include<conio.h>
#include<string.h>
 void main()
 {
   char str[10];
   clrscr();
   printf("Enter the string \n");
   scanf("%s",str);
   printf("Original string %s\n",str);
   printf("Converted string %s\n",strlwr(str));
   getch();
 }
```

Output:

```
Enter the string
MPSTME
Original string MPSTME
Converted string mpstme
```

EXPLANATION: strlwr ( ) converts all the characters into lower case of string given as its parameter. Its prototype is given in **string.h** header file.

char*strlwr (char*s);

8.13 STRUPR () FUNCTION

This function converts all the characters in a string from lower case to uppercase.

Syntax

strupr (string);

For example strupr ("exforsys") will convert the string to EXFORSY

```
/* Prog 8.26 Demo of strupr ( ) function */
#include <stdio.h>
#include<conio.h>
#include <string.h>
 void main()
 {
   char *string = "abcdefghijklmnopqrstuvwxyz", *ptr;
   clrscr();
   printf("This program shows the demo of strupr () function\n");
   /* converts string to upper case characters */
   ptr = strupr(string);
   printf("%s\n", ptr);
   getch();
 }
Output:
This program shows the demo of strupr () function
ABCDEFGHIJKLMNOPQRSTUVWXYZ
```

EXPLANATION: strupr ( ) converts all character of string given as its parameter. Its prototype is also given in **string.h**

8.14 STRCMPI () FUNCTION

This function is same as strcmp () which compares 2 strings but not case sensitive.

Example

strcmpi ("THE","the"); will return 0.

```
/*Prog 8.27 Demo of strcmpi ver 1*/
#include <string.h>
#include <stdio.h>
#include<conio.h>
 void main()
 {
   char *buf1="HARI", *buf2 = "hari";
   int ptr;
   clrscr();
   ptr = strcmpi(buf2, buf1);
   if(ptr>0)
```

```
        printf("buffer 2 is greater than buffer 1\n");
    if (ptr < 0)
        printf("buffer 2 is less than buffer 1\n");
    if (ptr == 0)
        printf("buffer 2 equals buffer 1\n");
    getch();
}
```

Output:

```
buffer 2 equals buffer 1
```

EXPLANATION: **strcmpi** (implemented as a **macro** that calls **strcmpi**) performs unsigned comparison of *s*1 and *s*2, **without casesansitivity.**

```
/* Prog 8.28 Demo of strcmpi */
#include<stdio.h>
#include<conio.h>
#include<string.h>
void main()
{
    char str1[]="MPSTME";
    char str2[]="mpstme";
    int c;
    clrscr();
    c=strcmpi(str1,str2);
    printf("c=%d\n",c);
    getch();
}
```

Output:

```
c=0
```

EXPLANATION: **strcmpi** compares two strings ignore the case *i.e.,* it does not distinguish between upper case and lower case that's why C contains a **0** value. **The *i* stand for ignore case in the strcmpi.** Its prototype is given in **string.h**

```
strcmpi ()
    ↑
i stand for ignore the case
```

8.15 STRNCAT ( ) FUNCTION

The general syntax for this function is given as follows:

char*strncat (char*des, const char* src, int max len)

strncat copies at most **maxlen** characters of **src** to the end of **dest** and then appends a **null character.**

The maximum length of the resulting string is **strlen (dest) + maxlen**

```
/*Prog 8.29 demo of strncat()function*/
#include<stdio.h>
#include<conio.h>
#include<string.h>
void main()
 {
   char str1[30]="I am proud of", str2[]="Indian";
   int s,len;
   clrscr();
   strncat(str1,str2,2);
   printf("str1=%s\n",str1);
   getch();
 }
```

Output

```
str1=I am proud ofIn
```

EXPLANATION: The prototype of **strncat** is given in **string.h** which is given as follows:

char*strncat (char*des, const char* src, int max len)

The function copies **maxlen** characters of **src string** and appends to the **des string** and adds null character at the end. In the program we append **"In"** by extracting first 2 characters from **str2.**

```
/*Prog 8.30 demo of strncat () function ver2 */
#include<stdio.h>
#include<conio.h>
#include<string.h>
void main()
 {
   char str1[30]="I am proud of", str2[]="Indian";
   int len;
   clrscr();
   len=strlen( strncat(str1,str2,2));
   printf("str1=%s\n",str1);
   printf("The maximum length of the resulting string=%d\n",len);
   getch();
 }
```

Output:

```
str1=I am proud ofIn
The maximum length of the resulting string=15
```

EXPLANATION: Here we apply **strlen** function for finding the maximum length of the resulting string and rest is similar to the previous program.

The maximum length of the resulting string is **strlen (dest) + maxlen**

8.16 STRNCPY ( ) FUNCTION

The general syntax for using strncpy ( ) function is given below:

char*strncpy (char *dest, const char*src, size_t maxlen);

strncpy copies up to maxlen character from src into dest, truncating or null-padding dest.The target string, dest, might not be null-terminated if the length of src is maxlen or more.

```
/*Prog 8.31 Demo of strncpy function */
#include<stdio.h>
#include<conio.h>
#include<string.h>
 void main()
 {
    char s1[10],s2[]="National";
    clrscr();
    strncpy(s1,s2,6);
    s1[6]='\0';        // added null character at the end.
    printf("s1=%s\n",s1);
    getch();
 }
Output:
s1=Nation
```

EXPLANATION: The prototype of the function strncpy is given in file **string.h** and rest is self-explanatory.

The function copies maxlen characters of src string and append s to the des string but does not add null character at the end. So in the program we have added null character at the end.

There are many more functions for string manipulation which you can explore at your own by using the help in turboc2/ turboc3. Some of the more functions in which you may be interested are given in the table form along with their purpose:

Functions	*Description*
strchr	Determine first occurrence of a given character in a string
strrchr	Determine last occurrence of a given character in a string.
strset	Sets all characters of a string with a given argument or symbol
strnset	Sets specified number characters of a string with a given argument or symbols
strstr	Determine first occurrence of given string in another string
strbrk	Search the first occurrence of the character in a given string and then it displays the string starting from that character.
strdup	Duplicates a string.
strtok	Find next token in a given string, token is specified by the user, may be space, tab, new line character or any user specified character.

Try all these functions yourself by taking turbo C/C++ help.

POINTS TO PONDER

In this section you have learned the following points.

- A string is a character array with a null character as the terminator at the last element.
- A string constant is a series of characters enclosed by double quotes.
- The C compiler automatically appends a null character to the array that has been initialized by a string constant.
- You cannot assign a string constant to a dereferenced char pointer.
- The **strlen()** function can be used to measure the length of a string. This function does not count the null character in the last element.
- You can copy a string from one array to another by calling the C function **strcpy().**
- The **gets()** function can be used to read a series of characters. This function stops reading when the newline character or **end-of-file (EOF)** is encountered. A null character is attached to the array that stores the characters automatically after the reading.
- The **puts()** function sends all characters, except the null character, in a string to the stdout, and appends a newline character to the output.
- You can read different data items with the **scanf()** function by using various format specifiers.

QUESTIONS AND ANSWERS

Q1. *What is a string? How do you know its length?*

Ans: In C, a string is a character array terminated by a null character. Whenever a null character is encountered in a string, functions, such as puts() or strcpy(), will stop printing or copying the next character.

The C function strlen() can be used to measure the length of a string. If it is successful, the strlen() function returns the total number of bytes taken by the string; however, the null character in the string is not counted.

Q2. *What are the main differences between a string constant and a character constant?*

Ans: A string constant is a series of characters enclosed by double quotes, while a character constant is a single character surrounded by single quotes. The compiler will append a null character to the array that is initialized with a string constant. Therefore, an extra byte has to be reserved for the null character. On the other hand, a character constant takes only 1 byte in the memory.

Q3. *Does the gets() function save the newline character from the standard input stream?*

Ans: No. The gets() function keeps reading characters from the standard input stream until a newline character or end-of-file is encountered. Instead of saving the newline character, the gets() function appends a null character to the array that is referenced by the argument to the gets() function.

Q4. *What types of data can the scanf() function read?*

Ans: Depending on the format specifiers indicated in the function, the scanf() function can read various types of data, such as a series of characters, integers, or floating-point numbers.

Unlike gets(), scanf() stops reading the current input item (and moves to the next input item, if there is one) when it encounters a space, a newline, a tab, a vertical tab, or a form feed.

EXERCISES

A. Answer the followings questions.

1. What is NULL character? Why is it important?
2. Why is it necessary to count NULL character while declaring string?
3. How a string is stored in C?
4. How a string is declared and initialized in C?
5. How a 2-D array of integers is different than a 2-D array of strings when scanned from keyboard.
6. List any 8 string manipulation function.
7. What is the difference between the functions **strcmp ( )** and **strcmpi ( )**? Explain with the help of suitable example for each?
8. What is the difference between NULL '\0' and 0?
9. What is the use of **strcpy ( )** and **strdup ( )** functions? Give example for each and explain the working of both the functions?
10. What is the difference between **strcpy ( )** and **strncpy( )** functions?

B. Brain Drill

1. Write a program to enter five full names of persons. Display their names, initials and last names.
2. Write a program to enter text through keyboard. Convert first character of each word in capital and display the text.
3. Write a program to encrypt the text **"INDIA"**. The output should be **KPFKC". ('A' is to be replaced with 'C', 'B' with 'D' and so on).**
4. Write a program to decrypt the text **"KPFKC"** to get original string **"INDIA"**.
5. Write a program to print given string from first occurrence of given character.
6. Write a program in C to compress any given string that the multiple blank present in it are replaced with single blanks.
7. Write a program which will read a string and output a list of ASCII codes of the characters present in it in tabular form.
8. Write a program in C to extract a substring from a specified position containing a specified number of characters, from an input string.

C. Match the following columns:

I	II
1. strlen	(*a*) compare two string.
2. strcmp	(*b*) finds length of string.
3. strlwr	(*c*) finds next token in string.
4. strcat	(*d*) joining two string.
5. strok	(*e*) converts all character to lower case.

D. Write True and False against each statements:

1. String and array of characters is same.

2. **strdup** is used to copy one string to another.
3. ASCII value of null character is **– 1.**
4. **gets** can read white space characters in the string.
5. **put(s)** is equivalent to **printf("%s", *s*)** where *s* is the string.

E. Fill in the blanks:

1. The function used to read a string with white space character is __________.
2. Whenever an error occurs function put s returns __________.
3. Every string ends with __________ whose ASCII value is __________.
4. A string is noting but __________ array.
5. For printing string using printf format specifier used is __________.
6. The function __________ is used to find length of the string.
7. The __________ of string is one more that __________ of string.

F. Predict the output of the following programs:

```
1. main ( )
   {
     char s1[ ] = "Hari";
     char s2[ ] = "Pandey";
     s1= s2;
     printf("%s",s1);
   }
2. main ( )
   {
     char nums[5][6]={"Four","Three","Two","One","zero"};
     printf("%s is %c\n", &nums[4][0],nums[0][0]);
   }
3. main ( )
   {
     char s[6] = "World";
     printf("%s",s[5]);
   }
4. main ( )
   {
     char name [10];
     strcpy(name ,"Ranjana");
     printf("%c%c%c",name[4],name[2],name[6]);
   }
5. main ( )
   {
     char ar = 'abc';
     printf("%c",ar);
```

```
   }
6. main ( )
   {
     char str[]= "hello \0 world";
     printf("%s",str);
   }
7. main ( )
   {
     char str [ ] =" hello\0world";
     printf("%s",sizeof(str));
   }
8. main ( )
   {
     char str [ ] = {'D','E','M','O',NULL};
     printf("str=%s \t size =%d\n", str, sizeof (str) );
   }
```

9

INTRODUCTION TO POINTERS IN 'C'

The chapter introduces you the most interesting and robust features of C programming language "**Pointers**".

The introduction teaches you the basics of the pointer:

1. What is a pointer?
2. How to declare pointer?
3. How to use pointer? Etc.

Initially two small programs are given to let you just acquaint with the use of pointers in C Programming examples show you how you can use them in varieties of programs.

Pointers and functions tell you how you achieve call by reference mechanism in C by passing address of a variable to the functions. Advanced topics like array and pointers, array and strings, array of pointers are discussed by giving suitable programming examples. Some not be done operation with pointers. Some not to be done operations with pointers are given. Generic pointer expressed as **void*** is discussed by giving just one example.

More advanced topic like functions returning pointers, pointers to functions are explained in brief.

9.1 INTRODUCTION

Pointer is most powerful and interesting features of C language. They are simple to use provided you understand the concept better. Each memory location has got some address represen in numeric or whole number. Pointers are special variables which store these addresses; hence we can say that a pointer is a valid address which is stored in a pointer type variable. A pointer variable is declared in the following manner:

int *pa;

The above declaration creates a pointer pa which can store address of an int type variable. In the pointer variable declaration an * has to precede variable name which is known as indirection operator. The expression following * must be an address. For address we use the operator **&**.

9.2 DESCRIPTION OF MEMORY IN TERMS OF CELL (ROW AND COLUMN)

We have already seen how variables are seen as memory cells that can be accessed using their identifiers. This way we did not have to care about the physical location of our data within memory, we simply used its identifier whenever we wanver1 to refer to our variable.

The memory of your computer can be imagined as a succession of memory cells, each one of the minimal size that computers manage (one byte). These single-byte memory cells are numbered in a consecutive way, so as, within any block of memory, every cell has the same number as the previous one plus one.

This way, each cell can be easily locaver1 in the memory because it has a unique address and all the memory cells follow a successive pattern. For example, if we are looking for cell 1776 we know that it is going to be right between cells 1775 and 1777, exactly one thousand cells after 776 and exactly one thousand cells before cell 2776.

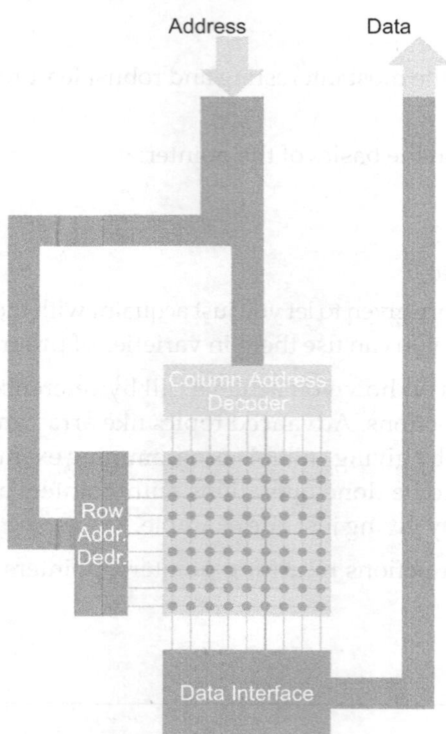

Fig. 9.1 *Description of memory in terms of cells.*

9.3 WHAT IS A POINTER?

A pointer is a variable whose value is used to point to another variable.

From this definition, you know two things:

1. First, that a pointer is a variable, so you can assign different values to a pointer variable.

2. Second, that the value contained by a pointer must be an address that indicates the location of another variable in the memory.

That's why a pointer is also called an **address variable.**

9.4 ADDRESS (LEFT VALUE) VERSUS CONTENT (RIGHT VALUE)

As you might know, the memory inside your computer is used to hold the binary code of your program, which consists of statements and data, as well as the binary code of the operating system on your machine.

Each memory location must have a unique address so that the computer can read from or write to the memory location without any confusion. This is similar to the concept that each house in a city must have a unique address.

When a variable is declared, a piece of unused memory will be reserved for the variable, and the unique address to the memory will be associaver1 with the name of the variable. **The address associaver1 with the variable name is usually called the left value of the variable.**

Then, when the variable is assigned a value, the value is stored into the reserved memory location as the content. The content is also called the right value of the variable.

For instance, after the integer variable x is declared and assigned to a value like this:

```
int x;
x = 7;
```

The variable x now has two values:

Left value: 1000

Right value: 7

Here the **left value, 1000,** is the address (base address) of the memory location reserved for *x*. The **right value, 7,** is the content stored in the memory location. Note that depending on computers and operating systems, the right value of *x* can be different from one machine to another.

You can imagine that the variable *x* is the mailbox in front of your house, which has the address (normally the street number) 1000. The right value, 7, can be thought as a letter delivered to the mailbox.

Note that when your C program is being compiled and a value is being assigned to a variable, the C compiler has to check the **left value** of the variable. If the compiler cannot find the **left value,** it will issue **an error message** saying that the variable is **undefined** in your program. That's why, in C, you have to declare a variable before you can use it. (Imagine a postal worker complaining that he or she cannot drop the letters addressed to you because you haven't built a mailbox yet.)

By using a variable's left value, the C compiler can easily locate the appropriate memory storage reserved for a variable, and then read or write the right value of the variable.

9.5 THE ADDRESS-OF OPERATOR (&)

The C language even provides you with an operator, &, in case you want to know the **left value** of a variable. This operator is called the **address-of operator** because it can return the address (that is, the left value) of a variable.

The following code, for example,

```
long int x, y;
y = &x;
```

Assigns the address of the long integer variable x to another variable, y.

As soon as we declare a variable, the amount of memory needed is assigned for it at a specific location in memory (its memory address). We generally do not actively decide the exact location of the variable within the panel of cells that we have imagined the memory to be - Fortunately, that is a task automatically performed by the operating system during runtime. However, in some cases we may be interesver1 in knowing the address where our variable is being stored during runtime in order to operate with relative positions to it.

The address that locates a variable within memory is what we call a ***reference*** to that variable. This reference to a variable can be obtained by preceding the **identifier** of a variable with an **ampersand sign (&), known as reference operator,** and which can be **literally translaver1 as "address of".** For example:

ver1= & ver2;

This would assign to **ver1** the address of variable **ver2,** since when preceding the name of the variable **ver2** with the reference operator **(&)** we are no longer talking about the content of the variable itself, but about its reference (*i.e.*, its address in memory).

For now on we are going to assume that ver2 is placed during runtime in the memory address **1776.** This number (1776) is just and arbitrary assumption we are inventing right now in order to help clarify some concepts, but in reality, we cannot know before runtime the real value the address of a variable will have in memory.

Consider the following code fragment:

```
ver2 = 25;
fred = ver2;          // (Assign the value of ver2 in fred)
ver1 = &ver2;         // Assign the address of ver 2 to ver1 by reference operator
```

The values contained in each variable after the execution of this, are shown in the following diagram:

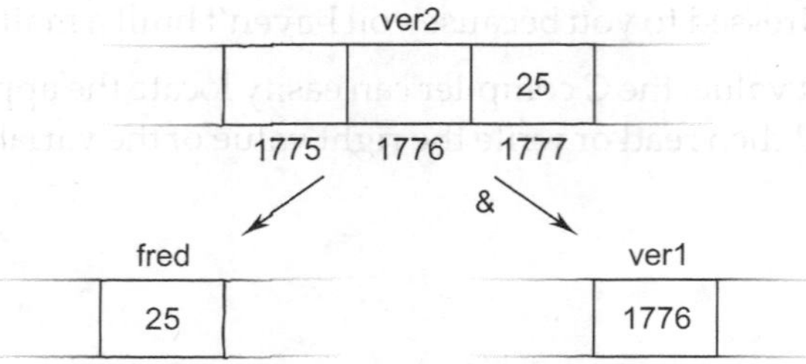

Fig. 9.2 *Functionality of reference operator/address operator (&).*

- First, we have assigned the value **25 to ver2** (a variable whose address in memory we have assumed to be **1776**).
- The second statement copied to **fred** the content of variable **ver2 (which is 25).** This is a standard **assignment operation,** as we have done so many times before.
- Finally, the third statement copies to **ver1** not the value contained in **ver2** but a **reference to it (*i.e.,* its address, which we have assumed to be 1776).** The reason is that in this third assignment operation we have preceded the identifier **ver2** with the **reference operator (&),** so we were no longer referring to the value of **ver2** but to its reference (its address in memory).

The variable that stores the reference to another variable (like ver1 in the previous example) is what we call a *pointer*. Pointers are a very powerful feature of the C/ C++ language that has many uses in advanced programming. Farther ahead, we will see how this type of variable is used and declared.

```
/*Prog 9.1 Demo of address operator/ reference operator & */
#include<stdio.h>
#include<conio.h>
 void main()
 {
   char c;
   int x;
   float y;
   clrscr();
   printf("c: address=0x%p, content=%c\n", &c, c);
   printf("x: address=0x%p, content=%d\n", &x, x);
   printf("y: address=0x%p, content=%5.2f\n", &y, y);
   c = 'A';
   x = 7;
   y = 123.45;
   printf("c: address=0x%p, content=%c\n", &c, c);
   printf("x: address=0x%p, content=%d\n", &x, x);
   printf("y: address=0x%p, content=%5.2f\n", &y, y);
   getch();
 }
```

Output:

```
c: address=0xFFF5, content=Å
x: address=0xFFF2, content=966
y: address=0xFFEE, content=-0.00
c: address=0xFFF5, content=A
x: address=0xFFF2, content=7
y: address=0xFFEE, content=123.45
```

EXPLANATION: The **printf** statement displays the address (that is, the **left value**) and the content (that is, the **right value**) of the character variable *c* on the screen. Here the **&*c*** expression returns the address of c. Note that the format specifier %*p* is used in the **printf ()** function displaying the address returned from **&*c***. Similarly the other printf ( ) print out the addresses of *x* and *y*, as well as the contents of x and y.

From the first part of the output, you see that the addresses (in **hex format**) of ***c*, *x*, and *y*** are **0*x*FFF5, 0*x*FFF2, and 0*x*FFEE.** Because these three variables have not been initialized yet, the contents contained in their memory locations are what are left there from the last memory writing.

However, after the initializations that is carried by the last three statement ***c*= 'A', *x* =7 and *y* = 123.45** the memory slots reserved for the three variables have the contents of the initial values. Then by printf display the addresses and contents of ***c*, *x*, and *y*** after the initialization.

You can see in the second part of the output, the contents of ***c*, *x*, and *y* is now 'A', 7, and 123.45, respectively, with the same memory addresses.**

NOTE: The format specifier %**p** used in the **printf ()** function is supporver2 by the **ANSI standard.** If, somehow, your compiler does not support %**p**, you can try to use %**u or** %**lu** in the **printf ()** function to convert and print out a **left value** (that is, an address).

Also, the addresses prinver2 out by the examples are obtained by running the examples on my machine. The values may be different from what you can get by running the examples on your machine. This is because the address of a variable may vary from one type of computer to another.

9.6 DEREFERENCE OPERATOR (*)

We have just seen that a variable which stores a reference to another variable is called a pointer. Pointers are said to **"point to"** the variable whose reference they store.

Using a pointer we can directly access the value stored in the variable which it points to. To do this, we simply have to precede the pointer's identifier with an **asterisk (*),** which acts as **dereference operator** and that can be literally translaver2 to **"value poinver2 by".**

Therefore, following with the values of the previous example, if we write:

ver1 = *ver2;

That we could read as: **"ver1 equal to value pointed by ver2"ver1** would take the value **25,** since **ver2** is **1776,** and the value pointed by **1776 is 25.**

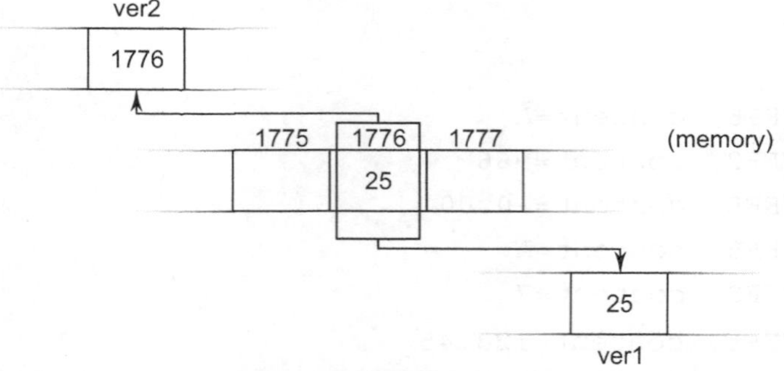

Fig. 9.3 *Demonstration of deference operator (*).*

You must clearly differentiate that the expression **ver2** refers to the value **1776,** while ***ver2** (with an asterisk * preceding the identifier) refers to the value stored at address **1776,** which in this case is **25.** Notice the difference of including or not including the dereference operator (I have included an explanatory commentary of how each of these two expressions could be read):

```
ver1 = ver2; // ver1 equal to ver2 (1776)
ver1 = *ver2; // ver1 equal to value pointed by ver2 (25)
```

Notice the difference between the references and dereference operators:

- & is the reference operator and can be read as "address of"
- * is the dereference operator and can be read as "value poinver2 by"

Thus, they have complementary (or opposite) meanings. A variable referenced with **&** can be dereference with *.

Earlier we performed the following two assignment operations:

```
ver3 = 25;
ver2 = &ver3;
```

Right after these two statements, all of the following expressions would give true as result:

```
ver3 = 25
&ver3 ==1776
ver2 == 1776
*ver2 == 25
```

The first expression is quite clear considering that the assignment operation performed on **ver3** was **ver3=25.** The second one uses the reference operator **(&),** which returns the address of variable **ver3,** which we assumed it to have a value of **1776.** The third one is somewhat obvious since the second expression was true and the assignment operation performed on ver2 was **ver2=&ver3.** The fourth expression uses the dereference operator (*) that, as we have just seen, can be read as **"value pointed by",** and the value pointed by *y* ver2 is indeed 25.

So, after all that, you may also infer that for as long as the address pointed by ver2 remains unchanged the following expression will also be true:

```
*ver2 == ver3
```

WARNING: Don't confuse the dereference operator with the multiplication operator, although they share the same symbol, *. The dereference operator is a **unary operator,** which takes only one operand. The operand contains the address (that is, left value) of a variable. On the other hand, the multiplication operator is a **binary operator** that requires two operands to perform the operation of multiplication.

Deference operator (*)	---→	**Unary Operator**
Multiplication Operator (*)	---→	**Binary Operator**

9.7 DECLARING POINTERS

As mentioned at the beginning of this lesson, a pointer is a variable, which means that a pointer has a left value and a right value as well. However, both the left and right values are addresses. The left value of a pointer is used to refer to the pointer itself, whereas the right value of a pointer, which is the content of the pointer, is the address of another variable.

The general form of a pointer declaration is:

```
data_type *pointer_name;
```

Here **data-type** specifies the type of data to which the pointer points. **Pointer_name** is the name of the pointer variable, which can be any valid variable name in C.

Note that right before the pointer name is an **asterisk (*)**, which indicates that the variable is a pointer. When the compiler sees the asterisk in the declaration, it makes a note in its symbol table so that the variable can be used as a pointer.

The following shows different types of pointers:

```
char *ptr_c; /* declare a pointer to a character */
int *ptr_int; /* declare a pointer to an integer */
float *ptr_flt; /* declare a pointer to a floating-point */
/*Prog 9.2 demo of pointer declaration and assigning value*/
#include <stdio.h>
#include<conio.h>
 void main()
 {
   char c, *ptr_c;
   int x, *ptr_x;
   float y, *ptr_y;
   clrscr();
   c= 'A';
   x = 7;
   y = 123.45;
   printf("c: address=0x%p, content=%c\n", &c, c);
   printf("x: address=0x%p, content=%d\n", &x, x);
   printf("y: address=0x%p, content=%5.2f\n", &y, y);
   ptr_c = &c;
   printf("ptr_c: address=0x%p, content=0x%p\n", &ptr_c, ptr_c);
   printf("*ptr_c => %c\n", *ptr_c);
   ptr_x = &x;
   printf("ptr_x: address=0x%p, content=0x%p\n", &ptr_x, ptr_x);
   printf("*ptr_x => %d\n", *ptr_x);
   ptr_y = &y;
   printf("ptr_y: address=0x%p, content=0x%p\n", &ptr_y, ptr_y);
   printf("*ptr_y => %5.2f\n", *ptr_y);
```

```
    getch();
  }
```

```
Output:
c: address=0xFFF5, content=A
x: address=0xFFF0, content=7
y: address=0xFFEA, content=123.45
ptr_c: address=0xFFF2, content=0xFFF5
*ptr_c => A
ptr_x: address=0xFFEE, content=0xFFF0
*ptr_x => 7
ptr_y: address=0xFFE8, content=0xFFEA
*ptr_y => 123.45
```

EXPLANATION: In the above given program, there are three variables, ***c, x, and y,*** and three pointer variables, ***ptr_c, ptr_c, and ptr_c,*** declared respectively. The ***c= 'A', x = 7 and y = 123.45;*** initialize the three variables ***c, x, and y.*** Then, **lines 13_15** print out the addresses as well as the contents of the three variables. In **line 16,** the left value of the character variable **c** is assigned to the pointer **variable ptr_c.** The output made by the statement in **line 17** shows that the pointer variable **ptr_c** contains the address of **c.** In other words, the content (that is, the right value) of **ptr_c** is the address (that is, the left value) of *c*. Then in **line 18,** the value referred to by the pointer ***ptr_c** is printed out. The output proves that the pointer ***ptr_c** does point to the memory location of **c.Line 19** assigns the left value of the integer *x* to the integer pointer variable **ptr_c.** The statements in **lines 20 and 21** print out the left value and right value of the pointer variable **ptr_c,** as well as the value referred to by the pointer ***ptr_x.** Similarly, the left value of the **float variable y** is assigned to the float pointer variable **ptr_y in line 22.** To prove that **ptr_c** contains the address of **y, and *ptr_y** gives the content held by **y, lines 23 and 24** print out the right values of **ptr_y and *ptr_y,** respectively. The statements in **lines 16, 19, and 22** show you how to assign the value of a variable to another—in an **indirect way.**

In other words, the left value of a variable can be assigned to another variable so that the latter can be used as a pointer variable to obtain the right value of the former. In this case, the variable name and the pointer refer to the same memory location. Accordingly, if either the variable name or the pointer is used in an expression to change the contents of the memory location, the content of the memory location has changed for the other.

```
/*Prog 9.3 demo of pointer ver1 */
#include<stdio.h>
#include<conio.h>
 void main()
 {
    int a;
    float b;
    clrscr();
    a=10;b=20.34;
```

```
    printf("Address of a=%u\n",&a);
    printf("Value of a=%d\n",a);
    printf("Address of b=%u\n",&b);
    printf("value of b=%f\n",b);
    getch();
  }
```

Output:

```
Address of a=65524
Value of a=10
Address of b=65520
value of b=20.340000
```

EXPLANATION: We have simply output the value and the address. For address we have used & operator (address operator) which prints address of the variable. Here in the program **%u** used for printing the address. If you put **%p** in place of **%u** then you will get the address of the variable in terms of **hex value.**

```
/*Prog 9.4 demo of pointer ver 2 */
#include<stdio.h>
#include<conio.h>
 void main()
 {
    int a;
    float b;
    clrscr();
    a=10;b=20.34;
    printf("Address of a=%p\n",&a);
    printf("Value of a=%d\n",a);
    printf("Address of b=%p\n",&b);
    printf("value of b=%f\n",b);
    getch();
 }
```

Output:

```
Address of a=FFF4
Value of a=10
Address of b=FFF0
value of b=20.340000
```

```
/*Prog 9.5 Demo of pointer ver 3 */
#include<stdio.h>
#include<conio.h>
 void main()
 {
```

```
  int a, *pa;
  float b,*pb;
  clrscr();
  pa=&a;
  pb=&b;
  *pa=50;
  *pb=45.25;
  printf("Address of a=%u\n",&a);
  printf("Address of a =%u\n",pa);
  printf("Address of a=%u\n",*(&pa));
  printf("Value of a=%d\n",a);
  printf("Value of a=%d\n",*pa);
  printf("Value of a=%d\n",*(&a));
  printf("Address of b=%u\n",&b);
  printf("Address of b=%u\n",pb);
  printf("Address of b=%u\n",*(&pb));
  printf("Value of b=%f\n",b);
  printf("Value of b=%f\n",*pb);
  printf("Value of b=%f\n",*(&b));
  getch();
}
```

Output:

```
Address of a=65524
Address of a =65524
Address of a=65524
Value of a=50
Value of a=50
Value of a=50
Address of b=65520
Address of b=65520
Address of b=65520
Value of b=45.250000
Value of b=45.250000
Value of b=45.250000
```

EXPLANATION: The declaration **int*pa** states that **pa** is a pointer to an **int** type variable. It means that pa will store address of an **int** type variable. The declaration **float * pb** states that **pb** is a pointer to a **float** type variable *i.e.,* it stores address of a **float type** variable. When we assign address of a variable say a we write **pa = &a;** and to access the value to which **pa** is pointing we use ***pa.** The * is known as **indirection operator.** It is always used with the address.

Note that pointers are always integer's *i.e.,* whole numbers. They are not of type float, int or char. Their type is determined by the fact that if we have a pointer which stores address of an int type variable we say the pointer is of type integer. Similar arguments for **float, char** and other data types. A pointer always stores address. In the statements **pa=&a** and **pb= &b** we store addresses of **a** and **b** into **pa** and **pb** respectively.

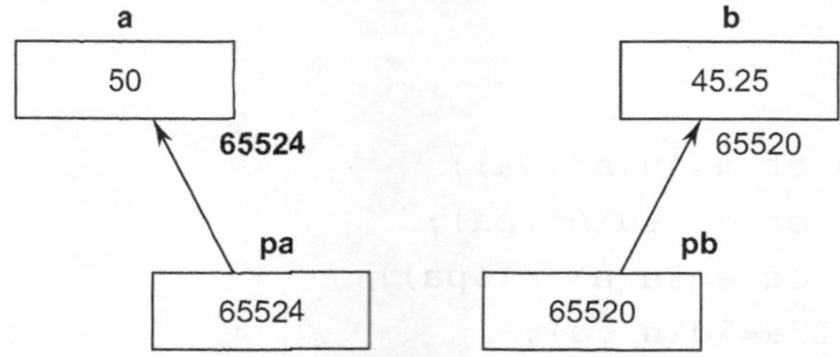

Fig. 9.4 *Demonstration of pointer.*

```
/*Prog 9.6 demo of pointer ver 3 */
#include<stdio.h>
#include<conio.h>
 void main()
 {
    int a,b,c,*pa,*pb,*pc;
    clrscr();
    pa=&a;
    pb=&b;
    pc=&c;
    printf("Enter value of a and b \n");
    scanf("%d%d",pa,pb);
    *pc=*pa+**pb;
    printf("a=%d\n",*pa);
    printf("b=%d\n",*pb);
    printf("c=%d\n",*pc);
    getch();
 }
```

Output:

```
Enter value of a and b
30 40
a=30
b=40
c=70
```

EXPLANATION: The new things is observe is that in the scanf we have simply used pa and pb instead of &a and &b as we have stored their addresses in pa and pb respectively. Rest is self-explanatory.

30	40	70
65234	65236	65238
pa	pb	pc
65234	65236	65238
66230	66232	66234

Fig. 9.5 *Reading value by using pointer.*

9.8 POINTERS TO POINTERS

C / C++ allow the use of pointers that point to pointers, that these, in its turn, point to data (or even to other pointers). **In order to do that, we only need to add an asterisk (*) for each level of reference in their declarations:**

```
char a;
char * b;
char ** c;
a = 'z';              // Assign z into a
b = &a;               // Assign the element which is at location a
c = &b;               // Assign the element which is at location b
```

This, supposing the randomly chosen memory locations for each variable of **7230, 8092 and 10502,** could be represented as:

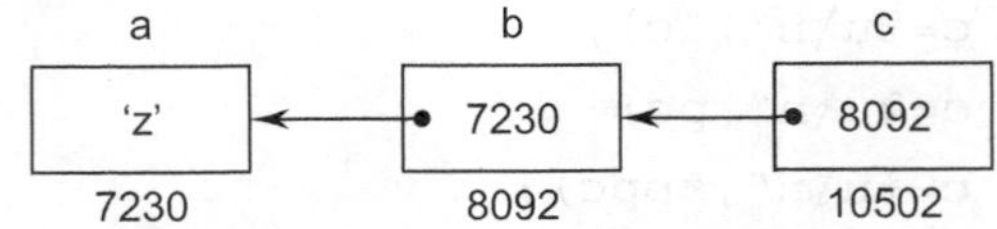

Fig. 9.6 *Demonstration of pointers to pointers*

The value of each variable is written inside each cell; under the cells are their respective addresses in memory.

The new thing in this example is variable c, which can be used in three different levels of indirection, each one of them would correspond to a different value:

- c has type char** and a value of 8092
- *c has type char* and a value of 7230
- **c has type char and a value of 'z'

```
/* Prog 9.7 pointer to pointer */
#include<stdio.h>
```

```
#include<conio.h>
 void main()
 {
  int a,*pa,**ppa;
  float b,*pb,**ppb;
  char c,*pc,**ppc;
  clrscr();
  pa=&a;ppa=&pa;
  pb=&b;ppb=&pb;
  pc=&c;ppc=&pc;
  a=10;
  b=34.56;
  c='p';
  printf("Address of a =%u\n",&a);
  printf("Address of a=%u\n",pa);
  printf("Address of a=%u\n",*ppa);
  printf("Value of a=%d\n",a);
  printf("Value of a=%d\n",*pa);
  printf("Value of a=%d\n",**ppa);
  printf("Address of b=%u\n",&b);
  printf("Address of b=%u\n",pb);
  printf("Address of b=%u\n",*ppb);
  printf("Value of b=%f\n",b);
  printf("Value of b=%f\n",*pb);
  printf("Value of b=%f\n",**ppb);
  printf("Address of c=%u\n",&c);
  printf("Address of c=%u\n",pc);
  printf("Address of c=%u\n",*ppc);
  printf("Value of c=%c\n",c);
  printf("Value of c=%c\n",*pc);
  printf("Value of c=%c\n",**ppc);
  getch();
}
```

Output:

```
Address of a =65524
Address of a=65524
Address of a=65524
Value of a=10
```

```
Value of a=10
Value of a=10
Address of b=65518
Address of b=65518
Address of b=65518
Value of b=34.560001
Value of b=34.560001
Value of b=34.560001
Address of c=65515
Address of c=65515
Address of c=65515
Value of c=p
Value of c=p
Value of c=p
```

EXPLANATION: Just like we store the address of a variable inside the pointer we can also store address of the pointer inside another pointer and this type of pointer variable is declared as:

int **ppa;

It declared a pointer to an int *i.e.,* it will hold an address of a pointer which already store an address of an int type variable. This is known as double indirection.

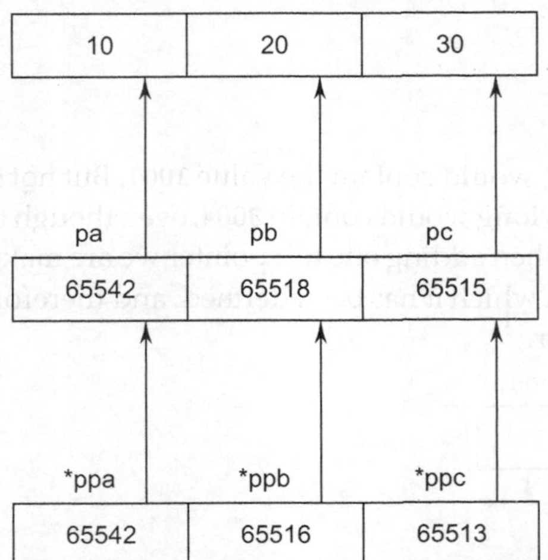

Fig. 9.7 *Demonstration of how pointer to pointer works*

From the figure given below we understand that:

1. Value of **pa** = address of ***a*** and value of ***pa** is = value of ***a.***
2. Value of **ppa** =address of **pa** and value of ***ppa** = value of **pa** = address of ***a***
3. Value of ****ppa** = value of ***pa** = **value** of ***a.***
4. Value of **&a** = **value** of **pa** = **value** of ***ppa.**
5. Value of ****ppa** is determined as (right to left)

6. When we want to find out value of ***&pa** then it will simply value of **pa** as * and & nullity each other in pointer expression and we are left with simply **pa.** Same is the case with & *pa

9.9 POINTER ARITHMETICS

To conduct arithmetical operations on pointers is a little different than to conduct them on regular integer data types. To begin with, only addition and subtraction operations are allowed to be conducted with them, the others make no sense in the world of pointers. But both addition and subtraction have a different behavior with pointers according **to the size of the data type to which they point.**

When we saw the different fundamental data types, we saw that some occupy more or less space than others in the memory. **For example, let's assume that in a given compiler for a specific machine, char takes 1 byte, short takes 2 bytes and long takes 4.**

Suppose that we define three pointers in this compiler:

```
char *mychar;
short *myshort;
long*mylong;
```

and that we know that they point to memory locations **1000, 2000 and 3000** respectively.

So if we write:

```
mychar++;

myshort++;

mylong++;
```

mychar, as you may expect, would contain the value **1001.** But not so obviously, **myshort** would contain the value **2002,** and **mylong** would contain **3004,** even though they have each been increased only once. The reason is that when adding one to a pointer we are making it to point to the following element of the same type with which it has been defined, and therefore the size in bytes of the type pointed is added to the pointer.

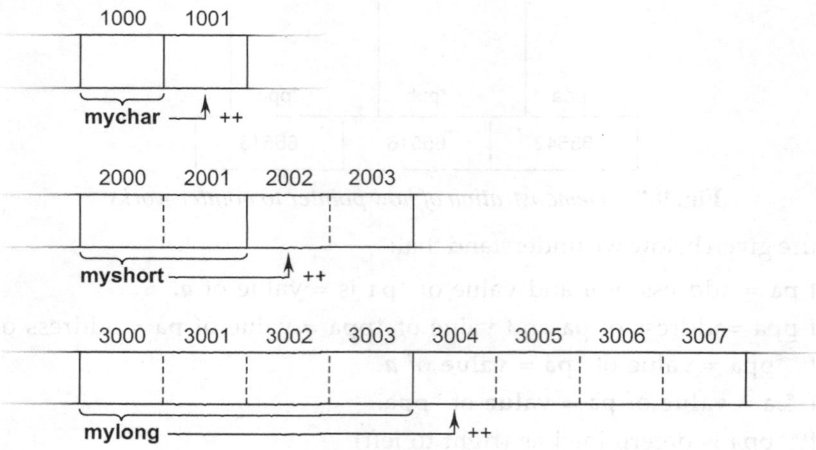

Fig. 9.8 *Demonstration of pointer arithmetic.*

This is applicable both when adding and subtracting any number to a pointer. It would happen exactly the same if we write:

```
mychar = mychar + 1;
myshort = myshort + 1;
mylong = mylong + 1;
```

Both the **increase (++)** and **decrease (--)** operators have greater operator precedence than the **dereference operator** (*), but both have a special behavior when used as suffix (the expression is evaluated with the value it had before being increased). Therefore, the following expression may lead to confusion:

```
*p++
```

Because ++ has greater precedence than *, this expression is equivalent to ***(p++).** Therefore, what it does is to increase the value of *p* (so it now points to the next element), but because ++ is used as postfix the whole expression is evaluated as the value pointed by the original reference (the address the pointer pointed to before being increased).

Notice the difference with:

```
(*p)++
```

Here, the expression would have been evaluated as the value pointed by *p* increased by one. The value of *p* (the pointer itself) would not be modified (what is being modified is what it is being pointed to by this pointer).

If we write:

```
*p++ = *q++;
```

Because ++ has a higher precedence than *, both *p* and *q* are increased, but because both increase operators **(++)** are used as postfix and not prefix, the value assigned to **p* **is** **q* before both *p* and *q* are increased. And then both are increased. It would be roughly equivalent to:

```
*p = *q;
++p;
++q;
```

Like always, I recommend you to use parentheses () in order to avoid unexpected results and to give more legibility to the code.

```
/*Prog 9.8 Arithmetic using pointer ver 1*/
#include<stdio.h>
#include<conio.h>
 void main()
 {
   float a,b,*pa,*pb;
   float a1,a2,a3,a4;
   clrscr();
   pa=&a;
```

```
   pb=&b;
   a=8.5;
   b=6.0;
   printf("Value of a=%f\n",*pa);
   printf("Value of b=%f\n",*pb);
   a1=*pa + *pb;
   a2=*pa - *pb;
   a3=*pa * *pb;
   a4=*pa / *pb;
   printf("a=%f\n",a);
   printf("b=%f\n",b);
   printf("Sum=%f\n",a1);
   printf("Sub=%f\n",a2);
   printf("Mul=%f\n",a3);
   printf("Div=%f\n",a4);
   getch();
 }
```

Output:

```
Value of a=8.500000
Value of b=6.000000
a=8.500000
b=6.000000
Sum=14.500000
Sub=2.500000
Mul=51.000000
Div=1.416667
```

EXPLANATION: Arithmetic using pointers is simple as can be seen from the code. The one thing you need to take care is that while division using pointer you will have to leave one space between / and pointer variable *i.e.,* if you write ***pa/*pb** the /* will be treated as beginning of comment and you will get error.

```
/*Prog 9.9 arithmetic using pointers ver 2*/
#include<stdio.h>
#include<conio.h>
 void main()
 {
   int a=10,*pa;
   clrscr();
   pa=&a;
   printf("Address=%u\n",pa++);
   printf("After pa++ address=%u\n",pa++);
```

```
   printf("After one more pa++ address=%u\n",pa);
   printf("Value of a=%d\n",*(pa-2));
   getch();
 }
```

Output:

```
Address=65524
After pa++ address=65526
After one more pa++ address=65528
Value of a=10
```

EXPLANATION: When a pointer is incremented it is advanced by *n* bytes where *n* depends upon type of pointer variable. If ***n*=2** for int then pointer advances by **2 bytes** and points to the next memory location. For ***n*=4 (float)** it advances by **4 bytes** and so on for other data types.

In the program it is clear that pointer advances by two bytes. We do this for twice and in the last expression we print the value by writing ***(pa-2)** to get the value at our original address. Similarly if you decrement a pointer it backwards by *n* bytes where *n* depends on the type of pointer variable. Try to modify the program for other data type such as **char, float and double etc.**

```
/*Prog 9.10 arithmetic using pointers ver 2*/
#include<stdio.h>
#include<conio.h>
 void main()
 {
   int a=10,*pa;
   clrscr();
   pa=&a;
   printf("Address=%p\n",pa++);
   printf("After pa++ address=%p\n",pa++);
   printf("After one more pa++ address=%p\n",pa);
   printf("Value of a=%d\n",*(pa-2));
   getch();
 }
```

Output:

```
Address=FFF4
After pa++ address=FFF6
After one more pa++ address=FFF8
Value of a=10
```

EXPLANATION: Here in the above given program I'm using **%p** as a formatted string to show the address of variable and as we know **%p** is used to show the address of any variable in terms of hex address that's why we get address in terms of **FFF4, FFF6 and FFF8.** Finally, by using **printf** we will print the value of a at location **(pa-2)**

9.10 POINTERS AND FUNCTIONS

In the earlier chapter we have studied about functions and how to pass parameters in them. Here we will see how to pass address to the functions and how is different from passing a value to function.

```
/*Prog 9.11 Demo of call by reference */
#include<stdio.h>
#include<conio.h>
 void main()
 {
    void change(int *);
    int a;
    clrscr();
    printf("Enter a number \n");
    scanf("%d",&a);
    printf("Before calling change function\n");
    printf("a=%d\n",a);
    change(&a);
    printf("After calling change function \n");
    printf("a=%d\n",a);
    getch();
 }
    void change(int *p)
    {
       *p=*p+10;
    }
```

Output:

```
Enter a number
15
Before calling change function
a=15
After calling change function
a=25
```

EXPLANATION: The declaration void change **(int *)** tells the compiler that change is a function which will accept only one argument address of an int type variable and returns nothing. When we call change we pass address of variable a into the function and the same is collected into pointer ***p***. Now in the function ****p*** represent the variable ***a*** in main and whatever change we perform through ****p*** will in turn changes the value of variable a or you can say that by passing the address to the function **(to pointer p)** we have given control of the variable ***a* to *p*.** This is just like giving the strings of the puppet to a person to move the strings in any manner he/she wants to control the puppet. Note the changes are done to the variable inside the function but how the changes are reflected back in the variable *a*. When we print the value of a after calling function change the value is taken from the memory location is known as call by reference or call by address.

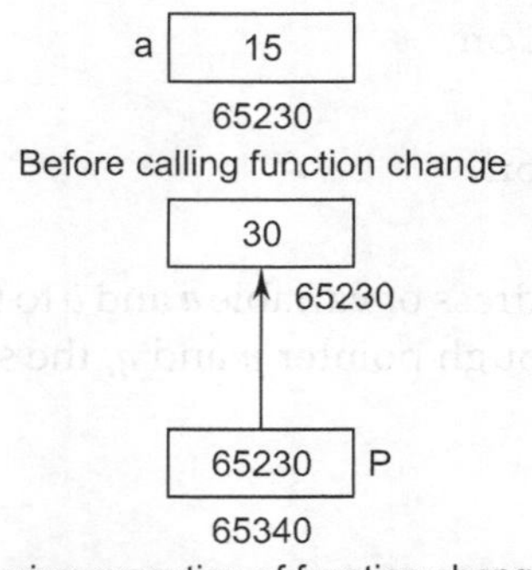

Fig. 9.9 *How pointer call value from function.*

```
/*Prog 9.12 swapping of two numbers */
#include<stdio.h>
#include<conio.h>
 void main()
 {
    void swap(int *,int*);
    int a,b;
    clrscr();
    printf("Enter two integer numbers \n");
    scanf("%d%d",&a);
    printf("Before calling swap function\n");
    printf("a=%d\tb=%d\n",a,b);
    swap(&a,&b);
    printf("After calling swap function \n");
    printf("a=%d\tb=%d\n",a,b);
    getch();
 }
    void swap(int *p,int*q)
    {
       int t;
       t=*p;
     *p=*q;
     *q=t
    }
```

Output:

```
Enter two integer numbers
45 90
Before calling swap function
a=45 b=90
After calling swap function
a=90 b=45
```

EXPLANATION: As we pass address of variable *a* and *b* to the function swap whatever changes we perform inside the function through pointer ***p*** and ***q***, the same is reflected back in the original actual parameters *a* and *b*.

Another may be:

```
Void swap (int*p, int*q)
{
  *p=*p+*q;
  *q=*p-*q;
  *p=*p-*p;
}
```

```
/*Prog 9.13 returning values without return statement */
#include<stdio.h>
#include<conio.h>
 void main()
 {
  void a_s_m_d(float,float,float*,float*,float*,float*);
  float a,b,sum,sub,div,mul;
  clrscr();
  printf("Enter two float numbers\n");
  scanf("%f%f",&a,&b);
  a_s_m_d(a,b,&sum,&sub,&mul,&div);
  printf("a=%f\tb=%f\n",a,b);
  printf("Sum=%f\n",sum);
  printf("Sub=%f\n",sub);
  printf("Mul=%f\n",mul);
  printf("Div=%f\n",div);
  getch();
 }
   void a_s_m_d(float p,float q,
                              float*sm,float*sb,float*ml,float*di)
   {
      *sm=p+q;
      *sb=p-q;
```

```
    *ml=p*q;
    *di=p/q;
}
```

```
Output:
Enter two float numbers
3.5 3.0
a=3.500000          b=3.000000
Sum=6.500000
Sub=0.500000
Mul=10.500000
Div=1.166667
```

EXPLANATION: Inside the function we pass two float values and addresses of 4 variables in which we want sum, mul, div and sub. In the function the operation performed on the two values is saved in respective variables through pointers.

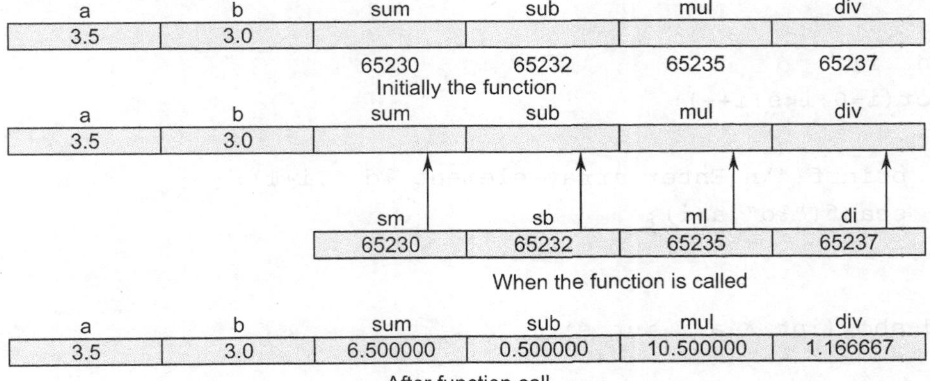

Fig. 9.10 *Demonstration of the functionality of the function.*

From the figure it is clear that initially we pass two float values into *a* and *b* and when function calling statement read by the compiler control then by using sm, sb, ml and di control reads the address of the sum, sub, mul and div. After function call you get the results.

9.11 ARRAYS AND POINTERS

Pointer to array is very simple. We just have to declare a pointer to data_type of the array. For example if we have an array like float arr[5]; we can declare a pointer float*ptr and can assign the base address of the array (*i.e.*, address of the first element of the array) to this pointer ptr by writing this

ptr = arr; or ptr = & arr[0];

After this address assignment arr[0] is equivalent to ptr[0] or *(ptr + 0) as ptr +0 gives address of first element of the array arr, ptr +1 address of second element of array arr and so on. In this regards note the following are sample ptr[*i*], *i*[ptr], *(ptr + *i*) and *(*i*+ptr). Same holds for array arr.

```
/*Prog 9.14 Demo of array and pointers ver 1*/
#include<stdio.h>
#include<conio.h>
 void main()
 {
    void input(int*,int);
    void show(int*,int);
    int p[5];
    clrscr();
    input(p,5);
    show(&p[0],5);
    getch();
    }
    void input(int*a,int s)
    {
       int i;
       for(i=0;i<s;i++)
       {
         printf("\n Enter array element %d:",i+1);
         scanf("%d",a+i);
       }
       }
    void show(int * a , int s)
    {
       int i;
       printf("Array elements are \n");
       for(i=0;i<s;i++)
       {
         printf("%d\n",*(a+i));
       }
       }
```

Output:

```
 Enter array element 1:10
 Enter array element 2:15
 Enter array element 3:20
 Enter array element 4:25
 Enter array element 5:39
Array elements are
10
```

```
15
20
25
39
```

EXPLANATION: In the function input and show we pass two parameters: one is address of an int and second an int type value.

Here you will have to recall **chapter-6** the name of array represents its base address *i.e., p.* Also address of first element is **&*p* [0].** Inside the function inputs we pass this address and size of the array *i.e.,* **5** in this case. This address is collected in pointer a so a now points to the original array. It means whatever input we take in function input will be stored in the original array. In the **show** function again we pass address of the first element and display array elements. From this we conclude that array is always passed by reference in the functions.

The function could also be written as

```
void input (int[],int);
```

but in the definition we have to specify size as:

```
void input (int a[5],int n)
```

```
/*Prog 9.15 Demo of double pointer to function */
#include<stdio.h>
#include<conio.h>
 void main()
 {
    int v=130;
    void show(int * *);
    int *p=&v;
    clrscr();
    show(&p);
    printf("Press any key to terminate.........\n");
    getch();
 }
    void show(int **pp)
    {
       printf("Value of v is %d\n",**pp);
    }
Output:
Value of v is 130
Press any key to terminate......
```

EXPLANATION: The function declaration of show says that it will accept an address of pointer to int as its argument so first declare an int pointer variable and store address of a inside **p**. We then pass address of pointer **p** to the function.

```
/*Prog 9.16 Demo of array and pointers ver 2*/
#include<stdio.h>
#include<conio.h>
 void main()
 {
    int a[]={10,20,30,40,50};
    void show(int**,int);
    int*p=a;
    clrscr();
    show(p,5);
    getch();
 }
    void show(int **pp,int s)
    {
      int i;
      printf("Array elements are:\n");
      for(i=0;i<s;i++)
      printf("%d\n",*(pp+i));
    }
```

Output:

```
Array elements are:
10
20
30
40
50
```


Fig. 9.11 *Demonstration for the working of double pointer.*

EXPLANATION: The program is similar to previous one with the difference that we are dealing with array. The base address of array we store in pointer *p* and address of this pointer *p* is passed the function which is collected in double pointer *pp*. The expression **pp* + 0 gives the address stored in *p* so *(**pp* + 0) gives first array element. Similarly, **pp* + 1 gives the address of second element of array and *(**pp* + 1) gives its value and so on.

```
/*Prog 9.17 Demo of sequence of pointers and 2-D array*/
#include<stdio.h>
#include<conio.h>
 void input(int**,int,int);
 void show(int**,int,int);
 void main()
 {
    int a[3][3];
    int row=3,col=3;
    clrscr();
    input((int**)a,row,col);
    show((int**)a,row,col);
    getch();
 }
    void input(int **p,int r, int c)
    {
       int i,j;
       for(i=0;i<r;i++)
       {
 for(j=0;j<c;j++)
 {
    printf("\n Enter p[%d][%d] element:",i,j);
    scanf("%d ",*(p+i)+j);
 }
       }
    }
    void show(int **p,int r, int c)
    {
       int i,j;
       printf("\n Matrix is \n");
       for(i=0;i<r;i++)
       {
          for(j=0;j<c;j++)
          printf("%d ",*(*(p+i)+j));
          printf("\n");
       }
    }
```

Output:

```
 Enter p[0][0] element:1
```

```
 Enter p[0][1] element:2
 Enter p[0][2] element:3
 Enter p[1][0] element:4
 Enter p[1][1] element:5
 Enter p[1][2] element:6
 Enter p[2][0] element:7
 Enter p[2][1] element:8
 Enter p[2][2] element:9
Matrix is
1 2 3
4 5 6
7 8 9
```

EXPLANATION: As explained in the **chapter-6** that a **2-D** array is collection of **1-D array.** So here we **have 3 1-D arrays** and to store addresses of these **3 1-D arrays** we need to have a **pointer to pointer.** To access address of any of the element of **any 1-D array (say 2nd row and 1st column)** we first have the address of the second **1-D array,** after that assuming that address as **base address** we find out address of element at **row 2 and column**

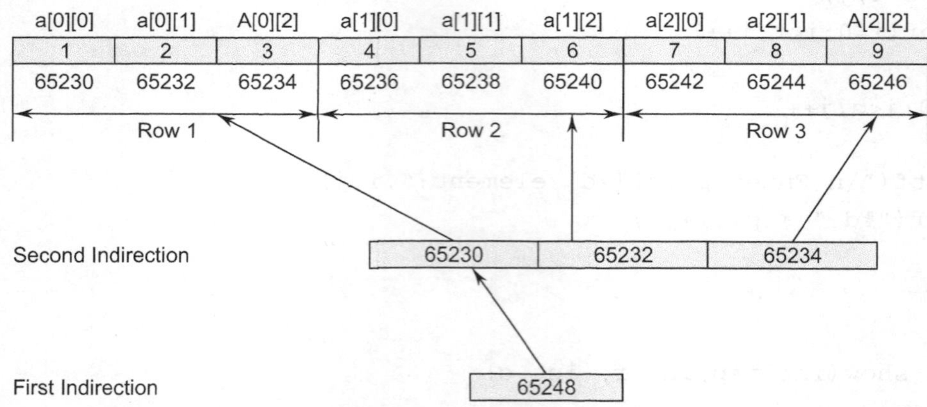

Fig. 9.12 *Demonstration of 2-D array in terms of 1-array (Row-major implementation)*

From the figure we observe the following things:

(*p*+0) or *(*p*+0) gives address of 1_{st} 1-D array *i.e.,* 65230

(*p*+1) or *(*p*+1) gives address of 2_{nd} 1-D array *i.e.,* 65236

(*p*+2) or*(*p*+2) gives address of 3_{rd} 1-D array *i.e.,* 65242

When we increment in *p* it is incremented by **sizeof(int) * number of columns** and when we increment ***(*p+i*)** say by 1 then it is only incremented by **2 bytes size of int data** type. As ***(*p+i*)** represent value at address **(*p+i*)** so **we conclude that *(*p+i*)+*j* gives address of element of *i*th row and *j*th column for example for *i*=1 and varying *j* from 0 to 2.**

*(*p*+1)+0 gives address 65236

*(*p*+1)+1 gives address 65238

*(p+1)+2 gives address 65240

((p+i)+j) gives element at p[i][j]

9.12 ARRAY OF POINTERS

The way we store elements of any type in array we can also store addresses in the array and that type of array is called array of pointers.

For creating a simple pointer to an int we write **int*p,** now to create an array of pointers to **5 int's** we simply write **int*p [5]** where each of the element of array *p i.e.,p* **[0], *p*[1], *p*[2] upto *p*[4] is a pointer.**

```
/*Prog 9.18 Demo of array of pointers */
#include<stdio.h>
#include<conio.h>
#define s 5
 void main()
 {
    int a[s];
    int *p[s];
    int i;
    clrscr();
    for(i=0;i<s;i++)
       p[i]=&a[i];
       for(i=0;i<s;i++)
       {
 printf("\n Enter a[%d] element:",i);
 scanf("%d",p[i]);
       }
    printf("Array elements are\n");
    for(i=0;i<s;i++)
     printf("a[%d]=%d\n",i,*(p[i]));
    getch();
 }
```

Output:

```
Enter a[0] element:11
Enter a[1] element:12
Enter a[2] element:13
Enter a[3] element:14
Enter a[4] element:15
```

```
Array elements are
a[0]=11
a[1]=12
a[2]=13
a[3]=14
a[4]=15
```

EXPLANATION: In the program we have stored first addresses of array *a* into pointer *p*. Now & *a* [*i*] and *p* [*i*] are equivalent expressions and we have used the later one in scanf. To print the array element we simply use the expression *(*p*[*i*]).

9.13 POINTERS AND STRINGS

Pointer to string is similar to pointer to array as seen earlier as string is nothing but a character array terminated with NULL character. We just have to declare a pointer to **char** type and put base address of the string in the pointer. For example if we have an array like **char str[15];** we can declare a pointer **char *ptr** and can assign the **base address** of array **(address of first element of array)** to this array **ptr** by writing this.

ptr = arr; or ptr = & arr [0];

After this address assignment **arr[0]** is equivalent to **ptr[0] or *(ptr + 0) as ptr + 0** gives address of first element of array arr, **ptr + 1** address of second element of array **arr** and so on. In this regard not the following are same **ptr[*i*], *i*[ptr], *(ptr + *i*).** Same holds for array arr.

```
/*Prog 9.19 Demo of pointers and strings ver1*/
#include<stdio.h>
#include<conio.h>
 void main()
 {
    char s[10];
    char *p=s;
    clrscr();
    printf("Enter the string\n");
    gets(s);
    printf("The string is %c\n",s);
    for(;p;p++)
        printf("%c",*p);
    getch();
 }
```

Output:

```
Enter the string
INDIAN
The string is
```

```
INDIAN
```

EXPLANATION: We store address of *s* into *p* and input the string in *s* using **gets.** In the for loop we start with *p* till *p*! =0 and print the whole string.

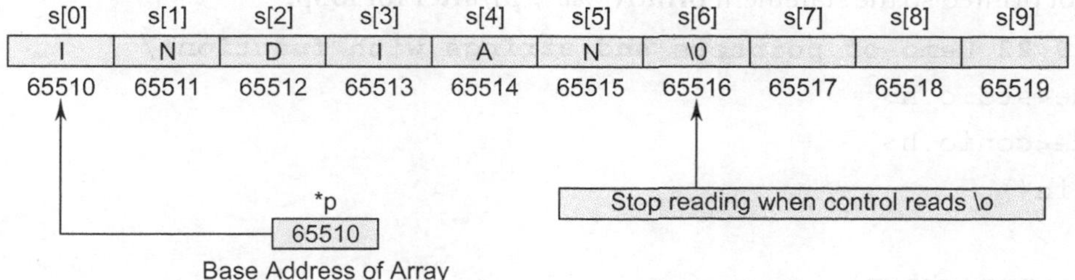

Fig. 9.13 *Demonstration of pointer and strings.*

In the above program if you want you can display the whole string at once by simply writing **printf("%s\n",b);.** Now if you write ***p=s+3*** it means p will hold address **65513** and when you print using pointer *p* you will get lysis as output. Similarly, if you want to reverse the string using pointer look at the following program.

```
/*Prog 9.20 Reversing a string using pointer*/
#include<stdio.h>
#include<conio.h>
 void main()
 {
   char s[15];
   char *p,*q=s;
   clrscr();
   printf("Enter the string up to size 15:");
   gets(s);
   printf("The reverse of the entered string is:");
   p=s+strlen(s)+1;
   for(;p!=q;p--)
   {
     printf("%c",*p);
   }
   getch();
 }
```

Output:

```
Enter the string up to size 15: UNIVERSITY
The reverse of the entered string is: YTISREVINU
```

EXPLANATION: We have used two pointers to point to the string *s*. Pointer ***q*** contain the address **65510.** We assume the string entered is **"UNIVERSITY"** (refer from the previous figure). The expression ***p* = *s* + strlen (*s*) – 1** become ***p* = *s* + 10** so ***p*** now points to the address **65519.**

To reverse the string we start from this pointer ***p*** and decrement it on iteration of the for loop. The testing condition is the starting address of string *s* which we have already stored in ***q***. In the expression ***p***! = ***q*** when ***p*** and ***q*** both are **65510** control comes out from the loop and character at address **65510** is not printed so the statement **printf("%c",*p); after for loop.**

```
/*Prog 9.22 Demo of pointers and strings with function*/
#include<stdio.h>
#include<conio.h>
void main()
{
  void input(char*);
  void show(char*);
  char s[20];
  clrscr();
  input(s);
  show(s);
  getch();
}
  void input(char *p)
  {
    printf("Enter the string \n");
    gets(p);
  }
  void show(char *p)
  {
    printf("The string is %s\n",p);
  }
```

```
Output:
Enter the string
WELCOME INDIA
The string is WELCOME INDIA
```

EXPLANATION: In the function **input and show** we simply pass the address of **char** type variable. Here we are passing the address of the **string *s***. The string entered is collected in ***p*** in the function input which is in turn collected in the original **string *s***. The function **show** displays the string.

```
/*Prog 9.22 Copy of two string using pointers and function */
#include<stdio.h>
#include<conio.h>
 void main()
 {
   void input (char *);
```

```
void copy (char*,char*);
void show(char*,char*);
char s[10];
char d[10];
clrscr();
input(s);
copy(d,s);
show("Your source string is:",s);
show("After copying string is:",d);
getch();
}
void input(char *s)
{
 printf("Enter the string:");
 gets(s);
}
void show(char *p, char*s)
{
  printf("%s\t%s\n",p,s);
}
 void copy(char *d, char *s)
 {
    while(*s!='\0')
    {
  *d=*s;
  d++;
  s++;
    }
  *d='\0';
 }
```

Output:

```
Enter the string: INDIAN
Your source string is: INDIAN
After copying string is: INDIAN
```

EXPLANATION: In the function **show** we pass **char** pointer variable. First is the hand-made string and second is the address of the string which we want to display.

In the **copy function** we pass address of the destination and **source string.** While source string does not come to an end we copy one character at a time from source string and assign to the destination string and increment both the pointers. In the end when **while** ends we put **null character at the end of destination string to mark end of the string.**

9.13.1 Pointer To Array of Strings

We have seen in the **chapter-7** that an array is declared as **char s [5] [10]** which declare **5 strings** each of **size 10.** Now suppose the array is initialized as:

`char s [5][10]={"NMIMS","MPSTME","PANDEY","INDIAN","VIJAY"};`

COLUMN →

ROW	S[0]	S[1]	S[2]	S[3]	S[4]	S[5]	S[6]	S[7]	S[8]	S[9]
S[0]	N	M	I	M	S	\0				
S[1]	M	P	S	T	M	E	\0			
S[2]	P	A	N	D	E	Y	\0			
S[3]	I	N	D	I	A	N	\0			
S[4]	V	I	J	A	Y	\0				

Fig. 9.14 *Demonstration of pointers to array of strings.*

As clear from the above figure that out of 50 bytes allocated only 6 +7 +7 + 7 + 6 =33 have been used. Remaining 17 bytes are unused. This wastage of memory can be avoided if we use pointer to array of strings as:

`char*ps_arr[]= {"NMIMS","MPSTME","PANDEY","INDIAN","VIJAY"};`

In this case only 5 pointers are stored in ps_arr [0] points to string "NMIMS", ps_arr [1] points to string"MPSTME" and son on. The total memory used in this case if 33 + 2 *5 = 43 bytes as compared to 50 bytes in the previous case. Thus array of pointers to string saves memory. Also manipulation of strings becomes quite easy as you have a look the program given below:

```
/*Prog 9.23 Demo of pointer and array of strings */
#include<stdio.h>
#include<conio.h>
 void main()
{
  char *s[5]={"DOS","WINDOS","LINUX","UNIX","SUN"};
  int i;
  clrscr();
  for(i=0;i<5;i++)
      printf("Address=%u\t value=%s\n",s[i],s[i]);
  getch();
  }
```

Output:

```
Address=180     value=DOS
Address=184     value=WINDOS
Address=191     value=LINUX
Address=197     value=UNIX
Address=202     value=SUN
```

EXPLANATION: From the declaration it is clear that there is an array pointer. **S [0]** contains address of string **"DOS"**, **s[1]** contains the address of **string "WINDOWS"** and so on. In the **printf** you can note that for printing address as well as printing strings we have used **s[*i*]**. It should be obvious as whenever we print say a string we simply write **printf("%s", *s*)** and *s* represents base address of **string *s*.**

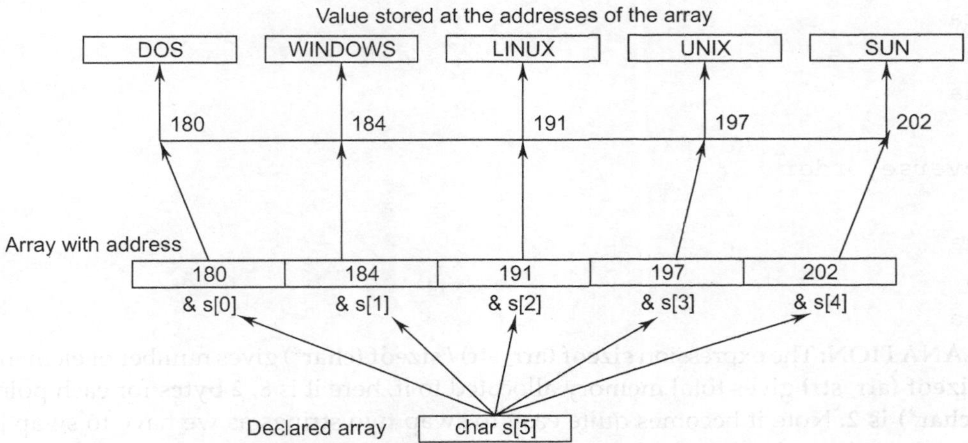

Fig. 9.15 *Demonstration of pointer and arrays of string.*

```
/*Prog 9.24 Reversing the order of string through pointer */
#include<stdio.h>
#include<conio.h>
 void main()
 {
   char* arr_str[]={"ruchika","anjana","ranjana","hari"};
   char *t;
   int i,n,j;
   clrscr();
   n=sizeof(arr_str)/sizeof(char*);
   printf("The original order\n");
   for(i=0;i<n;i++)
   printf("%s\n",arr_str[i]);
   for(i=0;i<n;i++)
   for(j=i+1;j<n;j++)
    {
      t=arr_str[i];
      arr_str[i]=arr_str[j];
      arr_str[j]=t;
    }
   printf("The reverse order\n");
   for(i=0;i<n;i++)
```

```
    printf("%s\n",arr_str[i]);
    getch();
  }
```

Output:

```
The original order
ruchika
anjana
ranjana
hari
The reverse order
hari
ranjana
anjana
ruchika
```

EXPLANATION: The expression **sizeof (arr_str) / sizeof (char*)** gives number of elements in the array. **Sizeof (arr_str)** gives total memory allocated to it, here it is **8, 2 bytes** for each pointer and **sizeof (char*) is 2.** Note it becomes quite easy to swap two strings as we have to swap just two pointers and not the entire string using **strcpy** as we did earlier sorting program. This feature is the main advantage of use of pointers in array of strings.

In the above program using array of pointers to string we initialized the array in the program itself. What if we first declare an array of pointer and store address of each string taken from the user in the array? How can we achieve this? One such code is given below but this doesn't work.

```
 char* arr[4];
 for(i=0; i<4; i++)
  {
         printf("Enter the string %d\n",i+1);
         gets(arr[i]);
  }
```

The memory for the strings have not allocated and we are trying to store their addresses into the array arr. This works well in case of array declared as char s[5][10] as the compiler allocates memory statically, but here we are dealing with the pointers, so memory for each string taken from user, has to be allocated specifically during execution of the program and this memory allocation is known as dynamic memory allocation. This is shown in the next program.

```
/*Prog 9.25 Demo of user entered strings into array of pointer*/
#include<stdio.h>
#include<conio.h>
#include<alloc.h>
#include<string.h>
#define s 4
 void main()
 {
```

```
    char*arr_str[s];
    char temp[20];
    int i,n,len;
    clrscr();
    for(i=0;i<s;i++)
    {
       printf("Enter a string %d\n",i+1);
       gets(temp);
       len=strlen(temp);
       arr_str[i]=(char*)malloc(len);
       strcpy(arr_str[i],temp);
    }
    printf("The entered strings are \n");
    for(i=0;i<s;i++)
     printf ("%s\n", arr_str[i]);
    getch();
 }
```

Output:

```
Enter a string 1
Work hard
Enter a string 2
Love is blind
Enter a string 3
I'm hari
Enter a string 4
You r Indian
The entered strings are
Work hard
Love is blind
I'm hari
You r Indian
```

EXPLANATION: In the **for loop** as each string is entered by the user it is stored in the temporary array **temp.** The length of this **(not the size)** array **temp** is find out and that much memory is allocated dynamically with the help of **malloc** function which allocates memory dynamically from heap. The allocated memory is returned and arr_str[0] points to that memory location. Next the entered string is copied from temp to this arr_str [0]. Similarly for *i*= 1, 2, and 3. In the end we display all strings through a for loop.

9.14 THINGS NOT TO BE DONE WITH POINTERS

The following things which we can not do with the pointers are given below:

1. Addition of two pointers
2. Subtraction of two pointers
3. Division of two pointers
4. Multiplication of two pointers.
5. Shifting or masking of two pointers
6. Addition of float or double to pointers.
7. Assignment of pointer of one type to another type.

As pointers are simply addresses so these above mentioned operation should not be performed. For example assuming *p*1 and *p*2 are two pointers so following should not be done.

*p*1+ *p*2;

*p*1 – *p*2;

*p*1 * *p*2;

*p*1 / *p*2;

*p*1 >> 1;

9.15 GENERIC POINTER

When a variable is declared as being a pointer to type void it is known as a generic pointer. Since you cannot have a variable of type void, the pointer will not point to any data and therefore cannot be referenced. That is to say, you can't use it with an asterisk before it to update a variable. It is still a pointer though, to use it just have to cast it to another kind of pointer first. Hence the term Generic pointer.

This is very useful when you want a pointer to point to data of different types at different times:

They are normally used for:

1. Passing generic pointers to functions and returning such pointers.
2. As an intermediate pointer type.
3. Used when the exact pointer type will be known at a later point of time.

```
/*Prog 9.26 Demo of generic pointer */
#include<stdio.h>
#include<conio.h>
void main()
{
  int i;
  char c;
  void *ptr;
  i=6;
```

```
  c='a';
  ptr=&i;
  clrscr();
  printf("ptr points to the integer value %d\n",*(int*)ptr);
  ptr=&c;
  printf("ptr now points to the character %c\n",*(char*)ptr);
  getch();
}
```

Output:

```
ptr points to the integer value 6
ptr now points to the character a
```

EXPLANATION: The variable ptr is a void pointer. A void pointer can store addresses of any data type. Initially we store the address of an int type variable and display it using void pointer. Note typecasting has been done. Next we put address of a char type variable and display it. Note dereferencing a void pointer is not allowed *i.e.*, if you write *ptr =10 then it will give you compile time error.

9.16 FUNCTION RETURNING POINTERS

Just we return int, char, float etc from a function we can also return address from a function. The declaration for that type of function would be.

Declaration:

```
            return_type *fun_name(parameters);
```

Definition:

```
            return_type * fun_mane(parameters)
            {
                 Statements;
                 Statements;
                 .........................;
                 .........................;
                 return &data;
```

Where data is the variable of return_type. Now see the program given below for better understanding.

```
/*Prog 9.27 Demo of function returning pointer ver 1*/
#include<stdio.h>
#include<conio.h>
 void main()
 {
   int *fun_sum(int,int);
   int x,y,*sum;
```

```
    clrscr();
    printf("Enter the first numbers\n");
    scanf("%d",&x);
    printf("Enter the second number\n");
    scanf("%d",&y);
    printf("The entered number by you \nx=%d\ty=%d\n",x,y);
    sum=fun_sum(x,y);
    printf("The sum of two numbers is %d\n",*sum);
    getch();
 }
  int*fun_sum(int p,int q)
  {
    static int c=p + q;
    return &c;
  }}
```

Output:

```
Enter the first numbers
50
Enter the second number
45
The entered number by you
x=50 y=45
The sum of two numbers is 95
```

EXPLANATION: The function **fun_sum** takes two parameters and return address of an int type variable. As the function **fun_sum** return the address we must have a pointer to **int** type to collect this returned address from function. Note in function **fun_sum** the variable declared is **static.** This is must as **static** variables are **hold time variables** and persist even after function is returned. Without static the variable ***c*** will be assumed as **auto** and will be destroyed when control returns from function. The rule of tumb is that never return address of local variable from a function. Always use **static storage** class if you want to do.

```
/*Prog 9.28 Demo of function returning pointer ver 2*/
#include<stdio.h>
#include<conio.h>
#include<string.h>
 void main()
 {
    char*revstr(char*);
    char * str,temp[20];
    clrscr();
    printf("Enter a string\n");
```

```
    gets(temp);
    printf("Orignal string %s\n",temp);
    str=revstr(temp);
    printf("Reverse string %s\n",str);
    getch();
  }
    char*revstr(char*s)
    {
 char*temp;
 temp=strrev(s);
 return temp;
    }
```

Output:

```
Enter a string
This is NMIMS
Orignal string This is NMIMS
Reverse string SMIMN si sihT
```

EXPLANATION: The function **char*revstr(char*)** accepts a pointer to **char** *i.e.,* a string and returned address of the **string.** Note in the function **revstr** no need to declare **temp** as **static** as pointer value are not allotted memory on **stack** (works on LIFO(Last in first out) principal). They persist till program does not come to end or a call to free is made.

9.17 POINTER TO FUNCTION

Just as we have pointer to variables of any type, pointers to array and structures (in the coming chapter) we can also have pointers to functions. Though not used in general but they are used in advanced C programming for accessing ROM-BIOS functions. For the time being you simply learn the basic: **How to define and use pointer to function?**

```
/*Prog 9.29 Pointers to function ver 1*/
#include<stdio.h>
#include<conio.h>
 void main()
 {
    void fun1(void);
    void (*pf)(void);
    void fun2(void);
    char p;
    clrscr();
    pf=fun1;
    printf("Calling fun1 through pointer\n");
```

```
    (*pf)();
    pf=fun2;
    printf("Calling fun2 through pointer\n");
    (*pf)();
    getch();
  }
    void fun1(void)
    {
      printf("In function fun1\n");
    }
    void fun2(void)
    {
      printf("In function fun2\n");
    }
```

```
Output:
Calling fun1 through pointer
In function fun1
Calling fun2 through pointer
In function fun2
```

EXPLANATION: For creating a pointer to a function we have to note the **prototype** of the function. In the program the return type of the function is **void** and function takes **void** argument *i.e.,* **no argument.** To create the pointer to this type of function we write in this manner.

void (*pf)(void)

Here, ***pf*** is a pointer to function whose **return type is void** and which takes **no argument.** Parenthesis around ****pf* is must otherwise it will become void **pf*(void); which means *pf* is function which takes void argument and which returns an address of type void.**

In the statement ***pf*= fun1** we are assigning the address of function **fun1 to *pf*.** We then call the function **fun1** through this pointer ***pf*** by **writing (**pf*) ().** Next we take the address of function **fun2 to *pf* and call the function fun2 by writing (**pf*) ().**

The above program has explained the concept of pointer to function. We present some more examples.

1. **int max(int, int);** For this function we write pointer to function as **int (*pmax) (int, int);** and to call the function after assigning address as **pmax = max** we **write** *x* = **(*pmax) (20, 30);** where *x* is any int type variable.
2. **char myfun(int, float);** For this function we write pointer to function as **char(*pfun) (int, float);** and to call the function after assigning address as ***pfun*= myfun** we write *x*= **(*pmax)(20, 30);** where *x* is any **char** type variable.

Some more complex examples can be given but I think for starting it is enough to understand the basics and explore the new things at their own to be expert in this field.

9.18 A QUICK REVIEW FOR POINTERS

Pointers: Definition

- Pointers provide an **indirect method** of accessing variables. The reason why pointers are hard to understand is because they aren't taught in a manner that is understandable. Think for a minute about a typical textbook. It will usually have a table of contents, some chapters, and an index. What if you were looking in the Weiss book for information on **printf?** You'd look at the index for **printf.** The index will tell you where information on **printf** is located within the book. ***Conceptually, this is how pointers work!* Re-read this analogy if you didn't get it the first time.** This is important. You must understand that pointers are indirect references.
- Because the **conceptual view** of a pointer is important in the understandability pointers, let's try to put this in terms that are more simple.
- Let's say you need some information about a secret party that's happening later in the day, but you only have one friend (Yes, I know that's sad). And your friend's name is **"Pointer"** However, he isn't very helpful directly because he doesn't really know anything about the party, but he tells you that he knows someone with that secret information. So any info you want, **"Pointer"(name of friend)** will just get from his friend. This is approximately how a **pointer works.**
- You may be wondering, what is the point of this (no pun intended)? Why don't I just make all variables without the use of pointers? It's because sometimes you can't. What if you needed an array of **ints,** but didn't know the size of the array before hand? What if you needed a **string,** but it grew dynamically as the program ran? What if you need variables that are persistent through function use without declaring them global (remember the swap function)? They are all solved through the use of pointers. Pointers are also essential in creating larger custom data structures, such as **linked lists.**
- So now that you understand how pointers work, let's define them a little better.
- A pointer when declared is just a reference. **DECLARING A POINTER DOES NOT CREATE ANY SPACE FOR THE POINTER TO POINT TO.** We will tackle this dynamic memory allocation issue later.
- A pointer is a reference to an area of memory in the heap. The heap is a dynamically allocated area of memory when the program runs.

Pointers: Declaration and Syntax

- Pointers are declared by using the * in front of the variable identifier. For example:

```
int *ip;
float *fp = NULL;
```

This declares a pointer, *ip*, to an integer. Let's say we want ip to point to an integer. The second line declares a pointer to a float, but initializes the pointer to point to the NULL pointer. The NULL pointer points to a place in memory that cannot be accessed. NULL is useful when checking for error conditions and many functions return NULL if they fail.

```
int x = 5;
int *ip;
```

```
ip = &x;
```

We first encountered the & operator first in the I/O section. The & operator is to specify the **address-of** *x*. Thus, the pointer, *ip* is pointing to *x* by assigning the address of *x*. **This is important.** You must understand this concept.

- This brings up the question, if pointers contain addresses, then how do I get the actual value of what the pointer is pointing to? This is solved through the * operator. The * **dereferences** the pointer to the value. So,

```
printf ("%d %d\n", x, *ip);
```

  Would print 5 5 to the screen.

- Remember the swap function? We can now simulate ***call by reference*** using pointers. Here is a modified version of the swap function using pointers.

```
void swap(int *x, int *y) {
    int tmp;
    tmp = *x;
    *x = *y;
    *y = tmp;
}
int main() {
    int a = 2, b = 3;
    swap(&a, &b);
    return EXIT_SUCCESS;
}
```

  This snip of swapping code works. When you call swap, you must give the address-of a and b, because swap is expecting a pointer.

- Why does this work? It's because you are giving the address-of the variables. This memory does not "go away" or get "popped off" after the function swap ends. The changes within swap change the values located in those memory addresses.

Pointers: Void Pointers

- Void pointers can be assigned to any pointer value. It sometimes necessary to store/copy/move pointers without regard to the type it references.
- You cannot dereference a void pointer.
- Functions such as malloc, free, and scanf utilize void pointers.

Pointers: Pointer Arithmetic

- C is one of the few languages that allow pointer arithmetic. In other words, you actually move the pointer reference by an arithmetic operation. For example:

```
int x = 5, *ip = &x;
ip++;
```

  On a typical 32-bit machine, **ip* would be pointing to 5 after initialization. But *ip++;* increments the pointer 32-bits or 4-bytes. So whatever was in the next 4-bytes, **ip* would be pointing at it.

- Pointer arithmetic is very useful when dealing with arrays, because arrays and pointers share a special relationship in C. More on this when we get to arrays!

POINTS TO PONDER

In this section you have learned the following points.

- A pointer is a variable whose value is used to point to another variable.
- A variable declared in C has two values: the left value and the right value.
- The left value of a variable is the address; the right value is the content of the variable.
- The address-of operator (&) can be used to obtain the left value (address) of a variable.
- The asterisk (*) in a pointer declaration tells the compiler that the variable is a pointer variable.
- The dereference operator (*) is a unary operator; as such, it requires only one operand.
- The *ptr_name expression returns the value pointed to by the pointer variable ptr_name, where ptr_name can be any valid variable name in C.
- If the right value of a pointer variable is 0, the pointer is a null pointer. A null pointer cannot point to valid data.
- You can update the value of a variable referred by a pointer variable.
- Several pointers can point to the same location of a variable in the memory.

QUESTIONS AND ANSWERS

Q1. *What are the left and right values?*

Ans: The left value refers to the address of a variable, and the right value refers to the content stored in the memory location of a variable. There are two ways to get the right value of a variable: use the variable name directly, or use the left value of the variable to refer to where the right value resides. The second way is also called the indirect way.

Q2. *How can you obtain the address of a variable?*

Ans: By using the address-of operator, &. For instance, given an integer variable *x*, the & *x* expression returns the address of *x*. To print out the address of *x*, you can use the %p format specifier in the printf() function.

Q3. *What is the concept of indirection in terms of using pointers?*

Ans: Before this hour, the only way you knew for reading from or writing to a variable was to invoke the variable directly. For instance, if you wanted to write a decimal, 16, to an integer variable *x*, you could call the statement *x* = 16;.

As you learned in this hour, C allows you to access a variable in another way-using pointers. Therefore, to write 16 to *x*, you can first declare an integer pointer (ptr) and assign the left value (address) of *x* to ptr—that is, ptr = &*x*;. Then, instead of executing the statement *x* = 16;, you can use another statement:

```
*ptr = 16;
```

Here the pointer *ptr refers to the memory location reserved by *x*, and the content stored in the memory location is updated to 16 after the statement is executed. So, you see, making use of pointers to access the memory locations of variables is a way of indirection.

Q4. *Can a null pointer point to valid data?*

Ans: No. A null pointer cannot point to valid data. This is so because the value contained by a null pointer is 0. You'll see examples of using null pointers in arrays, strings, or memory allocation later in the book.

EXERCISES

A. Answer the following questions:

1. What are pointers? Why are they important?
2. Explain the use of (*) indirection operator?
3. Explain the effect of ++ and – operator with pointer of all data types?
4. Why addition of two pointers is impossible?
5. Explain the relation between an array and a pointer?
6. Distinguish between the address stored in the pointer and the value at that address?
7. What is the base address? How is it accessed differentially for one-dimensional and two-dimensional arrays?
8. Explain the comparison of two pointers?
9. Explain the feature of pointers?
10. How strings are stored using pointer variables? Is it essential to declare length?
11. Why does an element counting of array always start at 0?
12. What is the relationship between an array name and pointer in C? How is an array name treated when it appears as a function argument?
13. What is an array of pointer? How is it declared?

B. Match the following columns:

I	II
1. void *x*;	(*a*) generic pointer.
2. void **x*;	(*b*) not allowed in C
3. Address of variable	(*c*) double indirection
4. int ***p*;	(*d*) pointer to function.
5. int (**p*)();	(*e*) &operator.

C. Write True or False against each statements:

1. An integer can be added to a pointer.
2. Pointers are not integer.
3. A pointer can be used as a scalar data type as well as derived data type.
4. The operand of address of operator & may be a register variable.
5. Call by reference is done with the help of pointer.
6. Pointers make execution of program faster.
7. void * is a generic pointer.
8. Address of functions can be taken and stored in a pointer.
9. Address of pointer can be applied to pointer variable only.

10. A 2-D array is nothing but a 1-D array of pointers.
11. Array of pointers can be used in C.

D. Fill in the blanks:

1. The two pointer operator are __________ and __________.
2. Pointer allows the direct access of __________.
3. Pointers are __________ numbers but not __________.
4. Indirection operator * returns __________.
5. The expression arr[*i*]+*j* is equivalent to __________.
6. The expression arr [*i*, *j*] is equivalent to __________.
7. The expression arr[*i*][*j*] is equivalent to __________.
8. The function name represents the __________ of the function.
9. A generic pointer cannot be __________.
10. Arrays are always passed by __________ into the function.

E. Brain Drill

1. Write a program using function to check whether characters +, –, * and / are present in the string or not.
2. Write a program to find k^{th} smallest element in an array using pointers.
3. Write a program to swap two string using pointer and function.
4. Write a program to reverse a number using pointer.
5. Write a program to find k^{th} element in an array of strings *i.e.*, string whose length is maximum.
6. Write a program to list all the strings whose initial letter starts with a given input character using function and pointer.
7. Write a program in C to find the area and perimeter of a circle using pointers.
8. Write a C program to arrange a list of names in ascending order using an array of pointers to strings.

F. Predict the output of the following programs:

```
1. main ( )
   {
        int a[5] , *p;
        for(p=a; p< &a[5]; p++)
        {
             *p= p-a;
             printf("%d",*p);
        }
   }
2. main ( )
   {
        char *cp;
        int *ip;
```

```
        cp = (char *) 0x100;
        ip= (int *)cp;
        ip++;
        cp++;
        printf("cp= %x\t ip=%x",cp,ip);
    }
3. main ( )
    {
            char *ptr ="Telco systems";
            (*ptr)++;
            printf("%s\n",ptr);
            ptr++;
            printf("%s\n",ptr);
    }
4. main ()
    {
        int i, b[] = {1,2,3,4,5}, *p;
        p=b;
        ++*p;
        printf("%d",*p);
        p+=2;
        printf("%d",*p);
    }
5. main ( )
    {
      char s1[] = "pointer";
      char *p;
      p=s1;
      p+=(p+5);
      printf("%s",p);
    }
6. main ( )
    {
        int a[5] = {-2,-1,3,4,5};
        int *b;
        b= &a[2];
        printf("%d\n",b[-1]);
    }
7. main ( )
    {
        char A1[20], A2[20], *p=A2;
        strcpy (A1, "Birthday");
        strcpy(A2,"Happy");
```

```
        p= A1;
        strcpy(A1,"Lover");
        *p= 'D';
        printf("%s\n",p);
    }
8. main ( )
    {
        int arr[4] = {6,7,8,9};
        int *ptr = arr + 2;
        printf("%d\n",ptr[1]);
    }
9. main ( )
    {
        char *p="name";
        void modify(char*);
        modify(p);
        printf("%s",p);
    }
   void modify (char *s)
    {
         char *n = "newname";
          s=n;
    }
10. main ( )
    {
         char buff [ ]= "This is a demo example";
         int i, *ptr;
         ptr = buff;
         for(i=0; *ptr; i++)
         printf("%c", ptr++);
     }
11. main ( )
     {
          char *ptr;
          ptr = "%d\n";
          ptr = ptr +2;
          printf(ptr-2, 275);
     }
12. main ( )
     {
        char *p="%d…%d\n";
        printf(p+4,97);
     }
```

10

Introduction to Structure and Union

The chapter starts with the introduction to the most important user defined data types which is also derived type, structures and unions in C.

The introduction tells you the following things:

(a) What is a structure?

(b) Why is it called a heterogeneous data type?

It gives you an answer by first giving you a very small example then explaining in step-by-step manner all the features of structure. It also compares it with array by telling how it is different from it. Programming examples present numerous examples of structures.

Array of structure have been covered by giving few programming examples. Nesting of structure then follows i.e., structure with in another.

Union are covered in section 10.6 which is a special type of structure. **Structure and union** are compared, programs containing both structures and union have been covered. An important concept in structure, bit field have been covered.

10.1 WHAT IS A STRUCTURE?

As you've learned, arrays can be used to collect groups of variables of the same type. **The question now is how to aggregate pieces of data that are not identically typed.**

The answer is that you can group variables of different types with a data type called a structure. In C, a structure collects different data items in such a way that they can be referenced as a single unit.

There are several major differences between an array and a structure. Besides the fact that data items in a structure can have different types, each data item has its own name instead of a subscript value. In fact, data items in a structure are called **fields or members** of the structure.

A structure is a derived data type which consists of collection of different data type which consists of collection of different data types such as int, char, float and even structure also. We see example of structure in our daily life. For keeping information about student we have to store his/her name registration number, age, address, class etc. Similarly for keeping information about employee we may have his/her employee code, date of joining, salary etc. All these attributes related to student or employee cannot be stored in array alone. Even if we wish to store these attributes using array we will have to use separate array for each attribute say one for salary, one for employee code and so on. Again managing this array separately won't be an easy task. In such situations we can use structure. We understand this new concept of C programming using programs.

The next two subsections teach you how to declare structures and define structure variables.

10.1.1 Declaring Structures

The general form to declare a structure is

```
struct struct_tag
{
      data_type1 variable1;
      data_type2 variable2;
      data_type3 variable3;
      ..................................................;
      ..................................................;
      ..................................................;
};
```

Here **struct** is the keyword used in C to start a structure declaration. **struct_tag** is the **tag name** of the structure. **variable1, variable2, and variable3** are the members of the structure. Their data types are specified respectively by **data_type1, data_type2, and data_type3.** As you can see, the declarations of the members have to be enclosed within the opening and closing braces ({and}) in the structure declaration, and a **semicolon (;)** has to be included at the end of the declaration.

The following is an example of a structure declaration:

```
struct automobile {
      int year;
      char model[8];
      int engine_power;
      float weight;
      };
```

Here **struct** is used to start a structure declaration. **automobile** is the **tag name** of the structure. In this example, there are three types of variables, **char, int, and float.** The variables have their own names, such as year, **model, engine_power, and weight.**

Note that a structure tag name, like automobile, is a **label to a structure.** The compiler uses the tag name to identify the structure labeled by that tag name

10.1.2 Defining Structure Variables

After declaring a structure, you can define the structure variables. For instance, the following structure variables are defined with the structure data type of automobile from the previous section:

```
struct automobile sedan, pick_up, sport_utility;
```

Here three structure variables, **sedan, pick_up,** and **sport_utility,** are defined by the structure of **automobile.** All three structure variables contain the four members of the structure data type of automobile.

Also, you can combine the structure declaration and definition into one statement like this:

```
struct automobile
{
    int year;
    char model[8];
    int engine_power;
    float weight;
}sedan, pick_up, sport_utility;
```

Here three structure variables, **sedan, pick_up, and sport_utility,** are defined with the structure data type of automobile in the single statement.

10.1.3 Referencing Structure Members with the Dot Operator

Now, let's see how to reference a structure member. Given the structure data type of automobile and the structure of sedan, for instance, I can access its member, year, and assign an integer to it in the following way:

```
sedan.year = 1997;
```

Here the structure name and its member's name are separated by the **dot (.) operator** so that the compiler knows that the integer value of **1997** is assigned to the variable called **year,** which is a **member of the structure sedan.**

Likewise, the following statement assigns the start address of the character array of model, which is another member of the structure **sedan, to a char pointer, ptr:**

```
ptr = sedan.model;
```

```
/*Prog 10.1 Access to structure members */
#include<stdio.h>
#include<conio.h>
main(void)
{
    struct computer
    {
        float cost;
        int year;
```

```
        int cpu_speed;
        char cpu_type[16];
    } model;
    clrscr();
    printf("The type of the CPU inside your computer?\n");
    gets(model.cpu_type);
    printf("The speed(MHz) of the CPU?\n");
    scanf("%d", &model.cpu_speed);
    printf("The year your computer was made?\n");
    scanf("%d", &model.year);
    printf("How much you paid for the computer?\n");
    scanf("%f", &model.cost);
    printf("Here are what you entered:\n");
    printf("Year: %d\n", model.year);
    printf("Cost: $%6.2f\n", model.cost);
    printf("CPU type: %s\n", model.cpu_type);
    printf("CPU speed: %d MHz\n", model.cpu_speed);
    getch();
}
```

Output:

```
The type of the CPU inside your computer?
Pentium
The speed(MHz) of the CPU?
156
The year your computer was made?
1999
How much you paid for the computer?
23459
Here are what you entered:
Year: 1999
Cost: $23459.00
CPU type: Pentium
CPU speed: 156 MHz
```

EXPLANATION: The purpose of the program is to show you how to reference members of a structure. As you can see from the program, there is a structure called **model** that is defined with a structure data type of computer in **lines 6_11.** The structure has one **float** variable, two **int** variables, and **one char array.**

The statement in **line 13** asks the user to enter the type of **CPU (Central Processing Unit)** used inside his or her computer. Then, **line 14** receives the string of the CPU type entered by the user and saves the string into the **char** array called **cpu_type.** Because **cpu_type** is a member of the model structure, the **model.cpu_type** expression is used in **line 14** to **reference the member** of the structure. Note that the **dot operator (.) is used to separate the two names in the expression.**

Lines 15 and 16 ask for the CPU speed and store the value of an **integer** entered by the user to another member of the model structure-the **int** variable **cpu_speed.** Note that in **line 16,** the **address-of operator (&)** is prefixed to the **model.cpu_speed** expression inside the **scanf ()** function because the argument should be an **int pointer.**

Likewise, **lines 17 and 18 receive** the value of the year in which the user's computer was made, and **lines 19 and 20** get the number for the cost of the computer. After the execution, the **int** variable year and the **float** variable cost in the model structure contain the corresponding values entered by the user.

Then, **lines 23_26** print out all the values held by the members of the model structure. From the output, you can tell that each member of the structure has been accessed and assigned a number or string correctly.

```
*Prog 10.2 Demo of structure ver1*/
#include<stdio.h>
#include<conio.h>
 struct person //declaration of structure
 {
    char name[10];
    int age;
 };
    void main()
    {
       struct person p;
       clrscr();
       printf("Enter name for person \n");
       scanf("%s",p.name);
       printf("Enter age for person\n");
       scanf("%d",&p.age);
       printf("Name=%s\n",p.name);
       printf("Age=%d\n",p.age);
       getch();
    }
```

Output:

```
Enter name for person
Ruchika Arora
Enter age for person
23
Name=Ruchika Arora
Age=23
```

EXPLANATION: Note several points about structure using above program:

1. Structure is a heterogeneous data structure. Remember array is a homogeneous data structure *i.e.,* all the elements of an array must be of the same type. You cannot mix int with float or float with char. This is not the case with structure *i.e.,* structure can have there elements of any data type even they may have other user defined data types as there elements.
2. Structure is defined by struct keyword. Following struct any valid identifier which conforms to identifier writing rules is allowed. In this program we have declared a structure named person. We could have chosen any other name also say student or employee.
3. The structure is opened using {and closed with} followed by a semicolon.
4. The structure declared above contains two member elements: first one is the character array name for length 20 and second one is age of type int. As we know int takes two bytes in memory (for DOS) so total size of the structure is 22 bytes.
5. The declaration alone does not reserve memory space. It simply tells the compiler about the prototype of the structure. The actual definition *i.e.,* creation of a variable of structure data type allocates memory.
6. The structure is an Abstract Data Type *i.e.,* following is only like a template.

   ```
   struct person
   {
           char name [20];
           int age;
   ```

   In order to use structure we have to create a variable of type structure just like we create variable of any other data type.
7. From statement struct **person** ***p;*** we actually creating ***p*** of type **struct person** type. We have to use **struct** keyword each time we create a variable of type **person** *i.e.,* you just can not write **person** ***p;*** before doing some changes which we will see later in the coming programs.
8. At the time of compilation 22 bytes will be allocated for this variable which consists of two parts:
   (*a*) 20 bytes for name
   (*b*) 2 bytes for age

   We can access these member elements by using membership operator or dot operator (). (Exact allocation of 22 bytes is compiler dependent)
9. Structure can be declared before main *i.e.,* global or it can be local to main or any other function or block.
10. The structure cannot be read as a whole. We have to store values into the individual members of the structure.
11. Diagrammatically we can show the structure as

Name	Age

Person

```
/*Prog 10.3 Demo of structure ver2*/
#include<stdio.h>
#include<conio.h>
 struct person
```

```
{
 char name[20];
 int age;
};
typedef struct person Per;
main()
{
 Per p;
 clrscr();
 printf("Enter name for person\n");
 scanf("%s",p.name);
 printf("Enter age for person\n");
 scanf("%d",&p.age);
 printf("Name=%s\n",p.name);
 printf("Age=%d",p.age);
 getch();
}
Output:
Enter name for person
hari
Enter age for person
12
Name=hari
Age=12
```

EXPLANATION: There is only one change in the program we have **typedefined** the **struct person** to **Per.** Now we can use **Per** any where we want to use **struct person** statement. It could be written in the following manner also.

```
typedef struct
{
  char name[20];
  int age;
}person ;
```

Meaning the whole

```
struct
{
   char name[20];
   int age;
};
```

Has been given a new name person. So now you can use simply person to declare variable as person type structure.

```
/*Prog 10.4 demo of structure ver3*/
#include<stdio.h>
#include<conio.h>
 main()
 {
  struct person
  {
    char name[10];
    int age;
  } p1, p2;
  clrscr();
  printf("Enter name and age for person 1\n");
  scanf("%s%d",&p1.name,&p1.age);
  printf("Enter name and age for person 2\n");
  scanf("%s%d",&p2.name,&p2.age);
  printf("Person 1Details are\n");
  printf("Name=%s\tAge=%d\n",p1.name,p1.age);
  printf("Person 2 Details are \n");
  printf("Name=%s\tAge=%d\n", p2.name, p2.age);
  getch();
 }
```

Output:

```
Enter name and age for person 1
Ranjana 22
Enter name and age for person 2
Anjana 27
Person 1Details are
Name=Ranjana    Age=22
Person 2 Details are
Name=Anjana     Age=27
```

EXPLANATION: Note we can declare variable just before putting **semicolon** to terminate structure declaration. Here we have created two variables ***p*1** and ***p*2** and rest is quite self explanatory.

10.1.4 Initializing Structures

A structure can be initialized by a list of data called **initializers. Commas** are used to separate data items in a list of data.

```
/* Prog 10.5 Demo of Initializing a structure ver1 */
#include <stdio.h>
#include <conio.h>
```

```
main(void)
{
    struct employee {
    int id;
    char name[32];
    };
   /* structure initialization */
   struct employee info = {
       1,
       "H.M.Pandey"
       };
       clrscr();
       printf("Here is a sample:\n");
       printf("Employee Name: %s\n", info.name);
       printf("Employee ID #: %04d\n\n", info.id);
       printf("What's your name?\n");
       gets(info.name);
       printf("What's your ID number?\n");
       scanf("%d", &info.id);
       printf("\nHere are what you entered:\n");
       printf("Name: %s\n", info.name);
       printf("ID #: %04d\n", info.id);
       getch();
}
```

```
Output:
Here is a sample:
Employee Name: H.M.Pandey
Employee ID #: 0001
What's your name?
Mr. Vijay Nath Pandey
What's your ID number?
0016
Here are what you entered:
Name: Mr. Vijay Nath Pandey
ID #: 0016
```

EXPLANATION: The purpose of the program is to initialize a structure and then ask the user to update the content held by the structure.

The structure data type, labeled as employee, is declared in **lines 6_9.** Then, the variable, **info,** is defined with the structure data type and initialized with the **integer 1** and the string **"H.M. Pandey"** in **lines 11_14.**

You can also combine the declaration, definition, and initialization of a structure into a single statement. Here's an example:

```
struct employee {
        int id;
        char name[32];
        } info = {
        1,
        "H.M.Pandey"
        };
```

The statements in **lines 17 and 18** display the initial contents stored by the two members of the info structure on the screen. Then, **lines 20_23** ask the user to enter his or her **name and employee ID number and save them into the two structure members, name and *id*, respectively.**

Before the end of the program, the updated contents contained by the two members are printed out by the statements in **lines 26 and 27.** Here again, the **dot operator (.)** is used in the program to **reference** the structure members.

```
/*Prog 10.6 Declaration and initialization simultaneously of structures ver2*/
#include<stdio.h>
#include<conio.h>
void main()
{
  struct person
  {
    char name[20];
    int age;
  };
    struct person p1={"Man Mohan",25};
    struct person p2={"Ranjana",23};
    clrscr();
    printf("Person1 Details\n");
    printf("Name=%s\tAge=%d\n",p1.name,p1.age);
    printf("Person2 Details\n");
    printf("Name=%s\tAge=%d\n",p2.name,p2.age);
    getch();
  }
```

Output:

```
Person1 Details
Name=Man Mohan Age=25
Person2 Details
Name=Ranjana Age=23
```

EXPLANATION: Here we have initialized both the structure variables at the place of declaration. Observe how we have defined both the structures. String members have to be enclosed within double quotes " ".

NOTE: The following will result into error.

```
struct person p1;
p1= {"Hari", 23};
```

```
/*Prog 10.7 Declaration and initialization of structures separately ver3*/
#include<stdio.h>
#include<conio.h>
 void main()
 {
   struct item
   {
    char iname[20];
    int icode;
    int iprice;
   };
   struct item i1;
   clrscr();
   strcpy(i1.iname,"Mouse");
   i1.icode=301;
   i1.iprice=300;
   printf("Item details\n");
   printf("Name=%s\t Code=%d",i1.iname,i1.icode);
   printf("\t Price=%d\n",i1.iprice);
   getch();
 }
```

Output:

```
Item details
Name=Mouse      Code=301      Price=300
```

EXPLANATION: In the previous program we declared and defined the members of structures at the same place. In this program we have initialized each member separately.

```
/*Prog 10.8 Copying one structure to another*/
#include<stdio.h>
#include<conio.h>
void main()
{
  typedef struct
```

```
{
  char cname[25];
  char model[20];
  int price;
}mobile;
mobile m1={"NOKIA","6600",12000};
mobile m2,m3;
m2=m1;
clrscr();
strcpy(m3.cname,"SONY_ERR");
strcpy(m3.model,"K700i");
m3.price=m1.price;
printf("Mobile Details\n");
printf("Company Name=%s\tModel=%s",m1.cname,m1.model);
printf("\tPrice=%d\n",m1.price);
printf("Company Name=%s\tModel=%s",m2.cname,m2.model);
printf("\tPrice=%d\n",m2.price);
printf("Company Name=%s\tModel=%s",m3.cname,m3.model);
printf("\tPrice=%d\n",m3.price);
getch();
}
```

Output:

```
Mobile Details
Company Name=NOKIA        Model=6600     Price=12000
Company Name=NOKIA        Model=6600     Price=12000
Company Name=SONY_ERR     Model=K700i    Price=12000
```

EXPLANATION: In the **mobile structure** we have taken three members **cname** for company name, **model** and **price.** Variable ***m1*** is initialized directly. The statement ***m2=m1*** copies structure ***m1* to *m2*.** All the member values of ***m1*** are assigned to ***m2*** in just a single statement. For ***m3*** we have given new values to **cname and model** but price. We have copied price from price member of ***m1*.**

10.2 ARRAY OF STRUCTURE

In C, you can declare an array of a structure by preceding the array name with the structure name. For instance, given a structure with the tag name of *x*, the following statement.

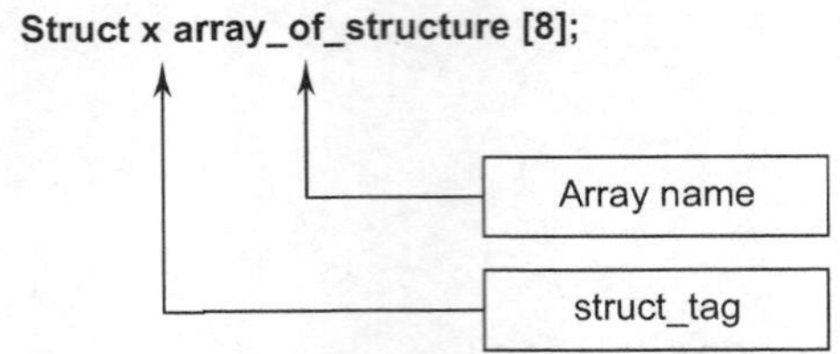

Fig. 10.1 *Basic syntax of array of structure.*

Declares an array, called **array_of_structure,** with the structure data type of ***x* (struct_tag).** The array has eight elements.

Similar to array of any data type an array of structure can also be created and will be very useful when processing of structure like book, person, employee, vehicle, item etc.

To declare an array of structure first you have to create a structure first. For example:

```
struct vehicle
{
    char vname [20];
    int now;
    char fuel_type;
};
struct vehicle varr[5];
```

This creates an array **varr** of structure type **vehicle.** Total **13*5 bytes** of memory will be allocated during compilation. See programs given below for more explanation.

```
/*Prog 10.9 Demo of array of structures */
#include<stdio.h>
#include<conio.h>
 void main()
 {
  typedef struct student
  {
    char sname[20];
    int rollno;
    char cname[20];
  }student;
  student sarr[5];
  int i;
  clrscr();
  for(i=0;i<5;i++)
  {
    printf("\n Enter name of student_no %d:",i+1);
    scanf("%s",sarr[i].sname);
```

```
    printf("\nEnter class name of student_no %d",i+1);
    scanf("%s",sarr[i].cname);
    printf("Enter the rollno");
    scanf("%d",&sarr[i].rollno);
  }
  printf("\n Student's Details\n\n");
  printf("\SName\tCName\tRollNo\n");
  for(i=0;i<5;i++)
  {
    printf("%s\t%s\t",sarr[i].sname,sarr[i].cname);
    printf("%5d\n",sarr[i].rollno);
  }
  getch();
}
```

Output:

```
Enter name of student_no 1:HARI
Enter class name of student_no 1 FF01
Enter the rollno123
Enter name of student_no 2:RUCHIKA
Enter class name of student_no 2 FF02
Enter the rollno124
Enter name of student_no 3:RANJANA
Enter class name of student_no 3 FF03
Enter the rollno125
Enter name of student_no 4: ANJANA
Enter class name of student_no 4 FF04
Enter the rollno126
Enter name of student_no 5:MADHURI
Enter class name of student_no 5FF05
Enter the rollno127
Student's Details
SName    CName     RollNo
HARI     FF01        123
RUCHIKA  FF02        124
RANJANA  FF03        125
ANJANA   FF04        126
MADHURI  FF05        127
```

EXPLANATION: The declaration student **sarr [5]** creates an array of **5** element of type structure student. The members of first array are accessed as **sarr [0].sname, sarr [0].rollno and sarr [0].cname.**

At the time of compilation **42*5 = 210** bytes are allocated **(42 is the size of structure).** We show this in the tabular format. In the parenthesis we have written number of bytes allocated.

As clear from the diagram 42 bytes are allocated for each array element.

Array	Sname [20]	Cname[20]	Rollno(2)
Sarr[0]	HARI	FF01	123
Sarr[1]	RUCHIKA	FF02	124
Sarr[2]	RANJANA	FF03	125
Sarr[3]	ANJANA	FF04	126
Sarr[4]	MADHURI	FF05	127

```
/*Prog 10.10 Merit list of student*/
#include<stdio.h>
#include<conio.h>
#define S 3
 void main()
 {
    typedef struct student
    {
       char sname[10];
       int rollno;
       int m1,m2,m3;
       float per;
    }student;
    struct student sa[S];
    int rno=101,i,s,j;
    int temp;
    clrscr();
    for(i=0;i<S;i++)
    {
     printf("\n Enter name and marks in threesubjects\n");
     scanf("%s%d%d%d",sa[i].sname,sa[i].m1, sa[i].m2,sa[i].m3);
     sa[i].rollno=rno;
     rno++;
     s=sa[i].m1+sa[i].m2+sa[i].m3;
     sa[i].per=(s/3.0);
   }
   for(i=0;i<S;i++)
   {
     for(j=i+1;j<S;j++)
```

```
        {
         if(sa[i].per<sa[j].per)
         {
        temp=sa[i].per;
        sa[i].per=sa[j].per;
        sa[j].per=temp;
         }
        }
    }
    printf("Student's Merit List \n\n");
    printf("\nName\tRollNo\t Per\n");
    for(i=0;i<S;i++)
    {
      printf("%s\t%d\t",sa[i].sname,sa[i].rollno);
      printf("%f\n",sa[i].per);
    }
 getch();
}
```

Output:

```
 Enter name and marks in three subjects
 Ramesh 89 97 90
 Enter name and marks in three subjects
 Akash 81 91 86
 Enter name and marks in three subjects
 Ravi 88 97 92
Student's Merit List
Name      RollNo     Per
Ramesh    101        92.34
Akash     102        92.00
Ravi      103        86.00
```

EXPLANATION: In the program we have modified the student structure and added three members for marks and one for percentage per. Here we assume that all the marks are from 100. We input name and marks for each student and find out percentage and assign to per field of each array element. We sort the array elements on the basis of per field. We apply the same logic as we applied to sort a simple 1D array. We have also taken a temporary structure variable temp to save array element while students are being swapped.

```
/*Prog 10.11 Sum of two duration ver1*/
#include<stdio.h>
#include<conio.h>
 typedef struct
```

```
{
 int day;
 int month;
 int year;
}duration;
 main()
 {
   duration d1,d2,d3;
   int d,m,y;
   clrscr();
     printf("Enter years,monthe and days for first duration\n");
   scanf("%d%d%d",&d1.year,&d1.month,&d1.day);
     printf("Enter years, month and days for second duration\n");
   scanf("%d%d%d",&d2.year,&d2.month,&d2.day);
   d= (d1.day+d2.day) %30;
   m=d1.month+d2.month+ (d/30);
   y=d1.year+d2.year+ (m/12);
   d3.day=d;
   d3.month=m;
   d3.year=y;
   printf("\nFirst duration\n");
   printf("%dyears%d months",d1.year,d1.month );
   printf("and %d days\n",d1.day);
   printf("\n Second duration \n");
   printf("%d years %d months",d2.year,d2.month );
   printf("and %d days\n",d2.day);
   printf("\n Sum of two durations \n");
   printf("%d years %d months",d3.year,d3.month );
   printf("and %d days \n",d3.day);
   getch();
 }
```

Output:

```
Enter years, month and days for first duration
8 10 12
Enter years, month and days for second duration
5 7 11
First duration
8years10 months and 12 days
Second duration
5 years 7 months and 11 days
```

```
Sum of two durations
14 years 17 months and 23 days
```

EXPLANATION: We have declared structure duration with three members' year, month and day of type integer. We input year, month and day for two structure variables and find out sum of two durations. We assume each month of 30 days.

Our calculation is based on the following logic:

1. We sum days of two structures and the mod of sum by 30 gives us total number of days.
2. Integer division of sum by 30 from step1 gives us extra months.
3. We add months of two structures with extra months from step 2 and mod by 12 this sum gives us total number of months.
4. Integer division of sum by 12 in step 3 gives us extra years.
5. We add year of two structures with extra year from step 4 and sum of these gives us total number of year.

```
/*Prog 10.12 Sum of two durations ver2*/
#include<stdio.h>
#include<conio.h>
 typedef struct
 {
   int sec;
   int min;
   int hour;
 }time;
  main()
  {
    time t1,t2,t3;
    int s,m,h;
    clrscr();
    printf("Enter hrs,mnts and secs for first time\n");
    scanf("%d%d%d",&t1.hour,&t1.min,&t1.sec);
    printf("Enter hrs,mnts and secs for second time\n");
    scanf("%d%d%d",&t2.hour,&t2.min,&t2.sec);
    s=t1.sec+t2.sec;
    m=t1.min+t2.min+s/60;
    h=t1.hour+t2.hour+m/60;
    t3.sec=s%60;
    t3.min=m%60;
    t3.hour=h;
    printf("\nFirst Time Value->\t");
    printf("%0d HRS: %0d MINS", t1.hour,t1.min);
    printf(":%0d SECS\n",t1.sec);
```

```
    printf("\n Second Time Value->\t");
    printf("%0d HRS : %0d MINS",t2.hour,t2.min);
    printf(": %0d SECS\n",t2.sec);
    printf("\n Sum of two time durations -> \t");
    printf("%0d HRS : %0d MINS", t3.hour,t3.min);
    printf(": %0d SECS\n",t3.sec);
    getch();
  }
```

Output:

```
Enter hrs,mnts and secs for first tim12 34 45
Enter hrs,mnts and secs for second time
7 23 67
First Time Value->               12 HRS: 34 MINS: 45 SECS
Second Time Value->              7 HRS: 23 MINS: 67 SECS
Sum of two time durations ->  19 HRS: 58 MINS: 52 SECS
```

EXPLANATION: This program is similar to the previous one except the duration is short now which consists of hours, minutes and seconds.

On the similar basis try to write program for subtraction of two durations.

```
/*Prog 10.13 Complex number arithmetic (sum and multiplication)*/
#include<stdio.h>
#include<conio.h>
 typedef struct
 {
   float real;
   float imag;
 }complex;
 void main()
 {
   complex c1,c2,c3,c4;
   float a,b;
   clrscr();
   printf("Enter the real part for first complexnumber\n");
   scanf("%f",&a);
   printf("Enter the imag part for first complex number\n");
   scanf("%f",&b);
   c1.real=a;
   c1.imag=b;
   printf("Enter the real part for sec complex number \n");
   scanf("%f",&a);
```

```
   printf("Enter the imag part for sec complex number \n");
   scanf("%f",&b);
   c2.real=a;
   c2.imag=b;
   c3.real=c1.real+c2.real;
   c3.imag=c1.imag+c2.imag;
   c4.real=c1.real*c2.real - c1.imag*c2.imag;
   c4.imag=c1.real*c2.imag + c1.imag*c2.real;
   printf("\t Complex Number 1\n");
   printf("\t %5.2f +j%5.2f\n",c1.real,c1.imag);
   printf("\t Complex Number 2\n");
   printf("\t%5.2f +%5.2f\n",c2.real,c2.imag);
   printf("\tSum of C1 & C2\n");
   printf("\t%5.2f + j%5.2f\n",c3.real,c3.imag);
   printf("\t Mul of C1 & C2\n");
   printf("\t%5.2f +j%5.2f\n",c4.real,c4.imag);
   getch();
 }
```

Output:

```
Enter the real part for first complex number
2.0
Enter the imag part for first complex number
1.4
Enter the real part for sec complex number
1.2
Enter the imag part for sec complex number
1.6
         Complex Number 1
          2.00 +j 1.40
         Complex Number 2
         1.20 + 1.60
        Sum of C1 & C2
         3.20 + j 3.00
         Mul of C1 & C2
         0.16 +j 4.88
```

EXPLANATION: In the program we have declared a complex structure. A complex number has two parts one is **real** and second is **imaginary.** Imaginary part is recognized by placing ***j* or *i*** before number and is called **iota.** When two complex numbers are added or subtracted their real parts are added or subtracted separately as well as imaginary part. When two complex numbers are multiplied the resultant complex is obtained as follows:

Assume two complex numbers are ($x1 + jy1$) and ($x2 + jy2$). Here j is called iota and $\surd j$ is – 1 so $j*j$ will be – 1. Now multiplication will be:

$$(x1 + j\,y1) * (x2 + j\,y2) = x1x2 + j\,x1y2 + j\,y1x2 - y1\,y2$$
$$= (x1x2 - y1y2) + j\,(x1y2 + x2y1)$$

Real part

Imaginary part

On the basis of this discussion I think it will be easy to understand the program presented above

10.3 NESTED STRUCTURES

A structure is called a nested structure when one of the members of the structure is itself a structure. For instance, given a structure data type of x, the following statement

```
struct y {
   int i;
   char ch[8];
   struct x nested;
   };
```

Declares a nested structure with a tag name of y, because one of the members of the y structure is a structure with the variable name of nested that is defined by the structure data type of x.

A structure can be nested within a structure. If this is done then nested structure act as a member of containing structure. Let's write few programs to understand this new concept.

```
/*Prog 10.14 Demo of nesting of structure ver1*/
#include<stdio.h>
#include<conio.h>
struct address
{
   char h_no[10];
   int s_no;
   char city[25];
   char state[30];
};
  struct person
  {
   char name[25];
   int age;
   struct address addr;
  };
  void main()
```

```
{
  struct person p;
  clrscr();
  printf("Enter the name and age for the person \n");
  scanf("%s%d",p.name,&p.age);
  printf("Enter the house_no,stree_no,city and state\n");
  scanf("%s%d",p.addr.h_no,&p.addr.s_no);
  scanf("%s%s",p.addr.city,p.addr.state);
  printf("Person Details\n\n");
  printf("Name:\t%s\tAge:\t%d\n",p.name,p.age);
  printf("Address:%s,%d\n",p.addr.h_no,p.addr.s_no);
  printf("\t%s,%s\n",p.addr.city,p.addr.state);
  getch();
}
```

Output:

```
Enter the name and age for the person
Vijay 54
Enter the house_no,stree_no,city and state
s17/127 6 varanasi UP
Person Details
Name:   Vijay    Age:   54
Address:s17/127,6
        Varanasi, UP
```

EXPLANATION: In the **address** structure we have stored the **house number, street number, city and state.** A variable of this structure is a number of **person** structures. Thus to access the members of address structure we have to use dot membership twice say for example ***p*.addr.city.** As ***p*** is a structure variable of person type and because of **addr** as a member of structure person we can write ***p*.addr.** This ***p*.addr** acts as a variable of structure address type and we can access any of its member using **dot operator.** Thus the following statements would be valid

```
struct address ar= p.addr;
```

```
/*Prog 10.15 Demo of nesting of structures ver2*/
#include<stdio.h>
#include<conio.h>
 struct address
 {
   char h_no[10];
   int s_no;
   char city[10];
   char state[10];
 };
```

```
 struct person
 {
  char name[10];
  int age;
  struct address addr;
 };
   main()
  {
      typedef struct person;
      person p={"Vijay" ,54,{"s17/127",5,"Varanasi","UP"}};
      clrscr();
      printf("Person Details\n\n");
      printf("Name:\t%s Age:\t%d\n",p.name,p.age);
      printf("Address:%s,%d\n",p.addr.h_no,p.addr.s_no);
      printf("\t%s,%s\n",p.addr.city.p.addr.state);
      getch();
  }
```

Output:

```
Person Details
Name:   Vijay  Age: 54
Address: s17/127, 5
        Varanasi, UP
```

EXPLANATION: As **person** contains a member as a structure **address,** so when initializing person all members of **address** structure are put into braces.

```
/*Prog 10.16 Nesting of structure date within employee structure*/
struct date
{
  int day;
  int month;
  int year;
};
 struct employee
 {
   char ename[20];
   char dept[20];
   struct date doj;
   char qual[15];
 };
#include<stdio.h>
```

```
#include<conio.h>
 void main()
 {
   struct employee e;
   clrscr();
   printf("Enter the emp name, qual, and dept.\n");
   scanf("%s%s%s",e.ename,e.qual,e.dept);
   printf("Enter the date of joining(dd/mm/yyyy)\n");
   scanf("%d%d%d",&e.doj,&e.doj.month,&e.doj.year);
   printf("Employee Details\n\n");
   printf("Name:\t%s\tDeptt:\t%s\n",e.ename,e.dept);
   printf("Qual:\t%s",e.qual);
   printf("\tDOJ:\t%2d/%2d/%2d\n",e.doj.day,e.doj.month,
           e.doj.year);
   getch();
 }
```

Output:

```
Enter the emp name, qual, and dept.
Hari BTECH CSE
Enter the date of joining (dd/mm/yyyy)
23 07 07
Employee Details
Name:   Hari     Deptt:   CSE
Qual:   BTECH    DOJ:     23/ 7/ 7
```

EXPLANATION: The program is quite simple. For date of joining of employee we have created a separate **date** which act as a member of structure **employee.** No **type checking** has been put for date so even if entered date is invalid program will work.

```
/* Prog 10.17 Demo Using nested structures */
#include <stdio.h>
#include<conio.h>
 struct department
 {
   int code;
   char name[32];
   char position[16];
 };
 typedef struct department DPT;
 struct employee
 {
   DPT d;
```

```
    int id;
    char name[32];
  };
  typedef struct employee EMPLY;
  void InfoDisplay(EMPLY *ptr);
  void InfoEnter(EMPLY *ptr);
  main(void)
  {
    EMPLY info = {
     {1,
       "Lecturer",
       "CSE"
       },
       1,
       "Hari Mohan Pandey"
     };
    clrscr();
    printf("Here is a sample:\n");
    InfoDisplay(&info);
    InfoEnter(&info);
    printf("\nHere are what you entered:\n");
    InfoDisplay(&info);
    getch();
  }
  /* function definition */
  void InfoDisplay(EMPLY *ptr)
  {
    printf("Name: %s\n", ptr->name);
    printf("ID #: %04d\n", ptr->id);
    printf("Dept. name: %s\n", ptr->d.name);
    printf("Dept. code: %02d\n", ptr->d.code);
    printf("Your position: %s\n", ptr->d.position);
  }
 /* function definition */
   void InfoEnter(EMPLY *ptr)
  {
    printf("\nPlease enter your information:\n");
    printf("Your name:\n");
    gets(ptr->name);
    printf("Your position:\n");
```

```
  gets(ptr->d.position);
  printf("Dept. name:\n");
  gets(ptr->d.name);
  printf("Dept. code:\n");
  scanf("%d", &(ptr->d.code));
  printf("Your employee ID #:\n");
  scanf("%d", &(ptr->id));
 }
```

Output:

```
Here is a sample:
Name: Hari Mohan Pandey
ID #: 0001
Dept. name: Lecturer
Dept. code: 01
Your position: CSE
Please enter your information:
Your name:
Vijay
Your position:
Lecturer
Dept. name:
CSE
Dept. code:
001
Your employee ID #:
0001
Here are what you entered:
Name: Vijay
ID #: 0001
Dept. name: CSE
Dept. code: 01
Your position: Lecturer
```

EXPLANATION: There are two structure data types in above given program. The first one, called **department,** is declared in **lines 4_8.** The second one, **employee,** declared in **lines 12_16,** contains a member of the department structure data type. Therefore, the employee structure data type is a **nested structure data type.**

Two synonyms, **DPT for the struct department data type,** and **EMPLY** for the struct employee data type, are created in two **typedef statements,** respectively, in **lines 10 and 18.** In the program, there are two functions, **InfoDisplay() and InfoEnter(),** whose **prototypes** are declared with a **pointer of EMPLY** as the argument (see lines 20 and 21).

The statement in **25_32 initializes a nested structure,** which is called **info** and defined with **EMPLY.** Note that the nested braces **({and}) in lines 26 and 29** enclose the initializers for the *d* structure of **DPT** that is nested inside the **info** structure.

Then, the statement in **line 35** displays the initial contents held by the nested **info** structure by calling the **InfoDisplay()** function. **Line 37** calls the **InfoEnter()** function to ask the user to enter his or her employment information and then save it into the **info** structure. The **InfoDisplay()** function is called again in **line 40** to display the information that the user entered and is now stored in the nested structure.

The definitions for the two functions, **InfoDisplay() and InfoEnter(),** are listed in **lines 45_52 and lines 54_67,** respectively.

10.4 STRUCTURES AND FUNCTION CALLS

The C language allows you to pass an entire structure to a function. In addition, a function can return a structure back to its caller. We can pass structure to function as parameters and have structure as return type for functions. We can also pass addresses of structures to the functions.

Let's write some programs which illustrate this.

```
/*Prog 10.18 Demo of structure with functions*/
 typedef struct
 {
   int ecode;
   char ename[30];
   int esal;
 }emp;
 #include<stdio.h>
 #include<conio.h>
  void main()
  {
    emp e={1023,"Vijay",25000};
    void show(emp);
    clrscr();
    show(e);
    getch();
  }
   void show(emp p)
   {
    printf("Details of Employee\n");
    printf("Name:\t%s\n",p.ename);
```

```
    printf("Ecode:\t%d\n",p.ecode);
    printf("Sal:\t %d\n",p.esal);
   }
```

Output:

```
Details of Employee
Name: Vijay
Ecode: 1023
Sal: 25000
```

EXPLANATION: The statement **voidshow(emp)** tells the compiler that show is function which takes one parameter of type **struct emp.** Had we not type defined the **emp** we would have to write **void show (struct emp);** we call the function **show and pass the variable *e*.** this is **call by value mechanism.** inside **show** we simply display the different fields associated with the structure. To modify any of the field of the structure we pass structure by reference as shown in the next program.

```
/* Prog 10.19 Passing a structure to a function */
#include <stdio.h>
#include<conio.h>
 struct computer
 {
   float cost;
   int year;
   int cpu_speed;
   char cpu_type[16];
 };
 /* create synonym */
   typedef struct computer SC;
 /* function declaration */
   SC DataReceive(SC s);
   main(void)
   {
     SC model;
     clrscr();
     model = DataReceive(model);
     printf("Here are what you entered:\n");
     printf("Year: %d\n", model.year);
     printf("Cost: $%6.2f\n", model.cost);
     printf("CPU type: %s\n", model.cpu_type);
     printf("CPU speed: %d MHz\n", model.cpu_speed);
     getch();
```

```
    }
  /* function definition */
    SC DataReceive(SC s)
    {
     printf("The type of the CPU inside your computer?\n");
     gets(s.cpu_type);
     printf("The speed(MHz) of the CPU?\n");
     scanf("%d", &s.cpu_speed);
     printf("The year your computer was made?\n");
     scanf("%d", &s.year);
     printf("How much you paid for the computer?\n");
     scanf("%f", &s.cost);
     return s;
    }
```

```
Output:
The type of the CPU inside your computer?
Pentium
The speed(MHz) of the CPU?
156
The year your computer was made?
1999
How much you paid for the computer?
25000
Here are what you entered:
Year: 1999
Cost: $25000.00
CPU type: Pentium
CPU speed: 156 MHz
```

EXPLANATION: The purpose of the program is to show you how to pass a structure to a function. The structure with the tag name of **computer** is declared in **lines 4_9.**

Note that in **line 11** the **typedef** keyword is used to define a **synonym, SC,** for structure computer. Then **SC** is used in the **sequential declarations.**

The **DataReceive()** function is declared in **line 13,** with the structure of computer as its argument (that is, the synonym **SC** and the variable **name s**), so that a copy of the structure can be passed to the function.

In addition, the **DataReceive()** function returns the copy of the structure back to the caller after the content of the structure is updated. To do this, **SC** is prefixed to the function in **line 13** to indicate the data type of the value returned by the function.

The statement in **line 17** defines the **structure model** with **SC.** The **DataReceive()** function is passed with the name of the model structure in **line 19,** and then the value returned by the function is assigned back to model as well. Note that if the **DataReceive()** function return value is not assigned to model, the changes made to **s** in the function will not be evident in model.

The definition of the **DataReceive()** function is shown in **lines 29_40,** from which you can see that the new data values entered by the user are saved into the corresponding members of the structure that is passed to the function. At the end of the function, the copy of the updated structure is returned in **line 39.**

Then, back to the **main()** function of the program, **lines 21_24** print out the updated contents held by the members of the structure.

10.5 POINTING TO STRUCTURES

As you can pass a function with a pointer that refers to an array, you can also pass a function with a pointer that points to a structure.

However, unlike passing a structure to a function, which sends an entire copy of the structure to the function, passing a pointer of a structure to a function is simply passing the address that associates the structure to the function. The function can then use the address to access the structure members without duplicating the structure. Therefore, it's more efficient to pass a pointer of a structure, rather than the structure itself, to a function.

For example: For the structure given below as

```
struct person
{
      char name[20];
      int age;
};
We can write
      struct person per, *ptr;
      ptr = &per
```

```
/* Prog 10.20 Demo of Pointing to a structure */
#include <stdio.h>
#include<conio.h>
struct computer
{
    float cost;
    int year;
    int cpu_speed;
    char cpu_type[30];
};
  typedef struct computer SC;
```

```
  void DataReceive(SC *ptr_s);
  main(void)
  {
  SC model;
  clrscr();
  DataReceive(&model);
  printf("Here are what you entered:\n");
  printf("Year: %d\n", model.year);
  printf("Cost: $%d\n", model.cost);
  printf("CPU type: %s\n", model.cpu_type);
  printf("CPU speed: %d MHz\n", model.cpu_speed);
  getch();
}
/* function definition */
    void DataReceive(SC *ptr_s)
    {
      printf("The type of the CPU inside your computer?\n");
      gets((*ptr_s).cpu_type);
      printf("The speed(MHz) of the CPU?\n");
      scanf("%d", &(*ptr_s).cpu_speed);
      printf("The year your computer was made?\n");
      scanf("%d", &(*ptr_s).year);
      printf("How much you paid for the computer?\n");
      scanf("%d", &(*ptr_s).cost);
    }
```

Output:

```
The type of the CPU inside your computer?
Pentium with HT
The speed (MHz) of the CPU?
156
The year your computer was made?
2002
How much you paid for the computer?
26000
Here are what you entered:
Year: 2002
Cost: $26000
CPU type: Pentium with HT
```

```
CPU speed: 156 MHz
```

EXPLANATION: The program shown above is almost identical to the one given earlier except that the argument passed to the **DataReceive()** function is a pointer defined with **SC**—that is, structure computer. **(Refer to lines 11 and 13.)** Also, the **DataReceive()** function does not need to return a copy of the structure because the function can access all members of the original structure, not the copy, via the pointer passed to it. That's why the **void** keyword is prefixed to the function name in **line 13.**

The statement in **line 17** defines the structure model. And in **line 19,** the address of the model structure is passed to the **DataReceive** function by applying the **address-of operator (&).**

When you look at the definition of the **DataReceive()** function in **lines 29_39,** you see that the **dereferenced pointer *ptr_s** is used to reference the members of the model structure. For instance, to access the **char array** of **cpu_type, (*ptr_s)** is used in the **(*ptr_s).cpu_type** expression to indicate to the compiler that **cpu_type** is a member in the structure pointed to by the pointer **ptr_s.** Note that the **dereferenced pointer *ptr_s** has to be enclosed within the parentheses **((and)).**

Another example is the **&(*ptr_s).cpu_speed** expression in **line 34,** which leads to the address of the **cpu_speed** variable that is a member of the structure pointed to by the pointer **ptr_s.** Again, the dereferenced pointer ***ptr_s** is surrounded by the parentheses ((and)).

The next subsection shows you how to use the arrow operator (->) to refer to a structure member with a pointer.

10.5.1 Referencing A Structure Member With → (Arrow Operator)

You can use the **arrow operator ->** to refer to a structure member with a pointer that points to the structure.

For instance, you can rewrite the (*ptr_s).cpu_type expression in above program with this:

```
ptr_s -> cpu_type
```

Or you could replace the **&(*ptr_s).cpu_speed** expression with this:

```
&(ptr_s->cpu_speed)
```

Because of its clearness, the **-> operator** is more frequently used in programs than the dot operator.

```
/*Prog 10.21 Demo of structure with function and pointer ver 1*/
#include<stdio.h>
#include<conio.h>
 struct emp
 {
   int ecode;
   char ename[30];
   int esal;
 };
 void main()
 {
```

```
    struct emp e={1023,"Vijay",25000};
    void modify(struct emp*);
    modify(&e);
    printf("Details of Employee\n");
    printf("Name:\t%s\n",p.ename);
    printf("Ecode:\t%d\n",p.ecode);
    printf("Sal:\t%d\n",p.esal);
    getch();
  }
    void modify(emp *p)
    {
       p->ecode=1025;
       p->ename="Hari";
        (*p).esal=30000;
    }
```

Output:

```
Details of Employee
Name: Hari
Ecode: 1025
Sal:30000
```

EXPLANATION: The statement **void modify(struct emp*)** tell the compiler that modify is a function which accepts address of variable of **struct emp** type. As we call the function by reference whatever changes performed inside the function they persist even if control comes out from the function so the next few **printf** statement display the modified displayed of the structure **emp.**

```
/*Prog 10.22 Demo of structure with function and pointer ver2*/
typedef struct
{
  int ecode;
  char ename[30];
  int esal;
}emp;
 void main()
 {
    emp e1,e2;
    void input(emp*);
    void show(emp);
    clrscr();
    input(&e1);
    input(&e2);
```

```
   show(e2);
   getch();
}
   void input(emp*ptr)
   {
      static int i;
      printf("Enter code, name and sal for Emp %d\n",++i);
      scanf("%d%s%d",&ptr->ecode,ptr->ename,&ptr->esal);
   }
   void show(emp p)
   {
      static int i;
      printf("\n Details of Employee %d\n",++i);
      printf("Name:\t%s\n",p.ename);
      printf("Ecode:\t%d\n",p.ecode);
      printf("Sal:\t%d\n",p.esal);
   }
```

Output:

```
Enter code, name and sal for Emp 1
1024 Hari 20000
Enter code, name and sal for Emp 2
1245 Ranjana 23000
Details of Employee 2
Name: Hari
Ecode: 1024
Sal: 20000
Details of Employee 1
Name:   Ranjana
Ecode:  1245
Sal:    23000
```

EXPLANATION: The **input** function accepts data from keyboard and stores in the structure variable. Calling function by reference ensures that data goes into *e*1 **and** *e*2 through pointer. In the **show** function we simply show the fields of the members so there is no need to pass the address of the structure variable. The use of **static** is self-explanatory.

```
/*Prog 10.23 Demo of structure with pointer ver 1*/
#include<stdio.h>
#include<conio.h>
typedef struct
```

```
{
    int icode;
    char iname[30];
    int quan;
    int uprice;
}item;
    void main()
    {
        item i1;
        item *p;
        clrscr();
        p=&i1;
        printf("Enter item code, item name, quan. and unit
        price\n");
        scanf("%d%s%d%d",&p->icode,p->iname,&p->quan,&p->uprice);
        printf("\nItem Code=%d\n",(*p).icode);
        printf("Item Name =%s\n",p->iname);
        printf("Item Quan=%d\n",(&i1)->quan);
        printf("Unit price=%d\n",i1.uprice);
        getch();
    }
```

Output:

```
Enter item code, item name, quan. and unit price
112 Mouse 20 200
Item Code=112
Item Name =Mouse
Item Quan=20
Unit price=200
```

EXPLANATION: In the item structure we have created four members item code,item name, number of items *i.e.,* quantity and unit price. The statement item **p* creates a pointer of item type and in it we assign the address of variable *i*1 of type item. To access the members of structure using this pointer *p* we use -> operator called pointer member operator. To access say icode we can follow any of the two approaches:

(*a*) p-> icode

(*b*) (*p).icode

We can also write (&*i*1)->icode or our usual method *i*1.code.

If we want we can create the pointer to structure in this manner also

```
struct item
{
    int icode;
```

```
    char iname[10];
    int quan;
    int uprice;
} i1,*p;
/*Prog 10.24 demo of structure with pointer ver 2*/
struct date
{
   int day;
   int month;
   int year;
};
   struct employee
   {
     char ename[15];
     char dept[15];
     struct date doj;
     char qual[20];
   };
#include<stdio.h>
#include<conio.h>
 void main()
 {
  struct employee e={"Vijay","Comp",{23,07,2007},"MTECH" };
  struct date *d=&e.doj;
  clrscr();
  printf("Employee details\n\n");
  printf("Name:\t%s\tDeptt:\t%s\n",e.ename,e.dept);
  printf("Qualification:\t%s",e.qual);
  printf("\tDOJ:\t%2d/%2d/%2d\n",d->day,d->month,d->year);
  getch();
 }
```

Output:

```
Employee details
Name:    Vijay    Deptt:  Comp
Qualification:    MTECH  DOJ:    23/ 7/2007
```

EXPLANATION: We have used the structure **employee and date** created earlier in programs. We have defined a pointer to **date** structure variable **doj** which is embedded in employee structure and printed the date of joining using this **pointer *d*.**

```
/*Prog 10.25 Complex number arithmetic using function and pointers*/
#include<stdio.h>
#include<conio.h>
typedef struct
{
  float real;
  float imag;
}complex;
void main()
{
  complex input();
  void show(char *,complex);
  complex sum(complex,complex);
  complex sub(complex,complex);
  complex mul(complex,complex);
  complex c1,c2,c3,c4,c5;
  clrscr();
  c1=input();
  c2=input();
  c3=sum(c1,c2);
  c4=sub(c1,c2);
  c5=mul(c1,c2);
  show("First Number: ",c1);
  show("Second Number: ",c2);
  show("Sum: ",c3);
  show("Sub: ",c4);
  show("Mul: ",c5);
  getch();
}
  complex input()
  {
    static complex temp;
    printf("Enter real and imaginary part\n");
    scanf("%f%f",&temp.real,&temp.imag);
    return temp;
  }
  void show(char *msg,complex c)
  {
   printf(msg);
   printf("%4.2f + j%4.2f\n",c.real, c.imag);
```

```
}
complex sum(complex A, complex B)
{
  static complex temp;
  temp.real=A.real + B.real;
  temp.imag= A.imag+B.imag;
  return temp;
}
complex sub(complex A, complex B)
{
  static complex temp;
  temp.real=A.real+B.real;
  temp.imag= A.imag+B.imag;
  return temp;
}
 complex mul(complex A, complex B)
 {
   static complex temp;
   temp.real= A.real*B.real-A.imag*B.imag;
   temp.imag= A.real*B.imag+A.imag*B.real;
   return temp;
 }
```

Output:

```
Enter real and imaginary part
1.0 2.0
Enter real and imaginary part
3.0 2.0
First Number: 1.00 + j2.00
Second Number: 3.00 + j2.00
Sum: 4.00 + j4.00
Sub: 4.00 + j4.00
Mul: -1.00 + j8.00
```

EXPLANATION: Do not go over the length of the program. The program is quite simple if you observe it carefully. We have **five functions** one for **input,** one for **display** and other three are for **addition, subtraction and multiplication** of complex number respectively.

The statement **complex input ()** tells the compiler that **input** is a function which returns a variable of complex type and accepts zero parameters.

Similarly **complex sum (complex, complex)** tells the compiler that **sum** is a function that accepts two parameters of **complex** type and return the value of **complex** type. The function show accepts two parameters one is the string which we want to display and second is the **complex number** which you want to show. The function definitions are quite self-explanatory as the logic has been clearly stipulated earlier in the program with the difference that now it is put into the functions.

10.6 UNION (WHAT IS A UNION?)

A union is a **block of memory** that is used to hold data items of different types. In C, a union is similar to a structure, except that data items saved in the union are **overlaid in order to share the same memory location.** More details on the differences between unions and structures are discussed in the latter sections.

In other words union is similar to structure with the difference that all the member share the same memory area allocated to the element having maximum memory size. In structure each member has its own memory area

Table 10.1 ***The difference between structure and union.***

Example of structure	Example of union

`struct student`
`{`
`int reg_no;`
`char sname[15];`
`char sex;`
`};`
When the above statement is compiled 18 bytes are allocated as:
1. **2 byte for int reg_no.**
2. **15*1=15 for char sname[15].**
3. **1 byte for char sex.**
Therefore, **2+15+1=18bytes**
	`union student`
	`{`
	`int reg_no;`
	`char sname[15];`
	`char sex;`
	`};`
	If the same code we define in terms of union as shown above the only **15 bytes** will be allocated **(size of sname)** and all the members will be sharing this allocated **15 bytes memory block**

Due to this peculiar characteristic of union only one member can be used at a time. That's why they are used in application where at a time one member is needed.

10.6.1 Declaring Unions

The syntax for declaring a **union** is similar to the syntax for a **structure.** The following is an example of a union declaration:

```
union automobile {
        int year;
        char model[8];
        int engine_power;
        float weight;
};
```

Here **union is the keyword** that specifies the union data type. **automobile is the tag name** of the union. The variables, such as **year, model, engine_power, and weight,** are **members** of the union, and are declared within the braces (**{ and }**). The union declaration **ends** with a **semicolon (;).**

Like a structure tag name, a union tag name is a **label** to a union, which is used by the **compiler to identify the union.**

10.6.2 Defining Union Variables

You can define union variables after declaring a union. For instance, the following union variables are defined with the union labeled with automobile from the previous section:

```
union automobile sedan, pick_up, sport_utility;
```

Here the three variables, **sedan, pick_up, and sport_utility,** are defined as the union variables.

You can declare a union and define variables of the union in a single statement. For instance, you can rewrite the previous union declaration and definition like this:

```
union automobile {
    int year;
    char model[8];
    int engine_power;
    float weight;
} sedan, pick_up, sport_utility;
```

Here three union variables, **sedan, pick_up, and sport_utility,** are defined by the union of **automobile** in which there are **four members of different data types.**

If you declare a union and define variables of the union in a single statement, and **there is no more union variable definition made with the union,** you can **omit the tag name** of the union. For instance, the tag name automobile can be omitted in the union definition like this:

```
union {
    int year;
    char model[8];
    int engine_power;
    float weight;
} sedan, pick_up, sport_utility;
```

Omit the tag name automobile if you declare a union and define variable of the union in a single statement and there is no more union variable made with the union.

10.6.3 Referring A Union With Dot (.) Or ->

As well as being used to reference structure members, the dot operator (.) can be used in referencing union members. For example, the following statement assigns the value of 1997 to one of the members of the sedan union:

```
sedan.year = 1997;
```

Here the dot operator is used to separate the union name sedan and the member name year. In addition, if you define a pointer ptr like this:

```
union automobile *ptr;
```

Then you can reference one of the union members in the following way:

```
ptr->year = 1997;
```

Here the **arrow operator (->)** is used to reference the union member year with the pointer ptr.

```
/*Prog 10.26 Demo of referencing a union */
 #include <stdio.h>
 #include <string.h>
 #include<conio.h>
  void main(void)
  {
   union menu {
 char name[23];
 double price;
   } dish;
   clrscr();
   printf("The content assigned to the union separately:\n");
   /* reference name */
   strcpy(dish.name, "Sweet and Sour Chicken");
   printf("Dish Name: %s\n", dish.name);
   /* reference price */
   dish.price = 75.95;
   printf("Dish Price: %5.2f\n", dish.price);
   getch();
  }
```

Output:

```
The content assigned to the union separately:
Dish Name: Sweet and Sour Chicken
Dish Price: 75.95
```

EXPLANATION: The purpose of the program is to show you how to **reference union members with the dot operator.**

Inside the **main ()** function, a union, **called dish,** is first defined with the **union data type of menu in lines 7_10.** There are two members, **name and price,** in the union.

Then the statement in **line 14** assigns the string **"Sweet and Sour Chicken"** to the character array name that is one of the union members. Note that the **dish. name** expression is used as the first argument to the **strcpy()** function in **line 14.** When the compiler sees the expression, it knows that we want to reference the memory location of **name** that is a member of the **dish union.**

The **strcpy()** function is a C function that copies the contents of a string pointed to by the function's **second argument** to the memory storage pointed to by the function's first **argument.** I included the header file **string.h** in the program before calling the **strcpy()** function. **(See line 2.)**

Line 15 prints out the contents copied to the name array by using the **dish.name** expression one more time.

The statement in **line 17** assigns the value **75.95** to the **double** variable **price,** which is another member for the **dish union.** Note that the **dish.price** expression is used to reference the union member. Then **line 18** displays the value assigned to price by calling the **printf()** function and passing the **dish.price** expression as an argument to the function.

According to the results shown in the output, the two members of the **dish union, name and price,** have been successfully referenced and assigned corresponding values.

```
/*Prog 10.27 Demo of union ver 1*/
#include<stdio.h>
#include<conio.h>
union person
{
  int id;
  char sex;
};
 void main()
 {
   union person p;
   clrscr();
   p.id=15;
   printf("Id is %d\n",p.id);
   p.sex='M';
   printf("Sex is %c \n",p.sex);
   printf("Size of union is %d\n",sizeof(union person));
   getch();
 }
```

Output:

```
Id is 15
Sex is M
Size of union is 2
```

EXPLANATION: In the program union person containing two members id of type int and sex of type char. As size of int is 2 (on turbo C) and size of char is 1 so when a variable of this union person is created 2 bytes will be allocated and both its members will share this 2 byte storage area. In the program we have first used id then after displaying it we have used sex. What will happen if we initialize both first and then display? See the next program.

```
/*Prog 10.28 Demo of union ver 2*/
#include<stdio.h>
#include<conio.h>
```

```
union person
{
  int id;
  char sex;
};
  void main()
  {
     union person p;
     clrscr();
     p.id=12;
     p.sex='M';
     printf("ID is %d\n",p.id);
     printf("SEX is %c\n",p.sex);
     getch();
  }
```

Output:

```
ID is 77
SEX is M
```

EXPLANATION: Note the program note ***p*.sex** is initialized id so this later will be stored in 2 byte memory area and id will have garbage value. If you reverse these two initializations sex will have garbage value.

A union can also be type defined and can also be declared and defined simultaneously.

```
  typedef union
 {
          char code;
          int quan;
  } item;
 item i1= { 'L',20};
```

However as only one member of union can be used at any time, this type of declaration and definition is not used with union.

An array of union is also possible but it is used rarely. See the next program.

```
/*Prog 10.29 Array of union */
#include<stdio.h>
#include<conio.h>
   union intchar
   {
       int no;
       char ch;
   };
   void main()
```

```
{
union intchar arr[5];
int i;
clrscr();
printf("Size of arr is %d\n",sizeof(arr));
for(i=0;i<=4;i++)
arr[i].no=i;
printf("Numbers are\n");
for(i=0;i<=4;i++)
printf("arr[%d].no=%d\n",i,arr[i].no);
for(i=0;i<=4;i++)
arr[i].ch='A'+i;
printf("Characters are \n");
for(i=0;i<=4;i++)
printf("arr[%d].ch=%c\n",i,arr[i].ch);
getch();
}
```

Output:

```
Size of arr is 10
Numbers are
arr[0].no=0
arr[1].no=1
arr[2].no=2
arr[3].no=3
arr[4].no=4
Characters are
arr[0].ch=A
arr[1].ch=B
arr[2].ch=C
arr[3].ch=D
arr[4].ch=E
```

EXPLANATION: We have created an array of union of **5** elements. Initially we have used the no field of each **union** member and after displaying them we have initialized them the **ch** field and displayed them.

10.6.4 Initializing a Union

As mentioned earlier in this chapter, data items in a union are overlaid at the same memory location. In other words, the memory location of a union is shared by different members of the union at different times. The size of a union is equal to the size of the largest data item in the list of the union members, which is large enough to hold any members of the union, one at a time. Therefore, it does not make sense to initialize all members of a union together because the value of the latest initialized member overwrites the value of the preceding member. You initialize a member of a union only when you are ready to use it. The value contained by a union is the value that is latest assigned to a member of the union.

For instance, if we declare and define a union on a 16-bit machine (that is, the int data type is 2 bytes long) like this:

```
union u {
   char ch;
   int x;
} a_union;
```

Then the following statement initializes the char variable **ch** with the character constant **'H'**:

```
a_union.ch = 'H';
```

And the value contained by the **a_union** union is the character constant **'H'. However, if the int** variable *x* is initialized by the following statement:

```
a_union.x = 365;
```

Then the value contained by the a_union union becomes the value of 365. Demonstrates the content change of the union during the two initializations.

According to the **ANSI C standard,** a union can be initialized by assigning the first union member with a value. For instance, in the following statement:

```
union u {
   char ch;
   int x;
} a_union = {'H'};
```

The **a_union** union is said to be initialized because the character constant **'H'** is assigned to the first union member, **ch.**

If the first member of a union is a structure, the entire structure has to be initialized with a list of values before the union can be said to have been initialized.

```
/*Prog 10.30 Demo of Memory sharing in unions */
#include <stdio.h>
#include <conio.h>
void main(void)
{
   union employee {
       int start_year;
       int dpt_code;
       int id_number;
   } info;
   clrscr();
   /* initialize start_year */
```

```
    info.start_year = 2007;
    /* initialize dpt_code */
    info.dpt_code = 12;
    /* initialize id */
    info.id_number = 2345;
    /* display content of union */
    printf("Start Year:   %d\n", info.start_year);
    printf("Dpt. Code:    %d\n", info.dpt_code);
    printf("ID Number:    %d\n", info.id_number);
    getch();
  }
```

Output:

```
Start Year:   2345
Dpt. Code:    2345
ID Number:    2345
```

EXPLANATION: As you can see in program, a union called **info** has three int variable members, **start_year, dpt_code, and id_number. (See lines 6_10.)** Then, these three union members are assigned with different values consecutively in **lines 13, 15, and 17.** And in **lines 20_22,** we try to print out the values assigned to the three members. However, the output shows that every member in the info union has the same value, 2345, which is the integer assigned to the third member of the union, **id_number.** Note that **id_number** is the member that is assigned with 2345 last; the **info union** does hold the latest value assigned to its members.

10.6.5 The Size of a Union

As we know that the members of a union share the same memory location. The size of a union is the same as the size of the largest member in the union.

In contrast with a union, all members of a structure can be initialized together without any overwriting. This is because each member in a structure has its own memory storage. The size of a structure is equal to the sum of sizes of its members instead of the size of the largest member.

How do we come to know that whether all these are true? Well, we can prove it by measuring the size of a union or a structure.

Now we show here a program that measures the size of a union as well as the size of a structure. The structure has exactly the same members as the union.

```
/* Prog 10.31 Demo for the size of a union */
#include <stdio.h>
#include <string.h>
#include<conio.h>
 void main(void)
 {
```

```
   union u {
 double x;
 int y;
   } a_union;
   struct s {
     double x;
       int y;
   } a_struct;
   clrscr();
   printf("The size of double: %d-byte\n", sizeof(double));
   printf("The size of int: %d-byte\n", sizeof(int));
   printf("The size of a_union: %d-byte\n", sizeof(a_union));
   printf("The size of a_struct: %d-byte\n", sizeof(a_struct));
   getch();
 }
```

Output:

```
The size of double: 8-byte
The size of int: 2-byte
The size of a_union: 8-byte
The size of a_struct: 10-byte
```

EXPLANATION: The purpose of the program is to show the difference between a **union memory allocation** and a **structure memory allocation,** although both the union and the structure consist of the same members.

A union, called **a_union,** is defined in **lines 7_10;** it has two members, a **double** variable *x* and an **int** variable *y.* In addition, a structure, called **a_structure** and defined in **lines 12_15,** also consists of two members, a **double variable x and an int variable *y*.**

The statements in **lines 17_20** first measure the **sizes** of the **double and int** data types on the host machine. For instance, on my machine, the **size** of the **double data type is 8 bytes long and the int** data type is **2 bytes** long.

Then **lines 22_25** measure the sizes of the **a_union** union and **the a_structure** structure, respectively. From the output, we see that the size of **a_union is 8 bytes long.** In other words, the size of the union is the same as the size of the largest member, ***x*, in the union.**

The size of the structure, on the other hand, is the sum of the sizes of two members, *x* and *y*, in the structure **(10 bytes in total).**

10.6.6 Using Unions (Applications of Union/ Why We Use Union ?)

Now let's focus on the applications of unions. Basically, there are two kinds of union applications, which are introduced in the following two sections.

(a) Referencing the Same Memory Location Differently

The first application of unions is to reference the same memory location with different union members.

To get a better idea about referencing the same memory with different union members, let's have a look at the program which is given below, which uses the two members of a union to reference the same memory location. (We assume that the **char** data type is **1 byte long,** and the **int data type is 2 bytes long,** which are true on many machines.)

```
/* Prog 10.32 Demo of referencing the same memory in different ways */
#include <stdio.h>
#include<conio.h>
union u{
    char ch[2];
    int num;
  };
 int UnionInitialize(union u val);// function declaration.
 main(void)
 {
    union u val;
    int x;
    clrscr();
    x = UnionInitialize(val);
    printf("The two character constants held by the union:\n");
    printf("%c\n", x & 0x00FF);
    printf("%c\n", x >> 8);
    getch();
 }
 /* function definition */
 int UnionInitialize(union u val)
 {
    val.ch[0] = 'H';
    val.ch[1] = 'i';
    return val.num;
}
```

Output:

```
The two character constants held by the union:
H
I
```

EXPLANATION: As you see from the program a union called **val** is defined in **line 13.** It contains two members: one is a **char array ch** and the other is an **int variable num.** If a char data type is **1 byte**

long and an int data type is **2 bytes** long, the **ch** array and the integer variable num have the same length of memory storage on those machines.

A function named **UnionInitialize()** is called and passed with the union name **val** in **line 16.** The definition of the **UnionInitialize()** function is shown in **lines 25_31.**

From the function definition, you can see that the two elements of the **char array ch** are initialized with two character constants, **'H' and 'i' (in lines 27 and 28).** Because the char array **ch** and the **int** variable **num** share the same memory location, we can return the value of **num** that contains the same content as the **ch array.** (See **line 30.**) Here we've used the two members, **ch and num,** in the val union to reference the same memory location and the same contents of the union.

The value returned by the **UnionInitialize()** function is assigned to an int variable *x* **in line 16 inside the main ()** function. The statements in **lines 19 and 20** print out the **2 bytes** of the int variable **num.** Each byte of num corresponds to a character that is used to initialize the **ch** array because num and **ch** are all in the same union and have the same content of the union. **Line 19** displays the low byte **of num** returned by the *x* **& 0x00FF** expression. In **line 20,** the high byte of **num** is obtained by shifting the *x* **variable to the right by 8 bits.** That is, by using the **shift-right operator in the x >> 8 expression.**

From the output, you can see that the content of the **val** union is shown on the screen correctly.

NOTE: There are two formats to store a multiple-byte quantity, such as the **int** variable **num** in program 10.31. One of the formats is called the **little-endian format;** the other is the **big-endian format.**

(*a*) Little-ending format.

(*b*) Big-endian format.

For the **little-endian format,** the high bytes of a multiple-byte quantity are stored at higher memory addresses and the low bytes are saved at lower addresses. The little-endian format is used by **Intel's 80x86 microprocessors.** My computer's CPU is a **Pentium microprocessor,** which is one of the members in the **80*x* 86 families.** Therefore, in the program 10.31, the character constant **'H',** which is a low byte, is stored at the lower address. ***'i'*** is stored at the higher address because it's a **high byte.**

The **big-endian** format is just opposite. That is, the high bytes are stored at lower addresses; the low bytes are stored at higher addresses. **Motorola's 68000 microprocessor** family uses the **big-endian format.**

(b) Making Structures Flexible

The second application of unions is to nest a union inside a structure so that the structure can hold different types of values.

For example, suppose we want to write a program that asks the user about the name of a cable company or a satellite dish company that provides service to the user. Assume that the user either uses a cable or a satellite dish at home, but not both. Then, if we define two character arrays to store the cable company and satellite dish company names respectively, one of the arrays will be empty due to the assumption. In this case, we can declare a union with the two character arrays as its members so that the union can hold either a cable company name or a satellite dish company name, depending on the user's input. The next section demonstrates how to write a program with such a union.

```
/*Prog 10.33 Demo of Using unions (Making structure more flexible) */
#include <stdio.h>
#include <string.h>
#include <conio.h>
  struct survey
  {
     char name[20];
     char c_d_p;
     int age;
     int hour_per_week;
     union {
      char cable_company[16];
      char dish_company[16];
    } provider;
  };
  void DataEnter(struct survey *s);
  void DataDisplay(struct survey *s);
  void main(void)
  {
   struct survey tv;
   DataEnter(&tv);
   DataDisplay(&tv);
   getch();
  }
  /* function definition */
  void DataEnter(struct survey *ptr)
  {
   char is_yes[4];
   printf("Are you using cable at home? (Yes or No)\n");
   gets(is_yes);
    if ((is_yes[0] =='Y') ||(is_yes[0] == 'y'))
    {
        printf("Enter the cable company name:\n");
        gets(ptr->provider.cable_company);
        ptr->c_d_p = 'c';
      }
    else
    {
```

```
    printf("Are you using a satellite dish? (Yes or No)\n");
      gets(is_yes);
   if ((is_yes[0] == 'Y')||(is_yes[0] == 'y'))
   {
    printf("Enter the satellite dish company name:\n");
     gets(ptr->provider.dish_company);
     ptr->c_d_p = 'd';
   }
   else
   {
      ptr->c_d_p = 'p';
   }
   }
   printf("Please enter your name:\n");
   gets(ptr->name);
   printf("Your age:\n");
   scanf("%d", &ptr->age);
   printf("How many hours you spend on watching TV per week:\n");
   scanf("%d", &ptr->hour_per_week);
  }
 /* function definition */
 void DataDisplay(struct survey *ptr)
 {
  printf("\nHere's what you've entered:\n");
  printf("Name: %s\n", ptr->name);
  printf("Age: %d\n", ptr->age);
  printf("Hour per week: %d\n", ptr->hour_per_week);
  if (ptr->c_d_p == 'c')
    printf("Your cable company is: %s\n",
    ptr->provider.cable_company);
  else if (ptr->c_d_p == 'd')
    printf("Your satellite dish company is: %s\n",
    ptr->provider.dish_company);
  else
    printf("You don't have cable or a satellite dish.\n");
    printf("\nThanks and Bye!\n");
  }
```

Output:

```
Are you using cable at home? (Yes or No)
```

```
Y
Enter the cable company name:
XYZ
Please enter your name:
HARI MOHAN PANDEY
Your age:
24
How many hours you spend on watching TV per week:
12
Here's what you've entered:
Name: HARI MOHAN PANDEY
Age: 24
Hour per week: 12
Your cable company is: XYZ
Thanks and Bye!
```

EXPLANATION: As you can see in **lines 5_14,** a structure data type with the tag name survey is declared, and in it a nested union called provider has two members, the cable_company array and the dish_company array. The two members of the union are used to hold the names of cable or satellite dish companies, depending on the user's input.

The statements in **lines 16 and 17** declare two functions, **DataEnter()** and **DataDisplay(),** in which a pointer with **struct survey** is passed to the two functions as the argument.

A structure called *tv* is defined in **line 21** inside the **main()** function. Then in **lines 23 and 24,** the **DataEnter() and DataDisplay()** functions are invoked with the address of the **tv** structure as their argument.

Lines 29_58 contain the definition of the **DataEnter()** function, which asks the user to enter proper information, based on the survey questions. Under the assumption we made earlier, the user can use either cable or a satellite dish, but not both. If the user does use cable, then **line 38** receives the cable company name entered by the user and saves it into the memory storage referenced by one of the members in the provider union, **cable_company.**

If the user uses a satellite dish, then **line 46** stores the satellite dish company name entered by the user into the same location of the provider union. But this time the name of another union member, **dish_company,** is used to reference the memory location. Now you see how to save the memory by putting two exclusive data items into a union.

In fact, the program supports another situation in which the user has neither cable nor a satellite dish. In this case, the **char** variable ***c_d_p*,** which is a member of the structure, is assigned with the character constant ***'p'*.**

Lines 60_75 give the definition of the **DataDisplay()** function that prints out the information entered by the user back to the screen.

10.7 STRUCTURE AND BIT FIELD

A bit field is one bit or set of adjacent bits that are grouped in a word. A word may be of 8-bits or 16 bits. These bit fields can be made member of structure and can be used independently just like any other member of structure. The number of bits in a bit field variable specifies the range of values which can be stored in the bit field variable. Again as usual we write few programs to understand bit fields.

As you know, char is the smallest data type in C. On many machines, the char data type is 8 bits long. However, with the help of the struct keyword, we can declare a smaller object—a bit field—which allows you to access a single bit. A bit is able to hold one of the two values, 1 or 0.

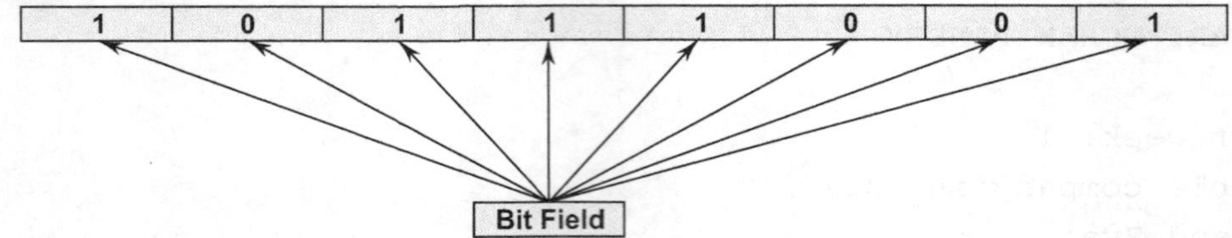

Fig. 10.2 *Description of Bit Field (each bit 1 or 0)*

The general form to declare and define **bit fields** is given below:

```
struct tag_name {
   data_type name1: length 1;
   data_type name2: length 2;
   . . .
   data_type nameN: length N;
} variable_list;
```

Here the struct keyword is used to start the declaration. **tag_name** is the tag name of the struct data type. **data_type,** which must be either **int, unsigned, or signed,** specifies the data type of **bit fields. names1, name2, and name** N are names of bit fields. **length1, length2, and lengthN** indicate the lengths of bit fields, which may not exceed the length of the int data type. **variable_list** contains the variable names of the bit field.

```
/*Prog 10.34 Demo of structure and bit field ver 1*/
#include <stdio.h>
#include <conio.h>
 struct bfield
 {
   unsigned a:3;
   unsigned b:1;
   signed c:2;
 };
 void main()
 {
   struct bfield var;
```

```
  clrscr();
  var.a=7;
  var.b=1;
  var.c=2;
  printf("Size of struct bfield is");
  printf("%d\n",sizeof(structbfield));
  printf("var.a=%d\nvar.b=%d\nvar.c=%d\n",
  var.a,var.b,var.c);
  getch();
}
```

Output:

```
Size of struct bfield is1
var.a=7
var.b=1
var.c=-2
```

EXPLANATION: In the program we have three bit-field members of structure **bfield.** Note how the structure is declared.

data type variable: number of bits

Only int, signed int or unsigned int can be used as data type. The meaning of each of the line within structure is explained below:

- **unsigned a: 3:** declares member *a* with 3 bits *i.e.,* we can store an unsigned number in the range **0 to 7** in ***a*** **.(0 to 2^3 – 1)**
- **unsigned b: 1:** declares member *b* with **1 bit** *i.e.,* we can store an unsigned number in the range **0** to **1in** ***b*****.(0 to 2^1 – 1).**
- **signed** ***a*****: 2:** declare member **c** with **3 bits** *i.e.,* we can store a signed number in the range **– 2 to 1.(– 2^2 – 1 to 2^{2-1} – 1)**

That the size of **var** is **1** ***i.e.,*** **1 byte.** This is because compiler does not allocate **6 bits** for this structure but it allocates one word which is one byte here. This is as shown below:

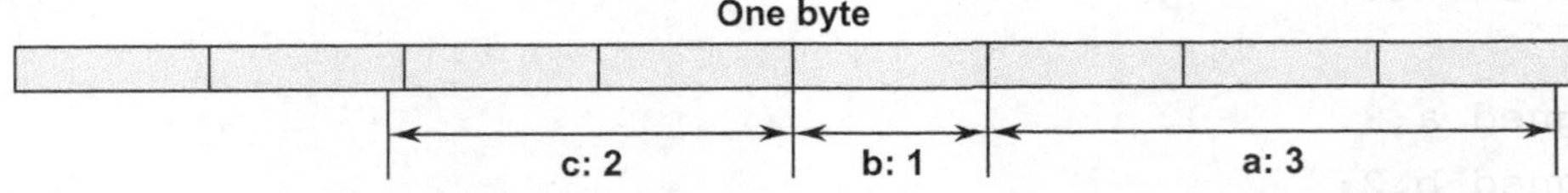

In the program we have 4 possible values for the third member *c* = –2,–1,0,1. We are trying to store 2 in this member. As this is not possible so the next value after 1 is stored in c. if you assign 3 to *c*–1 will be stored and for 5, 0 will be stored in c and so on.

```
/*Prog 10.35 Demo of structure and bit field ver 2*/
#include <stdio.h>
#include <conio.h>
 typedef struct
 {
```

```
    unsigned a:3;
    unsigned b:1;
    unsigned c:2;
    unsigned d:4;
  } bfield;
  void main()
  {
    bfield var = { 5,0,2,12};
    clrscr();
    printf("Size of struct bfiled is:=");
    printf("%d\n",sizeof(bfield));
    printf("var.a = %d\n var.b=%d\n", var.a, var.b);
    printf("var.c=%d\n var.d=%d\n",var.c, var.d);
    getch();
  }
```

Output:

```
Size of struct bfiled is:=2
var.a = 5
var.b=0
var.c=2
var.d=12
```

EXPLANATION: In the program the total number of bits are 10. If the word size happens to be 8 bits then while allocating bits for the member **d** 2 bits will be in the first word and remaining two bits will be in the next word. Whenever compiler sees this it automatically leaves 2 bits in the first word unused and stores the next field at the beginning of new word.

```
/* Prog 10.36 Demo of structure and bit field ver 3*/
#include <stdio.h>
#include <conio.h>
 typedef struct
 {
    unsigned a:3;
    unsigned b:2;
    unsigned :3;
    unsigned d:4;
 }bfield;
  void main()
  {
    bfield var={6,2,12};;
    clrscr();
    printf("Size of struct bfield is:");
```

```
    printf("%d\n",sizeof(struct bfield));
    printf("var.a=%d\nvar.b=%d\n",var.a,var.b);
    printf("var.d=%d\n",var.d);
    getch();
  }
```

Output:

```
Size of struct bfield is:2
var.a=6
var.b=2
var.d=12
```

EXPLANATION: Third line of the structure **bfield** denotes unnamed filed. This can be used to forces the compiler to start the new field at the beginning of the new word. In our case the sum of first two fields is **5 bits** so we have added an unnamed field of **3 bits.** This will result in **d** to start at the beginning of new word.

The same can be achieved by making width of the unnamed field equal to zero as unsigned: 0.

10.7.1 In Short We Summarize Following Points about Bit Field:

1. Bit fields do not have addresses.
2. Values cannot be assigned to them using scanf.
3. They can store values within their range.
4. They are not accessible using pointers.
5. They cannot be float.
6. They are typically used in applications where values within specified limits are permitted.
7. Assigning of bits to the bit field i.e., order of bits may be from left to right or right to left. We have ordered from right to left. This is compiler dependent.
8. Array of bit field is not permitted.
9. A function cannot return a bit field.
10. They may be used within arithmetic expressions.

```
/*Prog 10.37 Demo of applying bit fields */
#include <stdio.h>
#include <string.h>
 struct bit_field
 {
    int cable: 1;
    int dish: 1;
 };
 struct survey
 {
    char name[20];
    struct bit_field c_d;
```

```
   int age;
   int hour_per_week;
   union
   {
      char cable_company[16];
      char dish_company[16];
   } provider;
};
void DataEnter(struct survey *s);
void DataDisplay(struct survey *s);
void main(void)
{
   struct survey tv;
   clrscr();
   DataEnter(&tv);
   DataDisplay(&tv);
   getch();
}
/* function definition */
void DataEnter(struct survey *ptr)
{
   char is_yes[4];
   printf("Are you using cable at home? (Yes or No)\n");
   gets(is_yes);
   if ((is_yes[0] == 'Y') || (is_yes[0] == 'y'))
   {
      printf("Enter the cable company name:\n");
      gets(ptr->provider.cable_company);
      ptr->c_d.cable = 1;
      ptr->c_d.dish = 0;
   }
   else
   {
      printf("Are you using a satellite
      dish? (Yes or No)\n");
      gets(is_yes);
      if ((is_yes[0] == 'Y') ||(is_yes[0] == 'y'))
      {
       printf("Enter the satellite dish company name:\n");
```

```
        gets(ptr->provider.dish_company);
        ptr->c_d.cable = 0;
        ptr->c_d.dish = 1;
      }
      else
      {
        ptr->c_d.cable = 0;
        ptr->c_d.dish = 0;
      }
    }
   printf("Please enter your name:\n");
   gets(ptr->name);
   printf("Your age:\n");
   scanf("%d", &ptr->age);
   printf("How many hours you spend on watching
   TV per week:\n");
   scanf("%d", &ptr->hour_per_week);
 }
 /* function definition */
 void DataDisplay(struct survey *ptr)
 {
   printf("\nHere's what you've entered:\n");
   printf("Name: %s\n", ptr->name);
   printf("Age: %d\n", ptr->age);
   printf("Hour per week: %d\n", ptr->hour_per_week);
   if (ptr->c_d.cable && !ptr->c_d.dish)
     printf("Your cable company is: %s\n",
      ptr->provider.cable_company);
      else if (!ptr->c_d.cable && ptr->c_d.dish)
        printf("Your satellite dish company is: %s\n",
        ptr->provider.dish_company);
   else
     printf("You don't have cable or a satellite dish.\n");
     printf("\nThanks and Bye!\n");
  }
```

Output:

```
Are you using cable at home? (Yes or No)
y
Enter the cable company name:
abc
```

```
Please enter your name:
Hari Mohan Pandey
Your age:
24
How many hours you spend on watching TV per week:
45
Here's what you've entered:
Name: Hari Mohan Pandey
Age: 24
Hour per week: 45
Your cable company is: abc
Thanks and Bye!
```

EXPLANATION: The purpose of the program is to show you how to declare bit fields and how to use them. As you can see in **lines 5_8,** two bit fields, **cable and dish,** are declared with the **struct** data type. Each of the bit fields is **1 bit** long. Then a structure called ***c_d*** is defined with the two bit fields in **line 12,** which is within another structure declaration from **line 10** to **line 19.**

The bit fields **cable** and **dish** are used as **flags** to indicate whether the user is using cable or a satellite dish based on the answers made by the user. If the user has cable, then the cable bit field is set to **1** and the dish bit field is set to **0. (See lines 44 and 45.)** On the other hand, if the user has a satellite dish, then dish is set to **1** and cable is set to **0,** as shown in lines **53** and **54.** If, however, the user has neither cable nor a satellite dish, both cable and dish are set to 0 in **lines 56 and 57.**

So you see, we've used the combinations of the two bit fields, **cable and dish,** to represent the three situations: **having cable, having a satellite dish, or having neither cable nor a satellite dish.**

POINTS TO PONDER

In this section you have learned the following points:

- You can group variables of different types with a data type called a **structure.**
- The data items in a structure are called fields or members of the structure.
- The **struct** keyword is used to start a structure declaration or a structure variable definition.
- The **dot operator (.)** is used to separate a structure name and a member name in referencing the structure member.
- The **arrow operator (->)** is commonly used to reference a structure member with a pointer.
- A structure can be passed to a function, and a function can return a structure back to the caller.
- Passing a function with a pointer that points to a structure is more efficient than passing the function with the entire structure.
- Arrays of structures are permitted in C.
- You can enclose a structure within another structure. The latter is called a **nested structure.**

- It's legal to put a pointer into a structure even though the pointer may point to another structure that has not been declared yet.
- **A union is a block of memory** that is used to hold data items of different types.
- A union is similar to a structure, except that data items saved in the union are overlaid in order to share the same memory location.
- The size of a union is the same as the size of the largest member in the union.
- The **union keyword** has to be used to specify the union data type in a union declaration or a union variable definition.
- To reference a union member, you can use either a **dot operator (.)** to separate the union name and the union member name or an **arrow operator (->)** to separate the name of a pointer that points to the union and the union member name.
- The **ANSI C standard** allows you to initialize a union by assigning the first union member a value.
- You can access the same memory location with different union members.
- To make a structure flexible, you can nest a union inside a structure so that the structure can hold different types of values.
- You can define the bit fields, which can be a single bit or any number of bits up to the number of bits in an integer, by using the **struct** data type.
- If a member of a structure is a pointer to itself, it is a self-referential structure.
- Self referential union is also possible.
- A bit field is one bit or a set of adjacent bits within a word.
- Advantages of union are:
  (*a*) Structure can use as its member.
  (*b*) When a particular member alone is to be manipulated at a time, a union is a suitable structure.
  (*c*) Memory is economically used.

QUESTIONS AND ANSWERS

Q1. *Why do you need structures?*

Ans: In practice, you need to collect and group data items that are relevant but of different types. The structure data type provides a convenient way to aggregate those differently typed data items.

Q2. *Can you declare a structure and define a structure variable in a single statement?*

Ans: **Yes,** You can put the struct keyword, a tag name, a list of declarations of structure members, and a variable name into a single statement to declare a structure and define a structure variable. Then, the structure can be identified by the tag name; the variable is of the struct data type of the tag name.

Q3. *How do you reference a structure member?*

Ans: You can reference a structure member by prefixing the structure member's name with the structure variable name and a dot operator (.). If the structure is pointed to by a pointer, you can use the arrow operator (->), followed by the pointer name, to reference the structure member.

Q4. *Why is it more efficient to pass a pointer that refers to a structure to a function?*

Ans: When an entire structure is passed to a function, a copy of the structure is made and saved in a temporary block of memory called the stack. After the copy is modified by the function, it has to be returned and written back to the storage that holds the original content of the structure. Passing a function with a pointer that points to a structure, on the other hand, simply passes the address of the structure to the function, not the entire copy of the structure. The function can then access the original memory location of the structure and modify the content held by the structure without duplicating the structure on the stack. Therefore, it's more efficient to pass a pointer of a structure than to pass the structure itself to a function.

Q5. *What are the differences between a union and a structure?*

Ans: Basically, the difference between a union and a structure is that the members in a union are overlaid and they share the same memory location, whereas the members in a structure have their own memory locations. A union can be referenced by using one of its member names.

Q6. *What will happen if you initialize all members of a union together?*

Ans: The value that is assigned to a union member last will be the value that stays in the memory storage of the union until the next assignment to the union. In ANSI C, you can initialize a union by initializing its first member.

Q7. *How do you reference a union member?*

Ans: If the name of a union is used to reference the union members, then the dot operator (.) can be used to separate the union name and the name of a union member. If a pointer, which points to a union, is used to reference the union members, then the arrow operator (->) can be used between the pointer name and the name of a union member.

Q8. *Can you access the same memory location with different union members?*

Ans: Yes. Since all union members in a union share the same memory location, you can access the memory location with different union members. For example, in the program 10.31, two character constants are assigned to a union memory storage through one of the union members. The two characters saved at the memory location of the union are printed out with the help from another union member.

EXERCISES

A. Answer the following questions:

1. What is a structure in C? How is structure declared?
2. How are structured elements stored in memory? Explain with suitable example and also give the explanation of your example?
3. Explain nested structure? Give example for the support of your answer draw diagram to explain your example?
4. How structure elements are accessed using pointer? Which operator is used for accessing the element using pointer?
5. Is it possible to pass structure variable to function? Explain in detail the possible ways?

6. Explain the importance of bit field? How do bit fields save memory space?
7. Point out differences between union and structure? Explain with the help of example?
8. Distinguish between an array and a structure?
9. What is the need for a tag in a structure declaration? Demonstrate with a segment of program.
10. What is a union in C? How is data stored using union?
11. What are the applications of union? Explain with the help of example.

B. Match the following

1. Array	(*a*) can be self referenced
2. Structure	(*b*) homogeneous data structure.
3. Bit field	(*c*) heterogeneous data structure.
4. union	(*d*) adjacent bits in memory.
5. Self-referential structure	(*e*) contains a pointer to itself as a member.

C. Write True or False against each statement:

1. The data type of members of structure may be same.
2. A structure cannot contain the structure itself as its member.
3. Structure act as an Abstract Data Type (ADT).
4. During declaration of structure variable struct keyword is optional.
5. The structure can be read as a single entity.
6. Nesting of union is not allowed in C.
7. The exact size of a structure is compiler dependent.
8. The declaration and definition cannot be combined.
9. Two structure can be copied as a=b.
10. Pointer members are not copied during copying of two structures.

D. Fill in the blanks

1. A structure is a __________ type of data structure.
2. The keyword __________ is used to declare a structure.
3. Structure declaration describes the __________ of structure.
4. Initialization of a union variable can initialize its __________ only.
5. Only __________ data type can be used in a bit field.
6. A structure which contains a pointer to itself as a member is called.
7. The __________ operator is used to access the members of structure.

E. Brain Drill:

1. Write a program to define structure with tag state with field state name, number of districts and total population. Read and display the data.
2. Define a structure with tag population with fields Men and Women. Create structure within structure using state and population structure. Read and display the data.
3. Create user-defined data type equivalent to int. Declare three variables of its type. Perform arithmetic operations using these variables.

4. Declare the structure which will contain the following data for 5 employees:
   (*a*) Employee code (3 chars).
   (*b*) First name (20 chars).
   (*c*) Middle initial (1 char).
   (*d*) Last name (20 chars).

   The codes to be stored in this structure are E01, E02 and so on. Write a C program to input names for 5 employees and print out initials of each (*e.g.*, Swami K Puri should be printed as SKP) along with their code.

F. Predict the output of the following program:

```
1. main ( )
   {
      union
      {
         char a, b, c, d;
      } car;
      struct {
      int i, j;
      }in;
      long z;
      float f;
      double m;
   }mem;
   printf("%d", sizeof(mem) );
  }
2. main ( )
   {
      struct
      {
         int xx;
      } var1;
      (&var1)->xx=20;
      printf("%d",var1.xx);
   }
3. struct s1
   {
      int xx;
      }
      struct s1 *ptr, var;
       ptr = &var;
       ptr -> xx = 345;
```

```
        printf("%d", *ptr.xx);
    }
4. main ( )
    {
        struct temp
        {
            int xx;
        };
        struct temp temp;
        temp.xx = 90;
        printf("%d",temp.xx);
    }
5. main ( )
    {
        struct demo
        {
            int xx;
        };
        struct demo demo;
        int xx= 20;
        demo.xx=22;
        printf("%d,%d",x,demo.xx);
    }
```

11

Introduction to Storage Classes

The chapter discuss the attributes which all the variable in C possess *i.e.*, **storage class.** The introduction and second part discuss the basic idea of scope and lifetime variable. It also discusses local and global variable. It explains the meaning of scope by giving lots of examples which includes use of functions also. The side effects of use of **global variables** have been discussed. It gives a very brief idea of storage classes and what it tells about variables.

All 4 storage classes are illustrated as separate sections. Features of all the storage classes are discussed first by giving them as key points and later with lots of examples.**auto, exter, register and static,** the effect of using these storage classes on variables have been discussed. Some important points related with their usage in programming are mentioned by giving appropriate programming examples.

11.1 INTRODUCTION

A storage class is an attribute that changes the behavior of a variable. It controls the lifetime, scope, initial value and linkage for a variable. Storage classes are there for a variable which tells the following things:

(*a*) Where the variable will be stored (memory/ CPU register)?

(*b*) What will be the default initial value of the variable?

(*c*) What will be the scope of the variable?

(*d*) The lifetime of the variable?

Before delving into the topic of storage classes we first see by writing few programs to find out what is the meaning of scope of a variable?

11.2 SCOPE OF A VARIABLE

When we declare a variable within a function or a block **(A block can be created by enclosing statement within { })** that variable is accessible only to that block or function only. Other blocks/

functions cannot access that variable as they are local to that block/ functions only. **The area where the variable can be accessed is called the scope of the variable.** In other words, we can say portion of program where the variable may be visible or available.

```
/* Prog 11.1 Demo of scope of a variable */
#include<stdio.h>
#include<conio.h>
 void main()
 {
  int p=20;
  clrscr();
  printf("I am in main \n");
  printf("p=%d\n",p);
   {
     printf("Right now i'm in block\n");
     int y=25;
     printf("y=%d\n",y);
     printf("p=%d\n",p);
   }
  getch();
}
```

Output:

```
I am in main
p=20
Right now I'm in block
y=25
p=20
```

EXPLANATION: The variable *p* is local to the **main().** Its scope is the entire main function *i.e.,* it can be used anywhere within the **main().** The variable *y* is declared inside the block so its scope is local to that block only. Any access of *y* outside the block will result an error. Note *p* can be used **outside the block as block itself is contained within the main()**

```
/*Prog 11.2 Demo of global scope*/
#include<stdio.h>
#include<conio.h>
 int x;
 void main()
 {
   clrscr();
```

```
   printf("x=%d\n",x);
   getch();
 }
```

Output:

```
x=0
```

EXPLANATION: Any variable declared or defined outside main is treated as global variable. The default value of a global variable is 0. Its scope is entire program.

11.3 HIDING DATA

To solve a **complex problem** in practice, the programmer normally breaks the problem into smaller pieces and deals with each piece of the problem by writing one or two functions (or **routines**). Then, all the functions are put together to form a complete program that can be used to solve the complex problem.

In the complete program, there might be variables that have to be shared by all the functions. On the other hand, the use of some other variables may be limited to only certain functions. That is, the visibility of those variables is limited, and values assigned to those variables are hidden from many functions.

Limiting the scope of variables is very useful when several programmers are working on different pieces of the same program. If they limit the scope of their variables to their pieces of code, they do not have to worry about conflicting with variables of the same name used by others in other parts of the program.

In C, you can declare a variable and indicate its visibility level by designating its scope. Thus, variables with local scope can only be accessed within the block in which they are declared.

```
/*Prog 11.3 Global variable and function ver1*/
#include<stdio.h>
#include<conio.h>
 int x=20;
 void main()
 {
   void demo();
   clrscr();
   printf("In main\n");
   printf("x=%d\n",x);
   demo();
   getch();
 }
   void demo()
   {
```

```
      printf("In demo function \n");
      printf("x=%d\n",x);
   }
```

Output:
In main
x=20
In demo function
x=20

EXPLANATION: As explained in the previous program that a global variable's scope is the entire program so the *x* can be accessed within main as well as in the demo function. Note we have assigned initial value to the global variable 20.

The disadvantage of global variables is that any change performed by any of the function at any place propagated to the next function that will be using the same variable. See the next program given below.

/*Prog 11.4 Global variable and functions ver2*/

```
#include<stdio.h>
#include<conio.h>
 int x=30;
 void demo1();
 void demo2();
 void main()
 {
    clrscr();
    printf("In main\n");
    printf("x=%d\n",x++);
    demo1();
    demo2();
    getch();
 }
    void demo1()
    {
       printf("In demo1 function\n");
       printf("x=%d\n",x++);
    }
    void demo2()
    {
     printf("In demo2 function\n");
     printf("x=%d\n",x++);
    }
```

```
Output:
In main
x=30
In demo1 function
x=31
In demo2 function
x=32
```

EXPLANATION: The global variable *x* is accessed at three places in the program in **main (), in demo1 () and in demo2 ().** In main **x prints 30** and incremented by **1,** *x* is now **31.** When **demo1 ( )** is called prints *x* inside the function the **same *x*'s value 31** is used. *x* is then incremented by **1, *x* in now 32** which is used when **demo2()** is called. Note *x* has been changed at three places by three different functions. The main point to note here is that when one function is doing some modification the others are not aware that some modification is being done. Anybody is doing any changes at its own wish on poor variable *x*.

11.4 WHAT HAPPENS WHEN LOCAL VARIABLE AND GLOBAL VARIABLE HAVE THE SAME NAME?

When we have a local variable and a global variable with the same name, priority is given to local variable when the variable is accessed.

```
/*Prog 11.5 Local and global variable with same name ver1*/
#include<stdio.h>
#include<conio.h>
 int x =20;
 void main()
 {
    int x=20;
    clrscr();
    printf("x=%d\n",x);
    getch();
 }
Output:
x=20
```

EXPLANATION: *x* is global and x is local also. When used in main the priority is given to local x that belong to main ().

How do we access global variable then in the previous program? Simply by storing it in a new variable before declaring its local counterpart.

```
/*Prog 11.6Local and global variable with the same name ver 2*/
#include<stdio.h>
#include<conio.h>
 int x=20;
```

```
 void main()
 {
    int p=x;
    int x=30;
    clrscr();
    printf("Global x=%d\n",p);
    printf("Local x=%d\n",x);
    getch();
 }
```

Output:

```
Global x=20
Local x=30
```

EXPLANATION: The global *x*'s value is stored in the new variable *p* then local *x* is declared. Now we can have access to both local *x* and global *x* (through not access) in the form of *p*.

```
/*Prog 11.7 Local and global variable with same name ver3*/
#include<stdio.h>
#include<conio.h>
 char *x="Global";
 void main()
 {
   char *p=x;
   char *x="Local";
   clrscr();
   printf("%s\n",p);
   printf("%s\n",x);
   getch();
 }
```

Output:

```
Global
Local
```

EXPLANATION: The program is similar to previous one with the difference that we have worked with string instead of integer numbers.

11.5 BLOCK SCOPE

In this section, a block refers to any sets of statements enclosed in braces ({and}). A variable declared within a block has block scope. Thus, the variable is active and accessible from its declaration point to the end of the block. Sometimes, block scope is also called **local scope.**

For example, the variable **i** declared within the block of the following main function has block scope:

```
int main()
{
  int i; /* block scope */
  .
  .
  .
  return 0;
}
```

Usually, a variable with block scope is called a local variable.

11.6 NESTED BLOCK SCOPE

You can also declare variables within a nested block. If a variable declared in the outer block shares the same name with one of the variables in the inner block, the variable within the outer block is hidden by the one within the inner block for the scope of the inner block.

/*Prog 11.8 Printing out variables with different scope levels(Scopes in nested block)*/

```
#include <stdio.h>
#include<conio.h>
void main()
{
  int i = 32; /* block scope 1*/
  clrscr();
  printf("Within the outer block: i=%d\n", i);
  { /* the beginning of the inner block */
    int i, j;/* block scope 2, int i hides the outer int i*/
    printf("Within the inner block:\n");
    for (i=0, j=10; i<=10; i++, j--)
    printf("i=%2d, j=%2d\n", i, j);
  } /* the end of the inner block */
  printf("Within the outer block: i=%d\n", i);
  getch();
}
```

Output:

```
Within the outer block: i=32
Within the inner block:
i= 0, j=10
i= 1, j= 9
```

```
i= 2, j= 8
i= 3, j= 7
i= 4, j= 6
i= 5, j= 5
i= 6, j= 4
i= 7, j= 3
i= 8, j= 2
i= 9, j= 1
i=10, j= 0
Within the outer block: i=32
```

EXPLANATION: The purpose of the program in **PROGRAM 11.4** is to show you the different scopes of variables in nested blocks. As you can see, there are two nested blocks in program. The integer variable *i* declared in **line 6** is **visible** within the **outer block** enclosed by the braces **({and}) in lines 5 and 19.** Another two integer variables, ***i* and *j*,** declared in **line 11,** are visible only within the **inner block** from **line 10 to line 16.**

Although the integer **variable *i*** within the outer block has the same name as one of the integer variables within the inner block, the two integer variables can not be accessed at the same time due to their different scopes.

To prove this, **line 8 prints out the value, 32,** contained by ***i*** within the outer block for the first time. Then, the **for loop in lines 14 and 15** displays **10 pairs** of values assigned **to *i* and *j*** within the inner block. At this point, there is no sign showing that the integer variable *i* within the outer block has any effects on the one within the inner block. When the inner block is exited, the variables within the inner block are no longer accessible.

Finally, the statement **in line 17** prints out the value of ***i*** within the outer block again to find out whether the value has been changed due to the integer variable ***i*** within the inner block. The result shows that these two integer variables hide from each other, and no conflict occurs.

11.7 FUNCTION SCOPE

Function scope indicates that a variable is active and visible from the beginning to the end of a function.

In C, only the **goto** label has function scope. For example, the **goto** label, start, shown in the following code portion has function scope:

```
int main()
{
  int i; /* block scope */
  .
  .
  .
  start: /* A goto label has function scope */
```

.

```
  .
  .
  .
  goto start; /* the goto statement */
  .
  .
  .
  return 0;
}
```

Here the label **start** is visible from the beginning to the end of the **main ()** function. Therefore, there should not be more than one label having the same name within the **main ()** function.

11.8 PROGRAM SCOPE (GLOBAL VARIABLE)

A variable is said to have program scope when it is declared outside a function. For instance, look at the following code:

```
int x = 0;            /* program scope */
float y = 0.0;        /* program scope */
int main()
{
  int i;    /* block scope */
  .
  .
  .
  return 0;
}
```

Here the **int variable *x* and the float variable *y* have program scope.**

Variables with program scope are also called global variables, which are visible among different files. These files are the entire source files that make up an executable program. Note that a global variable is declared with an initializer outside a function.

The program 11.6 demonstrates the relationship between variables with program scope and variables with block scope.

```
/*Prog 11.9 Demo of program scope vs block scope */
#include <stdio.h>
#include<conio.h>
 int x = 1234;             /* program scope */
 double y = 1.234567;      /* program scope */
 void function_1()
```

```
{
  printf("From function_1:\n x=%d, y=%f\n", x, y);
}
void main()
{
  int x = 4321; /* block scope 1*/
  clrscr();
  function_1();
  printf("Within the main block:\n x=%d, y=%f\n", x, y);
  /* a nested block */
 {
   double y = 7.654321; /* block scope 2 */
   function_1();
  printf("Within the nested block:\n x=%d, y=%f\n", x, y);
 }
  getch();
}
```

```
Output:
From function_1:
  x=1234, y=1.234567
Within the main block:
  x=4321, y=1.234567
From function_1:
  x=1234, y=1.234567
Within the nested block:
  x=4321, y=7.654321
```

EXPLANATION: As you can see in **program 11.6,** there are two **global variables,** ***x*** **and** ***y*****,** with program scope; they are declared in **lines 4 and 5.**

In **lines 7_10,** a function, called **function_1( ),** is declared. The **function_1( )** function contains only one statement; it prints out the values held by both ***x*** **and** ***y*****.** Because there is no variable declaration made for ***x*** **or** ***y*** within the function block, the values of the global variables ***x*** **and** ***y*** are used for the statement inside the function. To prove this, the **function_1()** function is called twice in **lines 16 and 21,** respectively, from two nested blocks. The output shows that the values of the two global variables *x* and *y* are passed to **printf ()** enclosed in the **function_1( )** function body.

Then, **line 14** declares another integer variable, **x, with block scope,** which can replace the global **variable** *x* within the block of the **main()** function. The result made by the statement in **line 17** shows that the value of *x* is the value of the local variable *x* with block scope, while the value of *y* is still that of the global variable ***y*****.**

There is a **nested block in lines 19 and 23,** within which another double **variable** ***y*****,** with block scope, is declared and initialized. Like the **variable** *x* within the **main() block,** this variable, ***y*****,** within the nested block replaces the global variable *y*. The statement in **line 22 puts** the values of the local **variables *x* and *y*** on the screen.

```
/*Prog 11.10 local and global variable with functions ver1*/
#include<stdio.h>
#include<conio.h>
 int x=20;
 void demo1();
 void demo2();
 void main()
 {
    int x=5;
    clrscr();
    printf("In main\n");
    printf("x=%d\n",x);
    demo1();
    demo2();
    getch();
 }
  void demo1()
  {
     int x=30;
     printf("In demo1 function\n");
     printf("x=%d\n",x);
  }
  void demo2()
  {
     int x=40;
     printf("In demo2 function\n");
     printf("x=%d\n",x);
  }
```

Output:

```
In main
x=5
In demo1 function
x=30
In demo2 function
x=40
```

EXPLANATION: As stated earlier when local and global variable have same name priority is given to the local one. Though main () can have access to *x* by the trick given in earlier programs but demo1 () and demo2 () cannot and so the output.

How do we access the global variable inside the functions **demo1 ( ) and demo2 ( ).** Simply by passing a parameter of appropriate type to the function.

```
/*Prog 11.11 Local and global variables with functions ver2*/
#include<stdio.h>
#include<conio.h>
 int x=20;
 void demo1();
 void demo2();
 void main()
 {
   clrscr();
   demo1(x);
   demo2(x);
   getch();
 }
  void demo1(int temp)
  {
    int x=30;
    printf("In demo1 function\n");
    printf("Global x=%d\n",temp);
    printf("Local x=%d\n",x);
  }
   void demo2(int m)
   {
    int x=40;
    printf("In demo2 function\n");
    printf("Global x=%d\n",m);
    printf("Local x=%d\n",x);
   }
```

Output:

```
In demo1 function
Global x=20
Local x=30
In demo2 function
Global x=20
Local x=40
```

EXPLANATION: We have passed global variable as argument in the functions. Thus temp and *m* in demo1 () and demo2 () respectively represents global variable and local variable *x* can be used without any problem.

11.9 THE STORAGE CLASS SPECIFIERS

In C, the storage class of a variable refers to the combination of its spatial and temporal regions. You've learned about scope, which specifies the spatial region of a variable. Now, let's focus on duration, which indicates the temporal region of a variable.

There are four specifiers and two modifiers that can be used to indicate the duration of a variable. These specifiers and modifiers are introduced in the following sections:

1. Automatic (keyword is auto)
2. Static (keyword is static)
3. Register (keyword is register)
4. Extern (keyword is extern)

11.9.1 The Auto Specifier

The auto specifier indicates that the memory location of a variable is temporary. In other words, a variable's reserved space in the memory can be erased or relocated when the variable is out of its scope.

Only variables with block scope can be declared with the auto specifier. The auto keyword is rarely used, however, because the duration of a variable with block scope is temporary by default.

This is the default storage class *i.e.,* if you write int a then it is treated as auto int a. Automatic variables are always local to the function and declared inside the function *i.e.,* they cannot be global. Their scope is limited to the function in which they are declared. Any variable declared inside a function is treated as local and assumed to have auto storage class if no other storage class is specified. The entire variable we have used till now in all the programs are auto. Two variables with the same name declared in two different functions are independent of each other *i.e.*

```
void demo1()
{
    int x;
}
    void demo2()
{
    int x;
}
```

In the above functions both *x* are independent of each other:

These variables are local to the block in which they are declared. They come to life as soon control is transferred to these block and expires as soon as execution of that block comes to an end.

In short note the following points about auto storage class or variable.

1. Default initial value is garbage (computer generated)
2. Scope is local to the block in which declared.
3. Life is till control remains within the block.
4. Stored in the computer's memory (RAM)
5. Memory is economically used.
6. Built is protection as they are local.
7. They do not retain value once control has come out from the block. Each time control is entered into the block a new variable is created and the same dies when control exits.
8. They are created on stack.

```
/*Prog 11.12 Demo of auto storage class ver1*/
#include<stdio.h>
#include<conio.h>
 void main()
 {
    auto int x;
    auto float y;
    auto char c;
    clrscr();
    printf("x=%d\n",x);
    printf("y=%f\n",y);
    printf("c=%c\n",c);
    getch();
 }
```

Output:

```
x=-28819
y=0.000000
c=?
```

EXPLANATION: Default value of an auto variable is garbage value. Auto keyword can be omitted.

```
/*Prog 11.13 Demo of auto storage class ver2*/
#include<stdio.h>
#include<conio.h>
 auto int x;
 void main()
```

```
{
    clrscr();
    printf("x=%d\n",x);
    getch();
}
```

Output:

Error message: Storage class "auto" is not allowed here.

EXPLANATION: auto variable cannot be global. They can only be local.

11.9.2 The Static Specifier

The static specifier, on the other hand, can be applied to variables with either block scope or program scope. When a variable within a function is declared with the static specifier, the variable has a permanent duration. In other words, the memory storage allocated for the variable is not destroyed when the scope of the variable is exited, the value of the variable is maintained outside the scope, and if execution ever returns to the scope of the variable, the last value stored in the variable is still there.

For instance, in the following code portion:

```
int main()
{
    int i; /* block scope and temporary duration */
    static int j; /* block scope and permanent duration */
    .
    .
    return 0;
}
```

The integer variable *i* has temporary duration by default. But the other integer variable, *j*, has permanent duration due to the storage class specifier static.

A variable declared with this storage class has default initial value zero. A static variable can be internal static or external static. It depends upon where they are declared. If declared with in block or function they are internal static and have block scope and persistent storage. If they are declared as global then they are called external static. They have file scope and persistent storage.

In short, note the following points about static storage class:

1. Default initial value is zero.
2. Storage is memory (in the stack).
3. Internal static have no linkage.
4. External static have internal linkage.
5. Life till program execution is not over.
6. Static variable are initialized only once.
7. Static variables are initialized before the execution of program begins thus they are called load time variable.

8. They retain the value between different function calls.

```
/*Prog 11.14 Demo of static storage class ver 1*/
#include<stdio.h>
#include<conio.h>
 void main()
 {
    static int x;
    clrscr();
    printf("x=%d\n",x);
    getch();
 }
```

Output:

```
x=0
```

EXPLANATION: The default initial value of a static variable is zero.

```
/*Prog 11.15 Demo of static storage class ver2*/
#include<stdio.h>
#include<conio.h>
 void main()
 {
    void stat();
    void nonstat();
    int t;
    clrscr();
    for(t=1;t<=3;t++)
    {
       stat();
       nonstat();
    }
    getch();
 }
  void stat()
  {
     static int p=10;
     printf("In stat p=%d\n",p++);
  }
  void nonstat()
  {
    int p=10;
    printf("In nonstat p=%d\n",p++);
```

```
}
```

Output:

```
In stat p=10
In nonstat p=10
In stat p=11
In nonstat p=10
In stat p=12
In nonstat p=10
```

EXPLANATION: The function stat () and nonstat () are called thrice from the main (). In stat() the variable *p* is static and its initial value is 10 this is done when stat() is called for the first time. As control leaves this function for the first time value of *p* is 11, this value persist and stored in the stack. When control reaches to stat () second time *p* is not reinitialized instead it uses the stored value of *p* which is 11. In the third call it uses the value 12. (value of *p* was 12 when control quit the function stat () on second call). In nonstat () *p* is initialized each time the control enters into the function. The value of *p* does not persist in subsequent function call so each time 10 is printed.

```
/*Prog 11.16 Demo of static storage class ver3*/
#include<stdio.h>
#include<conio.h>
 void main()
 {
  void demo();
  clrscr();
  demo();
  demo();
  demo();
  getch();
 }
  void demo()
  {
     static int count;
     printf("Function called for %d times\n",++count);
  }
```

Output:

```
Function called for 1 times
Function called for 2 times
Function called for 3 times
```

EXPLANATION: The program is self-explanatory. We are simply counting how many times the function has called through the count variable as it is static and increments itself in each function call.

```
/*Prog 11.17 Demo of static and auto array*/
#include<stdio.h>
#include<conio.h>
 void main()
 {
  auto int notstat[10];
  static int stat[10];
  int t;
  clrscr();
  printf("Auto Array Default Values\n");
  for(t=0;t<5;t++)
  printf("notstat[%d]=%d\n",t,notstat[t]);
  printf("\n Static Array Defult Values \n");
  for(t=0;t<5;t++)
  printf("stat[%d]=%d\n",t,stat[t]);
  getch();
 }
```

Output:

```
Auto Array Default Values
notstat[0]=0
notstat[1]=1824
notstat[2]=0
notstat[3]=12291
notstat[4]=1824
Static Array Defult Values
stat[0]=0
stat[1]=0
stat[2]=0
stat[3]=0
stat[4]=0
```

EXPLANATION: auto array elements if not initialized by default contains garbage values whereas static array elements contains 0 as there default initial value.

```
/*Prog 11.18 Static as function argument*/
#include<stdio.h>
#include<conio.h>
 void main()
 {
   void demo(static int x);
   static int y=10;
   clrscr();
```

```
    demo(y);
    getch();
  }
  void demo(static int x)
  {
    printf("x=%d\n",x);
  }
```

Output:

ERROR MESSAGE: Storage class 'static' is not allowed here

EXPLANATION: You cannot apply static storage classes to arguments to the function.

```
/*Prog 11.19 Using the static specifier */
#include <stdio.h>
#include <conio.h>
  /* the add_two function */
 int add_two(int x, int y)
 {
      static int counter = 1;
      printf("This is the function call of %d,\n", counter++);
      return (x + y);
 }
 /* the main function */
 void main()
 {
     int i, j;
     clrscr();
     for (i=0, j=5; i<5; i++, j--)
      printf("the addition of %d and %d is %d.\n\n",
       i, j, add_two(i, j));
     getch();
 }
```

Output:

```
This is the function call of 1,
the addition of 0 and 5 is 5.
This is the function call of 2,
the addition of 1 and 4 is 5.
This is the function call of 3,
the addition of 2 and 3 is 5.
This is the function call of 4,
the addition of 3 and 2 is 5.
```

```
This is the function call of 5,
the addition of 4 and 1 is 5.
```

EXPLANATION: The purpose of the program 11.19 is to call a function to add two integers and then print out the result returned by the function on the screen. The function is called several times. A counter is set to keep track of how many times the function has been called.

This function, called add_two(), is declared in lines 4_10. There are two int arguments, *x* and *y*, that are passed to the function, and the addition of the two arguments is returned in line 9. Note that there is an integer variable, counter, that is declared with the static specifier in line 6. Values stored by counter are retained because the duration of the variable is permanent. In other words, although the scope of counter is within the block of the add_two() function, the memory location of counter and value saved in the location are not changed after the add_two() function is called and the execution control is returned back to the main() function.

Therefore, the counter variable is used as a counter to keep the number of calls received by the add_two() function. In fact, the statement of the printf() function in line 8 prints out the value saved by the counter variable each time the add_two() function is called. In addition, counter is incremented by one each time after the printf() function is executed.

The for loop, declared in lines 16_18 within the main() function, calls the add_two() function five times. The values of the two integer variables, *i* and *j*, are passed to the add_two() function for the operation of addition. Then, the return value from the add_two() function is displayed on the screen by the printf() function in lines 17 and 18.

From the output, you can see that the value saved by counter is indeed incremented by one each time the add_two() function is called, and is retained after the function exits because the integer variable counter is declared with static. Note that counter is only initialized once when the add_two() function is called for the first time.

11.9.3 File Scope and The Hierarchy of Scopes

In the first part of this chapter, I mentioned three of the four types of scopes:

1. Block scope
2. Function scope
3. Program scope.

It's time now to introduce the fourth scope-**file scope.**

In C, a global variable declared with the static specifier is said to have file scope. A variable with file scope is visible from its declaration point to the end of the file. Here the file refers to the program file that contains the source code. Most large programs consist of several program files.

The following portion of source code shows variables with file scope:

```
int x = 0;                /* program scope */
static int y = 0;         /* file scope */
static float z = 0.0;     /* file scope */
int main()
{
```

```
    int i; /* block scope */
    .
    .
    .
    return 0;
}
```

Here the int variable *y* and the float variable *z* both have file scope.

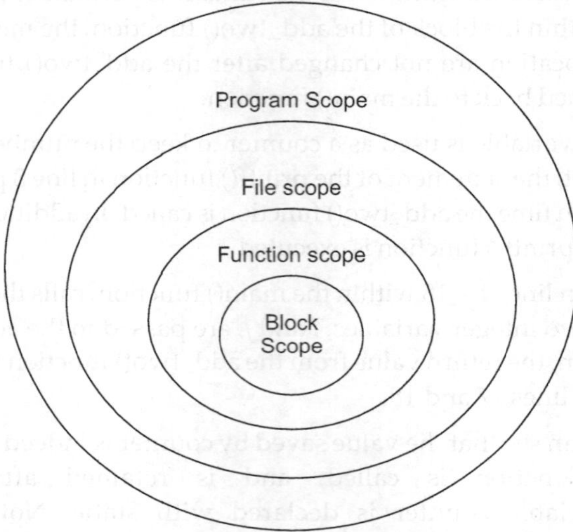

Fig. 11.1 *The hierarchy of scopes.*

The above **Figure** shows the hierarchy of the **four scopes.** As you can see, a variable with block scope is the most limited and is not visible outside the block within which the variable is declared. On the other hand, a variable with program scope is visible within all files, functions, and other blocks that make up the program.

11.9.4 The Register Specifier

The word register is borrowed from the world of computer hardware. Each computer has a certain number of registers to hold data and perform arithmetic or logical calculations. Because registers are located within the CPU (central processing unit) chip, it's much quicker to access a register than a memory location. Therefore, storing variables in registers may help to speed up your program.

The C language provides you with the register specifier. You can apply this specifier to variables when you think it's necessary to put the variables into the computer registers.

However, the register specifier only gives the compiler a suggestion. In other words, a variable specified by the register keyword is not guaranteed to be stored in a register. The compiler can ignore the suggestion if there is no register available, or if some other restrictions have to apply.

It's illegal to take the address of a variable that is declared with the register specifier because the variable is intended to be stored in a register, not in the memory.

In the following portion of code, the integer variable **i** is declared with the register specifier:

```
int main()
{
   /* block scope with the register specifier */
   register int i;
   . . .
   for (i=0; i<MAX_NUM; i++){
   /* some statements */
   }
   . . .
   return 0;
}
```

The declaration of **i** suggests that the compiler store the variable in a register. Because *i* is intensively used in the for loop, storing *i* in a register may increase the speed of the code shown here.

As we say Register are parts of the CPU and are considered as special storage areas. They are usually of size 4byte, 2 bytes or 1 byte (depend upon machine). Some of the registers may be AX, BX, CX, SP, PC etc. These registers are used for different purposes by the CPU. All the arithmetic and logical calculation are performed by using these registers. Usually all the variables are stored inside the memory (RAM) and CPU fetches them as required, stores them into the registers, does processing and in the end stores the values back into the memory. This all work could be reduced if variables were stored in the CPU registers and execution time could also be reduced.

In short note few points about register storage class:

1. Variable are stored within CPU registers.
2. Writing register storage class is simply a request to the compiler so variable may not be stored in CPU registers if they are not free/available.
3. You will never come to know whether variables are stored within register or within memory.
4. Number of registers is limited by the type of CPU.
5. They are usually limited to the char and int type variables though some compiler permits other type also.
6. Default initial value is garbage.
7. Scope is local to the block in which declared.
8. Life is block only.
9. You can not take address of a register class type variable.

```
/*Prog 11.20 Demo of register storage class*/
#include<stdio.h>
#include<conio.h>
 void main()
```

```
{
   register int a;
   clrscr();
   a=10;
   printf("a=%d\n",a);
   getch();
}
Output:
a=10
```

EXPLANATION: This is simple program to explain how to use register type variable.

```
/*Prog 11.21 Register to argument of function*/
#include<stdio.h>
#include<conio.h>
 void main()
{
   void demo(register int x);
   register int y=10;
   clrscr();
   demo (y);
   getch();
}
   void demo(register int x)
   {
      printf("x=%d\n",x);
   }
Output:
x=10
```

EXPLANATION: The aim of the program to simply show that you can apply register storage class to arguments to the functions.

11.9.5 The Extern Specifier

As stated in the section titled **"Program Scope,"** a variable with program scope is visible through all source files that make up an executable program. A variable with program scope is also called a global variable.

Here is a question: *How can a global variable declared in file A, for instance, be seen in file B?* In other words, *how does the compiler know that the variable used in file B is actually the same variable declared in file A?*

The answer is: Use the extern specifier provided by the C language to allude to a global variable defined elsewhere. In this case, we declare a global variable in file A, and then declare the variable again using the extern specifier in file B.

For instance, suppose you have two global int variables, *y* and *z*, that are defined in one file, and then, in another file, you may have the following declarations:

```
int x = 0;           /* a global variable */
extern int y;        /* an allusion to a global variable y */
int main()
{
    extern int z;    /* an allusion to a global variable z */
    int i;           /* a local variable */
    .
    .
    .
    return 0;
}
```

As you can see, there are two integer variables, *y* and *z*, that are declared with the extern specifier, outside and inside the main() function, respectively. When the compiler sees the two declarations, it knows that the declarations are actually allusions to the global variables *y* and *z* that are defined elsewhere.

Extern keyword is used for extern storage class. Whenever extern keyword is applied to variables they are treated as external variables or global variables.

They are generally used where a variable is to be shared among number of functions or in a multi file program where variable as well as functions are to be shared.

In short, note the following points about external variables. Extern storage class:

1. Default initial value is zero.
2. Scope is global from the point of definition to the rest of program or we can say they have file scope.
3. Extern keyword is used when a variable is declared and tells the compiler about the type of identifier.
4. The definition is outside the outermost block and it allocates memory storage.
5. The use of external variables provides a way so that information can be shared among number of functions.
6. The use of extern keyword is optional as external variables are recognized by the location of their definition within the program.
7. An external variable declaration cannot include the assignment of initial values.
8. Persistent storage of a variable retains the current value.
9. The value is globally available.

11.9.5.1 External Variable Definition Vs External Variable Declaration

1. Definition only creates variables whereas declaration refers to variable already defined.
2. Definition does allocates memory, declaration doesn't.
3. Definition appears only once whereas declaration can be at many places.
4. The keyword extern is used only in declaration.

```
/*Prog 11.22 demo of extern storage class ver1*/
#include<stdio.h>
#include<conio.h>
 void main()
 {
    extern int x;
    clrscr();
    x=150;
    printf("x=%d\n",x);
    getch();
 }
```

Output:

```
Linker Error: Undefined symbol x
```

EXPLANATION: extern int x; statement indicates that **x** has been defined somewhere else, so *x* after **clrscr()** is treated as new variable hence the error.

```
/*Prog 11.23 Demo of extern storage class ver 2*/
#isnclude<stdio.h>
#include<conio.h>
 void main()
 {
    extern int x;
    clrscr();
    x=150;
    printf("x=%d\n",x);
    getch();
 }
  x=150;
```

Output:

Compilation error: Type name expected

EXPLANATION: This time we get compilation error. This is so because we have forgotten to precede *x* with int. Put int before *x* and you will get the output *x*=150. Why 150? This is so as value of *x* is overwritten in the main ().

Had you have written int x only outside the main() the result would have been the same.

```
/*Prog 11.24 Demo of extern storage ver 3*/
#include<stdio.h>
#include<conio.h>
 int x=20;
 void main()
 {
   extern int x;
   clrscr();
   x=150;
   printf("x=%d\n",x);
   getch();
 }
  x=50;
```

Output:

```
Compilation Error: Type name expected
Compilation Error: Variable x initialized more than once.
```

EXPLANATION: While initialization extern variables extern keyword is optional and you cannot initialized extern variable more than once however changing values within function is permitted.

```
/*Prog 11.25 Demo of extern storage class ver 4*/
#include<stdio.h>
#include<conio.h>
 int x=90;
 void main()
 {
   extern int x;
   clrscr();
   printf("x=%d\n",x);
   getch();
 }
  int x;
  int x;
```

Output:

```
x=90
```

EXPLANATION: extern variable can be declared many numbers of times but can only be initialized once. This can not be applied to any other storage class.

NOTE: To make your program portable across different computer platforms, you can apply the following rules in your program when you declare or allude to global variables:

1. You can ignore the extern specifier, but include an initializer, when you declare a global variable.
2. You should use the extern specifier (without an initializer) when you allude to a global variable defined elsewhere.

11.10 THE STORAGE CLASS MODIFIERS

Besides the four storage class specifiers introduced in the earlier sections, C also provides you with two storage class modifiers (or qualifiers, as they're sometimes called) that you can use to indicate to the C compiler how variables may be accessed.

11.10.1 The Const Modifier

If you declare a variable with the const modifier, the content of the variable cannot be changed after it is initialized.

For instance, the following expression indicates to the compiler that circle_ratio is a variable whose value should not be changed:

```
const double circle_ratio = 3.141593;
```

Likewise, the value of the character array str declared in the following statement cannot be changed, either:

```
const char str[] = "A string constant";
```

Therefore, it's illegal to do something like this:

```
str[0] = 'a'; /* It's not allowed here. */
```

In addition, you can declare a pointer variable with the const modifier so that an object pointed to by the pointer cannot be changed. For example, consider the following pointer declaration with the const modifier:

```
char const *ptr_str = "A string constant";
```

After the initialization, you cannot change the content of the string pointed to by the pointer ptr_str. For instance, the following statement is not allowed:

```
*ptr_str = 'a'; /* It's not allowed here. */
```

However, the ptr_str pointer itself can be assigned a different address of a string that is declared with char const.

11.10.2 The Volatile Modifier

Sometimes, you want to declare a variable whose value can be changed without any explicit assignment statement in your program. For instance, you might declare a global variable that contains characters entered by the user. The address of the variable is passed to a device register that accepts characters from the keyboard. However, when the C compiler optimizes your program automatically, it intends to not update the value held by the variable unless the variable is on the left side of an assignment operator (=). In other words, the value of the variable is likely not changed even though the user is typing in characters from the keyboard.

To ask the compiler to turn off certain optimizations on a variable, you can declare the variable with the volatile specifier. For instance, in the following code portion, a variable, keyboard_ch, declared with the volatile specifier, tells the compiler not to optimize any expressions of the variable because the value saved by the variable may be changed without execution of any explicit assignment statement:

```
void read_keyboard()
{
   volatile char keyboard_ch; /* a volatile variable */
   .
   .
   .
}
```

POINTS TO PONDER

In this section you have learned the following points:

- A variable declared within a block has block scope. Such a variable is also called a local variable and is only visible within the block.
- The goto label has function scope, which means that it is visible through the whole block of the function within which the label is placed. No two goto labels share the same name within a function block.
- A variable declared with the static specifier outside a function has file scope, which means that it is visible throughout the entire source file in which the variable is declared.
- A variable declared outside a function is said to have program scope. Such a variable is also called a global variable. A global variable is visible in all source files that make up an executable program.
- A variable with block scope has the most limited visibility. On the other hand, a variable with program block is the most visible through all files, functions, and other blocks that make up the program.
- The storage class of a variable refers to the combination of its spatial and temporal regions (that is, its scope and duration.)
- By default, a variable with block scope has an auto duration, and its memory storage is temporary.
- A variable declared with the static specifier has permanent memory storage, even though the function in which the variable is declared has been called and the function scope has exited.
- A variable declared with the register specifier may be stored in a register to speed up the performance of a program; however, the compiler can ignore the specifier if there is no register available or if some other restrictions have to apply.
- You can also allude to a global variable defined elsewhere by using the extern specifier from the current source file.

- To make sure the value saved by a variable cannot be changed, you can declare the variable with the const modifier.
- If you want to let the compiler know that the value of a variable can be changed without an explicit assignment statement, declare the variable with the volatile modifier so that the compiler will turn off optimizations on expressions involving the variable.

QUESTIONS AND ANSWERS

Q1. *Can a global variable be hidden by a local variable with block scope?*

Ans: Yes. If a local variable shares the same name with a global variable, the global variable can be hidden by the local variable for the scope of the block within which the local variable is defined with block scope. However, outside the block, the local variable cannot be seen, but the global variable becomes visible again.

Q2. *Why do you need the static specifier?*

Ans: In many cases, the value of a variable is needed, even if the scope of the block, in which the variable is declared, has exited. By default, a variable with block scope has a temporary memory storage—that is, the lifetime of the variable starts when the block is executed and the variable is declared, and ends when the execution is finished. Therefore, to declare a variable with permanent duration, you have to use the static specifier to indicate to the compiler that the memory location of the variable and the value stored in the memory location should be retained after the execution of the block.

Q3. *Does using the register specifier guarantees to improve the performance of a program?*

Ans: Not really. Declaring a variable with the register specifier only suggests to the compiler that the variable be stored in a register. But there is no guarantee that the variable will be stored in a register. The compiler can ignore the request based on the availability of registers or other restrictions.

Q4. *When you declare a variable with the extern specifier, do you define the variable or allude to a global variable elsewhere?*

Ans: When a variable is declared with the extern specifier, the compiler considers the declaration of the variable as an allusion rather than a definition. The compiler will therefore look somewhere else to find a global variable to which the variable with extern alludes.

EXERCISES

A. Answer the following question:

1. What are automatic variables?
2. Why does register class not support all data types?
3. Can we declare a variable in different scopes with different data types? Answer in details.
4. Distinguish between static and extern variable?
5. What will be the initial values for the four storage classes of variables, if they are not given initial values?

6. What are the scope rules for the four storage classes?

B. Match the following:

I	II
1. auto	(*a*) can be defined using( )
2. extern	(*b*) same as global
3. static variable	(*c*) need not be stored in registers.
4. register variable	(*d*) load time variables
5. block	(*e*) default storage class.

C. Write True or False against each statements:

1. Internal static variables have temporary storage.
2. Address of registers type variable can be taken.
3. Between global and local variable having same name priority is given to global variable.
4. More than one storage class is allowed in a declaration.
5. The value of an auto variable persist when control goes out of a block.
6. External variable retail their values throughout the execution of the program.
7. Static variable are also called load time variables.
8. The default storage class is auto.

D. Fill in the blanks:

1. The storage class controls the __________, __________ and __________.
2. The auto variables have __________ scope.
3. __________ variable allocation does not allocate memory for a variable.
4. File scope is for __________ type of variable.
5. We cannot take address of __________ type of variable.
6. If the definition for an identifier does not have a storage class default storage __________ is assumed.

E. Brain Drill:

1. Write a program to calculate the sum of digits of the entered number. Create user-defined function sum_digit. Use static variable and calculate the sum of digits.
2. Write a program to create the for loop from 1 to 10000. Declare the loop variables of class register and auto. Observe the time required for completing the loop for both the type of variables. Find out in which class the execution time is minimum.

F. Predict the output of the following:

```
1. main ( )
   {
        auto int i= 10;
        {
             auto int i=5;
             printf("%d",i);
        }
```

```
            printf("%d",i+5);
            printf("%d",i);
        }
2. main ( )
        {
            extern int x;
            printf("%d",x);
        }
3. extern int x=20;
        main ( )
        {
            printf("%d",x);
        }
4. extern int x;
        main ( )
        {
            printf("%d",x);
        }
5. main ( )
        {
            void f(int);
            int i=1;
            f(i);
            f(i);
            f(i);
        }
        void f(int x)
        {
              static int y;
                y+=x;
             printf("%d\n",y);
            }
```

12

INTRODUCTION TO FILE HANDLING IN 'C'

The chapter provides detailed discussion of file handling in 'C'. A file is a means for the permanent storage of data.

The introduction part makes your basis by first telling you the normal working of program and data and its storage. Concept of file is then introduced by defining it and its **modus operandi**. Concept of stream, text and binary file, high and low level files is introduced.

Opening and closing of file is presented in the next section. It teaches you how to open close a file in C with the help of built-in data structure FILE. All the various modes for file manipulation is given in the form of table with their description. A lot of programming examples given which perform manipulation of data items stored in the file by opening in different modes.

Random access of file and related functions are converted. Command line arguments *i.e.* passing parameter to main functions with programming examples are covered in **section 12.5.** Saving and retrieving data to/ from file with complete menu driven program is covered in **section 12.7.** Some file error handling functions are covered in **section 12.8.**

12.1 INTRODUCTION

We all know that RAM is a volatile memory and any data stored in RAM is lost when PC is turned off. All the programs we have seen so far have made use of RAM. Any data variable that we define in our program is destroyed when the program execution is over. Also the outputs generated by the program are lost.

One solution may take printout of the program and outputs. They may help up to a certain extent but that is not appropriate for the practical purpose. Therefore in most real word applications data is stored in text files which is stored permanently on to the hard disk, floppy, compact disk or in any other persistent storage media. These files can be read back again, and can be modified also.

A data file is a collection of data items stored permanently in persistent storage area. The C language provides the facility to create these data files, write data into them, read back data, modify them and many more operations. The program data or output can be stored in these files and that persists even after program execution is over. The data can be read whenever necessary and can be placed back into the file after modification. The data remain safe provide storage media does not crash or corrupt.

From permanent storage point of view, a file is a region of memory space in the persistent storage media and it can be accessed using the built-in library functions available in the header files stdio.h or by the system calls of the operating systems. High level files are those files which are accessed and manipulated using standard library functions. For transfer of data they make use of stream. A stream is pointer to a buffer of memory which is used for transferring the data. In general stream can be assumed as a sequence of bytes which flow from source to destination. An I/O stream may be text stream or binary stream depending upon in which mode you have opened the file. A text stream contains lines of text and the characters in a text stream may be manipulated as per the suitability. But a binary stream is a sequence of unprocessed data without any modification. The standard I/O stream pointers are stdin (for reading), stdout (for output), and stderr (for error). By default stdin represent keyboard, stdout and stderr represents monitor or VDU.

Low level files make use of the system- calls of the operating system under which the program is run.

12.2 FILES VERSUS STREAMS

The C language provides a set of rich library functions to perform input and output (I/O) operation. Those functions can read or write any type of data to files. Before we go any further in discussing the C I/O functions, let's first understand the definitions of files and streams in C.

12.2.1 What Is a File?

In C, a file can refer to a disk file, a terminal, a printer, or a tape drive. In other words, a file represents a concrete device with which you want to exchange information. Before you perform any communication to a file, you have to open the file. Then you need to close the opened file after you finish exchanging information with it.

12.2.2 What is a Stream?

The data flow you transfer from your program to a file, or vice versa, is called a stream, which is a series of bytes. Not like a file, a stream is device-independent. All streams have the same behavior. To perform I/O operations, you can read from or write to any type of files by simply associating a stream to the file.

There are two formats of streams. The first one is called the text stream, which consists of a sequence of characters (that is, ASCII data). Depending on the compilers, each character line in a text stream may be terminated by a newline character. Text streams are used for textual data, which has a consistent appearance from one environment to another or from one machine to another.

The second format of streams is called the binary stream, which is a series of bytes. The content of an .exe file would be one example. Binary streams are primarily used for nontextual data, which is required to keep the exact contents of the file.

12.2.3 Buffered I/O

In C, a memory area, which is temporarily used to store data before it is sent to its destination, is called a buffer. With the help of buffers, the operating system can improve efficiency by reducing the number of accesses to I/O devices (that is, files).

By default, all I/O streams are buffered. The buffered I/O is also called the high-level I/O. Accordingly, the low-level I/O refers to the unbuffered I/O.

12.3 THE BASICS OF DISK FILE I/O

Now let's focus on how to open and close a disk data file and how to interpret error messages returned by I/O functions.

12.3.1 Pointers of File

The FILE structure is the file control structure defined in the header file stdio.h. A pointer of type FILE is called a file pointer, which references a disk file. A file pointer is used by a stream to conduct the operation of the I/O functions. For instance, the following defines a file pointer called fptr:

```
FILE *fptr;
```

In the FILE structure there is a member, called the file position indicator, that points to the position in a file where data will be read from or written to. You'll learn how to move the file position indicator in the coming section.

12.3.2 Opening and Closing a File

OPENING A FILE: The C I/O function **fopen ()** gives you the ability to open a file and associate a stream to the opened file. You need to specify the way to open a file and the filename with the **fopen ()** function.

The syntax for the **fopen ()** function is

```
#include <stdio.h>

FILE *fopen(const char *filename, const char *mode);
```

Here filename is a char pointer that references a string of a filename. The filename is given to the file that is about to be opened by the **fopen ()** function. Mode points to another string that specifies the way to open the file. The **fopen ()** function returns a pointer of type FILE. If an error occurs during the procedure to open a file, the **fopen ()** function returns a **null pointer.**

A file must be opened before you can perform any operation on it *i.e.* reading or writing. Before opening a file we have to create a pointer of structure FILE type which is defined in file stdio.h. Then the file is opened using fopen function. The function takes two arguments:

(*a*) First is the file name which is to be opened.

(*b*) Second is the mode in which we want to open the file.

For the time being remember *"r"* and *"w"* *i.e.* read and write mode respectively. A complete mode list which you can have as a second argument is given in the table. The function fopen returns a pointer of FILE type which actually represents the file. Any operation the file now on will be performed using this file pointer.

CLOSING A FILE: After a disk file is read, written, or appended with some new data, you have to disassociate the file from a specified stream by calling the **fclose** () function.

The syntax for the **fclose ()** function is

```
#include <stdio.h>
int fclose (FILE *stream);
```

Here stream is a file pointer that is associated with a stream to the opened file. If **fclose ()** closes a file successfully, it **returns 0.** Otherwise, the function returns **EOF.** Normally, the **fclose()** function fails only when the disk is removed before the function is called or there is no more space left on the disk.

Since all high-level I/O operations are buffered, the **fclose ()** function flushes data left in the buffer to ensure that no data will be lost before it disassociates a specified stream with the opened file.

Note that a file that is opened and associated with a stream has to be closed after the I/O operation. Otherwise, the data saved in the file may be lost; some unpredictable errors might occur during the execution of your program.

Now, let's create a small program which gives you an idea of file handling in C.

```
/*Prog 12.1 Demo of file handling, writing to file*/
#include<stdio.h>
#include<conio.h>
 void main()
 {
   FILE*fp;
   fp=fopen("demo1.txt", "w");
   fprintf(fp, "This is my first program of file handling in C\n");
   fclose(fp);
   getch();
 }
```

EXPLANATION: In the program we have created a file pointer fp of type FILE. Any valid identifier name can be used. The function fopen opens the file demo1.txt in write mode due to "*w*" If the file does not exist it will created. The function fprintf is used to write into the file whose first argument is the file pointer and second is the string which we want to the file. In the last statement we have closed the file using fclose function which accepts only argument the file pointer *fp*. An opened file must be closed which flushes all data in its related buffer and closes its link. More about file closing later on. As we have written data to the file, there will be no output on to the screen but the sole outcome of the program is the creation of file demo1.txt with some data written into it. The prototype of all the functions used is as follows:

```
#include<stdio.h>
```

```
int fprintf(FILE *stream, const char* format [arguments,....]);
FILE * fopen(const char * filename, const char *mode);
int fclose(FILE *stream);
```

Argument in square brackets are optional in function fprintf.

Now, the below table show lists of all the files modes and their associated meaning.

Table 12.1 *Various file opening modes*

File Mode	*Meaning*
"r"	Opens an existing text file for reading only, error if file does not exist
"w"	Open a new file for writing only. If file does not exist it will be created else existing file be destroyed and new file be created.
"r+"	Open an existing file for reading and writing purpose. Error if file does not exist.
"w+"	Open a new file for reading and writing. If file does not exist it will be created else existing file will be destroyed and new file will be created.
"a+"	Open an exiting file for reading and appending. If file does not exit it will be created else exiting file will be destroyed and new file will be created.
"rb"	opens an existing binary file for reading
"wb"	creates a binary file for writing
"ab"	opens an existing binary file for appending
"r+b"	opens an existing binary file for reading or writing
"w+b"	creates a binary file for reading or writing
"a+b"	opens or creates a binary file for appending

Note that you might see people use the mode ***"rb+"*** instead of ***"r+b"***. These two strings are equivalent. Similarly, ***"wb+"*** is the same as ***"w+b"***; ***"ab+"*** is equivalent to ***"a+b"***.

To read file in text mode we can append "t" to the existing modes. For example we can write ***"rt"***, ***"wt"***, ***"at"***, ***"r+t"***, ***"w+t"*** and ***"a+t"***. But writing ***"t"*** is optional as by default all files are opened in text mode and files created in this manner are also known as **ASCII** text files. For opening files in binary mode we can append ***"b"*** to the existing modes given in the table. They are discussed later in the chapter.

```
/*Prog 12.2 Demo of file handling, reading from the file*/
#include<stdio.h>
#include<conio.h>
 void main()
 {
  FILE*fp;
  char str[50];
  fp=fopen("demo1.txt", "r");
```

```
  fgets(str,sizeof(str),stdin);
  fprintf(stdout, "String read from file is \n");
  fprintf(stdout, "%s\n",str);
  fclose(fp);
 }
```

Output:

```
String read from file is
This is my first program of file handling in C
```

EXPLANATION: In the first program we had stored into the demo1.txt file. In this program we open the same file in read mode and read the string from the file. The string is read into the variable, good enough to hold the string read from file. The same string is displayed onto the screen using fprintf. Stdout represent the standard output stream that is our VDU or monitor. This is equivalent to file pointer pointing to screen and treating it as a file. The two fprintf statements can be simply replaced using printf but to give you a feel of how screen can be treated as a file we have given these statements. The alternate printf statements would be:

```
printf("String read from file is \n");
printf("%s\n",str);
```

The function fgets is equivalent to gets, with the difference that instead of just one argument it takes three arguments: pointer to char (say *p*), size of string in integer (say *n*), and file pointer (say *fp*). It simply read a string of *n* characters (second parameter) into *p* from file pointed by *fp*.

```
/* Prog 12.3 Opening and closing a file */
#include<stdio.h>
#include<conio.h>
  enum {SUCCESS, FAIL};
  void main(void)
  {
    FILE *fptr;
    char filename[]= "demo1.txt";
    int reval = SUCCESS;
    clrscr();
    if((fptr = fopen(filename, "r")) == NULL)
    {
     printf("Cannot open %s.\n", filename);
     reval = FAIL;
    }
    else
    {
     printf("The value of fptr: 0x%p\n", fptr);
```

```
        printf("Ready to close the file.");
        fclose(fptr);
    }
    return reval;
}
```

Output:

```
The value of fptr: 0x0152
Ready to close the file.
```

EXPLANATION: The purpose of the program 12.3 is to show you how to open a text file. From the expression in **line 12,** you can see that the **fopen()** function tries to open a text file with the name contained by the character array filename for reading. The filename array is defined and initialized with the name **demo1.txt** in **line 9.**

If an error occurs when you try to open the text file, the **fopen()** function returns a null pointer. **Line 13** then prints a warning message, and **line 14** assigns the value represented by the **enum name FAIL** to the int variable **reval.** From the declaration of the **enum** data type in **line 4,** we know that the value of **FAIL is 1.**

If, however, the **fopen()** function opens the text file successfully, the statement in **line 16** prints the value contained by the file pointer fptr. **Line 17** tells the user that the program is about to close the file, and **line 18** then closes the file by calling **the fclose() file.**

In **line 21,** the return statement returns the value of **reval** that contains **0** if the text file has been opened successfully or 1 otherwise.

From the output shown on my screen, I see that the value held by the file pointer fptr is **0x013E** after the text file is opened.

12.4 READING AND WRITING DISK FILES

The **program 12.3** does not do anything with the text file, **demo1.txt,** except open and close it. So how can you read any information from the file?

In C, you can perform I/O operations in the following ways:

- Read or write one character at a time.
- Read or write one line of text (that is, one character line) at a time.
- Read or write one block of characters at a time.

The following three sections explain the three ways to read and write to disk files.

12.4.1 One Character at a Time

Among the C I/O functions, there is a pair of functions, **fgetc() and fputc(),** that can be used to read from or write to a disk file one character at a time.

The syntax for the **fgetc()** function is

```
#include <stdio.h>
```

```
int fgetc(FILE *stream);
```

Here stream is the file pointer that is associated with a stream. The **fgetc()** function fetches the next character from the stream specified by stream. The function then returns the value of an int that is converted from the character.

The syntax for the **fputc()** function is

```
#include <stdio.h>
int fputc(int c, FILE *stream);
```

Here *c* is an int value that represents a character. In fact, the int value is converted to an unsigned char before being outputted. Stream is the file pointer that is associated with a stream. The **fputc()** function returns the character written if the function is successful; otherwise, it returns EOF. After a character is written, the **fputc()** function advances the associated file pointer.

To understand how to use the **fgetc() and fputc()** functions, let's have a look a program that opens a text file, and then reads and writes one character at a time.

```
/*Prog 12.4 Demo of Reading and writing one character at a time */
#include <stdio.h>
#include<conio.h>
 enum {SUCCESS, FAIL};
 void CharReadWrite(FILE *fin, FILE *fout);
 main(void)
 {
    FILE *fptr1, *fptr2;
    char filename1[]= "hari.txt";
    char filename2[]= "demo1.txt";
    int reval = SUCCESS;
    clrscr();
    if ((fptr1 = fopen(filename1, "w")) == NULL)
    {
       printf("Cannot open %s.\n", filename1);
       reval = FAIL;
       }
       else if ((fptr2 = fopen(filename2, "r")) == NULL)
       {
 printf("Cannot open %s.\n", filename2);
 reval = FAIL;
 }
  else
  {
```

```
    CharReadWrite(fptr2, fptr1);
    fclose(fptr1);
    fclose(fptr2);
    }
    return reval;
  }
  /* function definition */
  void CharReadWrite(FILE *fin, FILE *fout)
  {
    int c;
    while ((c=fgetc(fin)) != EOF)
    {
       fputc(c, fout); /* write to a file */
       putchar(c); /* put the character on the screen */
    }
}
```

Output:

```
This is my first program of file handling in C
```

EXPLANATION: The purpose of the **program12.4** is to read one character from a file, write the character to another file, and then display the character on the screen.

In program there is a function called **CharReadWrite(),** which has two file pointers as its arguments. (See the declaration of the **CharReadWrite() function in line 6.)**

The statement in **line 10** defines two file pointers, **fptr1 and fptr2,** which are used later in the program. **Lines 11 and 12** define two character arrays, **filename1 and filename2,** and initialize the two arrays with two strings containing filenames, **hari.txt and demo1.txt.**

In **line 15,** a text file with the name hari.txt is opened for writing. Hari.txt is contained by the filename1 array. The file pointer **fptr1** is associated with the file. If the **fopen()** function returns NULL, which means an error occurs, a warning message is printed out in **line 16.** Also, in **line 17,** the reval variable is assigned 1 and is represented by the enum name **FAIL.** If the file hari.txt is opened successfully, another text file, called demo1.txt, is opened for reading in **line 18.** The file pointer **fptr2** is associated with the opened text file.

If no error occurs, the **CharReadWrite()** function is invoked in **line 22** with two file pointers, **fptr1 and fptr2,** passed to the function as arguments. From the definition of the **CharReadWrite()** function in **lines 30 and 38,** we see that there is a while loop that keeps calling the **fgetc()** function to read the next character from the haiku.txt text file until the function reaches the end of the file. (See line 34.)

Within the **while loop,** the **fputc()** function in **line 35** writes each character read from the demo1.txt file to another text file, hari.txt, which is pointed to by **fout.** In addition, **putchar()** is called in **line 36** in order to put the character returned by the **fgetc()** function on the screen.

After the **CharReadWrite()** function finishes its job, the two opened files, which are associated with **fptr1 and fptr2,** are closed with a call to the **fclose()** function respectively in **lines 23 and 24.**

12.4.2 One Line at a Time

Besides reading or writing one character at a time, you can also read or write one character line at time. There is a pair of C I/O functions, **fgets() and fputs(),** that allows you to do so.

The syntax for the **fgets()** function is

```
#include <stdio.h>
char *fgets(char *s, int n, FILE *stream);
```

Here *s* references a character array that is used to store characters read from the opened file pointed to by the file pointer stream. ***n*** specifies the maximum number of array elements. If it is successful, the **fgets()** function returns the **char pointer *s*.** If **EOF** is encountered, the **fgets()** function returns a null pointer and leaves the array untouched. If an error occurs, the function returns a null pointer, and the contents of the array are unknown.

The **fgets()** function can read up to ***n*-1** characters, and can append a null character after the last character fetched, until a newline or an **EOF** is encountered. Note that if a newline is encountered during the reading, the **fgets()** function includes the newline in the array. This is different from what the **gets()** function does. The **gets()** function just replaces the newline character with a null character

The syntax for the **fputs()** function is

```
#include <stdio.h>
int fputs(const char *s, FILE *stream);
```

Here *s* points to the array that contains the characters to be written to a file associated with the file pointer stream. The **const** modifier indicates that the content of the array pointed to by *s* cannot be changed. If it fails, the **fputs()** function returns a nonzero value; otherwise, it returns zero.

Note that the character array must include a null character at the end as the terminator to the **fputs()** function. Also, unlike the **puts()** function, the **fputs()** function does not insert a newline character to the string written to a file.

We can modify the program 12.4 to read or write one character line at a time by calling the **fgets() and fputs()** functions. The modified version is shown the below given program.

```
/* Prog 12.5 Demo of Reading and writing one line at a time */
#include <stdio.h>
#include <conio.h>
 enum {SUCCESS, FAIL, MAX_LEN = 81};
 void LineReadWrite(FILE *fin, FILE *fout);
 main(void)
 {
   FILE *fptr1, *fptr2;
   char filename1[]= "hari.txt";
   char filename2[]= "demo1.txt";
```

```
    int reval = SUCCESS;
    clrscr();
    if ((fptr1 = fopen(filename1, "w")) == NULL)
    {
      printf("Cannot open %s for writing.\n", filename1);
      reval = FAIL;
    }
     else if ((fptr2 = fopen(filename2, "r")) == NULL)
     {
      printf("Cannot open %s for reading.\n", filename2);
      reval = FAIL;
     }
      else
      {
 LineReadWrite(fptr2, fptr1);
 fclose(fptr1);
 fclose(fptr2);
      }
  return reval;
 }
 /* function definition */
 void LineReadWrite(FILE *fin, FILE *fout)
 {
    char buff[MAX_LEN];
    while (fgets(buff, MAX_LEN, fin) != NULL){
    fputs(buff, fout);
    printf("%s", buff);
 }
 }
```

Output:

```
This is my first program of file handling in C
```

EXPLANATION: From the **program 12.5,** you can see that a function called **LineReadWrite()** has replaced the **CharReadWrite()** function.

The definition of the **LineReadWrite()** function is shown in **lines 30_38.** The **fgets()** function is called repeatedly in a **while** loop to read one character line at a time from the **demo1.txt** text file, until it reaches the end of the text file. In **line 34,** the array name **buff** and the maximum number of the array elements **MAX_LEN** are passed to the **fgets()** function, along with the file pointer fin that is associated with the opened **demo1.txt** file.

Meanwhile, each line read by the **fgets()** function is written to another opened text file called **hari.txt** that is associated with the file pointer **fout.** This is done by invoking the **fputs()** function in **line 35.**

12.4.3 One Block at a Time

If you like, you can also read or write a block of data at a time. In C, there are two I/O functions, **fread() and fwrite(),** that can be used to perform block I/O operations. The **fread()** and **fwrite()** functions are mirror images of each other.

- **fread () FUNCTION**

The syntax for the **fread()** function is

```
#include <stdio.h>
size_t fread(void *ptr, size_t size,size_t n,FILE *stream);
```

Here **ptr** is a pointer to an array in which the data is stored. **size** indicates the size of each array element. ***n*** specifies the number of elements to read. **stream** is a file pointer that is associated with the opened file for reading. **size_t** is an integral type defined in the header file **stdio.h.** The **fread()** function returns the number of elements actually read.

The number of elements read by the **fread()** function should be equal to the value specified by the third argument to the function, unless an error occurs or an **EOF (end-of-file)** is encountered. The **fread()** function returns the number of elements that are actually read, if an error occurs or an **EOF** is encountered.

- **fwrite() FUNCTION**

The syntax for the **fwrite()** function is

```
#include <stdio.h>
size_tfwrite(constvoid*ptr, size_tsize,size_tn,FILEstream);
```

Here **ptr** references the array that contains the data to be written to an opened file pointed to by the file pointer stream. **size** indicates the size of each element in the array. ***n*** specifies the number of elements to be written. The **fwrite()** function returns the number of elements actually written.

If there is no error occurring, the number returned by **fwrite ()** should be the same as the third argument in the function. The return value may be less than the specified value if an error occurs.

Note that it's the programmer's responsibility to ensure that the array is large enough to hold data for either the **fread ()** function or the **fwrite ()** function.

- **feof() FUNCTION**

In C, a function called **feof()** can be used to determine when the end of a file is encountered. This function is more useful when you're reading a **binary file** because the values of some bytes may be equal to the value of **EOF.** If you determine the end of a binary file by checking the value returned by **fread(),** you may end up at the wrong position. Using the **feof()** function helps you to avoid mistakes in determining the end of a file.

The syntax for the **feof()** function is

```
#include <stdio.h>
int feof(FILE *stream);
```

Here **stream** is the file pointer that is associated with an opened file. The **feof()** function **returns 0** if the end of the file has not been reached; otherwise, it returns a nonzero integer. The **program 12.6** shown below demonstrates how to read and write one block of characters at a time by calling the **fread() and fwrite()** functions. In fact, the **program 12.6** is another modified version of the **program 12.4.**

```
/*Prog 12.6 Demo of Reading and writing one block at a time */
#include <stdio.h>
#include <conio.h>
 enum {SUCCESS, FAIL, MAX_LEN = 80};
 void BlockReadWrite(FILE *fin, FILE *fout);
 int ErrorMsg(char *str);
 main(void)
 {
    FILE *fptr1, *fptr2;
    char filename1[]= "hari.txt";
    char filename2[]= "demo1.txt";
    int reval = SUCCESS;
    clrscr();
    if ((fptr1 = fopen(filename1, "w")) == NULL)
    {
       reval = ErrorMsg(filename1);
    }
     else if ((fptr2 = fopen(filename2, "r")) == NULL)
     {
       reval = ErrorMsg(filename2);
     }
      else
      {
BlockReadWrite(fptr2, fptr1);
fclose(fptr1);
fclose(fptr2);
      }
 return reval;
}
/* function definition */
 void BlockReadWrite(FILE *fin, FILE *fout)
 {
```

```
    int num;
    char buff[MAX_LEN + 1];
    while (!feof(fin)){
    num = fread(buff, sizeof(char), MAX_LEN, fin);
    buff[num * sizeof(char)] = '\0';/* append a null character */
    printf("%s", buff);
    fwrite(buff, sizeof(char), num, fout);
  }
  }
 /* function definition */
 int ErrorMsg(char *str)
 {
    printf("Cannot open %s.\n", str);
     return FAIL;
 }
```

```
Output:
This is my first program of file handling in C
```

EXPLANATION: The purpose of the **program12.6** is to show you how to invoke the **fread() and fwrite ()** functions in your program to perform block I/O operations. In the **program 12.6,** the **demo1.txt** file is read by the **fread()** function, and then the **fwrite()** function is used to write the contents read from **demo1.txt** to another file called **hari.txt** We call the two C I/O functions from our own function, **BlockReadWrite().**

From the definition of the **BlockReadWrite()** function in **lines 29_40,** you can see that a character array called **buff** is defined with the number of elements of **MAX_LEN + 1 in line 32,** although we only read **MAX_LEN** number of characters by calling the **fread()** function in **line 35.** The reason is that we append a **null** character in **line 36** after the last character read so that we ensure the block of characters saved in **buff** is treated as a string and can be printed out on the screen properly by the **printf()** function in **line 37.**

The **while** loop, shown in **lines 34_39,** keeps calling the **fread()** function to read a character block with **MAX_LEN** elements, until the **feof ()** function in **line 34 returns 0,** which means that the end of the text file has been reached. As shown in **lines 35 and 38,** we use the **sizeof** operator to measure the size of the **char data type** because the elements in the **buff** array are all characters.

```
/*Prog 12.7 Demo input output using stdin and stdout*/
#include<stdio.h>
#include<conio.h>
 void main()
 {
    char str[80];
    clrscr();
```

```
   fprintf(stdout, "Enter a string\n");
   fgets(str,sizeof(str),stdin);
   fprintf(stdout, "The string is %s\n",str);
   getch();
 }
```

Output:

```
Enter a string
This is Hari Mohan Pandey Lecturer Computer Science
The string is This is Hari Mohan Pandey Lecturer Computer Science
```

EXPLANATION: We have simply used **fprintf and fgets** functions to demonstrate that how **stdin** and **stdout** with these functions. Again they can be replaced by alternate **printf** statements.

```
/*Prog 12.8 Appending data to an exiting file*/
#include<stdio.h>
#include<conio.h>
 void main()
 {
  FILE*fp;
  char str[20];
  clrscr();
  fp=fopen("Demo1.txt", "a");
  fprintf(stdout, "Enter a string to append \n");
  gets(str);
  fprintf(fp, "%s",str);
  fclose(fp);
  getch();
 }
```

Output:

```
Enter a string to append
Append string
```

EXPLANATION: We have simply opened the file in the append mode. A string is taken from user through keyboard and append the same to the file demo1.txt. You can verify this by opening the file in any editor even turbo C.

For the next program we assume that there is a file demo2.txt whose contents are just one string **"EAT DRINK AND BE MARRY".**

```
/*Prog 12.9 Demo of r+ mode*/
#include<stdio.h>
#include<conio.h>
#include<stdlib.h>
 void main()
```

```
{
    FILE*fp;
    char str[30];
    clrscr();
    fp=fopen("demo2.txt", "r+");
    if(fp==NULL)
    {
        printf("File opening error");
        getch();
        exit(0);
    }
    fgets(str,sizeof(str),fp);
    fprintf(stdout, "The string read from file %s",str);
    fclose(fp);
}
```

Output

```
The string read from file EAT DRINK AND BE MARRY
```

EXPLANATION: The **mode *"r+"*** opens an existing file for reading and writing. To ensure that file exists prior to reading and writing we checked *fp* against **NULL.** If file does not found or any other error in opening the file occurs **fopen** function returns **NULL** which is defined in the file **stdio.h.** If this is so we have printed error message on to the screen and terminated the program. If everything is ok we read string from file and display on to the screen.

```
/*Prog 12.10 Writing and reading the same file ver1*/
#include<stdio.h>
#include<conio.h>
 void main()
 {
  FILE*fp;
  char str[50];
  clrscr();
  fp=fopen("temp1.text", "w");
  printf("Enter a string \n");
  gets(str);
  fprintf(fp,str);
  fclose(fp);
  fp=fopen("temp1.txt", "r");
  printf("String read from file is \n");
  fgets(str,sizeof(str),fp);
  printf("%s",str);
```

```
  fclose(fp);
  getch();
}
```

Output:

```
Enter a string
India is a great country
String read from file is
India is a great country
```

EXPLANATION: In the program we have opened the file first in write mode. A string is added to the file taking input from the user through the keyboard. The file is then closed. The same file is then opened in read mode and string is read back from file and displayed. Note the file is closed before opening it back in read mode. This is must as when a string is placed in the file the file pointer has advanced by the length of the string. To read the data back from the file we need to read it from the beginning. In both the mode, whenever the file is opened the file pointer is placed at the beginning of the file.

To read and write through the same file before closing at intermediate stage see the next program given below.

```
/*Prog 12.11 Writing and reading the same file ver2*/
#include<stdio.h>
#include<conio.h>
 void main()
 {
    FILE*fp;
    char str[50];
    clrscr();
    fp=fopen("temp1.txt", "w+");
    printf("Enter a string\n");
    gets(str);
    fprintf(fp,str);
    rewind(fp);
    printf("String read from file is \n");
    fgets(str,sizeof(str),fp);
    printf("%s",str);
    fclose(fp);
    getch();
 }
```

Output:

```
Enter a string
Honesty is the best policy
String read from file is
```

```
Honesty is the best policy
```

EXPLANATION: The program is similar to the previous one with the difference of **rewind** function. This function takes file pointer to the beginning of the file so we can now read without first closing and then opening in read mode. It takes just file pointer is its only argument. The file is opened initially in ***"w+"* mode.**

```
/*Prog 12.12 Writing and reading the same file using EOF as terminator*/
#include<stdio.h>
#include<conio.h>
void main()
{
  FILE*fp;
  char ch;
  clrscr();
  fp=fopen("demo2.txt", "w");
  printf("Enter a string, press F6 or ctrl-z to stop\n");
  ch=getchar();
  while(ch!=EOF)
  {
    putc(ch,fp);
    ch=getchar();
  }
  fclose(fp);
  fp=fopen("demo2.txt", "r");
  printf("Contents of file demo2.txt\n");
  ch=getc(fp);
  while(ch!=EOF)
  {
    putchar(ch);
    ch=getc(fp);
  }
  fclose(fp);
  getch();
}
```

Output:

```
Enter a string, press F6 or ctrl-z to stop
Only constant repitition will finally succeed in imprinting an idea on
the memory of the crowed
-Adolf Hitler.
^Z
```

```
Contents of file demo2.txt
Only constant repitition will finally succeed in imprinting an idea on
the memor
y of the crowed
-Adolf Hitler.
```

EXPLANATION: There is a lot of new material in this program. **EOF is a macro** defined in **stdio.h** which stand for **End Of File** and its **value is 26.** It is used to check for end of file character. We input from user and indefinite length of string character by character through **getchar ().** The function scan each character typed on the screen and checks it against **EOF** which will be generated when user presses **CTRL-Z of F6.** This is achieved through while loop. If the character is not **EOF** it is put into the file by **macro putc** which is used to put a single character into the file. When **EOF** is encountered in input **while** loop ends and file is closed. The file is then opened in read mode and reading is done again character by character basis. The macro **getc** is used to extract single character from file. As a null character denote end of string in C an end of file character denotes end of file. Note both the functions/macro advances file pointer to the next character while reading **(getc)** and while writing (putc)

The while loop in the above program can be written in the more compact way as follows:

```
/* for writing into file*/
while((ch = = getchar ( ))!=EOF)
putc(ch, fp);
/*for reading from file*/
while ((ch= =getc(fp))!=EOF)
putchar(ch);
```

The prototype of functions/ macros used in the program are as:

```
#include<stdio.h>
int getc(FILE*)
int putc(int c, FILE*);
int putc(int c,FILE*);
```

Both macros return EOF on error

In the above program getc and putc can be replaced by the following function **fgetc** and **fputc.** They differ from **getc and putc** that they are functions not **macros.**

```
/*Prog 12.13 writing and reading numeric data to/from file*/
#include<stdio.h>
#include<conio.h>
 void main()
 {
    FILE*fp;
    int i;
    clrscr();
    fp=fopen("num.txt", "w");
```

```
    for(i=0;i<=10;i++)
    putw(i,fp);
    fclose(fp);
    fp=fopen("num.txt", "r");
    while(1)
    {
     i=getw(fp);
     if(feof(fp)!=0)
        break;
     printf("%d",i);
    }
    fclose(fp);
    getch();
 }
```

Output:

012345678910

EXPLANATION: putw is used to put an integer into the file and **getw** to get one integer from file. First we have **put 10 integer** into the file through **putw** by opening the file in the write mode. Then by closing and opening in read mode we have extract the numbers through **getw.** This time for testing end of the file we have used built in function **feof** whose only argument is the file pointer. **This function returns zero value while reading from file. When end of file reaches it returns non- zero value.** So we run an infinite while loop and inside the loop check the value returned by feof(). If it returns non-zero we come out from loop.

The while can be written in the following manner also:

```
While (feof(fp)= = 0)
{
    i= getw(fp);
    printf("%d",i);
}
```

The prototype of the functions/macros used in the program is as :

```
#include<stdio.h>
int getw(FILE*);
int putw(int c, FILE*);
```

Both macros return EOF on error.

```
/*Prog 12.14 File copying*/
#include<stdio.h>
#include<conio.h>
 void main()
 {
```

```
    FILE*fp1,*fp2;
    char s1[15],s2[15],ch;
    clrscr();
    printf("Enter the source file name \n");
    scanf("%s",s1);
    fp1=fopen(s1, "r");
    if(fp1==NULL)
    {
     printf("Error in opening file %s\n",s1);
     getch();
     exit(0);
    }
    printf("Enter the destination file name\n");
    scanf("%s",s2);
    fp2=fopen(s2, "w");
    if(fp2==NULL)
    {
      printf("Enter the destination file name \n");
      getch();
      exit(0);
    }
    while(feof(fp1)==0)
    {
      ch=fgetc(fp1);
      fputc(ch,fp2);
    }
    fclose(fp1);
    fclose(fp2);
}
```

Output:

```
Enter the source file name
demo1.txt
Enter the destination file name
hari.txt
```

EXPLANATION: In the above program we are copying an entire file into another file character by character basis. We have opened the source file in read mode and destination file in write mode. The file names are taken as input. We have also checked that source file exist and if there is any error in opening the file we simply display the appropriate message and terminate the program, otherwise we read one character from source file and put into the destination file. This continues till source file ends. The end of file condition we have checked through **feof** function.

```
/*Prog 12.15 Working with two file at a time */
#include<stdio.h>
#include<conio.h>
 void main()
 {
    FILE *fp1,*fp2;
    char str[10];
    clrscr();
    fp1=fopen("names.txt", "w");
    fprintf(fp1, "Hari\n");
    fprintf(fp1, "Vijay\n");
    fprintf(fp1, "Ruchika\n");
    fprintf(fp1, "Ranjana\n");
    fprintf(fp1, "Anjana\n");
    fclose(fp1);
    fp2=fopen("sname.txt", "w");
    fprintf(fp2, "Pandey\n");
    fprintf(fp2, "Pandey\n");
    fprintf(fp2, "Arora\n");
    fprintf(fp2, "Pandey\n");
    fprintf(fp2, "Pandey\n");
    fclose(fp2);
    fp1=fopen("name.txt", "r");
    fp2=fopen("sname.txt", "r");
    while(1)
    {
       fscanf(fp1, "%s",str);
       printf("%s",str);
       if((feof(fp2)!=0) || (feof(fp1)!=0))
       {
          getch();
          exit(0);
       }
     fscanf(fp2, "%s",str);
     printf("%s\n",str);
    }
    fclose(fp1);
    fclose(fp2);
    getch();
```

```
}
Output:
Hari Pandey
Vijay Pandey
Ruchika Arora
Ranjana Pandey
Anjana Pandey
```

EXPLANATION: In the program we have used two file name.txt in which we have stored few names and sname.txt in which we have stored surname. We open the two files simultaneously and display the full name. If end of any of the file is encountered we terminate the program.

12.5 RANDOM ACCESS IN A FILE

Random access means reading data randomly from any where in the file. For this purpose we need to set the position of the file pointer in the file and then read the data. C provides a function **fseek** which we can use to access data in a random fashion. The declaration of **fseek** function as given in **stdio.h**

```
int fseek(FILE*fp,long offset,int wh_from);
```

First argument is the file pointer pointing to the concerned file, second is the long number which may be positive or negative or zero. Third argument is the position which tells the compiler where to search from. It may take one of the following three values:

Table 12.2 *Argument to fseek and its meaning*

Value	*Meaning*	*Macro Name*
0	Beginning of file	SEEK_SET
1	Current Position	SEEK_CUR
2	End of file	SEEK_END

Offset positive means move forwards, –ve means move backwards and 0 means stay at the current position. First byte in the file is at position 0. Some of the examples of fseek functions are as follows:

```
fseek(fp,2,SEEK_SET)→ Third byte from beginning
fseek(fp,6,SEEK_CUR)→ Forward by 6 bytes from current pos
fseek(fp,-5,1)→ Backward by 5 bytes from current pos.
fseek(fp,-4,2)→ Backward by 4 bytes from end.
fseek(fp,0,1)→ Stay at the current position.
```

For a good understanding of the fseek function follows the next program which uses a file alpha.txt whose contents A-Z. I have moved the file pointer forward and backward to get appropriate character to print **"HARI"**. You may try other name.

```
/*Prog 12.16 Random access of name CHINTU character by character*/
```

```
#include<stdio.h>
#include<conio.h>
 void main()
 {
  FILE*fp;
  char ch;
  clrscr();
  fp=fopen("alpha.txt", "w+");
  fprintf(fp, "ABCDEFGHIJKLMNOPQRSTUVWXYZ\n");
  rewind(fp);
  fseek(fp,2,SEEK_SET);
/*0 may be used as third argument*/
  ch=fgetc(fp);
  /*read 3rd character from begining i.e. C and pointer moved to D after reading*/
  printf("%c",ch);
  fseek(fp,4,SEEK_CUR);
  /*1 may be used as third argument */
  ch=fgetc(fp);
  /*read 4th character from current pos + 1 i.e. E, pointer moved to I after reading*/
  printf("%c",ch);
  fseek(fp,0,1);
  ch=fgetc(fp);
/* read charcater at current pos i.e. I, pointer moved to J after reading*/
  printf("%c",ch);
  fseek(fp,4,SEEK_CUR);
  /*read charcater from current pos+1 i.e. K, pointer moved to O after reading*/
  ch=fgetc(fp);
  printf("%c",ch);
  fseek(fp,-9,SEEK_END);
 /*read character from end, consider Z at -3 so T will be at -9, pointer moved to U after reading */
  ch=fgetc(fp);
  printf("%c",ch);
  fseek(fp,0,SEEK_CUR);
/*read character at current pos i.e. U*/
```

```
  ch=fgetc(fp);
  printf("%c",ch);
  fclose(fp);
  getch();
 }
```

Output:

CHINTU

EXPLANATION: The position is quite self explanatory as comments are inserted at appropriate places. When you place *n* inside the file as this is done in the program then start counting *z* from – 3 position else count *z* from position – 1(remove *n*).

There are two more functions related to random access to file. They are **rewind** which we have seen an **ftell.** The prototype of the function **ftell** is as given in **stdio.h.**

long ftell(FILE*);

ftell returns the current position of the file being pointed by the file pointer. For example in the following statements:

```
1. FILE*fp=fopen(demo.txt", "w");
   pos=ftell(fp);
```

Whenever a file is opened in read or writes mode the file pointer is placed at the beginning of the file *i.e.* at the first character which is at position **0** so **pos** will have **0** which **ftell** returns.

```
2. FILE*fp=fopen("demo.txt", "r");
   fseek(fp,0,2);
   pos=ftell(fp);
```

fseek move the pointer to the end of the file so pos will have number of characters in the file.

```
/*Prog 12.17 Counting number of character in a file*/
#include<stdio.h>
#include<conio.h>
 void main()
 {
  FILE*fp;
  long int n;
  clrscr();
  fp=fopen("demo1.txt", "r");
  fseek(fp,0,2);
  n=ftell(fp);
  printf("Number of characters in the file are %d\n",n);
  getch();
 }
```

Output:

```
Number of characters in the file are 85
```

EXPLANATION: The program is self-explanatory.

```
/*Prog 12.18 Counting number of character and lines in a files*/
#include<stdio.h>
#include<conio.h>
#include<errno.h>
 void main()
 {
   FILE*fp;
   int countl=0, countc=0;
   char ch;
   clrscr();
   fp=fopen("demo1.txt", "r");
   if(!fp)
   {
    printf("Error in opening file\n");
    getch();
    exit(0);
   }
   while(!feof(fp))
   {
    ch=fgetc(fp);
    if(ch=='\n')
    countl++;
    countc++;
   }
   printf("Number of charcters in the file=%d\n",countc);
   printf("Number of lines in the file=%d\n",countl);
   fclose(fp);
   getch();
 }
Output:
Number of characters in the file=81
Number of lines in the file=2
```

EXPLANATION: For counting number of lines in file we read whole file character by character and count number of '\n' which gives us number of lines.

```
/*Prog 12.19 Counting number of words in a file */
#include<stdio.h>
#include<conio.h>
```

```
#include<string.h>
 void main()
 {
  FILE*fp;
  int countw=0,check, i,len,words=0;
  char s[50];
  clrscr();
  fp=fopen("demo1.txt", "r");
  if(!fp)
  {
   printf("Error in opening file\n");
   getch();
   exit(0);
  }
  check=(int)fgets(s,sizeof(s),fp);
  while(check)
  {
   len=strlen(s);
   i=0;
   while(i<len-1)
   {
    if((s[i]==' '&&s[i+1]!=' ')||(s[i]!=' ' && s[i+1]=='\n'))
     words++;
    i++;
   }
   check=(int)fgets(s,sizeof(s),fp);
  }
  printf("Number of words in the file=%d\n",words);
  fclose(fp);
  getch();
 }
```

Output:

```
Number of words in the file=16
```

EXPLANATION: Through outer **while loop** we read a string of **16** characters at a time and run an inner while loop for the length of string read. For checking a word we check that **ith** character of string must be a space and **(*i*+1)th** character must be a space or ***i* th** character of string must not be a space and **(*i*+1)th** character must be a **'\n'.** You can check this logic against the contents of any file. The string length may be of any other size other than **16.**

/*Reversing a case of characters of a file and storing it i the new file*/

```
#include<stdio.h>
#include<conio.h>
#include<string.h>
 void main()
 {
   FILE *fp,*fp1;
   char ch;
   clrscr();
   fp=fopen("demo1.txt"."r");
   fp1=fopen("demo2.txt", "w");
   if(!fp)
   {
     printf("Error in opening file \n");
     getch();
     exit(0);
   }
   ch=fgetc(fp);
   while(ch!=EOF)
   {
     if(isupper(ch))
      fputc(tolower(ch),fp1);
      else if(islower(ch))
       fputc(toupper(ch),fp1);
     else
      putc(ch,fp1);
      ch=fgetc(fp);
   }
   fclose(fp);
   fclose(fp1);
   getch();
 }
```

EXPLANATION: The program is self-explanatory.

12.6 COMMAND LINE ARGUMENTS

In all the programs we have used so far we have written **main()** without arguments but in reality **main()** does not take arguments and also have a return type. The prototype of **main()** in C is :

```
int main(int argc, char*argv[])
or
```

int main(int argc, charargv)**

Number of parameters are passed are collected into the parameters argc which stands for arguments count. Value of each argument is stored in string array argv which stands for argument value. All arguments are of string type whether they are int, float or even a character. By default return type of any function if not specified int is assigned that's why int before main() is optional. For better understanding stand point see few program given below:

```
/*Prog 12.20 Demo of command line argument line arguments*/
#include<stdio.h>
#include<conio.h>
 main(int argc, char*argv[])
 {
   int i;
   clrscr();
   for(i=1;i<argc;i++)
   printf("Argument %d=%s\n",i+1,argv[i]);
   getch();
 }
```

Output:

```
Argument 2=this
Argument 3=is
Argument 4=hari
Argument 5=mohan
Argument 6=pandey
```

EXPLANATION: Type the above program on **Turbo C** editor and press **F9** which will make **.exe file (executable file) f21** assuming the file name is **f21.C.** Now come at the **DOS** prompt by using **DOS shell** option in file menu. At the **DOS** prompt type

C:\tc>f21 This is Hari Mohan Pandey

And then press **ENTER.** You will get the output as shown above.

Here total number of arguments is **6** stored in **argc** with a space between each command line argument. First argument is the file name itself we have not printed **f21** is stored in **argv[0],** second argument This is stored in **argv[1]** and so on. The parameter name **argc** and **argv** are not fixed. They may be something else.

```
/*Prog 12.21 Sum of command line arguments */
#include<stdio.h>
#include<conio.h>
#include<stdlib.h>
 main(int argc,char* *argv)
 {
```

```
   int i,sum=0;
   clrscr();
   for(i=1;i<argc;i++)
   sum=sum+atoi(argv[i]);
   printf("sum is %d\n",sum);
   getch();
 }
```

Output:

```
sum is 21
```

EXPLANATION: As mentioned in the previous program the argument supplied at command line are by default treated as strings. We run the program as:

C:\TC>f22 1 2 3 4 5 6

Now starting from second argument that 1 each argument is converted into integer with the help of built-in function **atoi** whose prototype is given in file **stdlib.h** and summed up in variable sum.

/*Prog 12.22 Max of float numbers supplied as command line arguments */

```
#include<stdio.h>
#include<conio.h>
#include<stdlib.h>
 main(int argc,char * *argv)
 {
  int i;
  float max,t;
  clrscr();
  max=atof(argv[1]);
  for(i=1;i<argc;i++)
  {
   t=atof(argv[i]);
   if(max<t)
   max=t;
  }
  printf("max is %f\n",max);
  getch();
 }
```

EXPLANATION: The program is self explanatory.

/*Prog 12.23 Copying of one file into another with file name supplied as command line argument*/

```
#include<stdio.h>
#include<conio.h>
```

```
#include<stdlib.h>
 main(int argc, char * *argv)
 {
  FILE*fp,*fp1;
  char ch;
  clrscr();
  if(argc!=2)
  {
   printf("Usage:<filename><source file><des file>");
   getch();
   exit(0);
  }
  fp=fopen(argv[1], "r");
  fp1=fopen(argv[2], "w");
  if(fp==NULL)
  {
   printf("File opening error");
   getch();
   exit(0);
  }
  while(!feof(fp))
  {
   ch=fgetc(fp);
   fputc(ch,fp1);
  }
  fclose(fp);
  fclose(fp1);
 }
```

EXPLANATION: In the program we take the source file and destination file as command line arguments. If number of arguments are not there we flash an error message. Similarly if there is error in opening source file we flash error. If all goes well we copy source file into destination character by character basis.

12.7 ENVIRONMENT VARIABLE

Environment variables are variables related with the present operating system environment. They provide different system settings and path to various directories in the current **OS.** The output may vary from **OS to OS.** They are utmost importance in **UNIX/ LINUX OS** but not so important in **DOS** environment. A program displays all environment variables in given below. You will be surprised to know that all environment variables are passed as a array of strings as a third argument to main function. Output again as I said may vary from **OS to OS.** Some of the environment variables are easy to understand like **PROMPT, HOMEDRIVE, OS etc.**

```
/*Prog 12.24 Display of environment variable*/
#include<stdio.h>
#include<conio.h>
 main(int argc,char*argv[],char*env[])
 {
  int i;
  clrscr();
  printf("Environment variables are \n");
  for(i=0;env[i];i++)
   printf("%s\n",env[i]);
  getch();
 }
```

Output:

```
MSDEVDIR=C:\Program Files\Microsoft Visual Studio\Common\MSDev98
NUMBER_OF_PROCESSORS=2
OS=Windows_NT
PATH=C:\WINDOWS\system32;C:\WINDOWS;C:\WINDOWS\system32\WBEM;c:\Xilinx\bin\nt;C:
\PROGRA~1\MICROS~3\Common\Tools\WinNT;C:\PROGRA~1\MICROS~3\Common\MSDev98\Bin;C:
\PROGRA~1\MICROS~3\Common\Tools;C:\PROGRA~1\MICROS~3\VC98\bin;C:\TCWIN45\BIN
PATHEXT=.COM;.EXE;.BAT;.CMD;.VBS;.VBE;.JS;.JSE;.WSF;.WSH
PROCESSOR_ARCHITECTURE=x86
PROCESSOR_IDENTIFIER=x86 Family 6 Model 15 Stepping 2, GenuineIntel
PROCESSOR_LEVEL=6
PROCESSOR_REVISION=0f02
PROGRAMFILES=C:\PROGRA~1
PROMPT=$P$G
SESSIONNAME=Console
SONICCENTRAL=C:\Program Files\Common Files\Sonic Shared\Sonic Central\
SYSTEMDRIVE=C:
SYSTEMROOT=C:\WINDOWS
TEMP=C:\WINDOWS\TEMP
TMP=C:\WINDOWS\TEMP
USERDOMAIN=NMIMS-52B70327A
USERNAME=Admin
USERPROFILE=C:\DOCUME~1\Admin
```

```
XILINX=c:\Xilinx
BLASTER=A220 I5 D1 P330 T3
```

EXPLANATION: The third argument in main receives array of strings as environment variables. With the help of for loop we have displayed environment variables till the last entry in **env** array is **null.**

12.8 STRUCTURE AND FILE

Till now we had been dealing with character data stored in file in the form of strings and numbers. Apart from this we can also write arrays and structure data to the file. The whole array and structure variables (better say a record) can be written and read from file. The functions used for the purpose can be **fprintf and fscanf,** but they are less efficient as we will see shortly.

```
/*Prog 12.25 Writing a structure into the file */
#include<stdio.h>
#include<conio.h>
typedef struct
{
  char iname[15];
  int u_price;
  int quan;
}item;
main()
{
  FILE*fp;
  char ch;
  item t;
  clrscr();
  fp=fopen("item.txt", "w");
  printf("Enter the item details\n");
  scanf("%s%d%d",t.iname,&t.u_price,&t.quan);
  fprintf(fp, "%s\t",t.iname);
  fprintf(fp, "%d\t",t.u_price);
  fprintf(fp, "%d\n",t.quan);
  fclose(fp);
}
```

Output:

```
Enter the item details
Processor 6000 15
```

EXPLANATION: In the program we have declared one structure called item which contains three members for item name, its unit price and quantity in order of declaration. Through input we have taken details of item and stored them into the file. The file is then closed you can verify that items are indeed written to the file by opening it in your editor.

In the last two programs we have written data to read data from the structure member by member. But we can write the whole structure into the file as well as can read whole structure at once. We use two functions whose prototype given in **stdio.h:**

int fwrite(const void *, int s, int n, FILE*);

int fread(void *, int s, int n, FILE*);

The first argument in the **fwrite** is the address of the location where a write has to perform, second is the number of bytes to be written say ***s***, and third is the number of such items whose size is a and fourth one is the file pointer ***fp***. If successful **fwrite** return number of such items of size **s**.

Similar arguments apply to fread with the difference that it reads instead of writing.

Numeric data including integer and floating point as well as character data, all are treated in terms of character data *i.e.* string "file" will take 4 bytes in memory, integer number 1245 will take 4 bytes in memory and even 1.23 will take 4 bytes in memory. But as these data stored in disk file they are stored in binary form and in this they are stored as per their type i.e. integer takes 2 bytes, float takes 4 bytes and character takes 1 byte. So if reading and writing is done when treating file as text file and it contains lots of numerical data it will require large amount of disk space. Hence fread and fwrite functions are used which used reads and write data in terms of binary data.

To read and write data to file in binary mode we can use mode *"rb"* for reading and ***"wb"*** for writing. Simialrly, we can use ***"r+b"* or *"rb+"*, *"w+b"* or *"wb+"*, *"a+b"* or *"ab+"*.**

In case of text mode file is saved on the storage media in binary form, as we read it back it is converted from binary to text mode. Against this no conversion is required in binary files.

Now, let's see few programs which make use of the functions explained above.

```
/*Prog 12.26 writing data to the file using fwrite*/
#include<stdio.h>
#include<conio.h>
 typedef struct
 {
   char iname[30];
   int u_price;
   int quan;
 }item;
 void main()
 {
   FILE*fp;
   char ch;
   item t;
```

```
   clrscr();
   fp=fopen("demo1.txt", "wb");
   printf("Enter the item details\n");
   scanf("%s%d%d",t.iname, &t.u_price,&t.quan);
   fwrite(&t, sizeof(t),1,fp);
   fclose(fp);
 }
```

Output:

```
Enter the item details
Keyboard 10 300
```

EXPLANATION: In the program we have written the whole structure at once with the use of **fwrite** function. First argument is the address of the structure and second is the size of this structure. Third argument is 1 that is we want to write only one structure at a time.

```
/*Prog 12.27 Reading structure data from file using fread */
#include<stdio.h>
#include<conio.h>
 typedef struct
 {
   char iname[20];
   int u_price;
   int quan;
 }item;
 void main()
 {
   FILE*fp;
   char ch;
   item t;
   clrscr();
   fp=fopen("demo1.txt", "rb");
   fread(&t, sizeof(t),1,fp);
   printf("\n");
   printf("Item details read from file\n");
   fprintf(stdout, "%s\t",t.iname);
   fprintf(stdout, "%d\t",t.u_price);
   fprintf(stdout, "%d\n",t.quan);
   fclose(fp);
   getch();
 }
```

Output:

```
Item details read from file
Keyboard 10 300
```

EXPLANATION: fread function reads the whole structure at once in *t* which is a variable of type item. Note prior to fread the variable *t* contains nothing. When fread returns successfully the members of t are filled with data which we display through **printf.**

```
/*Prog 12.28 Writing and reading array to\from file*/
#include<stdio.h>
#include<conio.h>
 void main()
 {
   FILE*fp;
   int a[10],i;
   clrscr();
   fp=fopen("arr.txt", "r+");
   for(i=0;i<=9;i++)
    a[i]=i+1;
    fwrite(a,sizeof(a),1,fp);
    for(i=0;i<=9;i++)
    a[i]=0;
    rewind(fp);
    fread(a,sizeof(a),1,fp);
    printf("Array is \n");
    for(i=0;i<=9;i++)
    printf("%d",a[i]);
    fclose(fp);
    getch();
   }
Output:
Array is
1 2 3 4 5 6 7 8 9 10
```

EXPLANATION: Not only structure we can also store array into the file. In the program we have first assigned numbers **1 to 10 into** the array *a* and stored the whole array into the file arr.txt by using just one statement **fwrite(a,sizeof(a),1,fp); a** is the **base address** of the array, sizeof a gives **20** and **1** means one such block of **20 bytes** is to be written to the file. We then make all the elements to array a to zero so that when we read back from file we get the original array. The array is read through **fread** and displayed.

```
/*Prog 12.29 Reading and writing structure data to/from file using
function*/
#include<stdio.h>
#include<conio.h>
```

```
typedef struct
{
  char sname[20];
  int collg_rno;
  char cls[5];
}student;
 char *fname="students.txt";
 void main()
 {
  char ch;
  student st;
  void input_data(student *);
  void show_data(student);
  input_data(&st);
  show_data(st);
    getch();
    }
   void input_data(student temp)
   {
    FILE*fp;
    fp=fopen(fname, "a+");
    printf("Enter the student name its college roll no and class\n");
    scanf("%s%d%s",temp.sname,&temp.collg_rno, temp.cls);
    fwrite(temp,sizeof(student),1,fp);
    fclose(fp);
   }
   void show_data(student temp)
   {
      FILE*fp=fopen(fname, "r");
      int n;
      printf("Student details read from file\n");
      n=fread(&temp, sizeof(temp),1,fp);
      while(n==1)
      {
     fprintf(stdout, "%s\t",temp.sname);
     fprintf(stdout, "%d\t",temp.collg_rno);
     fprintf(stdout, "%s\n",temp.cls);
     n=fread(&temp,sizeof(temp),1,fp);
     fclose(fp);
   }
```

```
Output:
Enter the student name its college roll no and class
Aman 2456 Isem
Student details read from file
Hari 2457 v sem
Ranjana 2347 VII sem
Ruchika 2567 V sem
```

EXPLANATION: In the program we have created on structure student which contains three members for **name, college roll no and class.** We have created two functions **input_data** for accepting input from the user and putting data into file through **fwrite.** In the **input_data ()** file is opened in the *"a+"* mode so we can append and read from the file. In the function show_data file is opened in read mode and we read one record at a time from the file through fread. As there may be more than one record into the file we have used **while** loop. Till fread returns 1(numbers of record at a time) we read from file and display on to the screen. We have assumed that file already contains some record. If it doesn't then you may call function **input_data** for *n* number of times (*n* is the number of records you want to write to the file).

In the following program we modify the previous one by adding two more functions for deleting a record and editing a record. I give you a complete menu driven program for management of student record. It's not a professional program but it gives a basic idea how to perform basic operation on record stored in the file.

```
/*Prog 12.30 Student database handling using files*/
#include<stdio.h>
#include<conio.h>
 typedef struct
 {
   char sname[15];
   int collg_rno;
   char cls[5];
}student;
   char *fname="stu.txt";
   void main()
   {
    char ch;
    student st;
    void input_data(student);
    void show_data(student);
    void edit_data(student,int);
    void del_data(student, int colno);
    void search_show(student,int colno);
    int rno,cno;
```

```
  clrscr();
  do
  {
   clrscr();
   printf("\n Welcome to student Database \n");
   printf("1.Add a record\n");
   printf("2.View records\n");
   printf("3.Search a record\n");
   printf("4.Delete a record\n");
   printf("5. Modify a record\n");
   printf("6.Exit\n");
   printf("Enter your choice (1 to 6)\n");
   scanf("%d",&ch);
   switch(ch)
   {
case 1:input_data(st);
       printf("Record is added\n");
       printf("Press any key to continue....\n");
       getch();
       break;
case 2:show_data(st);
       printf("Press any key to continue....\n");
       getch();
       break;
case 3: printf("Enter the college roll no of the student \n");
        scanf("%d",&cno);
        search_show(st,cno);
        printf("Press any key to continue....\n");
        getch();
        break;
case 4: printf("Enter the college roll no of the student \n");
        scanf("%d",&cno);
        del_data(st,cno);
        printf("Press any key to continue....\n");
        getch();
        break;
case 5: printf("Enter the record no u want to modify\n");
        scanf("%d",&rno);
        edit_data(st,rno);
        printf("Press any key to continue....\n");
```

```
        break;
  case 6: printf("Bye Bye\n");
        getch();
        exit(0);
    }
    }while(ch<=6 && ch>=1);
    getch();
  }
    void input_data(student temp)
    {
      FILE*fp;
      fp=fopen(fname, "a+");
      printf("Enter  the  student  name  its  college  roll  no  and
            class\n");
      scanf("%s%d%s",temp.sname,&temp.collg_rno,temp.cls);
      fwrite(&temp,sizeof(student),1,fp);
      fclose(fp);
    }
    void show_data(student temp)
    {
      FILE*fp=fopen(fname, "r");
      int n;
      printf("Student details read from file\n");
      n=fread(&temp,sizeof(temp),1,fp);
      while(n==1)
      {
    fprintf(stdout, "%s\t",temp.sname);
    fprintf(stdout, "%d\t",temp.collg_rno);
    fprintf(stdout, "%s\n",temp.cls);
    n=fread(&temp,sizeof(temp),1,fp);
      }
      fclose(fp);
      }
    void edit_data(student temp,int recno)
    {
      FILE*fp=fopen(fname, "r+");
      long int nmove;
      nmove=(recno-1)*sizeof(student);
      fseek(fp,nmove,0);
      printf("Enter  the  student  name  its  college  roll  no  and
```

```
   class\n");
   scanf("%s%d%s",temp.sname,&temp.collg_rno,temp.cls);
   fwrite(&temp,sizeof(temp),1,fp);
   fclose(fp);
}
void search_show(student temp,int cno)
{
 FILE*fp=fopen(fname, "r");
 int n,found=0;
 n=fread(&temp,sizeof(temp),1,fp);
 while(n==1)
 {
if(temp.collg_rno==cno)
 {
    printf("Record found\n");
    printf("%s\t%d\t%s\n",temp.sname,
             temp.collg_rno,temp.cls);
    getch();
   // break;
    found=1;
 }
n=fread(&temp,sizef(temp),1,fp);
 }
if(found==0)
printf("Record not found\n");
 }
 void del_data(student temp,int cno)
 {
FILE*fp1,*fp2;
int n;
fp1=fopen(fname, "r");
fp2=fopen("temp.txt", "w");
n=fread(&temp,sizeof(temp),1,fp1);
while(n==1)
{
 if(temp.collg_rno!=cno)
  fwrite(&temp,sizeof(temp),1,fp2);
  n=fread(&temp,sizeof(temp),1,fp1);
}
remove(fname);
```

```
    rename("temp.txt",fname);
    fclose(fp1);
    fclose(fp2);
 }
```

Output:

```
WELCOME IN STUDENT DATABASE
        1.Add a record
        2.View records
        3.Search a record
        4.Delete a record
        5.Modify a record
        6.Exit
        Enter your choice (1 to 6)
2
Student details read from file
Hari       12      1sem
Ranjana    13      2sem
Anjana     14      3sem
Man Mohan  15      4sem
Press any key to continue....
WELCOME IN STUDENT DATABASE
        1.Add a record
        2.View records
        3.Search a record
        4.Delete a record
        5. Modify a record
        6.Exit
        Enter your choice (1 to 6)
1
Enter the student name its college roll no and class
Vijay 17 Isem
Record is added
Press any key to continue....
WELCOME IN STUDENT DATABASE
        1.Add a record
        2.View records
        3.Search a record
        4.Delete a record
        5.Modify a record
```

```
        6.Exit
        Enter your choice (1 to 6)
2
Student details read from file
Hari        12      1sem
Ranjana     13      2sem
Anjana      14      3sem
Man Mohan   15      4sem
Vijay       21      Vsem
Press any key to continue....
```

EXPLANATION: To modify a record we initially reach to the location of that record. The location can be found out as follows:

loc=(n-1)*sizeof(structure student);

Then through **fseek** we reach to the loc in the file i.e. beginning of the record which is to be modified. We then accept the new data for the record and overwrite the existing record.

To search for a record we ask from the user the college roll no and scan the whole file for the record where **collg_no** matches with the user supplied **cno.**

For deletion of a record we move all the other records to a temporary file **temp.txt.** We then remove the original file using in built function remove which takes a single argument of const **char*** type, the file name to be removed. We then rename the temporary file **temp.txt** to the old stu.txt which is stored under variable **fname.**

12.9 ERROR HANDLING FUNCTION

In this section we discuss some of the error handling functions provided by C library which may be used in various programming situation involving file manipulations such as opening file, closing file, reading and writing a file, invalid path, invalid drive etc.

Check out programs given below:

```
/*Prog 12.31 Demo of ferror function*/
#include<stdio.h>
#include<conio.h>
 void main()
 {
   FILE*fp;
   int a[10];
   clrscr();
   fp=fopen("ar.txt", "w");
   fread(a,sizeof(a),1,fp);
   if(ferror(fp))
   {
```

```
    printf("Error reading from file\n");
    getch();
    exit(0);
  }
  fclose(fp);
  getch();
  }
```

Output:

```
Error reading from file
```

EXPLANATION: The **ferror** function is used to check error occurring on a read or write stream *i.e.* while reading or writing data from and to the file. It returns a nonzero number if error occurs. In the program we have opened the file in the write mode and trying to read it so **ferror** catches the error and we display the error message. The prototype of the function is:

```
#include<stdio.h>
int ferror(FILE*);
```

```
/*Prog 12.32 Demo of perror*/
#include<stdio.h>
#include<conio.h>
 void main()
 {
  FILE*fp;
  int a[10];
  clrscr();
  fp=fopen("a.txt", "r");
  fread(a,sizeof(a),1,fp);
  if(!fp)
  {
    perror("Error");
    getch();
    exit(0);
  }
  fclose(fp);
  getch();
 }
```

Output:

```
Error: No such file or directory
```

EXPLANATION: In the program we are trying to open a file in read mode that does not exist. The file pointer *fp* returns **zero** and **if** condition is true. The function **perror** displays system generated error message. It takes a single argument of **const char*** type say **msg.** The system generated error message is appended to this **msg** and displayed. By convention the file name is supplied as the argument.

```
/*Prog 12.33 Demo of errno*/
#include<stdio.h>
#include<conio.h>
#include<errno.h>
 void main()
 {
    FILE*fp;
    int a[10];
    clrscr();
    fp=fopen("a.txt", "r");
    fread(a,sizeof(a),1,fp);
    if(errno==ENOENT)
    {
       printf("File does not exist\n");
       getch();
       exit(0);
    }
    fclose(fp);
    getch();
 }
```

Output:

```
File does not exist
```

EXPLANATION: Whenever a system error occurs the global variable **errno** is set to a value to indicate the type of error. The error is extern int type variable declared in file **errno.h.** The value **ENOENT** indicates the error about non existent of file or directory. Some of the values given here along with error they represent.

```
/*Prog 12.34 Demo of clearerr */
#include <stdio.h>
#include <conio.h>
 int main(void)
 {
    FILE *fp;
    char ch;
    clrscr();
 /* open a file for writing */
    fp = fopen("DUMMY.FIL", "w");
 /* force an error condition by attempting to read */
    ch = fgetc(fp);
    printf("%c\n",ch);
```

```
    if (ferror(fp))
    {
       /* display an error message */
       printf("Error reading from DUMMY.FIL\n");
       /* reset the error and EOF indicators */
       clearerr(fp);
    }
 fclose(fp);
 getch();
}
```

EXPLANATION: In the above shown program we are using clearerr, which is used to reset the named stream's error and end-of-file indicators to 0. Once the error indicator is set, stream operations continue to return error status until call is made to clearer or rewind. The end -of -file (EOF) indicator is reset with each input operation.

In other words clearer resets error indication. The prototype of this function lies in stdio.h header file:

```
#include<stdio.h>
void clearerr(FILE*stream);
/*Prog 12.35 Demo of _strerror*/
#include <stdio.h>
#include<conio.h>
 int main(void)
 {
   FILE *fp;
   clrscr();
   /* open a file for writing */
   fp = fopen("TEST.$$$", "w");
   /* force an error condition by attempting to read */
   if (!fp) fgetc(fp);
   if (ferror(fp))
   /* display a custom error message */
   printf("%s", _strerror("Custom"));
   fclose(fp);
   getch();
}
```

EXPLANATION: **_strerror** builds a customized error message. With **_strerror,** if *s* is null, the return value points to the most recently generated error message. If *s* is not null, the return value contains the following:

(A) *s* (your customized error message)

(B) *a* colon

(C) *a* space

(D) the most-recently generated system error message

(E) *a* new line.

The prototype of **_strerror** exist in **string.h** header file:

```
#include<string.h>
char *_strerror (const char *s);
```

POINTS TO PONDER

In this section you have learned the following points:

- In C, a file can refer to a disk file, a terminal, a printer, or a tape drive.
- The data flow you transfer from your program to a file, or vice versa, is called a stream.
- A stream is a series of ordered bytes.
- Not like a file, a stream is device-independent.
- There are two stream formats: text stream and binary stream.
- The file position indicator in the FILE structure points to the position in a file where data will be read from or written to.
- The **fopen()** function is used to open a file and associate a stream to the opened file.
- You can specify different modes for opening a file.
- The **fclose ()** function is responsible for closing an opened file and disassociating a stream with the file.
- The **fgetc() and fputc()** functions read or write one character at a time.
- The **fgets() and fputs()** functions read or write one line at a time.
- The **fread() and fwrite()** functions read or write one block of data at a time.
- The **feof ()** function can determine when the end of a file has been reached.
- In a binary file, the feof () function should be used to detect EOF.

QUESTIONS AND ANSWERS

Q1. *What are the differences between a text stream and a binary stream?*

Ans: A text stream is a sequence of characters that may not have a one-to-one relationship with the data on the device. Text streams are normally used for textual data, which have a consistent appearance from one environment to another or from one machine to another. A binary stream, on the other hand, is a sequence of bytes that has a one-to-one correspondence to those on the device. Binary streams are primarily used for nontextual data that is needed to keep the exact contents on the device.

Q2. *Why do you need a file pointer?*

Ans: A file pointer is used to associate a stream with an opened file for reading or writing purposes. A pointer of the type FILE is called a file pointer. FILE is a typedef for a structure that contains overhead information about a disk file. A file pointer plays an important role in the communication between programs and disk files.

Q3. *What does the fclose() function do before it closes an opened file?*

Ans: As you know, all high-level I/O operations are buffered. One of the jobs of the **fclose ()** function is to flush data left in the buffer to ensure that no data is lost. For instance, when you finish writing several blocks of characters to an opened text file, you call the **fclose ()** function to disassociate a specified stream and close the text file. The **fclose ()** function will first flush all characters left in the buffer and write them into the text file before it closes the file. In this way, all characters you write to the file will be saved properly.

Q4. *What is the difference between fgets() and gets ()?*

Ans: The major difference between the **fgets () and gets ()** functions is that the **fgets ()** function includes a newline character in the array if the newline is encountered during the reading, whereas the **gets ()** function just replaces the newline character with a null character.

EXERCISES

A. Answer the following questions:

1. What is the difference between end of a file and end of a string?
2. How does an append mode differ from a write mode?
3. What is the use of **fseek ( )**? Explain it with the help of suitable example?
4. What are command line arguments? How are they used?
5. Compare **printf** and **fprintf?**
6. Write short notes on the following:
   (*a*) Low level disk operation.
   (*b*) Command line arguments.
   (*c*) Environment variable.
7. How re-direction of input and output is done? Explain in brief?

B. Match the following columns:

I	II
1. text files	(*a*) writing in binary.
2. system call	(*b*) takes 7 byes in memory.
3. beginning to the file	(*c*) takes 4 bytes in memory.
4. *"wb"*	(*d*) high level files.
5. *"wt"*	(*e*) rewind.
6. 12.345(binary mode)	(*f*) writing in text mode.
7. 23.4566(text mode)	(*g*) low level files.

C. Write True or False against each statement:

1. The main function allows command line arguments.
2. FILE is an example of structure data type .
3. Declaring a structure with const makes every element in it constant.
4. stdin represent keyboard.
5. ffind is used for random access in a file.
6. All command line arguments are treated as strings.
7. If you open a file in append mode, the file pointer is in the beginning of the file.

D. Fill in the blanks:

1. An I/O stream may be a __________ or a __________.
2. The standard input stream is __________.

3. The standard output stream is __________.
4. EOF is a __________ whose ASCII value is __________.
5. __________ function takes file pointer to the beginning of the file.
6. The function fopen() returns __________ if the open operation fails.
7. The feof ( ) returns __________ at the end of file.
8. There are total __________ standard stream pointers.

E. Brain Drill:

1. Write a program to create a data file and enter some text into it taken from the user. Now read the file and count number of blank and no blank line present in the file.
2. Modify the above program to count number of space, tabs and words.
3. Modify the program 1 to reverse each word present in the file.
4. Write a program to display contents of file on the screen. The program should ask for file name. Display the contents of the file in capital case.
5. Write a program to combine contents of two files in third file. Add line number at the beginning of each line.
6. Write a program to interchange the contents of the two files.
7. Write a program to find largest of three text files.
8. Write a program to generate a data file containing the list of cricket players, no. innings played highest run score and no. of hatricks made by them. Use structure variable to store the cricketer's name. no. of innings played, highest run score & number of hatricks.

F. Predict the output of the following programs:

1.
```
main ()
{
    FILE *fp;
     int c;
     fp= fopen("abc.txt", "r");
     while (c= fgetc(fp) != EOF)
     printf("%d" c);
     printf("\n");
     fclose(fp);
}
```

Assume abc.txt contains just three characters abc.

2.
```
main ( )
{
     unsigned char ch;
     FILE *fp;
     clrscr();
     fp= fopen ("myfile.c", "r");
     while((ch=fgetc(fp))!=EOF)
     putchar(ch);
     fclose (fp);
}
```

13

DYNAMIC MEMORY ALLOCATION

The chapter discusses one of the most important concepts in C programming, the concept of dynamic memory allocation. The introduction part covers the basics of static allocation and dynamic allocation. It also covers the run-time view of the program and explains how static and dynamic allocation is done.

The number of function used for the purpose of dynamic memory allocation / deallocation like:

(*a*) **malloc.**

(*b*) **Calloc.**

(*c*) **realloc**

(*d*) **free**

Are explained with their prototypes. A short example is then given of dynamic memory allocation with malloc function.

Dynamic memory allocation for string, arrays and structure have been covered by giving illustrative examples.

Reallocation of memory with the help of **realloc** function in the next section.

Concept of linked list with list –referential structure is explained by first giving a small program which shows you to create a linked list. A complete menu driven program is then given which performs all primitive operations on linked list like addition, deletion, sorting etc., in a linked list.

13.1 INTRODUCTION

When we declare variables, arrays, structure (in definition) etc. the memory for them is allocated at the compile time. This allocation is static allocation. When you declare the array say **int arr[10]** we give the size of array *i.e.* number of elements. We just cannot take input for *x* from user during program execution and declare the array by writing int arr[*x*]. Memory for array in the above declaration is allocated at compile time so compiler requires the size of the array. The size once fixed cannot be changed during the program execution. This may sometimes results in wastage of memory when size specified in the beginning is more than actually used in the program.

When you write your C program, the program's data and code is stored in the **RAM.** All the local and global variables used in the program are stored in a fixed area of memory allocated to that program. This area allocated is fixed and remained constant during the execution of the program. The local variable are always stored on the stack and are destroyed automatically as soon as control goes out of scope. Global and static variables are known as **load time variable** and they come into existence at the time of loading of the program. Thus we can say that global and local variables are efficiently handled by C compiler. But the programmer must know the amount of space required for every program.

The technique through which a program can be obtaining space in the RAM during the execution of the program and not during compilation is called dynamic memory allocation. In this method space for the variables (array, strings, structure etc.) is allocated from a free memory region which is known as **heap.** This area is not fixed in nature and keeps changing as the memory is allocated and deallocated from this region. The entire runtime view of memory for a program is given below.

Dynamic memory allocation is the allocation of memory at runtime *i.e.* when program executes then required memory is asked from the user and memory is allocated with the help of certain inbuilt functions which we explain shortly. There are four such functions which we can use for allocation, reallocation and for freeing the memory. The header file for the functions is **alloc.h**

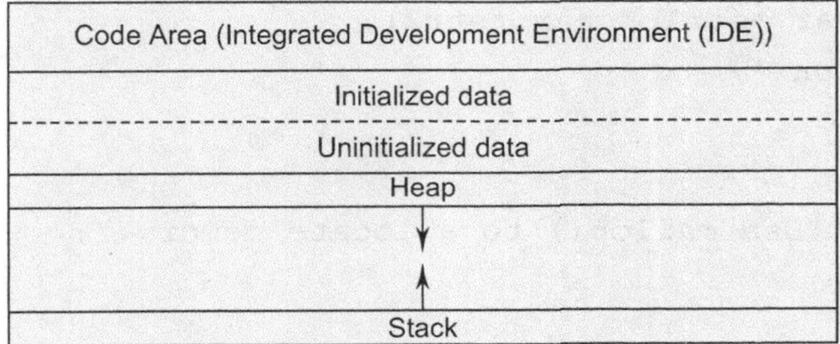

Fig. 13.1 *Run time memory area of a C program.*

13.2 ALLOCATING MEMORY AT RUNTIME

There are many cases when you do not know the exact sizes of arrays used in your programs, until much later when your programs are actually being executed. You can specify the sizes of arrays in advance, but the arrays can be too small or too big if the numbers of data items you want to put into the arrays change dramatically at runtime.

C provides you with four dynamic memory allocation functions that you can employ to allocate or reallocate certain memory spaces while your program is running. Also, you can release allocated memory storage as soon as you don't need it. These four C functions, **malloc (), calloc (), realloc (), and free ()**, are introduced in the following sections.

13.2.1 The Malloc () Function

You can use the **malloc ()** function to allocate a specified size of memory space. The syntax for the **malloc ()** function is given as:

```
#include <stdlib.h>
void *malloc(size_t size);
```

Here **size** indicates the number of bytes of storage to allocate. The **malloc ()** function returns a **void pointer.**

Note that the header file, **stdlib.h,** has to be included before the **malloc ()** function can be called. Because the **malloc ()** function returns a **void pointer,** its type is automatically converted to the type of the pointer on the left side of an assignment operator.

If the **malloc ()** function fails to allocate a piece of memory space, it returns a **null pointer.** Normally, this happens when there is not enough memory. Therefore, you should always check the returned pointer from **malloc ()** before you use it.

```
/* Prog 13.1 Using the malloc function */
#include <stdio.h>
#include <stdlib.h>
#include <string.h>
/* function declaration */
 void StrCopy(char *str1, char *str2);
/* main() function */
 main()
 {
   char str[] = "Use malloc() to allocate memory.";
   char *ptr_str;
   int result;
/* call malloc() */
   ptr_str = malloc( strlen(str) + 1);
   if (ptr_str != NULL)
   {
     StrCopy(str, ptr_str);
     printf("The string pointed to by ptr_str is:\n%s\n",ptr_str);
     result = 0;
   }
   else
   {
      printf("malloc() function failed.\n");
      result = 1;
   }
    return result;
 }
```

```
/* function definition */
  void StrCopy(char *str1, char *str2)
  {
     int i;
     for (i=0; str1[i]; i++)
     str2[i] = str1[i];
     str2[i] = '\0';
  }
```

Output:

```
The string pointed to by ptr_str is:
Use malloc() to allocate memory.
```

EXPLANATION: The purpose of the **program 13.1** is to use the **malloc()** function to allocate a piece of memory space that has the same size as a character string. Then, the content .of the string is copied to the allocated memory referenced by the pointer returned from the **malloc()** function. The content of the memory is displayed on the screen to prove that the memory space does contain the content of the string after the allocation and duplication.

Note that two more header files, **stdlib.h** and **string.h,** are included in **lines 3 and 4,** respectively, for the functions **malloc()** and **strlen(),** which are called in **line 14.**

Line 10 declares a **char** array, **str,** that is initialized with a character string of **"Use malloc() to allocate memory."**. A char pointer variable, **ptr_str,** is declared in **line 11.**

The statement in **line 14** allocates a memory space of **strlen(str)+1** bytes by calling the **malloc()** function. Because the **strlen()** function does not count the null character at the end of a string, adding 1 to the value returned by **strlen(str)** gives the total number of bytes that need to be allocated. The value of the returned pointer is assigned to the char pointer variable **ptr_str** after the **malloc()** function is called in **line 14.**

The **if-else** statement in **lines 15_24** checks the returned pointer from the **malloc()** function. If it's a null pointer, an error message is printed out, and the return value of the **main()** function is set to **1** in **lines 22 and 23.** (Remember that a nonzero value returned by the return statement indicates an abnormal termination.)

But if the returned pointer is not a null pointer, the start address of the **str** array and the pointer **ptr_str** are passed to a **subfunction** called **StrCopy()** in **line 16.** The **StrCopy()** function, whose definition is given in **lines 28_35,** copies the content of the **str** array to the allocated memory pointed to by **ptr_str.** Then, the **printf()** function in **lines 17 and 18** prints out the copied content in the allocated memory. **Line 19** sets the return value to **0** after the success of the memory allocation and string duplication.

The output on my screen shows that a piece of memory has been allocated and that the string has been copied to the memory.

There is a potential problem if you keep allocating memory, because there is always a limit. You can easily run out of memory when you just allocate memory without releasing it. In the next section, you'll learn how to use the **free()** function to free up memory spaces allocated for you when you don't need them.

13.2.2 Releasing Allocated Memory with Free ( )

Because memory is a limited resource, you should allocate an exactly sized piece of memory right before you need it, and release it as soon as you don't need it.

```
/*Prog 13.2 Using the free () function */
#include <stdio.h>
#include <stdlib.h>
/* function declarations */
void DataMultiply(int max, int *ptr);
void TablePrint(int max, int *ptr);
/* main() function */
main()
{
  int *ptr_int, max;
  int termination;
  char key = 'c';
  max = 0;
  termination = 0;
  clrscr();
  while (key != 'x')
  {
    printf("Enter a single digit number:\n");
    scanf("%d", &max);
    ptr_int= malloc(max * max * sizeof(int));/* call*/
                                        /* malloc() */
    if (ptr_int != NULL)
    {
       DataMultiply(max, ptr_int);
       TablePrint(max, ptr_int);
       free(ptr_int);
    }
    else
    {
       printf("malloc() function failed.\n");
       termination = 1;
       key = 'x'; /* stop while loop */
    }
```

```
    printf("\n\nPress x key to quit; other key to
    continue.\n");
    scanf("%s", &key);
  }
  printf("\nBye!\n");
  return termination;
}
/* function definition */
void DataMultiply(int max, int *ptr)
{
   int i, j;
   for (i=0; i<max; i++)
   for (j=0; j<max; j++)
   *(ptr + i * max + j) = (i+1) * (j+1);
}
/* function definition */
void TablePrint(int max, int *ptr)
{
   int i, j;
   printf("The multiplication table of %d is:\n",max);
   printf(" ");
   for (i=0; i<max; i++)
   printf("%4d", i+1);
   printf("\n ");
   for (i=0; i<max; i++)
   printf("----", i+1);
   for (i=0; i<max; i++){
   printf("\n%d|", i+1);
   for (j=0; j<max; j++)
   printf("%3d ", *(ptr + i * max + j));
  }
}
```

Output:

```
Enter a single digit number:
10
```

```
The multiplication table of 10 is:
          1   2   3   4   5   6   7   8   9  10
      --------------------------------------------
1|        1   2   3   4   5   6   7   8   9  10
2|        2   4   6   8  10  12  14  16  18  20
3|        3   6   9  12  15  18  21  24  27  30
4|        4   8  12  16  20  24  28  32  36  40
5|        5  10  15  20  25  30  35  40  45  50
6|        6  12  18  24  30  36  42  48  54  60
7|        7  14  21  28  35  42  49  56  63  70
8|        8  16  24  32  40  48  56  64  72  80
9|        9  18  27  36  45  54  63  72  81  90
10|      10  20  30  40  50  60  70  80  90 100
Press x key to quit; other key to continue.
5
Enter a single digit number:
5
The multiplication table of 5 is:
          1   2   3   4   5
      ----------------------
1|        1   2   3   4   5
2|        2   4   6   8  10
3|        3   6   9  12  15
4|        4   8  12  16  20
5|        5  10  15  20  25
Press x key to quit; other key to continue.
x
```

EXPLANATION: The purpose of the program13.2 is to build a multiplication table based on the integer given by the user. The program can continue building multiplication tables until the user presses the *x* **key** to quit. The program also stops execution if the **malloc()** function fails.

To show you how to use the **free()** function, the program allocates a temporary memory storage to hold the items of a multiplication table. As soon as the content of a multiplication table is printed out, the allocated memory is released by calling the **free()** function.

Lines 5 and 6 declare two functions, **DataMultiply()** and **TablePrint(),** respectively. The former is for performing multiplication and building a table, whereas the latter prints out the table on the screen. The definitions of the two functions are given in **lines 38_45** and **lines 47_64,** respectively.

Inside the **main()** function, there is a **while** loop in **lines 16_33** that keeps asking the user to enter an integer number **(see lines 17 and 18)** and then building a multiplication table based on the integer.

To hold the result of the multiplication, the statement in **line 20** allocates a memory storage that has the size of **max*max*sizeof(int),** where the **int** variable **max** contains the integer value entered by the user. Note that the **sizeof(int)** expression gives the byte number of the int data type of the computer on which the program is being run.

If the **malloc()** function returns a **null pointer,** the return value of the **main()** function is set to **1** to indicate an abnormal termination **(see line 28),** and the **while** loop is stopped by assigning the key variable with **'x' in line 29.**

Otherwise, if the **malloc()** function allocates a memory storage successfully, the **DataMultiply()** function is called in **line 22** to calculate each multiplication. The results are saved into the memory storage pointed to by the **ptr_int** pointer. Then the multiplication table is printed out by calling the **TablePrint()** function in **line 23.**

As soon as I no longer need to keep the multiplication table, I call the **free()** function in **line 24** to release the allocated memory storage pointed to by the **ptr_int** pointer.

If I did not release the memory, the program would take more and more memory as the user keeps entering integer numbers to build more multiplication tables. Eventually, the program would either crash the operating system or be forced to quit. By using the **free() and malloc()** functions, I am able to keep running the program by taking the exact amount of memory storage I need, no more and no less.

13.2.3 The Calloc ( ) Function

Besides the **malloc ( )** function, you can also use the **calloc ( )** function to allocate a memory storage dynamically. **The differences between the two functions are that the latter takes two arguments and that the memory space allocated by calloc ( ) is always initialized to 0.** There is no such guarantee that the memory space allocated by **malloc ( )** is initialized to **0.**

The syntax for the **calloc ( )** function is

```
#include <stdlib.h>
void *calloc(size_t nitem, size_t size);
```

Here **nitem** is the number of items you want to save in the allocated memory space. **size** gives the number of bytes that each item takes. The **calloc ( )** function returns a void pointer too.If the **calloc ( )** function fails to allocate a piece of memory space, it returns a **null pointer.**

```
/*Prog 13.3 Demo of using the calloc () function */
#include <stdio.h>
#include <stdlib.h>
/* main() function */
  main()
  {
    float *ptr1, *ptr2;
    int i, n;
    int termination = 1;
    n = 5;
    ptr1 = calloc(n, sizeof(float));
    ptr2 = malloc(n * sizeof(float));
    if (ptr1 == NULL)
    printf("malloc() failed.\n");
```

```
    else if (ptr2 == NULL)
    printf("calloc() failed.\n");
    else
    {
        for (i=0; i<n; i++)
        printf("ptr1[%d]=%5.2f, ptr2[%d]=%5.2f\n",i, *(ptr1 + i),
            i, *(ptr2 + i));
        free(ptr1);
        free(ptr2);
        termination = 0;
    }
   return termination;
 }
```

Output:

```
ptr1[0]= 0.00, ptr2[0]= 0.00
ptr1[1]= 0.00, ptr2[1]=-0.00
ptr1[2]= 0.00, ptr2[2]= 0.00
ptr1[3]= 0.00, ptr2[3]=575768100864.00
ptr1[4]= 0.00, ptr2[4]= 0.00
```

EXPLANATION: The purpose of the program13.3 is to use the **calloc ()** function to allocate a piece of memory space. To prove that the **calloc ()** function initializes the allocated memory space to **0,** the initial values of the memory are printed out. Also, another piece of memory space is allocated by using the **malloc ()** function, and the initial values of the second memory space is printed out too.

As you see in **line 12,** the **calloc ()** function is called with two arguments passed to it: the **int** variable ***n*** and the **sizeof (float)** expression. The **float** pointer variable **ptr1** is assigned the value returned by the **calloc ()** function.

Likewise, the **malloc ()** function is called in **line 13.** This function only takes one argument that specifies the total number of bytes that the allocated memory should have. The value returned by the **malloc ()** function is then assigned to another **float** pointer variable, **ptr2.**From **lines 12 and 13,** you can tell that the **calloc () and malloc ()** functions actually plan to allocate two pieces of memory space with the same size.

The **if-else-if-else** statement in **lines 14_25** checks the two values returned from the **calloc()** and **malloc()** functions and then prints out the initial values from the two allocated memory spaces if the two return values are not null.

I ran the executable program 13.3 several times. Each time, the initial value from the memory space allocated by the **calloc ()** function was always **0.** But there is no guarantee for the memory space allocated by the **malloc ()** function. The output shown here is one of the results from running the executable program on my machine. You can see that there is some **"garbage"** in the memory space allocated by the **malloc ()** function. That is, the initial value in the memory is unpredictable. (Sometimes, the initial value in a memory block allocated by the **malloc ()** function is **0.** But it is not guaranteed that the initial value is always **0** each time when the **malloc ()** function is called.)

13.2.4 The Realloc () Function

The **realloc ()** function gives you a means to change the size of a piece of memory space allocated by the **malloc ()** function, the **calloc ()** function, or even itself.

The syntax for the **realloc ()** function is

```
#include <stdlib.h>
void *realloc(void *block, size_t size);
```

Here block is the pointer to the start of a piece of memory space previously allocated. **size** specifies the total byte number you want to change to. The **realloc ()** function returns a **void** pointer. The **realloc ()** function returns a **null pointer** if it fails to reallocate a piece of memory space. The **realloc ()** function is equivalent to the **malloc ()** function if the first argument passed to **realloc ()** is **NULL.** In other words, the following two statements are equivalent:

```
ptr_flt = realloc(NULL, 10 * sizeof(float));
ptr_flt = malloc(10 * sizeof(float));
```

Also, you can use the **realloc ()** function as the **free ()** function. You do this by passing **0** to **realloc ()** as its second argument. For instance, to release a block of memory pointed to by a pointer **ptr,** you can either call the **free ()** function like this:

```
free(ptr);
```

or use the realloc() function in the following way:

```
realloc(ptr, 0);
```

```
/* Prog 13.4 Demo of using the realloc () function */
#include <stdio.h>
#include <stdlib.h>
#include <string.h>
  /* function declaration */
  void StrCopy(char *str1, char *str2);
  /* main() function */
  main()
  {
    char *str[4] = {"This is Hari Mohan Pandey;",
                    "Lecturer in Computer Science & Engg.;",
                    "This is the demo of realloc() function;",
                    "Be practical with C\n"
                   };
    char *ptr;
    int i;
    int termination = 0;
    clrscr();
    ptr = malloc((strlen(str[0]) + 1) * sizeof(char));
```

```
    if (ptr == NULL)
    {
      printf("malloc() failed.\n");
      termination = 1;
    }
    else
    {
      StrCopy(str[0], ptr);
      printf("%s\n", ptr);
      for (i=1; i<4; i++){
      ptr = realloc(ptr, (strlen(str[i]) + 1) * sizeof(char));
      if (ptr == NULL)
      {
         printf("realloc() failed.\n");
         termination = 1;
         i = 4; /* break the for loop */
      }
      else
      {
         StrCopy(str[i], ptr);
         printf("%s\n", ptr);
      }
    }
  }
 free(ptr);
 return termination;
}
/* function definition */
 void StrCopy(char *str1, char *str2)
 {
    int i;
    for (i=0; str1[i]; i++)
    str2[i] = str1[i];
    str2[i] = '\0';
 }
```

Output:

```
This is Hari Mohan Pandey;
Lecturer in Computer Science & Engg.;
This is the demo of realloc () function;
Be practical with C
```

EXPLANATION: The purpose of the program 13.4 is to allocate a block of memory space to hold a character string. There are **four strings** in the given program, and the length of each string may vary. I use the **realloc ()** function to adjust the size of the previously allocated memory so it can hold a new string. As you can see in **lines 10_13,** there are **four character strings.** Here I use an array of pointers, **str,** to refer to the strings.

A piece of memory space is first allocated by calling the **malloc ()** function in **line 20.** The size of the memory space is determined by the **(strlen (str[0])+1)*sizeof(char)** expression. As mentioned earlier, because the C function **strlen ()** does not count the null character at the end of a string, you have to remember to allocate one more piece of memory to hold the full size of a string. The **sizeof (char)** expression is used here for portability, although the **char** data type is **1** byte long on most computers.

If the **malloc()** function doesn't fail, the content of the first string pointed to by the **str[0]** pointer is copied to the block memory allocated by **malloc().** To do this, a function called **StrCopy()** is called in **line 26. Lines 45_52** give the definition of **StrCopy().** The **for** loop, in **lines 28_39,** copies the remaining **three strings,** one at a time, to the block of memory pointed to by **ptr.** Each time, the **realloc()** function is called in **line 29** to reallocate and adjust the previously allocated memory space based on the length of the next string whose content is about to be copied to the memory block. After the content of a string is copied to the memory block, the content is also printed out **(see lines 27 and 37).**

In this example, a block of memory space is allocated and adjusted based on the length of each of the four strings. The **realloc ()** function, as well as the **malloc ()** function, does the memory allocation and adjustment dynamically.

```
/*Prog 13.5 Demo of malloc and free*/
#include<stdio.h>
#include<conio.h>
#include<alloc.h>
 void main()
 {
   char *ch;
   int *p;
   float *f;
   clrscr();
   ch=(char*)malloc(sizeof(char));
   p=(int*)malloc(sizeof(int));
   f=(float*)malloc(sizeof(float));
   printf("Enter a character\n");
   *ch=getchar();
   printf("Enter an integer \n");
   scanf("%d",p);
   printf("Enter a float \n");
   scanf("%f",f);
```

```
   printf("U entered \n %c %d %f \n",*ch,*p,*f);
   free(ch);
   free(p);
   free(f);
   getch();
 }
```

Output:

```
Enter a character
A
Enter an integer
345
Enter a float
12.456
U entered
 A 345 12.456000
```

EXPLANATION: In the program we have allocated memory for an integer, a char, and a float variable dynamically. According to the type we have type casted the malloc function. The sizeof operator has been used to determine the size of each type which in turbo C turns out to be 1, 2 and 4 respectively. In the end we de-allocate the memory by apply the free function.

This was a very trivial example which simply demonstrate how to use malloc and free function. Usually you won't be allocating memory for simply a variable in this manner.

13.3 DMA FOR STRINGS

For dynamic allocation of string we just have to declare a pointer of type char and make use of malloc or calloc function. For example we can write:

```
Char*p;
p= (char*) malloc (sizeof (char)*20);
```

which allocates 20 bytes and starting address of this 20 bytes block is returned and assigned to p. From here onwards you can assume as if it were declared like char *p* [20]; .In case malloc fails to allocate memory it returns NULL. We give some examples.

```
/*Prog 13.6 Memory allocation for string*/
#include<stdio.h>
#include<conio.h>
 void main()
 {
  char *p;
  clrscr();
  p=(char *)malloc(sizeof(char)*20);
```

```
  printf("Enter your name\n");
  gets(p);
  printf("Hello %s\n",p);
  getch();
 }
```

Output:

```
Enter your name
Hari Mohan pandey
Hello Hari Mohan pandey
```

EXPLANATION: When the expression **p= (char*) malloc (sizeof (char)* 15);** executes **15** bytes of memory is allocated and *p* points to the first bytes of allocated block. Through **gets (*p*)** statement the string is stored at this address as shown.

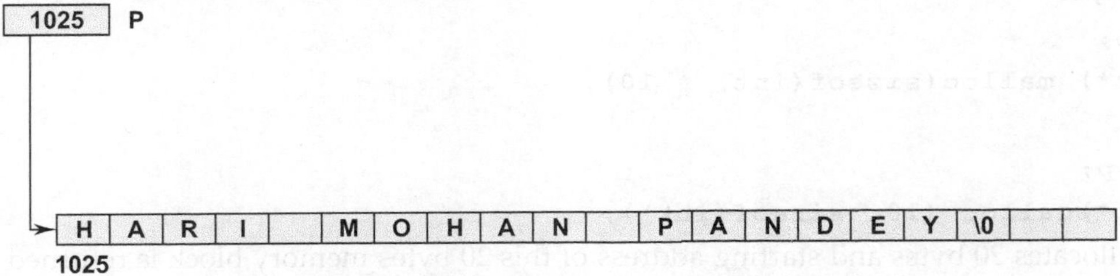

Fig. 13.2 *Implementation of malloc() function.*

```
/*Prog 13.7 Memory allocation for string ver2*/
#include<stdio.h>
#include<conio.h>
 void main()
 {
    char *p;
    clrscr();
    p=(char*)malloc(sizeof(char)* 20);
    printf("Enter your name \n");
    gets(p);
    printf("Hello");
    while(*p!=0)
    {
       printf("%c",*p);
       p++;
    }
   free(p);
   getch();
 }
```

Output:

```
Enter your name
Hari Mohan Pandey
Hello Hari Mohan Pandey
```

EXPLANATION: In the program we have allocated memory of 15 bytes and which is pointed by the pointer *p*. This name is taken from the user and stored in the *p*. The same is displayed by the treating *p* as a char array character by character using while loop. The memory is then freed by a call to free function.

13.4 DMA FOR ARRAYS

For dynamic allocation of arrays we just have to declare a pointer of type int float or any other data type depending upon what type of array we want to make, and make use of malloc or calloc function. For example we can write:

```
int *p;
p=(int*) malloc(sizeof(int) * 10);
or
 int* p;
p=(int*)calloc (10, sizeof(int));
```

which allocates 20 bytes and starting address of this 20 bytes memory block is returned and assigned to *p*. From here onwards you can assume as if array were declared like int *p*[10]; in case malloc or calloc fail to allocate memory it returns NULL.

Now, here we give some examples for better understanding the point.

```
/*Prog 13.8 Dynamic 1-D array*/
#include<stdio.h>
#include<conio.h>
 void main()
 {
   int *p,n,i;
   clrscr();
   printf("Enter the size of array\n");
   scanf("%d",&n);
   p=(int*)malloc(sizeof(int)*n);
   for(i=0;i<n;i++)
   {
     printf("\nEnter p[%d] element:",i);
     scanf("%d",p+i);
   }
   printf("Array elements are \n");
   for(i=0;i<n;i++)
   printf("p[%d]=%d\n",i,*(p+i));
```

```
   free(p);
   getch();
 }
```

Output:

```
Enter the size of array
10
Enter p[0] element:12
Enter p[1] element:13
Enter p[2] element:14
Enter p[3] element:15
Enter p[4] element:16
Enter p[5] element:17
Enter p[6] element:18
Enter p[7] element:19
Enter p[8] element:20
Enter p[9] element:21
Array elements are
p[0]=12
p[1]=13
p[2]=14
p[3]=15
p[4]=16
p[5]=17
p[6]=18
p[7]=19
p[8]=20
p[9]=21
```

EXPLANATION: There is nothing new in the program. Simply treat the *p* as integer array of size *n* given by the user. Rest is self- explanatory.

```
/*Prog 13.9 Demo of 2-D array*/
#include<stdio.h>
#include<conio.h>
 void main()
 {
  int **ptr,row,col,i,j;
  clrscr();
  printf("Enter number of row\n");
  scanf("%d",&row);
  ptr=(int**)malloc(sizeof(int)*row);
```

```
  printf("Enter number of col\n");
  scanf("%d",&col);
  for(i=0;i<row;i++)
  ptr[i]=(int*)malloc(sizeof(int)*col);
  for(i=0;i<row;i++)
  {
   for(j=0;j<col;j++)
   {
      printf("\n Enter p[%d][%d] element:",i,j);
      scanf("%d",(*(ptr+i)+j));
   }
  }
  printf("The matrix is \n");
  for(i=0;i<row;i++)
  {
    for(j=0;j<col;j++)
     printf("%d",ptr[i][j]);
     printf("\n");
  }
  for(i=0;i<row;i++)
  free(ptr[i]);
  free(ptr);
  getch();
 }
```

Output:

```
Enter number of row
3
Enter number of col
3
 Enter p[0][0] element:11
 Enter p[0][1] element:12
 Enter p[0][2] element:13
 Enter p[1][0] element:14
 Enter p[1][1] element:15
 Enter p[1][2] element:16
 Enter p[2][0] element:17
 Enter p[2][1] element:18
 Enter p[2][2] element:19
The matrix is
```

```
11 12 13
14 15 16
17 18 19
```

EXPLANATION: To create **2-D** array dynamically we will have to take a **double pointer.** Initially the pointer ***p*** points to memory allocated for **3-rows.** As each of the **row** will consists of a **1-D** array of **3** elements so using **for** loop for the number of **row** we allocated memory for the columns. We are having just three rows here so ***p*[0]** points to first 1-D array, ***p*[1]** points to the second **1-D** array and ***p*[2]** points to the third **1-D array.** Now the pointer ***p*** can be treated as a **2-D** array. To access any of the element we can write say ***p*[*i*][*j*]** or ***(*(*p* + *i*) + *j*).** For freeing the memory first we **free** the pointers **to 3 1-D** arrays and latter the pointer itself.

13.5 DMA FOR STRUCTURE

For dynamic allocation of structures we just have to declare a pointer of a particular type of structure and make use of malloc and calloc function. For example we can write:

```
struct person
{
 char name[10];
 int age;
};
 struct person *ptr;
ptr=(strcut person*) malloc(sizeof(struct person));
```

and for array of structure we can write:

```
ptr=(int*)calloc(10,sizeof(struct person));
```

Now, we give some example for the better understanding point of view:

```
/*Prog 13.10 Dynamic memory allocation for structure*/
#include<stdio.h>
#include<conio.h>
 void main()
 {
   typedef struct
   {
      char bname[20];
      int pages;
      int price;
   }book;
   book *ptr;
   clrscr();
   ptr=(book *)malloc(sizeof(book));
```

```
    printf("Enter the book name,pages and price\n");
    scanf("%s%d%d",ptr->bname, &ptr->pages,&ptr->price);
    printf("\n Book details\n");
    printf("Name=%s\n",(*ptr).bname);
    printf("Pages=%d\n",ptr->pages);
    printf("Price=%d\n",ptr->price);
    free(ptr);
    getch();
 }
```

Output:

```
Enter the book name,pages and price
Java 345 334
 Book details
Name=Java
Pages=345
Price=334
```

EXPLANATION: In the program we have allocated the memory for the structure book. Size of the structure book on **turbo C** turns out to be **24 (20 + 2 + 2 = 24).** So a block of 24 bytes is allocated (not necessary). Rest is similar to pointer to structure we did in **chapter structures and unions.**

```
/*Prog 13.11 dynamic array of structures*/
#include<stdio.h>
#include<conio.h>
#define NE 3
 void main()
 {
    type def struct
    {
       char bname[20];
       int pages;
       int price;
    }book;
    book *ptr;
    int i;
    ptr=(book*)calloc(NE,sizeof(book));
    clrscr();
    for(i=0;i<NE;i++)
    {
     printf("\n Enter the book name, pages and price\n");
     scanf("%s%d",(ptr+i)->bname,&(ptr+i)->pages);
```

```
     scanf("%d",&(ptr+i)->price);
     }
    printf("\nBook Details\n");
    for(i=0;i<NE;i++)
    {
      printf("Name=%s\t",ptr[i].bname);
      printf("Pages=%d\t",ptr[i].pages);
      printf("Price=%d\n",ptr[i].price);
    }
    free(ptr);
    getch();
  }
```

Output:

```
 Enter the book name, pages and price
Java 236 256
 Enter the book name, pages and price
C++ 567 346
 Enter the book name, pages and price
Unix 456 385
Book Details
Name=Java         Pages=236         Price=256
Name=C++          Pages=567         Price=346
Name=Unix         Pages=456         Price=385
```

EXPLANATION: With the help of calloc function memory is allocated for 3 structures (array of structure of size 3). It takes 2 parameters as explained in the beginning of the chapter, first is the number of elements and second is the size of each element of the array, here is the size of the structure book.

13.6 REALLOCATION OF MEMORY

In programming situation we may sometimes want to increase the size of the previously allocated memory so that we can store more data items. For this purpose C provides a function realloc which can be used for the reallocation of memory. In case reallocation fails it returns NULL. For example we first allocate memory using malloc or calloc.

int ***p*;**

***p*= (int*) malloc (sizeof (int)*10);**

Which allocates memory for **10** integers. To increase the size for **5** more integers we will write:

***p*= (int*) malloc (sizeof (int)* 10+5);**

Assume **realloc** does not fail, it returns a pointer to the newly allocated memory block.

Now see the programs given below for more explanation:

```
/*Prog 13.12 Demo of realloc ver 1*/
#include<stdio.h>
#include<conio.h>
 void main()
 {
   int *ptr,i,n;
   clrscr();
   printf("Enter the size of array\n");
   scanf("%d",&n);
   ptr=(int*)malloc(sizeof(int)*n);
   if(ptr==NULL)
   {
    printf("Allocation of memory failed \n");
    getch();
    exit(0);
   }
   for(i=0;i<n;i++)
   *(ptr+i)=i+1;
   printf("Original array is \n\n");
   for(i=0;i<n;i++)
   printf("Address:%u\t element:%d\n",ptr+i,*(ptr+i));
   printf("\n Reallocation memory for %d+4 elements\n",n);
   ptr=(int*)realloc(ptr,n+4);
   if(ptr==NULL)
   {
      printf("\n Reallocation of memory failed\n");
      getch();
      exit(0);
   }
```

Output:

```
Enter the size of array
3
Original array is
Address:2062         element:1
Address:2064         element:2
Address:2066         element:3
Reallocation memroy for 3+4 elements
After reallocation new array is
```

```
Address:2072        element:1
Address:2074        element:2
Address:2076        element:3
Address:2078        element:4
Address:2080        element:5
Address:2082        element:6
Address:2084        element:7
```

EXPLANATION: The function realloc is used for realloc the memory previously allocated by malloc or calloc. In the program we have allocated the memory for an array of size n. through realloc we have reallocated the memory for an increased array of size $n + 4$. As the new memory size is more than the previously allocated memory size it is possible that the new memory required is not contiguous to the previously allocated one. In this case a new memory block of new size **(in this case $n + 4$)** is allocated and the contents from the old memory block are copied to the new one. As clear from the output of the program the memory is reallocated (due to change of address). It is also possible that there may not be sufficient memory available to be allocated or reallocated. So we must check that the pointer returned from realloc or malloc or calloc is not NULL. This NULL checking code can be written in this earlier program also.

```
/*Prog 13.13 Demo of realloc ver2*/
#include<stdio.h>
#include<conio.h>
 void main()
 {
  int*ptr,i,n;
  clrscr();
  printf("Enter the size of array\n");
  scanf("%d",&n);
  ptr=(int*)malloc(sizeof(int)*n);
  if(ptr==NULL)
  {
   printf("Allocation of memory failed\n");
   getch();
   exit(0);
  }
  for(i=0;i<n;i++)
   *(ptr+i)=i+1;
  printf("Original array is \n\n");
  for(i=0;i<n;i++)
  printf("Address:%u\t element:%d\n",ptr+i,*(ptr+i));
  printf("\n Reallocating memory for %d-2 elements \n",n);
  ptr=(int*)realloc(ptr,n-2);
  if(ptr==NULL)
```

```
{
  printf("\n Reallocation of memory failed \n");
  getch();
  exit(0);
}
printf("\n after reallocation new array is \n\n");
for(i=0;i<n-2;i++)
printf("Address:%u\t element:%d\n",ptr+i,*(ptr+i));
getch();
free(ptr);
}
```

Output:

```
Enter the size of array
15
Original array is
Address:2066        element:1
Address:2068        element:2
Address:2070        element:3
Address:2072        element:4
Address:2074        element:5
Address:2076        element:6
Address:2078        element:7
Address:2080        element:8
Address:2082        element:9
Address:2084        element:10
Address:2086        element:11
Address:2088        element:12
Address:2090        element:13
Address:2092        element:14
Address:2094        element:15
Reallocating memory for 15-2 elements
after reallocation new array is
Address: 2066 element: 1
```

EXPLANATION: In this program the new size is less than the old size. When the new size of block is less than the size there will be a loss of data as it is visible from the output of the program .no error checking is performed for the input *n*. Better you insert your own code for the same.

13.7 LINKED LIST

A linked list is a dynamic data structure of elements which may be integer, float, string or a structure. The individual elements of linked list are called node and they are declared to be structure in C. The list is called linked list as the nodes are linked to each other with the help of pointers. It is called dynamic as we may add or delete node during program execution. Again for each node memory is allocated dynamically by malloc or calloc. In this section we will learn how to create a linked list and perform addition and deletion operation on it.

The structure of a node:

struct node

{

int data;

struct node*next;

};

We will have just one integer element data and a pointer of type struct node next to point to the next node. If no such node is present the next will have NULL.

The above declared structure is called self-referential structure as in the declaration it contains a pointer to itself.

When we declare array, the array name represents the base address and we can access all its elements if we know its base address. But in the linked list the difference node are created dynamically and their addresses may be contiguous that's why we have a struct node *next in the declaration of node. In this next pointer we store the address of next node. For the same reason we must have the starting address of the linked list *i.e.* address of the first node of the linked list. Therefore we declare a pointer start of type struct node to point to the first node of linked list. We have to be continuous about start as if we lost this address we won't be able to track the linked list.

```
/*Prog 13.14 Elementary linked list ver1*/
#include<stdio.h>
#include<conio.h>
#include<alloc.h>
 void main()
 {
   struct node
   {
   int data;
   struct node*next;
  };
  int d;
  struct node *start = NULL, *temp,*save;
  char ch;
```

```
  clrscr();
  printf("Enter the data for the node\n");
  scanf("%d",&d);
  start=(struct node*)malloc(sizeof(struct node));
  start->data=d;
  start->next=NULL;
  save= start;
  fflush(stdin);
  printf("Do you want to enter more(y/n)\n");
  scanf("%c",&ch);
  while(ch=='y'||ch=='y')
  {
    fflush(stdin);
    printf("Enter the data for the node\n");
    scanf("%d",&d);
    fflush(stdin);
    temp=(struct node*)malloc(sizeof(struct node));
    temp->data=d;
    temp->next=NULL;
    save->next=temp;
    save=temp;
    printf("Do you want to enter more(y/n)\n");
    scanf("%c",&ch);
  }
   while(start!=NULL)
   {
     printf("%d->",start->data);
     start=start->next;
   }
   getch();
 }
```

Output:

```
Enter the data for the node
10
Do you want to enter more(y/n)
y
Enter the data for the node
20
Do you want to enter more(y/n)
```

```
y
Enter the data for the node
30
Do you want to enter more(y/n)
y
Enter the data for the node
40
Do you want to enter more(y/n)
y
Enter the data for the node
50
Do you want to enter more(y/n)
y
Enter the data for the node
60
Do you want to enter more(y/n)
y
Enter the data for the node
70
Do you want to enter more(y/n)
y
Enter the data for the node
80
Do you want to enter more(y/n)
y
Enter the data for the node
90
Do you want to enter more(y/n)
n
10->20->30->40->50->60->70->80->90->
```

EXPLANATION: Initially we allocate memory for the first node and start point to it. We take input from user in *d* and assign *d* to data member of node and NULL to the next node and NULL to the next member field as this is our first node and there is no node following this node. This is as shown (here X shows NULL).

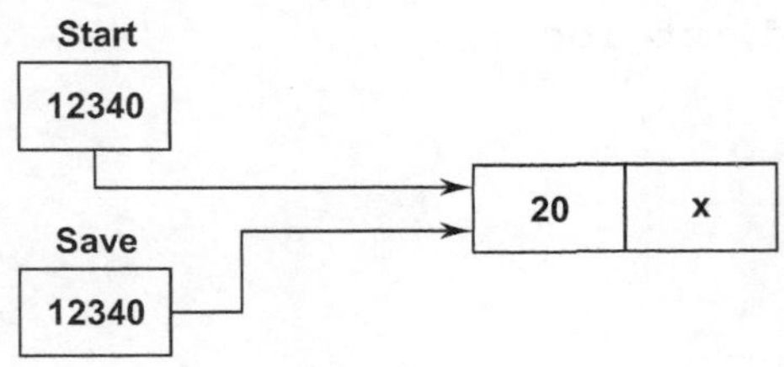

Next allocation of node depends upon user response. Next time when user presses y or Y.

```
save = temp (result in the figure)
```

13.7.1 Menu Driven Linked List

The next program is a complete program for the linked list with functions for addition, deletion, searching, counting and display etc. The whole program is made menu driven using switch-case and while loop. The following operations have been considered on the linked list:

1. **ADDITION**
   (A) Adding a node in the beginning.
   (B) Adding a node at the end.
   (C) Adding a node in between.
2. **DELETION**
   (A) Deleting at the first node.
   (B) Deleting the last node.
   (C) Deletion of node in between
3. **SEARCHING A NODE CONTAINING DATA**
4. **COUNTING NUMBER OF NODES**
5. **DISPLAY OF LINKED LIST.**

Each of the above listed operation is performed using functions, which are described in the explanation part. Do not go on to the length of the program. Understanding the function s one by one will help you.

```
/*Prog 13.15 Menu driven linked list*/
#include<stdio.h>
#include<conio.h>
#include<alloc.h>
 #include<ctype.h>
 struct node
   {
   int data;
   struct node*next;
 };
 typedef struct node*N;
 void add_end(N*, int);
 void add_beg(N*,int);
 void add_bet(N*,int d,int loc);
 void del_beg(N*);
 void del_end(N*);
 void del_bet(N*,int);
 void search(N*,int);
 void disp(N);
```

```
int count(N);
N alloc();
void main()
{
   int d,loc;
   N start,temp,save;
   int ch;
   char yesno;
   clrscr();
   start=NULL;
   do
   {
      clrscr();
      printf("\n\n\n*****Linked List Demonstration*****\n\n");
      printf("1.Add node at the start\n");
      printf("2.Add node at the end\n");
      printf("3.Add node in between\n");
      printf("4.Delete first node\n");
      printf("5.Delete last node\n");
      printf("6.Delete node containing data\n");
      printf("7.Search \n");
      printf("8.Display\n");
      printf("9.Count\n");
      printf("10.Exit\n\n");
      scanf("%d",&ch);
      switch(ch)
      {
       case 1:
              printf("Enter data for the node\n");
              scanf("%d",&d);
              add_beg(&start, d);
              printf("node added\n");
              printf("Press any key to continue\n");
              getch();
              break;
       case 2:
              printf("Enter data for the node\n");
              scanf("%d",&d);
              add_end(&start,d);
```

```
                printf("node added\n");
                printf("Press any key to continue\n");
                getch();
                break;
        case 3:
                printf("Enter data for the node\n");
                scanf("%d",&d);
                printf("Enter the location of the node after which
                   \n");
                printf("The new node to be inserted \n");
                scanf("%d",&loc);
                add_bet(&start,d,loc);
                printf("Press any key to continue\n");
                getch();
                break;
        case 4:
                fflush(stdin);
                printf("Are you sure (y/n)\n");
                yesno=getchar();
                if(tolower(yesno)=='y')
                del_beg(&start);
                else
                if(tolower(yesno)=='n')
                break;
                printf("Press any key to continue\n");
                getch();
                break;
        case 5:
                fflush(stdin);
                printf("Are you sure(y/n)\n");
                yesno=getchar();
                if(tolower(yesno)=='y')
                del_end(&start);
                else if(tolower(yesno)=='n')
                break;
                printf("Press any key to continue\n");
                getch();
                break;
```

```
  case 6:
          fflush(stdin);
           printf("Enter data for the node which u wnat to
                delete\n");
          scanf("%d",&d);
          del_bet(&start,d);
          printf("Press any key to continue\n");
          getch();
          break;
  case 7:
           printf("Enter data for the node which u ant to
                search\n");
          scanf("%d",&d);
          search(&start,d);
          printf("Press any key to continue\n");
          getch();
          break;
  case 8:
          printf("The linked list is \n");
          disp(start);
          printf("Press any key to continue\n");
          getch();
          break;
  case 9:
          printf("Number of elements=%d\n",count(start));
          getch();
          break;
  case 10:
          printf("Bye Bye\n");
          getch();
          exit(0);
  default:
           printf("Wrong choice \n");
  }
}while(ch>=1 && ch<=10);
 getch();
}
 N alloc()
 {
  return ((N)malloc(sizeof(struct node)));
```

```
  }
  void add_end(N*beg,int d)
  {
  N temp, save;
  save=*beg;
  if(*beg==NULL)
  {
   *beg=alloc();
   (*beg)->data=d;
   (*beg)->next=NULL;
  }
  else
  {
     while(save->next!=NULL)
       save=save->next;
       temp=alloc();
       temp->data=d;
       temp->next=NULL;
       save->next=temp;
  }
}
 void add_beg(N*beg,int d)
{
     N temp;
     temp=alloc();
     temp->data=d;
     temp->next=*beg;
     *beg=temp;
}
 void search(N*beg,int d)
 {
  N temp,save;
  int found=0;
  save=*beg;
  if(*beg==NULL)
  {
   printf("Linked list is empty\n");
   return;
  }
  else
```

```
{
 while(save!=NULL)
 {
  if(save->data==d)
   found=1;
   save=save->next;
  }
  if(found==1)
   printf("Element exist\n");
   else
   printf("Element does not exist\n");
   }
  }
  void add_bet(N*beg,int d,int loc)
  {
   N temp,save;
   int c,i;
   save=*beg;
   c=count(*beg);
   if(loc<=0||loc>c)
   {
     printf("Invalid location\n");
     getch();
     exit(0);
  }
 for(i=0;i<loc-1;i++)
 save=save->next;
 temp=alloc();
 temp->data=d;
 temp->next=save->next;
 save->next=temp;
 printf("node added\n");
 }
 void del_beg(N*beg)
 {
  N temp;
  if(*beg==NULL)
  {
    printf("Linked list is empty\n");
    return;
```

```
    }
   temp=(*beg);
   (*beg)=(*beg)->next;
   free(temp);
   printf("Node deleted \n");
  }
  void del_end(N*beg)
  {
   N temp,save=*beg;
   if(*beg==NULL)
   {
     printf("Linked list is empty\n");
     return;
   }
   while(save->next->next!=NULL)
   save=save->next;
   temp=save->next;
   free(temp);
   printf("Node deleted\n");
   }
   void del_bet(N*beg,int d)
   {
    N temp,save,prev;
    int c,i,found=0;
    save=*beg;
    if(save->data==d)
    {
      *beg=(*beg)->next;
      return;
    }
    while(save!=NULL)
    {
      if(save->data==d)
      {
       prev->next=save->next;
       free(save);
       found=1;
       break;
      }
```

```
    prev=save;
    save=save->next;
   }
   if(found==1)
   printf("Node deleted\n");
   else
   printf("Node does not exist\n");
  }
  int count(N ptr)
  {
    int num=0;
    while(ptr!=NULL)
    {
      num++;
      ptr=ptr->next;
    }
    return num;
  }
  void disp(N ptr)
  {
   while(ptr!=NULL)
   {
    printf("%d->",ptr->data);
    ptr=ptr->next;
   }
   printf("\n");
  }
```

Output:

```
**********************Linked List Demonstration*****************
1.Add node at the start
2.Add node at the end
3.Add node in between
4.Delete first node
5.Delete last node
6.Delete node containing data
7.Search
8.Display
9.Count
10.Exit
1
```

```
Enter data for the node
20
node added
Press any key to continue
*********************Linked List Demonstration*****************
1.Add node at the start
2.Add node at the end
3.Add node in between
4.Delete first node
5.Delete last node
6.Delete node containing data
7.Search
8.Display
9.Count
10.Exit
2
Enter data for the node
40
node added
Press any key to continue
*********************Linked List Demonstration*****************
1.Add node at the start
2.Add node at the end
3.Add node in between
4.Delete first node
5.Delete last node
6.Delete node containing data
7.Search
8.Display
9.Count
10.Exit
3
Enter data for the node
45
Enter the location of the node after which
The new node to be inserted
*********************Linked List Demonstration*****************
1.Add node at the start
2.Add node at the end
3.Add node in between
```

```
4.Delete first node
5.Delete last node
6.Delete node containing data
7.Search
8.Display
9.Count
10.Exit
4
Are you sure (y/n)
Y
Linked list is empty
Press any key to continue
```

EXPLANATION: The program can be well understood by taking one function at a time. The statement typedef struct node*N gives a new name N to struct node*. On the basis of we can say that N* means struct node**. To keep track of the start of the linked list we use a special pointer start whose initial value is NULL.

The function add_beg adds a new node in the linked list at the beginning .We call this function initially to create first for the linked list. The address of start and data for the node (after taking from user) is passed to the function. After a successful return from this function start points to the newly created node.

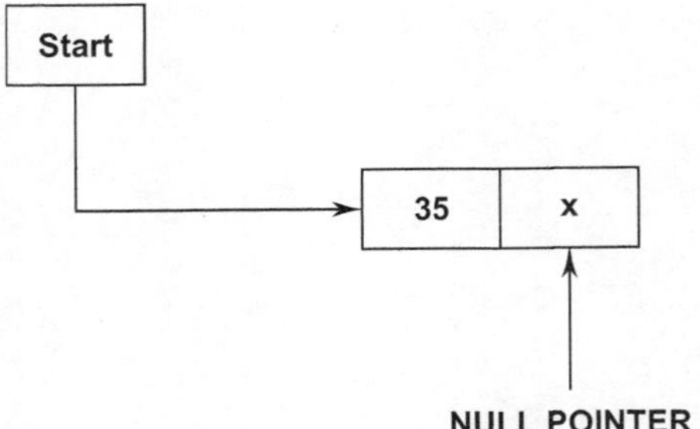

The function add_end adds a new node in the linked list at the end. If the linked list is empty then a new node is created and start point to the node else we reach up to the end of the linked list using while and a temporary pointer save and add the node there. Assuming that we have just one node in the linked list as shown in the above figure and we add a node at the end.

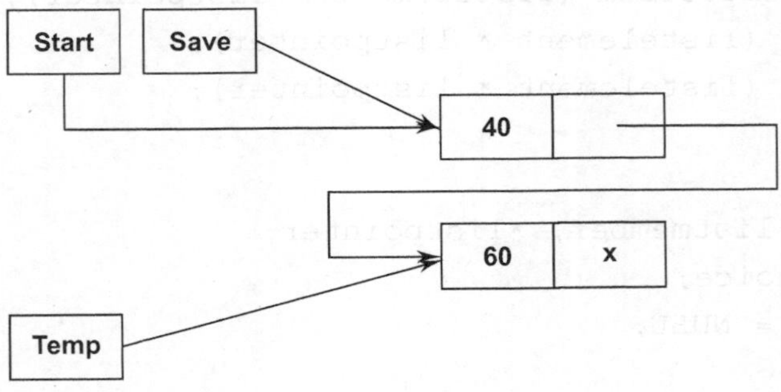

The function add_bet inserts a new node in between the linked list. It takes three parameters: address of the start, element to be inserted and the location of the node after which the new node is to be inserted.

The function del_beg deletes the first node of the linked list. It simply takes one parameter: address of the start pointer. The first node is deleted by making start to point to start ->next and freeing the node. For this starting node is first saved in a temporary variable and it is freed by a call to free.

The function del_end deletes the last the node of the linked list. For this we have to move to the end of the list and save the previous node in a temporary variable. The node is then deleted by a call to a free.

The function del_bet deletes a node with a given data which is input from the user. If the Data matches with the first node is deleted and function returns else we scan the whole linked list using while loop and delete the node by making next of the previous node to point to next of the node to be deleted.

In the figure second node with data 20 is to be deleted. The node previous to second after deletion points to third node with data value 30.

The function count is simple. It counts number of nodes in the linked list. For this we takes a variable count and increment it in the while loop.

The function search searches a node with a given data. The function is easy to understand.

```
/*Prog 13.16 Demo of dynamic data structures in to show the functional-
ity of queue in C*/
#include <stdio.h>
#include <conio.h>
#define FALSE 0
#define NULL 0
 typedef struct
  {
     int dataitem;
     struct listelement *link;
  }  listelement;
 void Menu (int *choice);
 listelement * AddItem (listelement * listpointer, int data);
 listelement * RemoveItem (listelement * listpointer);
 void PrintQueue (listelement * listpointer);
 void ClearQueue (listelement * listpointer);
 void main ()
 {
     listelement listmember, *listpointer;
     int data, choice;
     listpointer = NULL;
     do
```

```
  {
      Menu (&choice);
      switch (choice)
      {
        case 1:
                 printf ("Enter data item value to add ");
                 scanf ("%d", &data);
                 listpointer = AddItem (listpointer, data);
                 break;
        case 2:
                 if (listpointer == NULL)
                 printf ("Queue empty!\n");
                 else
                 listpointer = RemoveItem (listpointer);
                 break;
        case 3:
                 printQueue (listpointer);
                 break;
        case 4:
                 break;
                 default:
                 printf ("Invalid menu choice - try again\n");
                 break;
  }
} while (choice != 4);
  ClearQueue (listpointer);
}                     /* main ends here */
  void Menu (int *choice)
  {
  char local;
  printf("\nEnter\t1 to add item,\n\t2 to remove item\n\n\t3 to
    print queue\n\t4 to quit\n");
  do
  {
     local = getchar ();
     if ((isdigit (local) == FALSE) && (local != '\n'))
     {
      printf ("\nyou must enter an integer.\n");
      printf("Enter1to add,2toremove,3toprint,4 to quit\n");
```

```
    }
  } while (isdigit ((unsigned char) local) == FALSE);
    *choice = (int) local - '0';
}
  listelement* AddItem (listelement * listpointer, int data)
  {
    listelement * lp = listpointer;
    if (listpointer != NULL)
    {
      while (listpointer -> link != NULL)
      listpointer = listpointer -> link;
      listpointer->link=(structlistelement*)malloc
                  (sizeof(listelement));
      listpointer = listpointer -> link;
      listpointer -> link = NULL;
      listpointer -> dataitem = data;
      return lp;
    }
    else
    {
      listpointer = (struct listelement *) malloc (sizeof
             (listelement));
      listpointer -> link = NULL;
      listpointer -> dataitem = data;
      return listpointer;
    }
  }
   listelement * RemoveItem (listelement * listpointer) {
   listelement * tempp;
   printf ("Element removed is %d\n", listpointer -> dataitem);
   tempp = listpointer -> link;
   free (listpointer);
   return tempp;
}
   void PrintQueue (listelement * listpointer)
   {
     if (listpointer == NULL)
     printf ("queue is empty!\n");
     else
      while (listpointer != NULL)
```

```
        {
            printf ("%d\t", listpointer -> dataitem);
            listpointer = listpointer -> link;
        }
        printf ("\n");
    }
    void ClearQueue (listelement * listpointer)
    {
       while (listpointer != NULL)
       {
        listpointer = RemoveItem (listpointer);
       }
    }
```

Output:

```
Enter   1 to add item,
        2 to remove item
        3 to print queue
        4 to quit
1
Enter data item value to add 12
Enter   1 to add item,
        2 to remove item
        3 to print queue
        4 to quit
1
Enter data item value to add 13
Enter   1 to add item,
        2 to remove item
        3 to print queue
        4 to quit
1
Enter data item value to add 14
Enter   1 to add item,
        2 to remove item
        3 to print queue
        4 to quit
1
Enter data item value to add 12
Enter   1 to add item,
        2 to remove item
```

```
        3 to print queue
        4 to quit
1
Enter data item value to add 13
Enter   1 to add item,
        2 to remove item
        3 to print queue
        4 to quit
1
Enter data item value to add 14
Enter   1 to add item,
        2 to remove item
        3 to print queue
        4 to quit
3
12          13     14
Enter   1 to add item,
        2 to remove item
        3 to print queue
        4 to quit
2
Element removed is 12
Enter   1 to add item,
        2 to remove item
        3 to print queue
        4 to quit
```

EXPLANATION: Program is self-explanatory

POINTS TO PONDER

In this chapter you have learned the following points:

- In C, there are four functions that can be used to allocate, reallocate, or release a block of memory space dynamically at runtime.
- The **malloc ()** function allocates a block of memory whose size is specified by the argument passed to the function.
- The **free()** function is used to free up a block of memory space previously allocated by the **malloc(), calloc(), or realloc()** function
- The **calloc ()** function can do the same job as the **malloc ()** function. In addition, the **calloc ()** function can initialize the allocated memory space to **0.**

- The **realloc ()** function is used to reallocate a block of memory that has been allocated by the **malloc () or calloc ()** function.
- If a null pointer is passed to the **realloc ()** function as its first argument, the function acts like the **malloc()** function.
- If the second argument of the **realloc()** function is set to **0,** the **realloc()** function is equivalent to the free() function that releases a block of allocated memory.
- You have to include the header file stdlib.h before you can call the **malloc(), calloc(), realloc(), or free()** function.
- You should always check the values returned from the **malloc (), calloc (), or realloc ()** function, before you use the allocated memory made by these functions.

QUESTIONS AND ANSWERS

Q1. *Why do you need to allocate memory at runtime?*

Ans: Very often, you don't know the exact sizes of arrays until your program is being run. You might be able to estimate the sizes for those arrays, but if you make those arrays too big, you waste the memory. On the other hand, if you make those arrays too small, you're going to lose data. The best way is to allocate blocks of memory dynamically and precisely for those arrays when their sizes are determined at runtime. There are four C library functions, **malloc (), calloc (), realloc (), and free (),** which you can use in memory allocation at runtime.

Q2. *What does it mean if the malloc () function returns a null pointer?*

Ans: If the **malloc ()** function returns a null pointer, it means the function fails to allocate a block of memory whose size is specified by the argument passed to the function. Normally, the failure of the **malloc ()** function is caused by the fact that there is not enough memory to allocate. You should always check the value returned by the **malloc ()** function to make sure that the function has been successful before you use the block of memory allocated by the function.

Q3. *What are the differences between the calloc () and malloc () functions?*

Ans: Basically, there are two differences between the **calloc ()** and **malloc ()** functions, although both of them can do the same job. The first difference is that the **calloc ()** function takes two arguments, while the **malloc ()** function takes only one. The second one is that the **calloc ()** function initializes the allocated memory space to **0,** whereas there is no such guarantee made by the **malloc ()** function.

Q3. *Is the free () function necessary?*

Ans: Yes. The **free ()** function is very necessary, and you should use it to free up allocated memory blocks as soon as you don't need them. As you know, memory is a limited resource in a computer. Your program shouldn't take too much memory space when it allocates blocks of memory. One way to reduce the size of memory taken by your program is to use the **free ()** function to release the unused allocated memory in time.

EXERCISES

A. Answer the following questions:

1. Explain the concept of dynamic memory allocation?
2. Explain from the compiler's point of view difference between static allocation and dynamic allocation.
3. Discuss all the functions used for dynamic memory allocation and de-allocation?
4. What do you understand by a linked list? Discuss the advantages of it over array.
5. What happens when free is called?

B. Match the following questions:

I	II
1. static allocation	(*a*) dynamic data structure
2. reallocation	(*b*) deallocation of memory
3. free	(*c*) dynamic allocation.
4. linked list	(*d*) not at run time .
5. heap	(*e*) realloc function.

C. Write true or False against each statement:

1. Static allocation is done from stack.
2. dynamic allocation is also done from stack.
3. Delete function is used for the deallocation of previously allocated dynamic memory.
4. Without pointers, dynamic memory allocation cannot be done.
5. It is not necessary that **malloc ( ), calloc ( )** always returns successful.

D. Fill in the Blanks:

1. In dynamic memory allocation __________ data structure is used.
2. In static memory allocation __________ data structure is used.
3. Allocation done at compile time is known as __________ allocation.
4. Dynamic allocation is done from __________.
5. The function malloc takes __________ numbers of argument.
6. For the reallocation of memory we use of __________ function.
7. The memory allocated by **calloc ( )** function contains the storage initialized to __________.
8. The __________ is used to find out how much memory is to be allocated.
9. The function free takes just one argument of type __________.

E. Brain Drill:

1. Write a program to enter a string and remove all tabs with newline character? Memory for the string should be allocated dynamically.
2. Write a program to concatenate two string in to third string? Use dynamic memory allocation functions for all the strings.
3. Write a program which allocates memory for 200 strings of size 20 each. Reallocate memory for 300 strings and compare the memory addresses before and after reallocation.

4. Write your own version of malloc function which allocates memory for all built-in data types. In put to the function will be number of bytes and data type.

F. Predict the output of the following program:

```
1. main ( )
   {
          int *mptr, *cptr;
          mptr = (int*)malloc (sizeof (int));
          printf("%d",*mptr);
          cptr = (int*) calloc (sizeof(int),1);
          printf("%d",*cptr);
   }
2. main ( )
   {
          int i=10,j=20;
          int *pi=&i , *pj = &j;
          int k = *pi/*pj;
          printf("%d",k);
   }
3. main ( )
   {
          int *ptr;
          ptr = (int *) *400;
   }
```

14

INTRODUCTION TO 'C' PREPROCESSOR

This is the chapter which deals with C preprocessor is so depth which I think no book has ever dealt. Of course some compiler related macros have not been covered but I'm sure whatever I have covered is the best matter on C preprocessor you will get any where.

To start with, introduction of preprocessing given with a table of all preprocessor directives. A number of programming examples then given which makes use of some of the preprocessor directives. The difference between **#include"filename"** and **#include< filename>is** illustrated.

The notion of condition compilation is explained and various preprocessor directives used for the same are discussed.

Some special preprocessor directives like **___DATE___, ___FILE___** etc. have been explained. A brief introduction of the #pragma directive (used by the expert programmers) is given. Program to call a function first other than main is given with the help of this macro.

Difference between functions and macros are covered in the last section in an illustrative manner.

14.1 INTRODUCTION

The preprocessor is a program that processes the source program *i.e.* your C program file before it is passed to the compiler. A 'C' preprocessor is a collection of special statements called directives that are executed before the starting of the compilation process. Preprocessor directives are always initialized at the beginning of the program through it is not essential. They may appear any where within the program. All the preprocessor directives begins with a symbol hash (#). The following are preprocessor directives provides by C:

Table 14.1 *C preprocessor directives.*

#define	**#endif**	**#elif**
#ifndef	**#undef**	**#error**
#include	**#ifdef**	**#if**
#pragma	**#else**	**#line**
defined	**#(stringizing)**	**##(token-pasting)**

The preprocessor directives can be divided into three categories.

1. Macro substitution division
2. File inclusion division
3. Compiler control division

14.1.1 What Is the 'C' Preprocessor?

If there is a constant appearing in several places in your program, it's a good idea to associate a symbolic name to the constant, and then use the symbolic name to replace the constant throughout the program. There are two advantages to doing so:

1. First, your program will be more readable.
2. Second, it's easier to maintain your program.

For instance, if the value of the constant needs to be changed, find the statement that associates the constant with the symbolic name and replace the constant with the new one. Without using the symbolic name, you have to look everywhere in your program to replace the constant.

For this, C has a special program called the C preprocessor that allows you to define and associate symbolic names with constants. In fact, the C preprocessor uses the terminology **macro** names and **macro** body to refer to the symbolic names and the constants. **The C preprocessor runs before the compiler.** During preprocessing, the operation to replace a macro name with its associated macro body is called macro substitution or macro expansion. You can put a macro definition anywhere in your program. However, a macro name has to be defined before it can be used in your program.

In addition, the C preprocessor gives you the ability to include other source files. For instance, we've been using the preprocessor directive **#include** to include **C header files,** such as **stdio.h, stdlib.h, and string.h,** in the programs. Also, the C preprocessor enables you to compile different sections of your program under specified conditions.

14.1.2 The 'C' Preprocessor Versus The Compiler

One important thing you need to remember is that the C preprocessor is not part of the C compiler. The C preprocessor uses a different syntax. All directives in the C preprocessor begin with a **pound sign (#).** In other words, the pound sign denotes the beginning of a preprocessor directive, and it must be the first nonspace character on the line.

The C preprocessor is line oriented. Each macro statement ends with a newline character, not a semicolon. (Only C statements end with semicolons.) One of the most common mistakes made by a programmer is to place a semicolon at the end of a macro statement. Fortunately, many C compilers can catch such errors.

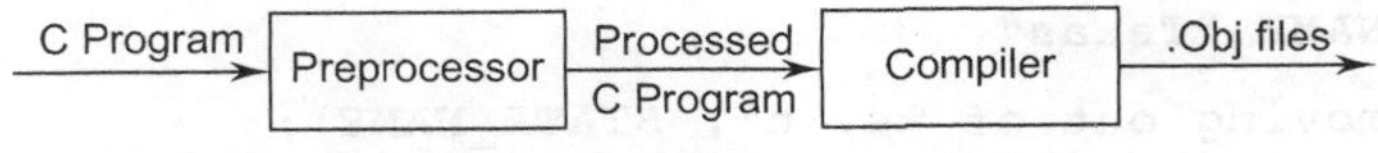

Fig. 14.1 *Preprocessing in C*

In the figure shown above input to the C preprocessor is the C program. The preprocessor replaces all the occurrences of macro template with their corresponding expansion then the processed file is passed to the C compiler for compilation.

Now I introduced you some points regarding macros:

1. Every macro template defined is treated as constant.
2. Before compilation macro template is searched by the preprocessor and expansion occurs at every place where is find, thus the length of program increases. In case of function, it is given affixed area of memory and function call transfers control to this area.
3. No type checking is performed while arguments to the macro i.e. whether arguments are integer, float, char, pointer etc.
4. They produce side effects.
5. They are faster in execution as function calling overhead, saving and retrieving of parameters and return address is not done.

These points will be clear to you as you move along with the chapter.

14.2 THE #DEFINE AND #UNDEF DIRECTIVES

The **#define** directive is the most common preprocessor directive, which tells the preprocessor to replace every occurrence of a particular character string (that is, a macro name) with a specified value (that is, a macro body).

The syntax for the **#define** directive is

```
#define macro_name macro_body
```

Here **macro_name** is an identifier that can contain letters, numerals, or underscores. **macro_body** may be a string or a data item, which is used to substitute each **macro_name** found in the program.

As mentioned earlier, the operation to replace occurrences of **macro_name** with the value specified by **macro_body** is known as macro substitution or macro expansion. The value of the macro body specified by a **#define** directive can be any character string or number. For example, the following definition associates **STATE_NAME** with the string **"Texas"** (including the quotation marks):

```
#define STATE_NAME "Texas"
```

Then, during preprocessing, all occurrences of **STATE_NAME** will be replaced by **"Texas"**. Likewise, the following statement tells the C preprocessor to replace **SUM** with the string **(12 + 8)**:

```
#define SUM (12 + 8)
```

On the other hand, you can use the **#undef** directive to remove the definition of a macro name that has been previously defined. The syntax for the **#undef** directive is

```
#undef macro_name
```

Here **macro_name** is an identifier that has been previously defined by a **#define** directive. The **#undef** directive **"undefines"** a macro name. For instance, the following segment of code:

```
#define STATE_NAME "Texas"

printf ("I am moving out of %s.\n", STATE_NAME);

#undef STATE_NAME
```

Defines the macro name **STATE_NAME** first, and uses the macro name in the **printf ()** function; then it removes the macro name.

14.3 DEFINING FUNCTION-LIKE MACROS WITH # DEFINE

You can specify one or more arguments to a **macro** name defined by the **#define** directive, so that the macro name can be treated like a simple function that accepts arguments. For instance, the following macro name, **MULTIPLY,** takes two arguments:

```
#define MULTIPLY (val1, val2) ((val1) * (val2))
```

When the following statement:

```
result = MULTIPLY (2, 3) + 10;
```

is preprocessed, the preprocessor substitutes the expression 2 for val1 and 3 for val2, and then produces the following equivalent:

```
result = ((2) * (3)) + 10;
```

```
/*Prog 14.1 Demo of using #define */
#include <stdio.h>
#define METHOD          "ABS"
#define ABS(val)        ((val) < 0 ? -(val) : (val))
#define MAX_LEN         8
#define NEGATIVE_NUM -10
 void main(void)
 {
   char *str = METHOD;
   int array[MAX_LEN];
   int i;
   clrscr();
   printf("The orignal values in array:\n");
   for (i=0; i<MAX_LEN; i++)
   {
      array[i] = (i + 1) * NEGATIVE_NUM;
      printf("array[%d]: %d\n", i, array[i]);
   }
   printf("\nApplying the %s macro:\n", str);
   for (i=0; i<MAX_LEN; i++)
   {
      printf("ABS(%d): %3d\n", array[i], ABS(array[i]));
   }
```

```
   getch();
}
```

Output:

```
The orignal values in array:
array[0]: -10
array[1]:-20
array[2]: -30
array[3]: -40
array[4]: -50
array[5]: -60
array[6]: -70
array[7]: -80
Applying the ABS macro:
ABS(-10): 10
ABS(-20): 20
ABS(-30): 30
ABS(-40): 40
ABS(-50): 50
ABS(-60): 60
ABS(-70): 70
ABS(-80): 80
```

EXPLANATION: The purpose of the **program 14.1** is to define different macro names, including a function-like macro, and use them in the program.

In **lines 4_7,** four macro names, **METHOD, ABS, MAX_LEN, and NEGATIVE_NUM** are defined with the **#define** directive. Among them, **ABS** can accept one argument. The definition of **ABS** in **line 5** checks the value of the argument and returns the absolute value of the argument. Note that the conditional **operator? :** is used to find the absolute value for the incoming argument.

Then, inside the **main ()** function, the **char** pointer **str** is defined and assigned with **METHOD in line 11.** As you can see, **METHOD** is associated with the string **"ABS".** In **line 12,** an int array called array is defined with the element number specified by **MAX_LEN.**

In **lines 16_19,** each element of array is initialized with the value represented by the **(*i* + 1) * NEGATIVE_NUM** expression that produces a series of negative integer numbers.

The **for** loop in **lines 22_24** applies the function-like **macro ABS** to each element of array and obtains the absolute value for each element. Also, all absolute values are printed on the screen. The output from the **program 14.1** proves that each **macro** defined in the program works very well.

```
/*Prog 14.2 Demo of macro*/
#define PI 3.14
#include<stdio.h>
```

```
#include<conio.h>
 void main()
 {
    float area,r,peri;
    clrscr();
    printf("Enter the radius\n");
    scanf("%f",&r);
    area=PI*r*r;
    peri=2*PI*r;
    printf("Radius=%f\n",r);
    printf("Area=%f\n",area);
    getch();
 }
```

Output:

```
Enter the radius
13.0
Radius=13.000000
Area=530.659973
```

EXPLANATION: The **#define** directive is used to define macro templates. In the above **program 14.2 PI** is the **macro** name or **macro** template and **3.14** is the **macro expansion.** There must not be = **(assignment operator)** between macro template and its corresponding expansion. There should be at least space between macro template and its expansion. During preprocessing the preprocessor searches for the macro templates in the program right after the first line after the **#define** directive in which macro template was created. It then replaces each occurrence of macro expansion but in some cases it may create problem. You may write macro template in small or capital letters but usually it is written in capitals to distinguish from variables which are generally written in lowercase.

```
/*Prog 14.3 macro is a constant*/
#define V 30
#include<stdio.h>
#include<conio.h>
 void main()
 {
    clrscr();
    printf("V=%d\n",V);
    V=V+1;
    printf("V now=%d\n",V);
    getch();
 }
```

Output:

```
Error message (Lvalue required)
```

EXPLANATION: Every macro template is treated as a constant so its value cannot be already by any means. So the above program given an error.

```
/*Prog 14.4 Demo of string macro-template ver 1*/
#define TEXT "This is macro template"
#include<stdio.h>
#include<conio.h>
 void main()
 {
    clrscr();
    printf(TEXT);
    getch();
 }
```

Output:

```
This is macro template
```

EXPLANATION: We have created a macro template **TEXT** whose vale *i.e.* expansion is a string so **printf (TEXT)** is replaced as **printf ("This is macro template")** after preprocessing.

```
/*Prog 14.5 Demo of string macro-template ver 2*/
#define TEXT " This is macro template"
#include<stdio.h>
#include<conio.h>
 void main()
 {
    clrscr();
    printf("TEXT");
    getch();
 }
```

Output:

```
TEXT
```

EXPLANATION: Macro is not expanded in double quotes.

```
/*Prog 14.6 Demo of string macro-template ver 3*/
#include<stdio.h>
#define TEXT "This is macro template"
#include<conio.h>
 void main()
 {
```

```
    char *p="TEXT";
    clrscr();
    printf(p);
    getch();
  }
```

Output:

TEXT

EXPLANATION: Same as given in the previous program.

```
/*Prog 14.7 demo of multiline string macro-template*/
#define TEXT "This is demo\of multiline\macro in C"
#include<stdio.h>
#include<conio.h>
 void main()
 {
    clrscr();
    printf(TEXT);
    getch();
 }
```

Output:

This is demo of multiline macro in C

EXPLANATION: Multi line macro can be written by placing a backslash \ at the end of the line as shown in the above program.

```
/*Prog 14.8 More on string macro ver 1*/
#define TEXT "This is macro demo"
#include<stdio.h>
#include<conio.h>
#include<string.h>
  void main()
  {
    char p[25];
    clrscr();
    strcpy(p,TEXT);
    printf(p);
    getch();
  }
```

Output:

This is macro demo

EXPLANATION: Because TEXT macro's expansion is a string it can be copied into another string *p* in the above program which is then displayed.

```
/*Prog 14.9 More on string macro-template ver 2*/
#define TEXT "This is demo"
#include<stdio.h>
#include<conio.h>
#include<string.h>
 void main()
 {
   char *p;
   clrscr();
   strcpy(p,TEXT);
   printf(p);
   getch();
 }
```

Output:

This is demo (Logical error)

EXPLANATION: This program produces a logical error. This is because memory for *p* has not allocated and we trying to copy "This is demo" (after processing) in it. In turbo C program produce an output:

This is demo

Null pointer assignment

```
/*Prog 14.10 more on string macro-template ver3*/
#include<stdio.h>
#include<conio.h>
#define TEXT "This is demo"
 void main()
 {
   char *p=TEXT;
   clrscr();
   printf(p);
   getch();
 }
```

Output:

This is demo

EXPLANATION: This program works fine because we have assigned address of string "This is demo" to pointer *p*.

```
/*Prog 14.11 Use of one macro for another*/
#define MAX 5
#define DMAX MAX*2
#include<stdio.h>
#include<conio.h>
 void main()
 {
    clrscr();
    printf("max=%d\n",MAX);
    printf("double of max=%d\n",DMAX);
    getch();
 }
```

Output:

```
max=5
double of max=10
```

EXPLANATION: Once a macro template is created it can be used in defining new macro templates.

```
/*Prog 14.12 Macro with argument*/
#define PI 3.14
#define TPI 2*PI
#define AREA(x)  (PI*x*x)
#define PERI(x)(TPI*x)
#include<stdio.h>
#include<conio.h>
 void main()
 {
 float area,r,peri;
 clrscr();
 printf("Enter the radius \n");
 scanf("%f",&r);
 area=AREA(r);
 peri=PERI(r);
 printf("Radius=%f\n",r);
 printf("Area=%f\n",peri);
 getch();
}
```

Output:

```
Enter the radius
12.0
Radius=12.000000
```

```
Area=75.360001
```

EXPLANATION: In the **AREA and PERI** macro template we have passed one argument. Value of that argument is put in the expansion where the macro template is used and value is calculated. Obviously **PI and TPI** macro must have been defined earlier.

```
/*Prog 14.13 macro for built in function*/
#define PRINT(s) printf(s)
#define INT int
#define FLOAT float
#define clear clrscr()
#define gkey getch()
#define takev scanf
#include<stdio.h>
#include<conio.h>
 void main()
 {
    INT a;
    FLOAT b;
    clear;
    PRINT("Enter an int number\n");
    takev("%d",&a);
    PRINT("Enter a float number \n");
    takev("%f",&b);
    printf("a=%d\n",a);
    printf("b=%f\n",b);
    gkey;
 }
Output:
Enter an int number
14
Enter a float number
23.56
a=14
b=23.559999
```

EXPLANATION: A number of macro templates have been created in the above program. Note we have given new name to the existing keywords and functions. This works fine because first preprocessing is performed then compilation.

```
/*Prog 14.14 Finding sqr and cube*/
#include<stdio.h>
#include<conio.h>
#define PRINT(s) printf(s)
```

```
#define CUBE(x) (x*x*x)
#define SQR(x) (x*x)
 void main()
 {
    float num,sq,cu;
    clrscr();
    PRINT("Enter a float number\n");
    scanf("%f",&num);
    sq=SQR(num);
    cu=CUBE(num);
    printf("Square of %f is %f\n",num, sq);
    printf("Cube of %f is %f\n",num,cu);
    getch();
 }
```

Output:

```
Enter a float number
12.34
Square of 12.340000 is 152.275604
Cube of 12.340000 is 1879.080933
```

EXPLANATION: We have created two macros with arguments. **CUBE (12.34)** is expanded as **(12.34*12.34*12.34) and SQR (12.34*12.34).** Note you may get wrong result if you use these **macro** as **CUBE (1+2).** Explanation is provided in the later programs. Try also with different data type.

```
/*Prog 14.15 Swapping of two numbers*/
#include<stdio.h>
#include<conio.h>
#define SWAP(a,b) a=a+b, b=a-b, a=a-b
 void main()
 {
    float a=2.4, b=3.5;
    clrscr();
    printf("Before swapping\n");
    printf("a=%f\tb=%f\n",a,b);
    SWAP(a,b);
    printf("After swapping \n");
    printf("a=%f\tb=%f\n",a,b);
    getch();
 }
```

Output:

```
Before swapping
a=2.400000      b=3.500000
After swapping
a=3.500000      b=2.400000
```

EXPLANATION: Logic of swapping has been put into macro SWAP. The logic has been discussed in the earlier chapter also. Try with different data types.

```
/*Prog 14.16 Max of two numbers*/
#define PRINT(s) printf(s)
#define MAX(a,b) (a>b?a:b)
#include<stdio.h>
#include<conio.h>
 void main()
 {
    float a,b,m;
    clrscr();
    PRINT("Enter two float numbers\n");
    scanf("%f%f",&a,&b);
    m=MAX(a,b);
    printf("max of %f and %f is %f\n",a,b,m);
    getch();
 }
```

Output:

```
Enter two float numbers
123.45 456.78
max of 123.449997 and 456.779999 is 456.779999
```

EXPLANATION: When **MAX (*a, b*)** is called it is expanded as **(*a*>*b*? *a* :*b*)** and maximum of **a** and **b** is stored in *m* which is displayed through **printf( )** statement.

```
/*Prog 14.17 Max of three number ver 1*/
#define PRINT(s) printf(s)
#define MAX(a,b,c) (a>b?(a>c?a:c):(b>c?b:c))
#include<stdio.h>
#include<conio.h>
 void main()
 {
    int a,b,c,m;
    clrscr();
    PRINT("Enter three integer number \n");
    scanf("%d%d%d",&a,&b,&c);
    m=MAX(a,b,c);
```

```
   printf("max of %d,%d and %d is %d\n",a,b,c,m);
   getch();
 }
```

Output:

```
Enter three integer number
234 567 143
max of 234,567 and 143 is 567
```

EXPLANATION: Logic to find out max of 3 numbers has been put into MAX macro which is expanded when used in expression during preprocessing. The logic has been explained in the earlier chapters.

```
/*Prog 14.18 Max of three number ver2*/
#define PRINT(s) printf(s)
#define MAX2(a,b) (a>b?a:b)
#define MAX3(a,b,c) (a>b?MAX2(a,c):MAX2(b,c))
#include<stdio.h>
#include<conio.h>
 void main()
 {
   int a,b,c,m;
   clrscr();
   PRINT("Enter three integer numbers\n");
   scanf("%d%d%d",&a,&b,&c);
   m=MAX3(a,b,c);
   printf("max of %d,%d and %d is %d\n",a,b,c,m);
   getch();
 }
```

Output:

```
Enter three integer numbers
1234 567 789
max of 1234,567 and 789 is 1234
```

EXPLANATION: The program is similar to the previous one except macros. Two macros are created and macro to find out max of 2 numbers is used in the macro to find out max of 3 numbers.

```
/*Prog 14.19 Max of two using if-else*/
#define PRINT(s) printf(s)
#define MAX2(a,b) if(a>b) c=a; else c=b;
#include<stdio.h>
#include<conio.h>
 void main()
```

```
 {
    float a,b,c;
    clrscr();
    PRINT("Enter two float numbers\n");
    scanf("%f%f",&a,&b);
    MAX2(a,b);
    printf("max of %fand %f is %f \n",a,b,c);
    getch();
 }
```

Output:

```
Enter two float numbers
456 123
max of 456.000000and 123.000000 is 456.000000
```

EXPLANATION: In this time for finding maximum of two numbers we have used if-else statement.

```
/*Prog 14.20 String macro and pointers*/
#define STRING "LOVABLE C"
#include<stdio.h>
#include<conio.h>
 void main()
 {
    clrscr();
    printf("%s\n",STRING);
    printf("%s\n",STRING+4);
    printf("%c\n",*(STRING+4));
    printf("%c\n",STRING[4]);
    getch();
 }
```

Output:

```
LOVABLE C
BLE C
B
B
```

EXPLANATION: After preprocessing the four printf statement will look like as:

```
printf("%s\n", "LOVABLE C");
printf("%s\n", "LOVABLE C"+ 4);
printf("%c\n", *("LOVABLE C" +4));
printf("%c\n", " LOVABLE C" [4]);
```

"LOVABLE C" means starting address of this string say ***p*** then we may write ***p*** = **"LOVABLE C "** so our printf becomes

```
printf("%s\n", p);
printf("%s\n",p+4);
printf("%c\n",*(p+4));
printf("%c\n",p[4]);
```

Now it is quite easy to tell the output.

```
/*Prog 14.21 changing the look of the program*/
#define MAIN main()
#define LBRACE {
#define RBRACE }
#define C clrscr()
#define G getch()
#define P(s) printf(s)
 MAIN
 LBRACE
 C;
 P("Hello macro!!");
 G;
 RBRACE
Output:
Hello macro!!!
```

EXPLANATION: The program is self-explanatory.

```
/*Prog 14.22 Side effects of macro ver1*/
#include<stdio.h>
#include<conio.h>
#define MUL(x) (x*x)
 main()
 {
    int x,y;
    clrscr();
    x=5;
    y=MUL(x);
    printf("y=%d\tx=%d\n",y,x);
    getch();
 }
Output:
y=25    x=5
```

EXPLANATION: The program is self explanatory.

```
/*Prog 14.23 Side effect of macro ver 2*/
#include<stdio.h>
#include<conio.h>
#define MUL(x)  (x*x)
 void main()
 {
  int x,y;
  clrscr();
  x=5;
  y=MUL(x+3);
  printf("y=%d\tx=%d\n",y,x);
  getch();
 }
```

Output:

```
y=23     x=5
```

EXPLANATION: The expansion of **MUL (*x* + 3)** is treated as **(*x*+3* *x*+3)** so output becomes **5+3*5+3 = 23.** If you want the desired output write macro **MUL as MUL(*x*) ((*x*)*(*x*)).** On expansions it becomes **= ((*x*+3)*(*x*+3))**

= ((8)*(8))

= 64

```
/*Prog 14.24 Side effects of macro ver3*/
#include<stdio.h>
#include<conio.h>
#define MUL(x)  (x*x)
 void main()
 {
   int x,y;
   clrscr();
   x=5;
   y=MUL(x++);
   printf("y=%d\tx=%d\n",y,x);
   getch();
 }
```

Output:

```
y=25     x=7
```

EXPLANATION: When macro is expanded it will be like **(*x*++ * *x*++)** so value of *x* will be incremented twice but for value of *y* original value of *x* will be taken.

```
/*Prog 14.25 Side effects of macro ver 4*/
```

```
#include<stdio.h>
#define MUL(x) (x*x)
 void main()
 {
    int x,y;
    clrscr();
    x=5;
    y=MUL(++x);
    printf("y=%d\tx=%d\n",y,x);
    getch();
 }
```

Output:

```
y=49     x=7
```

EXPLANATION: In this case the final value of x after post increment will be used for calculating the value of *y*.

/*Prog 14.26 Macro for a for loop ver1*/

```
#define MYFOR(a,b,c) for(i=a;i<b;i=i+c)
#include<stdio.h>
#include<conio.h>
 void main()
 {
    int i=1,c=10,ir=1;
    clrscr();
    MYFOR(i,c,ir)
    printf("%d\n",i);
    getch();
 }
```

Output:

```
1
2
3
4
5
6
7
8
9
```

EXPLANATION: Here **MYFOR** macro is for **for** loop. First argument of macro is the initialization condition for the **for** loop, second is the condition check and third one is the increment.

/*Prog 14.27 Macro for a for loop ver2*/

```
#define MYFOR(a,b,c) for(i=a;i<b;i=i+c)\
                        {\
                            printf("%d\t",i);\
                        }

#include<stdio.h>
#include<conio.h>
 void main()
 {
    int i=1,c=10,ir=1;
    clrscr();
    MYFOR(i,c,ir)
    getch();
 }
```

Output:

```
1
2
3
4
5
6
7
8
9
```

EXPLANATION: This program is very similar to the previous one but the only difference between the previous program **(program 14.26)** and this program is that the body of the **for** loop is made as part of the macro template **MYFOR.** As stated earlier back slash can be used for multi line macro.

14.4 THE # INCLUDE DIRECTIVE

From the very first program of this book we have been working with this include directive. This directive is used to load specific file in the current program. All the functions, variables, constants etc. of the include file can be used in the current program. The include file is also compiled with the current program. By this I want to say that if the include file contains some syntactical errors but your current program not, and then your program will not run.

There are basically two different syntax of using include directive:

1. **#include "stdio.h":**

   In this case the search for the file **"stdio.h"** is done in the current directory as well as in the directories in the specified path which might have been set up in options/ directories in turboC IDE (Integrated Development Environment). The syntax is used usually for the inclusion of user defined files. In double quotes you may also specify the complete path is file is in some other directory other than current directory.

2. **#include<stdio.h>:**

   In this case the search is done only in the directories in the specified path which might have been set up in option/ directories in Turbo C IDE.

For example create a file use.c and define following macro in that file:

```
/*File use.c*/

#define X 10

#define P " It works"

#define CUBE(x) ((x)*(x)*(x))
```

Now create a new file inuse.c as follows

```
/*Prog 14.28 Use of macro formt the other file*/
#include"use.c"
#include<stdio.h>
#include<conio.h>
 void main()
 {
    clrscr();
    printf("X=%d\n",X);
    printf(P);
    printf("\nCube of 3 is %d\n", CUBE(3));
    getch();
 }
```

Output:

```
X=10
It works
Cube of 3 is 27
```

EXPLANATION: The macro template **P** and **CUBE** are in file **use.c** which we have included. Make sure the file **use.c** is in the current directory in which the file **inuse.c** is there.

```
/*Prog 14.29 without #directive*/
#define print(s) printf(s)
#include<conio.h>
#include<stdio.h>
 void main()
 {
   clrscr();
   print("Welcome");
   print("\n In preprocessor");
   getch();
```

```
}
```

Output:

```
Welcome
In preprocessor
```

EXPLANATION: The program is self-explanatory.

```
/*Prog 14.30 Demo of #directive ver1*/
#define print(s) printf(#s)
#include<conio.h>
#include<stdio.h>
 void main()
 {
    clrscr();
    print(hello);
    print(\n Macro Next is integer\n);
    print(1234);
    getch();
 }
```

Output:

```
Hello
Macro Next is integer
1234
```

EXPLANATION: As stated in the beginning of the chapter is called stringizing operator. It allows a formal argument within a macro definition to be converted to a string. Note in the macro expansion the argument is preceded by this operator so on expansion the argument will be enclosed in the double quotes. Multiple spaces will be turned into single space in the string. Moreover the resulting string will automatically be combined with the adjacent string. Numbers may also be given but they will be treated as string.

```
/*Prog 14.31 Demo of # directive ver 2*/
#define print(s) printf(#s)
#include<conio.h>
#include<stdio.h>
 void main()
 {
    clrscr();
    print("hello");
    print("\n macro");
    getch();
 }
```

Output:

```
"hello"
```

```
"\n macro"
```

EXPLANATION: As argument to the macro is already in the double quotes it produces the above output.

```
/*Prog 14.32 demo of #directive ver3*/
#define print(s) printf(#s"Added")
#include<conio.h>
#include<stdio.h>
 void main()
 {
   clrscr();
   print(oops! I didnt know this);
   getch();
 }
```

Output:

```
oops! I didnt know this Added
```

EXPLANATION: Multiple spaces have turned into single and string "Added" has been added to argument string.

```
/*Prog 14.33 Demo of token pasting operator*/
#define print(i) printf("y" #i "= %d\n", y##i)
#include<conio.h>
#include<stdio.h>
 void main()
 {
   int y2=20;
   clrscr();
   print(2);
   getch();
 }
```

Output:

```
y2= 20
```

EXPLANATION: The ## operator is called token-pasting operator. It causes individual items within a macro definition to be concatenated, thus forming a single item.

Note in the statement **`printf("y" #i "=%d\n", y # # i)`**

"y" #i is turned into ***y*2** because value of ***i* is 2** then it is concatenated with **"=%d\n"** so resultant string becomes **"y2=%d\n"**. The expression ***y##i*** turns into *y*2 so complete statement after preprocessing becomes.

```
printf("y2=%d\n",y2);
/*Prog 14.34 # and ## in one program ver1*/
#define print(i) printf("y"#i "=%d\n",y##i)
```

```
#include<conio.h>
#include<stdio.h>
 void main()
 {
    int y2=20,x=2;
    clrscr();
    print(x);
    getch();
 }
```

Output:

Error

EXPLANATION: Constant value has to be given when using a token-posting operator. Use 2 in place of *x* to get the output similar to the previous program.

/*Prog 14.35 # and ## in one program ver2*/

```
#define print(s,i) printf(#s #i "=%c\n",s##i)
#include<conio.h>
#include<stdio.h>
 void main()
 {
    char t1='T',t2='O',t3='K';
    char t4='E',t5='N';
    clrscr();
    print(t,1);
    print(t,2);
    print(t,3);
    print(t,4);
    print(t,5);
    getch();
 }
```

Output:

```
t1=T
t2=O
t3=K
t4=E
t5=N
```

EXPLANATION: *#s* **and** *#i* are concatenated to form *t1, t2* and so on up to *t5* which again combined with *"=%c"* and *s##i* gives values for ***t1, t2, t3, t4, t5*. We just cannot write a simple loop perform the above operation why?**

/*Prog 14.36 Combining two to get one*/

```
#define combine(x,y) x##y
```

```
#include<conio.h>
#include<stdio.h>
 void main()
 {
    int ab=30;
    clrscr();
    printf("ab=%d\n",combine(a,b));
    getch();
 }
```

Output:

```
ab=30
```

EXPLANATION: The program is self-explanatory.

14.5 CONDITIONAL COMPILATION

Usually compilation is done from beginning of your program to end of program. Simple if else which we have seen in earlier chapter lets you control the execution of the program based on the condition. There are several directives which allow you to compile selected portion of code based on condition. This process is called conditional compilation. **#if, #ifdef, #ifndef, #else and #endif** are the most commonly used conditional compilation directives.

A preprocessor directive must be the only **instruction** on a line. Preprocessing directives are lines in your program that start with **'#'**. Whitespace is allowed before and after the **'#'**. The **'#'** is followed by an identifier that is the directive name. For example, **'#define'** is the directive The C language's preprocessor directives are given as follows:

(*a*) **#if**
(*b*) **#else**
(*c*) **#elif**
(*d*) **#endif**
(*e*) **#define**
(*f*) **#undef**
(*g*) **#warning**
(*h*) **#error**
(*i*) **#line**

Main uses of directives are:

1. **Conditional Compilation:** Using special preprocessing directives, you can include or exclude parts of the program according to various conditions.
2. **Line Control:** If you use a program to combine or rearrange source files into an intermediate file, which is then compiled, you can use line control to inform the compiler of where each source line originally came from.

3. **Error and Warning Reporting:** The directive **'#error'** causes the preprocessor to report a **fatal error** and the directive **'#warning'** is like the directive **'#error'**, but causes the preprocessor to issue a warning and continue preprocessing.

14.5.1 The #if, #elif, and #else Directives

The **#if** directive specifies that certain statements are to be included only if the value represented by the conditional expression is nonzero. The conditional expression can be an arithmetic expression.

The general form to use the **#if** directive is

```
#if expression
   statement1
   statement2
   . . .
   statementN
#endif
```

Here **expression** is the conditional expression to be evaluated. **Statement1, statement2, and statementN** represent the code to be included if expression is nonzero. Note that the **#endif** directive is included at the end of the definition to mark the end of the **#if** block, as it does for an **#ifdef** or **#ifndef** block.

In addition, the **#else** directive provides an alternative to choose. The following general form uses the **#else** directive to put **statement_1, statement_2, and statement_N** into the program if expression is zero:

```
#if expression
   statement1
   statement2
   . . .
   statementN
#else
   statement_1
   statement_2
   . . .
   statement_N
#endif   /* mark the end of #if block */
```

Again, the **#endif** directive is used to mark the end of the **#if** block. Also, a macro definition can be used as part of the conditional expression evaluated by the **#if** directive. If the macro is defined, it has a nonzero value in the expression; otherwise, it has the value 0.

For example, look at the following portion of code:

```
#ifdef DEBUG
   printf("The value of the debug version: %d\n", debug);
#else
   printf("The value of the release version: %d\n", release);
```

```
#endif
```

If **DEBUG** has been defined by a **#define** directive, the value of the debug version is printed out by the printf() function in the following statement:

```
printf("The value of the debug version: %d\n", debug);
```

Otherwise, if **DEBUG** has not been defined, the following statement is executed:

```
printf("The value of the release version: %d\n", release);
```

Now consider another example:

```
#if 1
 printf("The line is always printed out.\n");
#endif
```

The **printf()** function is always executed because the expression **1** evaluated by the **#if** directive never **returns 0.**

In the following example:

```
#if MACRO_NAME1 || MACRO_NAME2
   printf("MACRO_NAME1 or MACRO_NAME2 is defined.\n");
#else
   printf("MACRO_NAME1 and MACRO_NAME2 are not defined.\n");
#endif
```

The logical operator || is used, along with **MACRO_NAME1 and MACRO_NAME2** in the expression evaluated by the **#if** directive. If one of the macro names, **MACRO_NAME1 or MACRO_NAME2,** has been defined, the expression returns a nonzero value; otherwise, the expression returns **0.**

The C preprocessor has another directive, **#elif,** which stands for **"else if."** You can use **#if and #elif** together to build an **if-else-if** chain for multiple conditional compilation.

```
/*Prog 14.37 Demo of using #if, #elif, and #else */
#include <stdio.h>
#include <conio.h>
#define C_LANG      'C'
#define B_LANG      'B'
#define NO_ERROR  0
 void main(void)
 {
   clrscr();
   #if C_LANG == 'C' && B_LANG == 'B'
   #undef C_LANG
   #define C_LANG "I know the C language.\n"
   #undef B_LANG
   #define B_LANG "I know BASIC.\n"
    printf("%s%s", C_LANG, B_LANG);
```

```
    #elif C_LANG == 'C'
    #undef C_LANG
    #define C_LANG "I only know C language.\n"
     printf("%s", C_LANG);
    #elif B_LANG == 'B'
    #undef B_LANG
    #define B_LANG "I only know BASIC.\n"
     printf("%s", B_LANG);
    #else
     printf("I don't know C or BASIC.\n");
    #endif
    return NO_ERROR;
}
```

```
Output:
I know the C language.
I know BASIC.
```

EXPLANATION: The purpose of the **program 14.37** is to use the **#if, #elif, and #else** directives to select portions of code that are going to be compiled. Inside the **main()** function, the **#if** directive in **line 10** evaluates the conditional expression **C_LANG == 'C' && B_LANG == 'B'.** If the expression returns nonzero, then statements in **lines 11_15** are selected to be compiled.

In **line 11** the **#undef** directive is used to remove the **C_LANG** macro name. **Line 12** then redefines **C_LANG** with the string **"I know the C language.\n"**. Likewise, **line 13** removes the **B_LANG** macro name and **line 14** redefines **B_LANG** with another character string. The **printf()** function in **line 15** prints the two newly assigned strings associated with **C_LANG and B_LANG.**

The **#elif** directive in **line 16** starts to evaluate the expression **C_LANG == 'C'** if the expression in **line 10** fails to return a nonzero value. If the **C_LANG == 'C'** expression returns nonzero, the statements in **lines 17_19** are compiled.

If, however, the expression in **line 16** also fails to return a nonzero value, the **B_LANG == 'B'** expression in **line 20** is evaluated by another **#elif** directive. The statements in **lines 21_23** are skipped, and the statement in **line 25** is compiled finally if the **B_LANG == 'B' expression returns 0.**

In **line 26** the **#endif** directive marks the end of the **#if** block that starts on **line 10.** From the program14.36 you can tell that **C_LANG and B_LANG** have been properly defined in **lines 4 and 5.** Therefore, the statements **in lines 11_15** are selected as part of the program and compiled by the **C** compiled. The two character strings assigned to **C_LANG and B_LANG** during the redefinition are printed out after the **program 14.36** is executed.

14.5.2 Nested Conditional Compilation

According to the ANSI C standard, the **#if and #elif** directives can be nested at least **eight levels.** For example, the **#if** directive is nested in the following code segment:

```
#if MACRO_NAME1
   #if MACRO_NAME2
      #if MACRO_NAME3
         printf("MACRO_NAME1, MACRO_NAME2, and MACRO_NAME3\n");
      #else
         printf("MACRO_NAME1 and MACRO_NAME2\n");
      #endif
   #else
      printf("MACRO_NAME1\n");
   #endif
#else
   printf("No macro name defined.\n");
#endif
```

Here the **#if** directive is nested to **three levels.** Note that each **#else or #endif** is associated with the nearest **#if.**

```
/*Prog 14.38 Demo of nesting #if */
#include <stdio.h>
#include <conio.h>
/* macro definitions */
#define ZERO       0
#define ONE        1
#define TWO        (ONE + ONE)
#define THREE      (ONE + TWO)
#define TEST_1     ONE
#define TEST_2     TWO
#define TEST_3     THREE
#define MAX_NUM    THREE
#define NO_ERROR   ZERO
 /* function declaration */
void StrPrint(char **ptr_s, int max);
 /* the main() function */
main(void)
 {
   char *str[MAX_NUM] = {"The choice of a point of view", "is the
                              initial act of culture.", "--- by O.
                                   Gasset"};

   clrscr();
    #if TEST_1 == 1
        #if TEST_2 == 2 /*Nesting Apply */
```

```
          #if TEST_3 == 3
               StrPrint(str, MAX_NUM);
          #else
               StrPrint(str, MAX_NUM - ONE);
          #endif
       #else
          StrPrint(str, MAX_NUM - TWO);
       #endif
    #else
       printf("No TEST macro has been set.\n");
    #endif
    return NO_ERROR;
}
 /* function definition */
 void StrPrint(char **ptr_s, int max)
 {
    int i;
    for (i=0; i<max; i++)
    printf("Content: %s\n",ptr_s[i]);
}
```

Output:

```
Content: The choice of a point of view
Content: is the initial act of culture.
Content: --- by O. Gasset
```

EXPLANATION: The purpose of the program 14.38 is to print the content of character strings controlled by the **nested #if** directives. At the beginning of the program, **nine macro** names are defined in **lines 5_13.** The prototype of a function, **StrPrint(),** is given in **line 15. Lines 19_21** define and initialize an array of **char** pointers called **str.**

The **#if** directives in **lines 23_25** evaluate macro names, **TEST_1, TEST_2, and TEST_3,** respectively. If the **three** macro names all return nonzero values, then in **line 26, StrPrint()** is invoked to print the content of all character strings pointed to by the pointers in the **str** array.

If, however, only **TEST_1 and TEST_2** are nonzero, the statement in **line 28** prints out the content of the **MAX_NUM-ONE** strings. Likewise, if only **TEST_1** returns a nonzero value, the **StrPrint() function** is called in **line 31** to print out the content of the **MAX_NUM-TWO** strings.

The last case is that **TEST_1, TEST_2,** and **TEST_3** all return zero. Then the **printf()** function in **line 34** is executed to display the message No **TEST** macro has been set onscreen.

As you can tell from the **program 14.38 TEST_1, TEST_2, and TEST_3** are all defined with nonzero constants; the content of all character strings referenced by the pointers of the str array are printed out as the output from the program.

14.5.3 The #ifdef and #endif Directives

The **#ifdef** and **#endif** directives control whether a given group of statements is to be included as part of your program. The general form to use the **#ifdef** and **#endif** directives is:

```
#ifdef macro_name
   statement1
   statement2
   . . .
   statementN
#endif
```

Here **macro_name** is any character string that can be defined by a **#define** directive. **Statement1, statement2, and statementN** are statements that are included in the program if **macro_name** has been defined. If **macro_name** has not been defined, **statement1, statement2, and statementN** are skipped.

Because the statements under the control of the **#ifdef** directive are not enclosed in braces, the **#endif** directive must be used to mark the end of the **#ifdef** block. For instance, the **#ifdef** directive in the following code segment:

```
. . .
#ifdef DEBUG
   printf("The contents of the string pointed to by str: %s\n", str);
#endif
. . .
```

Indicates that if the macro name **DEBUG** is defined, the **printf()** function in the statement following the **#ifdef** directive is included in the program. The compiler will compile the statement so that the contents of a string pointed to by **str** can be printed out after the statement is executed.

14.5.4 The #ifndef Directive

The **#ifndef** directive enables you to define code that is to be executed when a particular macro name is not defined. The general format to use #ifndef is the same as for #ifdef:

```
#ifndef macro_name
   statement1
   statement2
   . . .
   statementN
#endif
```

Here **macro_name, statement1, statement2, and statementN** have the same meanings as those in the form of **#ifdef** introduced in the previous section. Again, the **#endif** directive is needed to mark the end of the **#ifndef** block.

```
/*Prog 14.39 Demo of using #ifdef, #ifndef, and #endif */
#include <stdio.h>
#include <conio.h>
#define UPPER_CASE 0
#define NO_ERROR 0
  main(void)
  {
     clrscr();
     #ifdef UPPER_CASE
       printf("THIS LINE IS PRINTED OUT,\n");
       printf("BECAUSE UPPER_CASE IS DEFINED.\n");
     #endif
     #ifndef LOWER_CASE
       printf("\nThis line is printed out,\n");
       printf("because LOWER_CASE is not defined.\n");
     #endif
     return NO_ERROR;
  }
```

Output:

```
THIS LINE IS PRINTED OUT,
BECAUSE UPPER_CASE IS DEFINED.
This line is printed out,
because LOWER_CASE is not defined.
```

EXPLANATION: The purpose of the program 14.39 is to use **#ifdef and #ifndef** directives to control whether a piece of message needs to be printed out. Two macro names, **UPPER_CASE** and **NO_ERROR,** are defined in **lines 4 and 5.**

The **#ifdef** directive in **line 9** checks whether the **UPPER_CASE** macro name has been defined. Because the macro name has been defined in **line 4,** the two statements in **lines 10 and 11** are executed before the **#endif** directive in **line 12** marks the end of the **#ifdef** block.

In line 13, the #ifndef directive tells the preprocessor to include the two statements in **lines 14** and **15** in the program if the **LOWER_CASE** macro name has not been defined. As you can see, **LOWER_CASE** is not defined in the program at all. Therefore, the two statements in **lines 14 and 15** are counted as part of the program.

The output from running the program 14.39shows that the **printf()** functions in **lines 10, 11, 14, and 15** are executed accordingly, under the control of the **#ifdef and #ifndef** directives.

```
/*Prog 14.40 Demo of conditional compilation ver1*/
#include<conio.h>
#include<stdio.h>
#define TEXT "working with conditional directives"
 void main()
```

```
{
 clrscr();
 #ifdef TEXT;
 printf(TEXT);
 #else
 printf("TEXT not defined");
 #endif
 getch();
}
```

Output:

```
working with conditional directives
```

EXPLANATION: Because TEXT is defined **#ifdef TEXT** is true so expansion of **TEXT** is displayed on execution after compilation. If **TEXT** was not defined **#else** block would have executed. The compiler ignores **#else** block even if errors are there in the **#else** block.

```
/*Prog 14.41 Demo of conditional compilation ver2*/
#include<conio.h>
#include<stdio.h>
#define TEXT "You are working with conditional directive"
 void main()
 {
   clrscr();
   #if defined TEXT
   printf(TEXT);
   #else
   printf("TEXT not defined");
   #endif
   getch();
 }
```

Output:

```
You are working with conditional directive
```

EXPLANATION: This program is similar to the previous one except we have used defined directive here. If macro name is previously defined the expression **#if** defined **macro_name** is true else otherwise. You are free to choose any of the type either **#ifdef** or **#if** defined.

```
/*Prog 14.42 Demo of condition compilation ver3*/
#include<conio.h>
#include<stdio.h>
#define ASG =
 void main()
 {
   int a,b;
```

```
   clrscr();
   #ifdef ASG
   a ASG 10;
   b ASG 20;
   #else
   a=10;
   b=20;
   c=a+b;
   printf("Sum is %d",c);
   getch();
 }
```

EXPLANATION: #ifdef statement is true because ASG is defined. Note we have intentionally made error in the #else block but that will be ignored because #else block would not be compiled.

```
/*Prog 14.43 demo of conditional compilation ver3*/
#include<conio.h>
#include<stdio.h>
 void main()
 {
   clrscr();
   #ifndef N
   #define N 250
   printf("N is %d\n",N);
   #else
   printf("N is %d\n",N);
   #endif
   getch();
 }
```

Output:

```
N is 250
```

EXPLANATION: Because N was not defined earlier **#ifndef N** is true. In the **#ifndef** block we now define **N** and print its value. Had **N** was defined earlier the **#else** block would have compiled and executed.

```
/* Prog 14.44 Demo of conditional compilation ver 4*/
#include<conio.h>
#include<stdio.h>
 void main()
 {
  clrscr();
```

```
 #if !defined N
 #define N 12345
 printf("N is %d\n",N);
 #else
 printf("N is %d\n",N);
 #endif
 getch();
}
```

Output:

```
N is 12345
```

EXPLANATION: We have one use of defined directive in the **program 14.38.** This is other use to check whether macro has been defined or not. The not **operator (!)** reverses the condition. Again you are free to choose whether to use **#ifndef** or **#if!defined.**

```
/*Prog 14.45 demo of conditional compilation ver5*/
#include<conio.h>
#include<stdio.h>
#define MAX 20
void main ()
{
  char str[MAX]="HARI MOHAN";
  #undef MAX
  int arr[MAX];
  getch();
}
```

Output:

Undefined symbol 'MAX'

'str' is assigned a value that is never used

EXPLANATION: The **#undef** directive removes any previously defined macro. So in the third line after **#undef MAX** is undefined and it produces error.

```
/*Prog 14.46 Demo of conditional compilation ver6*/
#include<conio.h>
#include<string.h>
#include<stdio.h>
#define F_MON "JANUARY"
#define S_MON "FEBRUARY"
#define T_MON "MARCH"
#define FR_MON "APRIL"
#define FA_MON "FAKE MONTH"
#define CURRENT _MONTH FA_MON
void main()
```

```
{
   clrscr();
   #if strcmp(CURRENT_MONTH,F_MON)==0
   printf("%s month has %d days \n",F_MON,31);
   #elif strcmp(CURRENT_MONTH,S_MON)==0
   printf("%s month has %d days\n",S_MON,28);
   #elif strcmp(CURRENT_MONTH,T_MON)==0
   printf("%s month has %d days\n",T_MON,31);
   #elif strcmp(CURRENT_MONTH,FR_MON)==0
   printf("%s month has %d days\n",FR_MON,30);
   #else
   printf("Oops I defined only four valid months");
   #endif
   getch();
}
```

Output:

```
Oops I defined only four valid months
```

EXPLANATION: Here in the above **program 14.43** we have defined **4** months using macro. The macro **CURRENT_MONTH** is defined by the value of any of the macros defined as months. In the **main** we are checking whether what the value of **CURRENT_MONTH** is. For this program this is equal to **F_MON** so **#if** expression is true and corresponding printf statement is executed. **#elif** is equal to **else-if** *i.e.* if first if condition fails then first **elif** will be checked and so on. Try changing value of **CURRENT_MONTH** macro and executes.

```
/*Prog 14.47 demo of conditional compilation ver 7*/
#include<string.h>
#include<conio.h>
#include<stdio.h>
#define BIN 2
#define OCT 8
#define DEC 10
#define HEX 16
#define RADIX HEX
 void main()
 {
  clrscr();
  #if RADIX==BIN
  printf("Number system is binary\n");
  #elif RADIX ==OCT
  printf("Number system is octal\n");
  #elif RADIX==DEC
```

```
 printf("Number system is decimal\n");
 #elif RADIX==HEX
 printf("Number system is haxadecimal\n");
 #else
  printf("Unknown number system");
  #endif
  getch();
}
```

Output:

Number system is haxadecimal

EXPLANATION: The program is self-explanatory.

```
/*Prog 14.48 Demo of conditional compilation ver 8*/
#include<stdio.h>
#include<conio.h>
#define DAMSEL "HARI MOHAN PANDEY"
 void main()
 {
   clrscr();
   #ifdef DAMSEL
   printf("DAMSEL is %s\n",DAMSEL);
   #else
   #error "DAMSEL UNDEFINED MACRO"
   #endif
   getch();
 }
```

Output:

DAMSEL is HARI MOHAN PANDEY

EXPLANATION: The **#error** directive is used to display user defined error messages during compilation of the program. It forces the compiler to stop compilation and display user defined error message along with some info defined by compiler. Usually they are used when a particular macro is not defined or for debugging purpose. In the program **DAMSEL** is defined so **#else** part will be ignored. Run the program by omitting it. You will get error message **DAMSEL UNDEFINED MACRO.** The message after **#errors** may be written without double quote.

14.6 SOME SPECIAL PREPROCESSOR DIRECTIVES

There are some special ANSI C preprocessor macros which start with __ and ends with __. They are used in special programming situations. From the usage the meaning will be clear. See the program given below and read the explanation.

```
/*Prog 14.49 Demo of some special directives */
#include <conio.h>
#include <stdio.h>
 void main()
 {
   clrscr();
   printf("The Date is:%s\n",__DATE__);
   printf("The time is :%s\n",__TIME__);
   printf("The File is :%s\n",__FILE__);
   printf("The line is :%d\n",__LINE__);
   getch();
 }
```

Output:

```
The Date is:Oct 20 2007
The time is :23:45:36
The File is :PRE\F49.C
The line is :10
```

EXPLANATION: All the macros used in the above program are ANSI C predefined macros. You can see that every macro name is defined with two underscores (__) as suffix and prefix. These macro can be used for finding out system date, file name, time and line number. As clear from the output of the program that:

__DATE__: macro prints current system date as string. Actually this is the date of the translation of the source file into object file.

__TIME__: macro prints current system time as string. This represents time at which programs was compiled in the form hour: minute: second.

__FILE__: macro prints current system file name as string *i.e.* name of the file being compiled.

__LINE__: macro prints current compiled line number as integer, first line of program is at line number.

```
/*Prog 14.50 Demo of line directive alone */
#include <stdio.h>
#include <conio.h>
#line 200 /*Line number reset to 200*/
 void main()
 {
   clrscr();
   printf("Current Line No:%d\n",__LINE__);/*Line no 204*/
   getch();
 }
```

Output:

```
Current Line No: 204
```

EXPLANATION: The **#line** directive changes the contents of **__LINE__** directive. As stated in the above program the **__LINE__** directive contains the line number of the current compiled line. With **#line 200** statement we have specified that line count should begin from **200** so the output display line number **204.**

```
/*Prog 14.51 use of __FILE__ directive to print the source file*/
#include <stdio.h>
#include <conio.h>
 void main()
 {
   FILE*fp;
   char ch;
   clrscr();
   fp=fopen(__FILE__,"r");
   while(!feof(fp))
   {
     ch=fgetc(fp);
     putchar(ch);
   }
   fclose(fp);
   getch();
 }
```

Output:

```
/*Prog 14.51 use of __FILE__ directive to print the source file*/
#include <stdio.h>
#include <conio.h>
 void main()
 {
   FILE*fp;
   char ch;
   clrscr();
   fp=fopen(__FILE__,"r");
   while(!feof(fp))
   {
     ch=fgetc(fp);
     putchar(ch);
   }
   fclose(fp);
   getch();
 }
```

EXPLANATION: The purpose of this program is to show that by using __FILE__ macro one can print the whole file on the output screen. The file is opened in the read mode and displayed. Rest is self explanatory.

14.7 THE #PRAGMA DIRECTIVE

This directive should be used by expert programmers only as most of the sub directives (options) that can be used with this **#pragma** directive are compiler specific. We will present only two of them here.

#pragma startup and #pragma exit

For the usage of the above two see the programs given below.

```
/*Prog 14.52 Demo of #pragma directive ver 1*/
#include <stdio.h>
#include <conio.h>
 void fun1(void);
#pragma startup fun1
 void main()
 {
    printf("Inside main\n");
    getch();
 }
  void fun1(void)
  {
    printf("Inside fun1\n");
  }
Output:
Inside fun1
Inside main
```

EXPLANATION: The **#pragma** startup directive is used to run any function before main. The syntax is **#pragma startup (func_name) (priority),** where **func_name** is the function name is the function name which must take argument of type void and return type must also be **void** and priority denotes priorities of the function in case we have more than one function of function of type as stated in the previous sentence. In the program we have written **#pragma** startup **fun1.** This line ensures that fun1 will be called before main function. Note we have not used **clrscr()** inside the **main,** if we do so then it will wipe out the screen and output generated by fun1 won't be visible.

```
/*Prog 14.53 Demo of #pragma directive ver 2*/
#include <stdio.h>
#include <conio.h>
 void fun1(void);
 void fun2(void);
#pragma startup fun1 2
```

```
#pragma startup fun2 1
 void main()
 {
    printf("Inside main\n");
    getch();
 }
  void fun1(void)
  {
     printf("Inside fun1\n");
  }
  void fun2(void)
  {
     printf("Inside fun2\n");
  }
```

Output:

```
Inside fun2
Inside fun1
Inside main
```

EXPLANATION: The program is similar to previous one but we have assigned priority in the startup. Small number represents higher priority, so **fun2** will be called first, then **fun1** and then **main.** Priority number **0 to 63** are reserved (should not be used), from **64 to 255** can be used by the user.

As seen in the above two programs we can call functions before main, we can also write functions which are called after execution of main is over. See the next program.

```
/*Prog 14.54 Demo of #pragma directive ver3*/
#include <stdio.h>
#include <conio.h>
 void fun1(void)
 void fun2(void)
#pragma exit fun1 2
#pragma exit fun2 1
 void main()
 {
    printf("Inside main\n");
    getch();
 }
   void fun1(void)
   {
      printf("Inside fun1\n");
   }
```

```
void fun2(void)
{
    printf("Inside fun2\n");
}
```

```
Output:
Inside main
Inside fun2
Inside fun1
```

EXPLANATION: Higher priority function will be called in the end.

14.8 MACRO V_S FUNCTIONS

1. In the macro code is substituted at the place of macro name. For example in the macro given #define X 100, 100 will be substituted by the preprocessor. In case of function, function is actually called and control jumps to the memory location where function definition is written.
2. In case of macro when a macro is called at several places in the program, the macro expansion is done at all places, thus if you have used the macro at 100 places in the program thus increasing the size of the code. In case of function the function is just written once at a memory location and control is transferred to that location. Thus function definition is written just once, no matter how many times you call the functions. In short macro increases the size of the program code whereas function not.
3. When you call a function overhead occurs due to saving of local variables, return address of the statement, saving register values in the stack and also when function is returned these saved values are popped back. This overhead makes execution of function slow. In case of macro no overhead occurs, just replacement need to be done. So execution of macro is faster as compared to functions.
4. In function strict type checking can be performed whereas no type checking can be done in case of macro. For example consider the declaration of macro:

   ```
   #define SUM (a, b) ((a) + (b))
   ```

   Macro will be expanded when you write **SUM (10,20) or SUM(10.0,20.0) or SUM (*'a','b'*)** *i.e.* it won't distinguish between the type of arguments being passed.

   In case of function **void sum (int, int);** type checking will be performed when function will be called as **sum (35.5, 76.8).**
5. Macros are processed by preprocessor whereas function is processed by compiler.
6. If the macro definition go like kind of *x*++ and *y*++. It is better to use functions and avoid macros. Use **typedef** instead of macros (while pointer declarations).
7. Macro names unlike function names cannot be passed as arguments to the function whereas a function can be a parameter for other function. It is for this reason that ANSI C requires each C compiler to implement each library function as a **"pure"** function even though a compiler may provide a macro implementation of the function.

POINTS TO PONDER

In this section you have learned the following points:

- The C preprocessor runs before the compiler. During preprocessing, all occurrences of a macro name are replaced by the macro body associated with the macro name.
- The C preprocessor also enables you to include additional source files to the program or compile sections of C code conditionally.
- The C preprocessor is not part of the C compiler.
- A macro statement ends with a newline character, not a semicolon.
- The **#define** directive tells the preprocessor to replace every occurrence of a macro name defined by the directive with a macro body that is associated with the macro name.
- The **#undef** directive is used to remove the definition of a macro name that has been previously defined.
- You can specify one or more arguments to a macro name defined by the **#define** directive.
- The **#ifdef** directive enables you to define code that is to be included when a particular macro name is defined.
- The **#ifndef** directive is a mirror directive to the #ifdef directive. The former enables you to define code that is to be included when a particular macro name is not defined.
- The **#endif** is used to mark the end of an **#ifdef, an #ifndef,** or an **#if** block.
- The **#if, #elif,** and **#else** directives enable you to select portions of code to compile.

QUESTIONS AND ANSWERS

Q1. *Is the C preprocessor part of the C compiler?*

Ans: No. The C preprocessor is not part of the C compiler. With its own line-oriented grammar and syntax, the C preprocessor runs before the compiler in order to handle named constants, macros, and inclusion of files.

Q2. *How do you remove a macro name?*

Ans: By putting a macro name after the **#undef** directive, the macro name can be removed. According to the ANSI C standard, a macro name has to be removed before it can be redefined.

Q3. *Why do you need the #endif directive?*

Ans: The **#endif** directive is used with an **#if, #ifdef, or #ifndef** directive because statements under the control of a conditional preprocessor directive are not enclosed in braces ({and}). Therefore, #endif must be employed to mark the end of the block of statements.

Q4. *Can the conditional expression following the #if directive be an arithmetic expression?*

Ans: Yes. The conditional expression evaluated by the **#if** directive can be an arithmetic expression. If the expression returns a nonzero value, the code between the **#if** directive and the next nearest directive are included for compilation. Otherwise, the code is skipped.

EXERCISES

A. Answer the following questions:

1. What is a preprocessor?
2. What are the advantages of preprocessor?
3. What are the two form of **#include** directive? Explain with the help of suitable example for each respectively?
4. What is the difference between token pasting and stringizing directive?
5. Describe the following:
   (*a*) Pre-processing.
   (*b*) Macro Vs. Functions

B. Match the following columns:

I	II
1. #define	(*a*) undefined a macro.
2. #if	(*b*) define a macro.
3. #	(*c*) conditional compilation.
4. /	(*d*) multiple macro.
5. #undef	(*e*) token pasting.

C. Write True or False against each statement:

1. The macro act as a symbolic constant.
2. Preprocessing is done before compilation.
3. The use of macro makes execution of program faster.
4. "stdio.h" is different from <stdio.h>.
5. The # is known as stringizing operator.
6. The #if is used during execution of the program.
7. Macros are processed inside the strings.

D. Fill in the blanks:

1. The _____ symbol is used in all preprocessor directives.
2. The symbol for token pasting operator is__________.
3. __________ is used to undefine a previously defined macro.
4. If a macro is not defined it takes __________ value.
5. For concatenation using preprocessor directives we can use ________.
6. # include "stdio.h" searches file stdio.h first in ________.
7. #if-#else is used for ______________.
8. We can use __________ to generate our own errors.

E. Brain Drill

1. Write a program in C with a macro to find the roots of quadratic question.
2. Write a program in C with a macro to find the area of the triangle.
3. Write a program with conditional compilation for finding out the are of a rectangle or the area of a square.

4. Write a program with conditional compilation for one of the following when called:
   (*a*) Divisible by 3.
   (*b*) Divisible by 5.

F. Predict the output of the following program:

1.
```
#define prn (a) printf("%d",a)
    #define print(a,b,c) prn (a), prn(b), prn(c)
    #define max(a,b) (a>b)?a:b
    main ( )
    {
        int x=1, y=2;
        printf(max(x++,y,y));
        printf(max(x++,y,x,y));
    }
```

2.
```
#define TOKEN(x) 1##x
main()
{
    printf("%d\n",TOKEN(5));
}
```

3.
```
#define STR(x,y) #x"Likes" #y
main()
{
    char s[ ] =STR (Hari, Programming);
    printf("%s \n",s);
}
```

4.
```
#define CHK(a) a+1
main()
{
    int i=2;
    int j=4 *CHK(i*3);
    printf("j=%d\n",j);
}
```

5.
```
#define str "Pandey"
#ifdef str
int x=20
#endif
main()
{
     int x=10;
     printf("%s\n",str);
}
```

15

MISCELLANEOUS BUILT-IN FUNCTION OF 'C'

The chapter discusses the usage of some of the most important functions along with their prototype, and header file used. The **printf** and **scanf** have been dealt rigorously as they are the most common functions used. Formatting with printf is discussed by giving it a separate heading as it is considered an important topic:

Functions for random generation of numbers like **rand, random, srand and randomized** are given. Depending upon suitability and requirement user can use them. Some time and date related functions, functions for printing colored text and background, some mathematical function, function for producing sound from speakers etc. are covered. Presence of a key hit from the keyboard through a function and function for the position of cursor at a given specified row and columns is covered.

15.1 PRINTF

The prototype of this function as given in the header file **stdio.h** is as follows:

```
int printf(const char *,............);
```

The first argument is a const string and second argument ……. denotes variable number of arguments which may be zero also. The function is used to print data on to the standard output i.e. screen. There are various formats of using printf. The most common use is

```
printf("Hello this is the demo for printf\n");
```

Here we have written only the first argument. Second argument is null over here. We can also write in the manner:

```
const char *p = "Hello this is the demo";
printf(p);
```

In the following given program we use second argument also.

```
/*Prog 15.1 Demo of printf ver1*/
#include <stdio.h>
```

```
#include <conio.h>
 void main()
 {
    int a=100,b=200;
    clrscr();
    printf("a=%d\tb=%d\n",a,b);
    getch();
 }
```

Output:

```
a=100 b=200
```

EXPLANATION: The program is self-explanatory.

```
/*Prog 15.2 Demo of printf ver2* /
#include <stdio.h>
#include <conio.h>
 void main()
 {
    int a=100,b=200;
    const char *p="a=%d\tb=%d\n";
    clrscr();
    printf(p,a,b);
    getch();
 }
```

Output:

```
a=100 b=200
```

EXPLANATION: Again the program is self-explanatory.

Now, I think arguments to printf must have been clear to you. Now we see that is the return type int means in printf statement. It returns number of characters printed in the first argument i.e. const string. Let's

Let's write some programs to make your concepts better.

```
/*Prog 15.3 Demo of printf ver 3*/
#include<stdio.h>
#include<conio.h>
 void main()
 {
    int count;
    clrscr();
    count=printf("Hello");
```

```
    printf("\nCount=%d\n",count);
 }
```

Output:

```
Hello
Count=5
```

EXPLANATION: Here count return 5, number of character printed. In this manner you can use printf to find the length of the string but string will also be printed. Based on the discussion so far can you predict the output of the following code given.

```
/*Prog 15.4 Demo of printf ver4*/
#include <stdio.h>
#include <conio.h>
 void main()
 {
    int count;
    clrscr();
    printf("%d\t%d\n",printf("one\n"),printf("Two\n"));
    printf("%d\n",printf("One Two\n"));
    getch();
 }
```

Output:

```
Two
one
4 4
One Two
8
```

EXPLANATION: The right most printf is processed first. The program is self-explanatory.

```
/*Prog 15.5 Demo of printf ver 5*/
#include <stdio.h>
#include <conio.h>
 void main()
 {
    int x;
    clrscr();
    printf("%d\n",printf("%d\n%d\n",100,200));
    getch();
 }
```

Output:

```
100
200
8
```

EXPLANATION: Counting %, *d* **and** *n* separately we have total **8** character in the formatted string of the **inner printf** so the output.

15.2 FORMATTED OUTPUT IN 'C'

Formatting means displays single piece of data item in different manner. For that we have used printf function and inside it we use different field width for displaying strings, integer and floating point numbers. Also we control the alignment of the output. Lot's examples are given for clarify the concept.

```
/*Prog 15.6 Demo of formatting the string*/
#include <dos.h>
#include <stdio.h>
#include <process.h>
 void main()
 {
    char *p="WELCOME IN C PROGRAMMING";
    clrscr();
    printf("|%s|\n",p);
    printf("|%10s|\n",p);
    printf("|%10.4s|\n",p);
    printf("|%-27s|\n",p);
    printf("|%27s|\n",p);
    getch();
 }
```

Output:

```
|WELCOME IN C PROGRAMMING|
|WELCOME IN C PROGRAMMING|
|WELC|
|WELCOME IN C PROGRAMMING|
|WELCOME IN C PROGRAMMING|
```

EXPLANATION: When %10s is used to format the string for output the string **printf** allocates a width of **10** characters and print the string but the length of string is more than **10** so the whole string is displayed.

For %**10.4s** a width of **10** characters is allocated and first four characters is printed left padded i.e. right justified.

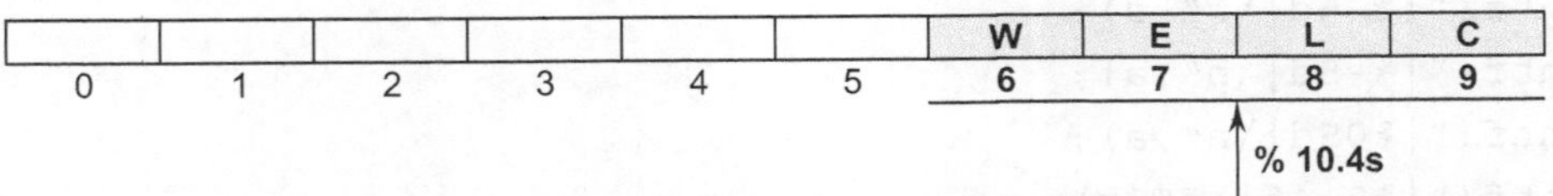

First four characters is printed left padded i.e. right justified

For %-10.4 s a width of 10 characters is allocated and first four characters are printed right padded i.e. left justified.

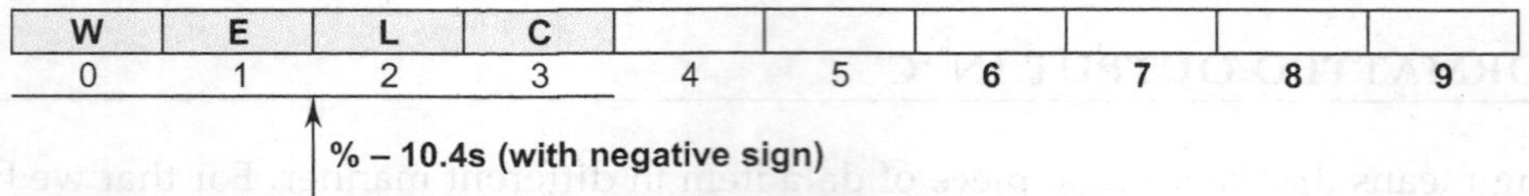

First four characters is printed right padded i.e. left justified

For %27s a width of 27 characters is allocated and whole string starting from left is printed *i.e.* **left padded.**

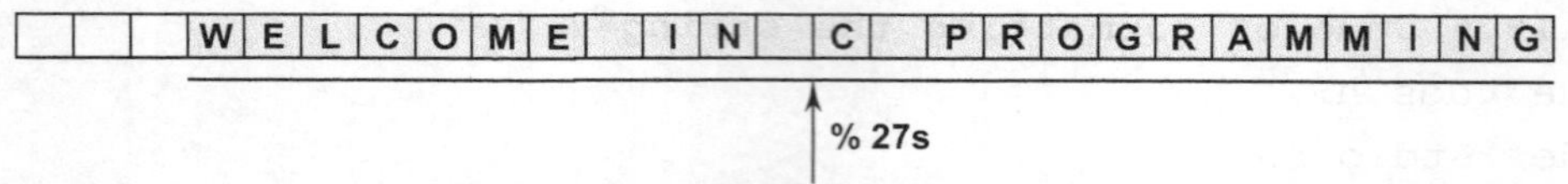

String starting from left is printed i.e. Left padded (right justified)

For %-27s a width of 27 characters is allocated and string is left justified.

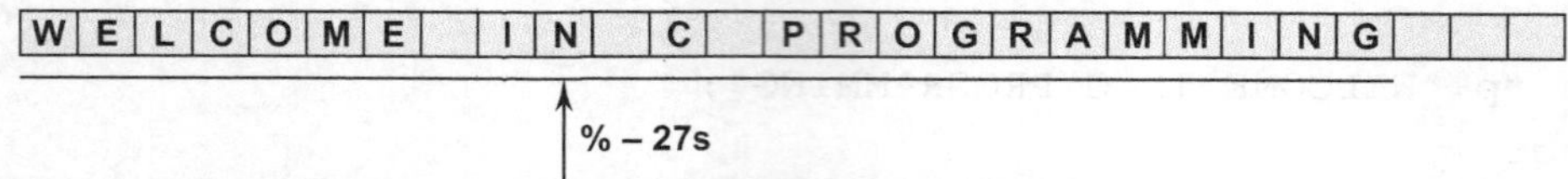

String starting from right is printed i.e. Left padded (left justified)

From the above discussion it is noticeable that:

1. When the field width is less than the length of string the whole string is displayed. When **flag** "-"is put before the width then it does not affect the output.
2. When the field width is more than the length of the string then output is right justified and left padded. When **flag** "-"is put before the width then output is left justified and right padded.

```
/*Prog 15.7 Demo of formatting the numbers*/
#include<stdio.h>
#include<process.h>
#include<stdio.h>
 void main()
 {
   int a=123;
   float b=23.456;
   clrscr();
   printf("|%2d|\n",a);
   printf("|%5d|\n",a);
   printf("|%-5d|\n",a);
   printf("|%-5d|\n",a);
   printf("|%05d|\n",a);
   printf("|%8.4f|\n",b);
   printf("|%-8.4f|\n",b);
```

```
  getch();
}
Output:
|123|
|  123|
|123  |
|123  |
|00123|
|  23.4560|
|23.4560  |
```

EXPLANATION: For width less than number of digits in the number output will be the whole number as it.

Case 1: for %5d output will be shown as

A width of 5 spaces is created and output is right justified.

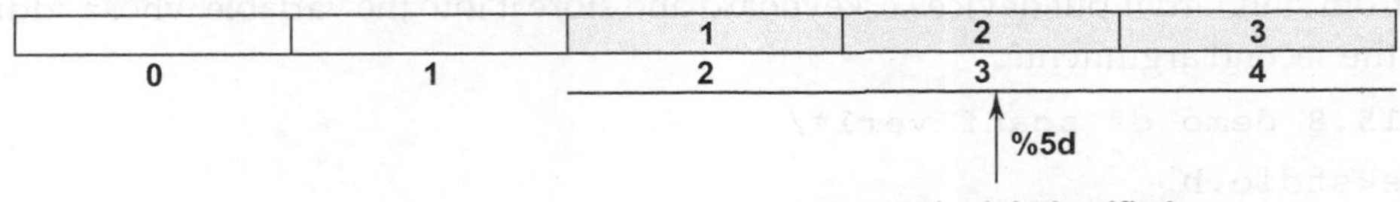

Case 2: for %-5d output will be shown as

A width of 5 spaces is created and output is left justified.

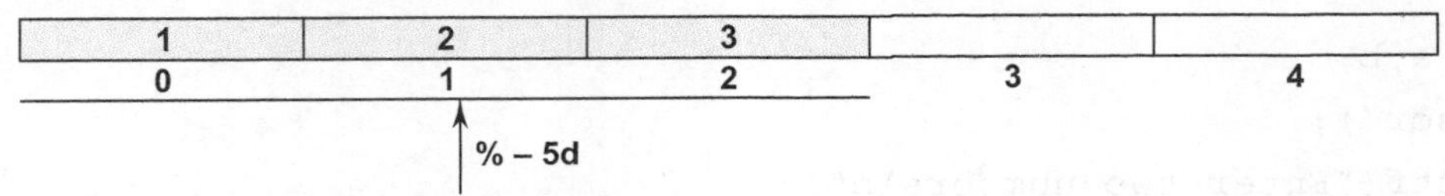

Case 3: for %05d output will be shown as

In this case the only difference in the output is that **empty spaces are filled with zero's and** output is right justified

0 0 1 2 3

0 1 2 3 4

% 5d

Empty spaces are filled with zero

Output is right justified

Case 4: For %8.4f output will be shown as:

Out of 8 spaces 4 spaces are after decimal, one for decimal and 3 before decimal sign. Output is right justified.

2 3 . 4 5 6 0

0 1 2 3 4 5 6 7

% 8.4f

Output is right justified

Case 5: For %-8.4 f output will be shown as:

Out of 8 spaces 4 spaces are after decimal, one for decimal and 3 before decimal sign. Output is left justified.

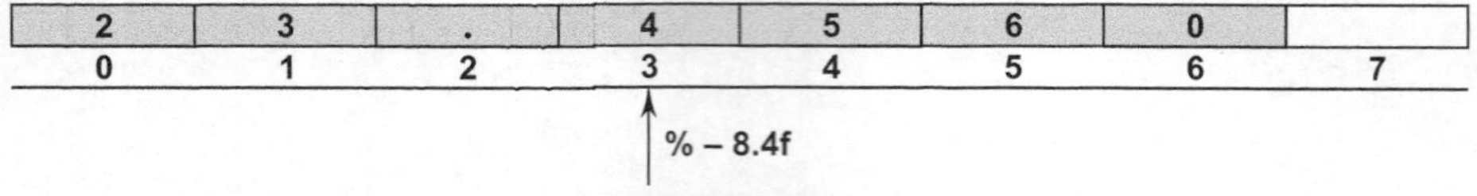

Output is left justified

15.3 SCANF

The prototype of this function is given in the stdio.h header file:

```
int scanf(const char *,..........................);
```

The first argument is a const string and second argument ....denotes variables number of arguments with may be zero also but argument does not make sense in scanf. The function is used to scan data from standard input device *i.e.* keyboard and store it into the variable whose addresses we supply as the second argument.

```
/*Prog 15.8 demo of scanf ver1*/
#include<stdio.h>
#include<conio.h>
 void main()
 {
    int a,b;
    clrscr();
    printf("Enter two numbers\n");
    scanf("%d%d",&a,&b);
    printf("a=%d\nb=%d\n",a,b);
    getch();
 }
```

Output:

```
Enter two numbers
12 34
a=12
b=34
```

EXPLANATION: The program is self-explanatory. The format string of scanf can be replaced if desired as:

```
const char *p="%d%d";
scanf(p,&a,&b);
```

Usually we do not give width in the scanf function. But what consequences it may leave on to the data lets check it out.

```
/*Prog 15.9 Field width in scanf ver1*/
#include <stdio.h>
#include <conio.h>
 void main()
 {
   int a,b;
   clrscr();
   printf("Enter two numbers of 4 digits each \n");
   scanf("%1d%4d",&a,&b);
   printf("You entered \n");
   printf("a=%d\tb=%d\n",a,b);
   getch();
 }
```

Output:

```
Enter two numbers of 4 digits each
3456 2567
You entered
a=3 b=456
```

EXPLANATION: %1d %4d in the format string of scanf means first number to be input in through scanf will be of 1 digit in length and second number will be of 4 digits of length. So the 4 from first number is assigned to a and remaining digits are assigned to b, second number 2567 is ignored.

We give some more examples with small code snippets.

```
scanf("%2d%4d",&a,&b);
i/p: 4567 8978
o/p: a = 45 b = 67
scanf("%4d%1d",&a,&b);
i/p: 12345 8978
o/p: a= 1234 b=5
```

The second number 8978 that is unread will be assigned to the first variable in the next scanf call as shown in the next program below.

```
/*Prog 15.10 field width in scanf ver2*/
#include <stdio.h>
#include <conio.h>
 void main()
 {
  int a,b,c;
  clrscr();
```

```
  printf("Enter two numbers of 4 digits each\n");
  scanf("%3d%4d",&a,&b);
  printf("Enter one more number\n");
  scanf("%3d",&c);
  printf("You entered \n");
  printf("a=%d\tb=%d\tc=%d\n",a,b,c);
  getch();
 }
```

Output

```
Enter two numbers of 4 digits each
2345 5678
Enter one more number
You entered
a=234 b=5 c=567
```

EXPLANATION: Because of the **%3d** in the first scanf **234** is assigned to **a, 5 to b and 567** is assigned to *c* from number **5678.** Note input did not wait to accept data through second **scanf** statement.

Conclusion from the above two programs is to use %**d** in the **scanf** statement as field specification *i.e.* the statement **scanf ("%d%d", &a, &b);** will accept correct values for **a and b. %3d** can be used when you want that user enters only number which has no more **3** digits in length. If you do not want remaining entered numbers assigned to variable in the next scanf statement simply use **fflush** function as in the next program.

```
/*Prog 15.11 field width in scanf ver3 */
#include <stdio.h>
#include <conio.h>
 void main()
 {
    int a,b,c;
    clrscr();
    printf("Enter two numbers of 4 digits each\n");
    scanf("%3d%4d",&a,&b);
    fflush(stdin);
    printf("Enter one more number \n");
    scanf("%3d",&c);
    printf("You entered \n");
    printf("a=%d\tb=%d\tc=%d\n",a,b,c);
    getch();
 }
```

Output:

```
Enter two numbers of 4 digits each
```

```
8978 2334
Enter one more number
275
You entered
a=897 b=8 c=275
```

EXPLANATION: The **fflush** function **flushes** the input buffer. Actually the unread value was there in the input buffer and **scanf** first look into this buffer for accepting value and later assigning it to the variable without waiting for the next input from keyboard. Once this buffer is cleared scanf read data from keyboard.

```
/*Prog 15.12 field width in scanf ver 4*/
#include <stdio.h>
#include <conio.h>
 void main()
 {
   int a,b,c;
   clrscr();
   printf("Enter three numbers\n");
   scanf("%*d%d%d",&a,&b,&c);
   printf("You entered \n");
   printf("a=%d\tb=%d\tc=%d",a,b,c);
   getch();
 }
Output:
Enter three numbers
23 45 67
You entered
a=45     b=67    c=-29329
```

EXPLANATION: As '*' in **scanf** before field width may be used to skip an input field. **This is known as assignment suppression.** In the above program due to star in the first %**d. 23** will be skipped and **45** will be assigned to **a** and **67** to *c*. *c* will contain some garbage value as on my **PC**.

If you change scanf statement as:

```
scanf("%d%*d%d",&a,&b,&c);
```

Assignment of input values to variables will be **a= 45, b=67, c=garbage value.**

The asterisk should be in between % and *d*. If you write as:

```
scanf("%*d%*d%*d",&a,&b,&c);
```

All three inputs will be ignored and *a, b, c* will have garbage values.

```
/*Prog 15.13 Field width in scanf ver 5*/
#include<stdio.h>
#include<conio.h>
```

```
 void main()
 {
  int a,b,c;
  clrscr();
  printf("Enter three numbers\n");
  scanf("%*3d%2d%d",&a,&b,&c);
  printf("You entered \n");
  printf("a=%d\tb=%d\tc=%d\n",a,b,c);
  getch();
 }
```

Output:

```
Enter three numbers
2343 456 678
You entered
a=3      b=456      c=-29329
```

EXPLANATION: Due to %***3d** only first three digits input will be skipped so **4th digit** ***i.e.*** **3** from first input will be assigned to ***a*****, 456 to b and garbage value to** ***c*****.**

We have seen that in order to take float input through scanf we have to use %*f* format specifier. But what if similar to field width specification for integer numbers we put restriction on floating point input.

Now, let's see some examples:

```
/*Prog 15.14 Use of %f and %g in scanf*/
#include <stdio.h>
#include <conio.h>
 void main()
 {
   float a;
   clrscr();
   printf("Enter a float number\n");
   scanf("%2g",&a);
   printf("You entered\n");
   printf("a=%f\n",a);
   getch();
 }
```

Output:

```
Enter a float number
346.789
You entered
a=34.000000
```

EXPLANATION: If you put field width while inputting **float** numbers it accepts only integer part and skip the **fractional part** but number will be treated as float as seen from the output of **printf** above.

Now, if we change the printf as:

```
printf("a=%g\n",a);
output you get will be a=34
```

Note scanning number by writing %**xx14.fff** will not work for *e.g.* **2.2f** will not work.

```
/*Prog 15.15 Use of %d and %g in scanf */
#include<stdio.h>
#include<conio.h>
 void main()
 {
    float a;
    int b;
    clrscr();
    printf("Enter a float and an int number\n");
    scanf("%2g%d",&a,&b);
    printf("You entered\n");
    printf("a=%g\tb=%d\n",a,b);
    getch();
 }
Output:
Enter a float and an int number
2345.56 3467
You entered
a=23     b=45
```

EXPLANATION: As it is clear from the output that **23** from first number is assigned to variable ***a*** and remaining digit **45** are assigned to variable ***b***. Second number **3467** is ignored here.

```
/*Prog 15.16 Use of %d, %c and %g in scanf*/
#include<stdio.h>
#include<conio.h>
 void main()
 {
    float a;
    int b;
    char c;
    clrscr();
    printf("Enter a float, an int and a character\n");
```

```
    scanf("%2g%d%c",&a,&b,&c);
    printf("You entered \n");
    printf("a=%g\tb=%d\tc=%c\n",a,b,c);
    getch();
 }
```

Output:

```
Enter a float, an int and a character
2345.56 57 s
You entered
a=23    b=45     c=.
```

EXPLANATION: Due to %2g, **23** will be assigned to ***a***, then **45** is assigned to ***b*** and a **dot (.)** is assigned to ***c***. If you input as **34.5678 67 *d*** then ***b*** and ***c*** contain garbage values.

```
/*Prog 15.17 Reading and displaying scientific data*/
#include<stdio.h>
#include<conio.h>
 void main()
 {
    float a,b;
    clrscr();
    printf("Enter two float numbers\n");
    scanf("%e%g",&a,&b);
    printf("You entered\n");
    printf("a=%e\tb=%e\n",a,b);
    getch();
 }
```

Output:

```
Enter two float numbers
1.25e-03 45.34
You entered
a=1.250000e-03 b=4.534000e+01
```

EXPLANATION: %*e* specifier is used to scan numbers represented in scientific notation. The same can be used in printf for printing scientific numbers. Even if the number is taken using %*g* or %*f* can be printed using %*e* format specifier.

```
/*Prog 15.18 Use of comma in input */
#include<stdio.h>
#include<conio.h>
 void main()
 {
    int a,b;
```

```
  clrscr();
  printf("Enter two integer numbers\n");
  scanf("%d,%d",&a,&b);
  printf("You entered\n");
  printf("a=%d\tb=%d\n",a,b);
  getch();
}
```

Output:

```
Enter two integer numbers
12 34
You entered
a=12    b=12803
```

EXPLANATION: Due to comma, in scanf second input is skipped and *b* contains garbage value. To get the correct input simply either remove comma, in scanf or input values as: 12, 34.

```
/*Prog 15.19 Input an int and output char*/
#include<stdio.h>
#include<conio.h>
 void main()
 {
   int a;
   char b;
   clrscr();
   printf("Enter an integer and a character\n");
   scanf("%2d%d",&a,&b);
   printf("You entered\n");
   printf("a=%d\tb=%c\n",a,b);
   getch();
 }
```

Output:

```
Enter an integer and a character
6566 b
You entered
a=65    b=B
```

EXPLANATION: Due to %2*d*, 65 from 6566 is assigned to *a* and 66 is assigned to *b* and *'b'* is skipped. In printf B is printed because type of *b* is char and it contains 66 which is the ASCII value of B.

```
/*Prog 15.20 Use of [] in scanf*/
#include<stdio.h>
```

```
#include<conio.h>
 void main()
 {
   char str[25];
   clrscr();
   printf("Enter a string\n");
   scanf("%[a-z]",str);
   printf("You entered %s\n",str);
   getch();
 }
```

Output:

(first run)

```
Enter a string
nmims
You entered nmims
```

(second run)

```
Enter a string
INDIA
You entered
```

EXPLANATION: %[] is used to accept selected input in a string. In the program we are accepting a string which contains only lower case letters from ***a* to *z*.** So in the first case we get the correct output, whereas in the second run because of upper case input the output is blank as nothing was scanned. The scanf will scan only lower case letters and will stop at the first uppercase letter.

So, if the input NMIMS output will be blank or if input is nmimS output will be nmim.

```
/*Prog 15.21 Use of [] in scanf ver 2*/
#include<stdio.h>
#include<conio.h>
 void main()
 {
   char str[25];
   clrscr();
   printf("Enter a string \n");
   scanf("%[a-z A-Z]",str);
   printf("You entered %s\n",str);
   getch();
 }
```

Output:

```
Enter a string
```

```
NMINMS Mumbai
You entered NMINMS Mumbai
```

EXPLANATION: You could simply use gets to scan a string including a space but knowing more than one way to perform a task is always better.

```
/*Prog 15.22 use of [] in scanf ver3*/
#include<stdio.h>
#include<conio.h>
 void main()
 {
   char str[10];
   clrscr();
   printf("Enter a string\n");
   scanf("%[ahir]",str);
   printf("You entered %s\n",str);
   getch();
 }
```

Output:

(first run)

```
Enter a string
hari
You entered hari
```

(Second run)

```
Enter a string
pandey
You entered
```

EXPLANATION: This program will accept only those string which contains only *'a' 'h' 'i' 'r'* character in lower case.

```
/*Prog 15.23 use of [] in scanf ver 4*/
#include<stdio.h>
#include<conio.h>
 void main()
 {
   char str[10];
   clrscr();
   printf("Enter a string \n");
   scanf("%[^i]",str);
   printf("You entered %s\n",str);
   getch();
 }
```

```
Output:
Enter a string
hari
You entered hari
```

EXPLANATION: The character specified after the ^ (caret or circumflex) are not permitted in the input string. The reading of the string will be terminated at the ecounter of such character in this case it is ***i***. You can put more than one character after ^ then termination will occur on the occurrence of any of the characters for e.g. for the following statement:

```
scanf("%[^ha]",str);
```

```
/*Prog 15.24 return type of scanf*/
#include<stdio.h>
#include<conio.h>
 void main()
 {
    char a;
    int b,check;
    char c[10];
    clrscr();
    printf("Enter a char,int and a string\n");
    check=scanf("%c%d%s",&a,&b,&c);
    if(check==1)
    {
       printf("Wrong sequence of input\n");
      .getch();
       exit(0);
    }
    printf("%d data items accepted correctly \n",check);
    printf("%c\t%d\t%s\n",a,b,c);
    getch();
 }
```

```
Output:
(first run)
Enter a char,int and a string
A 56 Vijay
3 data items accepted correctly
A    56       Vijay
(second run)
Enter a char,int and a string
23 s RAM
Wrong sequence of input
```

EXPLANATION: **scanf** returns 1 if it is able to scan all inputs correctly in ordered manner. If we input a char type value followed by an int type value and a string then scanf returns 3 the number of data items scanned correctly. If you are given any other order than scanf return 1 which you can check to inform user about the wrong order of inputs.

15.4 RAND

The prototype of this function as given in the header file **stdlib.h**

int rand(void);

This function returns random numbers in the range **0** to **RAND_MAX** which is defined in the file **stdlib.h** and whose value is **32767.**

```
/*Prog 15.25 Demo of rand function*/
#include<stdio.h>
#include<conio.h>
#include<stdlib.h>
 void main()
 {
    int i;
    clrscr();
    printf("five number between 1 and 5 using rand()\n");
    for(i=0;i<5;i++)
    printf("%d\t",rand()%5+1);
    printf("\n value of RAND_MAX is %d\n",RAND_MAX);
    getch();
 }
Output:
five number between 1 and 5 using rnad()
2       1       3       1       2
value of RAND_MAX is 32767
```

EXPLANATION: The rand function is used to generate random numbers in the range **0** to **RAND_MAX.** In the program we generat random numbers between 1 and 5 (inclusive both). If you want numbers between **0** to **9** you may write **rand () %10.** In the printf you write **rand()** instead of **rand%5+1,** you get five random numbers between **0 and 32767.**

One problem with this **rand()** is that each time you run the program you get the same set of random numbers. To get new set of number between a ranges see the next program.

```
/*Prog 15.26 Demo of randomize function*/
#include<stdio.h>
#include<conio.h>
#include<stdlib.h>
```

```
#include<time.h>
 void main()
 {
    int i;
    randomize();
    clrscr();
    printf("Five numbers between 90 and 95\n");
    for(i=0;i<5;i++)
    printf("%d\n",rand()%6+90);
    getch();
 }
```

Output:

(first run)

```
Five numbers between 90 and 95
95
91
94
95
94
```

(Second run)

```
Five numbers between 90 and 95
91
92
91
91
94
```

(Third run)

```
Five numbers between 90 and 95
92
94
90
93
92
```

(Fourth run)

```
Five numbers between 90 and 95
93
91
93
94
95
```

EXPLANATION: As can be seen from the outputs of the program that use of **randomize macro** has given four different sets of random numbers on each run of the program. The macro randomize internally uses **time** function for generating random numbers so your program must include header file **time.h**

15.5 SRAND

The prototype of this function is given in the header file **stdlib.h**

```
void srand(unsigned seed);
```

This function initializes random number generator *i.e.* it provides an unsigned value seed each time this function is used in the program which result in a new random number each time you run the program. Its effect is same as of **randomize** function. The **seed** value usually taken is the **system time.**

```
/*Prog 15.27 Demo of srand function*/
#include<stdio.h>
#include<conio.h>
#include<stdlib.h>
#include<time.h>
 void main()
 {
    int i;
    time_t t;
    clrscr();
    srand(time(&t));
    printf("Five number between 9 and 95 \n");
    for(i=0;i<5;i++)
    printf("%d\n",rand()%6+90);
    getch();
 }
```

```
Output:
(First run)
Five number between 90 and 95
94
92
95
90
92
(Second run)
Five number between 90 and 95
```

```
95
93
94
93
92
(Third run)
Five number between 90 and 95
90
94
92
95
93
```

EXPLANATION: **time_*t*** is the structure declared in **time.h** header file. We have created one variable *t* of this data type and passed the address of *t* in this time function which gives current time in seconds.

15.6 CTIME

The prototype of this function is given in the header file **time .h**

```
char* ctime(const time_t*time);
```

The function accepts the address of variable of type **time_*t*** and returns the current date and time in string form provided you use time function as **time(&*t*).**

```
/*Prog 15.28 demo of ctime function */
#include<stdio.h>
#include<time.h>
#include<conio.h>
 int main(void)
 {
   time_t t;
   clrscr();
   time(&t);
   printf("Today's date and time:%s\n",ctime(&t));
   getch();
 }
Output:
Today's date and time:Mon Oct 22 08:21:58 2007
```

EXPLANATION: without the use of **time (&t)** statement the output will be a constant string as on my PC

15.7 _DOS_ GETDATE

The prototype of this function as given in the header file **dos.h**

```
void _dos_getdate (struct dosdate_t*dateptr);
```

The function fills in the dateptr structure with the system's current date.

```
/*Prog 15.29 Prints today's day and date in DD/MM/YYYY format*/
#include<stdio.h>
#include<conio.h>
#include<dos.h>
 void main()
 {
   struct dosdate_t d;
   char *p;
   clrscr();
   _dos_getdate(&d);
   switch(d.dayofweek)
   {
     case 0:
          p="Sunday";
          break;
     case 1:
          p="Monday";
          break;
     case 2:
          p="Tuesday";
          break;
     case 3:
          p="Wednesday";
          break;
     case 4:
          p="Thursday";
          break;
     case 5:
          p="Friday";
          break;
     case 6:
          p="Saturday";
          break;
   }
```

```
    printf("Today is %s",d.day);
    printf("%02d/ %02d/ %04d\n",p,d.day,d.month,d.year);
    getch();
  }
```

Output:

```
Today is Monday 22/10/2007
```

EXPLANATION: In the function **_dos_getdate** we pass the address of variable of **struct dosdate_t** which is defined in the file **dos.h.** The structure has four fields namely **dayofweek, day, month and year. Dayofweek** is returned as number which is **0** for **Sunday, 1** for **Monday** and so on.

15.8 _DOS_GETTIMEC

The prototype of this function as given in the header file dos.h

```
Void _dos_gettime(struct dostime_t*timeptr);
```

The function fills in the values in the **timeptr** structure of **dostime_t** which can be used to display current system time.

```
/*Prog 15.30 Display current time ver1*/
#include<stdio.h>
#include<conio.h>
#include<dos.h>
 void main()
 {
    struct dostime_t t;
    clrscr();
    _dos_gettime(&t);
    printf("Current time is \t");
    printf(":%02d:%02d:%02d\n",t.hour,t.minute,t.second);
    getch();
 }
```

Output:

```
Current time is          : 09:55:43
```

EXPLANATION: The structure **dostime_t** contains four members **hour, minute, second and hseconds** which stand for **hundredth of second.** We pass the address of the variable *t* of structure **dostime_*t* type** which results in filling the values in its members. We than use member's **hour, minute and second** to display the current time.

```
/*Prog 15.31 Displaying current time ver2*/
#include<stdio.h>
#include<dos.h>
```

```
#include<conio.h>
 void main()
 {
    struct dostime_t t;
    int h;
    clrscr();
    _dos_gettime(&t);
    h=t.hour;
    printf("Current time is\t");
    if(h>=12)
    {
       h=h-12;
       printf(":%02d:%02d:%02d PM\n",h,t.minute,t.second);
    }
    else
        printf(":%02d:%02d:%02d AM \n",h,t.minute,t.second);
    getch();
 }
```

Output:

```
Current time is: 11:22:51 AM
```

EXPLANATION: The program is similar to previous one with the difference that the time shown is in 12 formats.

```
/*Prog 15.32 Greet user on the basis of current system time*/
#include<stdio.h>
#include<conio.h>
#include<dos.h>
 void main()
 {
    struct dostime_t t;
    int h;
    clrscr();
    _dos_gettime(&t);
    h=t.hour;
    if(h>=12 && h<=16)
       printf("\n GOOD AFTERNOON\n");
       else if(h>16 && h<=21)
        printf("\n GOOD EVENING\n");
        else if(h>=1 && h<12)
             printf("\nGOOD MORNING \n");
```

```
    getch();
  }
```

Output:

```
GOOD MORNING
```

EXPLANATION: The program is self-explanatory.

15.9 CEIL AND FLOOR

`double ceil(double x);`

The function does the routing of number *x* and returns smallest **integer** <*x*, where *x* is the argument to the argument to the function.

`double floor(double x);`

The function does the rounding of number *x* and returns largest **integer** > *x*, where *x* is the argument to the function.

```
/*Prog 15.33 demo of ceil and floor function*/
#include<stdio.h>
#include<conio.h>
#include<math.h>
 void main()
 {
    double num=234.56;
    clrscr();
    printf("Original number=%5.2f\n",num);
    printf("After applying ceil num=%5.2f\n",ceil(num));
    printf("After applying floor num=%5.2f\n",floor(num));
    getch();
  }
```

Output:

```
Original number=234.56
After applying ceil num=235.00
After applying floor num=234.00
```

EXPLANATION: The program is best understood by viewing the output.

15.10 FMOD

`double fmod(double x, double y);`

The function returns remainder of *x* and *y*.

```
/*Prog 15.34 Demo of fmod function*/
#include<stdio.h>
#include<conio.h>
#include<math.h>
void main()
{
    double x=34.6,y=6.0,m;
    clrscr();
    m=fmod(x,y);
    printf("Remainder of %4.2f by %4.2f is %4.2f\n",x,y,m);
    getch();
}
```

Output:

```
Remainder of 34.60 by 6.00 is 4.60
```

EXPLANATION: For finding integer remainder we use % operator and for floating point mod we use **fmod** function.

15.11 SYSTEM

```
int system (const char *command);
```

The function executes any dos command or exe file supplied as argument to it. The **exe** file must be present in the current directory. For example to execute dir command from within your C program file you write.

```
system("dir");
```

Similarly, to execute any C executable file we write:

```
system("filename.exe");
```

```
/*Prog 15.35 Demo of system function*/
#include<stdio.h>
#include<conio.h>
#include<stdlib.h>
void main()
{
    clrscr();
    printf("Launching notepad...");
    system("notepad");
    getch();
}
```

Output:

```
Launching notepad...
```

EXPLANATION: First make exe of the program and then run at the command prompt. Before running the program make sure you copy the file notepad.exe in the current working directory.

15.12 DELAY FUNCTION

Delay function causes the current execution of the program to be suspended by ms (milliseconds). With a call of delay function, the current program is suspended from execution for the time specified by the argument milliseconds. The prototype of this function is given in the dos.h header file.

```
void delay(unsigned ms);
```

It is not necessary to make a calibration call to delay before using it. delay is accurate to one millisecond.

```
/*Prog 15.36 Demo of delay function*/
#include <dos.h>
#include <stdio.h>
#include <conio.h>
 void main()
 {
   clrscr();
   sound(1500);
   delay(500);
   nosound();
   getch();
 }
Output:
A sound.
```

EXPLANATION: Due to **dealy(500)** the program suspended for 500 milliseconds (0.5 seconds) then resumes its execution.

```
/*Prog 15.37 Demo of delay function ver2*/
#include<stdio.h>
#include<conio.h>
#include<dos.h>
 void main()
 {
   int x=1;
   clrscr();
   for(;x<=10;x++)
   {
```

```
        printf("%d",x);
        sound(1000);
        delay(500);
        nosound();
    }
    getch();
}
```

Output:

1 2 3 4 5 6 7 8 9 10 (print 1 to 10 one by one with sound)

EXPLANATION: Due to **delay (500)** the program suspends for **500** milliseconds then resumes its execution during each iteration of for loop with sound because in the program we are using **sound** and **no sound** function too.

```
/*Prog 15.38 Demo of delay ver3*/
#include<stdio.h>
#include<conio.h>
#include<dos.h>
 void main()
 {
    int x=1;
    clrscr();
    for(;x<=10;x++)
    {
        printf("%d",x);
        delay(500);
    }
    getch();
 }
```

Output:

1 2 3 4 5 6 7 8 9 10 (print 1 to 10 one by one without sound)

EXPLANATION: Same as given above program only the difference is that here we are not using sound and no sound functions.

15.13 MODF FUNCTION

modf function splits double into integers and fraction parts. The prototype of this function is given in **math.h** header file.

```
double modf(double x, double *ipart);
```

modf breaks the **double** *x* into two parts:

1. **integer part.**
2. **Fraction part.**

It stores the integer in **ipart** and returns the fraction

```
/*Prog 15.39 Demo of modf function*/
#include <math.h>
#include <stdio.h>
#include <conio.h>
 void main(void)
{
   double fract, inte;
   double number = 12345.6789;
   clrscr();
   fract= modf(number, &inte);
   printf("The whole and fractional parts of %lf are %lf and
         %lf\n",number,inte,fract);
   getch();
}
```

Output

```
The whole and fractional parts of 12345.678900 are 12345.000000 and
0.678900
```

EXPLANATION: The **program 15.37** shows the functionality of **modf** function. Rest is self-explanatory.

15.14 MODFL FUNCTION

modfl function splits ling double into integer and fraction parts. The prototype of **modfl** function is in the **math.h** header file.

```
long double modfl(long double(x),long double *(ipart));
```

In other words we can define modfl as: **modfl** is the long double version of modf

15.15 SOUND AND NOSOUND FUNCTION

The sound function turns the PC speaker on at the specified frequency freq which is supplied as its argument. The prototype of sound function is given in header file dos.h:

```
void sound(unsigned freq);
```

The nosound function performs the reverse function of sound .The function turns off the PC speaker. The prototype of nosound function is in dos.h header file.

```
void nosound(void)
```

Here frequency specifies the frequency of the sound in **hertz (cycles per second).**

```
/*Prog 15.40 Demo of sound and nosound function*/
#include<dos.h>
#include<stdio.h>
 void main()
 {
    unsigned long l=390,m;
    for(m=l;m<=9456;m+=1000)
    {
      sound(m);
      delay(5000);
      nosound();
    }
    getch();
 }
```

Output:

```
Sounds of different-different frequencies.
```

EXPLANATION: The program produces sound of different frequencies starting from **390** with an increment of **1000.** You will hear sound at each frequency from **PC** speaker for a duration of **5** second due to **delay(5000).** The number **390** is chosen randomly. I have treated all the frequencies as you may not hear sound at some frequencies.

```
/*Prog 15.41 Demo of sound and nosound function*/
#include <dos.h>
int main(void)
{
    sound(7);
    delay(10);
    nosound();
    return 0;
}
```

Output:

```
Emits 7-hrtz tone for 10 second (PC may not be able to emit the tone)
```

EXPLANATION: This program will run successfully but you cannot here the sound because the PC may not be able to emit the 7-hrtz tone.

15.16 SLEEP FUNCTION

Sleep function is used to suspend execution for an interval .The prototype of this function is in **dos.h** header file. The declaration syntax for **sleep** function is given as follows:

void sleep(unsigned sec);

With a call of **sleep** function, the current program is suspended from execution for the number of seconds specified by **the argument seconds.** The interval is only accurate to the **nearest hundredth** of a second or the accuracy of the **DOS clock,** which ever is less accurate.

```
/*Prog 15.42 Demo of sleep function*/
#include <dos.h>
#include <stdio.h>
#include <conio.h>
 void main(void)
 {
    int i;
    clrscr();
    for (i=1; i<10; i++)
    {
       printf("Sleeping for %d seconds\n", i);
       sleep(i);
    }
  getch();
 }
```

Output:

```
Sleeping for 1 seconds
Sleeping for 2 seconds
Sleeping for 3 seconds
Sleeping for 4 seconds
Sleeping for 5 seconds
Sleeping for 6 seconds
Sleeping for 7 seconds
Sleeping for 8 seconds
Sleeping for 9 seconds
```

EXPLANATION: The program shown above shows the working style of sleep function. Rest is self-explanatory.

15.17 _DOS_GETDISKFREE FUNCTION

This function is used to find out how much space is free in disk. The prototype of this function is available in the dos.h header file. The declaration syntax for this function is as follows:

unsigned _dosgetdiskfree (unsigned char drive, struct diskfree_t, *dtable);

_dosgetdiskfree accepts a drive specifier in drive and fills in the **diskfree _t structure *dtable** with disk characteristics. Drive specifies a drive number as follows:

```
0= default
1= A-drive
2= B-drive
3= C-drive and soon.
```

On successful execution of **_dosgetdiskfree** returns **0** (zero) and on error given a non zero value and sets an **errno** (error number) to EINVAL (invalid drive specified)

```
/*Prog 15.43 Demo of _dos_getdiskfree function*/
#include <stdio.h>
#include <dos.h>
#include <process.h>
#include <conio.h>
 void main(void)
 {
  struct diskfree_t free;
  long avail;
  clrscr();
  if (_dos_getdiskfree(0, &free) != 0)
  {
    printf("Error in _dos_getdiskfree() call\n");
    exit(1);
  }
  avail = (long) free.avail_clusters
      * (long) free.bytes_per_sector
      * (long) free.sectors_per_cluster;
  printf("The current drive has %ld bytes available\n", avail);
  getch();
 }
```

Output:

```
The current drive has 1023932928 bytes available (On my PC)
```

EXPLANATION: Here in the program we are using a function **_dos_getdiskfree** function which shows the free space in the disk rest is self-explanatory,

15.18 getdfree FUNCTION

The function **getdfree** accepts a drive specifier in derive and fills the **dfree structure *dtable** with disk characteristics. The prototype of getdfree function available in the **dos.h** header file. The syntax of the **getdfree** function is given as:

```
void getdfree(unsigned char drive, struct dfree * dtable);
```

On unsuccessful (error) getdfree sets **df_sclus** in the dfree structure to **0xFFFF.**

```
/*Prog 15.44 Demo of getdfree function */
#include <stdio.h>
#include <stdlib.h>
#include <dir.h>
#include <dos.h>
#include <conio.h>
 void main(void)
 {
     struct dfree free;
     long avail;
     int drive;
     clrscr();
     drive = getdisk();
     getdfree(drive+1, &free);
     if (free.df_sclus == 0xFFFF)
     {
        printf("Error in getdfree() call\n");
        exit(1);
     }
        avail = (long) free.df_avail
              * (long) free.df_bsec
              * (long) free.df_sclus;
     printf("Drive %c: has %ld bytes available\n", 'A' + drive,
           avail);
     getch();
 }
```

Output:

```
Drive C: has 1023932928 bytes available
```

15.19 GETFAT FUNCTION

This function is used to get the information of **FAT (file allocation table).** The prototype of this function lies in **dos.h** header file. The syntax of **getfat** function is given as:

```
    void getfat(unsigned char drive, struct fatinfo* dtable);
```

```
/*Prog 15.45 Demo of getfat function */
#include <stdio.h>
#include <conio.h>
```

```
#include <dos.h>
 void main(void)
 {
   struct fatinfo diskinfo;
   int flag = 0;
   clrscr();
   printf("Please insert disk in drive A\n");
   getchar();
   getfat(0, &diskinfo);
   /* get drive information */
   printf("\n Default Drive c: is ");
   switch((unsigned char) diskinfo.fi_fatid)
   {
     case 0xFD:
           printf("360K low density\n");
           break;
     case 0xF9:
           printf("1.2 Meg high density\n");
           break;
     default:
           printf("unformatted\n");
           flag = 1;
   }
     if (!flag)
     {
    printf(" sectors per cluster %5d\n", diskinfo.fi_sclus);
    printf("number of clusters %5d\n", diskinfo.fi_nclus);
    printf(" bytes per sector %5d\n", diskinfo.fi_bysec);
     }
    getch();
 }
```

Output:

```
Please insert disk in drive A
c
Default Drive c: is unformatted (On my PC)
```

EXPLANATION: The program shows the demo of getfat function. Rest is self-explanatory

15.20 GETFATD FUNCTION

This function gets information from the **FAT (file allocation table)** for a certain drive and fill in a **fat info structure** with the information. The prototype of this function is also lies in the dos.h header file. The syntax for using **getfatd** function is given below:

```
void getfatd(struct fatinfo *dtable);
```

dtable points to the **fatinfo structure** to be filled in.

```
/*Prog 15.46 Demo of getfatd function*/
#include <stdio.h>
#include <dos.h>
#include <conio.h>
 void main()
 {
    struct fatinfo diskinfo;
    clrscr();
    /* get default drive information */
    getfatd(&diskinfo);
    printf("\nDefault Drive:\n");
    printf("sectors per cluster:  %5d\n",diskinfo.fi_sclus);
    printf("FAT ID byte: %5X\n",diskinfo.fi_fatid & 0xFF);
    printf("number of clusters   %5d\n",diskinfo.fi_nclus);
    printf("bytes per sector     %5d\n",diskinfo.fi_bysec);
    getch();
 }
```

Output:

```
Default Drive:
sectors per cluster: 127
FAT ID byte:         0
number of clusters 15747
bytes per sector   512
(On my PC)
```

EXPLANATION: The program shows the behavior of getfatd function which is used for getting the disk information. Rest is elf-explanatory.

15.21 KBHIT FUNCTION

The function kbhit is used to check for currently available key pressed. The prototype of this function lies in the conio.h header file. The syntax of this function is given:

```
int kbhit(void);
```

The key pressed can be retrieved using **getch () or getche ()** function.

```
/*Prog 15.47 Demo of kbhit function */
#include <conio.h>
 void main(void)
 {
   clrscr();
   cprintf("Press any key to continue:");
   while (!kbhit()) /* do nothing */ ;
   cprintf("\r\nA key was pressed...\r\n");
   getch();
 }
```

Output:

```
Press any key to continue:
A key was pressed...
```

EXPLANATION: The program shows the working of **kbhit** function. Rest is self-explanatory.

```
/*Prog 15.48 Demo of kbhit */
#include <stdio.h>
#include <conio.h>
 void main()
 {
   char ch;
   clrscr();
   while(!kbhit())
   {
      ch=getch();
      if(ch==27)
      break;
      printf("Key pressed is %c\n",ch);
   }
   getch();
 }
```

Output:

```
Key pressed is a
Key pressed is b
Key pressed is c
Key pressed is d
Key pressed is e
```

```
Key pressed is f
Key pressed is g
Key pressed is h
Key pressed is i
Key pressed is j
Key pressed is k
Key pressed is l
Key pressed is m
Key pressed is n
Key pressed is o
Key pressed is p
Key pressed is q
Key pressed is r
Key pressed is s
Key pressed is t
Key pressed is u
Key pressed is v
Key pressed is w
Key pressed is x
Key pressed is y
```

EXPLANATION: The **while** loop checks if a key is pressed or not. If it is then it is extracted using **getch ()** which is displayed through printf. If **Esc** key is pressed we exit from loop. The output continues till you don't press **Esc** key.

15.22 GOTOXY FUNCTION

The **gotoxy** function takes cursor to the position at **row r** and **column c** which are supplied as its argument. Row argument is from **0 to 24** and column from **0 to 79.** The prototype of **gotoxy** is given in the **conio.h** header file. The syntax of gotoxy is given as:

```
void gotoxy(int c, int r);
```

```
/*Prog 15.49 Demo of gotoxy */
#include <conio.h>
 void main(void)
 {
    clrscr();
    gotoxy(30,12);
    cprintf("WELCOME IN C PROGRAMMING");
    getch();
    getch();
 }
```

```
Output:
WELCOME IN C PROGRAMMING
```

EXPLANATION: The program is self-explanatory.

```
/*Prog 15.50 Demo of gotoxy */
#include<stdio.h>
#include<conio.h>
 void main()
 {
    clrscr();
    gotoxy(24,5);
    printf("Text at row 14 and column 46");
    getch();
 }
Output:
                                            Text at row 14 and column 46
```

EXPLANATION: The program is self-explanatory.

15.23 TEXTCOLOR

The prototype of the function is given in the header file **conio.h.** The syntax of the function is given as:

```
void textcolor(int col);
```

The function sets the character **foreground color.** The col may have value from **0 to 7.**

```
/*Prog 15.51 Demo of text color */
#include <conio.h>
 void main(void)
 {
    int i,j;
    clrscr();
    for(i=0;i<5;i++)
    {
        for(j=0;j<80;j++)
        cprintf("A");
        cprintf("\r\n");
        textcolor(i+1);
    }
    getch();
 }
```

```
Output:
(colorful text)
AAAAAAAAAAAAAAAAAAAAAAAAAAAAAAAAAAAAAAAAAAAAAAAAAA
AAAAAAAAAAAAAAAAAAAAAAAAAAAAAAAAAAAAAAAAAAAAAAAAAA
AAAAAAAAAAAAAAAAAAAAAAAAAAAAAAAAAAAAAAAAAAAAAAAAAA
AAAAAAAAAAAAAAAAAAAAAAAAAAAAAAAAAAAAAAAAAAAAAAAAAA
AAAAAAAAAAAAAAAAAAAAAAAAAAAAAAAAAAAAAAAAAAAAAAAAAA
```

15.24 TEXTBACKGROUND

The prototype of the function is given in the header file **conio.h.** The syntax for using textbackground is given as:

```
void textbackground(int col);
```

The function sets the character **background color.** The col may have value from **0 to 7.**

```
/*Prog 15.52 Demo of textbackground function color */
#include <conio.h>
 void main(void)
 {
     int i,j;
     clrscr();
     for(i=0;i<5;i++)
     {
         for(j=0;j<50;j++)
         cprintf("A");
         cprintf("\r\n");
         textcolor(i+1);
         textbackground(i);
     }
     getch();
 }
Output:
(colorful backgroud)
AAAAAAAAAAAAAAAAAAAAAAAAAAAAAAAAAAAAAAAAAAAAAAAAAA
AAAAAAAAAAAAAAAAAAAAAAAAAAAAAAAAAAAAAAAAAAAAAAAAAA
AAAAAAAAAAAAAAAAAAAAAAAAAAAAAAAAAAAAAAAAAAAAAAAAAA
AAAAAAAAAAAAAAAAAAAAAAAAAAAAAAAAAAAAAAAAAAAAAAAAAA
AAAAAAAAAAAAAAAAAAAAAAAAAAAAAAAAAAAAAAAAAAAAAAAAAA
```

EXPLANATION: Program is self-explanatory.

```
/*Prog 15.53 Demo of text color and background color */
```

```
#include <conio.h>
 void main(void)
 {
     int i,j;
     clrscr();
     for(i=0;i<5;i++)
     {
          for(j=0;j<50;j++)
          cprintf("A");
          cprintf("\r\n");
          textcolor(i+1);
          textbackground(i);
     }
     getch();
 }
```

Output:

```
(Colorful Text and back ground)
AAAAAAAAAAAAAAAAAAAAAAAAAAAAAAAAAAAAAAAAAAAAAAAAAA
AAAAAAAAAAAAAAAAAAAAAAAAAAAAAAAAAAAAAAAAAAAAAAAAAA
AAAAAAAAAAAAAAAAAAAAAAAAAAAAAAAAAAAAAAAAAAAAAAAAAA
AAAAAAAAAAAAAAAAAAAAAAAAAAAAAAAAAAAAAAAAAAAAAAAAAA
AAAAAAAAAAAAAAAAAAAAAAAAAAAAAAAAAAAAAAAAAAAAAAAAAA
```

EXPLANATION: Program is self-explanatory.

15.25 TEXTATTR FUNCTION

textattr sets both the **foreground** and **background** color in a single color. The prototype of this function is given in conio.h header file. The syntax of this function is given as:

void textattr(int attr);

```
/*Prog 15.54 Demo of textattr function*/
#include <conio.h>
 void main(void)
 {
    int i;
    clrscr();
    for(i=0;i<9;i++)
    {
          textattr(i + ((i+1) << 4));
          cprintf("This is a test\r\n");
    }
```

```
    getch();
}
```

Output:

(colorful text(foreground) and background with blinking text)

```
This is hari mohan pandey
This is hari mohan pandey
This is hari mohan pandey
This is hari mohan pandey
This is hari mohan pandey
This is hari mohan pandey
This is hari mohan pandey
This is hari mohan pandey
This is hari mohan pandey
```

15.26 CPRINTF FUNCTION

The **cprintf** function is similar to **printf** with the difference that we have to use ***\r\n*** sequence at the end of string to achieve the ***\n*** effect. Again to see the effect of **textcolor** and **textbackground** function we have to print string using **cprintf.** The prototype of the function is given in the **conio.h** header file. The syntax is given as:

```
int cprintf(const char*,[format string .......]);
```

With cprintf, the string is written directly to screen memory or by way of **BIOS** call, depending upon the value of **directvideo.**

```
/*Prog 15.55 demo of cprintf ver1*/
#include <conio.h>
 void main(void)
 {
    /* clear the screen */
     clrscr();
    /* create a text window */
     window(10, 10, 80, 25);
    /* output some text in the window */
     cprintf("Hello how r'u\r\n");
    /* wait for a key */
     getch();
 }
```

Output:

```
        Hello how r'u
```

EXPLANATION: This program shows the working of cprintf. Rest is self-explanatory.

```
/*Prog 15.56 Demo of cprintf(Marquee simulation) in C ver 2*/
#include<dos.h>
#include<time.h>
#include<stdio.h>
#include<stdlib.h>
 void main()
 {
   char ch;
   int r=12,c=0,i;
   clrscr();
   while(2)
   {
      gotoxy(c,r);
      textcolor(rand()%8);
      textbackground();
      cprintf("Hello C\r\n");
      delay(150);
      c++;
      if(c==77)
      c=0;
      if(kbhit())
       break;
       clrscr();
   }
   getch();
 }
```

```
Output:
(Colorful background with colorful text)
Hello C
```

EXPLANATION: The program displays **Hello C** at cursor position at **row 12 and col 0** in a random selected color. The **delay** causes delay of **150 millisecond** so that we can see hello **C** on to the screen. The column position *c* is incremented so that hello is displayed at **pos(1,12)** is second iteration of **while** loop. This continues at the net effect of this is that the next hello moves from left to right which is termed as **marquee (moving text).** When *c* reaches value of **77** it is made **0** again. The **clrscr()** function ensures that previous **Hello C** is erased. If any key is hit in between then we break from **while** loop.

```
/*Prog 15.57 Demo of cprint(Marquee simulation) in C ver 3*/
#include<dos.h>
#include<time.h>
```

```
#include<stdio.h>
#include<stdlib.h>
 void main()
 {
   char ch;
   int r=12,c=0,i;
   clrscr();
   while(2)
    {
     gotoxy(c,r);
     textcolor(rand()%8);
     textbackground(rand()%10);
     cprintf("Hello C\r\n");
     delay(150);
     c++;
     if(c==77)
     c=0;
     if(kbhit())
      break;
      clrscr();
    }
   getch();
 }
Output:
(Random text color and random background also)
```

EXPLANATION: The change with this program is in background color by applying **rand()** function. Rest is self-explanatory.

EXERCISES

A. Answer the following questions:

1. Why stdio.h header file is used so frequently?
2. What is the difference between printf and cprintf?
3. Can we use delay function under windows/Unix environment?
4. Use system function to run some commands of DOS from a C program?
5. Explore all other different functions available in different header files in C?

B. Match the following columns:

I	II
1. **system**	(*a*) system time
2. **fmod**	(*b*) run executable file
3. **rand**	(*c*) takes one argument
4. **ctime**	(*d*) finds mod of two float numbers.
5. **scanf**	(*e*) max number returned is 32767.
6. **random**	(*f*) variable number of arguments.

C. Write True or False against each statement:

1. For formatted output we use **printf** function.
2. **scanf** returns number of input data items successfully read.
3. **printf** can be used to find length of a string.
4. The value of **RAND_MAX** is **128.**
5. The **freq** function can be used to generate frequencies.
6. The function **rand** takes one parameter.
7. The **system** function is declared in **dos.h** header file.
8. The function **movexy** is used to set the cursor at desired row and column.
9. The parameter to **delay** is in second.
10. To check whether a key has been pressed or not we use **kbpress** function.

D. Fill in the blanks:

1. To move the cursor at a desired position on screen we use __________.
2. For random number generation we can use either __________ or __________.
3. For the execution of any executable file we can use __________.
4. Function __________ is used to generate sound.
5. For finding system time structure used is __________.
6. For finding system time function used is __________.
7. For printing colorful texts we can use __________ in conjunction with __________.
8. return type of printf and scanf function is __________.
9. The functions __________ and __________ takes variable number of arguments.
10. The function __________ can be used to find modulus of two float numbers.

E. Brain Drill:

1. Write a function similar to delay function in dos.h and use it in your program.
2. Write a program to display entered text at specified position given on the screen entered by the user.
3. Write a function which works similar to fmod function. Test it with some input.
4. Initialize an array with 10 elements and display all elements in a random manner without using any built-in function for randomization.

16

Introduction to Data Modifier and Math Functions in 'C'

In earlier chapter we have already discussed about "Data Types and Names in C," you learned about several data types, such as **char, int, float, and double,** in the C language. In this chapter, you'll learn about four **data modifiers** that enable you to have greater control over the data. The C keywords for the four data modifiers are given below:

1. **signed**
2. **unsigned**
3. **short**
4. **long**

16.1 ENABLING OR DISABLING THE SIGN BIT

As you know, it's very easy to express a negative number in decimal. All you need to do is put a minus sign in front of the absolute value of the number. But how does the computer represent a negative number in the binary format?

Normally, one bit can be used to indicate whether the value of a number represented in the binary format is negative. **This bit is called the sign bit.** The following two sections introduce **two data modifiers, signed and unsigned,** that can be used to **enable** or **disable** the **sign bit.**

16.2 THE SIGNED MODIFIER

For integers, the leftmost bit can be used as the sign bit. For instance, if the **int** data type is **16 bits** long and the rightmost bit is counted as **bit 0,** you can use bit **15** as a sign bit. When the sign bit is set to **1,** the **C compiler** knows that the value represented by the data variable is **negative.**

There are several ways to represent a negative value of the **float or double data types.** The implementations of the **float** and **double** data types are beyond the scope of this book. You can refer to **Kernighan and Ritchie's** book 'The C Programming Language' for more details on the implementations of **negative** values of the **float** or **double** type.

The C language provides a data modifier, **signed,** that can be used to indicate the compiler that the **int** or **char** data type uses the **sign bit.** By default, the **int** data type is a **signed quantity.** But the **ANSI** standard does not require the **char** data type be **signed;** it's up to the **compiler vendors.** Therefore, if you want to use a signed character variable, and make sure the compiler knows it, you can declare the character variable like this:

```
signed char ch;
```

So that the compiler knows that the character variable **ch** is signed, which means the variable can take a value in the range of **– 128 (that is, – 2^7) to 127 (that is, 2^7_1). (Remember that for an unsigned character variable, the range is 0 to 255; that is, 2^8_1.)**

EXAMPLE: To represent a negative number in the binary format, you can first get its equivalent positive value's binary format. Then you perform the complement operation on the binary, and finally, add one to the complemented binary.

For instance, given a negative integer -12345, how can you represent it in the binary format?

First, you need to find the binary format for the positive integer **12345,** which is **0011000000111001.** Then, you perform the complement operation on **0011000000111001;** that is, **~0011000000111001,** and obtain the following:

```
1100111111000110
```

And finally, adding **1** to **1100111111000110** gives you **1100111111000111,** which is the binary format of the negative integer **–12345.**

16.3 THE UNSIGNED MODIFIER

The C language also gives you the unsigned modifier, which can be used to tell the C compiler that no sign bit is needed in the specified data type.

Like the signed modifier, the unsigned modifier is meaningful only to the **int and char** data types. For instance, the declaration

```
unsigned int x;
```

Tells the C compiler that the integer variable *x* can only assume positive values from **0** to **65535 (that is, 2^{16}_1),** if the **int** data type is **16** bits long. In fact, **unsigned int** is equivalent to **unsigned** according to the **ANSI standard.** In other words, **unsigned int** ***x;*** is the same as **unsigned** ***x*;.**

Also, the ANSI standard allows you to indicate that a constant is of type unsigned by **suffixing** ***u*** **or U** to the constant. For instance,

```
unsigned int x, y;
x = 12345U;
y = 0xABCDu;
```

Here, the unsigned integer constants **12345U** and **0xABCDu** are assigned to variables *x* and *y*, respectively.

```
/*Prog 16.1 Demo of using signed and unsigned modifiers */
#include <stdio.h>
#include <conio.h>
  void main()
  {
      signed char ch;
      int x;
      unsigned int y;
      clrscr();
      ch = 0xFF;
      x = 0xFFFF;
      y = 0xFFFFu;
      printf("The decimal of signed 0xFF is %d.\n", ch);
      printf("The decimal of signed 0xFFFF is %d.\n", x);
      printf("The decimal of unsigned 0xFFFFu is %u.\n", y);
      printf("The hex of decimal 12345 is 0x%X.\n", 12345);
      printf("The hex of decimal -12345 is 0x%X.\n", -12345);
      getch();
  }
```

```
Output:
The decimal of signed 0xFF is -1.
The decimal of signed 0xFFFF is -1.
The decimal of unsigned 0xFFFFu is 65535.
The hex of decimal 12345 is 0x3039.
The hex of decimal -12345 is 0xCFC7.
```

EXPLANATION: The statement in **line 13** displays the decimal value of the **signed char** variable **ch.** The output on the screen shows that the corresponding decimal value of **0xFF** is **– 1** for the **signed char** variable **ch.**

Lines 14 and **15** print out the decimal values of the **int** variable *x* **(which is signed by default)** and the **unsigned int** variable *y*, respectively. Note that for the variable *y*, the **unsigned integer** format specifier *%u* is used in the **printf ()** function in **line 15.**

Based on the output, you see that **0xFFFF** is equal to **– 1** for the **signed int** data type, and **65535** for the **unsigned int** data type. Here, the **integer** data type is **16 bits** long.

Lines 16 and 17 print out **0x3039 and 0xCFC7,** which are the **hex** formats of the decimal values of **12345 and – 12345,** respectively. According to the method mentioned in the last section, **0xCFC7** is obtained by adding 1 to the complemented value of **0x3039.**

16.4 CHANGING DATA SIZES

Sometimes, you want to reduce the memory taken by variables, or you need to increase the storage space of certain data types. Fortunately, the C language gives you the flexibility to modify sizes of data types. The two data modifiers, **short and long,** are introduced in the following two sections.

16.4.1 The Short Modifier

A data type can be modified to take less memory by using the short modifier. For instance, you can apply the short modifier to an integer variable that is **32 bits long,** which might reduce the memory taken by the variable to as little as **16 bits.**

You can use the short modifier like this:

```
short x;

unsigned short y;
```

By default, a **short int** data type is a signed number. Therefore, in the **short** *x;* statement, *x* is a signed variable of **short integer.**

16.4.2 The Long Modifier

If you need more memory to keep values from a wider range, you can use the long modifier to define a data type with increased storage space. For instance, given an integer variable *x* that is **16** bits long, the declaration is defined as:

```
long int x;
```

Increases the size of *x* to **32 bits.** In other words, after the modification, *x* is capable of holding a range of values from **-2147483648 (that is, -2^{31}) to 2147483647 (that is, 2^{31}_1).** The **ANSI** standard allows you to indicate that a constant has type long by suffixing l or L to the constant. For instance:

```
long int x, y;

x = 123456789l;
y = 0xABCD1234L;
```

Here, the constants of the long int data type, **123456789l** and **0xABCD1234L,** are assigned to variables *x* and *y*, respectively. Also, you can declare a long integer variable simply like this:

```
long x;

long int x;
```

Now here I give program that can print out the numbers of bytes for different **modified data types.**

```
/* Prog 16.2 Demo of modifying data with using short and long modifiers
*/

#include <stdio.h>

#include <conio.h>

 void main()
```

```
{
    clrscr();
    printf("The size of short int is: %d.\n", sizeof(short int));
    printf("The size of long int is: %d.\n", sizeof(long int));
    printf("The size of float is: %d.\n", sizeof(float));
    printf("The size of double is: %d.\n", sizeof(double));
    printf("The size of long double is:%d.\n", sizeof(long double));
    getch();
}
```

Output:

```
The size of short int is: 2.
The size of long int is: 4.
The size of float is: 4.
The size of double is: 8.
The size of long double is: 10.
```

EXPLANATION: In **program 16.2** the **sizeof** operator and **printf()** function are used to measure the sizes of the modified data types and display the results on the screen. For instance, **lines 6 and 7** obtain the size of the **short int** data type and print out the number of the byte, **2,** on the screen. From the output, you know that the short int data type is **16 bits (that is, 2 bytes)** long on my machine. Likewise, **lines 8 and 9** find the size of the **long int** data type is **4 bytes (that is, 32 bits) long,** which is the same length as the **float** data type obtained in **lines 10 and 11. Lines 12 and 13** obtain the **size of the double data type,** which is **8 bytes (that is, 64 bits)** on my machine. Then, after being modified by the long modifier, the size of the **double** data type is increased to **10 bytes (that is, 80 bits),** which is printed out by the **printf() function in lines 14 and 15.**

16.4.3 Adding H, L, Or L To Format Specifiers

You can add *h* into the integer format specifier **(like this:** %*hd*, %*hi*, **or** %*hu*) to specify that the corresponding number is a **short int or unsigned short int.**

On the other hand, using %*ld* **or** %L*d* specifies that the corresponding **datum is long int.** %*lu* **or** %Lu is then used for the **long unsigned int** data.

The below given program shows the usage of %*hd*, %*lu*, **and** %*ld*.

```
/*Prog 16.3 Demo using %hd, %ld, and %lu specifiers */
#include <stdio.h>
#include <conio.h>
void main()
{
    short int          x;
```

```
    unsigned int        y;
    long int            s;
    unsigned long int t;
    clrscr();
    x = 0xFFFF;
    y = 0xFFFFU;
    s = 0xFFFFFFFFl;
    t = 0xFFFFFFFFL;
    printf("The short int of 0xFFFF is %hd.\n", x);
    printf("The unsigned int of 0xFFFF is %u.\n", y);
    printf("The long int of 0xFFFFFFFF is %ld.\n", s);
    printf("The unsigned long int of 0xFFFFFFFF is %lu.\n", t);
    getch();
  }
```

Output:

```
The short int of 0xFFFF is -1.
The unsigned int of 0xFFFF is 65535.
The long int of 0xFFFFFFFF is -1.
The unsigned long int of 0xFFFFFFFF is 4294967295.
```

EXPLANATION: There are four data types declared in program 16.3: the **short int** variable *x*, the **unsigned int variable** *y*, the **long int variable** *s*, and the **unsigned long int variable** *t*. The four variables are initialized in **lines 6_9.**

To display the decimal values of *x, y, s,* **and** *t,* the format specifiers *%hd, %u, %ld,* **and** *%lu* are used, respectively, in **lines 15_18** to convert the corresponding **hex** numbers to **decimal** numbers. The output from the program shows that values contained by *x, y, s,* **and** *t* have been correctly displayed on the screen.

16.5 MATHEMATICAL FUNCTIONS IN C

Basically, the **math functions** provided by the C language can be classified into **three groups:**

- Trigonometric and hyperbolic functions, such as a **cos(), cos(), and cosh().**
- Exponential and logarithmic functions, such as **exp (), pow (), and log10 ().**
- Miscellaneous math functions, such as **ceil (), fabs (), and floor ().**

You have to include the header file **math.h** in your C program before you can use any math functions defined in the header file.

The following two sections introduce several math functions and tell you how to use them in your programs.

16.5.1 Calling Sin (), Cos (), and Tan ()

You should appreciate that C gives you a set of functions to deal with trigonometric or hyperbolic calculations, if you think those calculations are very tough. For instance, given an angle *x* in radians, the **sin(*x*)** expression returns the **sine** of the angle.

The following formula can be used to convert the value of an angle in degrees into the value in radians:

```
radians = degree * (3.141593 / 180.0).
```

Here, **3.141593** is the approximate value of ***pi*.** If needed, you can use more decimal digits from ***pi*.** Now, let's have a look at the **syntax of the sin (), cos (), and tan () functions.**

(A) SYNTAX FOR SIN () FUNCTION

The syntax for the **sin ()** function is

```
#include <math.h>
double sin(double x);
```

Here, the **double variable** *x* contains the value of an **angle in radians.** The **sin ()** function returns the sine of *x* in the **double data type.**

```
/*Prog 16.4 Demo of sin() function*/
#include <stdio.h>
#include <math.h>
#include <conio.h>
  void main()
  {
    double res, angle= 0.5;
    clrscr();
    res= sin(angle);
    printf("The sin() of %lf is %lf\n", angle, res);
    getch ();
}
```

Output:

```
The sin() of 0.500000 is 0.479426
```

EXPLANATION: The **program 16.4** shows the demonstration of **sin ().** Here in the program I take **angle** in radian as **0.5** and **res** be the result. After applying **sin ()** I store the result into **res** and then by applying **printf** function we will display the result of **res.**

(B) SYNTAX FOR COS () FUNCTION

The syntax for the **cos ()** function is

```
#include <math.h>
double cos (double x);
```

Here, the **double** variable *x* contains the value of an angle in **radians.** The **cos ()** function returns the cosine of *x* in the **double data type.**

```
/*Prog 16.5 Demo of cos () function */
#include <stdio.h>
#include <math.h>
#include <conio.h>
 void main()
 {
   double res;
   double angle= 0.5;
   clrscr();
   res= cos(angle);
   printf("The cosine of %lf is %lf\n", angle, res);
   getch();
 }
```

Output:

```
The cosine of 0.500000 is 0.877583
```

EXPLANATION: Program is self-explanatory.

(C) TAN ( ) FUNCTION

The syntax for the **tan ()** function is

```
#include <math.h>
double tan (double x);
```

Here, the **double** variable *x* contains the value of an **angle in radians.** The **tan ()** function returns the **tangent** of *x* in the **double data type.**

```
/*Prog 16.6 Demo of tan() function*/
#include <stdio.h>
#include <math.h>
#include <conio.h>
 void main()
 {
   double res,angle;
   clrscr();
   angle = 0.5;
   res= tan(angle);
   printf("The tan of %lf is %lf\n",angle, res);
   getch();
 }
```

Output:

```
The tan of 0.500000 is 0.546302
```

EXPLANATION: Program is self-explanatory.

```
/* Prog 16.7 Demo of calculating trigonometric values using sin(),
cos(), and tan() functions */
#include <stdio.h>
#include <math.h>
#include <conio.h>
 void main()
 {
     double angle;
     clrscr();
     angle = 45.0;                           /* 45 degree */
     angle *= 3.141593 / 180.0;              /* convert to radians */
     printf("The sine of 45 is:              %f.\n", sin(angle));
     printf("The cosine of 45 is:            %f.\n", cos(angle));
     printf("The tangent of 45 is:           %f.\n", tan(angle));
     getch();
 }
Output:
The sine of 45 is:      0.707107.
The cosine of 45 is:    0.707107.
The tangent of 45 is:   1.000000.
```

EXPLANATION: Note that the header file **math.h** is included, which is required by the C math functions. The **double** variable *x* in program is initialized with **45.0** in **line 9.** Here, **45.0** is the value of the angle in **degrees,** which is converted into the corresponding **radians** in **line 10.**

Then, the statement in **line 11** calculates the **sine** of *x* by calling the **sin()** function and prints out the result on the screen. Similarly, **line 12** obtains the **cosine of** *x* and shows it on the screen as well. Because *x* contains the value of a **45-degree** angle, it's not surprising to see that both the **sine** and **cosine** values are the same, about **0.707107.**

Line 13 gives the tangent value of *x* by using the **tan()** function. As you might know, the tangent of *x* is equal to the sine of *x* divided by the cosine **of** ***x*****.** Because the sine of a **45-degree** angle is the same as the cosine of a **45-degree** angle, the tangent of a **45-degree** angle is equal to **1.** The result (in the floating-point format) of **1.000000,** in the third line of the listing's output, proves it.

You can declare a constant **PI** initialized to **3.141593,** and another constant initialized to **180.0.** Or, simply declare a single constant initialized to the result of **3.141593/180.0.**

16.5.2 Calling Pow () and Sqrt ()

The **pow() and sort()** functions are two other useful math functions in C.

(A) POW () FUNCTION

The syntax for the **pow ()** function is

```
#include <math.h>
double pow(double x, double y);
```

Here, the value of the **double variable** *x* **is raised to the power of** *y***.** The **pow ()** function returns the result in the double data type.

(B) SQRT () FUNCTION

The syntax for the **sqrt()** function is

```
#include <math.h>
double sqrt(double x);
```

Here, the **sqrt()** function returns the non-negative square root of *x* in the **double** data type. **The function returns an error if x is negative.**

In fact, if you set up the second argument in the **pow()** function to **0.5**, and *x* contains a non-negative value, the two expressions, **pow(*x*, 0.5) and sqrt(*x*), are equivalent.**

Now, take a look at how to call the pow() and sqrt() functions in the program shown below.

```
/*Prog 16.8 Demo of using pow() and sqrt() functions */
#include <stdio.h>
#include <math.h>
#include <conio.h>
 void main()
 {
    double x, y, z;
    clrscr();
    x = 64.0;
    y = 3.0;
    z = 0.5;
    printf("pow(64.0, 3.0) returns: %7.0f\n", pow(x, y));
    printf("sqrt(64.0) returns: %2.0f\n", sqrt(x));
    printf("pow(64.0, 0.5) returns: %2.0f\n", pow(x, z));
    getch();
 }
```

Output:

```
pow(64.0, 3.0) returns: 262144
sqrt(64.0) returns: 8
pow(64.0, 0.5) returns: 8
```

EXPLANATION: The three double variables in the above program ***x*, *y*, and *z*,** are initialized with **64.0, 3.0, and 0.5, respectively, in lines 9_11.**

The **pow()** function in **line 12** takes *x* and *y* and then calculates the value of *x* raised to the power of *y***.** Because the fractional part is all decimal digits of **0s**, the format specifier **%7.0f** is used in the **printf()** function to convert only the non-fractional part of the value. The result is shown on the screen as 262144. In **line 13**, the non-negative square root of *x* is calculated by calling the **sqrt()** function. As in **line 12,** the format specifier **%2.0f** is used in **line 13** to convert the non-fractional part of the value returned from the **sqrt()** function, because the fractional part consists of decimal digits of **0s.** As you see in the output, the non-negative square root **of *x* is 8.**

As I mentioned earlier, the **pow(*x*, 0.5)** expression is equivalent to the **sqrt(*x*)** expression. Thus, it's no surprise to see that **pow(*x*, *z*)** in the statement of **line 14** produces the same result as **sqrt(*x*)** does in **line 13.**

POINTS TO PONDER

In this section you have learned the following points.

- The signed modifier can be used to enable the sign bit for the char and int data types.
- All int variables in C are signed by default.
- The unsigned modifier can be used to disable the sign bit for the char and int data types.
- The memory space taken by a data variable can be reduced or increased by using the short, or long, data modifier respectively.
- There is a set of C library functions, such as sin(), cos(), and tan(), that can be used to perform trigonometric or hyperbolic computations.
- There is another group of math functions in C—for example, pow()—that can perform exponential and logarithmic calculation.
- The sqrt() function returns a non-negative square root. The expression sqrt(x) is equivalent to the pow(x, 0.5) expression, if x has a non-negative value.
- The header file math.h must be included in your C program if you call some math functions defined in the header file.

QUESTIONS AND ANSWERS

Q1. *Which bit can be used as the sign bit in an integer?*

Ans: The **leftmost bit can be used as the sign bit for an integer.** For instance, assume the int data type is **16 bits** long. If you count the bit position from right to left, and the first bit counted is bit **0**, then bit **15** is the leftmost bit that can be used as the sign bit.

Q2. *What can the %lu format specifier do?*

Ans: The %**lu** format specifier can be used to convert the corresponding **datum** to the **unsigned long int data type.** In addition, the %**lu format** specifier is equivalent to **%Lu.**

Q3. *When do I use short and long?*

Ans: If you need to save memory space, and you know the value of an integer data variable stays within a smaller range, you can try to use the short modifier to tell the C compiler to reduce the default memory space assigned to the variable, for instance, from 32 bits to 16 bits. On the other hand, if a variable has to hold a number that is beyond the current range of a data type, you can use the long modifier to increase the storage space of the variable in order to hold the number.

Q4. *Does the sin () function takes a value in degrees or in radians?*

Ans: Like other trigonometric math functions in C, the **sin()** function takes a value in radians. If you have an angle in degrees, you have to convert it into the form of radians. The formula is:

```
radians = degree * (3.141593 / 180.0)
```

17

INTRODUCTION TO TOP 'C' SECRETS

This chapter contains some ultimate C secrets. Each secrets is listed with some theory and some code, some are only as theory. Start reading, they are waiting for you.

17.1 SECRET-1

The range of all integral data types like **int, char, long** etc is defined in a herder file **limits.h** which you can use to find out range of these data types. For each type *i.e.* char, long, signed char etc range (only for signed) is given. For unsigned only maximum value is given. These values are given in terms of constants. For example **CHAR_MIN** and **CHAR_MAX** will give**-127** and **128** as output. Code for this may be:

```
#include<limits.h>
 main()
{
   printf("%d\t%d\n"CHAR_MIN,CHAR_MAX);
}
/*Prog 17.1 Program to display all the constants to display their ranges*/
#include <stdio.h>
#include <conio.h>
#include <limits.h>
 void main()
 {
   clrscr();
   printf("CHAR_MIN=%d\n",CHAR_MIN);
   printf("CHAR_MAX=%d\n",CHAR_MAX);
```

```
    printf("INT_MIN=%d\n",INT_MIN);
    printf("INT_MAX=%d\n",INT_MAX);
    printf("SHRT_MIN=%d\n",SHRT_MIN);
    printf("LONG_MIN=%ld\n",LONG_MIN);
    printf("LONG_MAX=%ld\n",LONG_MAX);
    printf("SCHAR_MIN=%d\n",SCHAR_MIN);
    printf("SCHAR_MAX=%d\n",SCHAR_MAX);
    printf("UCHAR_MAX=%d\n",UCHAR_MAX);
    printf("UINT_MAX=%ld\n",UINT_MAX);
    printf("USHRT_MAX=%ld\n",USHRT_MAX);
    printf("ULONG_MAX=%lu\n",ULONG_MAX);
    getch();
}
```

All the constants defined in the file are given in the table:

Table 17.1 *Introduction to data types and their ranges*

DATA TYPE	CONSTANT	VALUE
CHAR	CHAR_MIN	-127
	CHAR_MAX	128
INT	INT_MIN	-32768
	INT_MAX	32767
LONG	LONG_MIN	-2147483648
	LONG_MAX	2147483648
SHORT	SHRT_MIN	-32768
	SHRT_MAX	32768
SIGNED CHAR	SCHAR_MIN	-127
	SCHAR_MAX	128
UNSIGNED CHAR	UCHAR_MAX	255
UNSIGNED INT	UNIT _MAX	65535
UNSIGNED SHORT	USHART_MAX	65535
UNSIGNED LONG	ULONG_MAX	4294967295

```
Output:
CHAR_MIN=-128
CHAR_MAX=127
INT_MIN=-32768
INT_MAX=32767
SHRT_MIN=-32768
```

```
LONG_MIN=-2147483648
LONG_MAX=2147483647
SCHAR_MIN=-128
SCHAR_MAX=127
UCHAR_MAX=255
UINT_MAX=65535
USHRT_MAX=65535
ULONG_MAX=4294967295
```

17.2 SECRET-2

Whenever a program calls a function, vital information like the return address, the function's arguments, local variables etc. are stored on stack and this information is called stack-frame of that function. For every call to a function, the system creates a stack frame. Hence, the stack are contains a series of stack-frame. The stack- frame is also known as activation record.

17.3 SECRET-3

Consider the two programs given below:

```
#include <stdio.h>
#include <conio.h>
void main()
{
  clrscr();
  goto lab;
  {
    int a=10;
    lab: printf("%d",a);
  }
  getch();
}
```

Output:

```
-28685 (Garbage value)
```

```
#include <stdio.h>
#include <conio.h>
 void main()
 {
   clrscr();
```

```
   goto lab;
   {
      static int a =10;
      lab: printf("%d",a);
   }
   getch();
}
```

Output:

10

The program is free of compilation errors but the output produced is the garbage values and a warning is flashed by the compiler:

"Unreachable code in the function main"

This warning is due to the fact that the statement int a= 5; is completely by passed. Accidentally by passing initializations and branching into and out of the control loops are the chief dangers of the **"goto"** control statements.

The second program reduces this dangerous nature of **"goto"** by initializing the variable using the keyword static. **"goto"** does not create any problems as static variables are initialized during **load time.**

17.4 SECRET-4

Consider the following program as given below:

```
#include <stdio.h>
#include <conio.h>
 void cdecl c_func();
 void pascal pas_fun();
  void main()
  {
     int a=10, b=20, c=-30;
     clrscr();
     c_func(a,b,c);
     pas_func(a,b,c);
  }
  void cdecl c_func(int a,int b)
  {
     printf("C calling convention a=%d\tb=%d\n",a,b);
  }
  void pascal pas_func(int a,int c)
```

```
{
    printf("Pascal calling convetion a=%d\tc=%d\n",a,c);
}
```

Output:

```
C calling function a=10 b=20
Pascal calling convention a=20 c=30
```

In C when a function does not take any arguments during declaration (no void is written), then it can take any number of arguments. The keyword cdecl are used to change the behavior that how the parameters are passed to function, either from left to right or right to left. The keyword cdecl is for C convention and pascal is for pascal convention. In C convention as you are aware parameters are passed from left to right so 10 is passed into a, 20 is passed into b and 30 is ignored. Reverse happens in pascal convention 30 is stored in b, 20 in a as parameters are passed from right to left.

17.5 SECRET-5

(A) The keyword **"typedef"** can only be used with data types, whereas the preprocessor **#define** directive can replace any C statements.

(B) **"typedef"** statements are compiled by the C compiler while the preprocessor **#define** directives are handled by preprocessor.

(C) One should not end a **#define** directive with a semicolon, but **"typedef"** statements must end with semicolon.

17.6 SECRET-6

Modifying the constant value can be done with the help of pointer.

```
(A) void main()
    {
            const int xx = 20;
            xx = xx + 10;
            printf("%d", xx);
    }
```

On compilation an error will be generated by the compiler that you cannot modify the constant object.

Now see the next program.

```
(B) main()
    {
        const int xx=20;
        int *pc = &xx;
        (*pc)= 30;
        printf("%d",xx);
    }
```

This time it works fine and produces the output 30.

Volia! We modify the value of a constant with the help of pointers!.

17.7 SECRET-7

Consider the following program:

```
main()
{
    int x, y;
    clrscr( );
    x=20;
    y= sizeof(++x);
    printf("x=%d\ty=%d\n",x,y);
}
```

Output:

```
X= 20 y =2
```

When sizeof operator is applied to an expression, the compiler does not compile it for executable code. In other manner no expression but inside size will be evaluated. The value returned by the operator size of is determined at compilation time before executing the program.

17.8 SECRET -8

Consider the following program

```
main()
{
    float inf =3.7 E + 38;
    clrscr( );
    printf("%f\n", inf);
}
```

Output:

```
+INf
```

The range of a float variable is from 3.4E-38 to 3.4E +38. The value stored in variable in *f* is more than 3.4E + 38 and hence the result.

17.9 SECRET- 9

C compiler classifies all data types (scalar and derived) into two categories:

(*a*) Lvalue

(*b*) Rvalue.

Lvalue is an expression that refers to an object that can be examined as well as altered. The examples of this category are:

1. Variable names with data types int, char, float, double, long double etc.
2. Pointers.
3. Structures.
4. Unions and array elements.
5. The outcome from applying the indirection operator.

The second category Rvalue permits examination but not alteration. That is, the compiler assigns the read only storage to object under this category. The examples of this category are:

1. Constants.
2. Function name.
3. Array names.
4. Enumeration Data types.

In case of type modifier 'constant' and enumerated data types, a value can be assigned which cannot be later modified. In case of function and array names, the compiler itself assigns them values. The value is nothing but the address of the string location of a function or the address of the zeroth element of the array. Hence they cannot be changed.

Note the use of pointers can be change the value of constants. The complier does not notice this change because instead of the 'constant name, a pointer to address of the constant is used.

17.10 SECRET-10

Whenever you run a program, the operating system allocates a part of memory for that program and then copies the executable code (your .exe file) from disk to that memory area. The C compiler divides the allocated area in four parts:

1. The code area (code segment)
2. The data area (data segment)
3. The heap.
4. The stack

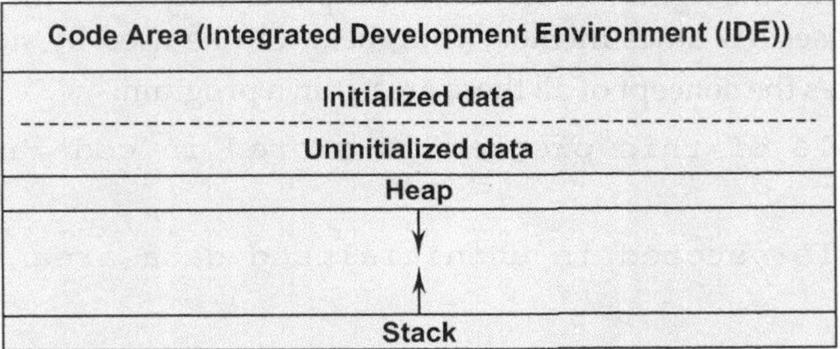

Fig. 17.1 *Run time memory area of a C program*

We briefly discuss each of the area.

1. **CODE AREA**
   (*a*) This area is fixed in nature as size of program is known at load time.
   (*b*) It contains the executable code of the program.
   (*c*) Contents of this memory area cannot be changed.
   (*d*) During compilation and linking size of this area is determined.
   (*e*) Any location of this code area can be accessed through pointers to functions.
2. **THE DATA AREA**
   (*a*) This area is also fixed in nature as size of program's data is known during load time.
   (*b*) It contains all global variables, arrays, structure etc. It also contains internal and external static data.
   (*c*) In the uninitialized data area global and static variables are stored and initialized by a value zero.
   (*d*) In the initialized data area variables are initialized by their respective values.
   (*e*) Static and global variables are called load time variables as during the program load their values are known.
   (*f*) **printf()** and **scanf()** functions uses the data area for storing and receiving the data.
3. **THE STACK AREA**
   (*a*) For functions this area is indispensable. Whenever we call a function a stack-frame for that function is generated in this area. This area used by the compiler to store auto and temporary variable, function parameters and return address of the function. The size of this area is dynamic i.e. changes throughout the execution of the program.
4. **THE HEAP AREA**
   (*a*) It's a special memory area which is used to allocate memory at runtime. Memory can be allocated from this area with the use of library functions **malloc ( ), calloc ( )** etc. and used memory can be returned back to this memory area with the help of library function **free( ).**
   (*b*) Its nature is dynamic.
   (*c*) This area is managed by the programmers and hence while allocating the memory one should check whether memory is available in the heap area or not.
   (*d*) As seen from the figure the stack and heap area may share the same memory region if need arises. At times memory from heap can be used by stack and vice-versa.

A program illustrates the concept of all these area as in a program.

```
/* executable file of this program is stored in code_area */
int x;
/* global variable: stored in uninitialized data area */
float y;
/*global variable :stored in uninitialized data area */
Char ch = 'A';
/* global variable: stored in initialized data area */
```

```
main()
{
    int xx;
     /* local variable: stored in stack area*/
    float kk=4.5;
     /* local variable: stored in stack area*/
    static int s;
     /* static variable: stored in uninitialzed data area */
    Static int ss =15;
     /* static variable: stored in uninitialized data area */
    int *p;
    p=(int*)malloc(20);
     /* memory is allocated from heap*/
}
```

17.11 SECRET-11

Functions that are called without a declaration, without in scope are assumed to be declared as:

extern int func();

That in C an undeclared function is assumed return an int type value and accept any number of arguments. If the function is later defined otherwise, the compiler complains the discrepancy. This may sometimes creates problem or may result in linking error. The safest way is to declare all the functions prior to their use.

17.12 SECRET-12

Structure cannot be compared using built-in = = and != operators as there is no single way for a compiler to implement structure comparison. A simple byte by byte comparison won't work as padding is used to keep the alignment of later correct. A field by field comparison might require a many repetitive codes for large structures. Any compiler generated comparison could not be executed to compare pointer fields. If you want to compare two structures, you will have to write your own function for the same.

17.13 SECRET-13

Many machines access values in memory most efficiently when the values are appropriately aligned. For example in a byte addressed machine long int of size might be placed at addresses that are multiplied of 4. In dos structures are aligned on a boundary that is completely divisible by 16 as 1 paragraph is of 16 bytes. Some machines cannot perform unaligned accesses at all and require that all data be appropriately aligned.

For example: if you declare structure like this

```
struct
{
    char c;
    int x;
};
```

The compiler will usually leave an unnamed unused hole between the **char** and **int** fields to ensure that the int field is properly aligned.

17.14 SECRET-14

C does not support pass by reference. C always use pass by value. C seems to have something like pass by reference in two situations:

(*a*) First when you pass pointers in functions and calling functions with & (address) operator.

(*b*) Second in array the compiler will essentially simulate if for you when you pass an array to a function.

17.15 SECRET-15

For each pointer type there is special value called **"null pointer"**. This **"null pointer"** is different from all other pointer values and is guaranteed to compare unequal to a pointer to any object or function. That is, a null pointer points no where and it does not contain address of any variable or functions. A null pointer is conceptually different from an uninitialized pointer. A null pointer is known not to point to any object or function whereas an uninitialized pointer might point any where.

17.16 SECRET-16

The array declaration char arr[6] requests that space for six characters be set aside, to be known by the name arr. That is there is a location named arr at which six character can sit. The pointer declaration char **p*, on the other hand requests a place that holds a pointer to be known by the name *p*. This pointer can point almost anywhere: to any char; to any contiguous array of chars or nowhere.

The declaration given below:

```
char arr[] = "hello";
char *p[ ] = " world";
```

Will result in the following figure:

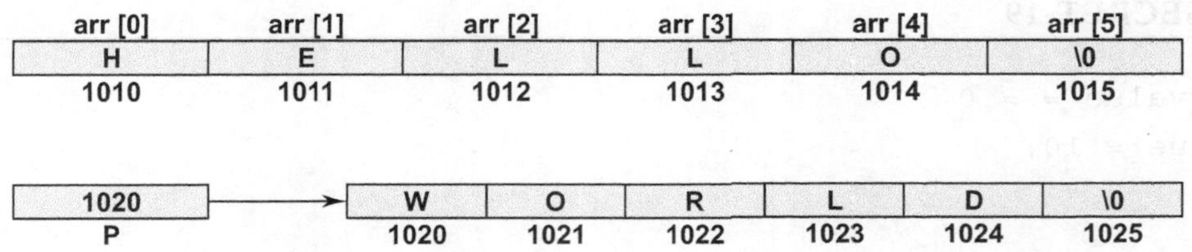

17.17 SECRET-17

For the following program:

```
main( )
{
   extern int i;
    i=10;
    printf("%d",i);
}
```

`The output produced is "Linker error: undefined symbol _i";`

extern storage class in the declaration **extern int *i*;** specifies to the compiler that the memory for I is allocated in some other file and that address of *i* will be known at the time of linking. But linker finds that no other variable of name *i* is available in any other program with memory space allocated to it. Hence an error message is issued by the linker.

17.18 SECRET-18

Consider the following program

```
main ( )
{
     float xx=2.2;
     long double yy=2.2;
     if(xx==yy)
     printf("Both are equal\n");
     else
     printf("Both are not equal\n")
}
```

Output:

```
Both are equal
```

For floating point numbers **(float, double, long double)** the exact values with which they are stored cannot be predicted. Depending on the number of bytes, the precision with which values are represented varies. **float** takes **4 bytes** and long double takes **10 bytes.** So **float** stores **0.5** with less precision than long double. The rule of thumb is that never compares or at least be cautious when using floating point numbers with relational operators.

17.19 SECRET-19

```
#if anyvalue = = 0
int value = 10;
#endif
 main()
{
   int val =20;
   printf("%d\t%d\n", value, val);
}
```

Output

10 203

This code is to show that preprocessor expressions are not the same as ordinary expressions. If a name is not known the preprocessor treats it to be equal to zero. So if condition becomes true and the program compiles and run successfully.

17.20 SECRET-20

```
main()
{
       int x=1;
       while(x<=3)
      {
           printf("%d\n",x);
           if(x>2)
         goto funlab;
         i ++;
      }
 }
 fun ()
 {
    funlab;
    printf("reached here\n");
 }
```

Output:

```
Complier error: Undefined lable funlab in function main.
```

The labels have **function scope.** In other words the scope of labels is limited to functions. The lable **funlab** is available only inside the function **fun ( ).** Hence, it is not visible in function **main ().**

17.21 SECRET-21

```
main()
{
   main()
}
```

Output:

Produced runtime error: stack overflow.

main () function calls itself again and again. Each time the function is called its return address is stored in the call stack. Since there is no condition to terminate the function call stack overflows at runtime. So it terminates the program and result in runtime error.

17.22 SECRET-22

```
main()
{
  void *vptr;
  int xx=20;
  int *x= &xx;
  printf("%d",(int*)*vptr);
}
```

Output:

Compile error: cannot apply indirection

C language does not allow pointer arithmetic on void pointers which is also termed as generic pointer. The argument being that we don't know the size of what is being pointed to with a **void *** and therefore can't known how far to seek the pointer to get to the next valid address. So no pointer arithmetic can be done on it.

17.23 SECRET-23

```
   int arr_dim(int arr [ ])
        {
              return sizeof(arr)/sizeof(int);
        }
        main( )
        {
              int arr[10];
              int size = arr_dim(arr);
```

```
        printf("size of array is %d\n",size);
    }
```

Output:

```
    1
```

Surprised by seeing the output. You expected **10.** How come this may be? Well the reason is very simple. Array cannot be passed to functions as arguments and only the pointers can be passed. So the argument is equivalent to **`int*arr`** in the function **`arr_dim`.** The return statement becomes **`sizeof (int *)/sizeof (int)`** and hence produces 1 as output.

17.24 SECRET-24

Endianness is the attribute of a system that indicates whether integers are represented from left to right or right to left. Endianness comes in two varieties:

(*a*) Big Endianness

(*b*) Little Endianness.

- Big endian means that the most significant byte of any multibyte data field is stored at the lowest memory address, which is also the address of the larger field.
- Little endian means that the least significant byte of any multibyte data field is stored at the lowest memory address, which is also the address of the larger field.

For example:

A 4 byte long int.

Byte 3 Byte2 Byte1 Byte0

Will be arranged in memory as follows:

```
Base Address + 0 Byte0
Base Address + 1 Byte1
Base Address + 2 Byte2
Base Address + 3 Byte3
```

Intel processor (those used in PC's) use **"Little endian"** byte order.

"Big Endian" means that the high-order byte of the number is stored in memory at the lowest address, and the low-order byte at the highest address. (The big end comes first).

Again long int, would then be stored as:

```
Base Address +0 Byte3
Base Address +1 Byte2
Base Address +2 Byte1
Base Address +3 Byte0
```

Motorola processors (those used in **Mac's**) use **"Big Endian"** byte order. All **INTEL** machines are **little endian** and all **AMD's** machines are **big endian.**

```
/*prog. 17.2 Demo to show machine is Big endian or little endian */
#include <stdio.h>
#include <conio.h>
 void main()
 {
    int word = 0x001;
    char *byte=(char*) &word;
    clrscr();
    if(byte[0]==1)
    printf("Machine is little endian\n");
    else
    printf("Machine is big endian\n");
    getch();
 }
```

```
Output:
Machine is little endian (On my machine)
```

The code assigns the value 001(hex) to a 2 byte integer. A char pointer extracts the first byte by the statement byte [0]. If value at this position happens to be 01 then the machine follows little endian (01 is the lower byte) and if the value is 00 then machine follows big endian (00 is the higher byte).

17.25 SECRET-25

```
main()
{
   int xx=258;
         int *pxx = &xx;
         printf("%d %d",*((char*)pxx),*((char*)ppx+1));
      }
```

```
Output:
2 1
```

The integer value **257** can be represented in binary as **0000000100000001.** The Intel machine are little endian machine. Little endian means that the lower order bytes are stored at lower address and higher order are stored at higher addresses. The integer value **258** represented in binary is **0000000100000010.** The lower byte is **00000010** and in decimal it is **2.** The higher byte is **00000001** and in decimal it is **1.**

17.26 SECRET-26

A dangling pointer arises when you use the address of an object (any variable of any type) after its lifetime is over. This may occur in situations like returning addresses of the automatic variables from a function or using the address of a memory block after it is freed.

17.27 SECRET-27

Consider the following program

```
char* fun1()
{
    char *p ="From fun1";
    return p;
    }
    char *fun 2()
    {
        char p[]="from fun2";
        return p;}
main()
{
  printf("%s\n",fun1());
  printf("%s\n",fun2());
}
```

Output:

```
From fun1
garbage value)
```

In the function **fun1( )** pointer is used and character constants are stored in the code/data area. In the second function **fun2()** value is allocated from the stack and on exiting the function it is destroyed so it prints garbage. The second case is of dangling pointer. The solution in this case to declare the array as static data is a load time data and variable even after control comes out from function.

17.28 SECRET-28

When you press key on the keyboard, pressed key is registered. After the keystroke has been registered, the controlled within the keyboard (keyboard controller) generates a special code to indicate what has been pressed. This is called a scan code. In fact, each key on the keyboard has two scan codes:

(*a*) **The first is called the make code, and is sent when the key is pushed down.**

(*b*) **The second is called the break code, and is sent when the key is released.**

The reason for having two codes is that it allows for much more flexibility than just a single code. Using two codes, the PC system can tell not only what keys were pressed, but for how long, and also which keys have been held down for a period of time. This dual-code system also facilities the multiple-Key combinations, such as **"<Ctrl>+A"**, or **"<Alt>+ <Tab>"**, that we are so used on the PC.

Each key on the keyboard has its own scan code make- break pair; this is true even if there are two keys that are the same. For example, the PC can tell the difference between the left and right **<shift>** keys (often used to control the flippers in pinball games! :^). It can also differentiate between the main **<Enter>** key and the one on the numeric keypad.

Any key pressed on the keyboard is of two bytes. First byte contains the ASCII code and second byte contains the scan code. For all function keys the scan code is **0.** To find out the scan code of any key program is given below is a complete program for finding out scan codes for function keys like all arrow keys, **F1 to F12,** shift, enter etc.

```
#include <stdio.h>
#include <conio.h>
  void main ( )
  {
       int ch;
       int s;
       clrscr( );
       ch= getch( );
       if(ch==0)
       s= getch();
       printf("The scan code is %d\n",s);
       getch();
  }
```

As an example scan code for arrow keys were found out with this program:

```
LEFT_ARROW_KEY-72
UP_ARROW_KEY-75
RIGHT_ARROW_KEY-77
DOWN_ARROW_KEY-80
```

Given below is the complete program which uses do-while loop and display you the key which you presses by their names. The program terminates when you press Esc key.

```
/*prog. 17.3 This program shows how to pick up the scan codes from a
keyboard*/
/*These define the scan codes (IBM)for the keys. All numbers are in
decimal*/
```

```
#define PAGE_UP 73
#define HOME 71
#define END 79
#define PAGE_DOWN 81
#define UP_ARROW 72
#define LEFT_ARROW 75
#define DOWN_ARROW 80
#define RIGHT_ARROW 77
#define F1 59
#define F2 60
#define F3 61
#define F4 62
#define F5 63
#define F6 64
#define F7 65
#define F8 66
#define F9 67
#define F10 68
#include <stdio.h>
#include <conio.h>
 void main()
 {
     char ch;
     printf("Press Escape to Quit\n");
     do
     {
       ch=getch();
       if(ch==0)
       {
 ch=getch();
 /*Even though there are 2 getch() it reads one keystroke*/
 switch(ch)
 {
   case PAGE_UP:
                 printf("PAGE UP\n");
                 break;
```

```
case PAGE_DOWN:
            printf("PAGE DOWN\n");
            break;
case HOME:
            printf("HOME\n");
            break;
case END:
            printf("END\n");
            break;
case UP_ARROW:
            printf("UP ARROW\n");
            break;
case DOWN_ARROW:
            printf("DOWN ARROW\n");
            break;
case LEFT_ARROW:
            printf("LEFT ARROw\n");
            break;
case RIGHT_ARROW:
            printf("RIGHT_ARROW\n");
            break;
case F1:
            printf("F1\n");
            break;
case F2:
            printf("F2\n");
            break;
case F3:
            printf("F3\n");
            break;
case F4:
            printf("F4\n");
            break;
case F5:
            printf("F5\n");
            break;
```

```
    case F6:
                    printf("F6\n");
                    break;
    case F7:
                    printf("F7\n");
                    break;
    case F8:
                    printf("F8\n");
                    break;
    case F9:
                    printf("F9\n");
                    break;
    case F10:
                    printf("F10\n");
                    break;
    default:
                    printf("Some other key \n");
  }
      }
       else
     putchar(ch);
      }
      while(ch!=27); /*27=Escape key*/
  }
```

17.29 SECRET-29

The **volatile** keyword acts as a data type qualifier. It alters the default way in which the compiler handles the variables and does not attempt to optimize the storage referenced by it. Volatile means the storage is likely to change anytime by code outside the control of the user program. This means that if you reference a variable, the program should always read from the physical address and not its cached value. A volatile keyword is an instruction to the optimizer to make sure that the variable or function is not optimized during compilation.

Consider the following code segment:

```
int check=1;
while (check);
```

In the above code on compilation the compiler assumes that the value of the check won't be changed during the execution of the program. So the compiler is free to ignore the while (check) loop instruction during optimization. However, if the check variable is changed outside the program control (say by an interrupt routine or by some thread) then it is advisable to declare the check as a **volatile** variable.

17.30 SECRET-30

In C a segment violation or segmentation fault occurs when an attempt is made to access memory whose address is well-formed, but to which access cannot be arranged. This might be due to either a protection fault or an invalid page fault. The most likely causes would be inadvertent use of null pointers or uninitialized pointer, corruption of malloc area and a mismatched function arguments especially involving pointers, two possible cases where this may happen when writing scanf("%d", x); and fprintf(invalid FILE* argument);

17.31 SECRET-31

The following code gives compilation error:

const int x=5;

int arr[x];

The reason is that const qualifier means "read-only"; An object so qualified (here int x) is a run time object that cannot normally be assigned to . The value of a const-qualified object is therefore not a constant expression in the full sense of term and cannot be used for array dimensions, case labels and the like.

NOTE:

```
#define X 5
int arr[X];
```

will work a constant defined with #define is considered a true compile time constant.

17.32 SECRET-32

The sizeof operator does not work in preprocessor #if directive because preprocessing happens during an earlier phase of compilation before type name have been parsed. Instead of using sizeof we can use constants defined in **"limits.h"** header file.

17.33 SECRET-33

Assertion is used during debugging to make sure the given condition is satisfied. They are actually macros. They test statements you pass to them and if the statement is false, they halt the program and inform you that the assertion has failed. If is defined in the header file **<assert.h>**. For example:

```
main()
```

```
{
    int i, j;
    for(i=0;i<=10;i++)
    {
        j=j+5;
        assesrt(i<5);
    }
}
```

The output of the above code will be:

Runtime error: Abnormal program termination. Assert failed (i<5)

In the program, when I gets the value 5, the condition i<5 becomes false and so the assertion fails. So the program terminates by issuing the message. After debugging we can use

#undef NDEBUG

And this will disable all the assertions from the source code. Assertion is a good debugging tool to make use of.

17.34 SECRET-34

Consider the following C code:

```
char *p1;
char p2[ ] ="A string";
p1=p2;
```

Now **p1** contains the address of the string constant. No copying of contents takes place. Only the address is copied. Still change made though **p1** affects the object it is pointing *i.e.*

P1[0] ='P'; makes string "P string"

This is called shallow copy. By default in C shallow copy is done for pointer assignment. Now consider the following code:

```
char *p1= malloc(strlen(p2)+1);
strcpy(p1,p2);
```

This is known as **deep copy.**

Here **p1** and **p2** both pointing to different memory locations and changes made to one doesn't affect another.

17.35 SECRET-35

Consider the following code:

```
char **strings;
strings[0] ="good always";
```

```
strings[1]="bad never";
strings[2]="venver good never bad;
for(i=0;i<3;i++)
printf("%s\t%d\n",string[i],strlen(string[i]));
```

This type of implementation is known as **ragged array** and it is useful in places where the string of variable size is used. The most common and popular method is to have dynamic memory allocation to be done on every dimension. The command line arguments for example, are passed only as **ragged arrays.**

An advantage of ragged array is that a fixed array of strings is not required as generally done while declaring array statistically. It may result in saving of memory substantially. Also when some of strings are particularly long, there is no need to worry about the maximum length of the string characters.

17.36 SECRET-36 (AVOID DEEPLY NESTED BLOCKS)

There are times when, for any number of reasons, you end up writing code that is **deeply nested.** Consider the following example:

Deeply nested code

```
void DeepNestFunction( void )
{
    if (test1) {
        (more code)
        if (test2) {
            (more code)
            if (test3) {
                (more code)
                if (test4) {
                    (more code)
                }
            }
        }
    }
} /* DeepNestFunction */
```

While this nesting is only four deep, we've had times when it would have gone ten deep. When nesting gets too deep, the code becomes harder to read and understand. There are two basic solutions to this problem.

Unroll the tests. The first solution is to create a Boolean variable that maintains the current success or failure status and to constantly retest it as follows.

Unrolling the deep nesting

```
void UnrollingDeepNesting( void )
{
    BOOL bVar= (test1);
    if (bVar) {
```

```
            (more code)
            bVar = (test2);
            }
        ifbVar) {
            (more code)
            bVar = (test3);
            }
        ...
} /* UnrollingDeepNesting */
```

Call another function. The second solution is to **package** the innermost tests into another function and to call that function instead of performing the tests directly.

17.37 SECRET-37 (KEEP FUNCTION SMALL)

The primary reason to keep functions small is that it helps you manage and understand a programming problem better. If you have to go back to the code a year later to modify it, you may have forgotten the small details and have to relearn how the code works. It sure helps if functions are small.

As a general rule, try to keep functions manageable by restricting their length to one page. Most of the time functions are smaller than a page and sometimes they are a page or two. Having a function that spans five pages is unacceptable.

> As a general rule, try to keep functions under one page.

If a function starts to get too large, step back a moment and try to break the function into smaller functions. The functions should make sense on their own. Remember to treat a function as a method that transitions an object from one valid state to another valid state. Try to come up with well-defined, discrete actions and write functions that perform these actions.

17.38 SECRET-38 (FUNCTIONS HAVE A SINGLE POINT OF EXIT)

This has more to do with writing functions that are easily maintainable than anything else. If a function has one **entry point,** a flow of control and **one exit point,** the function is easier to understand than a function with **multiple exit points.**

It also helps eliminate **buggy code** because using a return in the middle of a function implies an algorithm that does not have a straightforward flow of control. The algorithm should be redesigned so that there is only one exit point.

In a sense, a return in the middle of a function is just like using a **goto statement.** Instead of transferring control back to the caller at the end of the function, control is being passed back from the **middle of the function.**

17.39 SECRET-39(DO NOT USE THE GOTO STATEMENT)

I agree with the majority opinion that goto statements should be avoided. Functions with goto statements are hard to maintain.

Appendix-I

QUESTIONS FOR TECHNICAL INTERVIEWS

1. Difference between arrays and pointers?
2. What is the purpose of **realloc ( )**?
3. What is static memory allocation and dynamic memory allocation?
4. How are pointer variables initialized?
5. Are pointers integers?
6. What is a pointer variable?
7. What is a pointer value and address?
8. What is a method?
9. What are the advantages of the functions?
10. What is the purpose of main ( ) function?
11. What is an argument? Differentiate between formal arguments and actual arguments?
12. What is a function and built-in function?
13. What is modular programming?
14. When does the compiler not implicitly generate the address of the first element of an array?
15. What are the characteristics of arrays in C?
16. Differentiate between a linker and linkage?
17. What are advantages and disadvantages of external storage class?
18. Differentiate between an internal static and external static variable?
19. What are the advantages of auto variables?
20. What is storage class and what are storage variable?
21. Which expression always return true? Which always return false?
22. Write the equivalent expression for x%8?
23. Why n++ executes faster than n+1?
24. What is a modulus operator? What are the restrictions of a modulus operator?
25. What is the difference between a string and an array?
26. Is it better to use a pointer to navigate an array of values, or is it better to use a subscripted array name?
27. Can the sizeof operator be used to tell the size of an array passed to a function?
28. Is using exit() the same as using return?

29. Is it possible to execute code even after the program exits the main() function?
30. What is a static function?
31. Why should I prototype a function?
32. How do you print an address?
33. Can math operations be performed on a void pointer?
34. How can you determine the size of an allocated portion of memory?
35. What is a "null pointer assignment" error? What are bus errors, memory faults, and core dumps?
36. What is the difference between NULL and NUL?
37. What is the heap?
38. Can the size of an array be declared at runtime?
39. What is the stack?
40. When should a far pointer be used?
41. What is the difference between far and near?
42. Is it better to use malloc () or calloc()?
43. Why should we assign NULL to the elements (pointer) after freeing them?
44. When would you use a pointer to a function?
45. How do you use a pointer to a function?
46. Can you add pointers together? Why would you?
47. What does it mean when a pointer is used in an if statement?
48. Is NULL always defined as 0?
49. What is a void pointer?
50. What is a null pointer?
51. How many levels of pointers can you have?
52. What is indirection?
53. How do you print only part of a string?
54. How can I convert a string to a number?
55. How can I convert a number to a string?
56. What is the difference between a string copy (strcpy) and a memory copy (memcpy)? When should each be used?
57. How can you check to see whether a symbol is defined?
58. How do you override a defined macro?
59. What is #line used for?
60. What is a pragma?
61. What are the standard predefined macros?
62. How can type-insensitive macros be created?
63. How many levels deep can include files be nested?
64. Can include files be nested?
65. Can you define which header file to include at compile time?
66. What is the difference between **#include and #include** "file"?

67. Is it better to use a macro or a function?
68. How are portions of a program disabled in demo versions?
69. What is the benefit of using an enum rather than#define constant?
70. What is the benefit of using #defined to declare a constant?
71. Can a file other than a .h file be included with #include?
72. How can you avoid including a header more than once?
73. What will the preprocessor do for a program?
74. What is a macro, and how do you use it?
75. What is Preprocessor?
76. How can I make sure that my program is the only one accessing a file?
77. How can I open a file so that other programs can update it at the same time?
78. How do you determine whether to use a stream function or a low-level function?
79. What is the difference between text and binary modes?
80. How can you restore a redirected standard stream?
81. How do you redirect a standard stream?
82. How can I search for data in a linked list?
83. How can I sort a linked list?
84. What is hashing?
85. What is the quickest searching method to use?
86. What is the easiest searching method to use?
87. How can I sort things that are too large to bring into memory?
88. What is the quickest sorting method to use?
89. What is the easiest sorting method to use?
90. What is the benefit of using const for declaring constants?
91. Can static variables be declared in a header file?
92. What is the difference between declaring a variable and defining a variable?
93. Is it acceptable to declare/define a variable in a C header?
94. When should a type cast not be used?
95. When should a type cast be used?
96. How can you determine the maximum value that a numeric variable can hold?
97. How reliable are floating-point comparisons?
98. Can a variable be both const and volatile?
99. When should the volatile modifier be used?
100. When should the register modifier be used? Does it really help?

APPENDIX-II

FUNCTION PROTOTYPE AND THEIR PURPOSE

(A) HEADER FILE <STDIO.H>

1. **int fclose(FILE *fp);**
   Close file fp.Return 0 if file successfully closed.
2. **int feof(FILE *fp);**
   Determine if an end-of-file condition has been reached; if so return a non-zero value else return a 0 value.
3. **int fgetc (FILE *fp);**
   Enter a single character from file f.
4. **char *fgets (char *s, int n, FILE *fp);**
   Enter string s, containing n characters from file fp.
5. **FILE *fopen (const char *filename, const char *m);**
   Open a file filename in mode m; return a pointer to the file.
6. **int fputc(int n, FILE *fp);**
   Send a single character n to file fp.
7. **int fputs(const char *s, FILE *fp);**
   Send string s to file fp.
8. **int fread (void *ptr, int size, int n, FILE *fp);**
   Enter size data items each of size n from file fp to string s.
9. **int fscanf(FILE *fp, cont char * format[.......]);**
   Enter data items from f (for detail see chapter 12)
10. **int fseek(FILE *fp, long offset, int wh);**
    Move the file pointer for file fp distance offset bytes from location wh which may be beginning end of current location within the file.
11. **long ftell(FILE *fp);**
    Return the current file pointer position within file fp.
12. **int fwrite (void *ptr, int size ,int n, FILE *fp);**
    Send size data items each of size n from file fp to string s.
13. **int getc(FILE *fp);**
    Enter a single character from file fp.
14. **int getchar(void);**
    Enter a single character from the standard input device.

15. **char *gets(char *s);**
    Enter string s from the standard input device.
16. **int getw(FILE *fp);**
    Return the next integer from file fp.
17. **int printf(const char *format,.....);**
    Send data items to the standard output device (for more refer chapter-15).
18. **int putc(int c, FILE *fp);**
    Send a single character to file fp.
19. **int putchar(int c);**
    Send a single character c to standard output device.
20. **int puts(const char *s);**
    Send data c to file fp.
21. **int putw(int c, FILE *fp);**
    Send dara c to file fp.
22. **int remove(const char *fp);**
    Deletes the file fp.
23. **int rename(const char * oname, const char *nname);**
    Renames file from oname to nname.
24. **void rewind(FILE *fp);**
    Move the pointer to the beginning of the file fp.
25. **int scanf(const char *, ...) ;**
    Enter data items from the standard input device.

(B) HEADER FILE <MATH.H>

1. **double floor(double x);**
   Return a value rounded down to the next integer.
2. **double ceil(double x);**
   Return a value rounded up to next higher integer.
3. **double cos (double x);**
   Return the cosine of x (angle is in radian).
4. **double fabs(double x);**
   Return the absolute value x.
5. **double fmod(double x1, double x2);**
   Return the remainder of x1/x2 with same sign as x1.
6. **double labs(double x);**
   Return the absolute value of x;
7. **double pow(d1,d2);**
   Returnd1 raised to the power d2.
8. **double sin(double d);**
   Return the sine of d (angle is in radian).
9. **double tan(double d);**
   Return the tangent of d.

(C) HEADER FILE <STDLIB.H>

1. **double atof(char *s);**
   Convert string s into a double value.
2. **int atoi(char *s);**
   Convert string s into an int value.
3. **int atol(char *s);**
   Convert string s into a long int value.
4. **void exit(int status);**
   Close all files and buffers, and terminates the program.
5. **int rand(void);**
   Return a random positive integer.
6. **void srand (unsigned seed);**
   Initialize the random number generator.
7. **void free (void char *com);**
   Free a block of a allocated memory pointed by pointer block.
8. **int system(cont char *com);**
   Pass command com to the operating system, any .exe file can also be given.
9. **double abs(x);**
   Return the absolute value x.

(D) HEADER FILE <CTYPE.H>

1. **int isalnum(int c);**
   Determine if argument c is alphanumeric. Return a nonzero value if true, zero otherwise.
2. **int isdigit(int c);**
   Determine if argument c is a digit. Return a nonzero value if true, zero otherwise.
3. **int islower(int c);**
   Determine if argument c is a lowercase letter. Return a nonzero value if true, zero otherwise.
4. **int isodigit(int c);**
   Determine if argument c is an octal digit. Return a nonzero value if true, zero otherwise.
5. **int isspace(int c);**
   Determine if argument c is a whitspace character. Return a nonzero value if true, zero otherwise.
6. **int isupper(int c);**
   Determine if argument c is a digit. Return a nonzero value if true, zero otherwise.
7. **int isxdigit(int c);**
   Determine is argument c is a hex digit. Return a nonzero value if true, zero otherwise.
8. **int tolwer (int ch);**
   Convert letter ch to lower case.
9. **int toupper(int ch);**
   Convert letter ch to uppercase.

(E) HEADER FILE <TIME.H>

1. **clock_t clock(void);**
   Returns number of clock tick since program starts.
2. **char *ctime(cont time_t*time);**
   Converts a time_t value time into 26 character string.
3. **time_t time (time_t *timer);**
   Gives current time in seconds.

(F) HEADER FILE <ALLOC.H>

1. **void *malloc(int s);**
   Allocates bytes of memory. Return a pointer to the beginning of the allocated space.
2. **void *calloc(int nitems, int s);**
   Allocates memory for an array having nitems elements, each of length s bytes. Return a pointer to the beginning of the allocated block space.
3. **void *realloc (void *block, int s);**
   Realloc adjusts the size of the allocated block to s bytes.
4. **void free(void *ptr);**
   Releases the block of memory pointed by ptr.

(G) HEADER FILE <STRING.H>

1. **int strcmp(const char *s1, const char *s2);**
   Compare two strings lexicographically, return a negative value if s1<s2, 0 if s1 and s2 are identical, and a positive value if s1>s2.
2. **int strcmpi (const char *s1, const *s2);**
   Compare two strings lexicographically, irrespective of case. return a negative value if s1<s2, 0 if s1 and s2 are identical and a positive value if s1> s2.
3. **char*strcpy (char *des, const char *src);**
   Copy string src to dest.
4. **int strlen(cont char *s);**
   Return the length of string s.
5. **char *strset(char *s, int c);**
   Set all characters within s to c except null character.
6. **char *strcat(char *des, const char *src);**
   Strcat appends a copy of src to the end of dest.
7. **char *strchar(const char *s, int c);**
   Scans a string in the forward direction looking for a specific character c.
8. **char *strlwr(char *s);**
   Converts all uppercase letters in s to lower case.
9. **char *strupr (char * s);**
   Converts all lower case letters in s to uppercase.
10. **char *strrev(char *s);**
    Reverse the string.

APPENDIX-III

INTRODUCTION TO COMMON 'C' ERRORS

1. BEGINNER ERRORS

These are errors that beginning C students often make. However, the professionals still sometimes make them too!

1.1 Forgetting to Put A Break in A Switch Statement

Remember that C does not break out of a switch statement if a case is encountered. For example:

```
int x = 2;
switch(x)
{
    case 2:
            printf("u r in case 2 \n");
    case 3:
            printf("u r in case 3\n");
}
```

Output:

```
U r in case 2
U r in case 3
```

Put a break to break out of the switch:

```
int x = 2;
switch(x)
{
    case 2:
            printf("u r in case 2\n");
            break;
    case 3:
            printf("u r in case 3\n");
```

```
            break;/* not necessary, but good if additional
                     cases are added later */
}
```

1.2 USING = INSTEAD OF ==

C's = operator is used exclusively for assignment and returns the value assigned. The == operator is used exclusively for comparison and returns an integer value **(0 for *false*, not 0 for *true*).** Because of these return values, the C compiler often does not flag an error when = is used when one really wanted an ==.

For example:

```
int x = 5;
if ( x = 6 )
    printf("x equals 6\n");
```

This code prints out *x* equals 6! Why? The assignment inside the if sets x to 6 and returns the value 6 to the if. Since 6 is not 0, this is interpreted as *true*.

One way to have the compiler find this type of error is to put any constants (or any *r*-value expressions) on the left side. Then if an = is used, it will be an error:

```
if(6 = x)
```

1.3 SCANF () ERRORS

There are two types of common **scanf()** errors:

1.3.1 Forgetting to Put an Ampersand (&) on Arguments

scanf () must have the address of the variable to store input into. This means that often the ampersand address operator is required to compute the addresses.

Here's an example:

```
int x;
char * st = malloc(31);
scanf("%d",&x);/* & required to pass address to scanf() */
scanf("%30s", st);/*NO & here, st itself points to variable! */
```

As the last line above shows, sometimes no ampersand is correct!

1.3.2 Using the Wrong Format for Operand

C compilers do *not* check that the correct format is used for arguments of a **scanf()** call. The most common errors are using the %*f* format for doubles **(which must use the %lf format)** and mixing up %*c* and %*s* for characters and strings.

1.4 SIZE OF ARRAYS

Arrays in C always start at index 0. This means that an array of 10 integers defined as: int a[10]; has valid indices from **0 to 9** *not* **10!** It is very common for students go one too far in an array. This can lead to unpredictable behavior of the program.

1.5 INTEGER DIVISION

Unlike Pascal, C uses the / operator for both real and integer division. It is important to understand how C determines which it will do. If both operands are of an integral type, integer division is used, else real division is used.

For example:

```
double half = 1/2;
```

This code sets half to **0** not **0.5!** Why? Because **1** and **2** are integer constants. To fix this, change at least one of them to a real constant.

```
double half = 1.0/2;
```

If both operands are integer variables and real division is desired, cast one of the variables to double (or float).

```
int x = 5, y = 2;
double d = ((double) x)/y;
```

1.6 LOOP ERRORS

In C, a loop repeats the very next statement after the loop statement. The code:

```
int x = 5;
while( x > 0 );
   x--;
```

is an infinite loop. Why? The semicolon after the while defines the statement to repeat as the null statement (which does nothing). Remove the semicolon and the loop works as expected. Another common loop error is to iterate one too many times or one too few. Check loop conditions carefully!

1.7 NOT USING PROTOTYPES

Prototypes tell the compiler important features of a function: **the return type and the parameters of the function.** If no prototype is given, the compiler *assumes* that the function returns an **int** and can take any number of parameters of any type.

One important reason to use prototypes is to let the compiler check for errors in the argument lists of function calls. However, a prototype *must* be used if the function does not return an int. For example, the sqrt() function returns a double, not an int. The following code:

```
double x = sqrt(2);
```

will not work correctly if a prototype:

```
double sqrt(double);
```

does not appear above it. Why? Without a prototype, the C compiler assumes that **sqrt()** returns an **int.** Since the returned value is stored in a double variable, the compiler inserts code to convert the value to a double. This conversion is not needed and will result in the wrong value.

The solution to this problem is to include the correct **C header file** that contains the **sqrt()** prototype, **math.h.** For functions you write, you must either place the prototype at the top of the source file or create a header file and include it.

1.8 NOT INITIALIZING POINTERS

Anytime you use a pointer, you should be able to answer the question: *What variable does this point to?* If you can not answer this question, it is likely it doesn't point to any variable. This type of error will often result in a Segmentation fault/coredump error on **UNIX/Linux** or a general protection fault under Windows.

Here's an example of this type of error.

```
#include <string.h>
int main()
{
  char * st;/* defines a pointer to a char or char array */
  strcpy(st, "abc");/* what char array does st point to?? */
  return 0;
}
```

How to do this correctly? Either use an array or dynamically allocate an array.

```
#include <string.h>
int main()
{
  char st[20];     /* defines an char array */
  strcpy(st, "abc");   /* st points to char array */
  return 0;
}
OR
#include <string.h>
#include <stdlib.h>
int main()
{
  char *st = malloc(20);/* st points to allocated array*/
  strcpy(st, "abc");/* st points to char array */
  free(st);      /* don't forget to deallocate when done! */
```

```
    return 0;
}
```

Actually, the first solution is much preferred for what this code does. Why? Dynamical allocation should only be used when it is required. It is slower and more error prone than just defining a normal array.

2. STRING ERRORS

2.1 Confusing Character and String Constants

C considers character and string constants as very different things. Character constants are enclosed in *single quotes* and string constants are enclosed in *double quotes.* String constants act as a pointer to the actually string. Consider the following code:

```
char ch = 'A';      /* correct */
char ch = "A";      /* error */
```

The second line assigns the character variable ch to the address of a string constant. This should generate a compiler error. The same should happen if a string pointer is assigned to a character constant:

```
const char * st = "A";    /* correct */
const char * st = 'A';    /* error */
```

2.2 Comparing Strings With ==

Never use the == operator to compare the value of strings! Strings are char arrays. The name of a char array acts like a pointer to the string (just like other types of arrays in C). So what? Consider the following code:

```
char st1[] = "abc";
char st2[] = "abc";
if ( st1 == st2 )
  printf("Yes");
else
  printf("No");
```

This code prints out *no*. Why? Because the == operator is comparing the *pointer values* of st1 and st2, not the data pointed to by them. The correct way to compare string values is to use the **strcmp ()** library function. (Be sure to include string.h) If the if statement above is replaced with the following:

```
if ( strcmp(st1,st2) == 0 )
  printf("Yes");
else
  printf("No");
```

The code will print out *yes*. For similar reasons, don't use the other relational operators (<,>, *etc.*) with strings either. Use **strcmp ()** here too.

2.3 Not Null Terminating Strings

C assumes that a string is a character array with a terminating null character. This null character has ASCII value 0 and can be represented as just 0 or '\0'. This value is used to mark the end of meaningful data in the string. If this value is missing, many C string functions will keep processing data past the end of the meaningful data and often past the end of the character array itself until it happens to find a zero byte in memory!

Most C library string functions that create strings will always properly null terminate them. Some do not **(*e.g.*, strncpy ())**. Be sure to read their descriptions carefully.

2.4 Not Leaving Room for the Null Terminator

A C string must have a null terminator at the end of the meaningful data in the string. A common mistake is to not allocate room for this extra character. For example, the string defined below.

```
char str[30];
```

Only has room for only 29 (not 30) actually data characters, since a null *must* appear after the last data character.

This can also be a problem with dynamic allocation. Below is the correct way to allocate a string to the exact size needed to hold a copy of another.

```
char * copy_str = malloc( strlen(orig_str) + 1);
strcpy(copy_str, orig_str);
```

The common mistake is to forget to add one to the return value of **strlen()**. The **strlen()** function returns a count of the data characters which does *not* include the null terminator.

This type of error can be very hard to detect. It might not cause any problems or only problems in extreme cases. In the case of dynamic allocation, it might corrupt the *heap* (the area of the program's memory used for dynamic allocation) and cause the next heap operation (malloc(), free(), etc.) to fail.

3. INPUT/OUTPUT ERRORS

3.1 Using Fgetc (), Etc. Incorrectly

The **fgetc(), getc() and getchar()** functions all return back an ***integer*** value. For example, the prototype of **fgetc()** is:

```
int fgetc( FILE * );
```

Sometimes this integer value is really a simple character, but there is one very important case where the return value is **not** a character!

What is this value? **EOF** A common misconception of students is that files have a special EOF character at the end. There is no special character stored at the end of a file. EOF is an *integer* error code returned by a function. Here is the **wrong** way to use **fgetc()**:

```
int count_line_size( FILE * fp )
{
  char ch;
```

```
  int cnt = 0;
  while( (ch = fgetc(fp)) != EOF && ch != '\n')
     cnt++;
  return cnt;
}
```

What is wrong with this? The problem occurs in the condition of the while loop. To illustrate, here is the loop rewritten to show what C will do behind the scenes.

```
while( (int) ( ch = (char) fgetc(fp) ) != EOF && ch != '\n')
  cnt++;
```

The return value of **fgetc(fp)** is cast to char to store the result into ch. Then the value of **ch** must be cast back to an int to compare it with **EOF.** So what? Casting an int value to a **char** and then back to an int may not give back the original int value. This means in the example above that if **fgetc()** returns back the **EOF** value, the casting may change the value so that the comparison later with **EOF** would be false.

What is the solution? Make the ch variable an int as below:

```
int count_line_size( FILE * fp )
{
  int ch;
  int cnt = 0;
  while( (ch = fgetc(fp)) != EOF && ch != '\n')
     cnt++;
  return cnt;
}
```

Now the only hidden cast is in the second comparison.

```
while( (ch = fgetc(fp)) != EOF && ch != ((int) '\n') )
  cnt++;
```

This cast has no harmful effects at all! So, the moral of all this is: **always** use an int variable to store the result of the **fgetc(), getc() and getchar ().**

3.2 Using Feof ( ) Incorrectly

There is a wide spread misunderstanding of how C's **feof()** function works. Many programmers use it like Pascal's **eof()** function. However, C's function works differently!

What's the difference? Pascal's function returns true if the *next* read will fail because of end of file. C's function returns true if the *last* function failed. Here's an example of a misuse of **feof():**

```
#include <stdio.h>
int main()
{
  FILE * fp = fopen("test.txt", "r");
  char line[100];
```

```
  while( ! feof(fp) ) {
     fgets(line, sizeof(line), fp);
     fputs(line, stdout);
  }
  fclose(fp);
  return 0;
}
```

This program will print out the last line of the input file *twice*. Why? After the last line is read in and printed out, **feof()** will still **return 0** (false) and the loop will continue. The next **fgets()** fails and so the line variable holding the contents of the last line is not changed and is printed out again. After this, **feof()** will return true (since **fgets()** failed) and the loop ends.

How should this fixed? One way is the following:

```
#include <stdio.h>
int main()
{
  FILE * fp = fopen("test.txt", "r");
  char line[100];
  while (1) {
     fgets(line, sizeof(line), fp);
     if ( feof(fp) )        /* check for EOF right after fgets() */
       break;
     fputs(line, stdout);
  }
  fclose(fp);
  return 0;
}
```

However, this is not the best way. There is really no reason to use feof() at all. C input functions return values that can be used to check for EOF. For example, fgets returns the NULL pointer on EOF. Here's a better version of the program:

```
#include <stdio.h>
int main()
{
  FILE * fp = fopen("test.txt", "r");
  char line[100];
  while( fgets(line, sizeof(line), fp) != NULL )
  fputs(line, stdout);
  fclose(fp);
  return 0;
}
```

3.3 Leaving Characters in the Input Buffer

C input (and output) functions buffer data. Buffering stores data in memory and only reads (or writes) the data from (or to) I/O devices when needed. Reading and writing data in big chunks is much more efficient than a byte (or character) at a time. Often the buffering has no effect on programming.

One place where buffering is visible is input using scanf (). The keyboard is usually line buffered. This means that each line input is stored in a buffer. Problems can arise when a program does not process all the data in a line, before it wants to process the next line of input. For example, consider the following code:

```
int x;
char st[31];
printf("Enter an integer: ");
scanf("%d", &x);
printf("Enter a line of text: ");
fgets(st, 30, stdin);
```

The **fgets()** will not read the line of text that is typed in. Instead, it will probably just read an empty line. In fact, the program will not even wait for an input for the **fgets()** call. Why? The scanf() call reads the characters needed that represent the integer number read in, but it leaves the '\n' in the input buffer. The **fgets()** then starts reading data from the input buffer. It finds a '\n' and stops without needing any additional keyboard input.

What's the solution? One simple method is to read and dump all the characters from the input buffer until a **'\n'** after the **scanf()** call. Since this is something that might be used in lots of places, it makes sense to make this a function. Here is a function that does just this:

```
/* function dump_line
* This function reads and dumps any remaining characters on the current
input
* line of a file.
*   Parameter:
*      fp - pointer to a FILE to read characters from
*   Precondition:
*      fp points to a open file
*   Postcondition:
*       the file referenced by fp is positioned at the end of the next
line
*      or the end of the file.
*/
void dump_line( FILE * fp )
{
  int ch;
```

```
  while( (ch = fgetc(fp)) != EOF && ch != '\n' )
    /* null body */;
}
```

Here is the code above fixed by using the above function:

```
int x;
char st[31];
printf("Enter an integer: ");
scanf("%d", &x);
dump_line(stdin);
printf("Enter a line of text: ");
fgets(st, 30, stdin);
```

One incorrect solution is to use the following:

```
fflush(stdin);
```

This will compile but its behavior is undefined by the ANSI C standard. The **fflush ()** function is only meant to be used on streams open for output, not input. This method does seem to work with some C compilers, but is completely unportable! Thus, it should not be used.

3.4 Using The Gets () Function

Do not use this function! It does not know how many characters can be safely stored in the string passed to it. Thus, if too many are read, memory will be corrupted. Many security bugs that have been exploited on the Internet use this fact! Use the fgets () function instead (and read from stdin). But remember that unlike **gets (), fgets ()** does *not* discard a terminating **\n** from the input.

The **scanf ()** functions can also be used dangerously. The **%s** format can overwrite the destination string. However, it can be used safely by specifying a width. For example, the format **%20s** will not read more than **20** characters.

APPENDIX-IV

HOW TO DEBUG 'C' PROGRAMS ?

This document explains how to write computer programs that work and that are understandable to other intelligent beings! These two attributes are *not* independent! In general, programs that other programmers can not understand do not work very well. (Not to mention the fact that they are maintenance nightmares!)

Writing structured programs (structured code *and* data!) helps greatly in debugging the code. Here is a quick review of some of the features of a structured program.

1. *Lots* of well-defined functions!
2. Using structured loop constructs (*i.e.*, while and for) instead of goto.
3. Using variables that have *one* purpose and *meaningful names.*
4. Using structured data types to represent complex data.
5. Using the ADT (*Abstract Data Type*) or OOP (*Object-Oriented Programming*) paradigm of programming.

1. HOW TO START

The most common types of mistakes when programming are:

1. **Programming without *thinking***
2. **Writing code in an unstructured manner**

Let's take these in order

1.1 Thinking about Programming

When a real programmer (or programming team) is given a problem to solve, they do not immediately sit down at a terminal and start typing in code! They first design the program by thinking about the numerous ways the problem's solution may be found.

One of the biggest myths of programming is that: ***The sooner I start coding the sooner a working program will be produced.*** This is NOT true!! A program that is planned before coding will become a working program before an unplanned program. Yes, an unplanned program will be typed in and maybe compiled faster, but these are just the *first* steps of creating a *working* program! Next comes the debugging stage. This is where the benefits of a planned program will appear. In the vast majority of the time, a planned program will have less bugs than an unplanned program. In addition, planned programs are generally more structured than unplanned programs. Thus, finding the bugs will be easier in the planned program.

So how does one *design* a program before coding? There are several different techniques. One of the most common is called ***top-down design.*** Here an outline of the program is first created. (Essentially, one first looks at the general form of the **main ()** function and then recursively works down to the lowest level functions.) There are many references on how to write programs in this manner.

Top-down design divides the program into **sub-tasks.** Each sub-task is a smaller problem that must be solved. Problems are solved by using an algorithm. Functions (and data) in the program implement the algorithm. Before writing the actual code, take a very small problem and trace by hand how your chosen algorithm would solve it. This serves several purposes:

1. It checks out the algorithm to see if will actually work on the given problem. (If it does not work, you can immediately start looking for another algorithm. Note that if you had immediately starting coding you would probably not discover the algorithm would not work until many lines of code had been entered!)
2. Makes sure that *you* understand how the algorithm actually works! (If you can not trace the algorithm by hand, you will *not* be able to write a program to do it!)
3. Gives you the detail workings of a short, simple run of the algorithm that can be used later when debugging the code.

Only when you are confident that you understand how the entire program will look should you start typing in code.

1.2 Structured Programming

When a program is structured, it is divided into sub-units that may be tested separately. This is a *great* advantage when debugging! Code in a sub-unit may be debugged separately from the rest of the program code. I find it useful to debug each sub-unit as it is written. If no debugging is performed until the entire program is written, debugging is much harder. The entire source of the program must be searched for bugs. If sub-units are debugged separately, the source code that must be searched for bugs is much smaller! Storing the sub-units of a program into separate source files can make it easier to debug them separately.

The ADT and OOP paradigms also divide programs into sub-units. Often with these methods, the sub-units are even more independent than with normal structured code. This has two main advantages:

1. Sub-units are even easier to debug separately.
2. Sub-units can often be *reused* in other programs. (Thus, a new program can use a previously debugged sub-unit from an earlier program!)

Sub-units are generally debugged separately by writing a small ***driver program.*** Driver programs set up data for the sub-task that the sub-unit is supposed to solve, calls the sub-unit to perform his sub-task, and then displays the results so that they can be checked.

Of course, all the following debugging methods can be used to debug a sub-unit, just as they can be used to debug the entire program. Again, the advantage of sub-units are that they are only a part of the program and so are *easier* to debug than the entire program at once!

2. COMPILING PROGRAMS

The first step after typing in a program (or just a sub unit of a program) is to compile the program. The compiling process converts the source code file, you typed in, into machine language and is stored in an *object file.* This is known as *compiling*. With most systems, the object file is automatically *linked* with the system libraries. These libraries contain the code for the functions that are part of the languages library. (For example, the C libraries contain the code for the printf() function.)

2.1 Compiler Errors

Every language has syntax rules. These rules determine which statements are legal in the language and which are not. Compiler programs are designed to enforce these rules. When a rule is broken, the compiler prints an error message and an object file is not created. Most compilers will continue scanning the source file after an error and report other errors it finds. However, once an error has been found, the compiler made be confused by later perfectly legal statements and report them as errors. This brings us to the first rule of compiler errors:

- **First Rule of Compiler Errors:** The first listed compiler error is always a true error; however, later errors may not be true errors.

Succeeding errors may disappear when the first error is removed. So, if later error messages are puzzling, ignore them. Fix the errors that you are sure are errors and re-compile. The puzzling errors may magically disappear when the other true errors are removed.

If you have many errors, the first error may scroll off the screen. One solution to this problem is to save the errors into a file using redirection. One problem is that errors are written to stderr not stdout which the > redirection operator uses. To redirect output to stderr use the 2> operator.

Here's an example:

C:\tc\err.c>errors

C:\tc\more errors

The compiler is just a program that other humans created. Often the error messages it displays are confusing (or just plain *wrong!*). Do not assume that the line that an error message refers to is always the line where the true error actually resides. The compiler scans source files from the top sequentially to the bottom. Sometimes an error is not detected by the compiler until many lines below where the actual error is. Often the compiler is too stupid to realize this and refers to the line in the source file where it realized something is wrong. The true error is earlier in the code. This brings us to the second rule of compiler errors:

- **SECOND RULE OF COMPILER ERRORS:** A compiler error may be caused by any source code line above the line referred to by the compiler; however, it can not be caused by a line below.

In C (and C++), do not forget that the **#include** preprocessor statement inserts the code of a header file into the source file. An error in the header file, may cause a compiler error referencing a line in the main source file. Most systems allow the preprocessed code (that the C compiler actually compiles!) to be stored in a file. This allows you to see exactly what is being compiled. This file will also show

how each **C macro** was expanded. This can be *very* helpful to discover the cause of normally very hard to find errors.

A useful technique for finding the cause of puzzling compiler errors is to delete (or comment out) preceding sections of code until the error disappears. When the error disappears, the last section removed must have caused the error.

The compiler can also display ***warnings.*** **A warning is not a syntax error; however, it *may* be a logical error in the program.** It marks a statement in your program that is legal, but is suspicious. You should treat warnings as errors unless you understand why the warning was generated. Often compilers can be set to different warning levels. It is to your advantage to set this level as high as possible, to have the compiler give as many warnings as possible. Look at these warnings *very* carefully!.

Remember that just because a program compiles with no errors or warnings does *not* mean that the program is correct! It only means that every line of the program is **syntactically correct.** That is, the compiler understands what each statement says to do. The program may still have many ***logical errors!*** An English paper may be grammatically correct (*i.e.*, have nouns, verbs, *etc.* in the correct places), but be gibberish.

2.2 Linker Errors

The ***linker*** is a program that links object files (which contain the compiled machine code from a single source file) and libraries (which are files that are collections of object files) together to create an executable program. The linker matches up functions and global variables used in object files to their definitions in other object files. The linker uses the ***name (often the term symbol is used)*** of the function or global variable to perform the match.

The most common type of linker error is an unresolved symbol or name. This error occurs when a function or global variable is used, but the linker can not find a match for the name.

For example, on an **IBM AIX** system, the error message looks like this:

0706-317 ERROR: Unresolved or undefined symbols detected:

Symbols in error (followed by references) are dumped to the load map.

The -bloadmap :< filename> option will create a load map.

.fun

This message means that a function (or global variable) named fun (ignore the period) was referenced in the program, but never defined. There are two common causes of these errors:

Misspelling the Name of the Function

In the example, above there was a function named func. This is *not* a compiler error. Code in one source file can use functions defined in another. The compiler assumes that any function referenced, but not defined in the file that references it, will be defined in another file and linked. It is only at the link stage that this assumption can be checked. (Note that C++ compilers will usually generate compiler errors for this, since C++ requires prototypes for *all* referenced functions!)

The Correct Libraries or Object Files Where Not Linked

The linker must know what libraries and object files are needed to form the executable program. The standard C libraries are automatically linked. UNIX systems, like the AIX system, do *not* automatically link in the standard C math library! To link in the math library on the AIX system, use the -lm flag on the compile command. For example, to compile a C program that uses sqrt, type:

cc prog.c -lm

Remember that the #include statement only inserts text into source files. It is a common *myth* that it also links in the appropriate library! The linker *never* sees this statement!

There are also bugs related to the linker. One difficult bug to uncover occurs when there are two definitions of a function or global variable. The linker will pick the first definition it finds and ignores the other. Some linkers will display a warning message when this occurs (The AIX linker does not!)

Another bug related to linking occurs when a function is called with the wrong arguments. The linker only looks at the name of the function when matching. It does no argument checking. Here's an example:

```
File: x.c
int f( int x, int y)
{
  return x + y;
}
File: y.c
int main()
{
  int s = f(3);
  return 0;
}
```

These types of bugs can be prevented by using prototypes. For example, if the prototype:

int *f*(int, int);

is added to *y.c* the compiler will catch this error. Actually, the best idea is to put the prototype in a header file and include it in both *x.c* and *y.c*. Why use a header file? So that there is only one instance of the prototype that all files use. If a separate instance is typed into each source file, there is no guarantee that each instance is the same. If there is only one instance, it can not be inconsistent with itself! Why include it in *x.c* (the file the function is defined in)? So that the compiler can check the prototype and ensure that it is consistent with the function's definition. (Additional note: C++ uses a technique called *name mangling* to catch these types of errors.)

3. RUNTIME ERRORS

A runtime error occurs when the program is running and usually results in the program aborting. On a UNIX/Linux system, an aborting program creates a *coredump.* A coredump is a binary file named core that contains information about the state of program when it aborted. Debuggers like *gdb* and *dbx* can read this file and tell you useful information about what the program was doing when it aborted. There are several types of runtime errors:

3.1 Illegal Memory Access

This is probably the most common type of error. Under UNIX/Linux, the programs will coredump with the message `Segmentation fault (coredump).`

Using Win95 or NT, programs will also abort. However, traditional DOS does not check for illegal memory accesses; the program continues running, but the results are unpredictable. The DOS Borland/Turbo C/C++ compilers will check for data written to the NULL address. However, the error message `NULL pointer assignments` not displayed until the program terminates.

`DIVISION BY ZERO:` ALL operating systems detect this error and abort the program.

4. DEBUGGING TOOLS

Many methods of debugging a program compare the program's behavior with the correct behavior in great detail. Usually the normal output of the program does not show the detail needed. Debugging tools allow you to examine the behavior of the in more detail.

4.1 The Assert Macro

The assert macro is a quick and easy way to put debugging tests into a C/C++ program. To use this macro, you must include the **assert.h** header file near the top of your source file. Using **assert** is simple. The format is:

```
assert(boolean (or int) expression);
```

If the *boolean expression* evaluates to true (*i.e.*, not zero), the assert does nothing. However, if it evaluates to false (zero), assert prints an error message and aborts the program. As an example, consider the following assert:

```
assert( x != 0 );
```

If *x* is zero, the following will be displayed:

```
Assertion failed: x != 0, file err.c, line 6
Abnormal program termination
```

and the program will abort. Notice that the actual assertion, the name of the file and the line number in the file are displayed.

The assert macro is very useful for putting sanity checks into programs. These are conditions that should always be true if the program is working correctly. It should not be used for user error checking (such as when the file a user requested to read does not exist). Normal if statements should be used for these runtime errors.

Of course, in a commercial program, an assertion failure is not particular helpful to an end user. Also, checking assertions will make the program run at least a little slower than without them.

Fortunately, it is easy to disable the assert macro without even removing it. If the macro NDEBUG is defined (above the statement that includes assert.h!), the assert macro does absolutely nothing. If the assertions need to be enabled later, just remove the line that defines NDEBUG. (If this technique is used, be sure that the assert statements do not execute code needed for the program to run correctly. If NDEBUG is defined, the code would *not* be run!)

4.2 Print Statements

This time honored method of debugging involves inserting debugging print statements liberally in your program. The print statements should be designed to show both what code the program is executing and what values critical variables have.

4.3 Debuggers

The previous method of debugging by adding print statements has two disadvantages:

1. When new print statements are added, program must be recompiled.
2. Information output is fixed and can not be changed as program is running.

Source-level debuggers provide a much easier way to trace the execution of programs. They allow one to:

1. Look at the value of any variable as the program is running.
2. Pause execution when program reaches any desired statement. (This position in the program is called a *breakpoint*).
3. Single step statement by statement through a program.

I *strongly* recommend that you learn to use the debugger for whatever system you program on. A debugger can save *lots* of time when debugging your program!

4.4 Lint

The lint program checks C programs for a common list of bugs. It scans your C source code and prints out a list of possible problems. Be warned that lint is *very picky*! For example, the line:

```
printf("Hello, World ");
```

will produce a warning message because printf returns an integer value that is not stored. The return value of printf is often ignored, but lint still produces an warning. There are several ways to make lint happy with this statement, one is:

```
(void) printf("Hello, World ");
```

This says to ignore the return value.

4.5 Walk Through

A *walk through* is a process of hand checking the logic of a program. The programmer sits down with someone else (best if another programmer, but anybody will do) and walks through the program for an example case. Often it is the programmer himself who finds the bug in the process of explaining how the program is supposed to work and carefully looking at his code. However, it is easy for the programmer to *"know"* what the program *should be doing* and remain blind to what the program is *actually doing.*

Students need to be very careful using this approach with other students. Two students in the same class should not walk through a program together.

5. GENERAL TIPS

Here are some general tips for debugging programs.

5.1 Finding Bugs

Before bugs are removed they must be discovered!

- Aggressively test programs!
- Start with *small* problems that can be easily checked by hand. (You should already have one of these worked out from the planning stage!)
- Test every feature of the program at least once! And is once really enough? Test features in different ways if possible.
- Do not forget to test trivial problems.
- Do not make invalid assumptions about input data.

5.2 Determining the Causes of Bugs

A bug can only be caused by the code in the program that has already executed. Be sure you do not waste time searching through code that has not run yet. A debugger or print statements can be used to determine which code has executed and which has not.

Do not fix bugs by mindlessly changing code until it seems to work. You need to figure out why one statement does work and another does not. You should have a good reason for every line of code. *"It doesn't work without this line"* is not a good reason!

INDEX

A

B

C

D

E

F

G

H

I

J

K

L

M

N

O

P

Q

R

S

T

U

V

W